RELIGIOUS FOUNDATIONS *of* WESTERN CIVILIZATION

Judaism, Christianity, and Islam

JACOB NEUSNER, EDITOR

Abingdon Press
Nashville

RELIGIOUS FOUNDATIONS OF WESTERN CIVILIZATION
JUDAISM, CHRISTIANITY, AND ISLAM

Copyright © 2006 by Abingdon Press

This book is printed on acid-free paper.

Library of Congress Cataloging-in-Publication Data

Religious foundations of Western civilization : Judaism, Christianity, and Islam / Jacob Neusner, editor.
   p. cm.
   Includes bibliographical references and index.
   ISBN 0-687-33202-8 (binding: pbk. : alk. paper)
   1. Western countries—Religion. 2. Civilization, Western. 3. Christianity. 4. Judaism. 5. Islam.
   I. Neusner, Jacob, 1932-

BL689.R46 2005
200'.9182'1—dc22

2005019409

06 07 08 09 10 11 12 13 14 15—10 9 8 7 6 5 4 3 2 1
MANUFACTURED IN THE UNITED STATES OF AMERICA

CONTENTS

PREFACE

Religion defines the foundations of the West. Christianity, meeting at specific times and places with Judaism and Islam, from ancient times to the present day, has formed the basis for Western civilization. The confrontation between Islam and Christianity brought centuries of strife, the conflict between Judaism and Christianity precipitated an unending debate, full of recrimination. But the three religions that, in unequal proportions to be sure, defined for the West the human situation and determined the goals of the social order also engaged with one another in religious, not only in political, terms. They concurred that God is one and is made manifest to humanity through revealed books and through the prophets that write them or cause them to be recorded. And, as we shall see, Christianity acknowledged its beginnings in Judaism, and Islam accorded recognition to the prophets of Judaism and Christianity. So the religious traditions that form the foundations of Western civilization respond to one another and so define the issues of shared debate, the categories of culture.

Religiosity and Spirituality: The Public and the Personal

To understand the role of religion in the social order of the West, to begin with we have to distinguish spirituality from religion, and personal experience from public and shared enterprise. For that distinction will indicate not only what we study, but also what we do not study. We study public facts of the social order and cultural construction of groups of people, facts accessible to objective description, analysis, and interpretation. We do not study private affirmations or opinions, which are not available for public inquiry but can only be recorded.

Religion is public, a fact of society and culture, not private or personal. Spirituality refers to attitudes, experiences, and feelings that are private and individual. Religiosity is a matter not of attitude or personal conviction, but of public activity; it is what people do together. The difference is, we can study what a group does, but only acknowledge the report concerning what an individual believes in private. What a group affirms can be examined in context, derived from the interplay of contemporary opinion and the heritage of doctrine and normative deed through the ages. What an individual professes can only be noted. Of spirituality one may use the language "my 'Judaism'" or "my 'personal encounter with Christ,'" but of religion one speaks of what is shared and public: "Judaism teaches . . . ," "Christianity maintains . . . ," "Islam holds . . . ."

This leads to the definition of a religion in the setting of an entire civilization. A religion is a cultural system resting on belief in a supernatural being, a system composed by an account of (1) the way of life and (2) the worldview of (3) a group of people that sees itself as set apart for divine service. The group may call itself a people, a church, a community, or a nation; but it will always see itself as holy, distinct from the rest of humanity; and it will invariably regard its distinctive way of life and worldview as expressions of the sanctity of the group.

But if religions are public and shared in community, that does not mean defining them is simple. For over time world religions with long histories such as Judaism, Christianity, and Islam produce variation. There is no single "community of Judaism" or a uniform "community of Christianity" or a single monolithic Islam. The diversity of what Muslims understand as Islam has made its mark. In today's terms, Christianity encompasses Roman Catholic, Orthodox, and Protestant divisions, among many; and the same is so for diversity within Judaism, ancient and modern, and Islam in its complex history. Most people are aware that the communities of Judaism are divided, in modern times, into Reform and Orthodox Judaisms, among many, and Orthodox Judaism is itself diverse. Islam is divided into Sunni and Shiite branches with their various permutations.

In this book we will learn more about Reform and Orthodox Judaisms, Sunni and Shiite Islams, as well as the range of Christianities that have taken shape over time and shaped the character of Western civilization. Each community of a given religious tradition has its own narrative or worldview, its own distinguishing patterns of conduct or way of life, and its own account of itself as a social entity. Judaism, Christianity, and Islam each constitutes a species of the genus—religion—and each furthermore yields many subspecies.

The Religion Factor in Western Civilization

Religion has written much of the history of the West. Decisive events—the Crusades, the expansion of Europe to the Western hemisphere—invoked religious goals. The Crusades meant to recover for Christianity the once-Christian lands conquered by Islam. The goal of bringing Christianity to unknown lands animated the great explorations, Columbus to the west, the Portuguese to the east. Religious conflict provoked wars within Europe, for example, the wars of the Reformation.

Religion shaped the arts and architecture, the music and literature and culture and politics of the West. The Bible supplied facts deemed beyond dispute, and much of science began inquiry in dialogue with the Judeo-Christian Scriptures. The narrative of religions sustained long-term enterprises, for example, the building of cathedrals that required centuries of construction. Because great cathedral builders conceived of light as representing God, they struggled to admit light to their massive foundations. Representing scriptural narrative through light and shadow brought into being the sublime works of stained glass and fabric art characteristic of medieval architecture. Islamic mosques formed a principal medium of aesthetic experimentation and religious expression as well. Illuminated manuscripts of Judaic holy books formed a counterpart in Judaism to the aesthetic adventure of Christianity and Islam: representing God in the media of culture.

Learning—philosophy and science and technology alike—depended on the sponsorship of religious institutions, and universities began under religious auspices. The intellectual life of the West not only has been carried out by Christian, Judaic, and Islamic faithful. It also has been nourished by their convictions about God, the rationality conveyed by God's self-revelation in Scripture, and what God requires of the social order.

Religion and Politics in the West

Much of this book focuses on the shaping by religion of the institutions and ideas of politics in the West. That is because politics—the theory of legitimate violence—appeals to religious belief and narrative for legitimacy. We realize that many peoples have commonly defined themselves by appeal to shared religious loyalties, Orthodox Christianity in Romania, Greece, and Bulgaria; Roman Catholic Christianity in Hungary, Austria, Ireland, and Poland, for example. And in Islam and Judaism, no distinction was drawn between politics and religion, between institutions of this-worldly power and those that exercised the other-worldly kind.

Modern times brought new, secular approaches to both culture and politics. Until the eighteenth century, religion was the single decisive force shaping politics, culture, and society in the West. After that time, religion met competition from other sources of sensibility and intellect. In many parts of the world, and in much of the West, religion has more than held its own, and it remains a principal part of the consciousness and normative conduct of the West. Churches, synagogues, and mosques abound, and appeal to stories told by religion and imperatives imposed thereby define important components of the social order of the West. But even if religion played no role whatsoever in today's Western politics and culture, the landscape is studded with enduring monuments to its power. There is no understanding the world as we know it today without a clear account of what religion has been and has done, what it is and does today.

That is because, as a matter of fact, after two centuries of secularization, religion continues to fuel the engine of contemporary politics. Certain conceptions of jihad encourage battle with the Christian West and the state of Israel, and some leading figures in Islam preach anti-Semitism. Christianity fuels Serb attacks on Bosnian Muslims and defines issues of public debate in the United States and many other nations. Judaism forms one of the principal sources for the aspiration of the Jewish people to maintain the Jewish state, the State of Israel. But it also has inspired irredentist policies espoused by some in the conflict with Palestine. Similarly, Islam forms the ideological basis for the Shiite state of Iran, not to mention the founding of Pakistan in the division of the British Raj in India. Many of the intractable conflicts of the age—Islam and Hinduism in Pakistan and India, Hinduism and Buddhism in Sri Lanka, Islam and Christianity in the Balkans, the culture wars of the United States—

derive from religious convictions or at least use the vocabulary of religion. Nationality, religion, and culture converge and cause conflict.

That is not to assign to religion the unique position in shaping strife over public policy. For the past two centuries, Christianity, Judaism, and Islam, the three religions of Western civilization, have contended with secularism, nationalism, Nazism and Communism, Socialism and humanism, and other definitive bodies of social thought. But after seventy-five years of state-sponsored atheism, religion renews itself in Russia and the other former Soviet states. Orthodox Christianity survived in Russia, and Islam in Kazakhstan and the other Islamic possessions of the former USSR. So the fact remains that after two hundred years of struggle, in modern times religion has held its own and continues to shape the politics and culture of much of the West.

The Approach of This Book

This is a volume of description. We mean to give just the facts. We answer questions that describe, analyze, and interpret those facts. The editor and authors of this book engage in no act of advocacy in behalf of (or against) religion or a particular religion. The sole norm we espouse is an intellectual one: to tell the tale as objectively and descriptively as we are able. All concur that we cannot fully understand Western civilization without engaging with the religion factor, past and present, in its history and contemporary life too. We, therefore, have selected high points in the history of Western civilization that are defined by the religions of that civilization, Judaism, Christianity, and Islam. These define many of the decisive moments in Western civilization, from the beginning to the present.

That leads to the question systematically answered in these pages. What, specifically, are the religious traditions that have shaped the West? They are, in order of appearance, Judaism, Christianity, and Islam, covered in chapters 3, 4, and 5. And how are we to identify principal events in which those traditions made history? Here we have selected critical chapters in the history of the culture of the West, its philosophy, mysticism, and in the politics of the West as defined by competing religions, both in history and today. Finally, what role has religion defined for itself in the world today?

To answer those questions, this textbook accomplishes two tasks. First, we define the classical forms of Judaism, Christianity, and Islam. Since

Christianity has constituted the principal religious force in the shaping of the history of the West, we lay somewhat heavier emphasis on its history and cultural role than on those of Judaism or Islam, but Islam and Judaism do figure as well. Second, we outline some of the important points at which these religions have directly intersected with one another in the West.

Parts One and Two

The order of the presentation is simple and logical. After William Green's definition, in part 1, of the terms "religious," "foundations," West, and "civilization," in part 2, we present three systematic accounts of the origins and main traits of Judaism, Christianity, and Islam. These chapters presuppose no detailed knowledge of those religious traditions.

Part Three

Then we turn to the chapters in Western history written by the three religions in dialogue on common interests. They have shared a totalizing approach to society, philosophy, and mysticism, and the commonalities are portrayed. In philosophy they argued with one another about a common agendum of problems of thought. In mysticism they shared the direct encounter with God that mystics seek, and they told one another what they had learned, respectively, about meeting with God in prayer and in meditation. We want to know how in the past they have worked together and enriched one another. We invoke the medieval dialogue in philosophy as a model for the relationships, in the twenty-first century, of the three religions of the West.

Part Four

From shared cultural agenda, we proceed in part 4 to principal moments of conflict in politics among Christianity and Islam and Judaism, with special attention to the Crusades, the contest over Spain, the Islamic-Christian struggle for the Balkans, and the political contention among the three religions of the West in modern times, represented by issues of religion and nationalism: Christian imperialism, Judaic Zionism, and Islamic Jihad.

Part Five

We turn in part 5 to what has happened in modern times in Christianity and Judaism, and to the response of Islam to the challenges of modernity. Here Christianity defined the pattern, in the Renaissance, Reformation, and Enlightenment, with Judaism in Europe responding to the Christian model. Islam in the West has now begun to encounter those problems of modern sensibility and culture that Christianity and then Judaism have confronted for two hundred years.

Part Six

We conclude part 6, with accounts of how Judaism, Christianity, and Islam have formed theories of "the other," their competition. We answer the question, how has this religion thought about the neighboring one(s). We pay specific attention to efforts at forming a theological foundation for religious toleration in Judaism, Christianity, and Islam.

In this way we present the principal religions of the West in two ways. First, we see them as religious systems, each with its own traits and history. These we define and outline. Second, we trace how their interactions have shaped important chapters in the history of Western civilization. These two distinct tasks, the editor and authors hope, will make this textbook serviceable in courses in religion, history, Western civilization, and humanities courses in general education programs.

Each chapter contains a few study questions to focus class discussion.

As between exposition of topics and presenting the subject through primary sources, we have given the authors of the chapters leeway. The participants have presented their topics in more than a single way. Some authors stress systematic exposition, others illustration through sources. All the chapters contain both expositions and illustrations. But the proportions vary.

The vocabulary of the academic study of religion serves in these pages. One special use requires attention, the use of the word *myth*. Religions may express their truth claims in philosophical ways, as generalizations about God, or they may state those same claims in narrative form. In the academic study of religion, we use the word *myth* to mean "truth in narrative form," and not to mean "untruth."

Acknowledgments

Professors Neusner and Chilton used this book in its initial form as the textbook for their joint course, Religion 123, "Religious Foundations of Western Civilization," at Bard College in 2003–04 Semester Two. Professor Green presented the opening lecture. The students read the chapters in manuscript. They were asked to supply comments on each chapter, which the several authors considered in producing the final draft of their chapters, respectively. The students also alerted us to problems of clarity and accessibility that we otherwise would have missed. Not only so, but our colleague in the study of Islam at Bard College, Professor Nerina Rustomji, participated in three of the sessions, while other members of the Program in Religion and other programs at Bard College helped as called upon. Bard's Institute of Advanced Theology sponsored several public events in connection with the experimental course. Professors Karen Sullivan (medieval literature), Leon Botstein (musicology), Daniel Berthold (philosophy), Paul Murray (religion), and John Pruitt (cinema) helped us with the medieval and modern units of the course. The book reflects our experience in teaching a one-semester course on the foundations of its sixteen chapters.

The fact that such an investment of resources would go into this project attests to the commitment of Bard College to the academic study of religion. This textbook aims at realizing Bard College's larger goal of serving the public interest through the enlightened negotiation of social and cultural differences. Simply put, this college, like its counterparts through American higher education in the liberal arts, means to foster tolerance even when fiercely held conviction concerning God is concerned.

Jacob Neusner

PART ONE

DEFINING THE TERMS

CHAPTER 1

What Do We Mean by "Religion" and "Western Civilization"?

William Scott Green

On September 11, 2001, nineteen men hijacked four American airplanes and engaged in devastating terrorist attacks against basic governmental and commercial institutions and centers of the United States. The attacks resulted in the destruction of the World Trade Center in New York City and caused extensive damage to the Pentagon, the center of the American military. The fourth plane, which was forced down by American passengers, was believed to be destined for the White House. The attacks murdered more than three thousand people, from nearly all backgrounds and persuasions. All the evidence suggests that the people who sponsored and carried out the attacks did so because they deeply oppose what they see as the behavior and values of America and the West and that their opposition in significant ways was motivated by, and expressed in the religious language of, a particular strain of Islam. The events of September 11 made people in America and the West look at ourselves afresh. They show us how and why the questions in this book matter to our lives today.

In the aftermath of the September 11 attacks, the American author Robert Stone wrote in the *New York Times:* "We witnessed . . . the violent assault of one narrative system upon another. . . . The power of narrative is shattering, overwhelming. We are the stories we believe; we are who we believe we are."[1] Stone suggests that the events of September 11 are the result of divergent stories that recount and explain who America and the West and their enemies "are." That is, the events of September 11 are the result of conflicting narratives about our conceptions of ourselves and about the meaning of the way we conduct our lives. Stone's observations raise the key questions this book and this course intend to examine.

Because the "narrative" of the West is under assault, it is important to ask what is at stake in that narrative. What is Western civilization, and what is the story that it tells? Equally, since the assault on that civilization is in some basic sense religious, what is the place of religion in Western civilization? In what sense can we say religion grounds a Western worldview? Finally, since the assault on the Western narrative system was made in the name of Islam, how does Islam fit into the framework of Western civilization and Western religion?

Defining "Western Civilization"

To guide us in thinking about the meaning of Western civilization, we turn to Professor Samuel P. Huntington, whose book, *The Clash of Civilizations and the Remaking of World Order,* is among the most important meditations on the nature of today's global politics. Professor Huntington's basic theme is "that culture and cultural identities, which at the broadest level are civilization identities, are shaping the patterns of cohesion, disintegration, and conflict in the post–Cold War world."[2]

Huntington explains that we should think of civilization as an integrated "cultural entity." He writes, "Civilizations are the biggest 'we' within which we feel culturally at home as distinguished from all the other 'thems' out there." A civilization, therefore, grounds peoples' sense of who they are and provides a framework that helps them distinguish themselves from others. In Stone's terms, we might think of a civilization as people's most comprehensive story, their "big picture," what Huntington calls their "broadest level of identification." Being part of a civilization, therefore, is fundamental to being human. Huntington notes that civilizations are adaptable and long-lasting, though they can disappear. He explains that "the crucial distinctions among human groups concern their values, beliefs, institutions, and social structures, not their physical size, head shapes, and skin colors."[3] Therefore, civilizations transcend race, ethnicity, governments, and nations. He suggests that there are eight "major contemporary civilizations": Sinic, Japanese, Hindu, Islamic, Orthodox, Western, Latin American, and African. Of special importance for this book. Huntington points out that "religion is a central defining characteristic of civilizations."[4] In the pages to come, we will explore the meaning of this last generalization for the West.

What, precisely, is the meaning of "West" or "Western civilization"? Huntingon astutely observes that although "the West" sounds like a geographic location, it cannot be. Unlike "north" and "south," "east" and "west" have no fixed reference points. They are relative locations. Rather, "historically, Western civilization is European civilization," and "the West" refers to what was once called "Western Christendom." In modern times, "Western civilization is Euroamerican or north Atlantic civilization." This designation will serve as a useful guide for the rest of our study.

A useful corollary to Huntington is supplied by an author whose work we will read in the next chapter. Professor Harold Berman, perhaps the leading scholar of the Western legal tradition, has views similar to those of Huntington, with some additions particularly useful for this project. Berman's succinct statement follows:

> The West . . . is not to be found by recourse to a compass. . . . The West is, rather, a cultural term, but with a very strong diachronic dimension. It is not, however, simply an idea; it is a community. It implies both a historical structure and a structured history. For many centuries it could be identified very simply as the people of Western Christendom. Indeed, from the eleventh to the fifteenth centuries the community of those people was manifested in their common allegiance to a single spiritual authority, the Church of Rome.
>
> As a historical culture, a civilization, the West is to be distinguished not only from the East but also from "pre-Western" cultures to which it "returned" in various periods of "renaissance." Such returns and revivals are characteristics of the West. They are not to be confused with the models on which they drew for inspiration. "Israel," "Greece," and "Rome" became spiritual ancestors of the West not primarily by a process of survival or succession but primarily by a process of adoption: the West adopted them as ancestors. Moreover, it adopted them selectively—different parts at different times. Cotton Mather was no Hebrew. Erasmus was no Greek. The Roman lawyers of the University of Bologna were no Romans.
>
> Some Roman law, to be sure, survived in the Germanic folklaw and, more important, in the law of the church; some Greek philosophy also survived, also in the church; the Hebrew Bible, of course, survived as the Old

Testament. But such survivals only account for a small part of their influence on Western law, Western philosophy, and Western theology. What accounted for the major part of their influence were the rediscoveries, reexaminations, and receptions of the ancient texts. Even to the extent that the ancient learning may be said to have survived without interruption, it was inevitably transformed. . . .

The West, from this perspective, is not Greece and Rome and Israel but the peoples of Western Europe *turning* to the Greek and Roman and Hebrew texts for inspiration, and *transforming* those texts in ways that would have astonished their authors. Nor, of course, is Islam part of the West, although there were strong Arabic influences on Western philosophy and science—though not on Western legal institutions. . . .

Indeed, each of the ancient ingredients of Western culture was transformed by being mixed with the others. The amazing thing is that such antagonistic elements could be brought together into a single world view. The Hebrew culture would not tolerate Greek philosophy or Roman law; the Greek culture would not tolerate Roman law or Hebrew theology; the Roman culture would not tolerate Hebrew theology, and it resisted large parts of Greek philosophy. Yet the West in the late eleventh and early twelfth centuries combined all three, and thereby transformed each one.[5]

Professor Huntington suggests that "religion is a central defining characteristic of civilizations." He also observes that the West produced no "major religion" and developed a distinctive political system in which national political interests outweigh religious ones. If both of these statements are accurate, how can religion be a foundation of Western civilization? To address this question, let us turn first to Professor Huntington's important observation about politics and religion in Western civilization. He explains:

The great political ideologies of the twentieth century include liberalism, socialism, anarchism, corporatism, Marxism, communism, social democracy, conservatism, nationalism, fascism, and Christian democracy. They all share one thing in common: they are the products of Western civilization. No other civilization has generated a significant political ideology. The West, however, has never generated a major religion. The great religions of the world are all products of non-Western civilizations and, in most cases, antedate Western civilization. As the world moves out of its Western phase, the ideologies which typified late Western civilization decline, and their place is taken by religions and other culturally based forms of identity and commitment. The Westphalian separation of religion and international politics, an idiosyncratic product of Western civilization is coming to an end, and religion, as Edward Mortimer suggests, is "increasingly likely to intrude into international affairs." The intracivilizational clash of political ideas spawned by the West is being supplanted by an international clash of culture and religion.[6]

The Peace of Westphalia, 1648, ended the religious wars of Europe[7] and led to the emergence of the network of nation-states that define the modern West. After Westphalia, Europeans fought one another over national rather than theological concerns, secular political issues rather than religious ones. That is why the West produced political ideologies rather than a "major religion." Professor Huntington calls this "separation of religion and international politics"—what we might call the distinction between the religious and the secular—"an idiosyncratic product of Western civilization." In other words, it is both distinctive and specific to the West.

If all this is so, then in what sense can we say that Western civilization has a religious foundation? If the dominant intellectual and cultural product of Western civilization are secular ideologies rather than religious ones, and if the political and social structures of the West transcend religious structures, what sense does it make to say that religion founds Western civilization at all? Is the distinction between religion and secularity—which is distinctive to the West—a product of religion? Let us turn to these specific issues.

Defining Religion

To begin to answer them, it is important to be clear about what we mean by "religion." This term is so fundamental to the way Americans imagine our lives, that achieving some clarity about it is essential if we are to achieve useful results in our study. For this project, we will use the definition of religion developed by the anthropologist Melford Spiro. He defines religion as "an institution consisting of culturally patterned interaction with culturally postulated superhuman beings."[8] Let us unpack this definition to see what is at stake in it.

The definition speaks of "superhuman beings." A superhuman being is a being more powerful than humans but not necessarily qualitatively different from them. Superhuman is not the same as supernatural. A superhuman being can do things for, and to, humans.

Next, the definition speaks not of random superhuman beings, but of beings that are "culturally postulated." That is a concise academic way

of saying that different cultures, or different civilizations, envision different kinds of superhuman beings. For instance, some cultures envision
multiple superhuman beings; others envision only one. In some cultures,
people worship deceased ancestors; in others, it would make no sense to
do so. "Culturally postulated" is a way of saying that people cannot worship a being that everyone in the world they inhabit says is nonsensical.
The superhuman beings that people worship must fit within and reflect
the values of the culture.

According to the definition, religion entails a "culturally patterned"
interaction with the superhuman beings. This means that just as the
superhuman beings are conditioned by the cultures from which they
spring or in which people live, so too the ways of interacting with those
superhuman beings are conditioned by those cultures. Interaction can
mean a range of things. Interaction can be speech or ethical action. It can
be prayer or obedience. It can be anguish or contemplation. The gods are
known through such interaction. When Spiro's definition says "culturally
patterned interaction," it means a kind of interaction that people find
plausible and sensible. For example, in Western civilization, it does not
make sense to imagine people having sexual relations with God. But in
ancient Greece, the gods were believed to assume earthly forms, impreg-
nate humans, and produce people who are half god and half human.
Having sex with a god is a perfectly legitimate kind of interaction, but it
is culturally patterned for ancient Greece, not for Western civilization.
How people imagine their gods will interact with them, and what their
gods can expect from them, has much to do with how a religion can shape
a civilization.

For our purposes, Spiro's definition is important for two reasons.
First, it acknowledges that religions must fit and reflect the cultures in
which they exist. It does not suppose that religion looks the same
everywhere, any more than civilizations are the same everywhere.
Second, it uses the concept of "superhuman being" as the variable that
distinguishes religion from not-religion, from politics or philosophy, for
instance. In this definition, religion is not the same as the approach to
life one values most highly. If people structure their lives around ideas
or philosophies that do not involve superhuman beings, they are living
secular, not religious, lives. So when we ask about the religious foundations of Western civilization, we are asking how the interactions
between people and their deities shaped the values and institutions of
the culture.[9]

The Biblical Foundations of Religion in the West

Following on Spiro's definition, we can refine our inquiry to ask, "How do Western ideas of, and human interactions with, God shape the Western idea of the distinction between religion and state?"

To begin to answer that question, we must acknowledge that in Western civilization, religion is fundamentally and resolutely biblical. The foundation of religion in the West is the Hebrew Bible, known in Judaism as *Tanakh*, in Christianity as the Old Testament, and in Islam as *Tawrat*.[10] The Hebrew Bible depicts God's relationship to the People of Israel and Israel's interactions with God. It contains various kinds of writing. The Torah (the Pentateuch, which includes the books of Genesis, Exodus, Leviticus, Numbers, and Deuteronomy) recounts Israel's early history and contains the core of Jewish religious practice. Historical books[11] describe Israel's life in its land and the behavior of its kings. The works of the prophets[12] contain sayings and visions attributed to Israel's inspired preachers. Other books contain wisdom sayings, stories of the Jews in exile, and the account of their return to the land of Israel.[13] As a whole, the books of the Hebrew Bible tell the story of God's creation of the cosmos, selection of Israel, redemption of Israel from Egypt, revelation of commandments in the desert, the conquest of the land of Israel, formation of a unified monarchy under King David, a civil war in Israel, the destruction of part of Israel by Assyria, the destruction of the Temple (the center of Israel's worship) in 586 B.C.E. by the Babylonians, the return of the Jews in the Persian period to the Land of Israel to rebuild the destroyed temple (538–515 B.C.E.).

The contents of the Hebrew Bible reach far back in antiquity. Versions of all of its books except Esther were found among the Dead Sea Scrolls; so the manuscripts of the Hebrew Bible can be dated at least to the first century C.E., and some are two centuries earlier. The contents of the Hebrew Bible are even older. Although it strains historical credibility to trace Israel's tradition to the figure of Abraham, ca. around 2000 B.C.E., the foundation of the book of Deuteronomy was likely written in 621 B.C.E., and the contours of biblical monotheism were established by one of Israel's greatest prophets, Second Isaiah, by 540 B.C.E. In contrast, Socrates was tried in 399 B.C.E., and Plato and Aristotle followed later, more than two centuries after Deuteronomy and about 140 years after Second Isaiah. A charitable but responsible reckoning could take Israel's tradition back at least three thousand years, if we count to the time of King David.

The Hebrew Bible is Judaism's scripture, and Judaism both shaped and was shaped by the Hebrew Bible's contents. Early traditions of Israel grounded Judaism's worldview; and throughout antiquity Jews transformed those traditions into texts that have been used in Judaic worship and study unto today.[14] In this sense Judaism is the oldest continuous religion in the West. The scriptures of Christianity and Islam contain additional writings, the New Testament and the Qur'an, respectively,[15] which produce interpretations of the Hebrew Bible that are different from Judaism's and from one another's. But both Christianity and Islam accept the contents of Judaism's scripture as part of their own religious legacy and heritage. Both religions presuppose Judaism and its scripture, morphology, and rituals, even as they read that scripture differently and adopted novel forms and religious behaviors. Christianity and Islam are inconceivable without their Judaic foundation. In this precise and focused way, Western civilization draws on Judaism as it does on no other religion.

How does the Hebrew Bible depict God and the way humans should interact with the deity? In Spiro's terms, how does Israelite culture "postulate" its superhuman being, and what are some key elements of their "culturally patterned interactions" with that deity? For the purposes of our work, the answer comes in two parts. First, the Hebrew Bible supposes that there exists only one deity, who has created the cosmos and humanity. Second, it envisions that deity as willingly limiting his powers to enter into a relationship with the creatures he created. In the culture of the Hebrew Bible's world, God does not reveal divine teaching to humanity at random or as a whole. Rather, in the Hebrew Bible's worldview, there is one God, with one message, which the deity communicates through a single community. Thus, the sole deity, the creator of heaven and earth, selects Israel as the medium of divine communication to humanity. In other words, there is only one god, and that is Israel's. From a biblical perspective, the fate of the world in some fundamental way depends on and is a function of the relationship between God and Israel.

The form of the relationship between God and Israel is the covenant, an agreement in which God and Israel stipulate their obligations to each other. There are multiple covenants in the Hebrew Bible. In Genesis 17, God establishes the identity of Israel by entering into an "eternal covenant" with Abraham and his descendants. In Exodus 20:1-17, God defines the character of Israel as a covenanted community through the revelation of the Ten Commandments, which address both how Israel is to relate to God and how the Israelites are to relate to one another. Exodus 24 reports Israel's assent to participation in the covenant. The covenants thus establish both the nature of the divine-human relationship and the conditions of legitimate human community in the created order. The covenants make clear that God and Israel, and therefore humanity, are unfulfilled in isolation. Interrelatedness is the distinguishing mark of God's created order.

Professor Daniel Elazar spells out the implications of the Hebrew Bible's covenant agreements for the distinction between religion and politics that characterizes Western civilization.

> The covenants of the Bible are the founding covenants of Western civilization. Perforce, they have to do with God. They have their beginnings in the need to establish clear and binding relationships between God and humans and among humans, relationships that must be understood to be political far more than theological in character, designed to establish lines of authority, distributions of power, bodies politic, and systems of law. It is indeed the genius of the idea and its biblical source that it seeks both to legitimize political life and to direct it into the right paths; to use theopolitical relationships to build a bridge between heaven and earth—and there is nothing more earthly than politics even in its highest form—without letting either swallow up the other.
>
> The covenant idea has within it the seeds of modern constitutionalism in that it emphasizes the mutually accepted limitations in the power of all parties to it, a limitation not inherent in nature but involving willed concessions. This idea of limiting power is of first importance in the biblical worldview and for humanity as a whole since it helps explain why an omnipotent God does not exercise his omnipotence in the affairs of humans. In covenanting with humans, God at least partially withdraws from controlling their lives. He offers humans freedom under the terms of the covenant, retaining the covenantal authority to reward or punish the consequences of that freedom at some future date. By the same token, humans who bind themselves through the covenant accept its limits in Puritan terms, abandoning natural for federal liberty in order to live up to the terms of their covenants. Beyond that, the leaders of the people are limited in their governmental powers to serving the people under the terms of the covenant. Thus the idea of constitutional or limited government is derived from the idea of the covenant.[16]

11

To translate Elazar's observations into the terms of Spiro's definition of religion: The culture of the Hebrew Bible postulates a superhuman being who limits his powers in order to relate to his creation, and the Bible's cultural pattern of interaction with that superhuman being is humanity's free assent to the relationship and to the consequences for violating it. The covenantal relationship assumes that Israelites have a significant measure of control over themselves and, consequently, that their actions and motivations matter. Through concrete, this-worldly actions—moral and physical, ethical and ritual, individual and communal—Israel nurtures and maintains the covenant. This means, as Elazar suggests, that the Bible conceives the relationship between humans and God to be one of mutuality and choice, not of force or coercion. For the covenant to work, humans must be free to enter into it. For humans to be free, God must restrain his control over their lives and activities.

The idea that God restrains the exercise of omnipotence in order to allow humans the freedom to respond to God may help explain why the Hebrew Bible—and in this case the New Testament as well—do not imagine that religion must exercise political power in order to achieve its aims. Neither the Hebrew Bible, nor Judaism, nor Christianity assumes that the religious life requires political control as well.[17] The Torah, for example, depicts a cult without a kingdom—a pure religion in its own realm. In the Torah's narrative, the Israelites receive their revelation from God in the desert, which is the opposite of governed territory. Although they are a community and a nation, they constitute neither a state nor a kingdom. Indeed, the Torah barely mentions a king for Israel, and it assumes that the monarch will consult the Torah before acting. In the texts, Israel's king plays no role in Israel's worship or cult. More important, the Hebrew Bible as a whole supposes that although God can be king, the Israelite king cannot be a god. If the king could be god, his power would be absolute, not limited. In addition to this evidence from the Torah, the books of Esther and Daniel both assume that it is possible for a Jew to be a loyal subject of a pagan king and remain true to his or her religious convictions. The Hebrew Bible draws a clear distinction between the institutions and realms of religion and politics. Jesus' famous admonition (Matt 22:21), "Then pay Caesar what is due to Caesar, and pay God what is due to God," assumes and applies—but does not argue for—the Hebrew Bible's distinction. It assumes that Caesar is not (and cannot be) God and thus presupposes this biblical distinction.

Religion and Secularism:
Two Realms of Western Civilization

The Hebrew Bible's distinction between the realms of religion and politics was fundamental to Christianity, the dominant religion of Western civilization. As Professor Bernard Lewis points out, Christianity made "secularism"—"the idea that religion and political authority, church and state, are different, and can or should be separated"—fundamental in Western civilization. The idea was justified not only by Jesus' teaching cited above, but also by the experience of Christianity itself.

> For three centuries, Christianity was a persecuted religion—different from, sometimes opposed to, and often oppressed by the state authority. In the course of their long struggle, Christians developed a distinctive institution—the church, with its own laws and courts, its own hierarchy and chain of authority. Throughout Christian history, and in almost all Christian lands, church and state continued to exist side by side as different institutions, each with its own laws and jurisdictions, its own hierarchy and chain of authority. The two may be joined, or, in modern times, separated. Their relationship may be one of cooperation, of confrontation, or of conflict. Sometimes they may be coequal, more often one or the other may prevail in a struggle for domination of the polity. In the course of the centuries, Christian jurists and theologians devised or adapted pairs of terms to denote the dichotomy of jurisdiction: sacred and profane, spiritual and temporal, religious and secular, ecclesiastical and lay.[18]

Lewis points out that Islam has a different perspective from that of the Hebrew Bible and Christianity.

> The idea that any group of persons, any kind of activities, any part of human life is in any sense outside the scope of religious law and jurisdiction is alien to Muslim thought. There is, for example, no distinction between canon law and civil law, between the law of the church and the law of the state, crucial in Christian history. There is only a single law, the shari'a, accepted by Muslims as of divine origin and regulating all aspects of human life: civil, commercial, criminal, constitutional, as well as matters more specifically concerned with religion in the limited, Christian sense of that word.[19]

Lewis's description of the differences between Christianity and Islam on the matter of secularism shows how Islam can be Western in the sense that it shares texts with Judaism and Christianity, but also non-Western in its political and legal experience. Islamic teaching, the Qur'an in particular, has a distinct perspective on the biblical heritage that Judaism and Christianity understand differently.

This brings us back to the questions raised at the outset of this chapter: In what sense can we say that Western civilization has a religious foundation? If the dominant intellectual and cultural products of Western civilization are secular ideologies rather than religious ones, and if the political and social structures of the West transcend religious structures, what sense does it make to say that religion founds Western civilization at all? Is the distinction between religion and secularity—which is distinctive to the West—a product of religion? In the readings that follow, Professor Harold Berman, whom we met in the first chapter, addresses precisely these issues. He explains how the Christian distinction between the religious and the secular, which derives from the Hebrew Bible, became institutionalized in Western civilization in the institution of law.

The conversion of the Roman emperor Constantine to Christianity in the fourth century gave Christianity a political power—control of the secular realm—for which its theology had not prepared it and offered no instruction. The uneasy and often cloudy relationship between the religion and state began to achieve clarity in the eleventh century when Pope Gregory VII removed the church from state control and gave it an autonomous existence. As Berman observes, this change led to the development of the institutions of law that have come to define the West.

> Among the peoples of Western Europe in the period prior to the eleventh century, law did not exist as a distinct system of regulation or as a distinct system of thought. Each people had, to be sure, its own legal order, which included occasional legal enactments by central authorities as well as innumerable unwritten legal rules and institutions, both secular and ecclesiastical. A considerable number of individual legal terms and rules had been inherited from the earlier Roman law and could be found in the canons and decrees of local ecclesiastical councils and of individual bishops as well as in some royal legislation and in customary law. Lacking, however, in both the secular and the ecclesiastical spheres, was a clear separation of law from other processes of social control and from other types of intellectual concern. Secular law as a whole was not "disembedded" from general tribal, local, and feudal custom or from the general custom of royal and imperial households. Similarly, the law of the church was largely diffused throughout the life of the church—throughout its structures of authority as well as throughout its theology, its moral precepts, its liturgy—and it, too, was

primarily local and regional and primarily customary rather than central-ized or enacted. There were no professional judges or lawyers. There were no hierarchies of courts.

Also lacking was a perception of law as a distinct "body" of rules and concepts. There were no law schools. There were no great legal texts deal-ing with basic legal categories such as jurisdiction, procedure, crime, con-tract, property, and the other subjects that eventually came to form structural elements in Western legal systems. There were no developed theories of the sources of law, of the relation of divine and natural law to human law, of ecclesiastical law to secular law, of enacted law to custom-ary law, or of the various kinds of secular law—feudal, royal, urban—to one another.

The relatively unsystematized character of legal regulation and the rela-tively undeveloped state of legal science were closely connected with the prevailing political, economic, and social conditions. These included the predominantly local character of tribal, village, and feudal communities; their relatively high degree of economic self-sufficiency; the fusion of authorities within each; the relative weakness of the political and eco-nomic control exercised by the central imperial and royal authorities; the essentially military and religious character of the control exercised by the imperial and royal authorities; and the relative strength of informal com-munity bonds of kinship and soil and of military comradeship.

In the late eleventh, the twelfth, and the early thirteenth centuries a fundamental change took place in Western Europe in the very nature of law both as a political institution and as an intellectual concept. Law became disembedded. Politically, there emerged for the first time strong central authorities, both ecclesiastical and secular, whose control reached down, through delegated officials, from the center to the localities. Partly in connection with that, there emerged a class of professional jurists, including professional judges and practicing lawyers. Intellectually, Western Europe experienced at the same time the creation of its first law schools, the writing of its first legal treatises, the conscious ordering of the huge mass of inherited legal materials, and the development of the concept of law as an autonomous, integrated, developing body of legal principles and procedures.

The combination of these two factors, the political and the intellectual, helped produce modern Western legal systems, of which the first was the new system of canon law of the Roman Catholic Church (then regularly called for the first time *jus canonicum*). It was also at that time divided into "old law" (*jus antiquum*), consisting of earlier texts and canons, and "new law" (*jus novum*), consisting of contemporary legislation and decisions as well as contemporary interpretations of the earlier texts and canons. Against the background of the new system of canon law, and often in rivalry with it, the European kingdoms and other polities began to create their own secular legal systems. At the same time there emerged in most parts of Europe free cities, each with its own governmental and legal institutions, forming a new type of urban law. In addition, feudal (lord-vassal) and manorial (lord-peasant) legal institutions underwent systematization, and a new system of mercantile law was developed to meet the needs of merchants engaged in intercity, interregional, and international trade. The emergence of these systems of feudal law, manorial law, mercantile law, and urban law clearly indicates that not only political and intellectual but also social and economic factors were at work in producing what can only be called a revolutionary development of legal institutions. In other words, the creation of modern legal systems in the late eleventh, twelfth, and early thirteenth centuries was not only an implementation of policies and theories of central elites, but also a response to social and economic changes "on the ground."

Religious factors were at work, as well. The creation of modern legal systems was, in the first instance, a response to a revolutionary change within the church and in the relation of the church to the secular authorities. And here the word *revolutionary* has all the modern connotations of class struggle and violence. In 1075, after some twenty-five years of agitation and propaganda by the papal party, Pope Gregory VII declared the political and legal supremacy of the papacy over the entire Church and the independence of the clergy from secular control. Gregory also asserted the ultimate supremacy of the pope in secular matters, including the authority to depose emperors and kings. The emperor—Henry IV of Saxony—responded with military action. Civil war between the papal and imperial parties raged sporadically throughout Europe until 1122, when a final compromise was reached by a concordat signed in the German city of Worms. In England and Normandy, the Concordat of Bec in 1107 provided a temporary respite, but the matter was not finally resolved there until the martyrdom of Archbishop Thomas Becket in 1170.

The great changes that took place in the life of the Western church and in the relations between the ecclesiastical and the secular authorities during the latter part of the eleventh and the first part of the twelfth centuries have traditionally been called the Hildebrand Reform, or the Gregorian Reform, after the monk Hildebrand, who was a leader of the papal party in the period after 1050 and who ruled as Pope Gregory VII from 1073 to 1085. However, the term "*Reform*" is a serious understatement, reflecting in part the desire of the papal party itself—and of later Roman Catholic historians—to play down the magnitude of the discontinuity between what had gone before and what came after. The original Latin term, *reformatio*, may suggest a more substantial break in continuity by recalling the sixteenth-century Protestant Reformation. Another term used to denote the same era, namely, the Investiture Struggle, is not so much an understatement as an oblique statement: by pointing to the struggle of the papacy to wrest from emperor and kings the power to "invest" bishops with the symbols of their authority, the phrase connects the conflict between the papal and imperial (or royal) parties with the principal slogan of the papal reformers: "the freedom of the church." What was involved ultimately was, in Peter Brown's words, "the disengagement of the two spheres of the sacred and the profane," from which there stemmed a release of energy and creativity analogous to a process of nuclear fission.[20] 21

Berman then explains how Christian religious ideas served as the basis for secular law:

It is impossible to understand the revolutionary quality of the Western legal tradition without exploring its religious dimension. It has been said that the metaphors of the day before yesterday are the analogies of yesterday and the concepts of today. So the eleventh-century legal metaphors were the twelfth-century legal analogies and the thirteenth-century legal concepts. The legal metaphors that lay at the foundation of the legal analogies and concepts were chiefly of a religious nature. They were metaphors of the Last Judgment and of purgatory, of Christ's atonement for Adam's fall, of the transubstantiation of bread and wine in the sacrament of the Eucharist, of the absolution of sins in the sacrament of penance, and of the power of the priesthood "to bind and to loose"—that is, to impose of remit eternal punishment. Other legal metaphors were chiefly feudal, though they had religious overtones—metaphors of honor, of satisfaction for violation of honor, of pledge of faith, of reciprocal bonds of service and protection. All of these metaphors were part of a unified structure of rituals and myths. (The word "myth" is used here not in the old sense of "fable" but rather in the opposite, now widely accepted, sense of "sacred truth.")[22]

What such an exploration shows is that basic institutions, concepts, and values of Western legal systems have their sources in religious rituals, liturgies, and doctrines of the eleventh and twelfth centuries, reflecting new attitudes toward death, sin, punishment, forgiveness, and salvation, as well as new assumptions concerning the relationship of the divine to the human and of faith to reason. Over the intervening centuries, these religious attitudes and assumptions have changed fundamentally, and today their theological sources seem to be in the process of drying up. Yet the legal institutions, concepts, and values that have derived from them still survive, often unchanged. Western legal science is a secular theology, which often makes no sense because its theological presuppositions are no longer accepted.

A bizarre example may shed light on the paradoxes of a legal tradition that has lost contact with its theological sources. If a sane man is convicted of murder and sentenced to death, and thereafter, before the sentence is carried out, he becomes insane, his execution will be postponed until he recovers his sanity. Generally speaking, this is the law in Western countries and in many non-Western countries as well. Why? The historical answer, in the West, is that if a man is executed while he is insane he will not have had the opportunity freely to confess his sins and to take the sacrament of Holy Communion. He must be allowed to recover his sanity before he dies so that his soul will not be condemned to eternal hellfire but will instead have the opportunity to expiate his sins in purgatory and ultimately, at the Last Judgment, to enter the kingdom of heaven. But where none of this is believed, why keep the insane man alive until he recovers, and then kill him?

The example is, perhaps, of minor importance in itself; but what it illustrates is that the legal systems of all Western countries, and of all non-Western countries that have come under the influence of Western law, are a secular residue of religious attitudes and assumptions which historically found expression first in the liturgy and rituals and doctrine of the church, and thereafter in the institutions and concepts and values of the law. When these historical roots are not understood, many parts of the law appear to lack any underlying source of vitality. . . .

The Western law of crimes emerged from a belief that justice in and of itself, justice *an sich*, requires that a violation of a law be paid for by a penalty, and that the penalty should be appropriate to the violation. The system of various prices to be paid for various violations—which exists in all societies—was thought to justify itself; it was justice—it was the very justice of God. This idea was reflected not only in criminal law but in all branches of the new canon law from the twelfth century on, and it was reflected more and more in the various branches of the new secular legal systems that began to develop contemporaneously. Contracts, it was said, must be kept, and if they were not, a price must be paid for their breach. Torts must be remedied by damages equivalent to the injury. Property rights must be restored by those who had violated them. These and similar principles became so deeply embedded in the consciousness—indeed, in the sacred values—of Western society that it became hard to imagine a legal order founded on different kinds of principles and values. Yet contemporary non-Western cultures do have legal orders founded on different kinds of principles and values, and so did European culture prior to the eleventh and twelfth centuries. In some legal orders, ideas of fate and honor prevail, of vengeance and reconciliation. In others, ideas of covenant and community dominate; in still others, ideas of deterrence and rehabilitation.

Western concepts of law are in their origins, and there in their nature, intimately bound up with distinctively Western theological and liturgical concepts of the atonement and of the sacraments. The new church holiday, All Souls' Day, introduced in the eleventh century, symbolized Western man's vision of the Last Judgment as a universal "Law Day," when all souls that have ever lived are to come before Christ the Judge to account for their sins and to be eternally convicted or acquitted. On this foundation, there was built a new conception of purgatory: baptized Christians who had died penitent could be assured that their natural propensity to sin was already forgiven, and that their actual sins would be fully expiated by proportional punishment in this life and the next, prior to the final day. Christ, in this conception, was no longer seen primarily as the Judge but as the divine Brother whose sacrifice on the cross served to reconcile God and man. The new emphasis on atonement was linked, in turn, with a new symbolism in the celebration of the sacrament of the Eucharist: the performance of certain acts and the utterance of certain words by the priest were considered to effectuate the transformation of the bread into the spiritual body of Christ. Thus the atonement, with its paradoxical consequence of divine forgiveness and divine punishment, was repeatedly reenacted and incorporated in the lives of the faithful. With divine justice so understood, it seemed to be a natural step to create a parallel concept of human justice. As God rules through law, so ecclesiastical and secular authorities, ordained by him, declare legal principles and impose appropriate sanction and remedies for their violation. They cannot look directly into men's souls, as God can, but they can find ways to approximate his judgment.[23]

Finally, Berman shows how Protestant Christianity appropriated fundamental ideas of the Hebrew Bible and the New Testament and made them applicable to the secular law and ideologies of the modern West:

The Lutheran Reformation, and the revolution of the Berman principalities which embodied it, broke the Roman Catholic dualism of ecclesiastical and secular law by delegalizing the church. Where Lutheranism succeeded, the church came to be conceived as invisible, apolitical, alegal; and the only sovereignty, the only law (in the political sense), was that of the secular kingdom or principality. It was just before this time, in fact, that Machiavelli had used the word "state" in a new way, to signify the purely secular social order. The Lutheran reformers were in one sense Machiavellians: they were skeptical of man's power to create a human law which would reflect eternal law, and explicitly denied that it was the task of the church to develop human law. This Lutheran skepticism made

107

possible the emergence of a theory of law—legal positivism—which treats the law of the state as morally neutral, a means and not an end, a device for manifesting the policy of the sovereign and for securing obedience to it. But the secularization of law and the emergence of a positivist theory of law are only one side of the story of the contribution of the Lutheran Reformation to the Western legal tradition. The other side is equally important: by freeing law from theological doctrine and from direct ecclesiastical influence, the Reformation enabled it to undergo a new and brilliant development. In the words of the great German jurist and historian Rudolf Sohn, "Luther's Reformation was a renewal not only of faith but also of the world: both the world of spiritual life and world of law."[24]

The key to the renewal of law in the West from the sixteenth century on was the Lutheran concept of the power of the individual, by God's grace, to change nature and to create new social relations through the exercise of his will. The Lutheran concept of the individual will become central to the development of the modern law of property and contract. To be sure, there had been an elaborate and sophisticated law of property and of contract, both in the church and in the mercantile community, for some centuries, but in Lutheranism its focus was changed. Old rules were recast in a new ensemble. Nature became property. Economic relations became contract. Conscience became will and intent. The last testament, which in the earlier Catholic tradition had been primarily a means of saving souls by charitable gifts, became primarily a means of controlling social and economic relations. By the naked expression of their will, their intent, testators could dispose of their property after death, and entrepreneurs could arrange their business relations by contract. The property and contract rights so created were held to be sacred and inviolable, so long as they did not contravene conscience. Conscience gave them their sanctity. And so the secularization of the state, in the restricted sense of the removal of ecclesiastical controls from it, was accompanied by a spiritualization, and even sanctification, of property and contract.

Therefore it is not true to say that Lutheranism placed no limits on the political power of the absolute monarchs who ruled Europe in the sixteenth century. The development of positive law was conceived to rest ultimately upon the prince alone, but it was presupposed that in exercising his will he would respect the individual consciences of his subjects, and that meant respecting also their property and contract rights. This presupposition rested—precariously, to be sure—upon four centuries of history in which the church had succeeded in Christianizing law to a remarkable extent, given the level of the cultural life of the Germanic peoples in the beginning. Thus a Lutheran positivism which separates law from morals, denies the lawmaking role, and finds ultimate sanction of law in political coercion nevertheless assumes the existence of a Christian conscience among the people and state governed by Christian rulers.

A slightly later form of Protestantism, Calvinism, also had profound effects upon the development of Western law, especially in England and America. The Puritans carried forward the Lutheran concept of sanctity of the individual conscience and also, in law, the sanctity of the individual will as reflected in property and contract rights. But they emphasized two elements that were subordinated in Lutheranism: first, a belief in the duty of Christians generally, and not merely Christian rulers, to reform the world:[25] and second, a belief in the local congregations, under its elected minister and elders, as the seat of truth—a "fellowship of active believers" higher than any political authority.[26] The active Puritan congregations, bent on reforming the world, were ready to defy the highest powers of church and of state in asserting their faith, and they did so on grounds of individual conscience, also appealing to divine law, to the Mosaic law of the Old Testament, and to natural-law concepts embodied in the medieval legal tradition. As the early Christian martyrs had founded the church by their disobedience to Roman law, so the seventeenth-century Puritans, including men like John Hampden, John Lilburne, Walter Udall, and William Penn, by their open disobedience to English law laid the foundations for the English and American law of civil rights and civil liberties as expressed in the respective constitutions of the two countries: Freedom of speech and press, free exercise of religion, the privilege against self-incrimination, the Independence of the jury from judicial dictation, the right not be imprisoned without cause, and many other such rights and freedoms.[27] Calvinists congregationalism also provided the religious basis for the modern concepts of social contract and government by consent of the governed.[28]

Puritanism in England and America, and Pietism, its counterpart on the European continent, were the last great movements within the institutional church to influence the development of Western law in any fundamental sense. In the eighteenth and nineteenth centuries both the Roman Catholic Church and the various Lutheran denominations continued, of course, to exert pressures upon law in various directions. Undoubtedly, prophetic Christianity continued to play an extremely important part in bringing about law reform—for example, in the abolition of slavery, in the protection of labor, and in the promotion of welfare legislation generally. And undoubtedly, on the other side, organized religion continued to support the status quo, whatever it happened to be. But the significant factor in this regard—in the nineteenth century and even more in the twentieth—was the very gradual reduction of traditional religion to the level of a personal, private matter, without public influence on legal development, while other belief systems—new secular religions (ideologies, "isms")—were raided to the level of passionate faiths for which people collectively were willing not only to die but also to live new lives.

It was the American and French revolutions that set the stage for the new secular religions—that is, for pouring into secular political and social movements the religious psychology as well as many of the religious ideas that had previously been expressed in various forms of Catholicism and Protestantism. At first a kind of religious orthodoxy was preserved by means of deistic philosophy—which, however, had little of that psychology which is the heart of religious faith. What was religious, in fact, about the great revolutionary minds of the late eighteenth and nineteenth centuries—men like Rousseau or Jefferson—was not their belief in God but their belief in Man, individual Man, his Nature, his Reason, his Rights. The political and social philosophies that sprang from the Enlightenment were religions because they ascribed ultimate meaning and sanctity to the individual mind—and also, it must be added immediately, to the nation. The age of individualism and rationalism was also the age of nationalism: the individual was a citizen, and public opinion turned out to be not the opinion of mankind but the opinion of Frenchmen, the opinion of Germans, the opinion of Americans.

Individualism, rationalism, nationalism—Triune Deity of Democracy—found legal expression in the exaltation of the role of the legislature and consequent reduction (except in the United States) of the law-creating role of judiciary; in the freeing of individual actions from public controls, especially in the economic sphere; in the demand for codification of criminal and civil law; in the effort to make predictable the legal consequences of individual actions, again especially in the economic sphere. These "jural postulates" (as Roscoe Pound would have called them)[29] were considered to be not only useful but also just, and not only just but also part of the natural order of the universe. Life itself was thought to derive its meaning and purpose from these and related principles of legal rationality, whose historical sources in theological doctrines of natural law and of human reason are evident.

Liberal democracy was the first great secular religion in Western history—the first ideology which became divorced from traditional Christianity and at the same time took over from traditional Christianity both it sense of the sacred and some of its major values. But in becoming a secular religion, liberal democracy was very soon confronted with a rival: revolutionary socialism. And when, after a century of revolutionary activity throughout Europe, communism ultimately seized power in Russia in 1917, its doctrines had acquired the sanctity of authoritative revelation and its leadership the charisma of high priests. Moreover, the Communist Party had the intimacy, on the one hand, and the austerity, on the other, of a monastic order. It is not accidental that during the purges after World War II, loyal Communists in Europe used to say, "There is no salvation outside the Party."

The jural postulates of socialism, though they differ in many respects from those of liberal democracy, show a common ancestry in Christianity. The Soviet Moral Code of the Builder of Communism, for example, which Soviet school children must learn by heart and which is taken as a basis for Soviet legal policy, contains such principles as: "conscientious labor for the good of society—he who does not work, neither shall he eat"; "concern on the part of everyone for the preservation and growth of public wealth"; "collectivism and comradely mutual assistance—one for all and all for one"; "honesty and truthfulness, moral purity, modesty, and unpretentiousness in social and personal life"; "an uncompromising attitude toward injustice, parasitism, dishonesty, careerism, and money-grubbing"; "an uncompromising attitude toward the enemies of communism", "fraternal solidarity with the working people of all countries and with all people."[30] Soviet law is strikingly reminiscent of the Puritan code of Massachusetts Bay Colony, the Body of Liberties of 1641, in its punishment of ideological deviation, idleness, and personal immorality.[31] In addition, the Soviet system places a very strong emphasis on the educational role of law and on popular participation in legal proceedings and in law enforcement—through Comrades' Courts and People's Patrols and by placing persons in the care of collective of the factory or the neighborhood. Moreover, this is done in the name of an eschatology which foresees the ultimate disappearance of coercion and of law itself as a communist society is created in which every person will treat every other—again, in the words of the Moral Code of the Builder of Communism—as "comrade, friend, and brother." It is by no means inconsistent with this utopian vision that strong measures of coercion and of formal law may be used to bring it about.[32]

Conclusion

The readings in this chapter argue that the distinction and interprpetation between the realms of religion and secularity is basic to Western civilization. The distinction is not hostile to Western religion. Rather, it is the product of biblical religion, which postulated a God who limited his power in order to allow humans to interact with him and with one another in freedom.

Discussion Questions

1. Why did the West produce no major religion?

2. What is the political origin of the biblical view of religion?

3. How does the biblical distinction between religion and government become important in the development of the Western legal tradition?

4. How does the Western distinction between religious and secular enable religion to remain a force in Western civilization?

PART TWO

RELIGIONS OF THE WEST

CHAPTER 2

JUDAISM

Jacob Neusner

Defining Judaism: A Religion

The first question is, how are we to define Judaism in such a way that it can be categorically compared and contrasted with other religions? In line with the definition of religion given in the preface, how shall we know that we deal with an example of a community that embodies the religious tradition, Judaism? A religion is composed by a way of life, a worldview, and a theory of the social group that lives in accord with that way of life and explains itself in line with that worldview. To answer the question, in the case at hand, then, I have to specify the traits that must mark the way of life and the worldview of that social order accurately classified as Judaic.[1]

We start with a negative definition. By Judaism in this book we do *not* mean "the religion of the Jewish People." That is, we do not survey Jews' opinions on religious questions and call the result Judaism. That is because the Jews, now as in the past a diverse group, encompass large numbers of secular people who profess no religion but regard themselves, and are regarded by others, as part of the Jewish People, a community of fate but not of faith. Some identify "being Jewish" with religious propositions and practices, others do not. And many form a vast middle that mixes religiosity with ethnicity in entire indifference to what the holy books say and the law of Judaism requires. The distinction between the ethnic and the religious yields a choice of adjectives, *Jewish* for the ethnic, *Judaic* for the religious.

It follows that the things on which the Jewish People in general concur need not fall into the classification of a religious belief or practice. It may represent a secular, ethnic fact. Take hallah and the bagel for example, two kinds of bread, for example. The hallah, a sweet bread baked for the Sabbath (which we shall meet in due course) is Judaic because it is part of the tradition of Judaism and the observance of that religion; the bagel is (or once was) ethnic and bears no information pertinent to the study of Judaism. It is a kind of food Jews like to eat. Religious Jews who practice Judaism eat hallah on the Sabbath. Ethnic Jews eat bagels for breakfast. The one fact pertains to the practice of religion, the other to an ethnic preference. Hallah is encompassed by the narrative of Judaism; bagels (with lox and cream cheese) are not.

It follows that even if nearly all Jews concur on a given proposition, that does not signify the proposition belongs as a dogma to the religion Judaism. A single example suffices. Just as we do not regard the politics of Italians or Poles as components of a definition of Catholic Christianity, so also we do not regard the political preferences of Jews, formed for secular considerations of interest for example, as data in the study of Judaism. That is an example of the requirement to differentiate the ethnic from the religious when studying Judaism (or any other world religion closely linked to a particular ethnic or national group). Thus by *Judaism* we do not mean "the religion of the Jewish People," because religion is not a matter of ethnic identity.

How Christianity and Islam Define Judaism

An affirmative definition is now required, one based on incontrovertible facts. To provide such a definition, we ask, what do people in general mean when they refer to "Judaism"? (Later on we shall ask how Judaism defines itself.) The answer to that question yields a working definition readily accessible to a broad audience. We start with what they know, or think they know, about Judaism.

It is possible to ask the question, how do the other religions of the West, Christianity and Islam, define Judaism? If the principal religions of Western civilization simply ignored competing traditions or did not define themselves by contrast with kindred faiths, we should find it inopportune to ask what one tradition acknowledges about the others. Other religions define Judaism because Judaism forms part of the worldview of those other religions, a part out of all proportion to its numbers. Otherwise, the tiny community of Judaism would not play a part in the definition of Western civilization.

Now, when we turn to the companion religions of Western civilization and ask them to tell us what they mean when they speak of "Judaism," they acknowledge that Judaism came first, then Christianity, then Islam. Christianity and Islam afford to Judaism a place in the narrative of their *own* respective traditions. Jesus, Paul, and most of the earliest Christians represented by the writings of the New Testament regarded themselves as Jews. Islam views Moses and Jesus (among many) as prophets, whose message is completed by the prophet Muhammad. Judaic and Christian communities play a role in the Islamic narrative. Accordingly, Christianity and Islam claim to carry forward and complete Judaism. Not only so, but Islam maintains that it completes Christianity and other faiths as well. That is why we appropriately ask, what do Christianity and Islam mean when they speak of that "Judaism" that both Christianity and Islam continue, complete, and perfect?

The answer derives from the story that each continuator-religion tells about itself. That is because both Christianity and Islam explain what they are by narrating a story that begins in the beginning of humanity recorded in the biblical book of Genesis,[2] which tells the story of the beginnings of the community of Judaism founded by the patriarch and matriarch, Abraham and Sarah. They are recognized by Judaism as the founders of the family, the children of Israel, a term we shall define in a moment and Christianity and Islam recognize that they originate in the persons of Abraham and Sarah as well.

This leads to the definition of Judaism provided by Christianity and Islam. *If we ask Christians or Muslims to define Judaism, they respond by citing narratives of Scripture.*[3]

First comes Christianity. "Judaism," Christianity conceives, "is the religion of the Old Testament." That is, Christians asked to define Judaism speak of the biblical books that Christianity calls the Old Testament. So Christianity defined by the Bible and its two testaments regards Judaism as the religion of the Old Testament, superseded by Christianity and understood in the light of Christianity's New Testament. Christianity regards itself as the continuation of the faith of the group about which the Old Testament stories speak.

Islam concurs but expresses itself in its own way. The prophet Muhammad regarded the Jews and Christians as "the people of the book," a reference to the Bible, and Islam retells with new narrative elements some of the same biblical stories. Coming still later than Christianity and regarding the ancient Israelite prophets as true prophets, whose work is sealed and perfected by Muhammad, Islam accordingly takes up the biblical narrative. Islam reveres important figures in those same narratives.

To understand the way in which Christianity and Islam define Judaism, therefore, we briefly have to take up the narrative set forth by Genesis. Who are these figures, beginning with Abraham, and why is this family of Abraham identified with "Judaism"? The biblical narrative records that God has chosen to found an extended family: Abraham and Sarah and their successors, Isaac and Rebecca, Jacob and Leah and Rachel, and so through time. Jacob's name was changed by God to "Israel," and the heirs and descendants of Abraham, Isaac, and Jacob who is also known as Israel are called "the children of Israel," or simply "Israelites."[4]

The biblical narrative continues with the story of the children of Israel in time of famine leaving the land God promised them, the Holy Land, for Egypt, where they were enslaved. God freed them from Egyptian bondage, led them to Mount Sinai, in the wilderness between Egypt and the Holy Land, and there through the prophet Moses gave them instruction, in Hebrew called "the Torah," containing the laws and teachings that they were to follow as they formed a "kingdom of priests and a holy people" in obedience to God's will.

In the context of the study of the religion Judaism, "Israel" speaks of the community of the faithful, the "kingdom of priests and holy nation" (Exod 19:6 RSV). That is a community of the faithful comparable to "the Church, the mystical body of Christ" in Christianity, or "ummah," the extended community of Muslim believers. (Today *Israel* also refers to the state of Israel, situated in what Judaism calls "the land of Israel." That is a secular usage. In Judaism *Israel* always means, the people of Israel, children of Abraham and Sarah, whether by birth or conversion.)

This is where Christianity and Islam join the story. Christianity recognizes Abraham as the first human being to know God, and the children of Abraham as those who know God. It says that Jesus is able to raise up children of Abraham and sees his sacrifice on the cross as the re-enactment of Abraham's sacrifice of Isaac in the story told in the book of Genesis at chapter 22. There the story is told of God telling Abraham to take Isaac and bind him on an altar and offer him up as a sacrifice. That is known as "the binding of Isaac." Christianity sees Christ on the cross as the counterpart to Isaac bound on the altar.

Islam enters the narrative through the same family connection. Islam points to the children of Abraham, Isaac and his half-brother, Ishmael. Specifically, it knows Ishmael as a prophet; and the prophet Muhammad, founder of Islam and seal of prophecy, was told by God in Medina that, like all other Arabs, Ishmael was son of Abraham. There are hadith—traditions of Islam—in which Muhammad likens himself to Abraham, above all other prophets. Like Abraham, Isaac, and Jacob, Muhammad was one of the worshipers of God (Arabic: Allah). The Arabs descend from Ishmael. The specific connection is drawn through Genesis 22. The Qur'an's tale of the binding of Isaac (Sura 37:99-110) identified the son who was bound on the altar as Ishmael, not Isaac, from whom the Arabs are descended.

The upshot is, both Christianity and Islam take up the narratives of the Old Testament and connect their stories to those that concern the formation of the children of Israel. Each draws heavily upon the Old Testament and regards itself as the fulfillment and completion of the biblical narratives and prophecies.

The Torah: The Pentateuchal Narrative and the Books of Joshua, Judges, Samuel, and Kings

Clearly, the narrative of the Torah will play a critical part in the definition of Judaism. Hence, before we turn how to Judaism defines Judaism, we would do well to review the way in which the Pentateuch—the Five Books of Moses, continued by Joshua, Judges, Samuel, and Kings—tells the story. The Pentateuch is Genesis, Exodus, Leviticus, Numbers, and Deuteronomy. There we find the narrative of the beginnings of the people of Israel and their entry into the land of Israel. In due course we shall identify the episodes of that narrative that Judaism selects as the chapters of its story.

The Pentateuch begins at Genesis with the creation of the world, the making of man and woman (Adam and Eve) in God's image, after God's likeness; then the fall of humanity from Eden through disobedience; the ten generations of humanity from Eden to the flood that wiped out nearly all of humanity except for Noah, progenitor of all humanity; then the decline of humanity in the ten further generations from Noah to Abraham. All of this is spelled out in the first eleven chapters of the book of Genesis. Genesis 12 begins the story of the rise of humanity through Abraham, his son Isaac, and his grandson Jacob, then the departure of the twelve sons of Jacob to exile in Egypt and, ultimately, in Sinai. Jacob's name was changed to Israel—"the man who sees God"—and that is the biblical explanation for the name of the extended family, the children of Israel, beginning with the twelve sons of Jacob (Israel). The scriptural narrative continues in the book of Exodus, God revealed the Torah to Moses; and that revelation contained the terms of the covenant that God then made with Israel, the family of Abraham, Isaac, and Jacob.

The book of Leviticus portrays the founding of the priests' service of God through the sacrifice of the produce of the Holy Land to which God would bring Israel, specifies the rules and regulations to govern the kingdom of priests and the holy people.

The book of Numbers provides an account of the wandering in the wilderness.

The book of Deuteronomy then presents a reprise of the story, a long sermon by Moses looking back on the history of Israel from the beginnings through the point of entry into the promised land, followed by a restatement of the rules of the covenant, or contract, between Israel and God, and ending with a prophecy of the Israelite people's future. The narrative of the Pentateuch concludes with Israel at the border of the promised land, ready to enter the land and build God's kingdom there.

That is not the end of the narrative. The books of Joshua, Judges, Samuel, and Kings record the story of Israel in the land of Israel conducting its affairs, sometimes in accord with God's wishes, oftentimes not. Finally, after the prophets had warned that Israel would be punished by the loss of the land if it did not keep the covenant of the Torah, the Israelites were taken into exile by the Babylonians who conquered the Middle East and in 586 B.C.E. destroyed Jerusalem, the holy city in the land of Israel, and the temple built by King Solomon for the worship of God through sacrifices such as are called for in the book of Leviticus—animal offerings on the altar. The story has a happy ending: after three generations of exile from 586 to 538 B.C.E., the Israelites were restored to the land of Israel, where the scribe, Ezra, governed in accord with the Torah revealed by God to Moses at Sinai.

The stories of Scripture are taken by Judaism to convey not a one-time tale, but a pattern that pertains to all the circumstances and times through which the people, Israel, live. That pattern emerges in the three great moments of Scripture, as set forth in the Pentateuch: first, the creation of the world and the fall of Adam and Eve from paradise; second, the freeing of the Israelites from Egyptian bondage; and third, the gift to Moses of the Torah—divine instruction, covering law, narrative, and prophecy—at Sinai and the restoration of Israel to the promised land, the land of Israel, after forty years of wandering in the wilderness.

The narrative seen whole portrays the experience of losing the land and regaining it, *exile and return*, and that pattern would impose order and meaning on the history of the Israelites over time. The pattern is briefly stated in two chapters. They concern (1) humanity, represented by Adam and Eve, and then, repeated in Israel, (2) the portion of humanity that knows God through the Torah. Representing humanity without the Torah, Adam and Eve lost Eden by reason of rebellion against God. In this same pattern Israel possessed—and then lost—the land for the same reason. But Israel—the children of Abraham and Sarah—holds in the Torah the instruction of God on how to live in such a way as to merit restoration to the land, eternal life in paradise. The message of the Torah, in Leviticus 26 and Deuteronomy 32, for example, is explicit that instruction on how to live is the point of the story. With this information in hand, we are ready to address how Judaism defines itself; that is, what it means to practice Judaism.

How Judaism Defines Itself

To practice Judaism as a religion means to take personally the tale of the Torah: to regard oneself and the community of Judaism with which one identifies as the continuation of that same family, the "people of Israel" of which Scripture speaks. What then should we expect of any community of Judaism, however the community may diverge in important details from all other communities of Judaism? Are there norms of belief or of behavior or of the definition of the community of the children of Israel? What must an Israelite affirm, what must he or she practice in order to qualify?

If we attempt to answer in terms of a shared worldview—propositions of conviction and conscience, for example—we invite endless quibbling about meanings of words and readings of texts. Every effort to define a lowest common denominator to indicate what is authentic theology precipitates endless debates. And the outcome, the point on which all concur, proves trivial and commonplace. Were we to say, "all Judaic religious systems affirm belief in one God," we would have to identify the definition of the God that all Judaisms concur is the One and Only God. And if we attempt to respond to the question of who is a Jew in terms of definitions of Israel, we find ourselves paralyzed by the perennial problem, debated in every generation and decided in none of them, the question "who is a Jew?"

But we may describe the way of life of the diverse communities of Judaism and come up with *practices* common to them all. We can indeed identify some norms of behavior, if not of belief, activities if not attitudes, that characterize nearly all Judaic systems and define who belongs and who does not in each of them. These norms of right behavior originate in the Torah; however the Torah is interpreted by a given community of Judaism, and the rules will dictate what is to be done or not to be done in all or nearly all such communities, past and present.

To identify the universal norm that in secular, purely descriptive terms qualifies a given Judaism as authentic, we begin with the original definition. Judaism is that religion that carries forward the narratives, prophecies, and laws of the Torah. Of the three classes of instruction in the Torah—narrative, prophecy, and law—narrative may accommodate the broadest range of diverse reading. People readily identify with a story and find themselves in its unfolding. So we ask, what stories do all communities of Judaism narrate? How does telling these stories define the worldview, way of life, and definition of the community of Judaism?

Telling the Torah's Tale About Oneself: Acting Out Events

The answer to the question of definition through narrative—we are the story that we tell about ourselves—comes from the festivals of Judaism, each of which recapitulates an event in the Torah's narrative. Keeping those festivals, nearly all communities of Judaism appeal to the same story, even as each constructs that story in its own image. I cannot think of a single community of Judaism, either in historical times or in today's world, that ignores the sacred calendar, the festivals, and the Sabbath day. A community of Judaism therefore is a group that continues the story of Israel as told in the Torah and that acts out episodes of that story periodically, through the year. That definition does not exclude other shared beliefs and behaviors, but it serves as the minimum of the common, normative definition of Judaism.

What precisely is meant by "telling the Torah's tale about oneself"? An example of how a community of Judaism inserts itself into the Torah's narrative is provided by the Passover Seder, a banquet attended by families and communities formed for the occasion. Its liturgy—the prayers that people recite in worship—explicitly asks the participants to see themselves as players in the narrative of ancient Israel. The language of the Passover Seder, the home rite celebrated in commemoration of the freeing of the Israelite slaves from Egyptian bondage, is worth examining, since it expresses in so many words the participation, in the distant past, of those present:

> We were the slaves of Pharaoh in Egypt; and the Lord our God brought us forth from there with a mighty hand and an outstretched arm. And if the Holy One, blessed be He, had not brought our fathers forth from Egypt, then surely we, and our children, and our children's children, would be enslaved to Pharaoh in Egypt. And so, even if all of us were full of wisdom and understanding, well along in years and deeply versed in the tradition, we should still be bidden to repeat once more the story of the Exodus from Egypt; and he who delights to dwell on the liberation is one to be praised.

Here is a clear statement of doing, just taking personally the narratives of Scripture: if God had not saved them, "we" should still be slaves. The story of Israel—of the holy people—then is spelled out, and in the course of the narrative, Israel comes to definition:

> Long ago our ancestors were idol-worshipers but now the Holy One has drawn us to his service. So we read in the Torah: And Joshua said to all the people, "Thus says the Lord, God of Israel: From time immemorial your fathers lived beyond the river Euphrates, even to Terah, father of Abraham and of Nahor, and they worshiped idols. And I took your father Abraham from beyond the river and guided his footsteps throughout the land of Canaan. I multiplied his offspring and gave him Isaac. To Isaac I gave Jacob and Esau. And I set apart Mount Seir as the inheritance of Esau, while Jacob and his sons went down to Egypt. (Passover Haggadah)

All of it is deeply relevant to those present, for it says who the assembled family really are, and for whom they really stand. They in the here and now stand for "our ancestors," Abraham, Isaac, and Jacob.

> Blessed is he who keeps his promise to Israel . . . for the Holy One, set a term to our bondage, fulfilling the word which he gave our father Abraham in the covenant made between the divided sacrifice: Know beyond a doubt that your offspring will be strangers in a land that is not theirs, four hundred years they shall serve and suffer. But in the end I shall pronounce judgment on the oppressor people and your offspring shall go forth with great wealth.

So through reenacting the story Israel defines itself: a family, a people, saved by God from bondage. A single formula in words recited in the Passover narrative, or haggadah in Hebrew, captures the moment; and to understand how the "we" of the family become the "we" of Israel, how the eternal and perpetual coming of spring is made to mark a singular moment: "For ever after, in every generation, every Israelite must think of himself [or herself] as having gone forth from Egypt."

What is it that makes plausible for nearly all Jews all over the world to use the word *we* in the statement, "We went forth . . . " and why do people sit down for supper and announce, "It was not only our forefathers that the Holy One, blessed be he, redeemed; us too, the living, he redeemed together with them"? One theme stands out: we, here and now, are really living then and there. "We were slaves . . . " tells a story about those gathered around the Seder table. Lest we miss the point, we are told that we must repeat the story of the exodus, and repeating is praiseworthy. The symbols on the table—the unleavened bread (Hebrew: *massah*), the bitter herbs, the lamb bone, and the like—explicitly invoke the "then and there" in the here and now. First comes the unleavened bread:

> This is the bread of affliction, which our ancestors ate in the land of Egypt. Let all who are hungry come and eat with us, let all who are needy come and celebrate the Passover with us. This year here, next year in the land of Israel; this year slaves, next year free people.

Now lest we miss the point that "we" are present in the past, and the past lives in us—"we are there, Moses is here," the story tells about us, the living, not only the long-ago dead—the message is announced in so many words:

> This is the promise that has stood by our forefathers and stands by us. For neither once, nor twice, nor three times was our destruction planned; in every generation they rise against us, and in every generation God delivers us from their hands into freedom, out of anguish into joy, out of mourning into festivity, out of darkness into light, out of bondage into redemption.

Passover tells the story of Israel through time, not one time period only, but all time, and its message is, "God delivers us from their hands," and that is the point that the story of Passover registers:

> *For ever after, in every generation, every Israelite must think of himself [or her-self] as having gone forth from Egypt.* For we read in the Torah: "In that day thou shalt teach thy son, saying: All this is because of what God did for me when I went forth from Egypt." It was not only our forefathers that the Holy One, blessed be He, redeemed; us too, the living, He redeemed together with them, as we learn from the verse in the Torah: "And He brought us out from thence, so that He might bring us home, and give us the land which he pledged to our forefathers" (italics added).

This example of how Passover reenacts historical events clearly illustrates the general definition of Judaism given at the outset: that community that carries forward the laws, prophecies, and narratives of Scripture. Judaism is the religion—the only religion—that realizes the rules of the Torah by acting out its narrative and obeying the Torah's laws. Judaism takes the stories of the Torah to heart and aspires to keep the laws of the Torah.

How the Moon and the Sun Tell Chapters in the Torah's Story of the Community of Judaism Called Israel

Harmony marks the relationship between Israel's life on earth and God's abode in heaven. In the words of the Qaddish, the prayer repeated in synagogue worship that sanctifies God's name, "He who makes peace in the heights may make peace for us." The sacred calendar signaled by the sun (for seasons) and the moon (for months), coordinates Israel's life here on earth with the movement of the heavenly bodies. The movement of the sun and moon around the earth[5] is interpreted by nearly all communities of Judaism to attest to critical episodes in the Torah's narrative.

Thus, as we just saw in the case of Passover, every year on the first full moon after the vernal equinox of March 21, the communities of Judaism commemorate the liberation of the Israelite slaves from Egyptian bondage and their escape into the wilderness of Sinai. That illustrates how critical chapters of the story of Israel, commemorated as festivals, are timed to coincide with turnings in the year of nature.

Passover, marking the end of the winter rains and the liberation of the Israelite slaves from Egypt, finds its counterpart in Sukkot or Tabernacles ("huts"), indicating the advent of the winter rains and the wandering of the Israelites in the wilderness of Sinai. That festival is signaled by the first full moon after the autumnal equinox of September 21. The episode of the narrative that is acted out begins after the giving of the Torah at Sinai. Then the freed slaves, Torah in hand, turn to build God's kingdom in the land God promised. Approaching the promised land, the freed slaves did not have confidence in God's promises. They turned away from the land. Consequently, God condemned the generation of freed slaves to wander for forty years in the wilderness. Only their children would be worthy of entering the promised land. Leviticus 23:33-43 explicitly links the Festival of Tabernacles to Israel's dwelling in the wilderness for forty years: "You shall live in booths [Sukkot] for seven days; all that are citizens in Israel shall live in booths, so that your generations may know that I made the people of Israel live in booths when I brought them out of the land of Egypt: I am the LORD your God" (vv. 42-43).

In reverting to the wilderness, Israel is to take shelter in any random, ramshackle hut, covered with what humanity does not value—broken branches of trees and shards and remnants of leaves. Israel's dwelling in the wilderness is fragile, random, and transient. The Torah thus has the Festival of Tabernacles to commemorate Israel's condition in the wilderness. During the feast for a week's time, Israel moves from its permanent houses to impermanent huts, reenacting the fragility of its life in the wilderness.

The context of the Festval of Tabernacles is the lunar month of Tishré. The first day of Tishré is the New Year, when God sits in judgment on all the world and decides the fate of nations and individuals for the coming year. The tenth day following the New Year is the Day of Atonement, which atones for sin and brings forgiveness for sin. In Hebrew, the New Year is called Rosh Hashanah and the Day of Atonement is called Yom Kippur. Then the Feast of Tabernacles follows in sequence. It is the third part of the season of judgment and atonement marked by the New Year and Day of Atonement. We realize that these fall on the first and the tenth days of the lunar month of Tishré. Sukkot comes on the fifteenth through the twenty-second days of that same month. The Feast of Tabernacles, therefore, is integral to the penitential season of judgment, atonement, and forgiveness of sin. It marks the happy outcome. It celebrates the advent of the rainy season with prayers and activities meant to encourage the now-conciliated God to give ample rain to sustain the life of the land and its people. Israel has rebelled and sinned, but Israel has also atoned and repented.

Restoring Paradise

Feasts of Passover and Tabernacles share a common thread: Israel liberated from Egyptian bondage, brought to Sinai, given the Torah, and condemned by its own rejection of the land to wander in the wilderness until all the contumacious generation has died out.

There is another narrative that shapes the way of life, worldview, and definition of Israel, of nearly all communities of Judaism, and that concerns the creation of the world. On the seventh day of the week, the Sabbath, Israel rests, as God rested after making the world. The Sabbath recreates the condition of the world when God completed creation: "God blessed the seventh day and declared it holy, because on it God creased from all the work of creation that he had done" (Gen 2:3, my translation). With God Adam and Eve rested on the first Sabbath, and on the Sabbath day, by its repose, Israel restores the conditions that prevailed when God and Adam were last together—that perfect Sabbath when God, having perfected creation, blessed and sanctified the Sabbath day in celebration of the perfection of creation—and entered upon repose.

The Sabbath comes every Friday at sunset and leaves every Saturday at sunset. It is the climax of Judaism. On that day of the week, faithful Israelites refrain from servile labor. They devote themselves to prayer and Torah study, to enjoying their families, and to eating and repose. They assemble in festival clothing at home for meals and in synagogues to hear the Torah sung to the congregation. The Sabbath day envelops the life of the faithful with holiness.

How is the story of the restoration of Eden told? The following story, from the Talmud of the land of Israel (ca. 400 C.E.), in so many words, says that the world will be restored to its original perfection, as in Eden, when Israel keeps the Sabbath day. Thus we are told that Israel's perfect sanctification of a single Sabbath day represents that repair and perfection of the world that marks the recovery of Israel's Eden:

> The Israelites said to Isaiah, "O Isaiah, our Rabbi, What will come for us out of this night?"
>
> He said to them, "Wait for me, until I can present the question."
>
> Once he had asked the question, he came back to them.
>
> They said to him, "Watchman, what of the night? What did the Guardian of the ages say [a play on 'of the night' and 'say']?"
>
> He said to them, "The watchman says: 'Morning comes; and also the night. [If you will inquire, inquire; come back again]'" (Is. 21:12).

They said to him, "Also the night?"

He said to them, "It is not what you are thinking. But there will be morning for the righteous, and night for the wicked, morning for Israel, and night for idolaters."

Now comes the main point in the exchange: when will this happen? It will happen when Israel wants. Only Israel's arrogance, to be atoned for by Israel's remorseful repentance, is standing in the way:

They said to him, "When?"

He said to them, "Whenever you want, He too wants [it to be]—if you want it, he wants it."

They said to him, "What is standing in the way?"

He said to them, "Repentance: 'come back again'" (Is. 21:12).

This is stated in the clearest possible way: a single day of repentance will restore paradise.

R. Aha in the name of R. Tanhum b. R. Hiyya, "If Israel repents for one day, forthwith the son of David will come.

"What is the scriptural basis? 'O that today you would hearken to his voice!'" (Ps. 95:7).

Now comes the introduction of the Sabbath as a test case. Reference is made to "the son of David." The meaning is, the Messiah of the house of David, whom the Israelites believe will come at the end of days to raise the dead from their graves, and to restore Israel to the land of Israel, the temple to Jerusalem, the sacrificial rites to the altar of the temple:

Said R Levi, "If Israel should keep a single Sabbath in the proper way, forthwith the son of David will come.

"What is the scriptural basis for this view? 'Moses said, Eat it today, for today is a Sabbath to the Lord; [today you will not find it in the field]' (Ex. 16:25).

"And it says, '[For thus said the Lord God, the Holy One of Israel], 'In returning and rest you shall be saved; [in quietness and in trust shall be your strength.' And you would not]'" (Is. 30:15). By means of returning and [Sabbath] rest you will be redeemed.[6]

The main point, then, is the linkage of repentance to the coming restoration of Israel to the land, from death to life, by the Messiah. But the advent of the Messiah depends wholly upon Israel's will. If Israel will subordinate its will to God's will, all else will follow. And the Sabbath stands at the very center of the Judaic narrative.

No wonder then, that in the liturgy of home and synagogue, to the Sabbath-observing Israelite, the Sabbath is the chief sign of God's grace:

For thou hast chosen us and sanctified us above all nations, in love and favor has given us thy holy Sabbath as an inheritance. (Sabbath Prayer book)

So states the prayer over wine that marks the sanctification of the Sabbath at the Friday night meal. Likewise in the Sabbath morning prayers the congregation states:

You did not give it [Sabbath] to the nations of the earth, nor did you make it the heritage of idolaters, nor in its rest will unrighteous men find a place.

But to Israel your people you have given it in love, to the seed of Jacob whom you have chosen, to that people who sanctify the Sabbath day. All of them find fulfillment and joy from your bounty.

For the seventh day did you choose and sanctify as the most pleasant of days and you called it a memorial to the works of creation.

Here again we find a profusion of themes, this time centered upon the Sabbath. The Sabbath is (1) a sign of the covenant. It is (2) a gift of grace, which neither idolaters nor evil people may enjoy. It is (3) the testimony of the chosenness of Israel. And it is (4) the most pleasant of days. Keeping the Sabbath is (5) living in God's kingdom:

Those who keep the Sabbath and call it a delight will rejoice in your kingdom.

Keeping the Sabbath brings the Israelite into the kingdom of God. So states the additional Sabbath prayer. Keeping the Sabbath now is a foretaste of the redemption: "This day is for Israel light and rejoicing." As the sun set on the sixth day of creation, God completed the works of creation and sanctified them as perfect. To act like God on the Sabbath, the Israelite rests and goes home to Eden.

Observing as holy time specific days and appointed seasons, most communities of Judaism act out the same episodes in the Torah's narrative of Israel. That permits us to speak of Judaism as a coherent set of religious communities that have thrived in the West. The story Judaism tells brings the past into the present and imposes upon the present the pattern of the past. It is a story about eternity in time, made up of narratives conveying timeless verities. People living anywhere in creation, any time in history, in any realm of language and culture, tell that story about themselves and find a natural fit. The Judaic way of life acts out, chapter by chapter, the worldview of the sacred community—episodes that form a continuous, single narrative of timeless relationships and transactions with God.

The Normative Judaism of the West: Rabbinic Judaism

The Torah—the Five Books of Moses—together with the Prophets and the Writings, shared among all communities of Judaism, not only provided for diverse groups of Judaic faithful a shared corpus of narratives, but also defined a realm of debate. Different groups of Judaic faithful, affirming the same Torah, selected for reenactment diverse episodes, finding in Scripture more than a single message.

Indeed, one community of Judaism found in the prophets the center of Scripture's message, while another identified in the Pentateuch its narratives and laws, the focus of its system. Those stressing the Pentateuch—its laws and narratives—are represented by a group of sages called *rabbis*, who possessed, in addition to the Torah, an oral tradition that originated in God's revelation to Moses at Sinai. This too they regarded as part of the Instruction, or Torah, of Sinai. The community of Judaism that they defined is called Rabbinic Judaism. That religious system for the Judaic social order determined the norms of most communities of Judaism from the early centuries of the Common Era to modern times and continues to set the norm for the majority of those Jews who practice Judaism in any form.

Tracing their traditions to the revelation at Sinai, the ancient rabbis held that the Torah, Instruction, was set forth by God to Moses in two media, in writing and memory, and they possessed that memorized, or oral, part of the Torah. The written part of the Torah corresponds to the Old Testament. The oral part ultimately was recorded in a set of writings of law and theology shaped into commentaries to Scripture, called Midrashim, on the one side, and a law code called the Mishnah, on the other. The Mishnah, which came to closure in 200 C.E., was amplified in a collection of supplements called the Tosefta, around 300 C.E., and two systematic commentaries to topical expositions of the Mishnah called Talmuds, the first deriving from the land of Israel and called the

Yerushalmi, or Talmud of Jerusalem, around 400 C.E., the second from Babylonia, called the Bavli, or Talmud of Babylonia, around 600 C.E. We shall learn more about these documents presently.

The Theology of Rabbinic Judaism

Through its law code and commentaries as well as its amplification of the written Torah, Rabbinic Judaism set forth a systematic theology, contained within its canonical writings, those of the written and oral Torah alike. That theology is acted out in laws governing required deeds of commission and omission and embodied in narratives that portray who God is and what God does. It expounds in narrative form and practical deed the view that God is one, unique, loving, and just, a view that is called monotheism—belief in the one and only God. It is different from all other religions that recognize multiple gods or divinities. In addition the one God is deemed just and merciful. Hence the Rabbinic theology of monotheism is modified by the adjective *ethical,* thus: ethical monotheism. Christianity and Islam are the other two monotheist religions, also affirming that the one and only true God is just and merciful. As we noted at the outset, the three religions of Western civilization form a continuum and themselves recognize the kindred relationship that binds them together.

Theology in Rabbinic Judaism in its formative centuries—the first six centuries of the Common Era—was expressed in two ways. First, it took mythic form. That is to say, it conveyed its theological principles by retelling the Scripture's narrative. Second, it came to formulation in a pattern of actions that embodied in concrete ways right attitudes, rules of behavior that realized matters of belief. Scripture called for the sanctification of the Sabbath, for example, and the rabbis of the Torah laid out the details of what was required to be done. Rabbinic Judaism in theology accomplished the systematization of Scripture's laws and the Torah's oral traditions into laws that embodied principles. This we have already seen in connection with the propositions yielded by Passover, Tabernacles, and the Sabbath. These examples show how the Judaic system of the ancient rabbinic sages worked.

Monotheism

Monotheism by nature explains many things in a single way. One God rules. Life is meant to be fair, and just rules are supposed to describe what is ordinary, in the name of that one and only God. So in monotheism a simple logic governs to limit ways of making sense of things. But that logic contains its own internal contradictions. If one true God has done everything, then, since he is God all-powerful and omniscient, all things are credited to, and blamed on, him—both good and bad. In that case he can be either good or bad, just or unjust—but not both. All monotheisms concur on the justice and mercy of God.

This is the point at which Rabbinic Judaism makes its own statement. Responding to the provocative issue of monotheism, how can an all-powerful, just and merciful God allow the wicked to prosper and the virtuous to suffer, the ancient Rabbis through law and narrative constructed a system that cohered to explain God's justice and mercy in all things. That is, the sages' dual Torah, written as conveyed in the oral, systematically reveals the justice of the one and only God of all creation. God is not only God but also good. Three principles define the theology of the dual Torah are as follows:

God Formed Creation in Accord with a Plan, Which the Torah Reveals

World order can be shown to conform to a pattern of reason based upon justice. Those who possess the Torah—Israel—know God, and those who do not—the Gentiles, defined as idolaters—reject him in favor of idols. What happens to each of the two sectors of humanity, respectively, responds to their relationship with God. Israel in the present age is subordinate to the nations because God has designated the idolaters as the medium for penalizing Israel's rebellion, meaning through Israel's subordination and exile to provoke Israel to repent. Private life as much as the public order conforms to the principle that God rules justly in a creation of perfection.

Israel's Condition Marks Flaws in Creation

What disrupts perfection is the sole power capable of standing on its own against God's power, and that is the human will. What humanity controls and God cannot coerce is humanity's capacity to form intention and therefore choose either arrogantly to defy, or humbly to love, God. Because humanity defies God, the sin that results from human rebellion flaws creation and disrupts world order (theological theodicy). The act of arrogant rebellion led to exile from Eden, pain in childbearing for

Woman, hard labor for Man, and death for both—thus accounting for the condition of humanity. But God retains the power to encourage repentance through punishing humanity's arrogance. In mercy, moreover, God exercises the power to respond to repentance with forgiveness. Since, commanding his own will, humanity also has the power to initiate the process of reconciliation with God through repentance—an act of humility—man may restore the perfection of that order that through arrogance he has marred.

God Ultimately Will Restore That Perfection That Embodied God's Plan for Creation

In the work of restoration, death, which comes about by reason of sin, will die, the dead will be raised and judged for their deeds in this life, and most of them, having been justified, will go on to eternal life in the world to come. The pattern of humanity restored to Eden is realized in Israel's return to the land of Israel. In that world or age to come, however, that sector of humanity that through the Torah knows God will encompass all of humanity. Idolaters will perish, and the humanity that comprises Israel at the end will know the one true God and spend eternity in God's light.

These principles describe a cosmic reworking of the Pentateuch's pattern of exile and return. The theology of Judaism as set forth in Scripture forms one of the great motifs of Western civilization, the fall from paradise described in John Milton's *Paradise Lost* and in the Sistine Chapel in the Vatican, for example. The story begins with the fall of Adam and the loss of Eden, with its parallel in the fall of Israel and the loss of the Land, Jerusalem, and the temple. But, as prophecy insisted, the sages also underscored that through return to God, Israel would recover and keep its Eden. And, sages added, Israel, on certain occasions and through certain rites and practices even now, on the Sabbath, could regain Eden for a moment.

The Two Stages in the Formation of Rabbinic Judaism

The theological system that Rabbinic Judaism constructed on the foundations of a systematic reading of the Written Torah and of the Oral Torah unfolded in two stages. These are represented by the rabbinic writings that fall into two periods, from 70–312 C.E., and from the start of the fourth century to the seventh, 312–640 C.E. The difference between the two stages is marked by the advent of Christianity as the state-religion of the Roman Empire. The first stage set forth a Judaic religious system without reference to the challenge of Christianity; the second group of writings portrayed a revision of the initial system, in response to the challenge represented by the success of Christianity.

The first phase in the formation of Judaism was defined by two events, one in 70 C.E. and the other in 200. It began with the loss of the second temple in 70 C.E. at the climax of a national revolt against Rome. When the Roman armies took Jerusalem in August of that year, they burned the temple and stopped its rites. In the second century, Rome restored Jewish government in the land of Israel. That restoration came to a climax with the promulgation of the Mishnah in 200 C.E. A philosophy in the form of a law code, the Mishnah and the works of scriptural commentary that accompanied it set forth a philosophy in response to the issues of loss and restoration. It treated the events of the day as comparable to the loss of Jerusalem the first time, in 586 B.C.E., and the restoration of the temple in the century following.

The second phase commenced with the conversion of the Roman Empire to Christianity in the fourth century C.E. and was marked by the response to the issues of the age set forth in the Talmud of the land of Israel and related readings of the Torah in light of the new challenge. These writings, produced about a century later at the beginning of the fifth century, presented doctrines that dealt with the program of Christianity. Rabbinic Judaism successfully adapted to the challenge of Christianity (and later on of Islam) and so retained the loyalty of the great majority of Jews. So long as Christianity, and later on, Islam, set the critical issue confronting Israel, the holy people, Rabbinic Judaism was the paramount, norm-setting Judaism. Only when, in modern times, Christianity met competition in defining Western civilization did Rabbinic Judaism also confront other Judaic systems, as we shall see.

The First Phase of Rabbinic Judaism: Judaism Without Christianity

Ignoring Christianity altogether, the Mishnah, the foundation document of Rabbinic Judaism, is a philosophical law code composed of six tractates or divisions, which cover sixty-two topics, in systematic expositions of particular subjects. It presents laws systematically, as part of a logical, coherent statement of topics. Through the details of the information that it organizes, the Mishnah sets forth the principles for the perfection of Israel's social order. Some of the laws were practical. They concerned everyday realities in the here and now. Other laws covered rules for situations not then in existence or transactions not subject to the authority of the rabbinic sages. In the former category are civil laws concerning torts and damages: oxen goring oxen, market fraud, and the like. In the latter are laws about the temple, then in ruins, and the conduct of its offerings, suspended from 70 C.E. when the Romans destroyed the temple and ended its sacrifices. Laws not pertinent to everyday life are probably included to guide the restoration of holy Israel's sacred society in the end of days. That is because the Mishnah's principal interest is in the enduring sanctification of Israelite society.

In number of words, the cultic purity division of the six divisions of the Mishnah is about a fourth of the total number of words in the Mishnah. Topics of interest to the priesthood and the temple—such as priestly rations taken from the altar of God and priestly fees for the conduct of the cult on holy and on ordinary days and management and upkeep of the temple and the rules of cultic cleanness—predominate in the first, second, and fifth divisions as well. Thus approximately two-thirds of the law code had no bearing on practical affairs at the time of the completion of that code. Viewed whole, then, the Mishnah was meant as a design for the restoration of the temple, which the Israelites expected at the end of days, when the Messiah would raise the dead, restore Israel to the land of Israel, and institute the world to come. But it also legislated for the workaday world. Practical rules governing the social order form the bulk of the third and fourth divisions, devoted to family and civil law.

Portrayed by the Mishnah, the first phase of Rabbinic Judaism responded to the destruction of the temple by asking the critical question precipitated by the destruction: what is the implication of the loss of the temple? Is Israel still holy? The Mishnah focused on issues of holiness, maintaining that the holiness of of Israel, the people—a holiness that had formerly centered on the temple, the city of Jerusalem, and the land of Israel—still endured in the very social order of the people commanded to form a "kingdom of priests and a holy nation." The message of the Mishnah made clear that Israel's sanctification as a holy people transcended the physical destruction of the building and the cessation of sacrifices. Israel did not require the emple to mark it as holy or the sacrifices to sanctify it because, on its own, Israel, the people, was holy. It formed the medium in humanity and the instrument of God's sanctification. The

Mishnah's legal system then instructed Israel to act as if there were a new temple formed of Israel, the Jewish people.

But at issue was not simply an act of poetic imagination. Concrete sacrifices were to continue, but they were offered out of the very heart of the holy people. The sacrifices that people could now make were acts of self-less deeds of loving-kindness. The spirit of the times that produced the Mishnah is captured in a story told in a much later document about the Rabbinic sage who escaped from Jerusalem to build a circle of disciples to preserve and hand on the Torah, written and oral.

> The Fathers According to Rabbi Nathan IV:V.2
> One time [after the destruction of the Temple in August, 70] Rabban Yohanan ben Zakkai was going forth from Jerusalem, with R. Joshua following after him. He saw the house of the sanctuary lying in ruins.
> R. Joshua said, "Woe is us for this place that lies in ruins, the place in which the sins of Israel used to come to atonement."
> He said to him, "My son, do not be distressed. We have another mode of atonement, which is like [atonement through sacrifice], and what is that? It is deeds of loving-kindness.
> "For so it is said, 'For I desire mercy and not sacrifice, and the knowledge of God rather than burnt offerings' (Hosea 6:6)."

The upshot is, the loss of the temple and its offerings did not mean the end. Israel's way of life, beginning with ethics, would endure. Israel had another way of serving God and atoning for sin, such as the temple had provided. The people, Israel, defined in the Torah's narratives, now possessed, in the Mishnah, a full account of the Torah's way of life aimed at sanctifying the people in the here and now.

But what of history, and where were things heading? The Mishnah and related writings completed before 300 C.E. do not answer. The worldview of Judaism would be incomplete until that question found an answer. The question would be answered by the documents that commented on the Mishnah, particularly the Talmud of the land of Israel, at the end of the fourth century and the beginning of the fifth, a hundred years after Rome legalized Christianity and adopted it as the religion of the state. That was the critical turning point at which Western civilization began: the definitive status of Christianity as the dominant religion of Europe. Then Judaism prepared itself for its long symbiosis with Christianity in the West.

The Second Phase of Rabbinic Judaism: Judaism Despite Christianity

Each of the important changes in the documents that were produced from the end of the fourth century to the closure of the Talmud of Babylonia in the seventh century C.E.—the Talmud of the land of Israel, Genesis Rabbah (a commentary on the book of Genesis), Leviticus Rabbah (which treats the book of Leviticus), and the like—responds to a powerful challenge presented by the triumph of Christianity. Rabbinic Judaism met that challenge and continued to do so for nearly the whole history of the West. We may say that as much as Judaism through the written Torah/Old Testament set the issues of Christianity, so Christianity would reciprocate for Judaism.

To understand why Christianity challenged Judaism, we have to keep in mind two facts. First, Christianity confronted all heirs of the Written Torah/Old Testament with the claim that the promises of the prophets were realized by Jesus Christ. Second, Christianity had been ferociously persecuted but now was the state-sponsored religion of the Roman Empire. That validated Christianity's conviction that Christ is king. Christianity had suffered three centuries of persecution. The Roman Emperor, Constantine, first legalized Christianity in 312 C.E. then converted to it. His successors made Christianity the state religion of the Roman Empire. Christian theologians pointed to these events as evidence for the truth of Christianity. Jews should now give up Judaism and adopt Christianity as their religion.

Rabbinic Judaism faced a set of urgent questions defined by Christianity as it assumed control of the Roman Empire. Judaism provided as its reply a system deriving its power not from armies and governments of this world, but from the Torah, read by sages, embodied by sages, and exemplified by sages. Asking in a new way the original questions to which Rabbinic Judaism responded in the Mishnah and related writings, this Judaism remained predominant so long as, and wherever, Christianity and later on Islam defined the prevailing culture.

The first issue is the definition of the record of God's will: Bible or Torah. Christians claimed that they possessed the key to the Israelite scriptures: the New Testament showed the true meaning of the Old Testament. The Bible of Christianity was the consequence. For their part, the rabbinic sages set forth the view of the Mishnah as revealed by God to Moses as the oral part of the Torah of Sinai—an answer to the

Christian position on the same matter of God's teaching at Sinai. The rabbinic sages held that what Christianity lacked was the oral part of the Torah of Sinai. So the question arose, which takes priority, the teachings of the Written Torah—possessed by church and synagogue alike—or those of the Oral Torah? That question is raised in so many words:

> Talmud of the Land of Israel Hagigah 1:7.V
> R. Zeirah in the name of R. Eleazar: "'Were I to write for him my laws by ten thousands, they would be regarded as a strange thing' (Hosea 8:12). Now is the greater part of the Torah written down? [Surely not. The oral part is much greater.] But more abundant are the matters that are derived by exegesis from the written [Torah] than those derived by exegesis from the oral [Torah]."
> And is that so?
> But more cherished are those matters that rest upon the written [Torah] than those that rest upon the oral [Torah],
> R. Haggai in the name of R. Samuel bar Nahman, "Some teachings were handed on orally, and some things were handed on in writing, and we do not know which of them is the more precious. But on the basis of that which is written, "And the Lord said to Moses, Write these words; in accordance with these words I have made a covenant with you and with Israel' (Ex. 34:27), [we conclude] that the ones that are handed on orally are the more precious."

The sages interpret the language—"in accordance with these words I have made a covenant with you and with Israel"—to mean the covenant between God and Israel was realized in accord with these words, the oral traditions in particular. The fact that a tradition is handed on in oral tradition is a mark of priority. And now the Mishnah and other rabbinic writings are explicitly included within the oral tradition of Sinai, so the picture is complete.

> Talmud of the Land of Israel Hagigah 1:7.V
> R. Yohanan and R. Yudan b. R. Simeon —
> One [of the named authorities] said, "If you have kept what is preserved orally and also kept what is in writing, I shall make a covenant with you, and if not, I shall not make a covenant with you."
> The other said, "If you have kept what is preserved orally and you have kept what is preserved in writing, you shall receive a reward, and if not, you shall not receive a reward."

[With reference to Deut. 9:10: "And on them was written according to all the words that the Lord spoke with you in the mount,"] said R. Joshua b. Levi, "He could have written, 'On them,' but wrote, 'And on them.' He could have written, 'All,' but wrote, 'According to all.' He could have written, 'Words,' but wrote 'The words.' [These then serve as three encompassing clauses, serving to include] Scripture, Mishnah, Talmud, laws, and lore. Even what an experienced student in the future is going to teach before his master already has been stated to Moses at Sinai."

What is the Scriptural basis for this view?

"There is no remembrance of former things, nor will there be any remembrance of later things yet to happen among those who come after" (Qoh. 1:11).

If someone says, "See, this is a new thing," his fellow will answer him, saying to him, "this has been around before us for a long time."

Here we have absolutely explicit evidence that people believed part of the Torah had been preserved not in writing but orally.

That the Mishnah is part of the Torah, the oral part, is claimed in so many words in the Talmud of Babylonia, the final statement of the formative age of Rabbinic Judaism. In what follows it is alleged that the Mishnah's laws originate at Sinai, meaning, with God: an oral tradition of Sinai ultimately written down in the Mishnah in particular.

Talmud of Babylonia Tractate Erubin 54B/5:1.I.43

What is the order of Mishnah-teaching? Moses learned it from the mouth of the All-Powerful. Aaron came in, and Moses repeated his chapter to him and Aaron went forth and sat at the left hand of Moses. His sons came in and Moses repeated their chapter to them, and his sons went forth. Eleazar sat at the right of Moses, and Ithamar at the left of Aaron.

Rabbi Judah says, "At all times Aaron was at the right hand of Moses."

Then the elders entered, and Moses repeated for them their Mishnah chapter. The elders went out. Then the whole people came in, and Moses repeated for them their Mishnah chapter. So it came about that Aaron repeated the lesson four times, his sons three times, the elders two times, and all the people once.

Then Moses went out, and Aaron repeated his chapter for them. Aaron went out. His sons repeated their chapter. His sons went out.

> The elders repeated their chapter. So it turned out that everybody repeated the same chapter four times.

This explicit account of verbal revelation of the Mishnah tells word for word how the Mishnah originated at Sinai when Moses received the Torah from God. In that model the disciples received the Torah from their masters, in that same chain of tradition. The Torah that is under discussion is orally formulated and then orally transmitted. It is not written down on tablets. It is recorded in the word-for-word dictation of God to Moses, Moses to Aaron, Aaron to his sons Eleazar and Ithamar, then to the whole people, to the elders, and so on down. And the orally formulated and orally transmitted teaching is called the *Mishnah*. The root of the word is the Hebrew letters *S H N Y*, repeat, hence, generically, *mishnah* with a small M would mean, "that which is repeated," meaning, from memory.

So in this story the Mishnah is defined as the outcome of a chain of traditions beginning at Sinai and transmitted in a process of discipleship, memorizing of the words of the master and handing them on to a new generation of disciples. When God gave the Torah at Sinai, then, included in the Torah was the oral tradition ultimately embodied in the Mishnah and, by extension, in other teachings of the rabbinic sages who form links in the chain of tradition from Sinai. For the faithful of Judaism, the narrative of the dual Torah extending to the Mishnah and to the teachings of its rabbinic sages validated the Judaic counterpart to the Bible, just then coming into being.

But it was not the sole component of the rabbinic Judaic system that made a response to the challenge of Christianity.

The Messiah in the Model of the Rabbinic Sage

Christians believed that Jesus was Christ, the Messiah promised by ancient Israelite prophecy. Christianity interpreted the christianization of Rome as a triumph and proof of the kingship of Christ. The rabbinic sages responded by defining the anticipated Messiah instead as a master of the Torah. The rabbis took for granted that the Messiah would keep the laws of the Torah and would be in the model of a rabbinic sage.

To express this doctrine, in the following source, the Rabbis portrayed a prior claim to Messiahship, the one imputed to Bar Kokhba, a general who led a Jewish rebellion against Rome in 132–135 and explained why he was not the true Messiah. Some claimed him as a messiah. But the rabbis of the narrative below favor humility as the criterion for authenticity, and Bar Kokhba is shown arrogant. They want Israel to obey God's will in the Torah, and Bar Kokhba rejects God's will. His arrogance, they hold, resulted in the loss of Jerusalem and the permanent closure of the temple there, and that accords with their theology.

Lamentations Rabbah LVIII:ii.7-10 to Lamentations 2:2

When R. Aqiba saw Bar Koziba, he said, "This is the royal messiah."

R. Yohanan b. Torta said to him, "Aqiba, grass will grow from your cheeks and he will still not have come."

Eighty thousand trumpeters besieged Betar. There Bar Koziba was encamped, with two hundred thousand men with an amputated finger.

Sages sent word to him, saying, "How long are you going to produce blemished men in Israel?"

He said to them, "And what shall I do to examine them [to see whether or not they are brave]?"

They said to him, "Whoever cannot uproot a cedar of Lebanon do not enroll in your army."

He had two hundred thousand men of each sort [half with an amputated finger, half proved by uprooting a cedar].

When they went out to battle, he would say, "Lord of all ages, don't help us and don't hinder us!"

That is in line with this verse: "Have you not, O God, cast us off? And do not go forth, O God, with our hosts" (Ps. 60:12).

What did Bar Koziba do?

He could catch a missile from the enemy's catapult on one of his knees and throw it back, killing many of the enemy.

That is why R. Aqiba said what he said [about Bar Koziba's being the royal messiah].

For three and a half years [the roman emperor,] Hadrian besieged Betar.

R. Eleazar the Modiite was sitting in sack cloth and ashes, praying and saying, "Lord of all the ages, do not sit in judgment today, do not sit in judgment today."

Since [Hadrian] could not conquer the place, he considered going home.

There was with him a Samaritan, who said to him, "My lord, as long as that old cock [Eleazar] wallows in ashes, you will not conquer the city.

"But be patient, and I shall do something so you can conquer it today."

He went into the gate of the city and found R. Eleazar standing in prayer.

He pretended to whisper something into his ear, but the other paid no attention to him.

People went and told Bar Koziba, "Your friend wants to betray the city."

He sent and summoned the Samaritan and said to him, "What did you say to him?"

He said to him, "If I say, Caesar will kill me, and if not, you will kill me. Best that I kill myself and not betray state secrets."

Nonetheless, Bar Koziba reached the conclusion that he wanted to betray the city.

When R. Eleazar had finished his prayer, he sent and summoned him, saying to him, "What did this one say to you?"

He said to him, "I never saw that man."

He kicked him and killed him.

At that moment an echo proclaimed: "Woe to the worthless shepherd who leaves the flock, the sword shall be upon his arm and upon his right eye" (Zech. 11:17).

Said the Holy One, blessed be He, "You have broken the right arm of Israel and blinded their right eye. Therefore your arm will wither and your eye grow dark."

Forthwith Betar was conquered and Ben Koziba was killed.

They went, carrying his head to Hadrian. He said, "Who killed this one?"

They said, "One of the Goths [troops in Roman service] killed him," but he did not believe them.

He said to them, "Go and bring me his body."

They went to bring his body and found a snake around the neck.

He said, "If the God of this one had not killed him, who could have vanquished him?"

That illustrates the following verse of Scripture: "If their Rock had not given them over. . . ." (Deut. 32:30).

In this portrait, drawn in the Talmud of the land of Israel, the Messiah is transformed into a rabbinic sage. He is no longer the Messiah embodied in the figure of the arrogant Bar Kokhba (in the Talmud's representation of the figure). So the Messiah theme comes to the fore when through advent to power Christianity makes its claim stick. But in the rabbinic sages' hands the Messiah-theme reinforced the teaching of the way of life through acts of holiness. The conduct required by the Torah will bring the coming Messiah. We saw that claim in connection with the keeping of the Sabbath: if all Israel will keep one Sabbath, the Messiah will come. That explanation of the holy way of life focuses upon the end of time and the advent of the Messiah—both of which therefore depend upon the sanctification of Israel. So sanctification takes priority, salvation depends on it.

The Mishnah of 200 C.E. contains no trace of a promise that the Messiah will come if and when the law of the Torah, represented by the Sabbath, is fully realized. Here, in a document of 400 C.E., two hundred years later, we find an explicitly messianic statement that the purpose of the law is to attain Israel's salvation: "If you want it, God wants it too." Note the stress on the keeping of the law of the Torah and on the attitude of the Israelite toward the law—hence the priority accorded to repentance. The law of the Mishnah is now encapsulated within the frame of repentance: a change of heart brought about by keeping the covenant with God contained in the Torah. The one thing Israel commands is its own heart; the power it yet exercises is the power to repent. With the temple in ruins, there is no possibility of bringing offerings to expiate sin. Now, therefore, repentance can take place only within the heart and mind. That reminds us of the story of Yohanan ben Zakkai and Joshua walking in the ruins of the temple, which the reader met earlier: there are actions Israelites can carry out that serve to atone as sacrifices used to serve to atone. These are deeds of loving-kindness.

Israel bears responsibility for its present condition. So what Israel does makes history. Israel may contribute to its own salvation, by the right attitude and the right deed. Israel makes its own history and therefore shapes its own destiny. The key is Israel's relationship to the Torah, which God gave to humanity to repair and tame the rebellious heart of Adam and Eve. This lesson, the rabbinic sages maintained, derives from the very condition of Israel even then, its suffering and its despair. History taught moral lessons. Israel's own deeds defined the events of history. Rome's role, like Assyria's and Babylonia's role, depended upon Israel's own sins. Israel had provoked divine wrath. Then the great empire, acting as God's agent, punished Israel. Paradoxically, Israel kept Rome in charge. That is, God exalted Rome, as he had exalted Babylonia, Media, and Greece in times past, to punish Israel. When Israel repented, Rome would no longer be needed, and

Israel would succeed Rome, with God's Torah realized on earth. Then the end of time would be at hand, and the Messiah would raise the dead for judgment and life eternal. That is how, for the coming fifteen centuries, rabbinic Judaism would explain to the small and subordinate community of Judaism how and why it formed the very heart and soul of human history.

Thus the Talmud of the land of Israel's system of history and Messiah presents a paradox. It lies in the fact that Israel can free itself of control by other nations only by humbly agreeing to accept God's rule. The nations— Rome, in the present instance—rest on one side of the balance, while God rests on the other. Israel must then choose between them. There is no such thing for Israel as freedom from both God and the nations, total autonomy and independence. There is only a choice of masters, a ruler on earth or a ruler in heaven. In the Talmud's theory of salvation, therefore, the framers provided Israel with an account of how to overcome the unsatisfactory circumstances of an unredeemed present, so as to accomplish the movement from here to the much-desired future. When the Talmud's authorities present statements on the promise of the law for those who keep it, therefore, they provide glimpses of the goal of the system as a whole.

So from a force that moved Israelites to take up weapons on the battlefield, as in the war led by Bar Kokhba, the messianic hope and yearning were transformed into motives for spiritual regeneration and ethical behavior. The energies released in the messianic fervor were then linked to rabbinical government, through which Israel would form the godly society. When we reflect that the message "if you want it, he too wants it to be" comes in a generation confronting, in the political triumph of Christianity, a dreadful disappointment, its full weight and meaning become clear. In this doctrine Rabbinic Judaism prepared the people of Israel for a long history of subordination and transformed weakness into the mark of inner strength. It made a virtue of necessity and turned the situation of the Jews into a sustaining force for Judaism. Christianity and Islam, for their reasons, in general left room for Judaism, the initial monotheism, to endure in their midst.

The Success of Rabbinic Judaism in Western Civilization

[1] Christian and Muslim Toleration

Rabbinic Judaism, paramount in the community of Judaism, represents one of the successful religions of humanity: it endured and made a difference precisely where it aimed to. Christianity and Islam permitted the practice of Judaism and allowed for the presence of Jews. The fate of paganism in the fourth century and beyond under Christianity and under Islam shows the importance of that factor. In conquering pagan peoples, both monotheist religions offered the choice of conversion or death. But ordinarily, with exceptions in various places and times, Jews were permitted to practice Judaism.

From the time of Constantine to the nineteenth century, Jewry in Christendom sustained itself as a recognized and ordinarily tolerated minority. The contradictory doctrines of Christianity—the Jews as Christ-killers to be punished, the Jews as witnesses to be kept alive and ultimately converted at the second coming of Christ—held together in an uneasy balance. The pluralistic character of some societies (for instance, of Spain), the welcome accorded entrepreneurs in opening territories (for instance, of Norman England, Poland and Russia, White Russia and Ukraine, in the early centuries of development in medieval times) account still more than doctrine for the long-term survival of Jews in Christian Europe. The Jews, like many others, formed not only a tolerated religious minority, but something akin to a guild, specializing in certain occupations, for example, crafts and commerce in the East. True, the centuries of essentially ordinary existence in the West ended with the Crusades, beginning in the late eleventh century (1092), which forced German Jewry to migrate from the Rhineland—where they had lived for close to ten centuries—to Poland and the eastern frontier of Europe. Neverthe-less, until the twentieth century, the Jews formed one of the peoples permanently settled in Europe, first in the West, and later in the East.

The Christian emperors' policy toward Judaism afforded to Jews and their religion such toleration as they would enjoy then and thereafter. The religious worship of Judaism was never prohibited. Pagan sacrifice, by contrast, came under interdict in 341. Festivals of pagan gods went on into the fifth century, but the die was cast. The Jews were to be allowed to live until the second coming of Christ, at the end of days, at which point it was expected that they would convert. So too, when Islam conquered much of the Christian world, in the Near East, North Africa, Spain, and the Mediterranean islands, Judaism held its own in the formerly Christian, now Islamic, countries and cultures. Christianity was acutely aware of the loss of these vast territories and populations to Islam. In Spain and Portugal, for example, for seven centuries, from the seventh through the fourteenth century, Christians would undertake the reconquest of the peninsula, and the Crusades to Palestine, from 1096 forward for several hundred years, aimed to recover the Holy Land for Christianity.

A word on the situation of Judaism and Christianity within Islamic countries is in order. In them only free male Muslims enjoyed the rank of a full member of society. Jews and Christians could accept Islam or submit, paying a tribute and accepting Muslim supremacy, but continuing to practice their received religions. Bernard Lewis, a scholar of Islam, characterizes the Islamic policy toward the conquered people of the Book, or the Bible, Christianity and Judaism, in these terms:

> This pattern was not one of equality but rather of dominance by one group and, usually, a hierarchic sequence of the others. Though this order did not concede equality, it permitted peaceful coexistence. While one group might dominate, it did not as a rule insist on suppressing or absorbing the others. . . . Communities professing recognized religions were allowed the tolerance of the Islamic state. They were allowed to practice their religions . . . and to enjoy a measure of communal autonomy. . . . The Jews fell into the category of dhimmis; communities accorded a certain status, provided that they unequivocally recognized the primacy of Islam and the supremacy of the Muslims. This recognition was expressed in the payment of the poll tax and obedience to a series of restrictions defined in detail by the holy law.[7]

The Jews like the Christians were a subject group and had to accommodate themselves to that condition. But they had already learned to accept a subordinated position in society by reason of the remarkable success of Christianity in fourth-century Rome. So from the fourth century C.E. in Christendom, and from the seventh C.E. in Islam, Judaism remained stable and vital. Both Islam and Christendom presented a single challenge: the situation of subordination along with toleration. But the basic religiosity of the Christian and Islamic worlds, encompassing the story of Israel, the community of Judaism, as well, reinforced the convictions concerning God and God's will for humanity that Rabbinic Judaism affirmed. They did so by asking much the same questions that Judaism answered. When new questions emerged, other Judaic systems would arise to answer them, as we shall see in due course.

[2] The Power of the Ideas of Rabbinic Judaism to Answer Urgent Questions

The second reason, besides Christian and Islamic toleration, for the persistence of Rabbinic Judaism, is that the Jews wished it to persist. We have little evidence that mass conversions either to Judaism or to Islam decimated the Jewish community, and that strongly suggests that Judaism stood firm. The reason is clear. Power based on arms changed nothing. Judaism's power lay in its weakness. The conquering religions served God's purpose as much as the Babylonians had in 586 B.C.E. by reiterating the cycle of exile and redemption. Having dealt with the political triumph of Christianity, Judaism found itself entirely capable of coping with the military and therefore political victory of Islam as well. Western civilization itself replicated that very situation to which Rabbinic Judaism addressed itself from its origins before the destruction of Jerusalem in 70 C.E.: the situation of exile from Eden and the Holy Land, the restoration of holy Israel to Eden and the Holy Land in the resurrection of the dead at the end of days. And in the interim: humility, repentance, atonement for sin, above all, obedience to God's commandments, which sanctify Israel the holy people.

Indeed, the stability of the Jewish communities in the newly conquered Islamic countries is noteworthy. It contrasts with the decline of Christianity in those same, long-Christian territories, such as Syria, Palestine, Egypt, Cyrenaica, and the far-western provinces of North Africa, not to mention Spain. So we observe a simple fact. Judaism satisfactorily explained for Israel the events of the day, whereas Christianity for masses of Christians who accepted Islam did not.

What was the difference? Christianity was unprepared for a new age of subordination, having won the throne of Rome. Christianity, triumphant through the sword of Constantine, with difficulty withstood the yet-sharper sword of Muhammad. On that account the great Christian establishments of the Middle East and North Africa fell away. Both Judaism and Christianity enjoyed precisely the same political status. But Judaism prepared the Jews for a situation of defeat, while Christianity validated its truth by appeal to political and military success, beginning with the conversion of Rome to Christianity. The one religion could cope with subordination, the other found it difficult to do so.

How did Rabbinic Judaism construct for Israel a world in which the experience of the loss of political sovereignty and the persistence of the situation of tolerated subordination within Islam and Christendom attest to the importance of Israel? The very facts of the day proved the truth of the faith. That condition turned out to afford reassurance and make certain the truths of the Torah as taught by the rabbis. This is expressed in the following narrative, which has the destruction of Jerusalem and the prosperity of the idolaters turned into reassurance of the salvation of Israel and the downfall of idolatry:

Sifré Deuteronomy XLIII:iii.7-8

"for Mount Zion which lies desolate; jackals prowl over it" (Lamentations 5:18):

Rabban Gamaliel, R. Joshua, R. Eleazar b. Azariah, and R. Aqiba went to Rome. They heard the din of the city of Rome from a distance of a hundred and twenty miles.

They all began to cry, but R. Aqiba began to laugh.

They said to him, "Aqiba, we are crying and you laugh?"

He said to them, "Why are you crying?"

They said to him, "Should we not cry, that idolators and those who sacrifice to idols and bow down to images live securely and prosperously, while the footstool of our God has been burned down by fire and become a dwelling place for the beasts of the field? So shouldn't we cry?"

He said to them, "That is precisely the reason that I was laughing. For if those who outrage him he treats in such a way, those who do his will all the more so!"

There was the further case of when they were going up to Jerusalem. When they came to the Mount of Olives they tore their clothing. When they came to the Temple mount and a fox came out of the house of the Holy of Holies, they began to cry. But R. Aqiba began to laugh.

"Aqiba, you are always surprising us. Now we are crying and you laugh?"

He said to them, "Why are you crying?"

They said to him, "Should we not cry, that from the place of which it is written, 'And the ordinary person that comes near shall be put to death' (Num. 1:51) a fox comes out? So the verse of Scripture is carried out: 'for Mount Zion which lies desolate; jackals prowl over it.'"

He said to them, "That is precisely the reason that I was laughing. For Scripture says, 'And I will take for myself faithful witnesses to record, Uriah the priest and Zechariah the son of Jeberechiah' (Isa. 8:2).

"Now what is the relationship between Uriah and Zechariah? Uriah lived in the time of the first temple, Zechariah in the time of the second!

"But Uriah said, 'Thus says the Lord of hosts: Zion shall be plowed as a field, and Jerusalem shall become heaps' (Jer. 26:18).

"And Zechariah said, 'There shall yet be old men and old women sitting in the piazzas of Jerusalem, every man with his staff in his hand for old age' (Zech. 8:4).

"And further: 'And the piazzas of the city shall be full of boys and girls playing in the piazzas thereof' (Zech. 8:5).

> "Said the Holy One, blessed be He, 'Now lo, I have these two witnesses. So if the words of Uriah are carried out, the words of Zechariah will be carried out, while if the words of Uriah prove false, then the words of Zechariah will not be true either.'
>
> "I was laughing with pleasure because the words of Uriah have been carried out, and that means that the words of Zechariah in the future will be carried out."
>
> They said to him, "Aqiba, you have given us consolation. May you be comforted among those who are comforted."

Aqiba turns the disheartening facts into reassuring indications of what is coming, validation of prophecy of salvation. It signals the working of the rabbinic system over the whole of its history. The very condition of Israel, subordinated and uncertain, validates its claim to form God's people, subject to God's rule and plan.

The success of Judaism derives from this reciprocal process. Rabbinic Judaism restated for Israel in an acutely contemporary form—in terms relevant to the situation of Christendom and Islam—that experience of loss and restoration, death and resurrection, that the Pentateuch had set forth. Rabbinic Judaism taught the Jews the lesson that its subordinated position itself gave probative evidence of the nation's true standing: the low would be raised up, the humble placed into authority, the proud reduced, the world made right. So Rabbinic Judaism did more than react, reassure, and encourage. It acted upon and determined the shape of matters. Rabbinic Judaism for a long time defined the politics and policy of the community. It instructed Israel, the Jewish people, on the rules for the formation of the appropriate worldview and way of life, for it laid forth the design of attitudes and actions that would yield an Israel both subordinate and tolerated, on the one side, but also proud and hopeful, on the other. God values humility and despises arrogance, both in messiahs and in nations. Making a virtue of a policy of subordination, Rabbinic Judaism defined the Jews' condition and endowed them with a sense of the power to control what objective conditions told them they could in no way change.

The Dominance of Rabbinic Judaism from the Seventh to the Nineteenth Century and Beyond

Over the centuries, from the fourth century to the present time, derivative systems took shape, restating in distinctive ways the fundamental convictions of Rabbinic Judaism, or adding their particular perspective or doctrine to that system. So Rabbinic Judaism accommodated these changes and developments, new modes of thought, new quests for religious experience.

The power of Rabbinic Judaism is attested by two facts of the history of Judaism from the seventh century. First, Rabbinic Judaism absorbed within itself massive innovations in modes of thought. So Rabbinic Judaism had the confidence and inner stability to adapt as circumstances required. The philosophical movement, described by Professor Seymour Feldman in chapter 6 of this book, presents striking testimony to the power of the received system, for it took as its task the validation and vindication of the faith, the law and doctrine of Rabbinic Judaism. Another innovative Judaic system, mysticism, described by Professor Elliot Wolfson in chapter 7, made provision for kinds of religious experience involving direct encounter with God, that Rabbinic Judaism on its own accommodated but did not emphasize.

Second, Rabbinic Judaism dictated the program of public debate among diverse communities of Judaism. That is to say, it so effectively defined the issues of public debate that heresies took shape in explicit response to its doctrines. The paramount authority of rabbinic sages, the doctrine of the Oral Torah, the view that the Messiah would embody the Torah and live by it—these indicative traits of Rabbinic Judaism provoked heresies, one denying the authenticity of an Oral Torah deriving from Sinai, another that posited a Messiah exempt from the laws of the Torah. These developments show that Rabbinic Judaism predominated even to the extent of dictating the character of its critics and enemies.

Subsets of Rabbinic Judaism

The Advent of Philosophical Thinking

The rise of Islam brought important intellectual changes, based on the character of Islamic culture. Rabbinic Judaism accommodated that new mode of thought. Specifically, Muslim theologians, who could read Greek or who read Greek philosophy translated into Arabic, developed a mode of thought along philosophical lines, rigorous, abstract, and scientific, with special interest in a close reading of Aristotle, founder of the philosophical tradition (as chapter 6 will show us).

Rabbinic Judaism, embodied in the great authorities of the Torah, had naturalized philosophy within the framework of the dual Torah. The earlier method of the Mishnah matches that of natural philosophy: classifying data by topics and hierarchizing the data by appeal to indicative traits of the classifications. But the later sages of the Talmud did not follow that generalizing and speculative mode of thought. They read Scripture within a different framework altogether. As the Judaic intellectuals in Islam faced the challenge of rationalism and philosophical rigor that the Muslim philosophers derived from their encounter with Greek philosophy, they read the written Torah, Scripture, and the Oral Torah in a new way. The task at hand was to reconcile and accommodate reason and revelation. In medieval Islam and Christendom, no Judaic intellectuals could rest easy in the admission that Scripture and science, in its philosophical form, came into conflict.

That is why alongside a study of Torah a different sort of intellectual religious life flourished in classical Judaism, the study of the tradition through the instruments of reason and the discipline of philosophy. The philosophical enterprise attracted small numbers of elitists and mainly served their specialized spiritual and intellectual needs. But they set the standard, and those who followed it included the thoughtful and the perplexed—those who took the statements of the tradition most seriously and, through questioning and reflection, intended to examine and effect the revealed truths of the Torah as philosophically valid. The philosophers, moreover, were not persons who limited their activities to study and teaching; they frequently both occupied high posts within the Jewish community and served in the high society of politics, culture, and science outside the community of Judaism as well. Though not numerous, the philosophers exercised considerable influence, particularly over the mind of an age that believed reason and learning, not wealth and worldly power, were what really mattered. In chapter 7 we shall meet philosophy of Judaism in the context of Christianity and Islam.

Hasidism

Not only did Rabbinic Judaism draw strength from new modes of thought, it also accommodated thought that placed a higher value on direct encounter with God and on spiritual gifts than even upon knowledge of the Torah that the rabbinic system emphasized. Professor Wolfson in chapter 8 places Judaic mysticism into the context of Christian and Islamic mystical doctrine and experience. But mystical doctrine formed the basis for the organization of communities of Judaism within the larger rabbinic world. Small circles of mystics flourished through the ages, from the first through the eighteenth century. But mystical beliefs and practices became the basis for a mass movement only in the eighteenth and nineteenth centuries, continuing into our own times. That mass movement, popular in Eastern European Jewry before the Holocaust and rooted in American Judaism as well, is called Hasidism.

Beginning in mid-eighteenth century in Ukraine and Poland, Hasidism offered direct encounter with God on the part of holy men, who were called *zaddikim*, or righteous men, and bore the title Rebbe. They were qualified by their spiritual gifts and took priority over meeting God in the Torah on the part of sages. Ultimately Hasidism found for Torah study a central place in its piety. The root HSD, yielding Hasid, serves that word, Hesed, to which Yohanan ben Zakkai made reference in his lesson to Joshua that Israel has a means of atonement for sin as effective as sacrifice, "deeds of loving-kindness." Now *Hasid* stood for one who reached God through discipleship of a righteous holy man, an intermediary between humanity and heaven, able through his prayers to influence God.

The mystic circles in Ukraine and Poland in the eighteenth century, among whom Hasidism developed, carried on practices that marked them different from other Jews, for example, through special prayers, distinctive ways of observing certain religious duties, and the like. The first among the leaders of the Hasidic movement of ecstatics and anti-ascetics, Israel b. Eliezer Baal Shem Tov, "the Besht," worked as a popular healer. From the 1730s onward he undertook travels and attracted to himself circles of followers in Podolia (Ukraine), Poland and Lithuania, and elsewhere. When he died, in 1760, he left behind not only disciples, but also a broad variety of followers and admirers in southeastern Poland and Lithuania. Leadership of the movement passed to a succession of holy men, about whom stories were told and preserved. In the third generation, from the third quarter of the eighteenth century into the first of the nineteenth, the movement spread and took hold. Diverse *zaddikim*, holy men and charismatic figures, developed their own standing and doctrine.

Given the controversies that swirled about the movement, we should expect that many of the basic ideas would have been new. But that was hardly the case. The movement drew heavily on available mystical books and doctrines, which, as Professor Wolfson's chapter on mysticism will show us, from medieval times onward had won a place within the faith as part of the Torah. Emphasis on a given doctrine on the part of Hasidic thinkers should not obscure the profound continuities between the modern movement and its medieval sources. To take one example of how the movement imparted its own imprint on an available idea, the influential Hasidic Rebbe, Rabbi Menahem Mendel of Lubavich, notes that God's oneness means more than that God is unique. It means that God is all that is:

> There is no reality in created things. This is to say that in truth all creatures are not in the category of something or a thing as we see them with our eyes. For this is only from our point of view, since we cannot perceive the divine vitality. But from the point of view of the divine vitality which sustains us, we have no existence and we are in the category of complete nothingness like the rays of the sun in the sun itself. . . . From which it follows that there is no other existence whatsoever apart from his existence, blessed be he. This is true unification.[8]

The Rebbe concludes that, since all things are in God, the suffering and sorrow of the world cannot be said to exist. So to despair is to sin.

By the end of the eighteenth century, powerful opposition, led by the most influential figures of East European Judaism, characterized Hasidism as heretical. Its stress on ecstasy, visions, miracles of the leaders—these were seen as delusions, and the veneration of the *zaddik* was interpreted as worship of a human being. The stress on prayer to the denigration of study of the Torah likewise called into question the legitimacy of Hasidism. In the war against Hasidism it was declared heretical, its books burned, its leaders vilified. Under these circumstances, the last thing anyone would anticipate would have been for Hasidism to find a place for itself within what would at some point be deemed Orthodoxy. But it did.

By the 1830s Hasidism defined the way of life of the Jews in the Ukraine, Galicia, and central Poland, with offshoots in White Russia and Lithuania on the one side, and Hungary, on the other. The waves of emigration from the 1880s onward carried the Hasidism to the West, and, in the aftermath of World War II, to the United States and the State of Israel as well. Today Hasidism forms a powerful component of Orthodox Judaism, and that fact is what is central to our interest in the capacity of Rabbinic Judaism to find strength by naturalizing initially alien modes of thought and media of piety. Habad Hasidism, deriving from the Rebbe of Lubovitch, competes with the contemporary organizations of standard Orthodoxy as a completely Orthodox Judaism. The basis for that accommodation is the devotion of Habad Hasidism to study of the Torah and to the holy way of life prescribed by the Torah. The doctrines and practices that distinguish that Hasidic community from the rest of Orthodoxy are not to be ignored, but, in the opinion of some, do not separate Habad from the rest of Orthodoxy.

Rabbinic Judaism Defines Its Heretics: Karaism and Sabbateanism

From the fourth century to the nineteenth century, heresies in Judaism defined themselves against the program of Rabbinic Judaism. Rabbinic Judaism so predominated that its doctrines dictated the norm, and what deviated acknowledged that norm. We see that fact in the two most important heresies that arose in the long age of rabbinic dominance. One of these, Karaism, rejected the rabbinic doctrine of the dual Torah, oral as well as written, and maintained that the Torah was only the written one. The other, Sabbateanism, rejected the rabbinic doctrine of the Messiah as a humble master of the Torah and maintained that a man identified as the Messiah, Shabbetai Zvi, was the Messiah even though he deliberately violated the teachings of the Torah. Both heresies therefore mounted opposition to the normative system within the terms defined by Rabbinic Judaism. What made a heresy *heretical*, then, was the rejection of one or another of the definitive doctrines of the norm. A very brief examination of the principal heresies suffices to show the paramount status of Rabbinic Judaism. When we come to Judaism in modern times, we shall meet communities of Judaism that ignored entirely the rabbinic doctrines and practices and asked other questions altogether.

Karaism

Karaism denied that God revealed to Moses at Sinai more than the Written Torah and explicitly condemned belief in an oral one. Karaism rested on four principles: (1) the literal meaning of the biblical text; (2) the consensus of the community; (3) the conclusions derived from Scripture by the method of logical analogy; (4) knowledge based on human reason and intelligence. It advocated the return to Scripture as against tradition, inclusive of rabbinic tradition.

The sect originated in Babylonia in the eighth century, following the formation of the Talmud of Babylonia and the rise of Islam. The movement itself claimed to originate in biblical times and to derive its doctrine from the true priest, Zadok. The founder, Anan b. David, imposed rules concerning food that were stricter than those of the rabbis and in other ways legislated a version of the law more rigorous than the talmudic authorities admitted. The basic principle predominated that Scriptures were to be studied freely, independently, and individually. Given the stress of Rabbinic Judaism on the authority of the sages, resting on their mastery of the Talmud and related canonical documents that recorded the oral part of the Torah of Sinai, we could not expect a more precisely opposite theological statement: a debate over the definition of the Torah: only written versus written and oral. Karaism continues to this day, with communities situated in the state of Israel and elsewhere.

Sabbateanism

What is important about the Sabbatean movement—a seventeenth-century messianic movement organized around the figure of Shabbetai Zvi, 1626–1672—is that it defined the Messiah not as a sage who kept and embodied the law, but as the very opposite. Sabbateanism responded to the Torah of Rabbinic Judaism with the Messiah as a holy man who violated the law in letter and in spirit. It held that, in the end of days, the Torah would no longer pertain; the Messiah would take over the tasks that the Torah had carried out in the pre-messianic age. In positing a Messiah in the mirror image of the sage Messiah of Rabbinic Judaism, the Sabbatean movement, like Karaism, paid its respects to the received system.

Shabbetai Zvi, born in Smyrna/Ismir in 1626, mastered talmudic law and lore and enjoyed respect for his learning even among his opponents. Suffering from bipolar disorder, during his manic periods he deliberately violated religious law in deeds called "strange or paradoxical actions" in the doctrine of his movement. During depressed periods, he chose solitude "to wrestle with the demonic powers by which he felt attacked and partly overwhelmed." During a period of wanderings in Greece and Thrace, he placed himself in active opposition to the law, declaring the commandments to be null and saying a benediction "to Him who allows what is forbidden." In these ways he marked himself as the Messiah.

In this way he distinguished himself even before his meeting with the disciple who organized his movement, Nathan of Gaza. In 1665, the two met and Nathan announced to Shabbetai that the latter was the true Messiah. This independent confirmation of Shabbetai's own messianic dreams served to confirm the Messianic claim. In May 1665, Shabbetai announced himself as the Messiah, and various communities, upon hearing the news, split in their response to that claim. Leading rabbis opposed him; others took a more sympathetic view. Nathan proclaimed that the time of redemption had come. In 1666, the Turkish authorities offered

Shabbetai Zvi the choice of accepting Islam or imprisonment and death. On Sept. 15, 1666, Shabbetai Zvi converted to Islam. Nathan of Gaza explained that the apostasy marked a descent of the Messiah to the realm of evil, outwardly to submit to its domination, but actually to perform the last and most difficult part of his mission by conquering that realm from within.

The Messiah was engaged in a struggle with evil, and just as in his prior actions in violating the law, he undertook part of the labor of redemption. The apostate Messiah would then form the center of the messianic drama, which was meant to culminate, soon enough, in the triumph. Until his death in 1672 Shabbetai Zvi carried out his duties as a Muslim and also observed Jewish ritual. He went through alternating periods of illumination and depression and, in the former periods, founded new festivals and taught that accepting Islam involved "the Torah of grace," as opposed to Judaism, "the Torah of truth." The Sabbatean heresy found its focus and definition in its opposition to the rabbinic dogma that the Messiah would qualify as a great sage, in the model of Moses who was called by sages "our rabbi." What better revolt against Rabbinic Judaism than at the very heart of its doctrine, by labeling the Messiah an anti-sage? Again, that attests to the power of Rabbinic Judaism to shape the imagination of even its foes.

Modern Times: Rabbinic Judaism Meets Competition

The rabbinic Judaic system was built on the experience of exile and return, modified in Rabbinic Judaism to encompass the sanctification of the life of the people as the condition of the salvation of the nation at the end of time. It answered the question of why and how to form "Israel," the unique and holy people that dwells apart from the (other) nations. No one conceived that the Israelite could or should be anything other than that. But with the advent of political emancipation and the beginning of the nation-state, in which all persons were citizens before the law, the question arose, why and how can we be both "Israel" and something else, for example French or German or British or American? Rabbinic Judaism made no provision for a dual, or a multiple, identity for Israelites: it was all or nothing.

So long as Christianity defined the issues of Western culture and politics, Rabbinic Judaism defined the norm for Judaism. Then the question was, why are you not Christian? And the answer came back: because we are God's people, living by the Torah, holy unto God. As politics revised the urgent question facing the Jews of Christian Europe, Rabbinic Judaism began to face competition from other Judaic religious systems. These set forth different conceptions of the worldview, way of life, and definition, besides the rabbinic one, of the social entity Israel. Reform Judaism and Zionism represent two most significant competing systems. They are unlike Karaism and Sabbateanism because they stand outside the framework of rabbinic doctrine of the dual Torah and the Messiah, even though Reform Judaism set forth a doctrine concerning the Torah and Zionism adopted Messianic motifs. In emphasis and proportion, they represent categorically new communities of Judaism, not heresies within the framework of the rabbinic community.

Reform Judaism explained how Israelites could be Judaic in religion and German or French or British or American in nationality. Zionism recast the very conception of the people living apart: it was to form a Jewish nation-state, like other nation-states. Drawing on the rabbinic worldview and way of life to redefine *Israel,* Reform and Orthodoxy (dealt with in chapter 14) exemplify the Judaisms of continuation. Other systems utterly rejected the narrative structure and system of Rabbinic Judaism. These are represented by Zionism (dealt with in chapter 12).

Conclusion:
Judaism in Western Civilization

Judaism, along with Christianity and Islam, has formed an integral part of Western civilization. In defining the civilization of the West, Judaism has played its role in two fundamental ways.

First, Judaism contributed the Hebrew Scriptures of ancient Israel (a.k.a. the Old Testament). These were adopted and deemed authoritative by Christianity. And alongside, narratives of Scripture were confirmed in Islam, which took as valid prophecy the Torah or teaching of Abraham and Moses as well as the Gospels of Jesus.

Second, the Jewish people have found a place for itself in all parts of Europe and the European Diaspora as well as in the Islamic world. Judaism has been practiced in Europe from Roman times and in the European Diaspora in the Western Hemisphere from the sixteenth century. Judaism endures as a vital component of Western civilization, with an influence far out of proportion to the numbers of those who practice it.

As between the contribution made by Judaism's Scriptures and that made by Judaism's practitioners, the influence of the Hebrew Scriptures has been pervasive, that of the Jewish People episodic. But the effect of the presence of Judaism through the Jewish people has been more intense, as the Jews practicing Judaism always represented the alternative to Christianity and Islam. With their claim of the authentic reading of Scripture and possession of the entire divine revelation to humanity, Judaism has challenged the competing heirs of a common Scripture and shared narrative. And the West has responded and continues to respond to the challenge of Judaism.

Discussion Questions

1. Why do we ask Islam and Christianity to define Judaism, or Judaism to define Islam and Christianity? What is the role of comparative religion in defining religions?

2. What is the point of the pentateuchal narrative continued in Joshua, Judges, Samuel, and Kings? What holds them all together?

3. What is the relationship between the natural world of sun and moon and stars and the historical world of Israel, the holy people, on earth?

4. How did Rabbinic Judaism restate the main points of Scripture, and how did it add its own messages to the main points of Scripture?

CHAPTER 3

CHRISTIANITY: WHAT IT IS AND HOW IT DEFINES WESTERN CIVILIZATION

Bruce Chilton

Introduction

Christianity emerged as the pre-eminent religion of the West during the fourth century when the Roman emperor Constantine decided to tolerate what had been a persecuted religious movement. His decision ended a centuries-old and failed policy of suppressing Christians, granted them rights of worship, and established Christianity as the governing ideology of the West.

Constantine's new policy thrust Christianity into a position of influence for which it had no preparation. Until Constantine, the concerns of Christianity had been directed not to this world, but to "the kingdom of God," a heavenly realm of complete justice. Christians' view of secular authority had been skeptical and remained so. Yet now the Catholic (which means "universal") Church became an inclusive faith community in the Roman Empire and a unifying principle side by side with a single emperor and one God. We can understand the effect the church had on the West only by examining how Christian faith defined itself prior to Constantine, when Christianity emerged as a religion separate from Judaism, which set the stage for Constantine's revolution.

Israel Prior to Contact with the Romans

Roman contact with the people of Judea who were the descendants of the Israelites occurred as they were recovering from a series of crises that

71

threatened their survival. In the year 721 B.C.E., the Assyrian Empire completed its invasion of the Northern Kingdom of Israel, sending the most prominent people into exile. The country, and its king and customs, ceased to exist as a culture (see 2 Kgs 17:6). By that time, the Northern Kingdom, which bore the name Israel, had been divided from the Southern Kingdom, Judea, for the better part of two centuries; Israel was more powerful and prosperous than Judea, owing to its superior natural resources and its location closer to the great empires of the time. Ironically, that also made the Northern Kingdom a more likely target of conquest. The Assyrian destruction of Israel left Judea as the sole guardian of the heritage of the patriarchs.

Spurred on by the demise of Israel in the north, religious leaders in Judah called the prophets attempted to purify the life of their people. Their prophecies were preserved in writing, often with supplements, and have come down to us as the Prophetic Books of the Bible. Isaiah (who lived in Jerusalem during the eighth century B.C.E.) urgently argued against foreign alliances and insisted that fidelity to God alone would save Jerusalem; Jeremiah (another Jerusalem prophet, from the seventh century B.C.E.) ceaselessly denounced faithlessness and was prosecuted for his trouble; Ezekiel's enactments of the disaster that finally overcame Jerusalem in 587 B.C.E. won him a reputation as a crank. But one king, Josiah, stood out as an example of royal power backing the teaching of the prophets (cf. 2 Kgs 22:1–23:30; 2 Chr 34:1–35:27). Josiah restored worship in the temple according to what Moses had taught; he centralized sacrifice in Jerusalem; he tolerated no foreign incursions. In his program, he was guided by a scroll of the law, which was found in the temple during the course of restoration, a scroll that has, since antiquity, been associated with the present book of Deuteronomy. This book presses an agenda of radical centralization and separation from foreign nations such as impelled Josiah. But in 609 B.C.E., Josiah was killed in battle.[1]

The end of the kingdom of Judah came quickly after the death of Josiah. Culminating in 587–586 B.C.E., the Babylonian Empire, which had succeeded the Assyrians (cf. the book of Nahum), implemented a policy of exile, subsequent to their siege of Jerusalem and their destruction of the temple. The policy of exile involved the removal of royalty, priesthood, and aristocracy far from Jerusalem, with the intent that they would be absorbed by the culture of Babylon (see 2 Kgs 24:10-17; 25:27-30).

Paradoxically, however, the forces that must have seemed sure to destroy the religion of Israel instead assured its survival and provided for its international dimension. During the Babylonian exile, priests of the destroyed temple and followers of the prophets joined forces to form a united program of restoration, which put Israel back on the map within a generation. Even more influentially, they memorialized their vision of that Israel in a book, the Pentateuch. With the emergence of the Pentateuch during the fifth century, an ideal Israel attributed to the regulations of Moses emerged as a truly biblical standard of faith and life.

The exile of Judah to Babylon, then, contributed to the priestly and prophetic hegemony that made restoration possible. Although priestly concerns are represented in the Pentateuch, the prophetic movement also brought a distinctive message to the canon. The prophets agreed with their priestly confederates that the land promised to Israel was to be possessed again, and postexilic additions to the books of Isaiah (40–55), Jeremiah (23:1-8; 31), and Ezekiel (40–48) constitute propaganda of return. But the previous abuses of the kings and their retainers made the prophets insist that righteousness was necessary for God to be pleased with God's people and that the events of the recent past were a warning.

Eschatology—the expectation that God was about to wipe out this world and bring in a new order of being—became characteristic of the prophetic movement. This new theme of prophecy came to voice both in additions to prophetic books, such as Isaiah and Ezekiel, and in fresh works, such as Joel and Malachi and Zechariah. The governments of this world—successively Persian, Ptolemaic, and Seleucid—were provisional, until an anointed king and an anointed priest would rule properly. The image of a priestly orientation redefined by the prophets is projected into the career of Ezra in the books of Ezra and Nehemiah: prophet, priest, and scribe become one in their insistence on the vision of classic Israel, centered upon the restored temple.

The Babylonian Empire fell to Cyrus the Persian, who in 539 B.C.E. permitted the people of Judah to return to their land. Cyrus is even referred to as God's anointed, his "messiah," in Isaiah 45:1 because he allowed the temple to be rebuilt in Jerusalem (as happened around 515 B.C.E.). Ezra was a principal figure in this restoration.

Although the temple was restored, it was far from ideal. Some who remembered the splendor of Solomon's edifice are reported to have wept in disappointment when they saw the results of the first efforts of restoration (Ezra 3:10-13). Despite its imperfections, the temple attracted a permanent priesthood. At the same time, the prophetic movement consolidated its writings into a canon (a standard of authoritative literature). Now followers of the prophets could teach and guide the nation on the basis of a common inheritance of Scripture. Ezra's own ministry involved guiding Israel on the basis of scriptural interpretation: the scribe emerges as the dominant, religious personality, the warrant of true prophecy and the arbiter of priestly conduct (see Neh 8).

The hegemony of priestly and prophetic interests that has been described brought together the Pentateuch or Torah (the Law) along with what are called within Judaism the Former Prophets (the biblical books from Joshua–2 Kings) and the Latter Prophets (the books of principal prophets such as Isaiah, Jeremiah, and Ezekiel). But disagreements concerning the proper conduct of worship, and the proper personnel of the priesthood, raged during the period of restored Israel, and powerful movements produced literatures outside of scribal control. The category known as Writings (the last in the three biblical divisions of traditional Judaism, and including such works as Psalms, Proverbs, Job, and Daniel) best characterizes other facets of the religion.

Within the Writings, the book of Psalms represents folk worship, emphasizing aspects of devotion in the temple that the book of Leviticus in the Pentateuch does not engage: music, dance, poetry, prayer, and praise (the term *psalms, tehillim,* means "songs of praise"). The psalms speak more eloquently of the emotional affect of and popular participation in sacrificial worship than any other document in the Bible. The book of Proverbs also represents a non-priestly, non-prophetic focus of piety in restored Israel, defined by discovering the way of wisdom. Job and Ecclesiastes are other examples of the literature of divine wisdom within the canon. Initially, Wisdom is understood to be as aspect of God, so that by knowing Wisdom intimately, one can become familiar with God.

The Writings proved to be an elastic category. Outside of territorial Israel, where the Bible circulated in Greek translation, works that did not exist in Hebrew were even added. Some of these help us understand the rise of Christianity. The Wisdom of Solomon was composed in Greek during the first century B.C.E. and focuses on Wisdom as a fundamental means of access to God, his feminine consort. Influences from Egyptian and Babylonian conceptions of divine Wisdom probably date from the time of the Israelite and Judean kings. Although the prophets had denounced foreign practices such as making idols and taking multiple wives, Wisdom was embraced by Judaism as a suitable and fertile means of communion with God. In the case of Philo of Alexandria, a Jewish teacher and sage who lived in Egypt (25 B.C.E.–45 C.E.), the pursuit of Wisdom became a philosophical articulation of Judaism; he contributed an awareness of how Judaism and Hellenistic culture might be related. Philo is unusually learned in his representation of a basic development of the Judaism of his period. His simultaneously Greco-Roman and Judaic notion of the *Logos* (the "word" of God) is a case in point (see *On the Creation of the World*).

The question of the priesthood in the restored temple, meanwhile, became increasingly fraught, and different factions of Judaism came to be more at odds with one another. Alexander the Great and the dynasties of generals who succeeded him after his death in 323 B.C.E. largely maintained the tolerant settlement of Cyrus the Persian in regard to Israel. Antiochus IV is commonly portrayed as a great exception to the policy, and he did unquestionably occupy Jerusalem and arrange for a foreign cult in the sanctuary, which included the sacrifice of swine (a Hellenistic delicacy).[2] Yet Antiochus entered the city as the protector of one high-priestly family, in their dispute with another (Josephus, *The Jewish War* 1 §§31-35). Dispossessed, the group that lost moved to Egypt, where a temple was built at Heliopolis, in a form different from the restored temple in Jerusalem (*The Jewish War* 1 §33; 7 §§420-432). This cult appears to have been of limited influence, but its existence is proof of deep divisions within the priestly ranks and within Judaism as a whole.

Early Judaism and the Romans

"Early Judaism" may be dated from 167 B.C.E., with the entry of Antiochus IV into Jerusalem and his desecration of the temple, but it is evident that the radical pluralization of Judaism prior to Jesus is rooted in the disunity of restored Israel during the period after the temple was restored. The temple of Onias is only one example of a mounting pluralism, but one which shows how deep divisions had become.

While Onias's group fled to Egypt, within territorial Israel another group emerged, defined by a desire to remain faithful to sacrifice in Jerusalem by an appropriate priesthood and a resistance to the demands of Antiochus. This group was known as "the faithful" (the famous *chasidim*). Among them was Mattathias, a country priest from Modin. His son Judas Maccabeus ("the hammer") introduced the most powerful priestly rule Judaism has ever known.[3] He turned piety into disciplined revolt, including an alliance with Rome (1 Macc 8) and a willingness to break the Sabbath for military reasons (1 Macc 2:41), which resulted in the restoration of worship within the covenant in the temple in 164 B.C.E. (1 Macc 4:36-61).

Judas's treaty with the Roman Republic (as it then was) involved mutual defense (see 1 Macc 8). His success resided in his combination of priestly prerogatives and political acumen. That combination was too rapid for some and unacceptable in the view of others. In strictly familial terms, Judas could not claim the high priesthood, because that was a prerogative of a priestly family called the Zadokites. By taking the powers of kingship, his descendants also arrogated to themselves a promise that in the Bible belongs to the house of David alone. Moreover, the suspension of the Sabbath for military purposes seemed arrogant to many Jews (cf. Josephus, *Jewish War 1* §§70-84). Antiochus had sanctioned apostasy, but the Maccabees appeared to be compounding apostasy both in its initial resistance (breaking the Sabbath) and in its consolidation of power (compounding seizure of the high priesthood with the claim of monarchy).

In the case of the Essenes, who occupied the famous site near the Dead Sea where the Dead Sea Scrolls were found, opposition to the Maccabees became overt. They pursued their own system of purity, ethics, and initiation. They also followed their own calendar and withdrew into their own communities, either within cities or in isolated sites such as Qumran. There they waited for a coming apocalyptic war, when they, as "the sons of light," could triumph over anyone not of their vision (see *War Scroll* and *Manual of Discipline*).[4]

Most of those who resisted Antiochus, or who sympathized with the resistance, were neither of priestly families nor as separatist as the Essenes. Nonetheless, the unchecked rule of the Maccabees' priests in the temple was not acceptable to them. For that large group, the Pharisaic movement held a great attraction. In their attempt to influence what the Maccabees did, the Pharisees did not try to replace them definitively. Their focus was upon the issue of purity, as defined principally in their oral tradition and in their interpretation of Scripture. Since issues of purity were bound to be complicated in the Maccabean combination of secular government and sacrificial worship, disputes were inevitable. Paradoxically, the willingness of the Pharisees to consider the Maccabees in their priestly function involved them in vocal and bloody disputes. For example, King Alexander Jannaeus is reported to have executed by crucifixion eight hundred opponents, either Pharisees or those with whom the Pharisees sympathized, and to have slaughtered their families.[5]

The Pharisees accepted and developed the notion that, with the end of the canon, the age of prophecy had ceased (cf. 1 Macc 4:46). For that reason, they saw the work of Ezra in restoring the temple and establishing the law of Moses as the precedent of their own (cf. Aboth 1:118; 2 Esd 14). But they identified themselves with no specific priestly or political figure (Ezra included); their program was its own guide and was not to be subservient to any particular family or dynasty. Further, Pharisaic interpretation was not limited to the Scriptures, nor was its characteristic focus scriptural: the principal point of departure was the recollection of earlier teaching of those called "sages."

The Pharisees had to negotiate a treacherous political environment. Rival claimants to the high priesthood appealed to the Roman general Pompey, who obliged by taking Jerusalem for Rome and entering the sanctuary (*Jewish War* 1 §§120-154). From that time (63 B.C.E.), and all through the reign of Herod and his relatives, the Pharisees' attitude to the Roman government was ambivalent. Some of them engaged in principled opposition to Rome and its representatives, occasionally to the point of violence, while others did not.

Those Pharisees who did oppose the Romans are sometimes known as the Zealots today, but the term is a misnomer when applied in that way. The Zealots were a *priestly* group of revolutionaries during the revolt of 66–70 C.E., not rebellious Pharisees (*Jewish War* 2 §§564-565; 4 §§224, 225). The rebellious Pharisees are also to be distinguished from the movements of prophetic figures, who claimed divine inspiration for their efforts to free the land of the Romans (*Jewish War* 2 §§258-265; 7 §§437-446).

Many Pharisees normally accommodated to the new regime, but resisted Herodian excesses, such as Herod the Great's erection of a golden eagle on a gate of the temple (*Jewish War* 1 §§648-655). Nonetheless, an apparently Pharisaic group is called "the Herodians" (Matt 22:16; Mark 3:6, 12:13), which signals its agreement with the interests of the royal family as the best support of its teaching of purity. These Herodians enjoyed the protection of Herod and his house; the authorities referred to in rabbinic literature as the "sons of Bathyra" (see Baba Mesia 85a in the Talmud) may also have been such a group. Other Pharisees still largely cooperated with the Romans and with the priestly administration of the temple, although they might fall out regarding such questions as whether the priestly vestments should be kept under Roman or local control (*Antiquities* 18 §§90-95; 20 §§6-14).

The priesthood itself was fractured in its response to Roman governance. Some priests, especially among the privileged families in Jerusalem, were notoriously pro-Roman. Some of their sons endured the surgery called epispasm in order to restore the appearance of a foreskin so they could compete naked in Hellenistic gymnastic competitions (cf. 1 Macc 1:14, 15; *Antiquities* 12 §§239-241). Such families were not highly regarded by most Jews (see Pesachim 57a in the Babylonian Talmud). They are typically portrayed in a negative light because they did not teach the resurrection of the dead (see *Jewish War* 2 §165; Matt 22:23; Mark 12:18; Luke 20:27; Acts 23:8). Their concerns were much more immediate: the Torah had stressed that correct worship in the temple would bring with it material prosperity, and the elite priests attempted to realize that promise by methods ranging from collaboration with the Romans to revolt against them.

Many ancient Christian sources were written by and for non-Jews. They tended to cast priests, scribes, Pharisees, and lawyers into a single category of persecutors and hypocrites, whom they called "the Jews." That tendency is evident in the present text of the Gospels, and unfortunately it afflicts modern study of Christianity and Judaism, as well as many Christians today, with the assumption that the Jewish people as such are anti-Christian. But the realities of a radically pluralized Judaism in which Jesus was a vigorous participant became part and parcel of his movement.

Jesus, His Movement, and the Roman Response

References within the Gospels to groups and movements within Judaism become quite explicable within Judaic social history. Priests sometimes appear locally, in adjudications of purity, while high priests are essentially limited to Jerusalem or use Jerusalem as a base of power. Pharisees, however, reach into Galilee, where they frequently enter into argument and discussion with the principal figure of the Gospels, a Galilean teacher named Jesus.

Jesus is addressed by the title *rabbi*, which shows that he was skilled in the folk traditions of Galilean Judaism. These traditions were predominantly oral, rather than written, because the majority of Jews in Galilee were illiterate. (That ambient illiteracy is what made being a "scribe"—

capable of writing and therefore reading—an unusual achievement.) That did not prevent Jesus from crafting an announcement of "the kingdom of God," an expectation cherished by Galilean Jews that God would sweep away the powers of this world and install an eternal reign of justice. His disputes with Pharisees often concerned issues of purity, because Jesus taught that God was cleansing his people, removing the barriers that separated them from his kingdom, as part of the process of installing the divine reign. As a rabbi, Jesus had close followers, deliberately promulgated his teaching by travel and sending his disciples to teach, and attempted to influence the conduct of worship in the temple. In Jerusalem, Jesus and his sympathizers raided the holy precincts to expel animals and their sellers, which he considered unclean when introduced for purposes of trade in the temple (Matt 21–25; Mark 11–13; Luke 19:28–21:38).

High priests found Jesus guilty of blasphemy for infringing on their prerogatives and denounced him to Pontius Pilate—the Roman prefect of Judea—as a threat to public order (Matt 26:1–27:2; Mark 14:1–15:1; Luke 22:1–23:5). Pilate alone had the power to order Jesus' execution.

From the point of view of official Roman policies, religious conflicts among their occupied subjects were usually beside the point. Yet Rome had arranged a special provision for Jews during the time of the republic, and they honored it. Rome paid for sacrifices that Israelite priests accepted and offered in the Jerusalem temple. That amounted to having the priests pray for Roman prosperity, and in exchange Jews enjoyed liberty of worship. By this brilliant maneuver, Rome made the temple into a symbol of its own power as well as the worship of Israel. What the different groups did with and to one another only mattered from the point of view of the public order, particularly in the temple. The Roman attitude is accurately represented in the book of Acts, which was written around 90 C.E., in the scene when the Apostle Paul is denounced in Corinth by some Jewish opponents before the Roman official Gallio (see Acts 18:12-17). (In that Gallio left an inscription behind, we can date this event to the year 51–52 C.E.) Gallio explicitly and firmly refuses to adjudicate the dispute, on the grounds that his concerns are with breaches of the Roman law, not with the Torah. But however much the Romans may have wanted to avoid the controversy caused by the emergence of Jesus' movement, events pressed them into the center of conflict.

The emergence of a group of followers around a Galilean rabbi named Jesus occasioned no official concern from the Romans prior to Jesus' action in the temple, with one big exception. Herod Antipas ruled

Galilee and Peraea (east of the Jordan) as a client ruler of Rome in succession to his father, Herod the Great (who died in 4 B.C.E.). Antipas's reign was notably stable, largely because he assiduously repressed critics. John the Baptist had denounced Antipas's marriage to his brother's former wife, insisting that Antipas keep the Torah of purity as any person might understand it (see Lev 20:21). Antipas had him beheaded (see Matt 14:3-12; Mark 6:17-29; Luke 3:19-20; and *Antiquities* 18 §§109-119). Therefore when Jesus, who had been a disciple of John's for a time, enjoyed popular success, Antipas's suspicion naturally turned to him (see Matt 14:1-2; Mark 6:14-16; Luke 9:7-9).

The executions of John the Baptist by Herod Antipas and of Jesus by Pontius Pilate were not examples of religious oppression. In each case, the representative of Roman power was insisting (from his own point of view) upon recognition of the legitimacy of the Roman settlement. Herod's marriage—challenged by John the Baptist—was a public arrangement, and the good order of the temple—challenged by Jesus—was part and parcel of the Roman recognition of Judaism as a sanctioned religion. Provided routine worship in the temple continued, and imperial sacrifices were accepted there—the old alliance from the time of the Maccabees was remembered (see 1 Macc 8)—and Judaism enjoyed the status of *religio licita*, a legal religion.

Jesus' threat to the public order as symbolized by the temple could not be ignored in Pilate's judgment, and over time—as non-Jews joined Jesus' movement after his death—his followers lost the right of being a *religio licita*. The first followers of Jesus all practiced Judaism and naturally assumed that their meetings were as licit as Judaism itself. After the Sabbath closed at sunset (which was seen as the end of one day and the beginning of another), followers of Jesus would continue their observance, concluding at dawn on Sunday, the day and the time of the resurrection. The rising of the heaven's sun corresponded to the rising of God's son within this practice. But these groups increasingly came to believe that non-Jews could join them in the worship of Jesus.

To these disciples, Pilate's execution of Jesus did not put an end to his teaching, his influence, or his life. He was still alive in their midst, and they prophesied in his name, inspired by the same Holy Spirit that had moved the prophets of old (see Acts 2:1-42). They believed that as a part of this new, inrushing power of divine Spirit, God had authorized them to include Gentiles in their midst. They baptized people in water, as John the Baptist had done, but for a new purpose: so that believers, both Jews and Gentiles, could be immersed in the Holy Spirit (Acts 1:5) and become part of a new creation.

With the inclusion of non-Jews within their community by baptism, and with their refusal to require circumcision and their rejection (in some cases) of other laws of purity, followers of Jesus ran the risk of being denounced as followers of a *superstitio* (as people today would say, a "cult"), rather than as practitioners of a *religio licita*. The very name given to Jesus' followers, *Khristianoi*, was a sign of coming trouble. Adherents of the movement came to be known as "Christians" (meaning partisans of Christ) in Antioch by around the year 45 C.E., and they embraced that term of intended ridicule. The use of the term by outsiders highlights the marginal status of non-Jews who accepted baptism. Without conversion to Judaism, they were not Jews in the usual understanding; having rejected the gods of Hellenism by being baptized, they were also no longer representative of the Roman-Roman syncretism that was then fashionable. By calling disciples *Khristianoi* (Acts 11:26), a term analogous to *Kaisarianoi* (supporters of Caesar), outsiders compared the movement more to a political faction than to a religion.

This perilous situation for Christians could be exploited by their opponents or by those eager to find scapegoats to deflect hostility from themselves. In the year 64 C.E., Emperor Nero used the marginal status of Christians to get out of a difficult political situation of his own. In that year, a huge fire destroyed Rome, and it was rumored that the conflagration had been set at Nero's order. There is no doubt but that the opportunity for Nero to rebuild Rome along the lines he preferred was one he exploited to the greatest possible extent. Nero attempted to deflect suspicion from himself by fastening blame for the fire on Christians. They were rounded up, interrogated, and slaughtered, often with elaborate means of torture. Nero's excesses in regard to the Christians were obvious even to those who held that their religion was superstitious. The result seems to have been a reduction of attacks upon Christians for several decades (see Tacitus, *Annals* 15.37-44).

In Jerusalem, meanwhile, trouble of a different kind was brewing for both Judaism and Christianity. A new spirit of nationalism influenced the priestly aristocracy. Josephus, a Jewish historian of the period who lived during this time, began his career as a priestly nationalist, and ended it as Rome's protégé. He reports that James, the brother of Jesus, was killed in the temple around 62 C.E. at the instigation of the high priest Ananus during the interregnum of the Roman governors Festus and Albinus

(*Antiquities* 20 §§197-203). To have the most prominent leader within Christian Judaism removed was obviously a momentous event within Christianity, but arguably the execution was even more ominous for the prospects of Judaism within the empire. Ananus was deposed from the high priesthood for his action in response to popular opposition to his action in Jerusalem, and Josephus's account of the period makes it clear that, from the time of Albinus onward, Rome had to contend with a rising tide of nationalistic Jewish violence in and around Jerusalem.

The tide rose fatefully in the year 66 C.E., when Eleazar (the *sagan* or manager of the temple) convinced priests not to accept any offerings from non-Jews (*Jewish War* 2 §409). That new policy included the sacrifices paid for by Rome, so the authorities of the temple were breaching terms basic to the recognition of Judaism as *religio licita*. Jewish insurgents took the Antonia, the fortress adjacent to the temple, and killed the Roman soldiers within. War had been irrevocably declared, and the victor could only have been Rome. Consequently the temple itself was destroyed by fire in 70 C.E. after a protracted siege.

The strategy of the Roman Empire in the wake of the revolt was simple, direct, and punitive. Rome now demanded that the *fiscus Iudaicus*, a tax that adult males had paid for the maintenance of the temple, be paid directly to the temple of Jupiter Capitolinus in Rome. Moreover, the Roman version of *fiscus Iudaicus* was to be paid by *all* Jews, minors and women included, not only by adult males. It is not surprising that, in the wake of those events, Judaic hopes centered on the restoration of the temple. Works such as 2 Esdras (in the Apocrypha, also known as 4 Ezra), written around 100 C.E., openly represent the eschatological vindication that was the object of much prayer and action. Such hopes were in cruel contrast to the political reality that the *fiscus Iudaicus* was now the price of being considered *religio licita*.

The period after the Jewish War also saw much unrest among Jews outside of geographical Israel, especially during the reign of Trajan (98–117 C.E.). Trajan also had to deal with the question of what to do with Christians. Although Nero's cruelty had discredited vigorous persecution, the association of Christianity with Judaism raised the question of Christian loyalty to Rome anew. Even within Christian literature, there are hints of an unwillingness of the new community to pay the *fiscus Iudaicus* (see Matt 17:24-27, from a Gospel composed ca. 80 C.E.). Moreover, the Davidic descent of Jesus and his relatives could easily be understood as a challenge to Roman hegemony, since David represented the royal line of Israel. At the same time, the growing number of Gentile

Christians obviously could not claim the legal protections that remained in place for Judaism.

During the time of the Emperor Domitian (81–96 C.E.), surviving relatives of Jesus, grandsons of Jesus' brother Judas, were interrogated concerning their understanding of the kingdom preached by Jesus (see Eusebius, *History of the Church* 3.19-20). To the Romans Christians seemed part of the problem of Jewish insurrection, which broke out yet again in Jerusalem in 132 C.E.

In a letter written in 111 C.E. to Pliny, governor of Bithynia and Pontus in Asia Minor, Trajan sets out his policy. Recognition of the gods of Roman (including the Emperor as *divi filius*, son of God) is said by Trajan to be all that should be required of those denounced as Christians. The question was not their identity or their practice as such, only whether they were loyal to the empire. By this time, there is no question of simply identifying Christianity with Judaism.

Indeed, the empire may be said to have recognized a separation between Judaism and Christianity before Jews and Christians did. Nero never considered extending the rights of a *religio licita* to Christians in 64, although many followers of Jesus still worshiped in the temple in Jerusalem. Not until around 85 C.E. would the framers of a principal prayer of Judaism, the Eighteen Benedictions, compose a curse to be included, against the Nazoraeans, followers of Jesus. On the Christian side the claim formally to replace Judaism only came near the end of the first century, as we will see in a later section. Trajan simply takes the separation for granted, in effect treating Christianity as a mostly harmless superstition.

By the time Trajan wrote to Pliny, Christians outside Israel were reading the Gospels alongside the Scriptures of Israel in their Greek version. Each Gospel was composed in a different city of the Roman Empire in the years after 70 C.E. They reflect a desire to gather the memories concerning Jesus that had earlier circulated in an oral form. The book of Acts takes the story up from the time of Jesus' resurrection until just before Nero's pogrom against Christians in Rome. In addition, the letters of Paul, a Hellenistic Jew from Tarsus who converted to faith in Jesus, were widely read. This collection was based on what Paul himself said to early Christian communities he visited, but gradually his letters were supplemented by his followers, and letters other than Paul's were also added to the New Testament, as Christians called their addition to the Bible of Israel.

All the writings of the New Testament were composed in Greek; many of them reveal a deep ignorance of Judaism on the part of Gentile

Christians. The Gospels also begin the long process of Christians blaming the Jews and their leaders for Jesus' execution, in order to ingratiate themselves to their Roman governors. Yet even Paul, the most radical thinker in the New Testament, believed that faith in Jesus was a part of God's unbreakable promise to Israel. The New Testament reflects Christianity as it was about to emerge as a religion separate from Judaism, but that process was far from complete at the time its writings were first brought together.

Christianity in a Hostile Empire

A second great Jewish revolt against the Romans (132–135 C.E.) was better organized than the first, but its consequences were even more disastrous. The remnants of the temple were removed and a new temple erected—to the gods of Rome. Jerusalem was renamed Aelia Capitolina, and Jews were forbidden to live there. By this time Judaism could no longer center upon Jerusalem. After the first revolt, a rabbi named Yohanan ben Zakkai had been given permission to establish an academy of rabbis in Yavneh, near Jerusalem. But by the second century, even Yavneh was eclipsed by centers in prosperous Jewish Galilee. The farming communities of Galilee provided the support for the rabbinic enterprise of framing a philosophy out of the Pharisaic concern for the purity of Israel.

While Judaism continued as *religio licita*, its association with revolt and the definitive destruction of the temple (recognized as one of the greatest buildings of its time) vastly undermined the public standing of Judaism in the Roman world. At the same time, Roman attention focused more on Christians in any case.

Trajan's policy was relatively tolerant: he had nothing to do with the mass persecution that Nero indulged in, and he simply insisted upon the equivalent of an oath of loyalty from those accused of being Christians. But the loyalty oath was to the gods of Rome and to the emperor as divine son. The result of that requirement was the phenomenon of Christian martyrdom. In good conscience, Christians could not comply with the policy, since swearing allegiance to the emperor was an act performed before his image, with an oblation of wine and the burning of incense. It was an imperial sacrifice and an obvious example of idolatry. During the reign of Trajan, Bishop Ignatius of Antioch was put to death and encouraged others to follow his example of holy obstinacy. Devotion to the divine ideal of the empire could also lead to the use of the loyalty test to seek out Christians despite the policy established by Trajan. That occurred in 177 C.E. in the Rhone Valley, at the instigation of the emperor and noted Stoic philosopher Marcus Aurelius.

Increasingly, imperial policy tried without success to contain the new religion. Emperor Severus issued an edict against Christian and Jewish proselytism in 202 C.E. The Severine persecution that followed was severe, but short-lived. One unfortunate effect (from the Roman point of view) was that it provoked Christians in North Africa to encourage martyrdom and to utter words that were to prove prophetic, "the blood of the martyrs is the seed of the Church" (a saying attributed to Tertullian [*Apology*, 50.13] but probably an aphorism by this time). In 250 C.E., the emperor Decius decreed that all citizens were to take part in sacrifice to the gods, and the inevitable result was a widespread persecution of Christians. During that persecution, the greatest theologian of the time, Origen, was imprisoned and tortured.

Origen actually died during the reign of Valerian (253–260), who attempted to suppress Christian worship itself for the first time. But Valerian was captured and killed by Shapur, the Sassanid monarch. In important rescripts, his successor actually restored Christian churches and cemeteries. Valerian's death is therefore an important transitional point from the point of view of official policy toward Christianity: it marks the moment from which Christians will begin to acquire rights. At the same time, Valerian's death marks the importance of the Sassanid Empire as a counterweight to the Roman Empire.

Emperor Diocletian (284–305) was the last great persecutor of Christianity during the period of the Roman Empire. His motives appear to have been patriotic. After all, he branded as criminals a group called the Manichaeans (named after a teacher named Mani who taught that the world is a struggle between good and evil) before he acted against the Christians. But when his persecution came, it was systematic and savage. Beginning in 303, property was seized and clergy were arrested. Trajan's old test, of offering sacrifice to the gods, was resumed and made universal. Diocletian himself abdicated in 305, but the persecution went on until 313. It was the last gasp of the ideal of a universal civic religion of the Roman Empire based upon the ancestral gods.

The Constantinian Settlement

Rivalry for the imperial throne proved key to the emergence of Christianity as a major world religion. Among the contenders for the title of emperor was Constantine, whose mother Helena was a Christian. Constantine met his principal rival in battle at the Milvian Bridge in 312 C.E. Legend has it that as a result of a religious vision, Constantine permitted his soldiers to display crosses on their shields. His victory at Milvian Bridge, and his eventual emergence as the sole emperor of the united Roman Empire assured the restoration of Christian worship and Christian property. Technically, Constantine only insisted on the toleration of Christianity, but Christian symbols appear on coins from 315, and the older references to the gods disappear in 323.

Constantine himself chaired a council of the most important bishops of the church that met at Nicaea in Asia Minor in 325. That council addressed the most controversial issue of Christian theology in that time or any time: the relationship between Jesus and God. Should Jesus be regarded as fully equal in divinity to his Father, the creator of the universe, or should he be seen as subordinate to the Father? This dispute was fierce because it combined in one argument two difficult areas of contention. First, it obviously raises doubts about the belief in one God to think of Jesus being equal to the Father. But second, unless God has in some way actually taken on human flesh, humanity would have little hope of ever attaining eternal life with God. This great dispute about Christology (the nature of Christ) was framed in the philosophical language of the time, but it concerned central issues of Christian faith and life.

Under Constantine, the bishops at Nicaea adopted the principle that Father and Son are equal in their divinity. This new orthodoxy paved the way for the doctrine of the Trinity to emerge, according to which Father, Son, and Spirit are all united in their commonly divine being, although each has a distinctive character.

Following the practice of his time, Constantine only accepted baptism himself at the time of his death. Since it was impossible to achieve the benefit of baptism more than once (Heb 6:4-6), those whose professions implicated them in mortal sin often put off receiving this sacrament until they could promise to sin no more. Constantine's delay did not signal any cynicism on his part; there was no question but that Christianity was now the religion of the empire.

Part of Constantine's motivation in insisting upon a single orthodoxy for the church was that he believed it was crucial for the unity of the Roman Empire. That same concern for unity also caused him, in 330 C.E., to leave Rome and set up his capital in Byzantium, renaming it

Constantinople ("Constantine's City"), present-day Istanbul. This move east was both practical and strategic, putting the imperial court in the wealthier and more populous half of the empire and in a position to respond quickly to the military threat from the Sassanid dynasty in Persia.

A brief coda marks the extraordinary reversal of fortunes experienced by Judaism and Christianity between the first and the fourth centuries. Under Emperor Julian (361–363), a return to the old gods was attempted, and authorization for the rebuilding of the temple in Jerusalem was given. Here Judaism is treated as belonging to ancestral religion, rather than to one of the new movements such as Christianity or Manichaeanism. An earthquake greeted the attempt to bring the project off, which only encouraged the Christian mobs that resisted the policies of Julian. The emperor himself was killed in battle with the Sassanids. His death left Rome to the Christians, and Jewish hopes for the restoration of the temple in ruins. Babylonia, which had long offered a more congenial environment than Rome for a Judaism that wished to order its own affairs, now appeared to be a land of promise compared to a Jerusalem that could no longer host the temple.

The fourth century closed with Emperor Theodosius I (who ruled between 378 and 395) consolidating the inheritance of Constantine. He banned any Christian teaching that did not accord the regnant orthodoxy of Nicaea and outlawed the old paganism of Rome. He also came to an arrangement with the migrant people called the Visigoths, permitting them to remain in the Balkans in exchange for their military service. His policy proved fateful, because the Visigoths were then well positioned to be led by Alaric in a campaign of pillage that ended with the sacking of Rome itself in 410. The Roman Empire remained, but with an eastern capital city, and with a constitutional settlement that made church and empire virtually indistinguishable.

Autonomous Christianity

By the time of Constantine, Christianity had developed an identity separate from Judaism and distinct from the ancestral religions of the Roman Empire. Its newness promoted both the persecution of the movement (as a foreign innovation) and its embrace by Constantine (as proof of the emperor's toleration). A pivotal early moment in the development of this independent self-consciousness is marked by the publication of the

Epistle to the Hebrews (ca. 95 C.E.). Hebrews' argument turns on the presentation of the Day of Atonement, when the Bible prescribes sacrifice for the sins of the people of God. This sacrifice remains central to Judaism and Christianity, albeit in differing ways.

The superiority of what it calls a better covenant is spelled out in Hebrews through chapter 9, relying on the attachment to Jesus of God's promise in Psalm 110 (Heb 7:28, in the author's translation): "For the law appoints men having weakness as high priests, but the word of the oath which is after the law appoints a Son for ever perfected." Perfection implies that daily offerings are beside the point, and this became a perennial Christian theme. The Son sacrificed himself "once for all, when he offered himself up" (7:26-27, author's translation). Because his sacrifice involved his own life and was in complete obedience to God, it achieved a perfection that no other action could. Moses' prescriptions for the sanctuary were a pale imitation of the heavenly sanctuary that Jesus has actually entered (8:1-6). This basic idea is impossible to grasp, unless it is understood that early Christians did not think of Jesus simply as a person in history. He was rather the eternal Son of God, who existed for all time, so that the revelation to Moses was a partial disclosure of what Jesus perfectly embodied. Accordingly, the covenant mediated by Jesus is "better," the "second" replacing the "first," the "new" replacing what is now "obsolete" (8:6-13).

Hebrews develops a theory of the relationship between Jesus and the Scriptures of Israel. The Epistle has been compared to a homily and calls itself a "word of exhortation" in 13:22. *Word* here (*Logos*, as in John's Gospel) bears the meaning "discourse," and the choice of diction declares Hebrews' homiletic intent. It is a sustained argument on the basis of authoritative tradition that intends to convince its readers and hearers to embrace a fresh position and an invigorated sense of purpose in the world. Hebrews engages in a series of scriptural identifications of Jesus: both Scripture (in the form of the Septuagint, the Greek translation) and God's Son are the authoritative points of departure.

Chapter 9 puts the cap on this argument. The devotion to detail attests the concern to develop the relationship between Jesus and Scripture fully. The chapter begins with the "first" covenant's regulations for sacrifice, involving the temple in Jerusalem. They reach their climax on the Day of Atonement when the high priest made his single visit to the inner recess of the sanctuary called the holy of holies, to offer the sacrifice that only he could accomplish for sin (Heb 9:1-5).

That precise moment is only specified in order to be fixed, frozen forever. What was a fleeting movement, a single day, in the case of the high priest of Israel became for Hebrews an eternal truth in the case of Jesus. The movement of lesser priests—in and out of the holy place, the "first tabernacle" (9:6), while the high priest could only enter "the second tabernacle," the holy of holies (9:7), once a year—was designed by the Spirit of God as a parable: the way into the holy of holies could not be revealed while the first temple, the first tabernacle and its service, continued (9:8-10). That way could only be opened, after the temple was destroyed, by Christ, who became high priest and passed through "the greater and more perfect tabernacle" of his body (9:11) by the power of his own blood (9:12) so that he could find eternal redemption in the sanctuary.

This extended metaphor is characteristic of Catholic Christianity in its teaching that Jesus is God's eternal Son. Chapter 9 of Hebrews speaks as if Jesus' death and the destruction of the temple in Jerusalem coincided, although some forty years separated them. It is as if no significant time had passed between the crucifixion and the arson under Titus. Chronology dissolves in Hebrews' vision of eternity.

Hebrews takes it for granted that Jesus' own body was a kind of "tabernacle," an instrument of sacrifice (9:11), because the Gospels speak of his offering his body and his blood during the Last Supper with his disciples. The Epistle pursues the meaning of *body* and *blood* as Jesus' self-immolating means to his end as high priest. The temple in Jerusalem has in Hebrews been replaced by a purely theological construct. The true high priest, Jesus, has entered once for all (9:12) within the innermost recess of sanctity, so that no further sacrificial action is necessary or appropriate.

In the conception of Hebrews, the temple on earth was a copy and shadow of the heavenly sanctuary, of which Moses had seen "types." A type (*tupos* in Greek) is an impress, a derived version of a reality (the anti-type). Moses had seen in simulacrum the very throne of God, which was then approximated on earth. That approximation is called the "first covenant" (9:1), but the heavenly sanctuary into which Christ has entered (9:24) offers us a "new covenant" (9:15) that is the truth that has been palely reflected all along.

The concluding three chapters of Hebrews point what has preceded in order to influence the behavior of those who read and hear the Epistle. Literal sacrifice is to be eschewed (10:1-18), and the approach to God in purity is now by means of Jesus (10:19-22). Confession of faith in him is to be maintained, love and good works are to be encouraged, and communal gatherings are to continue as the day of the Lord approaches (10:23-25).

Above all, Hebrews says there is to be no turning back, no matter what the incentives (10:26-40). Faith in that sense is praised as the virtue of the patriarchs, prophets and martyrs of old, although they were not perfected (11:1-40). Jesus alone offers perfection, as "the pioneer and perfecter of our faith" (12:1-3). Many related commandments follow: do not be afraid of shedding your blood (12:4), do not become immoral or irreligious in leaving old ways behind (12:16), give hospitality and care for prisoners and those who are mistreated (13:1-3), honor marriage and do not love money (13:4-5), respect leaders and beware false teaching (13:7, 9, 17), remember to share and to pray (13:16, 18). Interesting as those commands are individually (especially in drawing a social profile of the community addressed), the overriding theme is evident and carries the weight of the argument (12:14):

> Pursue peace with all, and sanctification, apart from which no one will see God. Divine vision, the sanctification to stand before God, is in Hebrews the goal of human life, and the only means to such perfection is loyalty to Jesus as the great high priest.

The sense of finality, of a perfection to which one must remain true, is deliberately emphasized (12:22-24):

> But you have come to Mount Zion and the city of the living God, the heavenly Jerusalem, and to myriads of angels in festal gathering, and to the assembly of first-born enrolled in heaven, and to a judge—God of all, and to the spirits of the just who are made perfect, and to Jesus the mediator of a new covenant, and to sprinkled blood which speaks better than the blood of Abel (author's translation).

Jesus, the only mediator of perfection, provides access to that heavenly place, which is the city of the faithful, the heart's only sanctuary.

Hebrews so centrally locates Jesus as the locus of revelation that in due course it became inevitable to develop a theology concerning his natures—human and divine—and his consciousness. Hebrews reflects the development of a religious system that derives completely from Jesus. The ability of the author of Hebrews to relegate Israel to history (see 8:8, 10; 11:22) is related to the insistence, from the outset of the Epistle, that the Son's authority is greater than that of the Scripture. Scripture is only authoritative to the extent that it attests the salvation mediated by the son (1:14; 2:3-4). The theory of types (typology) that is framed later in the Epistle between Jesus and the temple derives directly from the conviction of the prior authority of the Son of God in relation to Scripture.

Hebrews relativizes Israel and Israel's Scriptures, so that it became fashionable among Christians to speak of the "Old Testament" or "old covenant" in contrast to the "New Testament" or "new covenant." Hebrews traces its theology into Christ's replacement of every major institution, every principal term of reference, within the Judaism of its time. Before Hebrews, there were Christian Judaisms, in which Christ was conceived of as the key to the promises to Israel in various ways.[6] Hebrews' theology proceeds from those earlier theologies, but it self-consciously develops a system of autonomous Christianity, because all that is Judaic is held to have been provisional upon the coming of the Son, after which point it is no longer meaningful. There is a single center within the theology of Hebrews. Christ is the beginning, middle, and end of theology, just as he is the same yesterday, today, and forever (Heb 13:8). This center is not Christ *with* Moses, Christ *with* temple, Christ *with* David, Christ *with* Abraham, Christ *with* Scripture, Christ *with* Israel. In the end, the center is not really even Christ with Melchizedek (a figure whose meaning is explored in Hebrews), because Melchizedek disappears in the glory of Jesus, his heavenly archetype. Everything else is provisional—and expendable—within the consuming fire that is God (12:29).

Hebrews forms the theological capstone of the New Testament canon. It marks the moment at which "Israel" is rendered obsolete for Christianity. With Hebrews' emergence, Christianity's scriptural resources were complete.

Christian faith is grounded in the Holy Spirit, God's communication of the divine self in all its richness. Access to the Holy Spirit is possible because in Jesus Christ God became human. The incarnation (God's becoming flesh; *caro* in Latin) is what provides the possibility of divine Spirit becoming accessible to the human spirit. The primal case for all time of a person being fully identified with God, according to the theology of the church, offers the possibility that every believer can share that divine nature with Jesus.

Documenting the Spirit

From the perspective of Christian faith, then, there is a single source of theology: the Holy Spirit that proceeds from the Father and Son. Because God's very nature is love itself, this procession outward to all those he created is the unique and indivisible means of revelation.

Human beings are created with the capacity to know the Spirit in this sense. Yet the inspiration of the Holy Spirit has been discovered and articulated by means of distinct kinds of literature in the history of the church. In the diversity of those sources, both the variety and the coherence of Christianity may be appreciated.

The Scriptures of Israel have always been valued within the church, primarily in the Greek translation used in the Mediterranean world. (The Greek rendering is called the Septuagint, after the seventy-two translators who were said to have produced it; see *The Letter of Aristeas*.) Those were the only Scriptures of the church in its primitive phase, when the New Testament was being composed. In their meetings for prayer and worship, followers of Jesus saw the Scriptures of Israel "fulfilled" by their faith. Their conviction was that the same Spirit of God active in the prophets was available to them through Christ in a way that realized the Spirit's power and constituted God's chosen people.

In addition to the Scriptures of Israel, Christians also assembled and read documents that had been composed within their own communities. The New Testament was produced in primitive churches to prepare people for baptism, to order worship, to resolve disputes, to encourage faith, and for like purposes. As a whole, it is a collective document of primitive Christianity. Its purpose is to call out and order the people of God in response to the triumphant news of Jesus' preaching, activity, death, and resurrection. The New Testament provides the means of accessing the Spirit spoken of in the Scriptures of Israel. Once the New Testament was formed, it was natural—as we have seen in assessing the Epistle to the Hebrews—to refer to the Scriptures of Israel as the "Old Testament."

The Old Testament remains classic for Christians because it represents the ways in which God's Spirit might be known. At the same time, the New Testament is normative. It sets out how believers actually appropriate the Spirit of God that is also the Spirit of Christ. That is why the Bible as a whole is accorded a place of absolute privilege in the Christian tradition; it is the literary source from which believers know both how the Spirit of God has been known and how they can appropriate it.

Christian thinkers in the first centuries after the New Testament—usually called "Early Christianity" today—have also been accorded a special status in the theology of the Catholic Church. Although Christians were under extreme—sometimes violent—pressure from the Roman Empire, the early Christian era was a time of unique creativity. From thinkers as different from one another as Bishop Irenaeus in second-century France and Origen, the speculative third-century teacher active first in Egypt and then in Palestine, a common Christian philosophy began to emerge. Early Christianity might also be called a "catholic" phase, in the sense that it was a quest for a "general" or "universal" account of the faith, but that designation may lead to confusion with Roman Catholicism at a later period.

After the Roman Empire itself embraced Christianity in the fourth century, the church was in a position formally to articulate its understanding of the faith by means of common standards. During this period correct norms of worship, baptism, creeds, biblical texts, and doctrines were established. From Augustine in the West to Gregory of Nyssa in the East, Christianity for the first and only time in its history approached being truly ecumenical, a single worldwide movement of Spirit.

Jesus and his movement clearly recognized the traditional grouping of the Hebrew canon of Scripture into the Torah, the Prophets (often distinguished between the Former Prophets [Joshua–2 Kings] and the Latter Prophets [Isaiah–Malachi]), and the Writings. That grouping is cited in as so many words in Luke 24:44. But the Gospels themselves were written in Greek, and the Bible of the church was also Greek in language and Hellenistic in conception.

A great deal of work has been done in recent years on the Greek text of the Septuagint;[7] less attention has been given to the actual order of books in the rendering, which amounts to a radical revision of the significance of the Hebrew Bible. The Septuagint truly creates an Old Testament by the time of the first extant manuscript of the whole (the Codex Vaticanus, dated in the fourth century C.E.). The sequence and structure of the canon follows a pattern in the Septuagint significantly different from that of the Hebrew Bible. The grouping of Law, Prophets, and Writings is changed in the Codex Vaticanus to become a new pattern and order in which the first group is seen as "historical," the second "poetical," and the third "prophetic."[8]

By this change of order, the Prophets immediately preceded the Gospels of the New Testament. Moreover, the Prophet books were put in an order that facilitated an eschatological interpretation. The septuagintal order, by commencing with the Minor Prophets, is able to finish off with the greatest of the literary Prophets: Isaiah, Jeremiah (with additions), and Ezekiel.

Even more strikingly, the Old Testament canon closes with Daniel, now emphatically and climactically one of the Prophets (rather than one of the Writings, as in the Hebrew Bible). Daniel refers to the resurrection of the dead explicitly (12:2), the only work in the Old Testament to do so. Further, Daniel speaks of an angelic figure said to be "like a Son of Man" (7:13; 9:21; 10:16), and Jesus is identified with that figure in the Gospels. Here, then, was an ideal transition into the story of Jesus. It is interesting that the canon of the New Testament, which was also solidifying during the fourth century, closes similarly on a strong note of prophecy, with the Revelation to John, the most eschatological book in the New Testament.

Christians in North Africa were especially attached to the prophetic character of the people's faith. The teacher named Tertullian reflects this strict attachment to divine Spirit and the imminent expectation of judgment, which characterized much of Christianity during the second century. He addressed a book he called an *Apology* (that is, a philosophical and legal defense) to those who might be called upon to judge Christians, but in fact it was intended to counter the common prejudice that Christianity endured. It is as effective an example of rhetoric as one will find, and at the same time it illustrates the legal situation and the popular reaction to the new religion in the time after Trajan. The *Apology* was written in 197 C.E., shortly after Tertullian's conversion to Christianity, and excoriates the "don't ask, don't tell" policy that Trajan began, insisting that believers should not be persecuted for testifying to the Spirit within them.

The enthusiasm for the power of Spirit within them caused some Christians to insist that special gifts—such as speaking in tongues, visions, and fasting, as well as believing in particular doctrines—made them superior to other Christians, or even the only true believers. Irenaeus, bishop of Lyons during the second century, countered this tendency with what was called by his time a "catholic" faith. Faith as catholic is "through the whole" *(kath holou)* of the church. It is faith such as you would find it commonly in Alexandria, Antioch, Corinth, Ephesus, Lyons, Rome—not just in exceptional communities. That construction of Christianity is designed to stop any particular, local belief or custom becoming a requirement imposed on Christians as a whole.

Irenaeus's attempt to join in establishing a generic or catholic Christianity called attention to four aspects of faith that have remained constant in classic definitions of Christianity. First, faith was to be expressed by means of the Scriptures as received from Israel; there was no question of eliminating the Old Testament. That was the program of many groups called gnostic, whose name comes from the word for "knowledge" (*gnosis* in Greek). Some gnostics believed that their special insight enabled them to see that this world and whatever powers controlled it (including the God of the Old Testament) were false, and that only their knowledge revealed a completely spiritual reality beyond this world. Catholics, in contrast, insisted that Jesus revealed the same God who created the world. Second, catholic faith was grounded in the preachers whom Jesus himself delegated to teach (the apostles), as instanced in their own writings and also in the creeds. Third, communities were to practice their faith by means of the sacraments—rituals that brought worshipers into the presence of God's Spirit—that were universally recognized among Christians at that time, baptism and Eucharist. Fourth, the loyalty of the church to these principles was to be assured by the authority of bishops and priests, understood as successors of the Jesus' apostles. Taken together, these were the constituents of "the great and glorious body of Christ." They made the church a divine institution: "Where the Spirit of God is, there is the church and all grace, and the Spirit is truth" (see Irenaeus, *Against Heresies* 4.33.7).

Although Irenaeus's conception of Catholicism was designed to be inclusive, it was deliberately at odds with emerging Gnosticism. The issue was not only the status of the Old Testament (which was typically contested by gnostics). Gnostics also cherished writings that were not apostolic, sacraments of initiation that were not universal, and leaders who were authorized by private revelation rather than by the Spirit moving communally in the church. Irenaeus's concern to establish this fourfold definition of the church is consonant with one of his most vivid observations. He says the fact that there are four Gospels corresponds to the four quarters of the heavens, the four principal winds that circle the world, and the four cherubims before the throne of God. Indeed, the number four corresponds to the four universal (or catholic) covenants between God and humanity: those of Noah, Abraham, Moses, and Christ (see Irenaeus, *Against Heresies* 3.9.8). The Gospels belong to the order of the very basics of life, and—what is equally important in Irenaeus's mind— the basics of life belong to the Gospels. That is axiomatic within catholic Christianity: when the word became flesh in the incarnation of Jesus, flesh was sanctified.

The incarnational emphasis of catholic Christianity is accurately conveyed by its most ancient, second-century confession of faith, which is still in use under the title Apostles' Creed. The form in which it is currently used, however, was considerably developed during a time beyond our period of interest. As a guide to its ancient formulation, the best source is *Apostolic Tradition* of Hippolytus.[9] Hippolytus sets out the three questions that candidates for baptism answered, "I believe."

> Do you believe in God the Father Almighty?
> Do you believe in Christ Jesus the Son of God,
>   born by the Holy Spirit of the Virgin Mary,
>   who was crucified under Pontius Pilate and died
>   and rose again on the third day, alive from the dead
>   and ascended into heaven
> and sat on the right hand of the Father
>   who will come to judge the living and dead?
> Do you believe in the Holy Spirit
>   and the holy Church and the resurrection of the flesh?

The division of the creed into three sections, corresponding to Father, Son, and Spirit, is evident. That marks the commitment of the early Christian church to the Trinity as a means of conceiving God. Its commitment necessitated a philosophical explanation, which Origen provided during the third century. Indeed, the Trinity correlates with the kind of incarnational faith that is expressed in the creed.

The incarnation refers principally to Jesus as the embodiment of God, from the time of the prologue of John's Gospel (1:1-18). In the creed, however, that view of the incarnation is developed further. In its focus on Jesus as God's eternal Son, the longest, middle paragraph shows that the ancient practice of Christian catechesis is at the heart of the creed, and that paragraph is a fine summary of the Gospels (compare Peter's speech in Acts 10:34-43, where baptism is also at issue). But the statement about Jesus does not stand on its own. His status as Son is rooted in the recognition of the Father, understood as the creator of the heavens and the earth. The creed begins with an embrace of the God of Israel as creator and with an equally emphatic (if indirect) rejection of gnostic dualism.

The last paragraph of the creed, devoted to the Holy Spirit, also recollects the catechesis of Christians, which climaxed with baptism and reception of the spirit. That basic understanding was rooted in the catechesis of Peter, one of Jesus' first followers and an apostolic leader (again, see Acts 10:34-43 and the sequel in vv. 44-48). But here the common reception of the Spirit is used to assert the communal nature of life in the Spirit. To be baptized is to share the Spirit with the Holy Church; that is where communion with God, forgiveness, and the promise of the resurrection are to be found.

Finally, the creed closes on a deeply personal and existential note. "The resurrection" here refers, not to Jesus' resurrection (which has already been mentioned), but to the ultimate destiny of all who believe in God. The creed does not spell out its understanding of how God raised Jesus and how he is to raise us from the dead, but it is unequivocal that all are raised as embodied personality. There is no trace here of joining an undifferentiated divine entity, or of some part of a person (a soul, an essence) surviving in a disembodied way.

Christianity's Prophetic Philosophy

From the second century onward, Christian literature emerged that engaged in a spirited, intellectual defense of Christianity. The defense was conducted in the midst of the diverse and competing philosophies and religions of the Roman Empire at the time. In that environment, in which adherents of diverse groups were attracted to Christianity, it was imperative to develop an account of the intellectual integrity of faith, an "apology" or intellectual defense in the philosophical sense.

Christianity and Gnosticism both challenged the religious sensibilities of the Greco-Roman world, and revolutionized the understanding of what religion is. During the second century, both of them had discovered the idiom of philosophy in order to develop and convey their claims. Particularly, each crafted a distinctive view of the divine *Word* (*Logos*) that conveys the truth of God to humanity. For most Christians, that *Logos* was Jesus Christ, understood as the human teacher who fully incarnated what philosophers and prophets had been searching for and had partially seen. Gnostics were inclined to see that *Word* as a fully divine, ahistoric revelation of the truth. But whether the *Logos* was understood with an incarnational or a gnostic meaning, it offered the Greco-Roman world the prospect of seeing the whole of reality from a divine perspective. With Christianity and Gnosticism, philosophy and religion joined forces, and in their common identity became a permanent component of civilization in the West.

Justin Martyr was the theologian who articulated the *Logos* most clearly from the perspective of Christianity on the basis of the Gospel according to John. In 151 C.E. he addressed his *Apology* to the emperor himself, Antonius Pius. Justin believed the "true philosophy" represented by Christ, attested in the Scriptures of Israel, would triumph among the other options available at the time. He had been trained within some of those traditions, and by his Samaritan birth he laid claim to represent something of the wisdom of the East.

Justin argued that the light of reason in people is put there by God and is to be equated with the Word of God incarnate in Jesus. His belief in the salvation of people as they actually are is attested by his attachment to millenarianism, the conviction that Christ would return to reign with his saints for a thousand years. That conviction, derived from Revelation 20, was fervently maintained by many catholic Christians during the second century.

In strictly religious terms, Christianity did not compete well within the second century. Greco-Roman preferences were for noble, ancient faiths, and the movement centered on Jesus was incontrovertibly recent and base-born. Moreover, it could and often did appear to be subversive of the authority of the emperor. After all, Christians did not accept the imperial title of *divi filius* and instead applied it to their rabbi, who had died as a criminal under Roman justice. Moreover, Jesus' status as a rabbi was challenged over time because the recognized authorities of Judaism did not accept Christians as among their numbers. The persecution of Christianity had been as established policy of the Roman Empire for nearly a century by the time Justin wrote.

The Christianity that Justin defended, however, was as much a philosophy as it was a religion. His claim was that the light of reason in humanity, which had already been indirectly available, became fully manifest in the case of Jesus Christ. Jesus, therefore, was the perfect sage, and Socrates as much as Isaiah was his prophet. In that sense, Christianity was older than humanity; it was only its manifestation that was recent.

To make out his case, Justin used arguments that had been employed when Philo of Alexandria defended Judaism. Philo also identified the *Logos*, the prophetic word articulated in Scripture, as the reason through which God created the world and animates humanity. (Unlike Justin, of course, Philo draws no conclusions about Jesus, his contemporary.) Philo even makes out the historical case that Moses was an influence on the Greek philosopher Plato, so that the extent to which Greek philosophy illuminates God's wisdom is quite derivative. Justin is even bolder, in that his argument does not rely on such an historical premise. Rather, Justin contended that in Jesus the primordial archetype of humanity and of the world itself, the *Logos*, became accessible and knowable in a way that it was not before.

The relationship between Philo and Justin shows the extent to which Judaism in the first century and Christianity in the second century relied upon the revival of Plato's thought to provide them with a way of expressing how their respective religions were philosophically the most appropriate. Philo's case, argued in his brilliant continuous commentary on the Pentateuch in Greek, identified the creative *Logos* behind our world and in our minds as the Torah that God revealed perfectly to Moses. Justin, in a less voluminous way, more the essayist than the scholar, insisted that our knowledge of the *Logos* implies that it is eternally human and that its human instance is Jesus. The Platonic picture of perfect intellectual models was their common axiom, invoked in Philo's rounded, elegant Greek, and in Justin's controversial, rhetorical Greek. Had Philo and Justin met and disputed, Judaism and Christianity would have been represented as approximate equals and on a level playing field for the only time in their history.

Unfortunately not only one hundred years divided Philo and Justine, but also watershed events. The temple in Jerusalem had been burned under the Roman general Titus in 70 C.E., and taken apart by Emperor Hadrian's order in 135. Judaism was still tolerated in a way Christianity was not, but it was a movement now under suspicion. Judaism needed to reconstitute itself in the wake of the failed revolts against Rome that resulted in the double destruction of the temple. The rabbis who reinvented Judaism during the second century did so not on the basis of Platonism, but on grounds of a new intellectual contention. They held that the categories of purity established in their oral teaching as well as in Scripture were the very structures according to which God conducted the world. Mishnah, the principal work of the Rabbis, is less a book of law (which it is commonly mistaken for) than a science of the purity that God's humanity—that is, Israel—is to observe.

So complete was the rabbinic commitment to systematic purity at the expense of Platonism that Philo's own work was not preserved within Judaism. It only became known as a result of the work of Christian copyists. So the very philosophical idiom that the Rabbis turned from as a matter of survival—philosophical argument on a Platonist basis—was what Justin turned to, also as a matter of survival. Somewhere between 162 and 168, however, Justin was martyred in Rome, a victim of the increasing hostility to Christianity under the reign of Marcus Aurelius.

Prior to his death, however, Justin put Christianity on the intellectual course it would follow for centuries, both in embracing Plato and in claiming to supersede Judaism. He sets his *Dialogue with Trypho, A Jew* in the period after the revolt under Simon called Bar Kokhba (*Dialogue*, chap. 1), which lasted between 132 and 135. Thematically, Justin disputes Judaism's conception of the permanent obligation of the law (chaps. 1–47), and he sees the purpose of Scriptures in their witness to Christ's divinity (chaps. 48–108), which justifies the acceptance of non-Jews within the church (chaps. 109–136). Justin argues that the systemic meaning of the Scriptures of Israel is Christ, not the law of Moses.

Justin describes his own development from Platonism to Christianity as a result of a conversation with an old man. The sage convinced him that the highest good that Platonism can attain, the human soul, should not be confused with God himself since the soul depends upon God for life (chap. 6). Knowledge of God depends rather upon the revelation of God's Spirit (chap. 7):

> Long ago, he replied, there lived men more ancient than all the so-called philosophers, men righteous and beloved of God, who spoke by the divine spirit and foretold things to come, that even now are taking place. These men were called prophets. They alone both saw the truth and proclaimed it to men, without awe or fear of anyone, moved by no desire for glory, but speaking only those things which they saw and heard when filled with the Holy Spirit. Their writings are still with us, and whoever will may read them and, if he believes them, gain much knowledge of the beginning and end of things, and all else a philosopher ought to know. For they did not employ logic to prove their statements, seeing they were witnesses to the truth. . . . They glorified the creator of all things, as God and Father, and proclaimed the Christ sent by him as his Son. . . . But pray that, before all else, the gates of light may be opened to you. For not everyone can see or understand these things, but only he to whom God and his Christ have granted wisdom.

Here is a self-conscious Christianity, which distinguishes itself from Judaism and proclaims itself the true and only adequate philosophy. Justin's account of the truth of the *Logos* depends upon two sources of revelation that resonate with each other: the prophetic Scriptures that attest the Spirit and the wise reader who has been inspired by the Spirit.

Justin is quite clear, then, that his concern is not with the immediate reference of Scripture or what we would call its historical or literal meaning. In his *Dialogue*, Justin portrays Trypho as being limited to the immediate reference of Scripture, enslaved by its specification of laws.

Justin is committed to a typological reading of Scripture, following the principles of interpretation developed in the Epistle to the Hebrews. This became the Christian norm during the second century. The prophets were understood to represent "types" of Christ, impressions on their minds of the heavenly reality, God's own son. Isaac, for example, was taken to be a type of Jesus; where Isaac was nearly offered by his father Abraham on Mount Moriah in Genesis chapter 22, Jesus was actually offered on Golgotha. Trypho, by contrast, is portrayed as becoming lost in the literal meaning of the prophetic text. Christians such as Tertullian called any limitation to the immediate reference of Scripture (its "literal meaning") the "Jewish sense."

Anyone who is familiar with the development of Judaism from the second century onward will see the irony of understanding Judaic interpretation as literal. The second century was the period when the Rabbis interpreted Scripture in terms of its eternal meaning and when any limitation to its immediate reference came to be overridden by an appeal to the significance of the eternal Torah. Genesis 22 is a case in point. From the second century onward, Jewish interpreters asserted that Isaac was slain on Moriah, that he accepted his fate as a fully grown adult, and that God raised him from the dead. In other words, Isaac was a type of martyr in Judaism, as well as in Christianity. But the meaning of the type was different, involving a martyr's obedience to the Torah rather than to a prophet's vision of Christ.

Therefore what Justin presented as a meeting of minds is in fact a missing of minds. Both Justin and Trypho make the immediate reference of Scripture subservient to its ultimate significance. But because Christianity was committed to the *Logos* as its systemic center, and Judaism was committed to the Torah as its systemic center, the two could not understand each other. In the absence of any language to discuss systemic relationships, the two sides disputed about which makes better sense of the immediate reference (the "literal meaning") of the texts concerned. What is billed as a dialogue is really a shadow play, in that learned leaders reinforce their own positions by arguing over what neither side believed really matters.

The enduring contribution of Justin does not reside in his confrontation with Trypho, but in his account of how Christianity discovers the meaning of Scripture. The reader's recognition of God's Spirit in the text on the basis of God's Spirit moving within the reader is a classic formulation. Justin's synthesis joined the prophets of Israel and the philosophers of Greece into a single system, insisting that believers could find life and meaning, not in this world, but in the world to come. That otherworldly emphasis continued until the moment of Constantine's conversion, when Christians found themselves influencing temporal forces they had learned for centuries to reject or ignore.

Conclusion

In this chapter we have seen how Judaism prior to the time of Jesus provided Jesus and his movement with the religious vocabulary they used in their expectation of "the kingdom of God." The power of the Roman Empire exerted an influence on the early Judaism that was the context of Christianity, and Roman persecution directly challenged the existence of Christianity. The Roman emperor Constantine's conversion to Christianity therefore introduced a change of revolutionary proportions. By the time that revolution came during the fourth century, Christianity had responded to the destruction of the temple in 70 C.E. and to continuing debates with Jewish teachers by means of their theology that Jesus, the eternal Son of God, was the inner meaning of all the institutions of Judaism. That conviction shaped the emergence of the New Testament, the creeds of Christianity, and the thought of its leading teachers. They believed that the Spirit of God, released by Jesus' resurrection from the dead, had placed the mantle of prophecy on every follower of Jesus.

Constantine's conversion meant that the values embodied in Christianity's emergence became the values of Western civilization. The Bible of both the Old and New Testaments is the preeminent classic of the West as well as the canon (the standard of faith) of the church. The means of reading that text set out by Justin and his colleagues, attending to the Spirit rather than the letter, remains a basic principle for the interpretation of the Bible and other foundational texts to this day.

Faith in Jesus as the "Son" of God, a term disputed as much today as during the fourth century, reaches beyond matters of definition. The belief that God in the case of Jesus became one with human flesh has posed the question whether human beings can rightly treat this world as a dispensable commodity. The West continues to struggle with the basically incarnational challenge of finding divine meaning embodied in earthen vessels.

Christian sacraments are celebrated all over world today, and not only tolerated, but also supported in the West. Even states that declare their separation from religious concerns embrace many of the symbols and practices of Christianity in the manner of Constantine. Western governments continually respond to the challenge of meeting moral standards set by the church in their conviction that it gives voice to the Spirit of God, confident that "Where the Spirit of God is, there is the Church and all grace, and the Spirit is truth" (see Irenaeus, *Against Heresies* 4.33.7).

Discussion Questions

1. How did Roman policies toward Israel affect the attitude of the empire toward Christianity?

2. Why did the issue of Christianity prove difficult for Roman emperors to resolve?

3. What influence did the prophetic movement exert on the development of Christianity?

4. When would you say that Christianity and Judaism became different religions?

CHAPTER 4

ISLAM: WHAT IT IS AND HOW IT HAS INTERACTED WITH WESTERN CIVILIZATION

Th. Emil Homerin

Introduction

For many Americans, the word *Muslim* invokes a host of images: a veiled woman, a robed bedouin on camelback, an angry black man, and, especially today, an Arab terrorist. Though such impressions have some basis in fact, they are limited and limiting when we recall that many Muslim women have never worn a veil; only 2 million of the 180 million Arabs in the world are nomads, and Muslim militants are a tiny faction denounced by most Muslims, too. Further, not all Arabs are Muslim, while most of the world's 1 billion Muslims are not Arabs, nor can the vast majority of Muslims read Arabic. It is crucial, then, that we interrogate our images and stereotypes regarding Muslims, especially in light of the fact that there are millions of Muslims living throughout Europe today; and over four million American Muslims, some of whom died as firemen, policemen, and workers at the World Trade Center on September 11, 2001. The following chapter examines Islamic religious experiences and how they have shaped Muslim thought, culture, and history. We begin with the development of Islam from its origins in pre-Islamic Arabia, the revelation of the Qur'an, and Muhammad's teachings, and then move on to discuss the classical Islamic tradition in its various forms including law, theology, philosophy, and mysticism. Of particular importance are historical and political developments, especially those between Muslim and European powers, and we will conclude with an overview of the living faith practiced in various forms by Muslims in the world today.

Origins and Predecessors

The religious center of the Muslim world has always been the Ka'bah, the holy shrine in the city of Mecca, in present-day Saudi Arabia. But even before the rise of Islam, this was a special place for the Arab people throughout the region and beyond. Since the ninth century B.C.E., Arabs were a visible presence in the ancient world. Arab merchants called at Mediterranean ports, while rulers of the great Arab cities of Petra, Palmyra, and Hatra aspired to political power. On three separate occasions, an Arab ruled the Roman Empire as Caesar, yet a successful Arab dynasty failed to materialize in the Arabian Peninsula. Nevertheless, Arab cities long served as important centers of international commerce linking east and west, facilitating trade in material goods, ideas, and religion. Religious beliefs, cults, and practices flourished in the urban and nomadic cultures of the Arabian Peninsula and among the neighboring Arab-speaking communities, from earliest recorded history until the spread of Islam in the seventh century C.E., and some of these beliefs and practices would influence the shape and content of Islam.

The Arabian religions were polytheistic and characterized by idol worship and a mixture of beliefs and practices, local and imported, public and private. The most famous rite was an annual tribal pilgrimage to circumambulate one or more sacred stones called *baetyl*, from *bet 'el*, "house of the god." One of the best known was the Black Stone in the Ka'bah at Mecca, which would later become the goal of Muslim pilgrims. However, other stones were also venerated prior to Islam. Sacred stones could be found in temples, niches, and in the open air, but they were generally part of a larger rectangular area. This sanctuary (*haram*) could be partially covered and usually contained an altar for sacrifice, a well or cistern for ablutions, and one or more sacred trees in which offerings might be hung. The trees and other objects of the sanctuary were inviolate, and this was also a place of refuge for fugitives and any animals there. Thus the sanctuaries served to protect the areas surrounding them, which often became staging posts for commerce and caravans. Specific tribes cared for particular sanctuaries in northern Arabia, while in the south, the sanctuaries and their temples were looked after by religious functionaries. Pilgrimage to these sanctuaries could include fasting, sexual abstinence, a moratorium on fighting, burnt offerings, and sacrifices. Public ceremonies with incense and libations and sacrificial banquets were also held in honor of the deities.

The particular deities worshiped by the Arabs varied, but they have been traditionally grouped as those of southern and northern Arabia. A triad of astral deities representing the moon, the sun, and Venus was worshiped in the cults of the southern Arabian kingdoms. In the northern regions of Arabia and its perimeter, El or Ilah ("god") was worshiped, as was a host of other deities, including Ba'al, Dusharra, Shamash, Wadd ("love"), Hubal, and many others. The goddesses al-Lat ("goddess"), al-ʿUzza ("the strong"), and Manat ("fate") appear to have been frequently venerated in northern and central Arabia on the eve of Islam. Manat was also worshiped by the Nabataens, who identified her with the Greek goddess Nemesis. Other indigenous deities served as local protectors of a particular place or tribe.

The private religious rites of the Arabs were usually led by older men, and only members or affiliates of the clan could participate. The clan religions, then, were particular to a specific kin group and were not considered universal. Individual devotions included the use of geometric and/or animal symbols with inscriptions, worship of household gods, and, in southern Arabia, the worship of astral deities from roof terraces. Arabian inscriptions and graffiti often deal with personal matters, including prayers that the deity grant health and prosperity; and give safety and booty in battle; take vengeance on enemies and curse the foes. Some inscriptions offer thanksgiving or request expiation for transgressions. These religious acts, like those of many other ancient tribal societies, primarily served the present life of the group and the clan or community, not the individual, assuring, then, the permanent and unfailing help of the deity providing that the rites and rituals were properly performed.

Groups of worshipers might refer to themselves as the children of their particular deity (e.g., the children of the god Wadd). Further, many personal and tribal names were derived from those of animals (e.g., children of the Wolf), suggesting that identification with animals (totemism) probably served as an important mode of social grouping at an early stage of Arabian society and religion. The ancient Arabs also believed in the presence of spirits (animism) and powerful objects (fetishism) that could influence human behavior and events. Jinnis, ghouls, and other supernatural beings were thought to inhabit desolate places, waiting to lead heedless travelers to destruction. The jinnis were also thought to inspire diviners and poets, and they were closely associated with certain kinds of animals such as the owl and snake. The teeth and bones of various animals and other objects were believed to be efficacious in warding off evil spirits, and amulets and assorted rites were used as preventative medicine. Diviners *(kahins)* might fall into trance and foretell the future in oracles or take omens from the flight and cries of birds, while the sudden appearance and movement of certain animals contained hidden portents.

Life appeared as a series of calamities governed by a blind and capricious fate, an unpredictable tyrant who appointed the time of every person's death. Though most Arabs probably did not acknowledge a resurrection, they appear to have believed in a kind of reduced existence for the dead, since the dead were buried with such items as water and wine. The deceased were often buried in graves, which ranged from a trench or pit in the desert to freestanding tombs and tomb-facades in the cliffs near Petra. Among the tribes, a dead man's riding camel might also be left to starve to death at the grave so as to serve her master in the netherworld. Some of the ancient Arabs also believed that a spirit could return from the dead as a savage thirsty owl demanding vengeance for an unjust death.

The ethos of the ancient Arabs might be termed a heroic humanism. In the face of life's uncertainties, the Arabs held to a code of "manliness" *(muruᶜah)*, much of it still practiced today, which created social standards regarding what was honorable, including hospitality, generosity, bravery, and courage. Of special importance was protecting the tribe's women and children whose continued existence and prosperity were to be ensured by the age-old rite of blood vengeance. However, taking vengeance could also lead to a prolonged vendetta and needless bloodshed, and the pre-Islamic period has often been referred to as the *al-Jahiliyah*, the "Age of Impetuosity," as quick tempers and generations of ill will overruled wisdom and restraint.

An Ode by Shahl ibn Shayban al-Zimmani:
We forgave the sons of Hind
　　and said: "The folk are brothers.
"Perhaps the days will restore
　　the tribe as they were."
But when the evil was plain and clear,
　　stripped bare to see,
And nothing remained but enmity,
　　then we paid back as they paid!
We strode like the stalking lion,
　　the furious lion,

> With a devastating, crunching,
>   crushing blow,
> And a thrust, gashing, spewing
>   like the mouth of a very full wineskin.
> A little restraint when quick action is called for,
>   tells of servitude.
> And in evil is salvation
>   when goodness can not save you.[1]

Arabian society was in close contact with ancient Egyptian, Hellenistic, and Indo-Iranian cultures; and monotheistic and messianic ideas gradually spread throughout the Arabian Peninsula a few centuries prior to Islam, often by missionaries and merchants from Syria, Mesopotamia, and Ethiopia. Several Arab tribes in the north converted to Christianity, and Christian communities grew up in Najran near Yemen. Similarly, groups of Jews also migrated into Arabia, perhaps, for some, to escape Roman persecution, and Jewish settlements flourished in southern Arabia at San°a, and further north in the towns of Khaybar, Yathrib (Medina), and Tayma' in the Hijaz region. Significantly, some Arabs apparently repudiated polytheism and worshiped one god alone, becoming monotheists without converting to Christianity or Judaism. Nevertheless, monotheism, in any form, was embraced by comparatively few Arabs prior to Islam, though its presence in Arabia presaged religious change.[2]

The Birth of Islam: Its Scripture and Major Tenets

The Prophet Muhammad

Muhammad was born around 570 C.E. in Mecca and was orphaned young. He was a member of the Banu Hashim clan of the Quraysh tribe, which regulated and oversaw the pilgrimage to the sanctuary containing the Ka°bah and its Black Stone. Muhammad was raised by an uncle, Abu Talib, and worked with him as part of the well-established Quraysh caravan trade. Muhammad married Khadijah, a prosperous widow, and together they had four daughters. Muhammad grew to be a respected member of the tribe, but he was troubled by social and religious concerns. The sixth and seventh centuries for this region were a time of transition that was marked by ongoing tribal disputes, oligarchic rule, and religious ferment. According to Muslim tradition, Muhammad thought deeply on the problems plaguing his society, and at times he would go alone to reflect on these matters in a cave on Mt. Hira' outside of Mecca. One day, perhaps in the year 610 C.E., Muhammad went to the cave and was shocked to receive a revelation from God, which began:

> Recite in the name of your Lord who created, created the human from a clot of blood. Recite, for your Lord is the most generous, who taught by the pen, taught humanity what it did not know! (96:1-5)[3]

This is regarded as the beginning of God's revelation to Muhammad, which culminated a time of introspection and initiated a period of public action. Muhammad returned to Mecca where he soon began to preach and call people to worship the one true God, *Allah*. During his early prophetic career in Mecca, Muhammad also denounced idolatry, called for economic and social justice for all, and warned of an awesome judgment day.

Surah 99: *The Earthquake*
In the Name of God, the Compassionate, the Merciful
When the earth is shaken, trembling,
And the earth brings forth her burdens,
And people say: "What is with her?"
Then she will relate her news
That God revealed to her.
Then people will stagger forth to see their deeds.
For, whoever does an atom's weight of good, will see it,
And whoever does an atom's weight of evil, will see it.

But powerful members of Muhammad's own tribe opposed him, some claiming that he was possessed by a jinni. They denied his revelations and persecuted those who followed him. Yet Muhammad wanted desperately to convert his Quraysh relatives, and according to Muslim tradition, he may have briefly accepted the earlier pre-Islamic deities by reciting verses that recognized some of them to be intercessors with God. However, the Qur'an denounced any such compromise of monotheism as the work of Satan.

Though Muhammad had hoped to convert his entire tribe to Islam, he was forced to leave Mecca with his followers in 622 and immigrate to the city of Yathrib, about 250 miles to the north. There, Muhammad took on the role of a mediator among a number of fractious tribes of Arab polytheists and Jews, who gave Muhammad and the Muslims their own tribal status. Thus this emigration, the *hijrah*, begins year 1 on the Muslim calendar as it marks an important turning point for the nascent Islam. For Muhammad would build his "community of believers" *(ummah)* not on the basis of blood ties, but primarily on religious affiliation. Many of the revelations coming in Yathrib, later called Medina, address such issues as diet, marriage, inheritance, and other matters essential for defining and regulating a community. Muhammad was both a prophet and statesman, and following several years of conflict with the Quraysh and other tribes, the Muslims triumphantly entered Mecca, whose inhabitants converted to Islam in 630, two years before the Muhammad's death in 632.[4]

The Qur'an and Its Major Themes

Probably collected and arranged within a generation of his death, Muhammad's revelations form the *Qur'an* (the "recitation"), in which God speaks to Muhammad through Gabriel, the spirit of revelation, over a period of twenty-two years until the prophet's death. It is important to note at the outset that the Qur'an exalts prophecy and faith, not reason and argumentation. Further, the Qur'an is not a theological treatise aiming to prove the existence of God, nor is it a book of laws, though some obligations and prohibitions are found there. As a book, the Qur'an is composed of 114 chapters *(surahs)*, ranging from 3 to 286 verses. Though the Qur'an tells a number of stories, it is not a single narrative recording the sacred history of a people, as in Genesis and Exodus, nor does it recount the career of its prophet, as do the Gospels. Rather, the Qur'an declares itself to be God's revelation aimed at humanity and human behavior, repeatedly calling itself "guidance for humanity."

Without a clear narrative structure, it is difficult to find a sure chronology for the individual revelations, though the Qur'an's major themes are clear. First and foremost is the notion of monotheism, that there is one god, *Allah*, a word best translated as "God" with a capital "G."

> Qur'an 1: *The Opening*
> *In the name of God the compassionate, the merciful*
> Praise be to God, lord of the worlds,
> The compassionate, the merciful,
> Master of the day of reckoning,
> You we worship, and to You we turn for aid.
> Guide us along the straight path,
> The road of those whom You have blessed,
> Not those with anger against them,
> Nor those who are astray!

As the Qur'an declares repeatedly, God is one, not one among many as was the case among the pagan Arabs, but the one and only. Any other deity is but a figment of the imagination as Joseph tells the people of Egypt in the Qur'an (12:40): "Besides God, you worship nothing but names that you and your father made up." As to the one true God, the Qur'an declares:

> Your lord is God who created the heavens and the earth in six days. Then, He sat upon the throne dispensing all affairs. Who can intercede with Him save by His permission? He is God, your Lord, so worship Him. Will you not take heed? (10:3)

Here is the familiar Judeo-Christian image of the all-knowing, all-powerful God as lord and master ruling over his creation. This is a prominent theme of the Qur'an, frequently reflected in the Qur'an's use of the royal "We" when God speaks (46:3): "We have not created the heavens and all that is between them save in truth and for an appointed time. But the ungrateful who were warned, turn away!"

> Qur'an 2:255: *The Throne Verse*
> God: there is no deity but Him, the living, the eternal. Drowsiness does not touch Him, nor sleep. To Him belongs what is in the heavens and on earth. Who can interceded with Him save by His permission? He knows what is before humans and what is behind them, yet they grasp nothing of His knowledge save as He wills. His throne extends over the heavens and the earth, and He never tires of protecting them for He is the supreme and tremendous!

This and similar verses resonate with the Bible, which is hardly a surprise given the presence of Jews and Christians in Arabia at this time, and the fact that the pre-Islamic Arabs, too, traced their lineage back to Abraham through his firstborn son Isma'il (Ishmael). Thus, Judaism, Christianity, and Islam share in a common religious heritage. They all claim to believe in one God, who has made a covenant with his people to whom he gives laws for leading a life of righteousness. Still, there are substantive differences in their interpretations of key themes, including the covenant and monotheism. It is clear from a number of Qur'anic passages that God's covenant is not with a single people, such as with the Jews, but with all of humanity. "Oh humanity, did We not make a covenant with you that you would not worship Satan, who is your clear enemy, but that you worship Me? This is the straight path!" (36:60-61).

As to different conceptions of monotheism, the Qur'an's states: "God: there is no deity but Him, the living, the eternal. Drowsiness does not touch Him, nor sleep." This may seem a strange assertion in light of the many Qur'anic declarations of God's omnipotence and awesome power. Why would the Qur'an stress that the Almighty was never tired? But at stake in the seventh century was the proposition that God was unique and not in anyway human, and so he did not need to rest on the seventh day of creation (Gen 2:3). Here the Qur'an differs markedly from Genesis, as it does when speaking of the creation of Adam. For instance, the Qur'an says (3:59): "[God] created him from earth and then said to him 'Be!' and he was." And again (40:64): "God created the earth as a dwelling for you and the sky as your roof, and he shaped you in the best of forms." But the Qur'an never says that God created man in his own image (Gen 1:28). Such talk might well undermine God's uniqueness and justify the very polytheistic practices that the prophet Muhammad opposed. The Qur'an is quite clear on this point when it declares: "This is God, my Lord, in whom I turn and place my trust, originator of the heavens and the earth. There is nothing like Him, the all-seeing, all-knowing!" (42:10-11).

Qur'an 112: *Sincerity*
In the name of God, the compassionate, the merciful
Say: He is God, one,
God everlasting!
He did not beget, nor was He begotten,
And to Him there is no equal!

This early chapter again declares God to be without equal, and it denies that God has offspring, a clear reference to Christian doctrines of Jesus as the son of God, something the Qur'an takes literally. The Trinity, too, is an unacceptable compromise with monotheism (5:73): "They are disbelievers who say: 'God is the third of the trinity,' for there is no deity but God, the one!" According to the Qur'an, some people believed that there was a trinity consisting of God, Jesus, and his mother Mary. Even though Jesus was a great prophet and his mother a virgin of impeccable reputation, the Qur'an rejects the trinity as a form of polytheism in which others are given a divine status equal to God:

> And when God asked Jesus son of Mary: "Did you tell the people to take you and your mother as deities with God?" Jesus replied, "God forbid that I would say something I had no right to say!" (5:116)

The Qur'an is unequivocal in declaring God's oneness, though it does mention other supernatural beings. God has created hosts of angels, which surround his throne and serve him as messengers and guardians. Jinnis, spirited creatures made of fire, fly through the heavens at times and, at other times, interact with humans. Some of them believe in God, while others, in their disobedience, will go to hell. Perhaps, the latter are the satans mentioned in the Qur'an, who are led by Iblis, also known as Satan, humanity's primordial enemy. Yet none of these creations, even Satan, has power over human beings, unless humans give it to them:

> Whoever does a good deed, whether they are male or female, and who believes, We will resurrect them in a sweet life, and reward them with something equal to the best that they did. So when you recite the Qur'an, seek refuge in God from Satan, the accursed. But he has no power over those who believe and trust in their Lord. His power is only over those who take him as their patron and over those who make him an equal [with God]. (16:97-100)

This passage reveals two frequent and important corollaries of monotheism: individual moral responsibility and personal immortality. This was in clear contrast to the polytheistic religion of Arabia that primarily served the present life of the tribe, not necessarily the individual worshiper. Moreover, by the sixth century, blood vengeance, which was to protect the tribe, appears to have become a major nemesis of both the tribe and its individual members. This chaotic situation undoubtedly contributed to Muhammad's successful attempts to transform society. As part of his prophetic mission, Muhammad brought Qur'anic revelations that forbade vendetta and stringently regulated blood vengeance to the murderer, and he replaced the primacy of tribal affiliation with membership in the larger community of believers. No longer was it necessary for a person to die for his tribe to gain an amorphous immortality. Instead, individual men and women who believe in the one God and perform good deeds will enter the gardens of paradise and be reunited with their believing loved ones. Islam and its monotheism valorized the individual and so reshaped Arab society and its images of immortality.

But to attain this immortality, individuals must submit to God and his will, hence, the name of the religion, *Islam,* "to submit," while one who submits is a *Muslim.* To believe in the one God is the covenant each human has with him. God also demands that persons do good deeds in a quest for social justice, and so establishing a just moral order is a point of central concern, for which the Qur'an gives general principles for guidance. Yet humanity tends to forget this charge due to basic human weaknesses including pride, greed, narrow-mindedness, and despair. Summing up all of these weaknesses is selfishness, making oneself a partner with God. Selfishness leads to acts of injustice, which strain and may even break the covenant with God and our fellow human beings, ultimately leading to destruction. This and other human weaknesses are exploited by Satan in order to lead humans astray. But God, in his mercy, has time and again sent messengers to humanity to remind us of the good news that God still cares for his creation, to reaffirm God's will, and to warn of an impending judgment day. The prophets try to instill a mindfulness of God *(taqwa)* into humanity, for although people are free to act, judgment of that action, and the standard by which it will be judged, belong to God. Thus to believe in God and to do good works are vital to prosperity in this life and the next, as is evident in the Qur'an's many warnings regarding the judgment day:

> Oh, you who believe, be mindful of God. Let each person consider what they have set aside for tomorrow. Be mindful of God, for He knows what you do. The residents of hell and those of heaven are not equal, for the residents of paradise will be the winners! (59:18-19)

This final judgment, however, should not be regarded as a promise of gleeful vengeance, so much as a present warning to mend our ways, to try to right the wrongs that we have committed, and to seek justice in the world while there is still time. Further, many passages reveal a God of mercy and compassion whose living presence is always around us.

> Say (to them Muhammad): "If you love God, then follow me, that He may love you and forgive your sins, for God is forgiving and merciful." (3:31)
> God loves those who depend upon Him completely. (3:159)
> Oh self at peace, return to your Lord, contented and pleasing. Enter among My servants and enter My garden. (89:27-30)
> The paradise promised to those mindful of God is like a garden flowing with rivers of ever pure water and delicious milk, with rivers of wine delightful to those who drink, and rivers of pure honey. Every kind of fruit is there for them, and forgiveness from their Lord. (47:15)

But humanity need not wait until the judgment day to encounter God's blessings, for he has revealed the Qur'an to guide them, while he generously showers his favors upon sincere believers, especially during the mysterious Night of Destiny when, according to tradition, the Qur'an was first revealed.

> Qur'an 97: *Destiny*
> *In the name of God, the compassionate, the merciful.*
> Truly, We sent it down on the night of destiny.
> What will convey to you what the night of destiny is?
> The night of destiny is better than a thousand months!
> The angels and the spirit descend then by permission of their Lord from every order.
> Peace there is until the rise of dawn![5]

Creeds and Pillars

According to Islamic tradition, Muhammad was the final prophet sent by God to reaffirm what had been declared by all of the other prophets, from Adam to Abraham, Moses to Jesus, namely, to believe in the one God, his angels, and his prophets, their revelations, and the judgment day. In addition to these themes and beliefs, the Qur'an includes important rituals and rules for regulating personal and public life. Restrictions include those against the consumption of pork and alcohol and the prohibition of gambling, prostitution, adultery, murder, and other criminal offenses. Muslim men and women are to act and dress modestly, and they are encouraged to marry and procreate. Polygamy is allowed, and a man may marry up to four women at a time, provided he can treat his wives equally. Wives may be drawn from the Muslim, Jewish, or other monotheistic Christian communities, but a Muslim woman may be married to only one Muslim man at a time, thus assuring the male bloodline and Muslim religion of any offspring. While Muhammad remained monogamous during Khadijah's lifetime, following her death in 619 C.E., the prophet entered into a number of marriages, some of which represented various alliances between the prophet and members of the Muslim community. Though it is discouraged by the Qur'an, Muslims are allowed to divorce their spouse, and both parties are permitted to marry others, as are widows and widowers.

As for religious rituals, Muslim jurists have often referred to them as the "Five Pillars of Islam." The first is the Muslim profession of faith *(al-shahadah)*: "I bear witness that there is no deity but God, and I bear witness that Muhammad is the apostle of God." Recited by millions of Muslims every day, the first part of this statement, "I bear witness that there is no deity but God," makes one a monotheist; the second part, "I bear witness that Muhammad is the messenger of God," makes one a Muslim. The second pillar is the five daily canonical prayers *(al-salah)*, which reaffirm a believer's personal relationship with God. Based on Muhammad's practice, these prayers are preceded by ablutions and require the recitation of particular religious statements and a series of bodily positions and prostrations. Prayers may be performed in private or in public gatherings, and particularly important is the Friday noon congregational prayer, followed by a sermon by a qualified preacher. Announcing the time for each prayer period is the call to prayer *(adhan)*, which is called out from every mosque.

> *The Call to Prayer*
> God is most great! God is most great!
> God is most great! God is most great!
> I bear witness that there is no deity but God!
> I bear witness the Muhammad is the messenger of God!
> Come to prayer. Come to prayer.
> Come to success. Come to success.
> God is most great! God is most great!
> There is no deity but God!

A third pillar is an annual tithe on one's possessions (*al-zakah*) to be used for the good of the Muslim community and for the poor, in particular. Thus, while prayer links the believer with God, alms binds one to fellow Muslims. Likewise, a forth pillar is the fast (*al-saum*) during the entire month of Ramadan, when Muslims are to refrain from eating, drinking, and sexual relations during daylight hours. This fast reminds Muslims of their dependence on God as well as the plight of those who are less fortunate. The end of Ramadan is celebrated with the Feast to Break the Fast (*ʿId al-Fitr*), which begins with a congregational prayer and often includes festive family gatherings and donations to the poor. The fifth pillar is the *Hajj*, or the canonical pilgrimage to Mecca, undertaken once during a lifetime if a Muslim is financially and physically able to do so. The *Hajj* occurs annually over several specific days during the first two weeks of Islam's twelfth lunar month, during which time pilgrims perform a number of required religious rites and rituals. The *Hajj* serves as a preview of the day of judgment when all of humanity will be gathered together before God, and it dramatically underscores the strength and unity of the Muslim community as pilgrims come from all parts of the world to worship together as one. The *Hajj* ends with the Feast of Sacrifice (*ʿId al-Adha*), which is joyously celebrated for three days throughout the Muslim world as families sacrifice an animal to be shared with others and consumed during their feast.

Though generally not regarded as a pillar, the Qur'an also permits *jihad*, or a "struggle" in order to defend Muslims from attack or oppression by non-Muslims. Jihad originally developed as a response to the continued persecution of Muslims by the Quraysh polytheists who sought to destroy the early Muslim community by exiling them from Mecca:

> Permission to fight is granted to those who have been oppressed. God has power to give them victory. They were driven out of their homes for no other reason than that they declared "God is our Lord." If God did not defend some people by means of others then surely monasteries, churches, synagogues, and mosques, where God's name is mentioned often, would be destroyed. God will surely help those who help Him, for He is powerful, mighty! (22:39-40)

The Qur'an frequently exhorts Muslims to defend their faith, and God promises his forgiveness and heavenly reward to those who sacrifice their property and lives for this cause. Although the above early passage suggests that monotheists, in general, should be protected, later passages appear to call for the political subjugation and social subordination of Jews, Christians, and other monotheists who, in some way, oppose Islam:

> Fight those who do not believe in God, the last day, and who do not forbid what God and His messenger have forbidden, and who do not practice the religion of truth among the people given the Book, until they pay tribute out of hand and are humbled. (9:29)

Jews and Christians in the Qur'an

Jews, Christians, Zoroastrians, and other non-Muslim monotheists have an ambiguous position in the Qur'an. The Qur'an often refers to them collectively as the "People of the Book" (*Ahl al-Kitab*), that is, those communities who have previously received a revelation from one of God's many prophets. These revelations, including the Qur'an, have all descended to humanity from a heavenly source or prototype called the "Mother of Books." Moreover, this pristine revelation of monotheism and social justice has been given to various communities in multiple forms and languages. God said to Muhammad: "We have sent you with the truth of good tidings and of warning. There has never been a community save that there was one to warn it" (35:24). To underscore this point, God commands Muhammad to say, "I believe in whatever book God has sent down!" (42:15), and the Qur'an specifically mentions the Psalms of David, the Torah brought by Moses, the Gospel of Jesus, and the Qur'an, which was revealed in clear Arabic.

The Qur'an, then, portrays Muhammad as the latest and, perhaps, final prophet in a long indivisible chain of prophecy. Yet, in spite of this underlying unity, the original revelations may be altered over time as humans ignore God's commands and tend toward their own desires. As a result, God's original revelation to a community may become corrupted, as was the case noted above when the followers of Jesus began to believe in the Trinity. In addition, sectarianism arises, further undermining the truth that God's covenant is with all of humanity, and not just with a single community, such as the Jews, Christians, or even Muslims.

> [Some Jews and the Christians] say: "Only the Jews" or "Only the Christians will enter the Garden." That is their wishful thinking. Say: "Bring your clear proof if you are truthful." Indeed, those who surrender

themselves to God and do good deeds will have their reward from their Lord. They have nothing to fear nor will they grieve. But the Jews say: "The Christians are wrong!" and the Christians say: "The Jews are wrong!" Yet they read the Book. Thus speak those who do not know. So God will judge among them on the Day of Resurrection about what they differ. (2:111-113)

Despite such disagreements, the Qur'an explicitly recognizes the existence and rights of Jews, Christians, and other non-Muslim monotheists who strive to lead a pious life."

Those who believe [i.e., Muslims], and those who are Jews, Christians, and Sabians, whoever believes in God, the Last Day, and does good deeds, they will have their reward from their Lord. They have nothing to fear nor will they grieve. (2:62)

This recognition of religious diversity, however, should not be construed as religious equality, and the Qur'an warns Muslims against aligning too closely with those of other faiths lest Islam be compromised.

The Jews and Christians will never be satisfied with you until you follow their way. Say: "God's guidance is the true guidance!" Indeed, if you follow their desires after what knowledge has come to you, then you will have no helper or ally from God! (2:120)

Oh, you who believe, do not take Jews or Christians as allies for some of them are allies of one another. For one who makes alliances with them, is one of them, and God does not guide an oppressive people. (5:51)

Indeed, you will find the Jews and the polytheists to be the most hateful people toward those who believe, while those closest to the believers in affection are those who say: "We are Christians," because among them are priests and monks who are not arrogant. (5:82)

According to Muslim tradition, the last two passages and the one above on jihad against Christians and Jews were revealed late in the prophet's life after several Jewish tribes allied with the pagan Quraysh, who violently opposed Muhammad's mission to expand and strengthen the Muslim community. Therefore, while the Qur'an acknowledges and respects the rights of other monotheistic religions based on past revelations, it asserts the superiority of the Muslim faith proclaimed by Muhammad.

Qur'an 5:44-50: *On Religious Diversity*

44. We sent down the Torah containing guidance and a light, by which the prophets who submitted to God judged those whom they guided, and the rabbis and the priests did likewise with what was entrusted to them of God's book to which they bore witness. So do not fear people, fear Me, and do not sell My revelations for a paltry price. Those who do not judge by what We have sent down are the ingrates!

45. And in the Torah, We proscribed for them a life for a life, an eye for an eye, a nose for a nose, an ear for an ear, a tooth for a tooth, and similarly for wounds, though one who is charitable will attain atonement. Those who do not judge by what We have sent down are the oppressors!

46. And We made Jesus son of Mary follow in their footsteps, confirming the Torah before him, and We gave him the Gospel containing guidance and a light, confirming the Torah before him, as a guidance and an admonition to those mindful of God.

47. So let the people of the Gospel judge by that which God has sent down in it. Those who do not judge by what God has sent down are the corrupters!

48. And We sent down to you [Muhammad] the book preserving the truth and confirming the books before it. So, judge among them with what God has sent down, and do not follow their desires concerning the truth that has come down to you. For each of you, We have made a law and a course of action. Had God wished, He would have made you one religious community. But He tests you by what He has given you. So vie with one another in doing good deeds! To God you all return that He may set you straight about what you differed.

49. So judge among them with what God has sent down and do not follow their desires and beware of them lest they tempt you away from some of what God has sent down to you. If they turn away, then know that God wants to smite them for some of their sins, and most of them are corrupters!

50. Do they desire the judgment of the impetuous (*al-jahiliyah*)? But who is a better judge than God for a people certain in their faith?

The Prophetic Tradition

The Qur'an has been the essential guide for Muslims who seek to live their lives in accordance with God's revelation. Those in a quest for a personal relationship with God have found inspiration in Qur'anic accounts of human and divine interactions, often found in stories of the prophets, including Moses on Sinai and his standing before the burning bush, Abraham's conversations with God, and Jesus' miracles. But of greater significance has been the life of the prophet Muhammad and Qur'anic references to his spiritual encounters.

> Blessed be he [i.e. God or Gabriel] who took his servant (Muhammad) by night from the sacred mosque to the furthest mosque, whose precincts We have blessed, that We might show him Our signs. (17:1)
>
> Truly this is a revelation inspired, taught to him [Muhammad] by one strong, powerful, possessing intellect, who set himself on the farthest horizon and then drew close and descended to within two bows' length or nearer, and he revealed to his servant what he revealed. The heart did not lie about what it saw, so will you wrangle about what he saw? He saw him descend again, near the furthest lote tree where the Garden of Sanctuary is, where there enveloped the lote tree what enveloped it. His vision did not turn away or transgress, and truly, he saw one the greatest signs of his Lord! (53:4-18)

For Muslims, these passages serve as sources for Muhammad's amazing night journey from Mecca to Jerusalem and his subsequent ascension to heaven (*al-Isra' wa-al-Mi'raj*). There, accompanied by the archangel Gabriel, Muhammad met with earlier prophets and, finally, with God. The Qur'an gives few details beyond the passages cited above, and, in fact, they do not speak of ascension at all. Yet later Muslim tradition meticulously details these events based on prophetic *hadith* (*al-hadith al-nabawi*), accounts of Muhammad's sayings and actions. The hadith are the second foundational source for the religion of Islam. As shown in the following example, a single hadith is composed of a chain of known, authoritative individuals (*isnad*), who bear witness to the truth and accuracy of its content (*matn*).

> Muhammad ibn al-Muthanna told us that Abu Ahmad al-Zubayri told him that Isma'il heard it from Mansur, who heard it from Ibrahim, who heard it from 'Alqamah, who got it from 'Abd Allah, who said: "We used to regard signs as a blessing, but you regard them as a fearful omen. We were on a journey with the Messenger of God, God bless him and give him peace,

and water was running short. So he said: 'Bring me what water is left.' So they brought a container with a little water in it. Then he placed his hand into the container and said: 'Come to the blessed purity, and the blessing is from God!' And then I saw water flowing from between his fingers!"[6]

These hadith traditions have been essential for elaborating on Muhammad's heavenly ascension and other archetypal aspects of his pious life, and when compiled together in a narrative form, they resemble a Christian gospel. But in addition to telling of Muhammad's life, the hadith collections also give instructions on religious ritual and legal matters, as well as aphorisms and advice for following the straight path to God.

(Muhammad) the Apostle of God—God's blessings and peace be upon him—said: "Sincerity is that you worship God as if you see Him, and if you do not see Him, know that He sees you."
　　The Prophet—God's blessings and peace be upon him—said: "Not one of you truly believes until you love for your brother what you love for yourself."
　　The Messenger of God—God's blessings and peace be upon him—said: "Be in this world as if you were a stranger or wayfarer."[7]

Along with the prophetic hadith is a smaller body of hadith traditions known as "Divine Sayings" *(al-hadith al-qudsi)*. Some Muslims regard them as the words of God revealed to Muhammad but not found in the Qur'an for various reasons.

The Messenger of God—God's blessings and peace be upon him—said: "God said: '. . . My servant draws near to Me by nothing more dear to Me than by the religious obligations that I have imposed upon him, and My servant continues to draw near to Me by willing acts of devotion such that I love him. Then, when I love him, I become the ear with which he hears, the eye with which he sees, the hand with which he grasps, and the foot with which he walks. Surely if he were to request something of Me, I would give it, and if he were to seek My protection, I would shelter him.' "[8]

Historical Developments (632–1000)

Sunni and Shi‘i

The hadith are extremely important for providing information about Muhammad's life, the revelation of the Qur'an, and specific religious beliefs and practices. Further, hadith may touch upon other important matters including the governance of the Muslim community. One controversial hadith highlights an essential split regarding leadership. In this hadith, Muhammad declares his cousin and son-in-law ʿAli ibn Abi Talib (d. 661) to be his successor as Commander of the Faithful. Many Muslims do not accept the authenticity of this tradition. Instead, most Muslims have claimed to follow the *sunnah*, or "custom," of Muhammad as found in the reliable hadith collections, and so they are known as Sunni Muslims. Following Muhammad's death they chose a new leader, Abu Bakr (d. 634), from among the prophet's closest companions, who then became the caliph, or vice-regent (*khalifah*).

However, a significant minority have always held that Muhammad had designated ʿAli and ʿAli's male descendants as his rightful heirs, and this group, or "party of supporters" (*shiʿah*) came to be called the Shiʿi or Shiite Muslims. Though the initial difference between Sunni and Shiʿi involved issues of succession and leadership, over time, many Shiʿi have ascribed spiritual authority and even sinlessness to these special descendants of ʿAli who were to govern the community and regulate religious life as the chosen *imam* ("leader"). Nevertheless, by the ninth century, the Shiʿi themselves became divided over the issue of succession and the correct number of their imams. The most prominent groups have asserted that there were either seven or twelve imams, at the time of the last one's disappearance or "occultation" (*ghaybah*) in the ninth century. Most Shiʿi have believed that this last hidden imam will return as the *mahdi*, the "rightly guided one," a messianic figure who will appear near the end of time. Many Sunnis, too, have looked forward to the coming of a mahdi, though he is not found in the Qur'an or early Muslim creeds. Some Muslim religious authorities have found the hadith supporting the mahdi to be suspect, while political officials have generally regarded them as a threat.

The Rightly Guided Caliphs (632–661)

In the years immediately following the death of the prophet Muhammad, the Muslim community was led by a succession of Muhammad's closest companions and relatives. First was Muhammad's father-in-law, the respected Abu Bakr who, in his two years as caliph, solidified Muslim rule in the Arabian Peninsula. He was followed by the strong willed ʿUmar ibn al-Khattab (d. 644), who extended Muslim conquest and rule over an empire including Egypt, Palestine, Syria, Iraq, and

Iran. ʿUmar was assassinated by a slave and was succeeded by ʿUthman ibn ʿAffan (d. 656). The Islamic empire continued to expand into North Africa and Afghanistan, but this may not have been ʿUthman's most significant contribution to Islam. For, according to tradition, ʿUthman called together a committee of experts who collected and codified all of Muhammad's revelations and arranged them into the standard text of the Qur'an. Though often portrayed as pious, ʿUthman was, nevertheless, assassinated by other Muslims enraged by his alleged nepotism of his Umayyad clan of the Quraysh.

Most Shiʿi Muslims regard the first three caliphs as usurpers, and they recognize Muhammad's cousin and son-in-law ʿAli ibn Abi Talib as the first true caliph. Eventually, he succeeded ʿUthman to assume the troubled caliphate. The Umayyad clan wanted revenge for ʿUthman's murder, and their case was forcefully pursued by ʿUthman's nephew Muʿawiyah (d. 680), the Muslim governor of Syria. His forces fought on several occasions with the supporters of ʿAli, but these battles as well as attempts at a negotiated settlement resolved little. Then ʿAli was assassinated by one of a group of his former supporters, later known as the "Seceders" or Kharijites *(al-Khawarij)*, who felt that any compromise with Muʿawiyah was unacceptable. ʿAli was mourned by many Muslims, and Sunni Muslims regard him as the last of the "four rightly guided caliphs," as they believe his death marked a transition from righteous rule to that of political expediency.

The Umayyads (661–750)

ʿAli's oldest son, al-Hasan (d. 670), was caliph for a brief time after his father's death, but al-Hasan soon abdicated to Muʿawiyah. Securely in control of the caliphate, Muʿawiyah moved the capital of the empire north to Damascus where he founded the Umayyad dynasty. Often regarded as a line of tyrannical Arab kings, the Umayyads generally viewed the public treasury as their own personal possession. Moreover, most of the Umayyad caliphs were not religious individuals. Perhaps the worst of them was Muʿawiyah's son Yazid (d. 683), who, in order to secure his own power as caliph, laid siege to Mecca, burned down the Kaʿbah, and had ʿAli's second son, al-Husayn (d. 680) murdered. Al-Husayn's martyrdom occurred on the tenth of the Muslim month Muharram at Kerbala in present-day Iraq. This tragic event is commemorated annually by Shiʿi Muslims as the day of *Muharram*, a day of fasting and mourning, frequently accompanied by passion plays that graphically reenact al-Husayn's bloody martyrdom. Yet despite their faults, the Umayyad caliphs were still quite important to the spread and stability of Islam. The Umayyads centralized political authority and created a more professional army, while insisting on the use of Arabic as the official language of state.

"Protected People"

Under the Umayyads, the Muslim empire continued to grow in territory, encompassing a largely non-Muslim population. Counter to Western stereotypes, Islam was not spread by the sword, as conversion to Islam was not required of the conquered people provided they were monotheists. At this time, the majority of the population was composed of Christians, Jews, and Zoroastrians. These subject peoples were classified as "protected people" (*ahl al-dhimmah; dhimmi*). In exchange for paying taxes on their land (*kharaj*) and a special tax (*jizyah*), which exempted them from military service in the Muslim army, the protected people where allowed great latitude in terms of their religious beliefs and practices. However, they were not allowed to spread their faith, and were required to recognize the authority of the Muslim state and abide by its civil laws. By contrast, matters involving religious ritual or laws regarding personal status, such as marriage and divorce, were usually regulated on the basis of the individual's religious community.

Shariᶜah: The Divine Law

In the seventh through ninth centuries, nascent Islam faced rapidly changing conditions, which generated a series of questions regarding not only "protected peoples," but nearly every aspect of life and society. Religious thinkers of the Umayyad period worked to establish and regulate proper ritual, the obligations of the faith, and law, in a more traditional sense, which was often an ad hoc affair aimed to aid in the administration of an ever-expanding empire. Similarly, faced with Christian denunciations of Islam and continued dissention within the Muslim community, these scholars undertook to defend the faith and more precisely determine what constituted correct belief. Of particular importance was the development of jurisprudence (*fiqh*) undertaken by religious experts (*ᶜalim*/pl. *ᶜulama'*).

As noted above, the Qur'an addresses important communal matters including marriage, divorce, and inheritance. These and other subjects became the focus of Muslim scholars as they attempted to codify laws for the community, in accordance with the Qur'an and the custom of Muhammad and the early Muslim community as found in hadith. These two fundamental sources, the Qur'an and hadith, were augmented by the use of analogical reasoning (*qiyas*) and by the consensus of the scholarly community on legal issues (*ijma^c^*). Legal scholars known as *muftis* relied on these sources to offer informed opinions (*fatwa*) on questions of law. These opinions, though not legally binding, could be of assistance to the judge (*qadi*) who heard and judged legal cases. Thus the Qur'an's monotheism became pervasive in the Muslim community particularly through the *shari^c^ah* or divine law, which encompassed personal, communal, and ritual life. However, this should not be construed as a system of arid legalism. Rather, for many Muslims, the shari^c^ah has embodied the moral and ethical norms that guide and shape society and that help individuals know right from wrong, which is essential for success in this life and the next.[9]

The ^c^Abbasids (750–1258)

Umayyad despotism and discrimination against non-Arab Muslims eventually fomented a revolt. In 750, the Umayyads were overthrown by a coalition of Muslims, including Sunnis and Shi^c^is, Arabs and non-Arabs, especially Persians. The new rulers were descendants of Muhammad's uncle ^c^Abbas, hence the name of the dynasty, the ^c^Abbasids. Recognizing the vast size and diversity of the Muslim community, the ^c^Abbasid caliphs built a new capitol, Baghdad, in present day Iraq, which was more centrally located within the Muslim Empire. This shift east also reflects the increasing influence of the Persian culture and language of Iran on Islam and its rulers, some of whom had Persian mothers. No longer would Islam be synonymous with Arab, as all Muslims were to be recognized as equal. Moreover, the scholarly community became more specialized; and by the ninth century, distinct religious disciplines formed to develop and advance various aspects of Islamic belief and practice. The ^c^Abbasid period witnessed the emergence of the major Sunni and Shi^c^i schools of law, along with the collection and codification of hadith. Distinctive schools of Qur'anic commentary (*tafsir*), theology (*kalam*), and philosophy (*falsafah*) also arose at this time, as did movements to explore and articulate more fully mystical ideas and practice.[10]

Developments in Islamic Culture

During the ᶜAbbasid period, Muslim culture became more cosmopolitan and confident as it flourished under the early ᶜAbbasid caliphs, and the glorious reign of the caliph Harun al-Rashid (764–809) was immortalized in *Arabian Nights*. The caliphs sponsored the translation of works on various branches of science and philosophy into Arabic. By so doing, they preserved much of the Greek heritage that would later pass to Europe from Muslim Spain. But Muslims also built upon this heritage to make their own discoveries, such as the first vaccine for small pox or the explanation of the rainbow in light's refraction through raindrops. Muslim scientists studied the skies and the world of nature for centuries in order better to understand their workings and find tracings of a divine plan. Muslim astronomers carefully mapped the heavens with their planets and other celestial lights, while light itself was a central focus of the science of optics, in which Muslims excelled for centuries. Their work, too, would find its way to Europe, and such was also the case for important ideas in theology, philosophy, and mysticism.

Islamic Theology

Theology in Islam is known as *kalam* ("speech") due to the language used to formulate and debate the essential questions concerning Muslim faith and belief, and to defend Islam against non-Muslim antagonists. Similar to the shariᶜah, Muslim theology sought to investigate the facts and contexts of the Qur'anic revelation, so as to understand its meaning and implications for the developing Muslim community. Theology became increasingly specialized in the eight and ninth centuries, concentrating on questions of God's unity, justice, and attributes, and their relation to human free will and the individual's ultimate fate.

One of the first theological issues raised in Islam was the status of the Muslim who had committed a grave sin. This issue was part of the political and religious conflicts that occurred following the arbitration between ᶜAli and Muᶜawiyah concerning the caliphate. The Kharijites declared that a grave sinner was no longer a Muslim and must be opposed, especially if that sinner was the head of the community. The Kharijites required a show of faith by deeds, and so, the status of anyone's faith was suspect on the basis of their actions. Another group called the *Murjiᶜah* ("those who postponed") put off judging the faith of others. They left matters of belief and unbelief to be decided by God on the judgment day, and so, a ruling dynasty should not be disobeyed since the decision in all affairs belonged to God alone. The Murji'ah took a neutral position in the political disputes, thus earning them the name *Mu'tazilah* ("neutralists"). Among the early Mu'tazilites was the famous ascetic al-Hasan al-Basri (d. 728) who ascribed all evil to humans, the majority of whom be believed were hypocrites, Muslims in name only. His disciple Wasil ibn ʿAta (flounshed eighth century), considered the founder of the Mu'tazilah school of theology, chose instead to call the Muslim sinner a transgressor, indicating a more rational and legal view of the problem than al-Hasan's pietistic view. Though some may consider this an arcane debate today, the problem is once again a hot issue, as Muslim militants kill other Muslims who they believe have violated the faith.

Mu'tazilah theology is often viewed as a more rational approach to various issues. The principle concerns and positions of the Mu'tazilah center on five theses, the first being God's unity *(tawhid)*. In order to safeguard God's divine transcendence, the Mu'tazilah denied the eternity of God's speech; therefore the Qur'an was a created word. There was no similarity between a human and God, though humanity could know with certainty what God is and does by sound reasoning *(ʿaql)*, when considering creation and its causal dependency. Second, the Mu'tazilah believed in God's justice *(ʿadl)*, a doctrine that originally developed out of notions of human free will and God's absolute goodness. This led to the assertion that God could not do the unreasonable or unjust, and thus, to the third thesis, the doctrine of promise and threat, which declared that the faithful person must enter paradise and the infidel the fire of hell. Fourth was the position of neutrality regarding the status of Muslims who sinned, and finally, there was the obligation to encourage good and forbid the reprehensible whether in public or private, involving an individual or the community. During the Umayyad caliphate, this doctrine was used to justify rebellion, while during the ʿAbbasid period, it justified forced acceptance of Mu'tazilah positions and the persecution of their opponents.

For a brief period in the ninth century, the Mu'tazilah received the official backing of the ʿAbbasid caliph, but their political and theological domination was brief. A reaction against them and their persecution of others was led by al-Ashʿari (d. 935), a former Mu'tazilite. He used rational argumentation to undermine Mu'tazilah positions, particularly those regarding God's attributes and divine will. Al-Ashʿari and his followers held that God's attributes and, therefore, the Qur'an were eternal, though humanity could not know how or why. Further, reason could not determine what God can or cannot do; God could condemn the faithful to hell if he so willed. Concerning human actions, the Ashᶜarites declared that God determines them, but creates their "acquisition" by the individual who is, then, responsible for them. This was compatible with God's omnipotence, though humanity no longer had free will as in the Muᶜtazilite view.

Al-Ashᶜari's and other reactions against the Muᶜtazilah stressed God's power, will, and, especially, his determinism, and theology began to have only an indirect relationship to living faith. Dissatisfied with the scholasticism of dialectical theology and jurisprudence, as well as philosophy's unproven metaphysical assertions, Abu Hamid al-Ghazali (d. 1111) successfully formulated a system of belief in which personal faith and religious morality were central. Al-Ghazali relegated theology to the role of a weapon useful for defending Islam from heresy, but ineffectual for discovering certain truth in any important matter. Another prominent theologian, Fakhr al-Din al-Razi (d. 1209) clearly distinguished between the province of reason and that of revelation. In so doing, al-Razi attempted to restate Muslim dogma with a new and more vigorous systematic theology, yet al-Ghazali had set the tone for later thinking on matters of Muslim theology and philosophy.

Islamic Philosophy

The origin and basis for Islamic philosophy (*falsafah*) were either Greek or of Greek inspiration. Translations of Hellenistic scientific works, including philosophy, from Greek and Syriac sources, became available to Muslim thinkers in the mid-ninth century as the ᶜAbbasid caliphs sponsored translations carried out largely by Christians and Sabians. Thus the major works of Greek philosophy, from Plato to the sixth-century Alexandrian commentaries, were preserved in Arabic translation. Muslim philosophers sought to understand and interpret this corpus and to further philosophic and scientific investigation within the Islamic religious and cultural environment.

Philosophy, however, was not to be the handmaiden of Islamic theology. Human reason was the only theoretical limit, and the philosophers believed that the truth discovered by reason would not disagree with that revealed by the Qur'an, once both were correctly understood. Thus, the

Hellenistic philosophical tradition and the Islamic monotheistic one confronted each other in the Muslim philosophers who sought points of contact and coincidence as reason would allow. Philosophy in Islam, then, although Hellenistic in origin, has a clear Islamic stamp, and its fundamental issues revolve around prophetic revelation and the divine law.

The first Muslim philosopher of note was al-Kindi (flourished early ninth century), who usually wrote on natural philosophy and mathematics. He attempted to define the nature of human knowledge, which he believed could know any and all things with the aid of logic, mathematics, and similar scientific devices. However, a supernatural way to the same knowledge was possible, and God bestowed it upon his prophets who, in turn, communicated it to the masses in a beautifully clear and comprehensive style. The prophets' knowledge was complete and without flaw, while the knowledge attained through purely human reason, while being the same knowledge, lacked the prophetic perfection and conciseness. Al-Kindi's work also contains a number of themes developed in later Islamic philosophy and Christian theology: God as the first being and first cause, creation as the giving of being and distinct from natural causation, the immortality of the soul, and the rational and metaphoric exegesis of scripture.

The great philosopher al-Farabi (d. 950) elaborated on revelation's role as a guide for establishing the virtuous community, which would ensure material happiness in this world and supreme bliss in the next. Within this framework, al-Farabi probed philosophically the constituents of the Muslim community and, so, attempted to clarify its foundations. Al-Farabi believed that religion and philosophy were analogous; the prophet-lawgiver would also be the ideal philosopher-king, though his various duties involving prophecy, law-giving, philosophy, and kingship would not be identical. Further, in his work, al-Farabi emphasized the public and political functions of philosophy as the benefactors of human society.

Ibn Sina (known in the West as Avicenna, d. 1037) developed many of al-Farabi's ideas, particularly those concerning the question of being. He distinguished between essence and existence, arguing that since the fact of existence cannot be inferred from the essence of an existent, then existence must be due to a necessary being that is the first cause upon which all creation is necessarily and eternally dependent; this being is God. The medieval Christian theologian Thomas Aquinas (d. ca. 1274) would later make a similar argument to prove God's existence. Ibn Sina, however, made one exception to this rule of inference, namely the human soul whose existence could be affirmed through self-consciousness. The soul survives physical death, retaining its individual traits, to be rewarded and punished on the basis of its past deeds and intellectual and spiritual development. Ibn Sina also followed al-Farabi concerning the relationship between reason and revelation, religion being useful primarily for improving the quality of life and happiness among the masses. Further, revealed religion could point the way for a select few to experience directly the truth that was beyond description, and this spiritual knowledge was the culmination of the mystic philosopher's quest.

Islamic philosophy developed later in Spain and North Africa during the twelfth century based on the works of al-Farabi, Ibn Sina, and the theologian al-Ghazali. The more conservative intellectual atmosphere then prevalent in the western Islamic lands diverted philosophical inquiry away from political and metaphysical matters, placing more emphasis on scientific concerns. Indicative of this trend was the work of Ibn Bajjah (d. 1138) who interpreted al-Farabi's political philosophy as an unattainable ideal. Instead, a philosopher should shun the herd and concentrate on his solitary quest for a state of enlightenment. This high state could be experienced only after the philosopher had disciplined his mind through theoretical science. Ibn Tufayl (d. 1185) similarly characterized the philosopher as a solitary seeker of truth in his allegorical tale *Hayy ibn Yaqzan* ("Alive Son of Awake"), which affirmed as well the vocation of revealed religion for clothing the naked truth in forms suited to the multitude.

The greatest philosopher of the Muslim west was undoubtedly Ibn Rushd (known in the West as Averroes, d. 1198) who is best known for his insightful commentaries on Aristotle, which would later have considerable influence on medieval Christian thinkers through their Latin translations of his works. Ibn Rushd, too, believed that the philosophers were an elite who should not disturb the religious life of the common folk by divulging the pure truth, which would only confuse them. Between the masses and the philosophers were the theologians who, Ibn Rushd believed, failed to use philosophical demonstration to discover the truth and who spread false interpretations of the Qur'an among the ignorant people.

Philosophy was eclipsed by a resurgence of the theology of al-Ashari's school and by traditionalism beginning in the thirteenth century, only to reemerge within Islamic mysticism as *hikmah* ("wisdom"), which claimed to explain God, creation, and their relationship in the context of mystical experience. Central to this new wisdom were notions of God being intimately joined with his creation (monism). Many of these monistic doctrines drew from Greek the philosophical theories of Plotinus (d. ca. 270) and his school in Alexandria, Egypt. Creation was viewed not as some instantaneous event, but rather as a process of emanation of God into various levels of the universe, culminating in the human being. These and other theories were an important part of Islamic mysticism, and the most important proponents of this new wisdom were Yahya al-Suhrawardi (d. 1190), Ibn al-ᶜArabi (d. 1240), and Mulla Sadra (d. 1640).[11]

Sufism

Islamic mysticism is known in Arabic as *tasawwuf*, "following the Sufi path." Commonly known in the West as Sufism, Islamic mysticism may be defined as the study of experiences within Islam characterized by ineffability and transience, and frequently by a positive sense of passivity, timelessness, and unity. Sufism also includes the methods to attain and refine these experiences, the theories and doctrines regarding their origin and significance, and the place of these experiences within the lives of individuals and their societies. Sufism shares much in common with other mystical traditions, and some similarities probably owe to the fact that Islam arose and flourished in an environment of religious diversity. Islamic mysticism was clearly influenced by ascetic and mystical practices in the region, such as wearing a simple frock of wool (*suf*), from which Sufism derives its name. Fear of transgressing God's commandments and divine punishment led some pious Muslims to undertake ascetic practices as penance. A variety of disciplines were pursued to restrain temptation, and these included fasting, late-night prayer vigils, and seclusion. Periods of celibacy were also practiced, but lifelong celibacy was regarded as a violation of the Qur'an and hadith. Asceticism has had only a limited appeal to most Muslims, though among the mystics it became an essential tool for purification, self-control, and spiritual enlightenment.

Sufism has always drawn its main sustenance from the Qur'an and the traditions of Muhammad. Qur'anic passages often speak of God's mercy and compassion, as he is ever-present with his creation:

> To God belongs the east and west; wherever you turn, there is the face of
> God. (2:115)
> If my servants inquire of you concerning Me, lo, I am near. (2:186)
> We are nearer [to the human being] than his jugular vein. (50:186)

By the early ᶜAbbasid period, mystically inclined religious scholars,
including the still popular al-Qushayri (d. 465/1037), composed Qur'anic
commentaries and guidebooks. Their works include mystical lexicons,
biographies, spiritual genealogies, and careful explanations and instructions regarding Sufi thought and practice. These and other Sufis detailed
some of the psychological states (*hal/ahwal*), and ethical and cognitive
stages (*maqam/maqamat*) that form the mystic path leading toward the
annihilation of selfishness (*fana'*) and, subsequently, abiding in accord
with the will and living presence of God (*baqa'*). True love and humility
are required to reach this ultimate goal, and for many Sufis, this entails
spiritual jihad, the struggle against selfishness (*nafs*) in order to discover
the divine spirit (*ruh*) within. Therefore, one must restrain base tendencies by developing a powerful conscience and by accepting God's guidance, so that one becomes at peace and pleasing to God.

> So be mindful of God as much as you can, and listen, obey, and spend (on
> charity) for your own good, for whoever is saved from his own selfishness
> will be among the prosperous. (64:16)

The Qur'an often exhorts humanity to *dhikr*, to be "mindful" of God
and his blessings to them, and the Sufis developed dhikr into a meditative
practice. Dhikr meditation revolves around the repetition of God's divine
names or religious formulas, especially the witness to faith that "there is no
deity but God." This and other formula may be recited aloud or in silence,
among a group or alone in seclusion. Moreover, the dhikr ritual generally
includes various procedures involving breath control, posture, movement,
and dance. The aim of the Sufi dhikr is to purify the believer of selfishness
so that one may be obedient to God and true to the covenant to worship
God alone, lest one fall victim to selfish desires. According to the great
Sufi al-Junayd (d. 910), this is God's test of humanity and the origin of
the human spirit's painful longing to return to its heavenly home. This
tribulation, however, is the necessary spark for the Sufi's spiritual quest to
rein in selfish tendencies so as to encounter exhilarating moments of
enlightenment stabilized within a selfless spiritual life. The celebrated
Egyptian poet ᶜUmar Ibn al-Farid (d. 1235) spoke of this quest in his
verse where he compares the emerging mystic to a baby:

Ibn al-Farid: *Mystic Longing*

When the infant moans
 from the tight swaddling wrap
  and restlessly yearns
 for relief from distress,
He is soothed by lullabies and lays aside
 the burden that covered him;
  he listens silently
 to one who calms him.
The sweet speech makes him
 forget his bitter state
  and remember a secret whisper
 of ancient covenants.
For when he burns with desire
 from lullabies,
  anxious to fly
 to his first abodes,
He is calmed
 by his rocking cradle
  as the hands of his nurse
 gently sway it.
I have found in gripping rapture
 when she is recalled
  in the chanter's tones
 and the singer's tunes,
What a suffering man feels
 when he gives up his soul,
  when the messengers of death
 come to take him.
One finding pain
 in being torn asunder
  is like one pained in rapture
 longing for fellow travelers.
The soul pitied the body
 where it first appeared,
  and my spirit rose
 to its high beginnings,
And my spirit soared past the gate
 opening to beyond my union
  where there is no veil
 in communion.[12]

Yet this illumined life is only possible if God totally eradicates the Sufi's selfish will and graces him with the experience of mystical union. For many Sufis, the true meaning of God's oneness (*tawhid Allah*) is not merely monotheism, but above all God's absolute oneness. Therefore, mystical union is not the joining of two separate and distinct essences or natures but, rather, the realization of the divine unity of all existence. Thus, this radical monotheism leads to monism, "where only God truly exists." Ibn al-Farid likens this underlying reality to a shadow puppet theatre, which veils an essential truth, namely that the creator only exists with his creation. Just as the puppeteer relies on his puppets to perform his play, God as creator is only revealed in his creation, which, paradoxically, conceals his oneness. Therefore, the mystic who is allowed by God to see behind the screen of multiplicity finds only him, one and alone. This is union's truth.

Ibn al-Farid: *Shadow-play*
In illusion's drowsy dream, the phantom shadow
    leads you to what shimmers through the screens.
You see the shapes of things in every display
    disclosed before you from behind the veil's disguise.
Silent, they seem to speak; still, they seem to move,
    shedding light, though dark,
And you see two armies on land, at times,
    other times, at sea, in great companies.
Courageous, dressed in iron mail,
    they stand their guard with swords and spears.
The soldiers of land—knights on horse
    or mainly manly infantry—
And the heroes at sea—riding the decks
    or climbing the lance-like masts—
Are violently striking with shining sword,
    thrusting the brown strong-shafted quivering spear,
Drowning in the fire of striking arrows,
    burning in the deluge of piercing hot blades . . .
You will watch other shapes I have not mentioned,
    but I will trust in these choice few.
All that you witnessed was the act of one
    alone within the cloistering veils,
But when he removes the screen,

> you see none but him;
> No doubt lingers about
>   the forms and figures,
> And you realize when the truth is shown
>   that by his light you were guided
> to his actions in the shadows.[13]

Over the centuries, Sufi scholars have composed detailed accounts of their thought and practice, carefully noting the Qur'anic and prophetic basis for Islamic mysticism. Further, their works attempt to systematize Sufism and to situate it within the larger Islamic tradition. Sufism's attention to personal experience has been invoked repeatedly by al-Ghazali and other scholars to give spiritual relevance to the letter of the law and to enliven the God of theology. Further, beginning in the twelfth century, Muslim scholars worked to harmonize the various parts of Islam into a balanced and meaningful faith in which each aspect held its proper place and value. Law (*sharicah*) was the foundation for any acceptable system, and respected Sufi masters have made adherence to it a requirement for any spiritual development. A person must first master the Muslim rules and obligations regulating such important matters as the canonical prayers, fasting, and proper behavior, before one can enter the Sufi path (*tariqah*), which necessitates additional regulations concerning mystical devotions, personal conduct, and communal life. However, even then, the adept requires God's special grace in order to experience union and a vision of creation in its relation to God (*haqiqah*). Thus, belief, ritual, law, and mystical experience are all essential for those who seek the inner truth (*batin*) behind the world of exterior form (*zahir*). From this perspective, all of creation when seen aright glows with love's supernal light, and here again, Sufis cite the Qur'an for proof.

Qur'an 24:35: *The Light Verse*

God is the light of the heavens and the earth. The semblance of His light is like a niche in which is a lamp, the lamp in a glass. The glass is like a shining star lit from a blessed tree, an olive, of neither east nor west, whose oil would seem to shine even if not touched by fire. Light upon light, God guides to His light whom He wills, and God strikes parables for humanity, for God knows everything![14]

Historical Developments (1000–1500)

At its height in the ninth century, ᶜAbbasid rule stretched from Spain in the east to India in the west, but central authority over such a vast empire was difficult and eventually eroded. In the tenth century, a new Umayyad caliphate arose in Spain, while a Shiᶜi movement from North Africa created another caliphate, the Fatimid caliphate, in Egypt and Syria. Regional governors in Iran, Afghanistan, and India also founded their own dynasties, and the ᶜAbbasid caliphs had little real power as they were often controlled by senior military commanders. Then, in the eleventh century, a Turkic people known as the Saljuqs migrated from the Asian steppes and quickly took control of the ᶜAbbasid's eastern provinces. In 1055, the Saljuq leader Toghril Beg entered Baghdad and declared himself *sultan* ("sovereign"). He recognized the caliph's significance as the spiritual head of the Muslim community, but Toghril Beg and his Saljuq successors managed political and military affairs as they sought to reunify and expand the Muslim empire. The Saljuq sultanate promoted Sunni Islam by founding schools for higher religious education (*madrasahs*), and they supported religious scholars and mystics. The Saljuqs period is also important demographically as Turkic peoples became a significant element of the Muslim population, while Turkish joined Arabic and Persian as major languages for the expression of Islam and its cultures.

Christian Confrontations

The Saljuq expansion, particularly against the Byzantine Christians to the north, was a cause for alarm to Christians throughout Europe. Muslim armies had continued to seize political power and established their rule, where Islam became the religion of state. Though few Jews or Christians were forced to convert, non-Muslims were clearly second-class citizens. From this point on, Arabs, Turks, and other Muslims would form the primary target of Christian attacks. Non-Muslims, especially Christians, struggled to retain their identities and their followers, and a first line of defense was to stress how different and foreign Muslims appeared to be. Islam's tolerance of other monotheistic faiths made this easy. As noted above, Christian and Jewish communities protected under Islam continued to regulate the personal status of their faithful in religious and community affairs; only in matters involving the state or Muslims were they required to submit to Islamic law. This situation encouraged different religious communities to maintain their own way of life, but it also led, at times, to insular communalism. Efforts to restrain conversion to Islam were also sustained by anti-Muslim legends and writings that were circulated by Christians.

In Christian eyes, Muslim beliefs and practices seemed strange if somewhat familiar. At best they appeared inexplicable, but more often, Muslims were viewed as heretics and hypocrites; Muhammad, the prophet of Islam, was transformed into an evil sorcerer, if not the Prince of Darkness in the flesh, then a perfect fraud who tricked Arabs in his lust for women and power. Islam was not only wrong, but it was so repugnant that conversion to it was almost unthinkable. Of course, that was the intention of such notions, which were "Christian projections for Christian consumption."[15] For these stories and writings were not used in disputes with Muslims, but read among Christians to shore up belief in Christian religious, if no longer political, superiority in the Middle East and North Africa. Yet, there was a nagging theological problem. Christians could explain away the presence of the Jews as a remnant of God's old covenant. With the coming of Christ, a new covenant had superseded the old. But now a new religion, Islam, had arisen making much the same claim that the original divine message revealed to the prophets of old, from Adam to Abraham, Moses to Jesus, had most recently been given the Muhammad, the last of the prophets. This was disturbing to Christians and had to be rejected. While Christians could appreciate and appropriate Jewish scriptures, beliefs, and rituals, albeit in light of their own faith, Islamic scripture and practice had to be totally rejected. There was little common ground.

Mongols Versus Mamluks

Continuing into the Middle Ages, Islam loomed large as a threat to Christian Europe. While European powers struggled, Islamic civilization flourished, fostering the study of science, medicine, and philosophy. In an effort to retake Jerusalem and the Holy Land from the Muslims, Christian Europe organized a number of crusades beginning in the late eleventh century. The First Crusade successfully captured Jerusalem, but the city was soon in Muslim hands again. Subsequently over the next several centuries with a few exceptions, Muslim armies continued to dispatch their Christian foes. The Muslim general Salah al-Din al-Ayyubi (known in the West as Saladin, d. 1193) used his success against the Crusaders to carve out his own Sunni sultanate in Egypt, Palestine, and Syria. However the Ayyubids would soon be challenged by a greater threat coming from the east. Beginning around 1220, Mongol armies began to harass, then, conquer the northeastern provinces in present-day Pakistan, Afghanistan, and Iran. Nearly unstoppable, the Mongol hordes led by Hulegu methodically pillaged and destroyed city after city until they reached Baghdad. There in 1258, the Mongols sacked and burned the Muslim capital, slaughtering thousands of people, including the ᶜAbbasid caliph, his family, and many descendants of the prophet Muhammad. The Muslim community was stunned, as they were now held hostage and ruled by pagans. Overwhelmed by a sense of desolation and despair, many Muslims felt that the end of time was near at hand.

> Ismaᶜil ibn Abi Yusar (fl. thirteenth century): A *Lamentation*
> Judgment Day befell Baghdad with its harsh command
>   to turn and flee when they arrived.
> The Prophet's folk were seized, the men of learning, too;
>   those left behind were swallowed by the hordes.
> I never wished to stay alive as others passed away,
>   but God decrees other than we choose.[16]

The Mongols continued their advance toward Syria and Egypt until 1260, when they were met and defeated by the Ayyubid army of predominately Turkish slave soldiers. The victorious commander Baybars (d. 1277) soon replaced the Ayyubids with a new dynasty known as the Mamluks, as many of its sultans were originally slaves (*mamluk*, "royal slave"). The Mamluks repeatedly defeated the Mongols, and so their domain became a safe haven for fleeing Muslims. The Mamluk capitals of Damascus and, especially, Cairo grew into major centers of Islamic learning and culture. Ruling until 1517, the Mamluk sultans reestablished the caliphate based on ᶜAbbasid survivors, and they took pride in defending Islam both as military men and as patrons of the arts and letters. The Mamluks gave Muslims hope that all was not lost, that God had not abandoned them. The religious crisis posed by the Mongols was eased further when several Mongol leaders converted to Islam in the early fourteenth century leading to the restoration of nominal Muslim rule in their provinces.

Nevertheless, the Mongol invasion had resulted in massive deaths and destruction among Muslims, who like the Europeans, were also devastated by plague in 1348, and in subsequent years. Less confident than in the past, the Muslim community felt threatened and feared that these many invasions, famines, and plagues were trials sent by God to test their faith. Still, the spread of Islam continued, particularly by merchants and Sufi missionaries who carried the faith south into Africa, from the Sudan to Nigeria, and east, through India and on to Indonesia, Malaysia, and even China, as large portions of many populations gradually became Muslim. Islamic mysticism was pervasive at the time, and the Sufi orders flourished. These orders (*tariqah*/pl. *turuq*, "path") had originally coalesced around venerated Sufi masters including ʿAbd al-Qadir al-Jilani of Baghdad (d. 1166), the Indian Sufi Muʿin al-Din al-Chisti (d. 1236), and many others. Thus Sufism enriched Muslim religious life, spiritually, intellectually, and socially, as Muslims of all classes regularly attended Sufi gatherings for meditation and worship.

The Prophet Muhammad and His Saintly Successors

A devotional spirit was particularly pronounced at this time, and many Muslims believed that God's divine light shone most brightly in the prophet Muhammad, whose birthday became a special day of celebration (*Mawlid al-Nabi*). Traditionally on his holiday, Muslims have recited poems praising their prophet, as they seek his intercession in the affairs of this world and on the day of judgment. Muslims have also sought the intercession of the Muhammad's spiritual heirs, the Muslim saints. Although the Qur'an does not propound a clear doctrine of sainthood, a number of Qur'anic verses contain the word most commonly used in later Arabic to refer to a saint, *wali* (pl. *awliya'*):

> God is the *wali* of those who believe; He takes them from darkness into light! (2:257)
> The *walis* of God! They have no fear nor do they grieve! (10:62)

Here *wali* is best translated as "protector," "protected friend," or "ally." A *wali* was a patron or guardian who, in seventh-century Arabia, was required to regard his wards, allies, and other clients as blood relatives, taking blood vengeance on their behalf if necessary. Therefore, in these and similar verses, the Qur'an asserts that God defends his special friends whom he will protect in this world and the next. God declares in a divine saying: "Whoever treats a *wali* of mine as an enemy, on him I declare war!"[17]

The Qur'an declares that all pious Muslims are his *walis* or protected friends (7:34), but by the ninth century, *wali* had become the specific term for those rare Muslims believed to possess God-given spiritual power (*barakah*), revealed by their ability to perform miracles (*karamat*). Muhammad, other prophets, and male and female members of their families have often been venerated, as have many Sufis and some martyrs. Still, Islam lacks an ecclesiastical hierarchy like that of the Catholic Church, and so a formal system of canonization never developed. As a result, debate has continued for centuries over who is or is not a saint. Central to this issue has been forming a consensus on appropriate models of social behavior and personal piety and, above all, the very basis of religious authority, since those closest to God were believed to act on his behalf. The saints may be inspired by God with new insights into the meaning of the Qur'an and divine law, and so they pose a persistent problem for conservative Muslims who wish to establish God's unchanging laws for society.

One Muslim conservative opposing the saints was the fourteenth theologian Ibn Taymiyah (d. 1328), who stressed the primacy of the shari'ah over any sort of metaphysical speculation. Ibn Taymiyah zealously opposed anything that he perceived as a harmful religious innovation, including the cult of the saints, and he preached jihad against Christians, Shiites, and Mongols. Ibn Taymiyah also felt that Muslim society was under attacked from within, especially from beliefs in saintly intercession, mystical union with the divine, and monism. Ibn Taymiyah asserted that such beliefs and doctrines undermine the essential distinction between God and his creation upon which true monotheistic religion was based. Thus he stridently condemned the cult of the saints as idolatry and warned that monism blatantly encouraged deviation from God's truth, which could only be found in the Qur'an, the traditions of Muhammad, and codified in the divine law. Other Muslims countered that one does not worship saints; rather, the saints are to be venerated as a means to attain God's grace and forgiveness. Like a king accompanied by his courtiers, God is surrounded by his favorite companions, the prophets and saints, who have the power to intercede with Him on behalf of others.

The Gunpowder Empires (1500–1800)

While Sufism and the veneration of the saints remained marked features of Islam for centuries, after the Mongol's sack of Baghdad in 1258, a conservative spirit began to appear in many writings as religious scholars sought to protect and preserve their Muslim heritage. This was especially the case for Spain and North Africa as Muslim supremacy was defiantly challenged by Christian efforts to return to power known as the *reconquesta*.

Muslims had controlled North Africa since 711, when the weak and divided Visigoth kingdom fell prey to a Muslim army. For the next two decades, Muslim forces methodically advanced and consolidated their positions. Lingering Arab tribal animosities threatened the nascent Muslim state, but they were suppressed by ᶜAbd al-Rahman I (730–788), a descendant of the Umayyad caliphate, who established his dynasty in Cordoba after the ᶜAbbasid revolution of 750. Over the next two centuries, ᶜAbd al-Rahman and his successors rooted out political opposition, whether Christian or Muslim, as they sought to control the empire through a rigorous centralization of power. Their political institutions, such as the caliphate, contributed to the growing urban nature of Arab Muslim Spain, which was known as Andalusia. Prosperous Muslims settled in the land and increasingly immigrated to growing cities, such as Granada and Cordoba, where a large royal court soon gathered around the caliph. In time, the Umayyad Empire was divided into a number of smaller kingdoms. Nevertheless, Arabic language and culture had become dominate in the peninsula, even, among non-Muslim populations, and Muslims, Christians, and Jews studied poetry, philosophy, medicine, and other subjects, sometimes together.

Still, by the eleventh century, the Muslim kingdoms of Spain were challenged by Muslim dynasties of North Africa, and by the emerging Christian kingdoms of Aragon and Castile. Gradually, the Christians grew stronger, pushing the Muslims further south in Spain. Then in 1492, the Spanish expelled all Muslims and Jews from Spain and threatened to invade North Africa. In other Muslim lands, however, from Egypt to India, new empires arose to defend and promote the faith. Known as the gunpowder kingdoms due to their use of canons and firearms, the Mughals, the Safavids, and the Ottomans left enduring religious, artistic, and political legacies, which continue to shape the world today.

The Mughals

Beginning in the seventh century, Muslim armies raided India for booty, but they did not take an active political role in ruling parts of the subcontinent. This changed in the twelfth and thirteenth centuries as Turkish and Afghan Muslims carved out their own domains, including the Delhi Sultanate, in northern India. Then in 1526, Babur (d. 1530), a soldier of Turkish and Mongol descent, incorporated some of these Muslim states into the Timurid or Mughal dynasty, which would rule major parts of India for nearly two centuries. Among the most illustrious

Mughal sultans was Babur's grandson Akbar (d. 1605), who expanded the empire to control nearly half of India. In an effort to rule this vast area with its large population of diverse peoples, languages, and religions, Akbar created an efficient government bureaucracy and a system of justice based on the shariᶜah. In addition, he actively promoted religious tolerance among his subjects based on Sufi notions of peace, brotherhood, and divine monotheism, as he encouraged religious dialogue and interreligious marriage.

Akbar and several of his successors maintained a relatively successful and prosperous rule. They actively patronized religion, scholarship, and the arts, including Persian literature and Hindu poetry, and especially architecture, as is evident in the beautiful Taj Mahal, a mausoleum constructed by the Sultan Shah Jahan (d. 1666) for his beloved wife Mumtaz Mahal. Such projects, however, were very costly, and this together with expensive military operations against rival Muslim and Hindu rulers, financially weakened the sultanate. Shortly after sultan Awrangzib's death in 1701, the Mughal Empire disintegrated into a number of smaller provincial Muslim and Hindu dynasties. Many of them were eliminated or absorbed by the British, especially after the Revolt of 1857, which effectively ended any Muslim rule in India.

During the Mughal period some Hindus converted to Islam particularly from the lower castes and out-castes; and migrations of Muslims, especially of Turkish and Afghan peoples, increased the size of the Muslim population of India. Over the centuries, this Muslim population soared along with that of the rest of the subcontinent such that, in the world today, India and Pakistan have the second and third largest Muslim populations, respectively. Nevertheless, the Muslims of the Mughal Empire would always remain a small elite ruling a much larger non-Muslim population. Generally, Muslims regarded the Hindus as "protected people" to be taxed, while the Hindu population appears to have viewed their Muslim rulers and neighbors as bringing yet another faith that became a part of the larger Indian social system. The Sufi orders and the veneration of the saints were quite popular, and they resonated with similar elements in Hinduism. By contrast, some Muslim scholars opposed any religious influence or cooperation (syncretism) between Hindus and Muslims that might compromise Muslim rule. Their more conservative interpretations of Islam gained ground in the nineteenth century as Muslim political and social domination was slowly eroded by British rule and Indian nationalism.

The Safavids

A distinctive feature of the Mughals was that they were a Sunni Muslim minority ruling a vast Hindu majority. By contrast, the Safavids of Iran and Iraq were Shiᶜi, and in time, Shiᶜism would become the religion of the majority of people in their empire. The Safavids rose to power in northern Iran in the late fifteen century. Their name derives from Safi al-Din, a thirteenth-century Sufi ancestor and descendant of ᶜAli ibn Abi Talib, the first Shiᶜi imam. Like the Mughals, they were largely a Turkish dynasty heavily influenced by Persian culture. The founder of the dynasty was Ismaᶜil I (d. 1524) who attracted a large following among the Turkish tribes of the region, some of whom may have regarded him as savior sent to revive Shiᶜism. He conquered all of present-day Iran and declared himself shah. Ismaᶜil also recognized Twelver Shiᶜism, that tradition accepting twelve divinely guided imams, as the official religion of his empire, which he expanded to encompass the holy Shiᶜi city of Kerbala in Iraq. Ismaᶜil's imperial designs, however, were thwarted by the Ottoman Turkish sultan Selim (d. 1520), who declared a jihad against this Shiᶜi uprising and defeated Ismaᶜil and his forces in 1514 at Chaldiran in northwestern Iran. Selim, however, had to return west and so could not advance further.

To save the Safavid dynasty, Ismaᶜil's son Tahmasp (d. 1576) waged numerous campaigns against the Ottomans in the west, the Georgian Christians to the north and the Sunni Uzbeg Turks in the northeast. Later, under Shah ᶜAbbas I (d. 1629), the Safavids enjoyed a period of great power and prosperity, politically and intellectually, as they patronized Shiᶜi religious scholarship, philosophy, mysticism, and the arts, including Persian poetry, music, painting, and architecture. Subsequent Safavid shahs were less fortunate, losing ground to their rivals, particularly the Ottomans. Mesopotamia generally served as the dividing line between these two great empires, as did religion, for the Ottomans were Sunni, the Safavids Shiᶜi. As a result, Muslim minorities in both empires were regarded with suspicion and, at times, persecuted as rebellious subjects. Though the last Safavid shah was deposed by the Afghans in 1722, by this time Shiᶜism was firmly established as the majority faith of Iran and southeastern Iraq.

The Ottomans

By far the oldest and probably most successful of the gunpowder empires was the Ottomans. Named after their chief Osman (Arabic: ᶜUthman, d. 1326), the Ottomans began as a Turkish tribe, which, in the wake of the Mongols, migrated in the thirteenth century to northeastern Anatolia on the border with Byzantium. The early Ottomans prided themselves on being "holy warriors" (*ghazi*), defending and spreading the Muslim faith, particularly among the Christians to the north. Though Constantinople initially resisted their attacks, the Ottomans methodically expanded their territories into the Balkans, inflicting devastating defeats on coalitions of the Christian forces of Europe, including at the Battle of Kosovo in 1389, where the Serbian king Lazar was decapitated. Fearful of the Muslim threat, Pope Boniface IX called for a crusade in 1394, but his crusader army was soundly defeated at Nicopolis in 1396, by the Ottomans led by Bayazid I (d. 1403). Some years later, Pope Eugene IV called for another crusade, but after some initial success, the crusaders were decisively defeated at Varna in 1444 by Sultan Murad II (d. 1451). Murad II was succeeded by his son Mehmet (d. 1481). Mehmet is known as the "Conqueror," since he captured Constantinople in 1453 and made it the new Ottoman capital of Istanbul.

The Ottoman sultans also extended their empire against other Muslim Turkish dynasties to the south and west, and despite a few setbacks, they succeeded in consolidating and stabilizing their rule. Sultan Selim I defeated the Safavids in 1514, and then in 1517, he defeated the Mamluks and added Syria, Palestine, and Egypt as well as the holy cities of Mecca and Medina to his domains. A key to the Ottoman success was the Janissary (Turkish: *yeni cheri*, "new troops"), a corps of elite soldiers. They were forcibly recruited as young boys under a system known as the *devshirme*, a periodic compulsory levy on Christian boys in the Ottoman provinces. Though enslaving "protected people" is illegal under the shari͗ah, some Ottoman officials argued that these boys were the sultan's rightful slaves taken from the Christians, who were at war with Muslims. The boys were converted to Islam, tested, and then educated to serve the state as soldiers, especially as infantry with firearms, and/or administrators, and many Ottoman viziers, or prime ministers, arose from the Janissary.

Perhaps the zenith of the Ottoman Empire was the long reign of Sulayman "the Magnificent" (d. 1566), also known as "the Law-giver." This last title underscores the importance of the shari͗ah to Ottoman rule. Perhaps more than any other Muslim dynasty in history, the Ottomans attempted to integrate the shari͗ah into society as an essential dimension of state authority. The Ottomans organized formal educational institutions, which, in turn, produced the needed scholars qualified for the justice system. The ͗ulama' were under the control of the sultan and state, which gave them substantial power within a clear hierarchy of judicial, religious, and scribal positions and powers. Thus these "men of the pen" joined the "men of the sword" in serving the sultan. Under Sulayman, Turkish art and culture blossomed as is evident in calligraphy and painting, in the elegant Turkish lyrical poetry of the period, and in the grand mosques designed for Sulayman by the great architect Sinan Pasha (d. 1588).

The Ottoman Empire reached from Baghdad in the east to Tunis in the west, from the Yemen in the south to near Austria in the north where the Ottomans first laid siege to Vienna in 1529. The Ottomans would try again in 1683, but Vienna did not fall, and during the two centuries after Sulayman's death the Ottomans defended their empire against the Safavids in the southeast, and in the north and northwest, against the rising Russian Empire and the Hapsburg Austro-Hungarian Empire. Significant Ottoman expansion was no longer possible and, over time, precious financial resources were consumed by fruitless military campaigns. Further, the meritocracy that once determined the ranks and power of the sultan's servants was slowly eroded by the interests of families entrenched in the military and bureaucracy. The government and judicial systems became corrupted, and the military was less prepared to face its European enemies who were growing more powerful. Ottoman victories in battle were no longer assured in the seventeenth and eighteen centuries, and in the Treaty of Kuchuk Kaynarja of 1774, the defeated Ottomans were forced to cede the Muslim lands of the Crimea to Catherine the Great of Russia. Then, in 1798, Napoleon invaded the Ottoman province of Egypt, and though he was repelled by a joint Anglo-Ottoman coalition two years later, the Ottoman Albanian commander Muhammad ʿAli (d. 1848) effectively declared his independence of Ottoman authority. The Ottomans lost other provinces with significant Muslim populations, too, especially Albania, Bosnia, and Bulgaria in the Balkans. As nationalism spread throughout Europe, the Greeks, then the Romanians revolted and created their own nations. Similarly, nationalism took hold throughout the Arab world, further undermining Ottoman rule, which officially came to an end in 1923 when Turkey was declared a secular republic.[18]

Old Fears and New Realities (Nineteenth Through Twenty-first Centuries)

In spite of its declining years, much of the Ottoman period was a time of deep crisis for Christian Europe. Islam would not go away; if anything it was coming closer. The steady encroachments by the disciplined Ottoman armies into eastern Europe over the centuries continued to fuel Christian fears and prejudice in a struggle for survival, and Europeans saw the Turks as a reflection of their earlier Arab brethren; they were godless tyrants who enslaved others. Added to this was a new heresy to a Europe defined by class stratifications, the Ottoman leveling of the social order in which birth generally secured no special privilege. This greater social equality and religious tolerance under Islam, however, occasionally earned the admiration of non-Muslims. Particularly attractive were more personal, spiritual aspects of Islam developed in Muslim philosophy and mysticism.

One Sufi, in particular, captured the attention of the West, the celebrated Persian mystic and poet Jalal al-Din Rumi (d. 1273). He was born in what is present-day Afghanistan, but his family was forced to flee before the invading Mongol hordes. Eventually his father settled in Konya, in today's Turkey, and he resumed his life as a religious scholar and teacher. Jalal al-Din likewise pursued the study of Islam and its law, but he was attracted most to Islam's mystical dimensions. Jalal al-Din soon became a respected scholar in his own right, and he held teaching sessions on mysticism that attracted many followers. Rumi stressed personal morality and the state of one's heart before God. People must put aside difference and selfish desire in order to find their divine spirit within, and immerse themselves in God. Indeed, God's love is supreme, and Rumi proclaims God's everlasting love is for all people, no matter what their outward religion.

Rumi: *The Beloved's Spirit*
What do you think, Muslims?
I don't know myself!
I'm not a Christian or a Jew,
Not a Magi or a Muslim.
Not of east or west,
land or sea,
not of nature or of heaven.
Not of earth or water, air or fire,
not of stardust or of dust,
not of time or place.
Not from India or China,
Bulgaria or Afghanistan,
not from Iraq or Iran.

I'm not of this world—
  or the next,
    not from paradise or hell.
I'm not from Adam,
  not from Eve,
    not from Eden or the garden.
My place, the placeless,
  the traceless, my trace,
    not a body, not a soul,
      I am my beloved's spirit!
Duality,
  I have put away,
    for I have seen
      two worlds as one.
One I seek,
  One I know,
    One I see,
      One I call.
He is the first,
  He is the last,
    He is the seen
      and the hidden.
I know no one else
  but Him, Oh Him,
    Oh Him!
I no longer see
  heaven or earth;
    I am drunk
      from the cup of love![19]

Rumi's sons formed a Sufi order around their father, known as the Mevlevi Order, from an expression meaning "our master." The order is celebrated for its Persian and Turkish poetry, moving flute music, and for the order's beautiful and reverential dance. Famous in the West as the Whirling Dervishes, the Mevlevi Order spread throughout the Ottoman Empire. A major feature of this order and of much Sufism at this time was the respect and appreciation for other faiths; and in the seventeenth century, some Protestant groups claimed that tolerant Ottoman rule was preferable to Catholic persecutions. Further, a few observant European travelers attempted to give more positive accounts of Islam, but their voices were rarely heard. Far more popular than balanced accounts of Islam and Muslim life were elaborate reports of Muslim's "heathen ways." Polygamy, in particular, drew western reprobation, though few listened when an experienced French traveler reported in the eighteenth century: "There are fewer polygamous Muslims, than Catholic priests with mistresses."[20]

Orientalism

The Ottomans and Muslims were feared in Europe, yet admired by some for their achievements. This was indicative of a larger Western ambivalence with the Muslim world, which is evident in the work of the French painter Jean-Leon Gerome (1824–1904). Gerome lived and traveled extensively in the Middle East, beginning with his expedition to Turkey in 1855 and his year-long stay in Egypt in 1856. From his many sketches and studies, Gerome assembled meticulous scenes of domestic life, whether of *Arab Street Musicians* and happy children, or the more quiet and serene painting of peasant women drawing water at *Medinat el-Fayyoum* (1870), an oasis west of Cairo. At times, the Muslim men in his paintings reveal a stoic quality and a certain religious nobility as in the *Muezzin* (1864) in Cairo. Similarly, in his *Interior of a Mosque* (ca. 1875), Gerome is careful to note the various positions and gestures of the daily prayer ritual, which begins in the upright position with folded hands and continues with the bending at the waist and full prostration. After praying, Muslims often sit in silent reflection, and Gerome heightens the contemplative mood of his painting with a contrasting play of light and shadow. The lighted interior beneath the mosque's dome is balanced by the shaded recesses where Muslims pray on straw mats and in the background with the wooden screen before the prayer niche.

Gerome has often been called the finest of the Orientalist painters, and his orient was a place of "marvelous skies, resplendent colors, and barbaric and motley races of men."[21] Such evaluations of Muslim lands are characteristic of what is now called "Orientalism," in which Western romantic and racial notions were projected on to the European powers' colonized subjects in the "East," from North Africa and Turkey, to India and China. In nineteenth century Europe, sensational adventures were said to be reported firsthand recounting Muslim cruelty and debauchery. Even though seclusion and the harem prevented European contact with respectable Muslim women, this was no barrier to the imagination, and the lives of polygamous husbands with their wives and concubines were detailed, if discreetly. Perhaps succumbing to popular tastes and stereotypes, Gerome reproduced these Western fantasies in a series of paintings centering on the bath and slave markets. These many paintings include *The Narghile Lighter* (1898) with its naked, languishing beauties, *The Snake Charmer* (1880), with its decadent and homosexual suggestions, and the *Slave Market* (1866), with an exposed maiden flanked by leering Muslim men. In these and other paintings, Muslims and the Middle East form the background for Western projections, whether of sexual conquest, as in Gerome's *Woman of Cairo at Her Door* (1897) or of outright military victory and domination as in his *Napoleon in Egypt* (1867–1868).

A Changing World

This last painting also reveals how Muslim political fortunes had turned, and with the coming of European colonialism in the eighteenth century, Christians' fear of Islam was displaced by contempt. By the nineteenth century, various European powers occupied or controlled many Muslim lands; England ruled Egypt and India, France influenced parts of North Africa and Syria, while the Russians continued to incorporate former Ottoman lands into its own growing empire. Many Europeans believed this to be their right. Over the preceding centuries, the conviction had firmly taken hold that Muslims, in character, appearance, and lifestyle, were so different as to be almost nonhuman. This made an imperial relation easy. Western scientific and technical advances produced a strong belief in cultural superiority and a distinct sense of moral excellence that veiled ignoble intentions. Rich and powerful became synonymous with good and right. Arabs, Muslims, and other colonized people were regarded as backward, lazy, and licentious, children in need of discipline, sexual and brutish animals to be domesticated. So many in Europe were stunned when Muslims and other colonized people had the audacity to demand their independence as equals in a world free of colonial oppression. That Muslim religious leaders of the nineteenth and twentieth centuries supported these movements for independence only strengthened persistent Western perceptions of Islam as militant and violent.

Though most Third World nations today have been independent since 1948, they have inherited colonial legacies including economic dependence on the West and an enduring Western discrimination against them, whether based on color, ethnicity, religion, or, in the case of many Muslims, all three. This is also the case for the millions of Muslims and their families who have lived in Western Europe and who came to

England, France, Germany, and other countries as guest workers begin-ning in the 1960s. Further, populations of Muslims who have lived in Eastern Europe since the Ottoman period have repeatedly faced persecu-tion and oppression from ultra-nationalist states, such as Serbia and Bulgaria. The significant Muslim populations of Canada and the United States have faired far better. Some Muslims have been in North America since the 1800s, though the vast majority of Muslim immigrants came to America after WWI, especially during the 1960s in search of higher edu-cation and employment. Further, many African Americans converted to Islam after WWII, asserting that they were returning to the religion of their ancestors. While Muslims have been a visible part of American society for decades, they continue to be the targets of suspicion and racism, particularly in times of international crisis involving other Muslims.

Due, in part, to the Iranian revolution, the Palestinian independence movement, and the immoral actions of militant extremists, especially the destruction of the World Trade Towers on September 11, 2001, the over-whelming majority of Western images of Muslims today are not Gerome's enticing slaves or peasant women drawing water, but raging, reaction-aries who seize political power and oppress others. As for the Arabs, we generally find images of "camel riding, terroristic, hook-nosed, venal lechers whose undeserved wealth is an affront to civilization."[22] These and similar images underscore a persistent neocolonial stance on the part of many in the West that it is their "prerogative not only to manage the non-white world but also to own it, just because 'it' is not quite as human as 'we' are."[23]

However, and this is another crucial point, Arabs and Muslims have their "others" too, their notions, fantasies, and prejudice which, more often then not, focus on the West. During the Iranian Revolution in the 1980s, the religious leader Ayatollah Khomeini (d. 1989) denounced the great Satan of the United States, while radical Arab ideologues, includ-ing Saddam Hussein and Osama bin Laden, have long rallied against the "corrupt," "imperialist," and "Zionist" West. Much of the Arab and Muslim hostility toward the West undoubtedly stems from colonial expe-riences, but not all of it. Over the centuries, many Muslims have viewed non-Muslims as not only spiritually inferiors, but as deviants. Although the Qur'an expresses great respect for numerous biblical figures, including Moses and Jesus, it sometimes portrays Jews and Christians as obstinate ingrates who have corrupted God's message for their own selfish ends.

Further, from the outset, Muhammad was inextricably both prophet and statesman, and Islam's political and material success over the centuries gave Muslims little reason to doubt the truth and supremacy of their faith. Although there was often a tacit separation between the ruling and religious elites, various Muslim dynasties looked to Islam for their legitimization; it led them on to victory and supported their domination and rule over non-Muslim subjects. Riches and power were proof of what was good and right. But, beginning in the eighteenth century, new Western nations grew in power and formally victorious Muslim armies fell in defeat. Colonialism and its persistent legacies have pushed Muslims deeper into a defensive position such that, today, many feel impotent and humiliated. Thus, although Muslims in a dominant position have been able to tolerate other faiths, many are inexperienced in respecting others as equals in a world that they no longer control.

For many Muslims today, religious life continues to follow the ways of their ancestors. They pray daily, give to the poor, fast during Ramadan, and hope that, one day, they will be able to make the pilgrimage to holy Mecca. Millions of Muslims in Egypt, Pakistan, Indonesia, and elsewhere still venerate Muhammad and the saints and seek their intercession. Yet elsewhere, as in Saudi Arabia, religious tolerance and many traditional religious practices are scorned as more literal-minded clerics influenced by Ibn Taymiyah set the tone for religious practice. A recent poll on religion found that 80 percent of Muslims in the Kingdom of Saudi Arabia believe Islam is the only true religious path, suggesting a disregard, if not intolerance of other religions.[24] This has been a persistent problem in most religious traditions, especially monotheistic ones. Regarding others as inferior or evil, some have evoked the revelation from one true god to justify the use of power and coercion against followers of other faiths or dissenters within their own tradition. Thus, Islamic militants such as Osama bin Laden have declared jihad to be an ever-expanding struggle to destroy the "Christian-Zionist" West and to rule by Muslim law. Significantly, they have also targeted those Muslims, undoubtedly the Muslim majority, who do not share their view of the world as enflamed in a righteous cosmic war of good against evil, true religion against infidelity.[25]

Unfortunately, such political and militant rhetoric drowns out Islam's message of justice and compassion that is still to be found throughout the contemporary Muslim world, as Muslims have joined their voices to those calling for peace and cooperation. Though less visible than its Catholic counterpart, there is a nascent movement of liberation theology among

Muslims today who actively espouse religious pluralism and social justice for the oppressed majority of the world. In this context, jihad is not a holy war against non-Muslims, but a struggle to bring liberation to the oppressed and marginalized, particularly women and religious minorities, and to establish the social justice and economic balance called for by the Qur'an. The great American Muslim Malcolm X (d. 1965) was a pioneer for this movement when he declared that racism could only be cured by honestly accepting that all people were created by the same God. Here, God is the God of all, not just of self-righteous militants.[26] Fared Esack, a South African Muslim, elaborates:

> According to the Qur'an, it is not labels that are counted by God, but actions that are weighed. . . . The fact of group identity should not be allowed to subvert the principle of personal accountability that the Qur'an repeatedly affirms.[27]

In fact, an extraordinary passage in the Qur'an, cited earlier, justifies the need for religious diversity:

> For each of you, We have made a law and a course of action. Had God wished, He would have made you one religious community, but He tests you by what He has given you. So vie with one another in doing good deeds! (5:48)

Such movements for liberation face formidable odds in Third World nations, often characterized by totalitarian regimes and conservative clerics, fragmented civil societies and economies in collapse. Yet, committed Muslims have always known that the roads to truth are long and hard, and so they hold fast to the Qur'an, where God declares:

> As for those who strive hard in Our cause, We shall most certainly guide them on the paths that lead unto Me. (29:69)

Discussion Questions

1. Who was the prophet Muhammad? What was his life like before the revelation of the Qur'an? What was his life like after the revelation first, in Mecca, then later in Medina?

2. Describe the Qur'an. When was it revealed and in what language? How many chapters does it have and how were they arranged? What are some of the major themes of the Qur'an? In what ways do Meccan chapters differ from those revealed in Medina?

3. Describe and discuss the Five Pillars of Islam. What is the significance of each pillar in light of individual and collective Muslim concerns?

PART THREE

HISTORIC COMMON INTERESTS

RELIGION, POLITICS, CULTURE, LAW, AND SOCIETY

RELIGION, POLITICS, CULTURE, LAW, AND SOCIETY: JUDAISM

Alan J. Avery-Peck

Judaism encompasses the modern concepts of religion, politics, culture, and law under a single rubric, Torah, a Hebrew word from a root meaning "teaching" that denotes the sum total of God's revelation to the people of Israel. While people today commonly imagine this revelation to comprise primarily the Ten Commandments, Judaism, in it classical formulation, understands it to have been much broader. Alongside the entirety of the legal and narrative contents of the Hebrew Bible, God's Torah—revelation—is understood within Judaism to encompass legal and theological statements on a broad range of topics that have emerged over the course of post-biblical history. As a result of this encompassing idea of divine revelation, what the world today knows as merely a religion, Judaism is defined not so much by statements of creed and fundamental belief—though such statements certainly exist—as by a system of laws and ritual practices that, within classical Judaism, controlled all aspects of culture, economics, and politics. The content of Judaism thus is denoted by the word *Halakhah*, a term that refers to the sum total of the Torah's laws and so defines the entirety of the Jewish way of life. From the Hebrew root meaning "to walk," the *Halakhah* describes the proper path a Jew is to follow in matters of personal piety and religious devotion, in traits of culture and community, and in relationships with others both within and outside of the Jewish community. Appropriate modes of everything from business practices to political governance are understood to be included in God's revelation and so are controlled by the *Halakhah*, which phrases that revelation in the form of specific statements of what is permissible and prohibited.

In line with its theory of Torah, at the heart of Judaism stands the idea that decisions regarding the practice of Judaism made by religious authorities long after the original revelation depicted in Scripture comprise aspects of that revelation. This means that, just as the written Scriptures represent God's exact words and will, so subsequent teachings and laws developed by Jews in each generation constitute God's revelation to and will for the Jewish people. Judaism formalizes this conception in the idea that, at Sinai (see Exod 19ff.), Moses received from God two separate teachings. One was the Written Torah, embodied in the text of the Pentateuch and transmitted in writing and, from the beginning, made accessible to all of the people of Israel. The other part was an Oral Torah, which Judaism holds God taught orally to Moses, who repeated it to Joshua, who repeated it to elders, and so on through a long chain of tradition and into the hands of the rabbinic authorities who, in the first centuries C.E. emerged as leaders of the Jewish community in both the land of Israel and the Diaspora. Formulated for memorization, this aspect of revelation was transmitted orally until it reached the hands of the rabbis, who, to assure it would not be lost as a result of war, national strife, or other physical or intellectual calamity, began in the second century C.E. to codify and preserve it in written form.

In this theory, the Written and Oral Torahs are part of a single, uniform revelation and are, accordingly, of equal authority and importance. When a second-century rabbi in the Mishnah, the earliest document of Rabbinic Judaism, a fifth-century sage in the midrash or Talmud, or even a modern-day rabbi responds to a discussion or question from his (or, now, her) own day, his judgment does not simply comprise his own thinking and analysis. Rather, it is part and parcel of the divine revelation of Torah at Sinai. One effect of this conception of revelation is that all aspects of life—social, cultural, and political as well as ritual and theological—are understood to fall under the rubric of revelation and so to express an aspect of God's plan for the Jewish people. Judaism accordingly encompasses all that Jews think and do, finding within its theory of God and God's teaching an association between human intellect and divine truth.

Judaism's Theory of Torah

To understand this idea of Torah and its implications for the encompassing nature of Judaism, we turn to Mishnah Tractate Abot, which dates to early in the third century C.E. Here we find both the definition of revelation that shapes all subsequent Jewish thought about God and an illustration of the extent to which, in Judaism, the study of Torah produces a direct encounter with God that reveals how we are to live all aspects of our life.

Tractate Abot 1:1-18[1]

1:1   A. Moses received Torah at Sinai and handed it on to Joshua, Joshua to elders, and elders to prophets.

B. And prophets handed it on to the men of the great assembly.

C. They said three things:

(1) "Be prudent in judgment.

(2) "Raise up many disciples.

(3) "Make a fence for the Torah."

1:2   A. Simeon the Righteous was one of the last survivors of the great assembly.

B. He would say: "On three things does the world stand:

(1) "On the Torah,

(2) "and on the Temple service,

(3) "and on deeds of lovingkindness."

1:3   A. Antigonos of Sokho received [Torah] from Simeon the Righteous.

B. He would say,

(1) "Do not be like servants who serve the master on condition of receiving a reward,

(2) "but [be] like servants who serve the master not on condition of receiving a reward.

(3) "And let the fear of heaven be upon you."

1:4   A. Yose b. Yoezer of Seredah and Yose b. Yohanan of Jerusalem received [it] from them.

B. Yose b. Yoezer says,

(1) "Let your house be a gathering place for sages.

(2) "And wallow in the dust of their feet.

(3) "And drink in their words with gusto."

1:5   A. Yose b. Yohanan of Jerusalem says,

(1) "Let your house be wide open.

(2) "And seat the poor at your table ['make . . . members of your household']."

(3) "And don't talk too much with women."

B. (He spoke of a man's wife, all the more so is the rule to be applied to the wife of one's fellow. In this regard did sages say, "So long as a man talks too much with a woman, he (1) brings trouble on himself, (2) wastes time better spent on studying Torah, and (3) ends up an heir of Gehenna.")

1:6 A. Joshua b. Perahiah and Nittai the Arbelite received [it] from them.

B. Joshua b. Perahiah says,

(1) "Set up a master for yourself.

(2) "And get yourself a fellow disciple.

(3) "And give everybody the benefit of the doubt."

1:7 A. Nittai the Arbelite says,

(1) "Keep away from a bad neighbor

(2) "And don't get involved with a wicked man.

(3) "And don't give up hope of retribution."

1:8 A. Judah b. Tabbai and Simeon b. Shatah received [it] from them.

B. Judah b. Tabbai says,

(1) "Don't make yourself like one of those who make advocacy before judges [while you yourself are judging a case].

(2) "And when the litigants stand before you, regard them as guilty.

(3) "And when they leave you, regard them as acquitted (when they have accepted your judgment)."

1:9 A. Simeon b. Shatah says,

(1) "Examine the witnesses with great care.

(2) "And watch what you say,

(3) "lest they learn from what you say how to lie."

1:10 A. Shemaiah and Abtalion received [it] from them.

B. Shemaiah says,

(1) "Love work.

(2) "Hate authority.

(3) "Don't get friendly with the government."

1:11 A. Abtalion says,

"Sages, watch what you say, lest you become liable to the punishment of exile, and go into exile to a place of bad water, and disciples who follow you drink [bad water] and die, and the name of heaven be thereby profaned."

1:12　A. Hillel and Shammai received [it] from them.

　　　B. Hillel says,

　　　　　"Be disciples of Aaron, loving peace and pursuing peace, loving people and drawing them near to the Torah."

1:13　A. He would say [in Aramaic],

　　　　　(1) "A name made great is a name destroyed.

　　　　　(2) "And one who does not add subtracts.

　　　　　(3) "And who does not learn is liable to death.

　　　　　(4) "And the one who uses the crown passes away."

1:14　A. He would say,

　　　　　(1) "If I am not for myself, who is for me?

　　　　　(2) "And when I am for myself, what am I?

　　　　　(3) "And if not now, when?"

1:15　A. Shammai says,

　　　　　(1) "Make your learning of Torah a fixed obligation.

　　　　　(2) "Say little and do much.

　　　　　(3) "Greet everybody cheerfully."

1:16　A. Rabban Gamaliel says,

　　　　　(1) "Set up a master for yourself.

　　　　　(2) "Avoid doubt.

　　　　　(3) "Don't tithe by too much guesswork."

1:17　A. Simeon his son says,

　　　　　(1) "All my life I grew up among the sages, and I found nothing better for a person [the body] than silence.

　　　　　(2) "And not the learning is the main thing but the doing.

　　　　　(3) "And whoever talks too much causes sin."

1:18　A. Rabban Simeon b. Gamaliel says, "On three things does the world stand:

　　　　　(1) "on justice,

(2) "on truth,

(3) "and on peace."

B. "As it is said, 'Execute the judgment of truth and peace in your gates' (Zech. 8:16)."

The first point of importance is right at the beginning: Torah, an aspect of God's revelation distinct from "the" Torah, by which Judaism always means the Pentateuch, was transmitted by God to Moses and from Moses through a succession of authorities until it rested in the mouths of the rabbis of the first centuries C.E. Their teachings, accordingly, derive from God's revelation and so also constitute Torah. Their authority is equal to that of any statement found in Scripture itself.

Let us be clear. The stature of sages—their authority to dictate correct practice for all areas of life—derives from their position in the chain of tradition. They are recipients of the Torah transmitted by God to Moses and from Moses through the generations into the rabbis' own hands and minds. More than knowing Torah, they embody Torah, so that their own statements, phrased in their own words long after the events of the revelation at Mt. Sinai, are commensurate with God's own teachings.[2] This means that, at the heart of the rabbinic approach is the idea that humans gain knowledge of God's will not solely through God's explicit revelatory acts. Such knowledge, rather, emerges from the Jews' own active engagement with the details of revelation. According to Rabbinic Judaism, with thinking about Torah comes the possibility of knowing the entirety of God's will for humanity. Following this will, expressed in *Halakhah,* we then can shape the world into the condition God always meant it to have. Communal governance, business activity, social interactions, personal relationships, individual piety, and all other aspects of life are encompassed by God's will and revealed through human engagement with Torah.

The specific teachings included in this selection from Tractate Abot underscore this point. On the one hand, Abot presents a series of moralistic statements on the conduct of the sage, who is charged regarding the proper conduct of the school house and study and who is chastened to maintain the highest level of respect for the master-disciple relationship. At the same time, however, a central role of the sage is to bring the knowledge gained in the rabbinical academy into the community at large. This occurs not just through the sages' visibility as models of proper behavior. More important, it is the result of their concrete societal function as judges who assure that all aspects of communal life are governed according to the laws of Torah. Abot thus unites the familiar idea that religion concerns spiritual piety (e.g., 1:3: "Let the fear of heaven be upon you") with the concept, frowned upon today, that a religious leadership must play a central role within the structure of communal governance, holding the concrete political power necessary for it to impose upon the community the distinctive social ethic understood to be demanded by God. Illustrative of how classical Judaism combines these two aspects of communal life is the statement of Simeon (1:17). Even as he encourages the kind of withdrawal into silence that we often associate with religious asceticism, he asserts that action, not learning, is of central importance. Judaism demands a life lived in the community, a community that in all of its aspects is governed by observance of the precepts of Torah.

Within classical Judaism, the rabbi thus was distinguished by the power he acquired through mastery of Torah. This mastery gave him the right and the ability to lead the community in all aspects of its life, both in areas we commonly include under the rubric religion and in areas we today generally deem appropriately controlled only by civil law and civil authorities. But classical Judaism knows no such distinction. Certainly, today the rabbi is primarily a synagogue functionary, charged with offici-ating at worship services, delivering sermons, performing pastoral coun-seling, and, in general, serving as the executive officer of a synagogue. But this is not the model of the rabbi within classical Judaism. That individ-ual had as his central function rendering legal decisions that would shape communal life overall. He was a judge and bureaucratic functionary with a wide range of responsibilities within the classical community.

The Rabbi and Communal Governance

The communal functions of the classical rabbi are illustrated by a pas-sage from the Babylonian Talmud that discusses the daily activities of a third century C.E. Babylonian rabbi, Huna. Huna's activities reflect the way in which, in this period, the rabbi increasingly became a communal functionary whose goal was to assure the appropriate operation of all aspects of communal life under the terms understood to have been set by the Torah. The rabbi thus was responsible for community safety and eco-nomic welfare as much as he was responsible for matters we today under-stand properly to be the focus and concern of the clergy.

Babylonian Talmud Taanit 20b-21a

A. Said Raba to Rafram b. Papa, "Tell us, Master, some of the good deeds R. Huna used to do."

B. He said to him, "[What he did] in his childhood, I do not remember, [but] of his old age I do [recall]. On cloudy days, they used to drive him about in a golden carriage, and he would tour every part of the city, and he would order the demolition of any wall that was unsafe; if the owner was able to do so, he rebuilt it himself; but if not, [Huna] would rebuild it at his own expense."

C. "On every Sabbath eve, he would send a messenger to the market, and any vegetables the [market] gardeners had left over, he bought and threw into the river."

D. [At D-F, the anonymous voice of the Talmud interjects, explaining C:] Should he not have distributed these [foods] to the poor? [He did not do that since he was afraid] lest [the poor] would [come to] rely upon him and would not [any longer] buy any [food] for themselves.

E. Then, [instead of destroying the vegetables] should he not have given the vegetables to domestic animals? [He did not do this because] he held that one does not give to animals food fit for human consumption [since this would be treating food disrespectfully].

F. Then he should not have purchased [the vegetables] at all! [The reason he did so was that not buying them] might lead [the gardeners] to do wrong in the future.[3]

G. [Rafram continues:] "Whenever he came upon some [new] medicine, he would fill a water jug with it and suspend it above the doorstep of his house and say, 'Whosoever wants it, let him come and take some.'"

H. And some say, "He knew from tradition a medicine for that disease, Sibetha, and he would suspend a jugful of water and say, 'Whosoever needs some, let him come [and wash his hands] so that he may save his life from danger.'"

I. [Rafram continues:] "When he had a meal, he would open the door wide and say, 'Whosoever is in need, let him come and eat.'"

J. Raba said, "All these things I could myself do except this [last one], which I could not perform, because there are so many poor people [where I live], in Mahuza."

Huna, a rabbi and scholar of the Torah, functions as a communal administrator. He is a building inspector (A-B), an economic policy maker (C-

D), a public health administrator (E-F), and a welfare coordinator (G). What brings all of these activities under the purview of the religion, Judaism is the understanding that, through such bureaucratic activities, Huna assures that the community adheres to standards established by God and expressed in Torah. All aspects of social and economic life, that is to say, must be controlled according to the laws that define the proper conduct of the holy community.

This point is made concrete by the explanation, at C+D-F, for Huna's policy of buying up and then destroying surplus food. The first point of interest, C+F, is Huna's determination that farmers should be prevented from doing what natural economic processes dictate. At the heart of his understanding is not simply that such market forces will hurt the community at large, a recognition that still in our own day leads to governmental intervention in the marketplace. Judaism, rather, goes much further than this. For the Talmud's assertion, F, is that, if left to follow market forces, the vegetable farmers will wind up sinning. Rather than simply committing a social wrong, they will have strayed from the path Judaism knows God to intend for the world. Within classical Judaism, matters of communal economic policy thus come to be phrased as issues of religious law. An economic misdeed is no less a sin against God than is a ritual infraction.

Along these same lines, a second point of interest is the Talmud's explanation, E, of why Huna insists the surplus vegetables be destroyed rather than being giving to animals. Here again the passage shifts from economic theory to what we generally comprehend as theological thinking: Huna insists that food that is fit to be eaten by humans may not be fed to animals, since this would constitute an affront to God, who created the food specifically for human consumption. Why Huna considers it a sin to feed the food to animals but appropriate to destroy it eludes explanation. What deserves emphasis, rather, is the extent to which we see that, as portrayed in the Talmud, Huna's work as a community administrator is deeply informed by his understanding of Torah, which has precedence over the laws of market forces and economic processes. Instead, Huna's actions are shaped by his strong sense of the divine will and his knowledge that what is or is not permissible is controlled by that will rather than simply by what is humanly reasonable. Within this comprehension of the world it is absolutely appropriate, even necessary, that a rabbi should be a community leader—not just a "religious" leader—and that his leadership should enforce what he knows to be God's desire for humankind, revealed in Torah.

A World Marked by the Pervasive Presence of God

We see that Judaism associates all aspects of communal economic life and governance with the divine will, expressed in the Torah and codified in the *Halakhah*. Under this system of governance, from antiquity and through the period of Jewish emancipation in the eighteenth and nineteenth centuries, when Jews were first granted citizenship rights within the countries of their residence, Jewish communities were governed under the terms of Jewish law. Within this setting, the community's courts, markets, and system of public welfare, as much as its "religious" institutions, the schoolhouse and synagogue, operated under Jewish law and the rabbis' leadership. The community's culture, shaped by its exclusively Jewish population, similarly was controlled by Jewish notions of piety: how one dresses, the language one uses, the leisure activities deemed appropriate or prohibited, how one conducts one's business and relates to family and neighbors—all this was defined by the *Halakhah* and shaped by conceptions of piety derived from the study of Torah.

Within this setting, all that the Jews experienced in the world was understood to reflect the will and purposes of God. Aspects of nature and natural events as well as the results of human endeavor all were recognized as testifying to God's power and plan. As much as possible, therefore, the individual was to be cognizant of and, as appropriate, thankful to God for God's gifts to humankind. This idea is reflected in the idea that each Jew should find occasion to recite one hundred blessings every day. These blessings marked the individual's carrying out of commanded activities. Donning prayer garb, engaging in study, or a myriad of other commonplace actions thus entailed specific benedictions that recognized the individual's fulfilling of God's will. But, as we shall see, similar benedictions also praised God for all aspects of the world that the Jew encountered. Meir, an important second-century authority, spelled the matter out as follows (Tosefta Berakhot 6:24-25).[4]

6:24   F. R. Meir used to say, "There is no man in Israel who does not perform one hundred commandments each day [and thereby recite one hundred benedictions].

          G. "He recites the *shema'* and recites benedictions before and afterwards, eats his bread and recites benedictions before and afterwards, and recites three times the [Prayer] of Eighteen

170

Benedictions, and performs all the other commandments and recites benedictions over them."

6:25 A. And so would R. Meir say, "There is no man in Israel who is not surrounded by commandments [which protect him].

B. "[He has] phylacteries on his head; phylacteries on his arm; a *mezuzah* on his doorpost, and four fringes [on his garment] around him,

C. "and concerning them [the commandments], David said, 'Seven times a day I praise thee for thy righteous ordinances' (Ps. 119:164).

D. "He enters a bathhouse [and sees the mark of] circumcision in his flesh,

E. "as Scripture states, 'To the choirmaster according to the Sheminith' [that is, the eighth, here taken as a reference to circumcision on the eighth day after birth] (Ps. 12:1),

F. "and Scripture states, 'The angel of the Lord encamps around those who fear him, and delivers them' (Ps. 34:8)."

Clothes we wear, food we eat, the condition of our body—all these things continually remind us that all of life is lived under the protection of and in response to the divine will. Blessings provided the individual an opportunity to recognize the presence of God in aspects of life that in our age are deemed part of the mundane world, separate from religion. The point is clear in the following examples.

BENEDICTIONS FOR VARIOUS OCCASIONS

Before eating:
> *Blessed are you, O Lord our God, King of the universe,* . . .
> Before bread: *who brings forth bread from the earth.*
> Before wine: *who creates the fruit of the vine.*
> Before grains not made into bread: *who creates various kinds of food.*
> Before other foods: *by whose word all things exist.*
> On hearing bad news:
> *Blessed are you, O Lord our God, King of the universe, the true judge.*

On hearing good news:
> *Blessed are you, O Lord our God, King of the universe, who is good and dispenses good.*

On seeing individuals distinguished in secular knowledge:
> *Blessed are you, O Lord our God, King of the universe, who has given your wisdom to human beings.*

On seeing a king and his court:
> *Blessed are you, O Lord our God, King of the universe, who has given his glory to flesh and blood.*

On seeing lightning, falling stars, mountains, or deserts:
> *Blessed are you, O Lord our God, King of the universe, who has created the universe.*

On hearing thunder:
> *Blessed are you, O Lord our God, King of the universe, whose strength and might fill the world.*

On seeing the sea:
> *Blessed are you, O Lord our God, King of the universe, who made the great sea.*

On seeing trees blossoming the first time in the year:
> *Blessed are you, O Lord our God, King of the universe, who has made your world lacking in nothing and has produced therein good creatures and good trees to delight human beings.*

On smelling fragrant wood or bark:
> *Blessed are you, O Lord our God, King of the universe, who created fragrant woods.*

On deliverance from peril, recovery from sickness, or after a long journey:
> *Blessed are you, O Lord our God, King of the universe, who does good to the undeserving and who has rendered all good to me.*

Through benedictions such as these, the individual continually brings to consciousness the divine blessings that shape all aspects of life. Some of the benedictions recognize aspects of nature viewed as directly reflecting the existence and power of God. Thus we find blessings for the miracle of an earth that brings forth food and benedictions that reflect on the glory of nature, represented in mountains, seas, thunder, blossoming trees, and the like. But in its system of blessings, Judaism moves far beyond such matters to recognize all aspects of human experience as somehow reflecting God's presence. Thus both good and bad tidings, that is, everything that happens, are cause for recognition of the divine. Not just Torah learning but even learning that appears to be unrelated to Torah earns its benediction, representing equally with Torah study a legacy of God, the source of all wisdom. Even a king and his court, the opposite of the leadership informed by Torah offered by the rabbis, is seen to reflect God's interaction with humanity.

Within classical Jewish culture, a distinction between religious and mundane, between that which is guided by the precepts of faith and that which is controlled by secular intellect, thus does not exist at all. All aspects of life are under the purview of the God who created the world and all it contains. Everything the Jew experiences within life attests to the existence and glory of God.

Medieval Judaism and the Life of Torah

By the medieval period, the idea that God was reflected in all things, and thus in all learning, would lead Jewish legal experts and philosophers to rethink the foundational ideas of Judaism within the philosophical framework presented by the same Aristotelian and neoplatonic thought that was the focus of Islamic philosophers in Muslim Spain. This meant that complete knowledge and understanding of the Torah would require not simply knowledge of the Torah per se, but also a grounding in all aspects of the learning of this Golden Age of science, medicine, math, and, of course, the philosophical thought and literary works being created in Arabic.

In this period of intense Jewish philosophical thinking, Judah ibn Tibbon (1120–ca. 1190) translated from Hebrew into Arabic Judah Ha-Levi's major philosophical treatise, *The Book of Argument and Proof in Defense of a Despised Faith* (better known by its Hebrew title: *Sefer HaKuzari*). In a passage of Judah ibn Tibbon's own writing from the end of his life, he chastises his son for failing to dedicate himself sufficiently to the study not only of Torah, which is to be primary, but, equally, of science, including both ethics and physics, and of Arabic language and literature.[5] The point for our purposes is that, in Judah's view, all aspects of learning—theological and scientific—contribute to the formation of the educated Jew. It deserves note that, contrary to the concern expressed here, Judah ibn Tibbon's son, Samuel b. Judah, went on to become the translator of Moses Maimonides' most famous medieval philosophical work, *The Guide of the Perplexed*. Samuel's Hebrew and Arabic studies, as well as his philosophical knowledge, did not, in the end, fall short of the standards demanded by his father.

Judah Ibn Tibbon on Education[6]

My son, listen to my precepts, neglect none of my injunctions. Set my admonition before thine eyes, thus shalt thou prosper and prolong thy days in pleasantness. . . .

Thou knowest, my son, how I swaddled thee and brought thee up, how I led thee in the paths of wisdom and virtue. I fed and clothed thee; I spent myself in educating and protecting thee, I sacrificed my sleep to make thee wise beyond thy fellows, and to raise thee to the highest degree of science and morals. These twelve years I have denied myself the usual pleasures and relaxations of men for thy sake, and I still toil for thine inheritance.

I have assisted thee by providing an extensive library for thy use and have thus relieved thee of the necessity of borrowing books. Most students must wander about to seek books, often without finding them. But thou, thanks be to God, lendest and borrowest not. Of many books, indeed, thou ownest two or three copies. I have besides procured for thee books on all the sciences, hoping that thy hand might "find them all as a nest." Seeing that thy creator had graced thee with a wise and understanding heart, I journeyed to the ends of the earth and fetched for thee a teacher in secular sciences. I neither heeded the expense nor the danger of the ways. . . .

But thou, my son, didst deceive my hopes! Thou didst not choose to employ thine abilities, hiding thyself from all the books, not caring to know them or even their titles. . . .

. . . Seven years and more have passed since thou didst begin to learn Arabic writing but, despite my entreaties, thou hast refused to obey. . . .

. . . Nor hast thou acquired sufficient skill in Hebrew writing, though I paid, as thou must remember, thirty golden pieces annually to thy master. . . .

Therefore, my son! stay not thy hand when I have left thee, but devote thyself to the study of the Torah and to the science of medicine. But chiefly occupy thyself with the Torah. . . .

. . . Awake, my son! from thy sleep; devote thyself to science and religion; habituate thyself to moral living, for "habit is master over all thing." As the Arabian philosopher holds, there are two sciences, ethics and physics. Strive to excel in both!

> ... My son! If thou writest aught, read it through a second time, for no man can avoid slips. ... A man's mistakes in writing bring him into disrepute; they are remembered against him all his days.
>
> ... See to it that thy penmanship and handwriting are as beautiful as thy style. The beauty of a composition depends on the writing, and the beauty of the writing, on pen, paper and ink; and all these excellencies are an index to the author's work.
>
> ... Examine thy Hebrew books at every new moon, the Arabic volumes once in two months, and the bound codices once every quarter. Arrange thy library in fair order. ...
>
> Never refuse to lend books to anyone who has not means to purchase books for himself. ... If thou lendest a volume make a note of it. ... Every Passover and Tabernacles call in all books out on loan.
>
> Make it a fixed rule in thy house to read the Scriptures and to peruse grammatical works on Sabbaths and festivals, also to read Proverbs and the Ben Mishle.

Judah instructs his son regarding all aspects of learning. Study of Torah is only one part of what true education demands. Beyond this, one is to be devoted to areas we today imagine as secular, not just grammar and skills directly pertinent to the study of Judaic texts, but also Arabic, physics, and medicine, aspects of the larger intellectual world in which Judah and his son Solomon lived. In Judah's mind, these diverse areas of study—Torah, on the one side, science, on the other—seem hardly to be distinguished from each other at all. All learning ultimately is learning about God and about the world God created. Judaism, a religion that encompasses law, philosophy, culture, and governance, naturally demands training in all fields of knowledge.

Conclusion

In the perspective of classical Judaism, God revealed Torah as a guide to the proper conduct of human life in all of its aspects. Torah encompasses all knowledge, that which was recorded in the written revelation at Sinai and that which emerges from age to age, when the sage engages in the study of Torah. The rabbis' ability to discern Torah and thus to know God's plan for the world means that all aspects of human society appropriately are under his control. Classical Judaism thus holds that the rabbi, in contemporary terms a "religious" authority, rightly governs society, shaping all aspects of cultural, economic, and political life on the model presented by Torah. Codified in the *Halakhah* into specific rules and required practices, Torah thus presents an ideal for human society and the individual. To live according to Torah is to live according to the divine will, according to the norm by which God created the originally perfect world. That world is given now to humankind, who, under the guidance of Torah, can reshape it into its original perfection.

Discussion Questions

1. Judaism's theory of revelation asserts that, through their own reasoning and argumentation, rabbis participate in an ongoing process of divine revelation; their ideas have the same status as what God said explicitly to Moses at Sinai. Think about this conception of revelation. What does it say about the nature of human intellect and the connection between the human and the divine? How does it relate to other conceptions of revelation, in particular to those found in Islam and Christianity?

2. Judaism in its classical formulation takes as axiomatic that "religious" leaders will also be political and social leaders, shaping all aspects of communal governance and lifestyle. This is an idea foreign in today's secular culture, but it clearly worked well over thousands of years of Jewish history. Under what conditions might the association of religious and political power be societally appropriate and effective? What kind of society does this association create? How might you feel living in such a setting and under such conditions of religious leadership?

3. Classical Judaism demands that, through benedictions, individuals recognize the power and presence of God in all aspects of the created world, including in the accomplishments of human beings. At the same time, we have seen how the medieval philosopher and translator Judah Ibn Tibbon demanded that his son engage in what we would call secular learning. How does Judaism coordinate these two at least superficially contradictory impulses, one toward human empowerment and the other toward seeing God's hand in everything? To what extent does Jewish thinking in this area also explain the larger Judaic attitude toward revelation?

RELIGION, POLITICS, CULTURE, LAW, AND SOCIETY: CHRISTIANITY

Bruce Chilton

Introduction

From resources in the Scriptures of Israel as well as the teachings of Jesus and about Jesus, Christian teachers well before the time of Constantine enabled the church in the Greco-Roman world to develop a sense of its own identity. Christianity's prophetic philosophy overpowered persecution and made the toleration of the new faith politically expedient by the fourth century.

Yet toleration or recognition as the religion of the same Roman Empire that once was dedicated to destroy Christianity posed a deep challenge. Christians needed to have a theory of and attitude toward the society that now accepted them, if they were to relate productively to it. They could influence politics and culture within a year of having been victims of them both, because Christian clergy under Constantine were accorded the powers of magistrates. Within a century, Christian thinkers provided the church with theological models of history and society that thrive to this day. Their accomplishment was only possible, however, because Christian teachers had earlier endorsed the human world as the place of divine revelation despite the persecution of the Romans.

The Eternal *Logos* and Human Flesh: Irenaeus and Origen

Ancient Christianity, in the New Testament and in the thought of its earliest teachers, offered a deliberately ahistorical perspective: "Jesus Christ yesterday today the same—and forever," as Hebrews (13:8, in the author's translation) states and Justin Martyr explained. But faith during the long centuries of persecution prior to Constantine was won or lost on the battlefield of this life rather than in eternity. That is why Hebrews also emphasized Jesus' experience during what it called "the days of his flesh" (Heb 5:7), his life in historical circumstances. Hebrews insisted upon the significance of salvation for people who continued to live in the flesh.

The struggle with Gnosticism enhanced that emphasis upon life in the flesh during the second century. The clearest, most creative representative of this insistence is Irenaeus. In his treatise *Against Heresies*, Irenaeus pressed the case for the fulfillment of ancient prophecies in Christ: typology in Irenaeus's thought became a general theory of the relationship between the Scriptures of Israel, Jesus, and human experience. It is no coincidence that the second century saw the rise and triumph of the use of the phrase *New Testament* to refer to the canon of the Gospels, the letters of Paul, and the other writings generally received within the Church. That phrase implies another, *Old Testament*, which embodies the theory that the Scriptures of Israel are to be understood as types that are fulfilled in Christ.

Irenaeus contributed one of the most daring ideas of his time, and he did so within his general theory of the Scriptures. Just as he argued for the unity of the Old and the New Testament on the basis of the typology of Hebrews, Irenaeus also developed the relationship between Adam and Christ on the basis of what he read in Paul (especially in Rom 5). The description offered by Henry Chadwick can scarcely be improved upon:

> The divine plan for the new covenant was a "recapitulation" of the original creation. In Christ the divine Word assumed a humanity such as Adam possessed before he fell. Adam was made in the image and likeness of God. By sin the likeness became lost, though the image remained untouched. By faith in Christ mankind may recover the lost likeness. Because Irenaeus regarded salvation as a restoration of the condition prevailing in paradise before the Fall, it was easy for him to accept Justin's terrestrial hopes for the millennium. Because he believed that in the Fall only the moral likeness to God was lost, not the basic image, he was able to regard the Fall in a way very different from the deep pessimism of the Gnostics.[1]

For all his stress upon the authority of apostolic tradition, Irenaeus here shows himself to be a synthetic philosopher of early Christianity.

Irenaeus's attitudes comported with his own background. He was not a recent convert to Christianity, but a native product of Christian culture in Asia Minor. Irenaeus was nurtured in a milieu that anticipated the immediate fulfillment of biblical promises in Christ, and his theory of recapitulation is no historical survey, but an answer to the single question: how is it that faith in Jesus Christ will ultimately transform humanity?

In a single theory he elevated the flesh to the realm of what may be saved, set out a general approach to the relationship between the Testaments of the Scriptures, and articulated a symmetrical theology of primordial sin and eschatological hope. "God became man that man might become divine" (*Against Heresies* 3.10.2; 3.19.1; 4.33.4, 11). Christianity ever since (consciously and not) has been exploring the implications of Irenaeus's insight. His conviction that human beings were subject to sin and yet susceptible of being transformed, so as to turn the inheritance of Adam into the glory of Christ, became a staple of early Christian preaching.

But for all the daring profundity of Irenaeus's contribution, he did not articulate a theory of history. The consequence of the incarnation was absolute, but by definition it did not emerge from any sequence of events that were determined by the terms and conditions of this world, which we today call history. History speaks of sequence as well as of consequence. From the time of the Gospels until the present, Christian faith indeed speaks of events, but of events that are without precedent, literally unsequential. For Irenaeus, as for Hebrews and Justine Martyr, the incarnation told the real meaning of Israel's Scriptures out of the order of what we call real time. Chronology did not have any theological significance for thinkers who believed the Son of God was eternal. Within such a perspective, history does not even have the significance of a footnote.

Since recapitulation, like typology, is a theory of salvation rather than an historical argument, Irenaeus is able to make statements about Jesus without recourse to information about him, openly contradicting a literal reading of the Gospels. Because Jesus sums up our humanity in his flesh, Irenaeus holds he must have died around the age of fifty, the supposed time of complete human maturity (*Against Heresies* 2.22.1-6). The only reference in the New Testament to Jesus' age comes in the Gospel according to Luke, where he "began to be about thirty" (Luke 3:23, in the author's translation). Although that statement is vague, only abstract speculation can turn Jesus' age at his death into fifty.

The operative point in the distinction between Irenaeus and the gnostics he opposed is not that Irenaeus was historically minded while they embraced philosophy. That once fashionable generalization has virtually no merit, because the whole of Christianity articulated itself philosophically. The contrast between them is more basic. Irenaeus's speculation involved the flesh in its beginning in types, in its recapitulation in the case of Jesus, and in its fulfillment in paradise. Gnostic speculation, by contrast, referred to flesh as ancillary, an accident in the overall unfolding of spiritual essence. It is for that reason that Jesus must have been fifty when he died for Irenaeus, much as Hebrews can invent elements in Jesus' struggle for obedience. Hebrews' invention of circumstance (the "loud cry" in Gethsemane; 5:7) is less substantial than Irenaeus's, but each is motivated by the concern for what must have been the case. And what must have been in the flesh is a projection of what eternally is in heaven.

This procedure of thinking on the basis of God's nature and relating that to human nature, pioneered in the Epistle to the Hebrews and by Irenaeus, is best instanced by Origen of Alexandria. Born in 185, Origen knew the consequences that faith could have in the Roman world: his father died in the persecution under Septimus Severus in 202. Origen accepted the sort of renunciation demanded of apostles in the Gospels, putting aside his possessions to develop what Christians of the time called the philosophical life, a life consistent with the wisdom of the Gospels (see Eusebius, *History of the Church* 6.3). His learning resulted in his appointment to the catechetical school in Alexandria. Eusebius also reports that Origen castrated himself (*History of the Church* 6.8), inspired by Jesus' teaching in Matthew 19:12, but it seems likely Eusebius is repeating a calumny by Demetrios, bishop of Alexandria, who objected to Origen's ordination by the bishops of Jerusalem and Caesarea.[2] Origen moved from Alexandria to Caesarea in Palestine, to some extent as a result of bitter dispute with Demetrios, his episcopal nemesis. During the Decian persecution (250 C.E.) Origen was tortured, and he died of consequent ill health in 254.

Origen was the most powerful Christian thinker of his time. His *Hexapla* pioneered the compared study of texts of the Old Testament, while his commentaries and sermons illustrate the development of a conscious method of interpretation. His most characteristic work, *On First Principles*, is the earliest comprehensive Christian philosophy extant. It offers a systematic account of God, the world, free will, and Scripture. His *Against Celsus* is a classic work of apologetics, and his contribution to the theory and practice of prayer (represented in the classic source of meditation edited by Basil the Great during the fourth century, the *Philokalia*) is unparalleled. Throughout, Origen remains a creative and challenging thinker. Condemned by later councils of the church for his daring assertion that even fallen angels could theoretically one day repent and be saved (see *Apology* I.6), Origen remains the most controversial theologian in the Christian tradition.

Unlike Irenaeus, Origen insisted upon the transformation of existence from earth to heaven as a radical spiritualization of the human body. The line of demarcation between millennial expectations of eschatology (such as that of Justin and Irenaeus) and spiritual expectations of eschatology (such as that of Paul and Origen) is quite clear in classical Christianity, and the difference has not been resolved to this day.

For those sympathetic with Origen, the role of history was severely limited, because spiritual realities were vastly more important than the circumstances of this world. He himself was inclined to see the writings of Moses as an example of *historia* (see *On First Principles* 4.2.6, 8, 9; 4.3.4), a matter for literal reading. The aim of deeper interpretation was to find the allegorical or spiritual meaning that provides insight into the restoration *(apokatastasis)* of all things in Christ, a transformation that can only occur outside the terms and conditions of this world. Any limitation to the realm of literal history was for Origen the most dangerous self-deception.

The difference between Irenaeus and Origen is instructive on several levels. They both invested what happened to Jesus in the flesh with profound meaning, but in different ways. In Irenaeus's millennial perspective, what happened in the case of one person of flesh has consequence for all people of flesh, and vice versa. According to Origen's philosophical mode of thought, Jesus' flesh is important as the occasion to reveal the divine nature of the spiritual body, a reality that only the restoration of all things will manifest fully.

The difference between the *recapitulatio* of Irenaeus and the *apokatastasis* of Origen is more than a matter of nomenclature. It also reflects the dividing line between millennial and philosophical views of eschatological transformation and distinctive assessments of the value of the flesh. Yet for Irenaeus and Origen both, the appropriate interests of theology are only partially historical. Flesh is the medium of revelation in Irenaeus, while it is more loosely related to revelation in Origen. Although both views recognize the flesh of Jesus and one's own flesh as consequential, neither attributes sequential or chronological significance to flesh.

Neither writer imagines history as being started and then methodically pushed along by God in order to lead up to the kingdom of heaven.

Their views are antithetical to widespread modern assumptions. During the twentieth century, many Christians adhered to a movement called "the social Gospel." That movement invoked the model of a linear sequence of progress in divine revelation. This idea invoked a progressive and inevitable revelation of more and more knowledge of God, more and more incorporation of Jesus' teaching, But in classical Christianity as illustrated in the approaches of Irenaeus and Origen there could be no such picture of the unfolding of history, because there was not even an agreement that history existed as a category of divine action.

From the perspective of early Christianity, God had given flesh consequence: that followed immediately from any understanding of the incarnation, whether along the lines of an Irenaeus or an Origen. The consequentiality of flesh had been donated by God himself in the case of Jesus. Yet flesh was not held to have an inherent value, such that any human event, leading to another necessarily revealed divine purpose. Sequence and chronology in early Christianity proved to be difficult to explain in terms of the revelation of Christ. The confidence that the passage of time leads to progress, a commonplace in modern thought, is the inheritance of two influential Christian theologians who lived after Irenaeus and Origen.

The Christian Invention of History and Society: Eusebius and Augustine

Constantine's settlement prompted Christian thinkers to discover the significance of sequence or chronology within history. Even prior to his policy of official toleration, Christians had long become accustomed to the ethic of mutual care, which followed their commitment to Jesus' teaching, and that promoted resilient practices of help for the poor and related activities that easily translated into social programs, once Christianity has been embraced by the Roman Empire. In politics, however, Christians had virtually no experience of leadership until Constantine, although they had already started to think through the relationship between secular power and eternal salvation.

Now history—specifically, history as a sequence of events—could scarcely be ignored or slighted. The conversion of the Roman emperor seemed actually to validate the claims of the Gospel because the preeminent power of this world acknowledged the kingdom of the world to come. There was a before Constantine and an after Constantine in a way there has not been a before and after Marcus Aurelius, or even Augustus. Something happened that demanded a sequential explanation. That explanation, in turn, involved a Christian theory of society.

The beginning of Christian history as a way of looking at the world came with Eusebius (260–340), bishop of Caesarea. Through Pamphilus, his martyred teacher and model, Eusebius had been deeply influenced by the thought of Origen. So even before there was a consciously Christian history, we are confronted with an irony of history: from the least historical perspective there was provided the first comprehensively historical account of the meaning of Christ. Eusebius's prominence in the ecumenical church at various councils from Nicaea onward, as well as his friendship with Constantine, go a long way toward explaining why Eusebius should have made the contribution that makes him to ecclesiastical history what Herodotus is to Greco-Roman history.

As Eusebius attempted to express the startling breakthrough under Constantine, he portrayed the new emperor as chosen by God himself. The most famous result of his meditation on the significance of the new order in which Christianity was vindicated is his *History of the Church*, a vitally important narrative that takes up the Christian story from the time of Christ. The settlement under Constantine is Eusebius's goal, however, and his glowing portrayal of the emperor is most vividly conveyed in his *Praise of Constantine*. After speaking of Christ, the Word of God that holds dominion over the whole world, Eusebius goes on to make a comparison with Constantine (*Praise of Constantine*, 1.6): "Our Emperor, beloved of God, bearing a kind of image of the supreme rule as it were in imitation of the greater, directs the course of all things upon earth." Here the old pagan idea of the rule of the emperor as commensurate with the divine rule is provided with a new substance: the emperor who obeys Christ himself imitates Christ's glory.

Eusebius was inclined to describe himself as moderately capable (*History of the Church* 1.1; 10.4), and that may be an accurate assessment of him as a theologian and historian. But as a political theorist, Eusebius is one of the most potent thinkers in the West. He provided the basis upon which the Roman Empire could later be presented as the Holy Roman Empire, and the grounds for claiming the divine rights of rulers. At the same time, his reference to the conditional nature of those rights, as dependent upon the imitation of Christ, has provided a basis upon which political revolution may be encouraged on religious grounds.

Part of Eusebius's argument was that Constantine restored the united form of the empire that had been the ideal of Augustus (*History of the Church* 10.9.6-9). After a preface that sets out Christ's divine and human natures, Eusebius carefully places Christ's birth during Augustus's reign, after the subjugation of Egypt (*History of the Church* 1.5). The pairing of Augustus and Christ, and then Christ and Constantine is therefore symmetrical and defines the scope of the work. The result is to present a theologically structured political history.

The extent of that history is determined by its political horizon, much as in the case of Eusebius's predecessors in classical history. Whether we think of Herodotus in his explanation of the Persian War, or of Thucydides in the case of the Peloponnesian War, the impetus of writing history seems to be the experience of political change and dislocation. The scope of such work would be extended by such writers as Polybius (the apologist for Rome) and Josephus (the apologist for Judaism), but the desire to learn from the past in the effort to construct a politically viable present is evident throughout.

Eusebius's apology for Constantine, written as political history in form, often seems to descend into flattery. Some readers have wondered how Eusebius could so thoroughly fail to be critical, whether as historian or as theologian. As an historian, he knew that kings and their flatterers were transient; as a theologian in the line of Origen, he knew that perfection eluded human flesh. The key to understanding Eusebius's argument lies in his conviction that Christ was at work in Constantine's conversion (*History of the Church* 10.1):

> From that time on a day bright and radiant, with no cloud overshadowing it, shone down with shafts of heavenly light on the churches of Christ throughout the world, nor was there any reluctance to grant even those outside our community the enjoyment, if not of equal blessings, at least of an effluence from and a share in the things that God had bestowed on us.

The sharp change from being persecuted and all that involved was as disorienting for Eusebius as the Peloponnesian War had been to Thucydides, and an explanation was demanded. In that explanation, ecclesiastical history was born: that is, not simply the anecdotes of experience, but a rational account of God's activity within human events, chronologically ordered. Eusebius himself, who had once been imprisoned for his faith, now found himself at the center of a sympathetic empire.

The sequence of flesh met the consequence of flesh, and history was the offspring. The victory of Constantine and his colleague Licinius (who at first reigned with Constantine) was thought to be nothing less than the appointed plan of God within a definite sequence of events. Eusebius reminds the reader of the terrible tortures Christians had experienced, and then proceeds to describe the difference that Constantine made (*History of the Church* 10.4):

> But once again the Angel of the great counsel, God's great Commander-in-Chief, after the thoroughgoing training of which the greatest soldiers in his kingdom gave proof by their patience and endurance in all trials, appeared suddenly and thereby swept all that was hostile and inimical into oblivion and nothingness, so that its very existence was forgotten. But all that was near and dear to Him He advanced beyond glory in the sight of all, not men only but the heavenly powers as well—sun, moon, and stars, and the entire heaven and earth.

Only the language of apocalypse and of the sequenced revelation of God himself in Christ can explain to Eusebius's satisfaction how the former agony can so quickly have been transformed into festivity. The promised future had begun under Constantine, and there was no room for a return to the past.

The picture that Eusebius draws of the contemporary scene might have been drawn from an apocalyptic work, but it describes the Greco-Roman world of his day (*History of the Church* 10.9, after the narrative of the removal of Licinius):

> Men had now lost all fear of their former oppressors; day after day they kept dazzling festival; light was everywhere, and men who once dared not look up greeted each other with smiling faces and shining eyes. They danced and sang in city and country alike, giving honor first to God our Sovereign Lord, as they had been instructed, and then to the pious Emperor with his sons, so dear to God.

History for Eusebius was not just an account of the past, it was apocalypse in reverse. His account was designed to set out the sequence of events that brought about the dawn of a definitive new age.

Even before Eusebius, Origen had written that Rome would prosper better by worshiping the true God than even the children of Israel had

(*Against Celsus* 8.69). For Origen, this argument was hypothetical because the Roman Empire was not about to embrace Christianity during his time; for Eusebius, this surreal hypothesis had become a reality. The new unity of the empire, under God, in Christ, and through the piety of the emperor himself, constituted for Eusebius a divine polity (*politeia* or *politeuma*), literally a breath away from paradise.

Christian history was born under the pressure of success; its baptism of fire was the experience of an unimaginable failure. In 410 C.E., Alaric sacked the city of Rome itself at the head of the Visigoth armies. That event was a stunning blow to the empire generally, although its capital was now Constantinople rather than Rome. The pillage occurred while the Roman Empire was Christian; two centuries before, Tertullian had argued that idolatry brought about disaster (see *Apologeticus* 41.1), and now Christianity could be said to do so. Latin-speaking Christianity—especially in North Africa—had been particularly attracted to a millenarian eschatology. How could one explain that the triumphant end of history, announced by Eusebius and his followers, seemed to be reversed by the Visigoths?

Augustine, a man whose very life embodied the tortured dream of a peacable Christian empire, devoted himself to explaining that dilemma. Augustine was born in 354 in Tagaste in North Africa, the son of a petty administrator and his Christian wife. A benefactor from Tagaste enabled him to continue his studies in rhetoric in Carthage, where he was deeply influenced by his reading of Cicero, and then accepted the popular philosophy of Manicheanism. Its conception of the struggle between good and evil as two masses opposed to each other appealed to him deeply. Further study in Rome and Milan led to Augustine's conversion to Christianity. Rome brought him into contact with thinkers who showed him that Manicheanism was based upon unproved dogma, while in Milan he heard the sermons of Bishop Ambrose. Ambrose demonstrated to Augustine that the authority of faith did not contradict reason. At the same time, a reading of Platonist thinkers enabled Augustine to conceive of God as immaterial, beyond time and space.

Philosophy was the first expression of Augustine's faith. Even while he was preparing for baptism, he wrote treatises, and he continued doing so in Rome afterward. Then he returned to Tagaste, living and writing with a few friends. A visit to Hippo Regius proved fateful, however. He was made a priest and later became bishop of the small town. He continued to write extensively, but in a more pointed way against those who attacked the church. He particularly concerned himself with Manicheanism. In addition, he criticized two viewpoints that demanded perfection of Christians. The Donatists attempted to force from the church those who had cooperated with Roman authorities during the period of persecution, while the Pelagians argued that human effort was sufficient to attain redemption.

In addition, Augustine wrote on how to instruct new members of the church and composed homilies that were the basis of his popular fame. Three profoundly innovative works have influenced the world of letters and Christian doctrine ever since. His *Confessions* (finished in 400) are the epitome of his introspective method: the analysis of his own life enables him to lay out the forces at work in the human soul. The *City of God*, occasioned by the sack of Rome in 410, sets out the pattern of redemption within the tides of global history. *On the Trinity*—his great synthetic work begun in 400—is a meditation on the imprint of God's image within us and around us. He died in 430, while Hippo was under siege by the Vandals, whose advent presaged the dissolution of the empire in the West.

Augustine's *City of God*, a tremendous work of twenty-three books, responds to the perceived decay of the Roman Empire. From the outset, he sounds his theme, that the City of God is an eternal city that exists in the midst of the cities of men; those two cities are both mixed and at odds in this world, but they are to be separated by the final judgment (*City of God* 1.1). That thesis is sustained through an account of Roman religion and Hellenistic philosophy, including Augustine's critical appreciation of Plato (books 1-10).

In the central section of his work, Augustine sets out his case within a discussion of truly global history, starting with the story of the creation in Genesis. From the fall of the angels, which Augustine associates with the separation of light and darkness in Genesis 1:4, he speaks of the striving between good and evil. But the distinction between those two is involved with the will of certain angels, not with any intrinsic wickedness (*City of God* 11.33). People, too, are disordered in their desire, rather than in their creation by God (*City of God* 12.8).

The difference between the will God intends for his creatures and the will they actually evince attests the freedom involved in divine creation. But the effect of perverted will, whether angelic or human, is to establish two antithetical regimes (*City of God* 14.28):

> So two loves have constituted two cities—the earthly is formed by love
> of self even to contempt of God, the heavenly by love of God even to

contempt of self. For the one glories in herself, the other in the Lord. The one seeks glory from man; for the other God, the witness of the conscience, is the greatest glory. . . . In the one the lust for power prevails, both in her own rulers and in the nations she subdues; in the other all serve each other in charity, governors by taking thought for all and subjects by obeying.

By book 18, Augustine arrives at his own time and repeats that the two cities "alike enjoy temporal goods or suffer temporal ills, but differ in faith, in hope, in love, until they be separated by the final judgment and each receive its end, of which there is no end" (*City of God* 18.54).

Even now, in the power of the Catholic Church, God is represented on earth, and in the present, the Christian epoch (*Christiana tempora*) corresponds to the millennium promised in Revelation 20 (*City of God* 20.9). This age of dawning power, released in flesh by Jesus and conveyed by the church, simply awaits the full transition into the city of God, complete with flesh itself.

In his adherence to a kind of millenarianism and to the resurrection of the flesh in the Latin creed, Augustine is very much a product of North Africa and Italy (where he was active as a teacher of rhetoric prior to his conversion and his return to North Africa). But his *City of God* creates the greater frame, primordial and eschatological, within which history becomes a theological discipline. History, he argues, is more than a lesson in how to avoid war and create order. And here there is certainly more than the superficial enthusiasm that comes of histories written by the winners. Rather, history for Augustine—and from Augustine—is the interplay of those two forces that determine the existence of every society and every person.

Augustine died in Hippo while the city was actually under siege by the people called the Vandals. His passing, and the sack of his church and his city, was a curious witness to his *Christiana tempora*. But his conception that his history and every history reflected the struggle between the two cities prepared him and the global church for that disaster, and for much worse. He had turned back to the Eusebian model of history as apocalypse, and he took its apocalyptic dimension even more seriously than Eusebius himself had. No apocalyptic seer ever promised an easy transition to the reign of Christ, and to that moment when God would be all in all (1 Cor 15:28, which Augustine quotes). Smooth, unhampered progress is a model of history that only recommends itself to those in the line of Eusebius and historians since the nineteenth century. If history is apocalyptic, because the times of the church are millennial, then human flesh has indeed been blessed, but humanity's history is equally dedicated to struggle.

The struggle, however, is not ultimately between good and evil, but between the love of God and the love of self. That is the key to Augustine's ceaseless, pastoral ministry, as well as to his remarkably broad intellectual horizon. In every time and in every place, there is the possibility that the city of God will be revealed and embraced; now, in the *Christiana tempora*, we at last know its name, and can see the face of that love that would transform us all.

History after Augustine could be painted on canvasses of indeterminate size because he established the quest to integrate the historical task with philosophical reflection. At the same time, in his *Confessions*, he established the genre of autobiography as an investigation of the dynamics of universal salvation within the life of the individual he knew best, himself. Written large in nations and written small in persons, history attested the outward-working and inward-working power of God, if only one's eyes could see with the love of God and be freed of the blindness of self-love.

Christianity's Classical Society

Eusebius and Augustine together provided the classic program for Christianity's survival of the decay of the Roman Empire. A political theory of divine right and an historical perspective of the two cities would provide the matrix for the remains of the empire in the East and the petty kingdoms in the West to construct successive, variant, sometimes conflicting models of Christ's kingdom of earth. Without reference to those two ideologies, an understanding of the Middle Ages is simply impossible.

The contribution of Eusebius is frequently overlooked, because the triumphalist model of government, of which he was the chronicler, has long been out of fashion, whether within the church or without. But a commitment to a monarch who is Christ's regent in fact survived both the Reformation and the Renaissance; only the age of the Enlightenment saw it superseded. Even so, the Enlightenment committed itself to a cognate idea: that nationally constituted people could and should assert their inherent rights, as "endowed by their Creator," in the words of the American Declaration of Independence.

Augustine's influence is more widely recognized than Eusebius's, and it is unquestionably deeper. Global history and personal history have perennially been seen as revelatory; echoes of the *City of God* and the *Confessions* are heard in books, seen in movies, resonant in political arguments and personal disclosures. It may not be too much to say that with Augustine the human being in historical experience was invented. And he redefined what he meant by history; its time was for him not just one temporal segment after another. Time for Augustine was rather our remembrance of the past, our expectation for the future, our attention in the present (see *Confessions* 11). History, in today's jargon, was "constructed" in his understanding.

Considerable attention has been given in recent years to the eclipse of the view of history as objective events, the story of what "really happened." Facts, to be sure, remain at the end of this debate: there are data that can be verified, and there are mistakes that cannot be verified. But the arrangement of verifiable data into a sequenced account, and the determination of the scope of the inquiry cannot be decided by anything approaching an objective standard. Augustine provides self-conscious answers to the questions of the sequence (including the scope) and the consequence of history. And he shows how confronting the past belongs to the human task, personal and collective, of living in the present and fashioning a future with a society that can address its challenges.

Discussion Questions

1. Why did Irenaeus develop his theology of "recapitulation," and what is its importance for early Christian thought?

2. Explain the significance of the difference between the *recapitulatio* of Irenaeus and the *apokatastasis* of Origen.

3. What influence has Eusebius exerted on the conception of government in the Christian West?

4. Is Augustine better understood as a successor or as a critic of Eusebius?

RELIGION, POLITICS, CULTURE, LAW, AND SOCIETY: ISLAM

Th. Emil Homerin

Bismillah al-rahman al-rahim
"In the name of God, the compassionate, the merciful"

This phrase is spoken by Muslims innumerable times each day as they begin their prayers, read the Qur'an, and go about many other activities, such as starting to work in the morning, signing a contract, or writing a letter. This simple ritual is indicative of the pervasiveness of Islam in the lives of millions of people throughout the world since the seventh century C.E. until today. Similarly, the mosque has structured Muslim life for centuries, and religious ideas and functions have inspired the forms of many buildings fashioned in a diversity of regional styles. Islamic architecture conveys a sense of confidence, authority, and, at times, tranquillity, as seen in the Umayyad Mosque in Cordoba, Spain, in the mausoleum of the conqueror Timur (Tamerlane, d. 1405) in Samarqand, Uzbekistan, in the many gardens of Safavid Iran and Mughal India, and in the more recent Shah Alam Mosque in Malaysia and the Islamic Center of Greater Toledo in Perrysburg, Ohio.

The mosque is a central feature of nearly any Muslim neighborhood throughout the world, and often the inscriptions found in them and in other Muslim buildings are verses from the Qur'an. These verses are a source of inspiration to many and a form of protection to others, and Muslim taxi drivers may keep a copy of the Qur'an in their cabs to protect them in traffic. Daily, the Qur'an is publicly recited throughout the Muslim world, and some radio stations in Egypt and other Muslim countries are devoted to broadcasting only the Qur'an. The popularity of the Qur'an is evident from chanting competitions in Indonesia that draw great attention and crowds comparable to major sporting events in the Western nations, as religious beliefs and practice continue to shape the lives of many Muslims.[1]

Elements of Islamic mysticism also play their parts in popular culture. Sufism has long cultivated devotion to the prophet Muhammad through dance, verse, and music. Recordings by several Muslim artists, especially Nusrat Fateh Ali Khan (d. 1997), have recently become popular in Europe and America. A number of U.S. and British jazz and rock musicians have been influenced by this music, while contemporary rock songs from Pakistan and elsewhere may refer to Sufism, the saints, and, of course, the prophet Muhammad.[2] In their own way, these songs continue a long tradition of praising the prophet and his life in verse, similar to Christmas hymns about Jesus. Noteworthy among those who have praised Muhammad are the Egyptian poet al-Busiri (d. 694/1295), with his famous poem the *al-Burdah* ("The Prophet's Cape"), and Jaᶜfar al-Barzanji of Medina (d. 1766), whose *Mawlid al-Nabi* ("Nativity of the Prophet") has been translated into Swahili and other languages.

Similarly, a woman Sufi from Damascus, ᶜA'ishah al-Baᶜuniyah (d. 1516), composed love poems for the prophet. ᶜA'ishah was from a scholarly family with a long line of religious scholars and officials from Syria, and she received an excellent education from her father, uncles, and other teachers. ᶜA'ishah wrote a number of books and composed hundreds of poems, and she may have been the most prolific woman author in Arabic prior to the twentieth century. Much of her writing centers on the life of the prophet Muhammad, and this may have been due in part to a vision she had of him when she went on pilgrimage to Mecca as a young woman with her father. ᶜA'ishah tells us:

> God, may He be praised, granted me a vision of the Messenger [Muhammad] when I was residing in holy Mecca. An anxiety had overcome me by the will of God most high, and so I wanted to go to the holy sanctuary. It was Friday night, and I reclined on a couch on an enclosed veranda overlooking the holy Kaᶜbah and the sacred precinct. It so happened that one of the men there was reading a poem on the life of God's Messenger, and voices arose with blessings upon the Prophet. Then, I could not believe my eyes, for it was as if I was standing among a group of women. Someone said: "Kiss the Prophet!" and a dread came over me that made me swoon until the Prophet passed before me. Then I sought his intercession and, with a stammering tongue, I said to God's Messenger, "O

my master, I ask you for intercession!" Then I heard him say calmly and deliberately, "I am the intercessor on the Judgment Day!"[3]

ᶜA'ishah begins the following poem in praise of Muhammad with an invocation to the supernatural Light which, legend says, God used to bring about creation. According to tradition, God was a hidden treasure who desired to be known, and so the Light came forth from his knowledge as the first emanation. God made the Light shine in Adam and the other prophets, culminating in Muhammad, the most beloved of God and humanity's intercessor on the judgment day. ᶜA'ishah traces Muhammad's extraordinary lineage from the Light though his righteous ancestors until he appears on earth as the noble prophet. In the fourth verse, she refers to Muhammad as Taha, one of his common honorific titles, which some Muslims believe stands for "the pure, the guide" (*tahir hadin*). In the final verse, ᶜA'ishah mentions the nightingale, which, in Arabic, Persian, Turkish, and Urdu poetry, sings at night to his beloved rose. Some Muslim poets have called Muhammad a nightingale, as he spoke of his love for God, and this, too, points to the great respect and devotion that Muslims continue to feel for their prophet.

> ᶜA'ishah al-Baᶜuniyah (d. 1516): *Muhammad's Light*
> The light of the sun, the beautiful moon
>   vanish in the shining glow
>   of his noble line.
> Compassion's Lord robed him
>   in the cloak of splendor,
>   and all eyes were blind before it.
> He grew strong, righteous and good,
>   always descending
>   through the chaste and pure.
> Then he came forth, Taha,
>   a full moon high in his sky,
>   so to him is all glory, honor and pride.
> God's prayers be upon him
>   as long as noon day is bright,
>   and the nightingale sings on branches at night![4]

Even beyond this overtly religious verse, Islam has echoed within the larger body of poetry composed over the centuries in many languages, as can be heard in the following Somali love poem by Cilmi Bowdheri (d. 1941), a herdsman and baker. Cilmi asks the wind to carry his message to his beloved faraway. He repeatedly begs the wind to swear by the ever-lasting God and to make haste as if sent by God himself, for the poet needs a miracle to save his lost love.

Cilmi Bowdheri (d. 1941): *The Messenger*
Winds that posses the power of speech
Are something new in this world, perhaps,
But you must swear to me, O Wind, by the Everlasting One
That you will receive the impress of my words!

Indeed I would have gone to the sailing ships
And handed them my letters in a packet
But ships may tarry on their journeys
And nights may pass before they come to port,
So it is you, O Wind, whom I have chosen,
You who have the speed that I demand.
Swear to me then by the Everlasting One
That you will receive the impress of my words!
You pass above the ground,
Above the settlements of men,
Never resting, you run and run
As if sent by God on everlasting errands.
Weariness is not for you,
It is only the living whose breath gives out.
I have heard that other men have stepped forward
To claim the girl on whom my mind is set—
Wind swear to me by the Everlasting One
That you will carry my words through the air!

Daaroole is where I found my solace,
That is the place that you must find,
And nothing must stop you—
Not bad roads, nor screens of matting,
Muuse knows the country well
And he knows where she is to be found.
There is a man who looks at her admiringly—
O this world is a precipitous mountain path!

Tell her that stone houses and walls would have felt the pain
Tell her that termite hills would have sprouted green grass
If they had but heard these words of mine![5]

Poetry, song, chant, architecture, and the other arts of Muslim cultures can help others better understand and appreciate the depth and breadth of religion in the lives of Muslims. Indeed, many believers over the centuries have viewed Islam as encompassing their entire life, particularly as embodied in the *shariʿah*, the code of divine ethics, virtues, and laws, discussed briefly in chapter 5. In the following essay, the noted Iranian scholar Seyyed Hossein Nasr (b. 1933) provides a more focused discussion of this crucial aspect of Islam. Author of numerous books on Islam, Islamic philosophy, mysticism, and civilization, Dr. Nasr elegantly combines the sincere insights of a believing Muslim with the reasoned observation of a scholar of religion. Dr. Nasr has held a number of prestigious positions in higher education and is currently University Professor of Islamic Studies at George Washington University.

The *Shariʿah*
Divine Law—Social and Human Norm[6]

Sayyed Hossein Nasr

The *Shariʿah* is the Divine Law by virtue of accepting which a person becomes a Muslim. Only he who accepts the injunctions of the *Shariʿah* as binding upon him is a Muslim although he may not be able to realize all of its teachings or follow all of its commands in life. The *Shariʿah* is the ideal pattern for the individual's life and the Law which binds the Muslim people into a single community. It is the embodiment of the Divine Will in terms of specific teachings whose acceptance and application guarantees man a harmonious life in this world and felicity in the hereafter.

The word *Shariʿah* itself is derived etymologically from a root meaning road. It is the road which leads to God. It is of great symbolic significance that both the Divine Law and the Spiritual Way or *Tariqah*, which is the esoteric dimension of Islam, are based on the symbolism of the way or journey. All life is a sojourn, a journey through this transient world to the Divine Presence. The *Shariʿah* is the wider road which is meant for all men by virtue of which they are able to attain the total possibilities of the individual human state. The *Tariqah* is the narrower path for the few who have the capability and profound urge to attain sanctity here and now and seek a path whose end is the full realization of the reality of Universal Man transcending the individual domain.

The *Shariᶜah* is Divine Law, in the sense that it is the concrete embodiment of the Divine Will according to which man should live in both his private and social life. In every religion the Divine Will manifests itself in one way or other and the moral and spiritual injunctions of each religion are of Divine origin. But in Islam the embodiment of the Divine Will is not only a set of general teachings but of concrete ones. Not only is man told to be charitable, humble or just, but how also to be so in particular instances of life. The *Shariᶜah* contains the injunctions of the Divine Will as applied to every situation in life. It is the Law according to which God wants a Muslim to live. It is therefore the guide of human action and encompasses every facet of human life. By living according to the *Shariᶜah*, man places his whole existence in God's 'hand.' The *Shariᶜah*, by considering every aspect of human action, thus sanctifies the whole of life and gives a religious significance to what may appear as the most mundane of activities.

The lack of understanding of the significance of the *Shariᶜah* in the Western world is due to its concrete and all-embracing nature. A Jew who believes in Talmudic Law can understand what it means to have a Divine Law whereas for most Christians, and, therefore, for secularists with a Christian background, such an understanding comes with difficulty, precisely because in Christianity there is no clear distinction between the law and the way. In Christianity the Divine Will is expressed in terms of universal teachings such as being charitable, but not in concrete laws which would be stated in the New Testament.

The difference between the conception of Divine Law in Islam and in Christianity can be seen in the way the word canon (*qanun*) is used in the two traditions. This word was borrowed in both cases from the Greek. In Islam it has come to denote a man-made law in contrast to the *Shariᶜah* or divinely inspired Law. In the West the opposing meaning is given to this word in the sense that canonical law refers to laws governing the ecclesiastical organization of the Catholic and Episcopal churches, and has a definitely religious color.

The Christian view concerning law which governs man socially and politically is indicated in the well-known saying of Christ, "Render therefore unto Caesar the things which are Caesar's." This phrase has actually two meanings of which only one is usually considered. It is commonly interpreted as leaving all things that are worldly and have to do with political and social regulations to secular authorities of whom Caesar is the outstanding example. But more than that it also means that because Christianity, being a spiritual way, had no Divine legislation of its own, it had to absorb Roman Law in order to become the religion of a civilization. The law of Caesar, or the Roman Law, became providentially absorbed into the Christian perspective once this religion became dominant in the West, and it is to this fact that the saying of Christ alludes indirectly. The dichotomy, however, always remained. In Christian civilization law governing human society did not enjoy the same Divine sanction as the teachings of Christ. In fact this lack of a Divine Law in Christianity had no small role to play in the secularization that took place in the West during the Renaissance. It is also the most important cause for the lack of understanding of the meaning and role of the *Shari*ᶜ*ah* on the part of Westerners as well as so many modernized Muslims.

With regard to the Divine Law, therefore, the situation of Islam and Christianity differ completely. Islam never gave unto Caesar what was Caesar's. Rather, it tried to integrate the domain of Caesar itself, namely, political, social and economic life, into an encompassing religious worldview. Law is therefore in Islam an integral aspect of the revelation and not an alien element. Of course Roman Law also possessed a religious colour in the Roman religion itself, and the function of "The Divine Caesar" was to establish order on earth, through this law. But from the point of view of Christianity it was a foreign component without the direct sanctifying authority of revelation. In the Christian West law was thus from the beginning something human to be made and revised according to the needs and circumstances of the times. The Western attitude towards law is determined totally by the character of Christianity as a spiritual way which did not bring a revealed law of its own.

The Semitic notion of law which is to be seen in revealed form in both Judaism and Islam is opposite of the prevalent Western conception of law. It is a religious notion of law, one in which law is an integral aspect of religion. In fact religion to a Muslim is essentially the Divine Law which includes not only universal moral principles but details of how man should conduct his life and deal with his neighbor and with God; how he should eat, procreate and sleep; how he should buy and sell at the market place; and of course and above all else how he should pray and perform other acts of worship. It includes all aspects of human life and contains in its tenets the guide for a Muslim to conduct his life in harmony with the Divine Will. It guides man towards an understanding of the Divine Will by indicating which acts and objects are from the religious point of view obligatory (*wajib*), which are meritorious or recommended (*mandub*), which are forbidden (*haram*), which reprehensible (*makruh*), and which indifferent (*mubah*). Through this balance, the value of human acts in the sight of the Divine are made known to man so that he can distinguish between the "Straight Path" and that which will lead him astray. The *Shariʿah* provides for him the knowledge of right and wrong. It is, however, by his free will that man must choose which path to follow.

Such a Law contains the norm of the ideal human life. It is a transcendent Law which is at the same time applied in human society, but never fully realized because of the imperfections of all that is human. The *Shariʿah* corresponds to a reality that transcends time and history, and yet can be applied to new conditions and circumstances. Each generation in Muslim society should seek to conform to its teachings and apply it anew to the conditions in which it finds itself. The creative process in each generation is not to remake the Law but to reform men and human society to conform to the law. According to the Islamic view religion should not be reformed to conform to the ever changing and imperfect nature of men but men should reform themselves so as to live according to the tenets of revelation. In accordance with the real nature of things it is the human that must conform to the Divine and not the Divine to the human.

The movement of reform throughout Islamic history has been to seek to recreate and reshape human attitudes and social institutions so as to make them harmonious with the *Shariʿah*. It has been to revivify and revitalize human society by continuously infusing its structure with the principles of the revelation which are providentially sent as its guide and which alone provide a criterion for its own worth and value. Those modern movements which seek to reform the Divine Law rather than human society are, from the Islamic point of view, in every way an anomaly. Such movements are brought about to a great extent not only through the weakening of religious faith among certain men but also because the modern mentality, which originated in the West with its Christian background, cannot conceive of an immutable Law which is the guide of human society and upon which man should seek to model his individual and social life. There is no better proof of how deeply rooted man's religious heritage is than the modern Western attitude towards law which is the same as that of Christianity, although so many who have created and who uphold the modern view do not consider themselves as Christians and some even are opposed to Christianity.

The *Shari'ah* is for Islam the means of integrating human society. It is the way by which man is able to give religious significance to his daily life and be able to integrate this life into a spiritual center. Man lives in multiplicity; he lives and acts according to multiple tendencies within himself, some of which issue from animal desires, others from sentimental or rational or yet spiritual aspects of his being. Man faces this multiplicity within himself and at the same time lives in a society of which he is a part and with whose members he has an indefinite number of contacts and relations. All of these activities, these norms of doing and existing in the human condition, cannot be integrated and cannot find meaning save in the *Shari'ah*. The Divine Law is like a network of injunctions and attitudes which govern all of human life and in their totality and all-embracing nature are able to integrate man and society according to the dominating principle of Islam itself, namely unity or *tawhid*. The *Shari'ah* is the means by which unity is realized in human life.

Seen from the outside, this role of the *Shari'ah* may be difficult to understand. On the surface it seems to contain laws about how to marry, trade, divide inheritance or conduct the affairs of state. These are all acts performed in the world of time and multiplicity. How can they then be integrated so as to reflect unity? The answer is that these actions are still actions whether they are performed according to the *Shari'ah* or not. But the effect that such actions leave on the souls of men is completely different depending on whether the act is performed simply according to man-made laws or whether it follows the teachings of the *Shari'ah*. In the latter case the religious context in which the act is placed and the inner connection that the teachings of the *Shari'ah* have to the spiritual life of man transform an otherwise secular act into a religious one. Instead of the soul scattering itself over countless forms of action, the action itself leaves a positive imprint upon the soul and aids towards its integration.

There is a *hadith* according to which when a man works to feed his family he is performing as much an act of worship as if he were praying. This statement may be difficult to understand by one not acquainted with the traditional way of life. In modern society it is not possible to find religious significance in most actions and except for a few offices directly connected with the administration of religious needs, most professions through which men gain their livelihood are devoid of a direct religious significance. The breaking up of traditional Christian society, in which every act was endowed with a religious significance, long ago secularized a large domain of human life in the West. A contemporary who wishes to integrate all of his life finds great difficulty in giving religious significance to the daily work which he must of necessity perform.

The *Sharīʿah* makes the act of earning one's daily bread a religious act, one which a Muslim should perform with the awareness that he is performing an act that is pleasing in the sight of God and is as obligatory as specifically religious duties. The *Sharīʿah*, in fact, gives a religious connotation to all the acts that are necessary to human life, and of course not those which are simple luxuries. In this way the whole of man's life and activities become religiously meaningful. Were it to be otherwise man would be a house divided unto itself, in a condition of inner division and separation which Islam tries to avoid. By placing his life in the channels ordained by the *Sharīʿah*, man avoids many unseen catastrophes and assures himself a life of wholeness and meaning.

Some may object that accepting the *Sharīʿah* totally destroys human initiative. Such a criticism, however, fails to understand the inner workings of the Divine Law. The Law places before men many paths according to his nature and needs within a universal pattern which pertains to everyone. Human initiative comes in selecting what is in conformity with one's veritable needs and at the same time living according to the Divine norm as indicated by the *Sharīʿah*. Initiative does not come only in rebelling against the Truth which is an easy task since stones fall by nature; initiative and creativity come most of all in seeking to live in conformity with the Truth and in applying its principles to the conditions which destiny has placed before man. To integrate all of one's tendencies and activities within a divinely ordained pattern requires all the initiative and creative energy which man is capable of giving.

To the Muslim the *Sharīʿah* is an eternal and transcendent Law and the question of how it became codified and systematized in detail historically has not been of central interest until modern times. The studies of orientalists, which are usually historical, have directed attention to the gradual process by which the *Sharīʿah* became codified into the form in which the Islamic world has known it for the past millennium. It is therefore not without interest for us to consider how this process took place, although it must be made clear that the fact that the Divine Law was explicitly formulated and codified in its final form after several stages does not in any way diminish from its Divine nature and the immutability of its injunctions.

In essence all of the *Shariʿah* is contained in the Qur'an. The Holy Book, however, contains the principle of all the Law and not all of its details. It contains the Law potentially but not actually and explicitly, at least not all the different aspects of the *Shariʿah*. There was therefore, a gradual process by which this Law became promulgated in its external form and made applicable to all domains of human life. This process was completed in about three centuries during which the canonical books of Law in both Sunni and Shiʿite Islam were written, although the exact process is somewhat different in the two cases.

The principles of the Law contained in the Qur'an were explained and amplified in the prophetic *Hadith* and *Sunnah*, which together constitute the second basic source of Law. These in turn were understood with the aid of the consensus of the Islamic community *(ijmaʿ)*. Further, according to some schools, these sources of Law were complemented by analogical human reasoning *(qiyas)* where necessary. According to the traditional Islamic view therefore (as codified by Imam Shafiʿi [d. 819]), the sources of the *Shariʿah* are the Qur'an, *Hadith*, *ijmaʿ* and *qiyas*. The first two of these sources are the most important and are accepted by all schools of Law while the other two are either considered of lesser importance or rejected by some of the schools, while some jurists have added certain other principles such as that of the common good.

The meaning of the Qur'an and *Hadith* is clear enough, but a few words must be said about the other two sources. As far as *ijmaʿ* is concerned, it means the consensus of the Islamic community on some point of the Law and is considered important on the authority of the *hadith*: "My community shall never agree in error." Some modernized Muslims, who instead of wanting to substitute for the kingdom of God for the kingdom of man, especially Twentieth century man, have tried simply to equate *ijmaʿ* with parliamentary "democracy." This, however, is not exactly the case because first of all *ijmaʿ* can operate only where the Qur'an and *Hadith* have not clarified a certain aspect of the Law, so that its function is in this sense limited, and secondly it is a gradual process through which the community over a period of time comes to give its consensus over a question of Law. Finally, the view of Muslims over the centuries has been that giving direct opinion on problems of Law should be the function of the *ʿulama'* who alone are well-versed in the science of Law. The sciences connected with the *Shariʿah* are complex and require study before one can claim to be an authority on them. One could do no more than ask the consensus of a body of laymen on the diagnosis of a certain disease than on the legitimacy of a certain Law. The concept of *ijmaʿ* has always implied the consensus of those qualified in matters of Law combined with an inner interaction with the whole of the community whose results are felt only gradually.

As for *qiyas* it means essentially to use human reason to compare an existing situation with one for which legislation already exists. If the Qur'an has banned wine, it means that by analogy it has also banned any form of alcoholic drink whose effect is like wine, namely one which causes intoxication. The use of *qiyas* again is not a license for rationalism but an exercising of reason within the context of the revealed truths which are the basis of the *Shariʿah* and the prophetic utterances and practices which have made these truths known and have clarified them for the Muslim community.

Both *ijma* and *qiyas* are closely connected to the function of the *ʿulama'* as authorities on Law, of those who, having spent their lives studying this particular subject, are in a position to pass judgment upon it. There is no priesthood in Islam and every Muslim can perform the functions which in other religions are placed in the hands of the priesthood. But to pass judgment upon the Law is not the right of every Muslim, for no other reason than that not everyone is qualified from the scholarly point of view to do so. Not everyone can pass judgments upon the *Shariʿah* for the same reason that not everyone can give an opinion on astronomy or medicine unless he be qualified in these fields by having studied them. The *ʿulama'* are the custodians of the Law only because they have undertaken the necessary studies and mastered the required disciplines to make them acquainted with its teachings. . . .

The four important schools of Sunni law, the Maliki, Hanafi, Shafiʿi and Hanbali, that constitute the accepted schools of *Shariʿah* to the present day in the Sunni world, thus came into being in the third Islamic century. Of those, the one with the least number of followers is the Hanbali school which for long had its center in Egypt and Syria and from whose background the Wahhabi movement began. The Shafiʿi school has always been strong in Egypt and among the Malay people and to a certain extent in Syria. The Maliki school is completely dominant in North Africa and its followers constitute the most homogeneous body in the realm of Sunni Law. As for the Hanafi school, it was the official school of the Ottomans and is widespread in Turkey, the eastern part of the Arab world and the Indo-Pakistani Sub-continent.

As far as Law in the Shiᶜite world is concerned, its formation goes back to the fifth and sixth Imams, especially the sixth Imam Jaᶜfar al-Sadiq so that Twelve-Imam Shiᶜite Law is often called Jaᶜfari Law. There is here one difference with Sunni law in that in both Twelve-Imam Shiᶜism and Ismaᶜilism the Imams are the interpreters of the Law and their words and sayings form a part of the *Hadith* literature in addition to the utterances of the Prophet although the distinction between the two is preserved. The Law is, therefore, in principle, continuously being made in as much as the Imam is always alive. The Imam of Ismaᶜilism continues to live on earth from generation to generation while in Twelve-Imam Shiᶜism the Imam is in occultation *(ghaybah)* although he is alive and rules the world, being in inner contact with the *mujtahids* or those who provide fresh codifications and views of the Law. . . .

As far as the specific teachings of the *Shariᶜah* are concerned the Sunni and Shiᶜite schools are nearly the same except in the question of certain religious taxes and inheritance where, according to Shiᶜite Law, in certain cases the female line inherits more than in Sunni law. Otherwise, there is little disagreement between them. As for the different Sunni schools each emphasizes a certain aspect of the Law. For example, the Hanafis rely more on *qiyas*, and the Hanbalis on *Hadith* but the deviations are slight and one can go from one school to another without any difficulty. It is also of interest to cite in this context the attempt of the Persian king Nadir Shah who two centuries ago tried to make Jaᶜfari Law a fifth school of Law in Islam and thereby bring about a concordance between Sunnism and Shiᶜism. Mainly for political reasons, however, his plan was not accepted by the Ottoman caliph and did not bear any fruit. A similar attempt is being made in certain quarters today as seen by the teaching of Jaᶜfari Law at al-Azhar and different movements for the rapprochement between Sunnism and Shiᶜism.

More essential than the process of codification of the *Shariᶜah* is its actual content and substance. The *Shariᶜah* possesses the quality of totality and comprehensiveness. It encompasses the whole of man's life so that from the Islamic point of view there is no domain that lies outside of it, even if such an ideal be not easy to realize completely in human society. The lack of words in Arabic, Persian and other languages of the Islamic people for temporal or secular matters is due to this total nature of the Shariʿah and of course Islam as a whole.

Nevertheless, the Divine Law is comprised of branches depending on the particular aspect of life with which it is concerned. Some of the traditional scholars have divided it into two branches, one dealing with acts of worship (ʿibadat) and the other treating of transactions (muʿamalat). This classical division has led certain modernists to the conclusion that the first part of the Shariʿah can be preserved while the second can be secularized or at least changed as one sees fit. From the point of view of the Shariʿah, however, these two branches cannot be completely divorced from each other. Such acts of worship as the congregational prayer or fasting have a definite social aspect and involve the whole of the community, whereas how one deals in the market-place directly affects the quality and intensity of one's worship. There is no way to separate completely what concerns the relation between man and God from man's relation to other men. The two are inextricably intertwined and the spirit of the Shariʿah is precisely to preserve the unity of human life, albeit it has branches which apply to different domains, individual as well as social. To understand the content of the Shariʿah, it is therefore best to analyze its injunctions as they pertain to each particular domain of human life.

Politically, the Shariʿah contains definitive teachings which form the basis of Islamic political theory. In the Islamic view God is ultimately the only legislator. Man has no power to make laws outside the Shariʿah; he must obey the laws God has sent for him. Therefore, any ideal government from the point of view of the Shariʿah is devoid of legislative power in the Islamic sense. The function of the government is not to legislate laws but to execute God's laws. The cardinal reality is the presence of a Divine Law which should be administered in society.

As to the question of who the ruler in Islamic society should be, classical Sunni and Shiʿite theories differ. For Twelve-Imam Shiʿism there is no perfect government in the absence of the Mahdi or Twelfth Imam. In such a situation a monarchy or sultanate that rules with the consent of the ʿulama' is the best possible form of government in circumstances which by definition cannot be perfect. In Sunnism it is the caliphate that is considered as the legitimate form of rule. The caliph is the khalifah or vice-regent not of God but of His

Prophet and then only of that aspect of the function of the Prophet which was concerned with administering the Divine Law. The function of the caliph was to guard and administer the *Shariᶜah*, and he stood as the symbol of the rule of the *Shariᶜah* over human society. Islam is not technically speaking a theocracy but a nomocracy, that is a society ruled by a Divine Law. . . .

In a more general sense the economic teachings of the *Shariᶜah* are based on the respect for private property and, at the same time, opposition to extreme concentration of wealth in the hands of a single person or group. Usury is specifically forbidden and the paying of *zakah* itself has the function of "purifying" one's wealth (*zakah* itself being derived from the root *zky* meaning "purify") and also distributing some of it among the rest of the members of society through the "Muslim public treasury" *(bayt al-mal al-muslimin)*. The emphasis on the sacrosanct nature of private property is also clearly stated in the Qur'an. In fact the economic legislation of the Qur'an could not be applied were there to be no private property. According to the *Shariᶜah* man is given the right to own property by God and the possession of property is necessary for the fulfillment of his soul in this world provided he keeps within the teachings of the *Shariᶜah*. Those who interpret the teachings of Islam in a purely socialistic sense oppose the very text of the Qur'an which instructs man as to what he should do with his possessions. The Qur'an could not legislate about property if it did not accept the legitimacy of private property.

Altogether, of all the aspects of the *Shariᶜah* its political and economic teachings are perhaps those that have been least perfectly realized throughout Islamic history. But they have always stood as the ideal to be reached although they cannot be fully achieved considering the imperfections of human nature. The general spirit of *Shariᶜite* teachings, however, is deeply ingrained in the economic life of Muslims. For example, although specific forms of taxation may not have been followed and non-*Shariᶜite* taxes may have been levied, the general economic principles of the *Shariᶜah* have been realized to a great extent throughout history among traditional merchants and in craft guilds.

As far as the social teachings of the *Shariᶜah* are concerned, they comprise a vast subject which one cannot treat fully here. Altogether the *Shariᶜah* envisages a "dynamic" society, not in the modern proletarian sense, but in a traditional one. Before the rise of Islam there was an Arab aristocracy as well as a Persian one. Islam, by remolding society, did not destroy quality but made faith itself the criterion of man's worth according to the well-known Qur'anic verse, "Lo! the noblest of you, in the sight of Allah, is the best in conduct" (49:13).

By upholding the primary value of religion Islam made it possible for man to climb the scale of social "classes" through mastery in the religious sciences. A person who was gifted could become one of the *ulama'* and enjoy a respect greater than that afforded to a prince. Likewise, the Sufi orders have preserved a spiritual hierarchy in which the rank of a person depends upon his spiritual qualifications and not upon his social standing. The Sufi masters and saints have been the most venerated of men, respected by king and beggar alike. . . .

From the point of view of social structure, the teachings of the *Shari'ah* emphasize the role of the family as the unit of society, family in the extended sense not in its atomized modern form. The greatest social achievement of the Prophet in Medina was precisely in breaking the existing tribal bonds and substituting religious ones which were connected on the one hand with the totality of the Muslim community and on the other with the family. The Muslim family is the miniature of the whole of Muslim society and its firm basis. In it the man or father functions as the imam in accordance with the patriarchal nature of Islam. The religious responsibility of the family rests upon his shoulders. He is in a sense the priest in that he can perform the rites which in other religions are reserved for the priestly class. In the family the father upholds the tenets of the religion and his authority symbolizes that of God in the world. The man is in fact respected in the family precisely because of the sacerdotal function that he fulfils. The rebellion of Muslim women in certain quarters of the Islamic society came when men themselves ceased to fulfill their religious function and lost their priestly and patriarchal character. By becoming themselves denatured they caused the ensuing reaction of revolt among certain women who no longer felt the authority of religion upon themselves.

The traditional family is also the unit of stability in society, and the four wives that a Muslim can marry, like the four-sided Ka'bah, symbolize this stability. Many have not understood why such a family structure is permitted in Islam and attack Islam for it, as if polygamy belongs to Islam alone. Here again modernism carries with it the prejudice of Christianity against polygamy to the extent that some have even gone so far as to call it immoral and prefer prostitution to a social pattern which minimizes all promiscuous relations to the extent possible. The problem of the attitude of Western observers is not as important as that segment of modernized Muslim society which itself cannot understand the teachings of the *Shariʿah* on this point, simply because it uses as criteria categories borrowed from the modern West.

There is no doubt that in a small but significant segment of Muslim society today there is a revolt of women against traditional Islamic society. In every civilization a reaction comes always against an existing force or action. The Renaissance adoration of nature is a direct reaction to the dominant medieval Christian conception of nature as a domain of darkness and evil to be shunned. In Islam also the very patriarchal and masculine nature of the tradition makes the revolt of those women who have become aggressively modernized more violent and virulent than let us say in Hinduism where the maternal element has always been strong. What many modernized Muslim women are doing in rebelling against the traditional Muslim family structure is to rebel against fourteen centuries of Islam itself, although many may not be aware of the inner forces that drive them on. It is the patriarchal nature of Islam that makes the reaction of some modernized women today so vehement. Although very limited in number they are in fact, more than Muslim men, thirsting for all things Western. They seek to become modernized in their dress and habits with an impetuosity which would be difficult to understand unless one considers the deep psychological factors involved. Such women must, moreover, be clearly distinguished from pious women in the Islamic world who are seeking to regain their rights according to the *Shariʿah* in situations where, because of local customs, such rights have been denied or partially compromised.

From the Islamic point of view the question of the equality of men and women is meaningless. It is like discussing the equality of a rose and jasmine. Each has its own perfume, color, shape and beauty. Man and woman are not the same; each has particular features and characteristics. Women are not equal to men. But then neither are men equal to women. Islam envisages their roles in society not as competing but as complementary. Each has certain duties and functions in accordance with his or her nature and constitution . . .

The *Shariʿah* therefore envisages the role of men and women according to their natures which are complementary. It gives the man the privilege of social and political authority and movement for which he has to pay by bearing heavy responsibilities, by protecting his family from all the forces and pressures of society, economic and otherwise. Although a master in the world at large and the priest of his own family, man acts in his home as one who recognizes the rule of his wife in this domain and respects it. Through mutual understanding and the realization of the responsibilities that God has placed on each other's shoulders, traditional Muslim man and woman have been able to fulfill their personal lives and create a firm family unit which is the basic structure of Muslim society.

Besides its political, economic and social teachings, the *Shariᶜah* concerns itself with what is most essential to every religion, namely the relation between man and God. The most central aspect of the *Shariᶜah* is in fact concerned with the rites or acts of worship which every Muslim must perform and which constitute the ritual and devotional practices of Islam. . . .

In the Islamic perspective God has revealed the *Shariᶜah* to man so that through it he can reform himself and his society. It is man who is in need of reform not divinely revealed religion. The presence of the *Shariᶜah* in the world is due to the compassion of God for his creatures so that he has sent an all-encompassing Law for them to follow and thereby to gain felicity in both this world and the next. The *Shariᶜah* is thus the ideal for human society and the individual. It provides meaning for all human activities and integrates human life. It is the norm for the perfect social and human life and the necessary basis for all flights of the spirit from the periphery to the Center. To live according to the *Shariᶜah* is to live according to the Divine Will, according to a norm which God has willed for man.

Discussion Questions

1. What is the meaning and function of the *shariᶜah*? Discuss its historical development and administration from the time of the prophet Muhammad until the formulation of Islamic jurisprudence in the ninth century.

2. How does the *shariᶜah* differ from Western notions of law?

3. The cult of the saints and veneration of the prophet Muhammad were two important developments in medieval Islam. Discuss their possible origins and their importance to Muslim devotional life.

CHAPTER 6

PHILOSOPHY: AVERROES, MAIMONIDES, AND AQUINAS

Seymour Feldman

The Middle Ages is often characterized as "dark," implying the absence of intellectual culture other than the religious. It is also depicted as a period of persecution and conflict, the age of the Crusades. Yet there was one area where the various Western religions could and did find peace and repose—philosophy. At first sight this seems somewhat puzzling. After all, philosophy is the unhampered activity of raising questions and rigorously looking for answers, no matter where they lead or what they imply. Sometimes these answers and the methods used to reach them seem to be incompatible with religion. Yet, during the medieval period there existed a continuous and mutually profitable conversation amongst some of the intellectual giants of Judaism, Christianity, and Islam. This was made possible by the willingness of some religious thinkers to "cross over" and make use of what the pagan Greeks had to offer. Although at first there was some reluctance to borrow from alien sources, the depth and scope of Greek philosophy could not be ignored or resisted. And so theology began to philosophize in Greek.

This was made possible by the survival of many of the works of the leading Greek philosophers, either in the original Greek or in translation, along with later commentaries upon them. At first Western Christianity had to be content with a relatively small library of Greek philosophers—not much Plato (ca. 427–347), a little more Aristotle (ca. 384–322). But with the Arab-Muslim conquest of the Near East and North Africa, where there had been centers of Greek learning and culture, more of the

Greek heritage became available to the West through Arabic and Hebrew translations of the Greek texts, which were eventually rendered into Latin. By the middle of the twelfth century almost the entire body of Aristotelian philosophy and science had become part of the intellectual world of Judaism and Islam; in the middle of the thirteenth century Aristotle's philosophy had already reached Western Christianity.

I. The Intersection of Philosophy and Revealed Scripture

This philosophical import posed several serious challenges to religion: some philosophical doctrines were provocative and controversial, forcing thinkers to provide answers to questions that were perceived to be critical of certain religious dogmas; others offered philosophers and philosophically minded theologians the vocabulary and the principles whereby they could formulate and defend more articulately their religious beliefs. In the latter case, this can be seen in the ways in which religious thinkers quickly adopted philosophical arguments provided by Plato or Aristotle to defend their belief in the unity of God. But in the former case, there were some problems. For example, Aristotle claimed that the universe was eternal, a thesis that seems to deny the opening sentence of the Bible and goes against the Qur'an as well. Who is right: Moses or Aristotle? Is the world created or is it eternal? Further, the Western religions all have some kind of belief in human immortality along with individual reward and punishment. Here they were able to find support in Plato's theory of the soul's incorruptibility. But what about his doctrine of transmigration of souls? Plato believed that human souls not only preexist the bodies they eventually inhabit, but also survive bodily death and will occupy other bodies, perhaps even of other animals, according to their individual merits.

Aristotle followed a different path. Not only did he reject transmigration, but he also proposed and pursued a biological orientation in psychology that did not provide a clear-cut answer to the question of the soul's immortality. Since Aristotle's thought became the dominant intellectual force throughout most of the Middle Ages by virtue of its depth and scope, religious thinkers in all the Western traditions had to confront controversial doctrines that seemed to undermine some of their basic beliefs. They responded by composing their own philosophical or theological works of considerable originality and vitality.

It is remarkable that in facing this challenge, religious thinkers were often in accord on some fundamental questions and that their philosophical writings exhibit a common vocabulary and orientation. In many cases it is not easy or even possible to determine whether a particular text is written by a Christian, Jew, or Muslim. Sometimes the answer to a philosophical question supplied by a medieval thinker is religiously neutral; sometimes the answer, although particular to specific religion, stems from purely philosophical reasons, having little, if any, religious motivation. Medieval philosophy, regardless of its particular religious origin, can be considered as an intellectual drama, written in a mutually comprehensible language, whose protagonists present and represent philosophical theses and countertheses, whose religious significance is not always evident. Indeed, sometimes it is hidden or minimal.

II. Averroes, the "Commentator"

The most influential of the medieval Muslim philosophers in the West was the philosopher ibn Rushd (1126–1198), or Averroes, as he was commonly called by Christians. Born in Cordoba, Spain, where he lived for most of his life, he achieved distinction in many intellectual disciplines, most notably in law and philosophy. His writings, especially his commentaries upon Aristotle, had a tremendous impact upon Jewish and Christian thinkers, so much so that he was called "the Commentator." Many of these works were translated into Hebrew and Latin; some of them did not survive in Arabic but only in their Hebrew or Latin versions. Some later medieval philosophers derived their knowledge of Aristotle and other Greek philosophers primarily from Averroes's commentaries and continued the tradition of Aristotelian interpretation by writing commentaries upon Averroes's commentaries. When the collected works of Aristotle were first printed in Venice (1562–1574) in Latin translation, Averroes's commentaries were included. To study Aristotle was to read Averroes.

Although Averroes saw himself primarily as a philosopher, in some of his writings he considered issues of a more religious nature. Indeed, in one particular work he addressed the problem of the very compatibility of philosophy and Islam, a question that had vexed Muslim thinkers for several centuries. As a philosopher, he understandably believed in their compatibility, but he was careful to define their harmony within certain bounds. Averroes claimed that the Qur'an cannot teach anything that is false, since it is a divinely revealed text and God is the source of truth. Nor does this text forbid the study of philosophy, for God is the source of human reason. How could God forbid us to use what He has given us? Now, for Averroes, this divinely given reason had reached the height of perfection in the philosophy of Aristotle. So there cannot be any real contradiction between the truth of the Qur'an and what Aristotle has taught us. Averroes's attempt to prove the compatibility, indeed the identity, of the two teachings is based upon two fundamental principles, one derived from Aristotle's logic, the other from an already existing Islamic tradition.

Aristotle's logic teaches that there are different modes of argumentation, each differing in the strength of its conclusion. The strongest, and hence the best, type of argument is the demonstration, in which the conclusion is validly inferred from premises that are known to be true. A weaker type of argument is the dialectical proof, in which the premises are just assumed to be true. The weakest argument is the rhetorical one, in which truth itself is not the issue but only the power to persuade the audience, especially if the belief in question is politically useful or necessary.

Averroes takes this logical distinction and applies it to the question of the harmony between religion and philosophy. Philosophy is based upon demonstration, at least ideally, although at times it must be content with dialectical arguments so long as there is some evidence for their premises. Theology and religious law, however, employ dialectical arguments: they *assume* the truth of the Qur'an and then proceed to construct arguments to support religious dogmas or laws. Although Averroes had no problems with dialectical arguments in the law, he was opposed to the use of dialectic in the discussion of religious dogma, especially by those whose training in logic and philosophy was deficient. Thus, he had no use for the theologians who, he believed, had introduced confusion and obscurity in Islam by attempting to prove certain dogmas, whereas in truth their arguments were just dialectical, and thus dubious. For example, the Muslim theologians set out to prove philosophically the concept of creation *ex nihilo*, which is found in the Qur'an. According to Averroes, their arguments were all dialectical and thus conveyed no certain conviction. It would have been better had they refrained from philosophizing altogether.

But suppose the Muslim philosopher proves by a demonstrative argument that God has no corporeal qualities, such as anger? Although the Qur'an describes Allah as angry at the sinners, the Muslim philosopher, Averroes claims, is entitled to a considerable amount of interpretative freedom in dealing with religious texts. Revealed Scripture is given to all humans, not just to the philosophers or theologians. Accordingly, it must employ language that is easily understood by all. The philosophically educated will know that Allah is really not subject to anger; but they recognize that rhetorical language is effective in persuading the masses to abandon their evil ways. So no harm results from the anthropomorphic language in the Qur'an so long as its proper role is understood. In many cases, however, the philosophical interpretation of the text should not be disclosed to the uneducated, since it would only cause confusion, perhaps even heresy. In this respect, religion has a political purpose: it teaches all the members of a polity a common set of beliefs and regulations, so that an orderly and peaceful society results. That some of these beliefs are in fact not literally true need not worry the philosopher as long as they have desirable practical consequences.

If it was relatively easy for Averroes to employ the principle of interpretative freedom on the question of divine attributes, it was more difficult for him when he had to deal with the issues of creation of the world and human immortality. Having accepted the truth of Aristotle's theory of the eternity of the world, how could he incorporate this doctrine into the Qur'anic belief in divine creation of the world? Building upon but not fully accepting some of the ideas of earlier Muslim philosophers such as Al-Farabi (870–950) and Avicenna (980–1037), Averroes developed a version of a theory known as "eternal creation," an idea that goes back to some of the later interpreters of Plato, especially Plotinus (205–271). According to Averroes, insofar as the world is infinite in duration, both in the past and in the future, as proved by Aristotle, it is eternal. But insofar as it is caused by God, who is the first efficient cause of everything, it is created. Indeed, Averroes maintains, this was the teaching of Aristotle when he said that the movements of the heavenly bodies, whose motions determine terrestrial change, are brought about by the ultimate Unmoved Mover, God. So there is no real conflict between Aristotle and the Qur'an. The precise details of creation are not matters of real concern for religious practice. They can be left to the philosophers, but not the theologians, to determine.

The issue of immortality was even more difficult for Averroes. Since Aristotle's own views on this matter were far from clear, an entire interpretative tradition evolved, attempting to fill in the gaps and clarify the obscurities. On this subject Averroes wrote much and eventually reached a conclusion that seemed to be heretical. As a result of what he thought was the correct reading of Aristotle, Averroes concluded that essentially there was just one human intellect for all of us, even though as it is present in individual men it is particularized by our subjective perceptions, imaginations, and emotions. When the latter disappear at corporeal death, this unitary intellect is "purified" from any particularity, and thus exhibits its essential immortality as an incorporeal substance that is intellect perfectly actualized. True, at this level there is no longer any individuality, no personal persistence. But what is lost in subjectivity is gained in eternity. It is no wonder that some of his writings on this subject are no longer extant in Arabic and that subsequent medieval philosophers and theologians spent considerable effort in attempting to refute Averroes's theory.

III. Moses Maimonides, the "Second Moses"

A few years younger than Averroes, Moses Maimonides (1135–1204), was also born in Cordoba; however, he and his family were forced to flee Spain while still in his teens as a result of the conquest of southern Spain by a fanatical Muslim tribe from North Africa. Eventually Maimonides settled in Egypt, where he became both the chief physician to the Sultan of Egypt as well as the leader of the Jewish community. A deep student of philosophy and science he wrote the *Guide of the Perplexed*, originally in Arabic. In its Hebrew translations it became the most influential work upon subsequent Jewish thinkers even to this day. It also had a considerable effect upon Christian theologians such as Thomas Aquinas.

Like Averroes, Maimonides attempts to reach some kind of accommodation with philosophy, especially with Aristotle. His *Guide* is designed to show the philosophically educated Jew that in many areas Aristotle and the Torah are in agreement. And like Averroes he employs interpretative liberty to demonstrate this concord. Maimonides proposes the following principle: "The gates of interpretation are not closed." However, he does not believe that on every issue of philosophical or religious significance agreement between Aristotle and Moses can be attained. This will be true in the case of creation of the universe, as we shall see, and on several other questions, such as divine omniscience and providence.

Maimonides devotes most of Part 1 of the *Guide* to a close analysis of biblical language in the attempt to cleanse Scripture of any anthropomorphic connotations, which would suggest to the naive reader that God has corporeal characteristics. To believe this is to succumb to idolatry. Throughout this analysis Maimonides stresses the multiple semantic levels of the biblical text, pointing out the true meaning of such anthropomorphic expressions as "God is a rock." Just as a rock is the source of iron, so is God the source of all reality. These linguistic-philosophical analyses lead up to a definition of belief that reveals the essential thrust of Maimonides' religious orientation. For Maimonides, belief in general is a matter of intellectual conception, not just verbal utterance. This means that the believer must be able to form a *coherent* concept of what he or she believes. As he makes plain, Maimonides has in mind certain "beliefs" of the Christians and Muslims, doctrines that he considers to be unintelligible, such as the Christian doctrine of the Trinity. Once it is clear that the belief is logically coherent, it is then incumbent upon the believer to support this belief with evidence, to attempt to show that it is true. If the believer succeeds in proving his belief, he or she has attained the highest level of cognition. It is clear from this account that Maimonides subscribed to an evidentialist notion of belief that stresses the responsibility to base one's beliefs upon the best available information. "Blind faith" is not for him a virtue.

Almost at the very center of the *Guide* Maimonides discusses the crucial question of creation, but reaches a different conclusion from that of Averroes. As Maimonides sees it, the believer in the Torah, or for that matter any revealed religion, is faced with an "either-or" dilemma: either the world has been freely created by God such that it has a temporal beginning and manifests some design or purpose; or it emanates eternally and necessarily from God without any specific purpose. If the former is the case, then miracles are possible. If the latter is true, then they are not. Since the Torah narrates many instances of miracles, indeed it is itself the greatest miracle, creation is the very foundation of belief in the Torah. A world that is the eternal and necessary effect of God is a world that obeys fixed laws of nature that are inviolable, thus precluding the possibility of miracles.

But Maimonides is not content to appeal to authority or the prior assumption of biblical truth. In several closely argued chapters he shows that the various arguments brought forth against creation are invalid; indeed, he claims that Aristotle himself believed that they were just dialectical. Some of these arguments employed by the Aristotelians presuppose a principle that Maimonides considers to be unwarranted. These arguments assume that the act of creating the world must take place within a fixed framework of physical laws. But, Maimonides claims, it is this very framework that was created along with the creation of the world! One cannot retrodict what is the case now to the very first instant of time, or creation; for that moment is, for the creationist, unique. It is, so to speak, "free," or unbounded. Once the laws of nature are set, then "nature follows it course."

It should be noted, however, that Maimonides does not claim here more than the logical possibility of creation. As he himself clearly admits, he has not proved creation; all he has shown so far is that the biblical belief in creation is logically coherent insofar as it has not been shown to be absurd by the standard arguments against it. His next task is to show that the thesis of creation is more *plausible* than the theory of eternity as advocated by Aristotle and his medieval followers. To do this Maimonides highlights certain "anomalies," or scientific surds, that Aristotelian science is unable to account for. Remember that for the Aristotelian all natural events necessarily follow fixed laws; they should be *explicable* in terms of these laws. But consider the case of Mars' red color and Venus' bluish-silver hue. According to Aristotle's physics all the heavenly bodies are of the same matter; in other words, they should not have different colors. The fact that they, as well as other natural phenomena, exhibit features that are not explicable within the framework of Aristotelian science shows that the latter is not an adequate theory. On the other hand, if we posit that the world has been freely created by God, these apparently anomalous facts turn out to be explicable within the framework of a creator who has "particularized" these facts for some purpose or reason. In this sense apparent irregularity is evidence for creation.

Several cautionary notes: (1) Maimonides' argument in favor of creation is not an argument for creation *ex nihilo* ("from nothing"); on that issue Maimonides has no philosophical argument, just an appeal to tradition. He admits that if Plato's theory of creation from eternal formless matter were to be philosophically proved, he would admit it and interpret the Torah accordingly, since this theory is consistent with the biblical belief in miracles. But since Plato's thesis has not been proved, one need not go against authoritative tradition. (2) Although Maimonides stresses the role of miracles in evaluating the arguments for eternity of the world, it should be noted that in general he naturalizes miracles. They are part of the original plan for creation and were established at the very creation of the world such that when they do occur, nothing really new takes place. (3) Maimonides' intentional use of vague language and even contradictory statements has led some scholars to claim that his defense of creation *ex nihilo* was not his own view; rather, he held either some version of the eternity theory or of Plato's theory. On this reading of the Guide, Maimonides' explicit view is just a politically useful belief that does the ordinary believer no harm, although the philosophically sophisticated believer knows otherwise. This is one of several controversial issues in the interpretation of the *Guide*.

As we have seen, immortality was also a disputed question. Unfortunately, Maimonides' philosophical treatment of immortality is not as clear or detailed as we would like. He rarely refers to this topic in his *Guide*, only insisting that it is a matter of *intellectual perfection*, that it is the intellect alone that survives. Whether Maimonides thought that this intellect is individualized is unclear. It is possible that he believed that there is no personal, or particularized, immortality. Yet, in his most explicit and extensive discussions of this topic, which appear in his earlier legal works and the later Letter on Resurrection of the Dead, he seems to incline to the more traditional view of individual immortality. This is another of the more perplexing problems of the *Guide of the Perplexed*.

IV. Thomas Aquinas, the "Angelic Doctor"

Coming after both Averroes and Maimonides, Thomas Aquinas (1225–1274) was able to benefit from these thinkers' contributions to their common philosophical-theological enterprise. He wrote several critical treatises dealing with Averroes's more controversial doctrines and explicitly refers to Maimonides in his major work the *Summa Theologiae*. He also shared their admiration of and debt to Aristotle, and he wrote commentaries on many of the Aristotle's works. Nevertheless, in spite of his acute and deep philosophical mind and understanding of Aristotle, Aquinas was more of a theologian than Averroes and Maimonides. Perhaps this is partly to be explained by certain Christian doctrines that required him to distinguish sharply, more so than his Muslim or Jewish counterparts were obliged to do, between philosophy and theology. Several of these doctrines, for example, the Trinity and the Incarnation, are, he admits, not amenable to philosophical analysis and proof: they are "above reason," not inconsistent with reason, yet not demonstrable by means of philosophy. Here faith and authority are decisive. Aquinas labels such beliefs as "the Articles of Faith." Nevertheless, like Averroes and Maimonides, Aquinas believes that there are certain propositions that constitute the common domain of both philosophy and religion, for example, the existence of God and God's unity. Such doctrines are the "Preambles of Faith." These beliefs can be demonstrated by philosophy, and the theologian has much to learn from philosophical discussions of these topics.

Underlying this distinction is a concept of belief, or faith, that differs from the definition of belief proposed by Maimonides. Whereas the latter defined belief in intellectualist terms such that no significant difference exists between belief and faith, Aquinas distinguishes sharply between beliefs proposed and proved by reason and those that are revealed to us through revelation. The latter are believed through *faith*. Faith, then, is proper to religion. Moreover, faith involves an element of will as well. Religious beliefs contain voluntary assent essentially. One doesn't have faith conditionally or tentatively; it is an affirmation based upon the firm conviction that the proposition assented to be true beyond any conceivable doubt, even though there are no rational considerations favoring such a proposition other than those given through authoritative revelation. In this sense, faith is "free."

This distinction is nicely illustrated in Aquinas's treatment of the problem of creation. Similar to Maimonides, Aquinas maintains that the universe is not eternal and rejects the validity of the arguments of the Aristotelians. However, his definition of creation is different from Maimonides' notion and it is closer to that of Averroes, for whom creation simply means produced by God, having no explicit temporal connotations. In short, creation for Averroes and Aquinas is a temporally neutral concept. Moreover, creation in this sense is provable; it is then a Preamble of Faith. Nevertheless, that the universe is not eternal, that it is finite in duration in the past, is another matter. This is what the Bible teaches, but it is an Article of Faith, not capable of philosophical proof. Unlike Maimonides, however, Aquinas did not offer any philosophical argument in favor of this belief; instead, he simply based it upon theological authority.

On the issue of immortality Aquinas differs radically from both Averroes and Maimonides, in spite of his common debt to Aristotle's psychology. He is unwilling to abandon the traditional religious belief in individual reward and punishment after death, and thus argues for personal immortality. Indeed, for Aquinas it is not just the intellect that is the subject of immortality; it is the whole human soul as an individual substance that endures. Its substantial character—its being the kind of thing to persist as an independent entity—accounts for the soul's capacity to endure after corporeal corruption. Moreover, the soul as such contains nonintellectual features, such as sense perceptions, that individuate each person, and these particularizing factors remain even after the death of the body. Each of us then gets what we individually deserve.

V. Conclusion

If time travel were possible and we could go back to the Middle Ages, we would find ourselves in a cultural world considerably different from our own. Not only were the vernacular languages different from our own modern versions of these languages, but many medieval thought patterns would be strange to us. Yet, some of their intellectual concerns are our own. We too worry about the relationship between science and philosophy to religion, or the most rewarding way to read a religious text, or the proper mode of discourse to use in speaking about the divine. On these and other issues we find the medievals speaking a common language, not only amongst themselves, no matter their specific religious allegiances, but one that can be made intelligible to us as well. Cultures do differ; but some of these differences can be transcended or minimized. It was philosophy that enabled Averroes, Maimonides, and Aquinas to talk to one another. Perhaps we too can learn from these medieval masters how to converse with each other.

Averroes's Decisive Treatise, Determining the Nature of the Connection Between the Law and Wisdom

Averroes wrote this essay in 1179–1180, evidently as a response to a widespread belief in some Muslim circles that philosophy was dangerous to Islam. Both as a jurist and a philosopher he felt obliged to answer this challenge. He did so by showing that the Qur'an not only permits but requires the study of philosophy and that there is no real conflict between philosophy and Islam so long as (1) the Qur'an is properly interpreted, (2) that the interpretation be guided by philosophy, and (3) and that the interpreters and their audience be defined by philosophical competence.

The Decisive Treatise Determining the Connection Between the Law and Wisdom[1] (excerpts)

Averroes

In the name of God, the Merciful and the Compassionate.
May God be prayed to for Muhammad and his family,
And may they be accorded peace.

[I. Introduction]

(1) The jurist, imam, judge, and uniquely learned [Abu al-Walid Muhammad ibn Ahmad ibn Rushd] Averroes (may God be pleased with him) said: Praise be to God with all praises, and a prayer for Muhammad, His chosen servant and messenger. Now, the goal of this statement is for us to investigate, from the perspective of Law-based reflection, whether reflection upon philosophy and the sciences of logic is permitted, prohibited, or commanded—and this as a recommendation or as an obligation—by the Law.

[II. That philosophy and logic are obligatory]

[A. *That philosophy is obligatory*]

(2) So we say: If the activity of philosophy is nothing more than reflection upon existing things and consideration of them insofar as they are an indication of the Artisan—I mean insofar as they are artifacts, for existing things indicate the Artisan only through cognizance of the art in them, and the more complete cognizance of the art in them is, the more complete is cognizance of the Artisan—and if the Law has recommended and urged consideration of existing things, then it is evident that what this name indicates is either obligatory or recommended by the Law.

That the Law calls for consideration of existing things by means of the intellect and for pursuing cognizance of them by means of it is evident from various verses in the Book of God (may He be blessed and exalted). There is His statement (may He be exalted), "Consider, you who have sight" [59:2]; this is a text for the obligation of using both intellectual and Law-based syllogistic reasoning. And there is

His statement (may He be exalted), "Have they not reflected upon the kingdoms of the heavens and the earth and what things God has created?" [7:185]; this is a text urging reflection upon all existing things. . . .

[B. The case for syllogistic reasoning]

(3) Since it has been determined that the Law makes it obligatory to reflect upon existing things by means of the intellect and to consider them; and consideration is nothing more than inferring and drawing out the unknown from the known; and this is syllogistic reasoning or by means of syllogistic reasoning, therefore, it is obligatory that we go about reflecting upon the existing things by means of intellectual syllogistic reasoning. And it is evident that this manner of reflection the Law calls for and urges is the most complete kind of reflection by means of the most complete kind of syllogistic reasoning and is the one called "demonstration."

(4) Since the Law has urged cognizance of God (may He be exalted) and of all of the things existing through Him by means of demonstration; and it is preferable—or even necessary—that anyone who wants to know God (may He be exalted) and all of the existing things by means of demonstration set out first to know the kinds of demonstrations, their conditions, and in what [way] demonstrative syllogistic reasoning differs from dialectical, rhetorical, and sophistical syllogistic reasoning; and that is not possible unless, prior to that, he sets out to become cognizant of what unqualified syllogistic reasoning is, how many kinds of it there are, and which of them is syllogistic reasoning and which not. . . .

It is not for someone to say, "Now, this kind of reflection about intellectual syllogistic reasoning is a heretical innovation, since it did not exist in the earliest days [of Islam]." For reflection upon juridical syllogistic reasoning and its kinds is also something inferred after the earliest days, yet is not opined to be a heretical innovation. So it is obligatory to believe the same about reflection upon intellectual syllogistic reasoning—and for this there is a reason, but this is not the place to mention it. Moreover, most of the adherents to this religion support intellectual syllogistic reasoning, except for a small group of strict literalists, and they are refuted by the texts [of the Qur'an].

(5) Since it has been determined that the Law makes reflection upon intellectual syllogistic reasoning and its kinds obligatory, just as

it makes reflection upon juridical syllogistic reasoning obligatory, therefore, it is evident that, if someone prior to us has not set out to investigate intellectual syllogistic reasoning and its kinds, it is obligatory for us to begin to investigate it and for the one who comes after to rely upon the one who preceded, so that cognizance of it might be perfected. For it is difficult or impossible for one person to grasp all that he needs of this by himself and from the beginning, just as it is difficult for one person to infer all he needs to be cognizant of concerning the kinds of juridical syllogistic reasoning. Nay, this is even more the case with being cognizant of intellectual syllogistic reasoning.

(6) If someone other than us has already investigated that, it is evidently obligatory for us to rely on what the one who has preceded us says about what we are pursuing, regardless of whether that other person shares our religion or not. For when a valid sacrifice is performed by means of a tool, no consideration is given, with respect to the validity of the sacrifice, as to whether the tool belongs to someone who shares in our religion or not, so long as it fulfills the conditions for validity. And by "not sharing [in our religion]," I mean those Ancients who reflected upon these things before the religion of Islam.

[III. That demonstration accords with the Law]

[A. *The Law calls to humans by three methods*]

(11) Since all of this has been determined and we, the Muslim community, believe that this divine Law of ours is true and is the one alerting to and calling for this happiness—which is cognizance of God (Mighty and Magnificent) and of His creation—therefore, that is determined for every Muslim in accordance with the method of assent his temperament and nature require.

That is because people's natures vary in excellence with respect to assent. Thus, some assent by means of demonstration; some assent by means of dialectical statements in the same way the one adhering to demonstration assents by means of demonstration, there being nothing greater in their natures; and some assent by means of rhetorical statements, just as the one adhering to demonstration assents by means of demonstrative statements. . . .

[B. Demonstration does not differ from the Law]

(12) Since this Law is true and calls to the reflection leading to cognizance of the truth, we, the Muslim community, know firmly that demonstrative reflection does not lead to differing with what is set down in the Law. For truth does not oppose truth; rather, it agrees with and bears witness to it.

(13) Since this is so, if demonstrative reflection leads to any manner of cognizance about any existing thing, that existing thing cannot escape either being passed over in silence in the Law or being made cognizable in it. If it is passed over in silence, there is no contradiction here; it has the status of the statutes passed over in silence that the jurist infers by means of Law-based syllogistic reasoning. If the law does pronounce about it, the apparent sense of the pronouncement cannot escape either being in agreement with what demonstration leads to, or being different from it. If it is in agreement, there is no argument here. And, if it is different, that is where an interpretation is pursued. The meaning of interpretation is: drawing out the figurative significance of an utterance from its true significance without violating the custom of the Arabic language with respect to figurative speech in doing so—such as calling a thing by what resembles it, its cause, its consequence, what compares to it, or another of the things enumerated in making the sorts of figurative discourse cognizable.

(14) Since the jurist does this with respect to many of the Law-based statutes, how much more fitting is it for the one adhering to demonstrative science to do so. The jurist has only a syllogism based on supposition, whereas the one who is cognizant has a syllogism based on certainty. And we firmly affirm that, whenever demonstration leads to something differing from the apparent sense of the Law, that apparent sense admits of interpretation according to the rule of interpretation in Arabic.

No Muslim doubts this proposition, nor is any faithful person suspicious of it. Its certainty has been greatly increased for anyone who has pursued this idea, tested it, and has as an intention this reconciling of what is intellected with what is transmitted. Indeed, we say that whenever the apparent sense of a pronouncement about something in the Law differs from what demonstration leads to, if the Law is considered and all of its parts scrutinized, there will invariably be found in the utterances of the Law something whose apparent sense bears witness, or comes close to bearing witness, to that interpretation.

Because of this idea, Muslims have formed a consensus that it is not obligatory for all the utterances of the law to be taken in their apparent sense, nor for all of them to be drawn out from their apparent sense by means of interpretation, though they disagree about which ones are to be interpreted and which not interpreted. . . .

The reason an apparent and an inner sense are set down in the Law is the difference in people's innate dispositions and the variance in their innate capacities for assent. The reason contradictory apparent senses are set down in it is to alert "those well grounded in science" to the interpretation that reconciles them. This idea is pointed to in His statement (may He be exalted), "He it is who has sent down to you the Book; in it, there are fixed verses . . . " on to His statement, "and those well grounded in science" [3:7]. . . .

It has been transmitted that many in the earliest days [of Islam] used to be of the opinion that the Law has both an apparent and an inner sense and that it is not obligatory for someone to know about the inner sense if he is not an adept in knowledge of it nor capable of understanding it. There is, for example, what al-Bukhari relates about [c in original text] Ali ibn Abu Talib (may God be pleased with him), saying, "Speak to the people concerning what they are cognizant of. Do you want God and His messenger to be accused of lying?" And there is, for example, what is related of that about a group of the early followers [of Islam]. So how is it possible to conceive of consensus about a single theoretical question being transmitted to us when we firmly know that no single epoch has escaped having learned men who are of the opinion that there are things in the Law not all of the people ought to know in their true sense? That differs from what occurs with practical matters, for everybody is of the opinion that they are to be disclosed to all people alike; and, for consensus about them to be reached, we deem it sufficient that the question be widely diffused and that no difference [of opinion] about it be transmitted to us. Now, this is sufficient for reaching consensus about practical matters; but the case with scientific matters is different.

[C. Whether the philosophers are guilty of unbelief]

(16) If you were to say: "If it is not obligatory to charge with unbelief one who goes against consensus with respect to interpretation, since consensus with respect to that is not conceivable, what do you

say about the philosophers among the adherents of Islam like Abu Nasr [al-Farabi] and Ibn Sina [Avicenna]? For in his book known as *The Incoherence [of the Philosophers]*, Abu Hamid [al-Ghazali] has firmly charged both of them as unbelievers with respect to three questions: the argument about the eternity of the world, that the Exalted does not know particulars—may He be exalted above that—and the interpretation of what is set forth about the resurrection of bodies and the way things are in the next life," we would say: "The apparent sense of what he says about that is that he does not firmly charge them with unbelief about that, for he has declared in the book *The Distinction* that charging someone with unbelief for going against consensus is tentative. And it has become evident from our argument that it is not possible for consensus to be determined with respect to questions like these because of what is related about many of the first followers [of Islam], as well as others, holding that there are interpretations that it is not obligatory to expound except to those adept in interpretation. . . . "

(17) In addition to all of this, we are of the opinion that Abu Hamid [al-Ghazali] was mistaken about the Peripatetic sages[2] when he accused them of saying that He (Holy and Exalted) does not know particulars at all. Rather, they are of the opinion that He knows them (may He be exalted) by means of a knowledge that is not of the same kind as our knowledge of them. That is because our knowledge of them is an effect of what is known, so that it is generated when the known thing is generated and changes when it changes. And the knowledge God (glorious is He) has of existence is the opposite of this: it is the cause of the thing known, which is the existing thing.

So, whoever likens the two kinds of knowledge to one another sets down two opposite essences and their particular characteristics as being one, and that is the extreme of ignorance. If the name "knowledge" is said of knowledge that is generated and of knowledge that is eternal, it is said purely as a name that is shared, just as many names are said of opposite things—for example, *al-jalal*, said of great and small, and *al-sarim*, said of light and darkness. Thus, there is no definition embracing both kinds of knowledge, as the dialectical theologians of our time fancy. . . .

(18) As for the question whether the world is eternal or has been generated, the disagreement between the Ashʿarite dialectical

theologians[3] and the ancient sages almost comes back, in my view, to a disagreement about naming, especially with respect to some of the Ancients. That is because they agree that there are three sorts of existing things: two extremes and one intermediate between the extremes. And they agree about naming the two extremes but disagree about the intermediate.

One extreme is an existent thing that exists from something other than itself and by something—I mean, by an agent cause and from matter. And time precedes it—I mean, its existence. This is the case of bodies whose coming into being is apprehended by sense perception—for example, the coming into being of water, air, earth, animals, plants, and so forth. The Ancients and the Ashᶜarite in original text]arites both agree in naming this sort of existing things "generated."

The extreme opposed to this is an existent thing that has not come into existence from something or by something and that time does not precede. About this, too, both factions agree in naming it "eternal." This existent thing is apprehended by demonstration: it is God (may He be blessed and exalted) who is the Agent of the whole, its Giver of Existence, and its Sustainer (glorious is He, and may His might be exalted).

The sort of being between these two extremes is an existent thing that has not come into existence from something and that time does not precede, but that does come into existence by something—I mean, by an agent. This is the world as a whole.

Now, all of them agree on the existence of these three attributes with respect to the world. For, the dialectical theologians admit that time does not precede it—or, rather, that is a consequence of their holding that time is something joined to motions and bodies. They also agree with the Ancients about future time being infinite and, likewise, future existence. And they disagree only about past time and past existence. For the dialectical theologians are of the opinion that it is limited, which is the doctrine of Plato and his sect, while Aristotle and his faction are of the opinion that it is infinite, as is the case with the future.

(19) So it is evident that this latter existent thing has been taken as resembling the existing things that truly comes into being and the eternally existing thing. Those overwhelmed by its resemblance to the eternal rather than to what is generated name it "generated." But,

in truth, it is not truly generated, nor is it truly eternal. For what is truly generated is necessarily corruptible, and what is truly eternal has no cause. Among them are those who name it "everlastingly generated"—namely, Plato and his sect, because time according to them if finite with respect to the past.

(20) Thus, the doctrines about the world are not all so far apart from one another that some of them should be charged as unbelief and others not. Indeed, for opinions [vertical line in original text] to be such that this should happen, it is obligatory that they be excessively far apart—I mean, that they be opposites of each other, as the dialectical theologians suppose they are with respect to this question—that is, that the name "eternity" and that of "generated" with respect to the world as a whole are opposites of each other. And it has already become evident from our statement that the matter is not like that. . . .

Maimonides's *Guide of the Perplexed*

Maimonides completed the following treatise in 1190 after devoting most of his earlier literary activities to Jewish law and medicine. Like Averroes, Maimonides strives to show the compatibility of philosophy with the Mosaic Law. But the work is written in the form of a letter in response to some questions posed by one of his former pupils concerning the proper way to understand certain biblical words and passages. Again, philosophy serves as the code by means of which we come to understand what the Bible teaches. The fact that Maimonides is addressing a philosophically qualified reader is made evident in his definition of **belief** in chapter 50 of part 1. Genuine belief requires rational reflection and verification. A "true believer" is not the naïve fundamentalist, but the philosophically educated thinker about his or her religious commitments. Maimonides, again like Averroes, considers creation of the world to be a basic belief of revealed scripture; however, unlike his fellow Cordoban Maimonides realizes that the follower of Moses will have to part company with the disciple of Aristotle. On this issue there can be no compromise or accommodation.

The Guide of the Perplexed[4] (excerpts)

Moses Maimonides

Part I

CHAPTER 50

Know, thou who studiest this my Treatise, that belief is not the notion that is uttered, but the notion that is represented in the soul when it has been averred of it that it is in fact just as it has been represented. If you belong to those who are satisfied with expressing in speech the opinions that are correct or that you deem to be correct, without representing them to yourself and believing them, you take a very easy road. In accordance with this, you will find many stupid people holding to beliefs to which, in their representation, they do not attach any meaning whatever. If, however, you belong to those whose aspirations are directed toward ascending to that high rank which is the rank of speculation, and to gaining certain knowledge with regard to | God's being One by virtue of a true Oneness, so that no composition whatever is to be found in Him and no possibility of division in any way whatever—then you must know that He, may He be exalted, has in no way and in no mode any essential attribute, and that just as it is impossible that He should be a body, it is also impossible that He should possess an essential attribute. If, however, someone believes that He is one, but possesses a certain number of essential attributes, he says in his words that He is one, but believes Him in his thought to be many. This resembles what the Christians say: namely, that He is one but also three, and that the three are one. Similar to this is the assertion of him who says that He is one but possesses many attributes and that He and His attributes are one, while he denies at the same time His being corporeal and believes in His absolute simplicity; as if what we aimed at and investigated were what we should say and not what we should believe. For there is no belief except after a representation; belief is the affirmation that what has been represented is outside the mind just as it has been represented in the mind. If, together with this belief, one realizes that a belief different from it is in no way possible and that no starting point can be found in the mind for a rejection of this belief or for the supposition that a different belief is possible, there is certainty. When you shall have cast off desires and habits, shall have been endowed with understanding, and shall reflect on what I shall say in the following chapters, which shall treat of the negation of attributes, you shall necessarily achieve certain knowledge of it. Then you shall be one of those who represent to themselves *the unity of the Name* and not one of those who merely proclaim it with their mouth without representing to themselves that it has a meaning. With regard to men of this category, it is said: *Thou art near in their mouth, and far from their reins.* But men ought rather to belong to the category of those who represent the truth to themselves and apprehend it, even if they do not utter it, as | the virtuous are commanded to do—for they are told: *Commune with your own heart upon your bed, and be still. Selah.*

Part II
CHAPTER 13

There are three opinions of human beings, namely, of all those who believe that there is an existent deity, with regard to the eternity of the world or its production in time.

The first opinion, which is the opinion of all who believe in the Law of *Moses our Master, peace be on him,* is that the world as a whole—I mean to say, every existent other than God, may He be exalted—was brought into existence by God after having been purely and absolutely nonexistent, and that God, may He be exalted, had existed alone, and nothing else—neither an angel nor a sphere nor what subsists within the sphere. Afterwards, through His will and His volition, He brought into existence out of nothing all the beings as they are, time itself being one of the created things. For time is consequent upon motion, and motion is an accident in what is moved. Furthermore, what is moved—that is, that upon the motion of which time is consequent—is itself created in time and came to be after not having been. . . .

This is one of the opinions. And it is undoubtedly a basis of the Law of *Moses our Master,* peace be on him. And it is second to the basis that is the belief in the unity [of God]. Nothing other than this should come to your mind. It was *Abraham our Father, peace be on him,* who began to proclaim in public his opinion to which speculation had led him. For this reason, he made his proclamation *in the Name of the Lord, God of the world;* he had also explicitly stated this opinion in saying: *Maker of heaven and earth.*

The second opinion is that of all the philosophers of whom we have heard reports and whose discourses we have seen. They say that it is absurd that God would bring a thing into existence out of nothing. Furthermore, according to them, it is likewise not possible that a thing should pass away into nothing; I mean to say that it is not possible that a certain being, endowed with matter and form, should be generated out of the absolute nonexistence of that matter, or that it should pass away into the absolute nonexistence of that matter. To predicate of God that He is able to do this is, according to them, like predicating of Him that He is able to bring together two contraries in one instant of time, or that He is able to create something that is like Himself, may He be exalted, or to make Himself corporeal, or to create a square whose diagonal is equal to its side, and similar impossibilities. What may be understood from their discourse is that they say that just as His not bringing impossible things into existence does not argue a lack of power on His part—since what is impossible has a firmly established nature that is not produced by an agent and that consequently cannot be changed—it likewise is not due to lack of power on His part that He is not able to bring into existence a thing out of nothing, for this belongs to the class of all the impossible things. Hence they believe that there exists a certain matter that is eternal as the deity is eternal; and that He does not exist without it, nor does it exist without Him. They do not believe that it has the same rank in what exists as He, may He be exalted, but that He is the cause of its existence; and that it has the same relation toward Him as, for instance, clay has toward a potter | or iron toward a smith; and that He creates in it whatever He wishes. Thus He sometimes forms out of it a heaven and an earth, and sometimes He forms out of it something else. The people holding this opinion believe that the heaven too is subject to generation and passing-away, but that it is not generated out of nothing and does not pass away into nothing. For it is generated and passes away just as the individuals that are animals are generated from existent matter and pass away into existent matter. The generation and passing-away of the heaven is thus similar to that or all the other existents that are below it.

The people belonging to this sect are in their turn divided into several sects. But it is useless to mention their various sects and opinions in this Treatise. However, the universal principle held by this sect is identical with what I have told you. This is also the belief of Plato.

For you will find that Aristotle in the "Akroasis"[5] relates of him that he, I mean Plato, believed that the heaven is subject to generation and passing-away. And you likewise will find his doctrine plainly set forth in his book the *Timaeus*.[6] But he does not believe what we believe, as is thought by him who does not examine opinions and is not precise in speculation; he [the interpreter] imagines that our opinion and his [Plato's] opinion are identical. But this is not so. For as for us, we believe that the heaven was generated out of nothing after a state of absolute nonexistence, whereas he believes that it has come into existence and has been generated from some other thing. This then is the second opinion.

The third opinion is that of Aristotle, his followers, and the commentators of his books. He asserts what also is asserted by the people belonging to the sect that has just been mentioned, namely, that something endowed with matter can by no means be brought into existence out of that which has no matter. He goes beyond this by saying that the heaven is in no way subject to generation and passing-away. His opinion on this point may be summed up as follows. He thinks that this being as a whole, such as it is, has never ceased to be and will never do so; | that the permanent thing not subject to generation and passing-away, namely, the heaven, likewise does not cease to be; that time and motion are perpetual and everlasting and not subject to generation and passing-away; and also that the thing subject to generation and passing-away, namely, that which is beneath the sphere of the moon, does not cease to be. I mean to say that its first matter is not subject in its essence to generation and passing-away, but that various forms succeed each other in it in such a way that it divests itself of one form and assumes another. He thinks furthermore that this whole higher and lower order cannot be corrupted and abolished, that no innovation can take place in it that is not according to its nature, and that no occurrence that deviates from what is analogous to it can happen in it in any way. He asserts—although he does not do so textually, but this is what his opinion comes to—that in his opinion it would be an impossibility that will should change in God or a new volition arise in Him; and that all that exists has been brought into existence, in the state in which it is at present, by God through His volition; but that it was not produced after having been in a state of nonexistence. He thinks that just as it is impossible that the deity should become nonexistent or that His essence should undergo a change, it is impossible that a volition should undergo a change in Him or a new will arise in Him. Accordingly it follows necessarily that this being as a whole has never ceased to be as it is at present and will be as it is in the future eternity.

This is a summary and the truth of these opinions. They are the opinions of those according to whom the existence of the deity for this world has been demonstrated. Those who have no knowledge of the existence of the deity, may He be held sublime and honored, but think that things are subject to generation and passing-away through conjunction and separation due to chance and that there is no one who governs and orders being, are Epicurus, his following, and those like him, as is related by Alexander.[7] It is useless for us to mention these sects.| For the existence of the deity has already been demonstrated as true. . . .

After we have expounded those opinions, I shall begin to explain and summarize the proofs of Aristotle in favor of his opinion and the motive that incited him to adopt it.

CHAPTER 16

This is a chapter in which I shall explain to you what I believe with regard to this question. After that I shall give proofs for what we desire to maintain. I say then with regard to all that is affirmed by those Mutakallimun[8] who think that they have demonstrated the newness of the world, that I approve of nothing in those proofs and that I do not deceive myself by designating methods productive of errors as demonstrations. If a man claims that he sets out to demonstrate a certain point by means of sophistical arguments, he does not, in my opinion, strengthen assent to the point he intends to prove, but rather weakens it and opens the way for attacks against it. For when it becomes clear that those proofs are not valid, the soul weakens in its assent to what is being proved. It is preferable that a point for which there is no demonstration remain a problem or that one of the two contradictory propositions simply be accepted. I have already set forth for your benefit the methods of the Mutakallimun in establishing the newness of the world, and I have drawn your attention to the points with regard to which they may be attacked. Similarly all that Aristotle and his followers have set forth in the way of proof of the eternity of the world does not constitute in my opinion a cogent demonstration, but rather arguments subject to grave doubts, as you shall hear. What I myself desire to make clear is that the world's being created in time, according to the opinion of our Law—an opinion that I have already explained—is not impossible and that all those philosophic proofs from which it seems that the matter is different from what we have stated, all those arguments have a certain point through which they may be invalidated and the inference drawn from them against us shown to be incorrect. Now inasmuch as this is true in my opinion and inasmuch as this | question—I mean to say that of the eternity of the world or its creation in time—becomes an open question, it should in my opinion be accepted without proof because of prophecy, which explains things to which it is not in the power of speculation to accede. For as we shall make clear, prophecy is not set at naught even in the opinion of those who believe in the eternity of the world.

After I have made it clear that what we maintain is possible, I shall begin to make it prevail likewise, by means of speculative proof, over any other affirmations; I refer to my making prevail the assertion of creation in time over the assertion of eternity. I shall make it clear that just as a certain disgrace attaches to us because of the belief in the creation in time, and even greater disgrace attaches to the belief in eternity. I shall now start to bring into being a method that shall render void the proofs of all those who prove by inference the eternity of the world.

CHAPTER 17

In the case of everything produced in time, which is generated after not having existed—even in those cases in which the matter of the thing was already existent and in the course of the production of the thing had merely put off one and put on another form—the nature of that particular thing after it has been produced in time, has attained its final state, and achieved stability, is different from its nature when it is being generated and is beginning to pass from potentiality to actuality. It is also different from the nature the thing had before it had moved so as to pass from potentiality to actuality. For example, the nature of the feminine seed, which is the blood in the blood vessels, is different from the nature of this seed as it exists in the state of pregnancy after it has encountered the masculine sperm and has begun to move toward the transition from potentiality to actuality.

And even at the latter period, its nature is different from the nature of an animal that, after having been born, achieves perfection. No inference can be drawn in any respect from the nature of a thing after it has been generated, has attained its final state, and has achieved stability | in its most perfect state, to the state of that thing while it moved toward being generated. Nor can an inference be drawn from the state of the thing when it moves toward being generated to its state before it begins to move thus. Whenever you err in this and draw in inference from the nature of a thing that has achieved actuality to its nature when it was only in potential, grave doubts are aroused in you. . . .

. . . [T]his is exactly our position with regard to Aristotle. For we, the community of the followers of *Moses our Master and Abraham our Father,* may peace be on them, believe that the world was generated in such and such manner and came to be in a certain state from another state and was created in a certain state, which came after another state. Aristotle, on the other hand, begins to contradict us and to bring forward against us proofs based on the nature of what exists, a nature that has attained stability, is perfect, and has achieved actuality. As for us, we declare against him that this nature, after it has achieved stability and perfection, does not resemble in anything the state it was in while in the state of being generated and that it | was brought into existence from absolute nonexistence. Now what argument from among all that he advances holds good against us? For these arguments necessarily concern only those who claim that the stable nature of that which exists, gives an indication of its having been created in time. I have already made it known to you that I do not claim this.

Now I shall go back and set forth for your benefit the principles of his methods and shall show you that nothing in them of necessity concerns us in any respect, since we contend that God brought the world as a whole into existence after nonexistence and formed it until it has achieved perfection as you see it. He said that the first matter is subject to neither generation nor passing-away and began to draw inferences in favor or this thesis from the things subject to generation and passing-away and to make clear that it was impossible that the first matter was generated. And this is correct. For we do not maintain that the first matter is generated as man is generated from the seed or that it passes away as man passes away into dust. But we maintain that God has brought it into existence from nothing and that after being brought into existence, it was as it is now—I mean everything is generated from it, and everything generated from it passes away into it; it does not exist devoid of form; generation and corruption terminate in it; it is not subject to generation as are the things generated from it, nor to passing-away as are the things that pass away into it, but is created from nothing. And its Creator may, if He wishes to do so, render it entirely and absolutely nonexistent. We likewise say the same thing of motion. For he has inferred from the nature of motion that motion is not subject to generation and passing-away. And this is correct. For we maintain that after motion has come into existence with the nature characteristic of it when it has become stable, one cannot imagine that it should come into being as a whole and perish as a whole, as partial motions come into being and perish. This analogy holds good with regard to everything that is attached | to the nature of motion.

Thomas Aquinas's *Summa Theologica*

Aquinas devoted many years to the composition of this theological encyclopedia of the Christian religion, as he understood it. Completed two years before his death in 1274, the Summa encompasses the whole range of traditional Roman Catholic religious belief and practice, and as such has served as theological textbook for centuries. Written in a traditional medieval academic style of question and answer, the work attempts to provide definitive solutions to problems that were or could be asked by students of Christian belief. First the negative claims are presented concerning the question under discussion; then Aquinas states the authoritative belief of Scripture and church tradition. Once this has been made clear, he then proceeds to explain this belief often employing philosophical concepts and arguments based upon philosophers, such as Aristotle and Averroes, and theological authors, not only Christian but Jewish as well, such as Maimonides.

Like Maimonides, he is not a slavish follower of Aristotle or earlier religious authorities. He often reaches his own conclusions that he maintains are more in harmony with authentic Christian belief. His use of philosophy, however, has limits, which he carefully states. Note how he distinguishes between *preambles of faith and articles of faith* (*Summa Theologica*, Part 1 Question 1, articles 1, 2, and 8.). Whereas the former is a domain in which philosophy and religion meet and can work together, the latter is the proper province of theology, whose job is to show that certain Christian dogmas, unprovable and perhaps ultimately not fully comprehensible to philosophy, are nevertheless not absurd and thus are credible, at least to the Christian. On the one hand, this distinction is clearly evident in his claim that the world has been created by God, which the thesis is for him philosophically provable; on the other hand, the belief that the world began, that there was a first moment of time, is an article of faith not philosophically provable. Here we have to rely upon Scripture and Christian authorities.

The Summa Theologica[9] (excerpts)

Thomas Aquinas
Part One

Question 1: The Nature and Domain of Sacred Doctrine
(In Ten Articles)

To place our purpose within definite limits, we must first investigate the nature and domain of sacred doctrine. Concerning this there are ten points of inquiry: —
(1) Whether sacred doctrine is necessary? (2) Whether it is a science? . . . (8) Whether it is argumentative? (9) Whether it rightly employs metaphors and similes? (10) Whether the Sacred Scripture of this doctrine may be expounded in different senses?

First Article
Whether, Besides the Philosophical Disciplines, any further Doctrine Is Required?

We proceed thus to the First Article:
Objection 1. It seems that, besides the philosophical disciplines, we have no need of any further doctrine. For man should not seek to know what is above reason: *Seek not the things that are too high for thee* (*Ecclus. iii. 22*). But whatever is not above reason is sufficiently considered in the philosophical disciplines. Therefore any other doctrine besides the philosophical disciplines is superfluous.

Objection 2. Further, doctrine can be concerned only with being, for nothing can be known, save the true, which is convertible with being. But everything that is, is considered in the philosophical disciplines—even God Himself; so that there is a part of philosophy called theology, or the divine science, as is clear from Aristotle. Therefore, besides that philosophical disciplines, there is no need of any further doctrine.

On the contrary, it is written (2 Tim. iii. 16): *All Scripture inspired of God is profitable to teach, to reprove, to correct, to instruct in justice.* Now Scripture, inspired of God, is not a part of the philosophical disciplines discovered by human reason. Therefore it is useful that besides the philosophical disciplines there should be another science—*i.e.,* inspired of God.

I answer that, It was necessary for man's salvation that there should be a doctrine revealed by God, besides the philosophical disciplines investigated by human reason. First, because man is directed to God as to an end that surpasses the grasp of his reason: *The eye hath not seen, O God, besides Thee, what things Thou hast prepared for them that wait for Thee* (Isa. lxiv. 4). but the end must first be known by men who are to direct their intentions and actions to the end. Hence it was necessary for the salvation of man that certain truths which exceed human reason should be made known to him by divine revelation. Even as regards those truths about God which human reason can investigate, it was necessary that man be taught by a divine revelation. For the truth about God, such as reason can know it, would only be known by a few, and that after a long time, and with the admixture of many errors; whereas man's whole salvation, which is in God, depends upon the knowledge of this truth. Therefore, in order that the salvation of men might be brought about more fitly and more surely, it was necessary that they be taught divine truths by divine revelation. It was therefore necessary that, besides the philosophical disciplines investigated by reason, there should be a sacred doctrine by way of revelation.

Reply Obj. 1. Although those things which are beyond man's knowledge may not be sought for by man through his reason, nevertheless, what is revealed by God must be accepted through faith. Hence the sacred text continues, *for many things are shown to thee above the understanding of man* (Ecclus. iii. 25). And in such things sacred doctrine consists.

Reply Obj.2. Sciences are diversified according to the diverse nature of their knowable objects. For the astronomer and the physicist both prove the same conclusion—that the earth, for instance, is round: the astronomer by means of mathematics (*i.e.*, abstracting from matter), but the physicist by means of matter itself. Hence there is no reason why those things, which are treated by the philosophical disciplines, so far as they can be known by the light of natural reason, may not also be treated by another science so far as they are known by the light of the divine revelation. Hence the theology included in sacred doctrine differs in genus from that theology which is part of philosophy.

Second Article
Whether Sacred Doctrine Is a Science?

We proceed thus to the Second Article:

Objection 1. It seems that sacred doctrine is not a science. For every science proceeds from self-evident principles. But sacred doctrine proceeds from articles of faith which are not self-evident, since their truth is not admitted by all: *For all men have not faith (2 Thess.* iii. 2). Therefore sacred doctrine is not a science. . . .

On the contrary, Augustine says[10] that *to this science alone belongs that whereby saving faith is begotten, nourished, protected and strengthened.* But this can be said of no science except sacred doctrine. Therefore sacred doctrine is a science.

I answer that, Sacred doctrine is a science. We must bear in mind that there are two kinds of sciences. There are some which proceed from principles known by the natural light of the intellect, such as arithmetic and geometry and the like. There are also some, which proceed from principles known by the light of a higher science: thus the science of optics proceeds from principles established by geometry, and music from principles established by arithmetic. So it is that sacred doctrine is a science because it proceeds from principles made known by the light of a higher science, namely, the science of God and the blessed. Hence, just as music accepts on authority the principles taught by the arithmetician, so sacred doctrine accepts the principles revealed by God.

Reply Obj.1. The principles of any science are either in themselves self-evident, or reducible to the knowledge of a higher science; and such, as we have said, are the principles of sacred doctrine. . . .

Eighth Article
Whether Sacred Doctrine Is Argumentative?

We proceed thus to the Eighth Article:

Objection 2. It seems this doctrine is not argumentative. For Ambrose says: *Put arguments aside where faith is sought.* But in this doctrine faith especially is sought: *But these things are written that you may believe* (*Jo.* xx. 31). Therefore sacred doctrine is not argumentative.

Obj. 2. Further, if it is argumentative, the argument is either from authority or from reason. If it is from authority, it seems unbefitting its dignity, for the proof from authority is the weakest form of proof according to Boethius.[11] But if from reason, this is unbefitting its end, because, according to Gregory, *faith has no merit in those things of which human reason brings its own experience.* Therefore sacred doctrine is not argumentative.

On the contrary, The Scripture says that a bishop should *embrace that faithful word which is according to doctrine, that he may be able to exhort in sound doctrine and to convince the gainsayers* (*Tit.* i. 9).

I answer that, As the other sciences do not argue in proof of their principles, but argue from their principles to demonstrate other truths in these sciences, so this doctrine does not argue in proof of its principles, which are the articles of faith, but from them it goes on to prove something else; as the Apostle argues from the resurrection of Christ in proof of the general resurrection (*1 Cor.* xv. 12). However, it is to be borne in mind, in regard to the philosophical sciences, that the inferior sciences neither prove their principles nor dispute with those who deny them, but leave this to a higher science; whereas the highest of them, viz., metaphysics, can dispute with one who denies its principles, if only the opponent will make some concession; but if he conceded nothing, it can have no dispute with him, though it can answer his arguments. Hence Sacred Scripture, since it has no science above itself, disputes argumentatively with one who denies its principles only if the opponent admits some at least of the truths obtained through divine revelation. Thus, we can argue with heretics from texts in Holy Scripture, and against those who deny one article of faith we can argue from another. If our opponent believes nothing of divine revelation, there is no longer any means of proving the articles of faith by argument, but only of answering his objections—if he has any—against faith. Since faith rests upon infallible truth, and since the contrary of a truth can never be demonstrated, it is clear that the proofs brought against faith are not demonstrations, but arguments that can be answered.

Reply Obj.1. Although arguments from human reason cannot avail to prove what belongs to faith, nevertheless, this doctrine argues from articles of faith to other truths.

Reply Obj. 2. It is especially proper to this doctrine to argue from authority, inasmuch as its principles are obtained by revelation; and hence we must believe the authority of those to whom the revelation has been made. Nor does this take away from the dignity of this doctrine, for although the argument from authority based on human reason is the weakest, yet the argument from authority based on divine revelation is the strongest. But sacred doctrine also makes use of human reason, not, indeed, to prove faith (for thereby the merit of faith would come to an end), but to make clear other things that are set forth in this doctrine. Since therefore grace does not destroy nature, but perfects it, natural reason should minister to faith as the natural inclination of the will ministers to charity. Hence the Apostle says: *Bringing into captivity every understanding unto the obedience of Christ* (2 *Cor.* x. 5). Hence it is that sacred doctrine makes use also of the authority of philosophers in those questions in which they were able to know the truth by natural reason, as Paul quotes a saying of Aratus: *As some also of your own poets said: For we are also His offspring* (Acts xvii. 28). Nevertheless, sacred doctrine makes use of these authorities as extrinsic and probable arguments, but properly uses the authority of the canonical Scriptures as a necessary demonstration, and the authority of the doctors of the Church as one that may properly be used, yet merely as probable. For our faith rests upon the revelation made to the apostles and prophets, who wrote the canonical books, and not on the revelations (if any such there are) made to other doctors. . . .

Question 46:
On the Beginning of Creatures

Article 2: Whether It Is An Article of Faith That the World Began?

We proceed thus to the Second Article:
Objection 1. It would seem that it is not an article of faith but a

demonstrable conclusion that the world began. For everything that is made has a beginning of its duration. But it can be proved demonstratively that God is the producing cause of the world; indeed this is asserted by the more approved philosophers. Therefore it can be demonstratively proved that the world began. . . .

Obj. 5. Further, it is certain that nothing can be equal to God. But if the world had always been, it would be equal to God in duration. Therefore it is certain that the world did not always exist.

Obj. 6. Further, if the world always was, the consequence is that an infinite number of days preceded this present day. But it is impossible to traverse what is infinite. Therefore, we should never have arrived at this present day; which is manifestly false. . . .

On the contrary, the articles of faith cannot be proved demonstratively because faith is of things *that appear not.* But that God is the Creator of the world in such a way that the world began to be is an article of faith; for we say *I believe in one God, etc.* And again, Gregory says that Moses prophesied of the past, saying, *In the beginning God created heaven and earth* in which words the newness of the world is stated. Therefore the newness of the world is known only by revelation and hence it cannot be proved demonstratively.

I answer that, That the world did not always exist we hold by faith alone: it cannot be proved demonstratively; which is what was said above of the mystery of the Trinity. The reason for this is that the newness of the world cannot be demonstrated from the world itself. For the principle of demonstration is the essence of a thing. Now everything, considered in its species, abstracts from *here and now;* which is why it is said that *universals are everywhere and always.* Hence it cannot be demonstrated that man, or the heavens, or a stone did not always exist

Likewise, neither can the newness of the world be demonstrated from the efficient cause, which acts by will. For the will of God cannot be investigated by reason, except as regards those things which God must will of necessity; and what He wills about creatures is not among these, as was said above. But the divine will can be manifested by revelation, on which faith rests. Hence that the world began to exist is an object of faith, but not of demonstration or science. And it is useful to consider this, lest anyone, presuming to demonstrate what is of faith, should bring forward arguments that are not cogent; for this would give unbelievers the occasion to ridicule, thinking that on such grounds we believe the things that are of faith.

Reply Obj. 1. As Augustine says, the opinion of philosophers who asserted the eternity of the world was twofold. For some said that the substance of the world was not from God, which is an intolerable error; and therefore it is refuted by proofs that are cogent. Some, however, said that the world was eternal, although made by God. *For they hold that the world has a beginning, not of time, but of creation; which means that, in a scarcely intelligent way, it was always made. And they try to explain their meaning thus: for just as, if a foot were always in the dust from eternity, there would always be a foot print which without doubt was caused by him who trod on it, so also the world always was, because its Maker always existed.*[12] To understand this we must consider that an efficient cause which acts by motion of necessity precedes its effect in time; for the effect exists only in the end of the action, and every agent must be the beginning of action. But if the action is instantaneous and not successive, it is not necessary for the maker to be prior in duration to the thing made, as appears in the case of illumination. Hence it is held that it does not follow necessarily that if God is the active cause of the world, He must be prior to the world in duration, because creation, by which He produced the world, is not a successive change, as was said above. . . .

Reply Obj. 5. Even supposing that the world always was, it would not be equal to God in eternity, as Boethius says, for the divine Being is all being simultaneously without succession, but with the world it is otherwise.[13]

Reply Obj. 6. Passage is always understood as being from term to term. Whatever by gone day we choose from it to the present day there is a finite number of days which can be traversed. The objection if founded on the idea that, given two extremes, there is an infinite number of mean terms. . . .

Third Article: Whether the Creation of Things Was in the Beginning of Time?

We proceed thus to the Third Article:

Obj. 2. Further, the Philosopher[14] proves that everything which is made was being made. Hence, to be made implies a *before* and *after*. But in the beginning of time, since it is indivisible, there is not *before* and *after*. Therefore, since to be created is a kind of *being made*, it appears that things were not created in the beginning of time. . . .

On the contrary, it is said (*Gen*. i. 1): In the beginning God created heaven and earth.

I answer that, The words of Genesis, *In the beginning God created heaven and earth*, are interpreted in a threefold sense in order to exclude three errors. For some said that the world always was and that time had no beginning; and to exclude this the words *In the beginning* are interpreted to mean *the beginning of time*.

And some said that there are two principles of creation, one of good things and the other of evil things, against which *In the beginning* is expounded—*in the son*. For as the efficient principle is appropriated to the Father by reason of power, so the exemplary principle is appropriated to the Son by reason of wisdom; in order that, according to the words *(Ps. ciii. 24)*, *Thou hast made all things in wisdom*, it may be understood that God made all things in the beginning—that is, in the Son. As it is said by the Apostle (*Col*. i. 16), *In Him*—viz., the Son—*were created all things*.

But others said that corporeal things were created by God through the medium of spiritual creatures; and to exclude this the words of Genesis are interpreted thus: *In the beginning—i.e., before* all things— *God created heaven and earth*. For four things are stated to be created together—viz., the empyrean heavens, corporeal matter, by which is meant the earth, time, and the angelic nature. . . .

Reply Obj. 2. This saying of the Philosopher is understood *of being made* by means of movement, or as the term of movement. For since in every motion there is *before* and *after*, before any one point in a given motion—that is, while anything is in the process of being moved and made,—there is a *before* and also an *after*, because what is in the beginning of motion or in its term is not in the state of *being moved*. But creation is neither motion nor the term of motion, as was said above. Hence a thing is created in such a way that it was not being created before.

Discussion Questions

Averroes

1. How does Averroes justify the study and use of philosophy to an audience committed to belief in the authority of a divinely revealed text, the Qur'an?

2. Does Averroes replace the authority of the Qur'an with the authority of philosophy?

3. To what extent, according to Averroes, are we allowed to interpret a sacred text?

4. Is Averroes's attempt to reconcile the religious belief in creation of the world with the philosophical theory of the eternity of the world convincing?

Maimonides

1. Maimonides defines belief as involving argument and evidence. Does this eliminate faith?

2. Must religious beliefs be supported by rational arguments?

3. Maimonides believed that he had refuted the philosophers' arguments for the eternity of the world. Is his refutation successful?

Aquinas

1. Why should a philosophically educated person accept Aquinas' sharp distinction between the *preambles of faith* and the *articles of faith*?

2. Aquinas maintains that "sacred science," or theology, is a genuine science. Is he justified in this claim?

3. Aquinas believes that the createdness of the world is philosophically provable but that its being temporally created from nothing is not. What is the difference between these two theses, and why does he maintain this distinction?

CHAPTER 7

MYSTICISM AS A MEETING GROUND: SEEING THE UNSEEN

Elliot R. Wolfson

Mysticism and the Encounter with Ultimate Reality

Mysticism is considered a ubiquitous phenomenon, present in one form or another in all religious traditions. However, as is the fate of every key term used to study human culture, there is no consensus with respect to the precise meaning of the term *mysticism*, and a good deal of effort on the part of scholars has been to come up with a definition that is both comprehensive and flexible enough to account for the manifold manifestations of the mystical phenomenon in diverse religious traditions. Indeed, there is even debate regarding the legitimacy of seeking such a definition. The major camps on this issue are divided into the essentialist and contextualist. Essentialism is an orientation that presumes the sameness of the experiences that are deemed mystical in nature. The further assumption is that human nature itself does not change over time or in accord with different geographical milieu, and thus it is legitimate for the scholar to delineate common characteristics. The contextualist orientation, by contrast, denies the notion of a perennial philosophy or unchanging essence and focuses instead on the specific cultural context that gives way to the particular experience tagged with the label "mysticism."

In spite of this fundamental divergence in approach, representatives of the two schools share a working understanding of mysticism that allows one to speak of the selfsame phenomenon that is affirmed in essentialist terms or challenged in contextualist terms. In the most generic terms, the mystical element presumed in the case of one and the other is linked to consciousness of ultimate reality, identified as God in theistic religions or as the Absolute in nontheistic systems of belief. The unique state of mindfulness that this state of consciousness calls forth—the mindful overcoming of mindfulness, that is, the seemingly singular capacity of human thought to think the unthinkable—affords the individual the opportunity to be in contact with the being that is inaccessible to the human mind in its ordinary waking state. Even for the contextualist who argues that epistemologically all human experience and knowledge is mediated by linguistic and cultural factors, that which is distinctive in the mystical state is neither an object of sense perception nor a logically deduced rational truth. Some scholars use the word *transcendence* to capture the truth that lies beyond human comprehension, though clearly even this word is too limited to demarcate the being that has no limit. The mystical experience, we might say, involves an encounter with what is believed to be the ground of reality outside the grasp of human perception and knowledge.

Etymologically, the word *mystic* has its origin in the ancient Greek mystery cults into which an individual was initiated and thereby gained knowledge of cosmic and divine secrets. The one initiated into these cults was redeemed from history and time and reborn into eternity. The word *mystery*, whence the term *mystic* is derived, is from the root *myein*, which means to close the eyes, presumably chosen for the one initiated into the mysteries apprehended the invisible realities by closing his eyes to matters of the mundane, physical world. The enduring legacy in Western religions of the origin of the term *mysticism* in the mystery cults is the emphasis placed on the secretive nature of the knowledge attained by the mystic as a result of his or her experience of the absolute. The occult nature of this knowledge is twofold: first, it is not to be readily disclosed to the masses who are unworthy, and, second, reason or intellect cannot grasp this wisdom.

Although it is fashionable today to avoid positing a general definition of mysticism that ignores the specific sociocultural context within which the given mystical phenomenon takes shape, it still seems reasonable to speak taxonomically of mysticism as the quest to have a direct encounter with the one true source of all being. Mystical consciousness lays claim to an encounter of/with/in ultimate reality, the absolute ground of being, not through empirical observation or logical deduction, but through an experience of immediacy, a *tasting*, as Sufis are fond of saying, whereby all intermediaries—words, images, and concepts—are rendered transparent in the absolute, a luminal darkness beyond distinction and discrimination, a coincidence of opposites, where black is white and white, black, where night is day and day, night, where truth is deception and deception, truth, where good is evil and evil, good. It is precisely with respect to this mode of mindfulness that Jewish, Christian, and Muslim mystics in the late Middle Ages, by all accounts a time of strife and division, were able to express an ideal of union that transcends the boundaries of religious and cultural differences separating the different liturgical communities. What is striking in the teachings of mystics is the insistence of maintaining the difference of identity even in the face of the identity of difference.

Plotinus and the Ideal of Mystical Union

As it happens, the critical figure who influenced the contours of mystical spirituality in the three monotheistic traditions was the third-century pagan philosopher Plotinus. According to Plotinus, for the human mind to contemplate the first principle, the unknowable, nameless One, a tenet traceable to Plato's description of the Good as that which is "beyond being" (*Republic* 509B9-10), it must become like the One. The logic underlying this assumption rests on the ancient Hellenistic wisdom espoused in the adage of Anaxagoras that things of similar nature are attracted to one another, or, in the related formulation of Empedocles that wisdom consists of "like by like" since it is "either identical with or closely akin to perception."[1]

Even more pertinent for understanding Plotinus is his utilization of the Aristotelian formula, which is based on the aforementioned pre-Socratic principle, that the knower must become like the thing to be known (*De Anima* 429a13-17). One passage, in particular, worthy of citation is from a relatively early treatise in the Plotinian corpus, in which Plotinus sets out to explain the "inner sight" by which one can apprehend the true form of "inconceivable beauty," a way of seeing that is awakened when the eyes are shut (*Enneads* I.6.8).[2] If the mind is sufficiently purified from corporeal matters, then in turning inward, which is also depicted as an ascent to the intelligible realm, it will see the "true light" that cannot be measured by metric dimensions. In the speculum of inner vision, the mind's eye sees what is without within and what is within without, and hence spectator and spectacle can no longer be differentiated. "For one must come to the sight with a seeing power made akin to and like what is seen. No eye ever saw the sun without becoming sun-like, nor can a soul see beauty without becoming beautiful. You must become first all godlike and all beautiful if you intend to see God and beauty" (*Enneads* I.6.9).

In the continuation of the passage, Plotinus distinguishes the vision of the Intellect, the place of forms or ideas characterized as the intelligible beauty, and the vision of the Good, the "primary beauty," the origin that is beyond the "screen" of beauty. If, however, the One is utterly unique, it can be like no other thing. Indeed, in its absolute simplicity, the One can have no form or substance, and hence the only way to become "like" the One is to be assimilated into the One. However, to be assimilated into what is "beyond being"—a designation, Plotinus reminds us, that makes no positive statement about the One but only implies that it is "not this," that is, that it is not a particular something and thus cannot be compared to anything (*Enneads* V.3.14, V.4.1-2, V.5.6, VI.7.38)—the mind must transcend the specificity of its own being by disposing the filters of intellection, the categories of reason by which we comprehend and classify the data of sense experience.

> It would be absurd to seek to comprehend that boundless nature . . . but just as he who wishes to see the intelligible nature will contemplate what is beyond the perceptible if he has no mental image of the perceptible, so he who wishes to contemplate what is beyond the intelligible will contemplate it when he has let all the intelligible go. . . . But we in our travail do not know what we ought to say, and are speaking of what cannot be spoken, and give it a name because we want to indicate it to ourselves the best we can. (*Enneads* V. 5.6)

An iconoclastic breaking of all form occasions contemplative envisioning of the formless.

For Plotinus, there are three stages to the ascent of mind, which can be seen as a progressive attempt to apprehend beauty. The first stage is the rising from discursive knowledge appropriate for the sensible world, that is, reasoning from premise to conclusion and transitioning from one object of thought to another. The second stage brings an inner vision of intellect and the world of ideal forms wherein the distinction between subject and object is transcended. Finally, in the third stage, one sees the formless, the Good that is the source of ultimate beauty, radiant darkness beyond intellect and language. Plotinus conceives the ascent in accord with a major impulse in the Platonic understanding of the philosophical life, as a way to attain knowledge of self, "to face death before we die."[3] Central in the Plotinian scheme is a fundamental paradox. The higher one ascends on the ladder of self-knowledge, climbing from the multiplicity of the sensible to the complexity of the intelligible and beyond to the simplicity of the One, and the more one loses awareness of self, the more one gains knowledge of self.

The path of contemplation that Plotinus bestowed on the history of mystical pietism in the three religions is a process of purification, emptying the mind of images, concepts, and words. In the final stage, however, in the return of the "alone" to the "Alone," the purging culminates in a vision, albeit a seeing in which the difference between seer and seen is no longer viable; the eye that sees is the eye that is seen and the eye that is seen is the eye that sees. In this paradoxical teaching, one can find the experiential basis for the ecstatic ideal cultivated in Christian, Jewish, and Islamic mysticism. In the meditative state in which thinking, thinker, and thought can no longer be discriminated, the mind stretches beyond its own limits to be absorbed in the mindless but fully conscious source of all being. Intellect is the most perfect image of the One, but even that image must be transcended if one is to see the imageless light about which we cannot speak adequately (*Enneads* V.8.18).

Concerning the One it must be said that it is all things "by and in himself," since it contains all things in itself and they exist only by participation in it, but it is also none of them, since its being is in no way dependent on them. Inasmuch as the One "is all things and not a single one of them" (V.2.1), Plotinus insists that when we speak or think about it, we must dispense with every name; at best, we can "make signs (*sêmainein*) to ourselves about it" (V.3.13) in the manner of Egyptian hieroglyphs, a nondiscursive language based on ideogrammatic symbols rather than words and propositions (V.8.6).

> When you have put away all things and left only himself, do not try to find what you can add, but if there is something you have not yet taken away from him in your mind. For even you can grasp something about which it is not possible any more to say or apprehend anything else; but it is something which has its place high above everything, this which alone is free in truth, because it is not enslaved to itself, but is only itself and really itself, while every other thing is itself and something else. (V.8.21)

Paradoxically, that which is known and named to be truly itself and nothing else cannot be known or named, as knowing and naming entail relating a thing to other things, but only experienced in the vision of that which is invisible, a seeing that sees nothing, not even not-seeing, the mind's eye gazing in the darkness of seeing light (V.5.7) wherein nothing is seen and nobody sees.

Even the term *one* is to be interpreted, at best, negatively as denial of multiplicity. If it were to be taken positively "it would be less clear than if we did not give it a name at all: for perhaps this name [One] was given it in order that the seeker, beginning from this which is completely indicative of simplicity, may finally negate this as well, because, though it was given as well as possible by its giver, not even this is worthy to manifest that nature; since that nature cannot be heard, nor may it be understood by one who hears, but, if at all, by one who sees. But if the seer tries to look at a form, he will not know even that" (V.5.6). Not-seeing is previewed by abandoning all concepts and images, a seeing through the glass darkly (V.3.17). From this vantage point apophasis and mystical envisioning go hand in hand.

The Mystic Quest: Representing the Unrepresentable

The apophatic orientation, briefly outlined above, greatly informed the mystical speculation in the three monotheistic faiths and thereby transformed their respective theological sensibilities. At the same time, the theistic legacy of ancient Israelite prophecy imparted to Jewish, Christian, and Muslim mystics a tradition abounding with positive characteristics attributed to a deity whose grounding lay in revelatory experience. As I intimated above, it is difficult, if not impossible, to offer a definition of mysticism that can be applied to the different historical manifestations of any particular religion let alone comparatively to different religions. However, it is accurate to assert that a recurrent theme in the various mystical expressions within Judaism, Christianity, and Islam has been the desire to experience what prophets of yore experienced, envisioning the presence, the glory of God, in forms forbidden for priests and other Israelites to worship iconically, though seemingly permissible for poets to depict imaginally. Ancient Israelite culture was distinguished from other Near Eastern societies of its time by the explicit injunction against worshiping idols, but this did not stop poetic souls from depicting God in graphic form, thereby substituting mental icons for material forms of configuration.

It is precisely the aniconic spirit that fostered remarkable imaginative representations of the nonrepresentable in circles of Jewish, Christian, and Muslim mystics where specific meditational practices were cultivated for the stated aim of attaining a vision of the invisible. Like the prophets of old, albeit in fundamentally different historical circumstances, medieval visionaries simultaneously cultivated a rich iconography and vigorous iconoclasm—an unyielding and aggressive rejection of the physical representation of God, on the one hand, and an amplification of bold mythical imagery to depict God, on the other. The locus of that vision was typically situated in the heart/imagination of the visionary, the site where the division between inside and outside is dissolved in the play of double mirroring, the heart mirroring the image that mirrors the image of the heart. From that vantage point we can speak accurately of theistic mysticism as *speculative* theosophy, that is, a wisdom of God that is discerned in the mirror (*speculum*) of the enlightened mind/heart that reflects the immanence of the divine refracted in the world of discriminate beings as well as the transcendence of the one true divine being, which is without image or form.

In the terminology used by historians of religion, the mystical element in the three monotheisms ensues from the juxtaposition of image mysticism and apophatic mysticism, that is, a mysticism predicated on the possibility of envisioning the shape of God in conjunction with a mysticism that steadfastly denies the possibility of ascribing any form to the being beyond all configuration, indeed the being to whom we cannot even ascribe the attribute of being without denying the nature of that (non)being. In mystical accounts of scriptural religious cultures, which, needless to say, is the case with Judaism, Christianity, and Islam, the most important way that the visionary and unitive experiences are mediated is through study of canonical texts. The experiences themselves may surpass the limits of language, but it is only through language that those limits are surpassed. The apophatic tendency to submerge all forms of sentient imaging in the formlessness of pure consciousness cannot be completely severed from the kataphatic insistence on the possibility of being in the presence of the divine. The juxtaposition of the kataphatic and apophatic, affirmative and negative theology, has fostered the awareness

251

on the part of the ones initiated in the secret wisdom that mystical utterance is an unsaying, which is not the same as silence or not-speaking, but rather that which remains ineffable in being spoken, that which remains unknown in being known, that which remains invisible in being seen. Just as unsaying is to be contrasted with not-speaking and unknowing with not-knowing, so unseeing is to be distinguished from not-seeing.

Gregory of Nyssa and the Vision of Unseeing

An important mystical theologian of the early church in the fourth century who set out to expound the apophatic way was Gregory of Nyssa, a man of letters who studied Scripture and Platonic writings as well as the treatises of the fathers Origen and Clement of Alexandria. For Origen, the soul pursues a path of light on the way to God, whereas for Gregory, the journey is one from light to darkness, a darkness that is more fully light, so luminous it cannot but be dark. Gregory distinguishes three levels of vision of the invisible God, which we may call the cosmological, the anthropological, and the theophanic. According to the first level, the divine is seen in the contemplation of his energies or his potencies that act in the world, that is, vision by way of analogy. According to the second, God is seen through the human being who is created with the divine image, that is, an internal seeing of the mind. The third is exemplified by the theophany at the burning bush. Moses divested himself of the earthly covering and beheld the light from the bush, which symbolizes that the radiance, the one true being, "the transcendent essence and cause of the universe,"[4] shines through the thorny flesh, a foreshadowing of the mystery of the incarnation of the son who is the image of the father. The vision of the father consists of beholding "the ineffable and mysterious illumination which came to Moses,"[5] the vision of unseeing, the dark luminosity of the luminous darkness, the source of being beyond all being.

The life of Moses portrays the mystical journey, epitomized in the biblical image of his entering the dark cloud *(arafel)* on Mount Sinai (Exod 20:21), which is a figurative account of true vision, seeing that one cannot see.[6] The desire to see God, therefore, cannot be fulfilled since God cannot be seen except as the invisible, formless being. This, according to Gregory, is the spiritual meaning of God's saying to Moses, "No one shall see me and live" (Exod 33:20); that is, life is marked by the quest to envision the divine, which translates into the desire always to see more since what one seeks to see is forever inaccessible to one's visual grasp (John 1:18). The attainment of the quest to see God is realized in death.[7] The characteristic of God is to transcend all characteristics and hence one who thinks God is something knowable has no knowledge. To see the divine is ultimately to see that one cannot see, to discern one's own blindness in the constant yearning to attain the vision of the invisible.

Dionysius the Areopagite and the Knowing of Unknowing

The intertwining of affirmative and negative theology was expounded in more intricate philosophical detail by the sixth-century Syrian monk known as Dionysius the Areopagite, a figure who was to have a profound influence on the mystical spirituality in Eastern and Western Christianity as well as in Islamic and Jewish mysticism. Combining the rigor of logical analysis and the passion of poetic sensibility, Dionysius sought to articulate a mystical theology that was true to the kataphasis of scriptural faith and to the apophasis of philosophical contemplation. According to Dionysius's formulation in the *Divine Names* (588A-B),

> We must not dare to resort to words or conceptions concerning the hidden divinity which transcends being, apart from what the sacred scriptures have divinely revealed. Since the unknowing of what is beyond is something above and beyond speech, mind, or being itself, one should ascribe to it an understanding beyond being. . . . Indeed the inscrutable One is out of the reach of every rational process. Nor can any words come up to the inexpressible Good, this One, this source of all unity, this supra-existent Being. Mind beyond mind, word beyond speech, it is gathered up by no discourse, by no intuition, by no name.[8]

God is hidden and transcendent and thus technically "surpasses all discourse and all knowledge" (593A).[9] The only positive attributions that are legitimately ascribed to God are the characteristics derived from the language of Scripture. In this manner, Dionysius established a model employed subsequently by mystical exegetes in Judaism, Christianity, and Islam who sought to combine the apophatic and kataphatic, remaining faithful to the philosophical insight regarding the unknowability and ineffability of the One and to the revealed word of God predicated on a plethora of affirmative statements about the divine nature.

The juxtaposition of these distinct orientations to the texture of religious experience resulted in a paradox expressed by Dionysius and reiterated in one form or another by numerous mystic visionaries in the three monotheistic faiths: "God is therefore known in all things and as distinct from all things. He is known through knowledge and through unknowing" (872A).[10] In more conventional terms, God is both transcendent and immanent, "the cause of everything" but not identical to any one thing "since it transcends all things in a manner beyond being" (593C).[11] Insofar as there can be nothing outside God, God is "all things in all things," and thus it must be the case that God is known in all things. Yet, God is "no thing among things, (872A)"[12] for the one cannot be delimited or contained in any single entity and remain the one that is boundless, and hence God is apart from everything and is not known. It is in this *unknowing* that God is most truly known, a matter that is considered to be secret that ought not be divulged to the uninitiated (597C). In his *Mystical Theology*, Dionysius follows Gregory of Nyssa and ascribes to Moses the status of having freed himself from "what sees and is seen," plunging "into the truly mysterious darkness of unknowing. Here, renouncing all that the mind may conceive, wrapped entirely in the intangible and the invisible, he belongs completely to him who is beyond everything. Here, being neither oneself nor someone else, one is supremely united to the completely unknown by an inactivity of all knowledge, and knows beyond the mind by knowing nothing" (1001A).[13]

For Dionysius, the mystical agnosticism—the inherent inability to know, which is the highest level of knowledge—is attained in the last of the three stages of the path, purgation, illumination, and union *(henosis)*. The ideal of union is appropriated from Plotinus, but in Dionysius it should be rendered more precisely as divinization *(theosis)*. The way that one rises to this state is by unknowing *(agnosia)*, that is, by stripping the mind of all positive knowledge related to sense data and rational concepts, one is unified with the "intellectual light" (700D), that transcends all being and knowledge. "But again, the most divine knowledge of God, that which comes through unknowing, is achieved in a union far beyond mind, when mind turns away from all things, even from itself, and when it is made one with the dazzling rays, being then and there enlightened by the inscrutable depth of Wisdom" (872A-B).[14] The mandate of the contemplative life is to move beyond all images to the imageless. As Dionysius put it in the first of the letters to Gaius, "Someone beholding God and understanding what he saw has not actually seen God. . . . He is completely unknown and nonexistent. He exists beyond being and he is known beyond the mind. And this quite positively complete unknowing is knowledge of him who is above everything that is known." The author leads his reader once again to the mystical paradox: "complete unknowing is knowledge of him who is above everything that is known" (1065A).[15]

Sufism and the Vision of the Heart

If we turn now to the mystical traditions of Islam, there is ample evidence that Sufi masters embraced a similar paradox, placing at the summit of their path the vision of the divine face that cannot be seen. In spite of the unequivocal denial of the possibility of seeing God in Muslim faith, based firmly on the Qur'anic precedent to associate the word *unseen* (*ghayb*) with Allah (Q 11:31, 123; 13:9; 16:77; 35:18; 53:35), it is precisely the Sufi mandate, following the teaching of Muhammad, to worship God "as if you see him." This stands in contrast to Q 2:3 where belief in the unseen (*ghayb*) precedes the establishment of prayer (*salât*), one of the five fundamental pillars of Islam. On the other hand, the nexus between seeking God's face and prayer is attested in several verses (Q 6:52, 13:22, 18:28).

Also relevant is the polemic in Q 4:153 against the children of Israel, referred to as the "people of the book," which, closely following the unfolding of the narrative plot in Exodus, links idolatry, exemplified in the worship of the golden calf, to the desire to see God; in the Qur'anic version, the request is attributed to the Israelites as a whole, thus misreading the account in the Torah in which the petition to see the glory frontally (Exod. 33:12-16) is describing Moses alone, though, to be sure, the petition is intricately connected to the fate of the national collectivity. The Sufi mandate, following the teaching of Muhammad, is "worship God as if you see him," the mystical interpretation thereby lending support to the claim that prayer in a theistic tradition requires iconic representation of the divine within the imagination, a theme that is attested as well in medieval Jewish and Christian mystical piety. In a manner consonant with the neoplatonic tradition, moreover, the Sufi perspective

255

presumes an intricate connection between the unitive experience and envisioning; one sees the face only when one has become the face.

In Sufism, witnessing *(shahada)*, another of the five fundamental pillars, is connected more specifically with vision *(ru'ya)*, the locus of which is the heart *(ru'yat al-qalb)*—in part reflective of Q 53:12, "The heart did not lie in what it saw, will you then dispute with him on his vision?" The affirmation of the prophet's vision becomes the scriptural anchor to legitimate the heart as the vehicle of spiritual vision and mystical knowledge, as we see, for example, in the interpretation of Ja'far: "No one knows what he saw except the seer and the seen. The lover has come near to the beloved, as intimate and confidant to him."[16] The full visionary implication of this text, the nexus between vision, eros, death, and union, is drawn out by Ja'far in his commentary on the reworking of Exodus 33:20 in Q 7:143-144. According to the verse in Exodus, the request of Moses to see the glory resulted in his seeing the back, not the front; in the Qur'anic version, Moses did not see God at all, for when the glory appeared on the mountain it turned into dust, thereby indicating that God's response to Moses that he should look upon the mountain and if it abides his demand would be answered positively was, in effect, a way of saying that seeing the unseen consists of not-seeing. With respect to that which cannot be seen, for there is no/thing to be seen, not-seeing can be accounted as seeing. In Ja'far's paraphrase, God says to Moses, "you are not able to see me because you pass away. How can that which passes away *(fânin)* find a way to that which abides *(bâqin)*? . . . The Lord's face-to-face vision in respect to the servant is the annihilation of the servant. The servant's face-to-face vision of the Lord and in the Lord is enduring."[17]

In this text, we are introduced to two key technical terms utilized in Sufi teaching to express the goal of mystical union, *fanâ* and *baqâ*, passing-away and enduring. The scriptural foundation for these terms is Q 55:26, "All that dwells upon the earth is perishing *(fânin)*, yet still abides *(fa-yabqa)*, the face of your Lord, majestic, splendid." The one abiding reality is the divine essence, metaphorically depicted as the face of God, a usage attested in other verses as well such as "There is no god but he. Everything will perish except his own face" (Q 28:88). According to the mystical interpretation, by undoing the bonds that tie the soul to matters of the body, passing-away from the impermanent self, the higher self abides with the beloved; significantly, persisting in that which abides is expressed as seeing the unseen, beholding the face that has no visible form to behold. According to the eleventh-century Iranian mystic, Abû Hâmid Muhammad al-Ghazâli, the inner meaning of the verse relates to the removal of the veil, the symbolic act that signifies the declaration of unity *(tawhîd)* on the part of the "elect of the elect," the supreme mystical state of the annihilation of self as an entity distinct from the One; the mimetic figuration gives way to the ecstatic vision in which the self vanishes. There is nothing but vision, a seeing without seer or seen. In al-Ghazâli's own words, "They become extinct from themselves, so that they cease observing themselves. Nothing remains save the One, the Real. . . . This is the ultimate end of those who have arrived."[18]

Unveiling of the Veil

From a relatively early period the image of lifting the veil—seeing the face without impediment—was used by Sufis to convey mystical enlightenment or awakening, based on verses in the Qur'an (50:22; 53:57-58; 82:1-6) in which this activity is associated with the vision that will be manifest on the day of reckoning *(yawm ad-dîn)*. Consider the following example: Muhammad Ibn 'Abd al-Jabbâr Ibn al-Hasan al-Niffarî, a Sufi active in the tenth century, expressed the matter laconically in words he attributes to God in his *Kitâb al-Mawâqif*: "My moment has come / The time has come for me to unveil my face and manifest my splendor."[19] The revelatory experience, the unveiling of the face *(wajh)*, results in gnosis *(ma'rifa)*, illumination *(ishrâq)*, intuition *(dhawq)*, knowledge by presence *(al-'ilm al-hudûrî)*, the momentous apprehension of the "oneness of existence" *(wahdat al-wujûd)* in which the particularity of beings is annihilated like water dissolving in water or flame bursting into flame. In general, it may be said that Sufis removed the image of unveiling from its eschatological context and applied it to the inner journey of the seeker *(sâliq)* to see the truth *(al-haqq)* behind the veil, the visionary formulation of the mystical quest for union with the One. This does not mean to say that there is a categorical rejection of traditional eschatology on the part of Sufis, but only that their spiritual propensity for inwardness opened the way to a mystical interpretation that renders the eschaton more immediately present. In this sense, Sufism can be spoken of as having embraced an eschatology of and in the moment, mystical illumination in the present, the epiphany of the one true reality in the durationless instant *(ân* or *waqt)* that has no before or after, the interval that endures as that which elapses and elapses as that which endures.

Unveiling denotes the mystical awakening of the heart to the one true reality, a gnosis that is intricately connected to the secret of union. In one of the oldest and most celebrated Persian treatises on Sufism, *Kashf al-Mahjûb*, Abu al-Hasan al-Hujwîrî contrasts "absence" and "presence" by stating that the former "involves the sorrow of being veiled" and the latter "involves the joy of revelation."[20] In a second passage, he notes, the veils that obstruct one's knowledge of God are a result of ignorance; when ignorance is annihilated, veils vanish.[21] Apparently, this is the meaning of al-Hujwîrî's comment that "revelation (*mukâshafat*) implies the possibility of a veil (*hijâb*)";[22] that is, we can speak meaningfully of the revelation of truth only if it were previously veiled. In another passage, al-Hujwîrî uses a slightly different nomenclature to mark the two states of being: contraction of the heart is synonymous with agitation of longing in a state of occultation (*hijâb*), expansion of the calm of contemplation in a state of revelation (*kashf*).[23] The master of esoteric gnosis, accordingly, is one who peers beyond the veil of the veil-keepers in the quest for a vision of the face. By contrast, *majhub*, "veiled," assumes the negative connotation of one that is not spiritually illumined and therefore does not perceive the divine light without the veils of sentient and rational forms.

A plethora of other sources could have been cited to substantiate the point that the objective for one who walks the path is to rend the veil, to behold truth (*al-haqq*) in its naked form. If, however, truth has no image and no form, rending the veil conceals the face it reveals by revealing the face it conceals. Sufi masters, accordingly, conceived the image of lifting the veil along the lines of the ever-growing acceptance of the philosophical premise (rooted in the neoplatonic tradition discussed above) that the divine essence is unknowable and hence invisible. What would one see when one lifts the veil hiding the invisible if not another veil rendering the invisible visible? The conundrum yielded far-reaching paradoxical statements that enlighten the listener by way of silencing reason and shutting the mouth. Thus, al-Niffarî discerned that rending the veil—the ostensible goal of the mystical path—results in an overpowering of light that baffles the mind of created beings. "Knowings of the veil / cannot bear what appears / when the veil is torn."[24] To see the face behind the veil, one must be veiled from the unveiling; indeed, the one adroit in lifting the veils knows full well that throwing off the veil is itself a form of donning the veil. The paradox is articulated by al-Niffarî in a series of gnomic pronouncements:

> One you have seen Me, unveiling and the veil will be equal.
> You will not stand in vision until you see My veil as vision and My vision as veil.
> There is a veil that is not unveiled, and an unveiling that is not veiled. The veil that is not unveiled is knowledge through me, and the unveiling that is not veiled is knowledge through me.
> No veil remains: Then I saw all the eyes gazing at his face, staring. They see him in everything through which he veils himself. He said to me: They see me, and I veil them through their vision of Me from Me.[25]

Several centuries later—precisely in the period when kabbalah began to flourish in southern France and northern Spain—Muhyiddin Ibn al-'Arabî (1165–1240) elaborated the paradoxical mystery of the veil and its unveiling in a somewhat more technical philosophic tone commensurate with his speculative gnosis. "There is nothing in existence but veils hung down. Acts of perception attach themselves only to veils, which leave traces in the owner of the eye that perceives them."[26] Ephemeral contingencies are but veils hiding the eternal being, the necessary of existence, but it is through the concealment of these veils that the invisible is rendered visible. "Thus the Real becomes manifest by being veiled, so He is the Manifest/the Veiled. He is the Nonmanifest because of the veil, not because of you, and He is the Manifest because of you and the veil."[27] In another passage, Ibn al-'Arabî expresses the matter as a commentary on the *hadîth* that God possesses seventy veils of light and darkness:

> The dark and luminous veils through which the Real is veiled from the cosmos are only the light and the darkness by which the possible thing becomes qualified in its reality because it is a middle. . . . Were the veils to be lifted from the possible thing, possibility would be lifted, and the Necessary and the impossible would be lifted through the lifting of possibility. So the veils will remain forever hung down and nothing else is possible. . . . The veils will not be lifted when there is vision of God. Hence vision is through the veil, and inescapably so.[28]

The veil thus signifies the structure of secrecy basic to Sufism, envisioning the hidden secret revealed in the concealment of its revelation and concealed in the revelation of its concealment. Accordingly, the task is to discard the veils to reveal the truth, but if the veils were all discarded,

there truly would be no truth to see. The mandate to lift the veils, therefore, does not result in discarding all possible veils; indeed, there can be
no "final" veil to lift as there must always be another veil through which
the nonmanifest will be made manifest. In this respect, the Sufi sensibility remained faithful to the Qur'anic declaration that it is not fitting for
God to speak to a human "except by inspiration, from behind a veil, or
by the sending of a messenger" (Q 42:51), that is, by way of an intermediary that renders the unseen visible. What is unveiled in the unveiling
is not the face behind the veil but the veil before the face; that is, unveiling is the metaphorical depiction of removing the shells of ignorance that
blind one from seeing the truth of the veil in the veil of truth: God and
world are identical in their difference.

Kabbalistic Piety and Envisioning the Invisible

In consonance with the teachings of mystic visionaries in Islam and
Christianity, medieval kabbalists saw their primary task as imagining
what is without image, embodying that which is not a body. The faculty
that serves as the locus of the *coincidentia oppositorum* of form and formlessness, is the imagination, identified most frequently as the heart.
Through images in the heart, the divine, whose essence is incompatible
with all form, is manifest in the formlessness of the imaginal presence. As
the matter is expressed in one passage in the *Zohar*, the major compila-
tion of kabbalistic doctrine that began to take shape in the latter part of
the thirteenth century in Castile, a region of northern Spain, the *sefirot*,
the luminous emanations of the divine, are "ten holy crowns of the holy
name" (*asarah kitrin qaddishin di-shema qaddisha*).[29] In a second zoharic
passage, the sefirotic emanations are depicted as the multiple lights,
which collectively are the name of God, revealing the infinite radiance
that cannot be revealed:

> Thus I have seen sparks that glisten from the supernal spark, hidden of the
> hidden *[temira de-khol temirin]*. . . . [A]nd in the light of each and every gra-
> dation is revealed what is revealed *[itggalyya mah de-itggalyya]*, and all the
> lights are united . . . and one is not separated from the other. Each and
> every light of all the sparks, which are called arrayments of the king
> *[tiqqunei malka]* and crowns of the king *[kitrei malka]*, radiates and is united

with that innermost light that is within [*nehora dilego lego*] and is not separated from without, and thus everything rises to one gradation and everything is crowned in one matter, and one is not separated from the other, he and his name are one. The light that is revealed [*nehora deitggalyya*] is called the garment of the king [*levusha de-malka*], the innermost light that is within [*nehora dilego lego*] is the concealed light [*nehora satim*], and within it dwells the one that is not separate and is not revealed [*u-veih sharya hahu de-lo itpperash we-lo itggalyya*], and all of these sparks and all of these lights radiate from the holy ancient One [*atiqa qaddisha*], concealed of all concealed [*setima de-khol setimin*], the supernal spark [*botsina ila'ah*]. When all the lights that have emanated are contemplated, nothing is found but the supernal spark that is hidden and not revealed [*we-khad misttakkelan kullehu nehorin de-itppashshetan lo ishttekhah bar botsina ila'ah de-atmar we-lo itggalyya*].[30]

The name, which is comprised of the sefirotic gradations, the "glorious garments" (*levushin diqar*), "veritable garments" (*levushin qeshot*), "true arrayments" (*tiqqunei qeshot*), and "true sparks" (*botsinei qeshot*) that reveal the hidden light of the infinite, the "supernal spark" (*botsina ila'ah*), is configured in the imagination in potentially manifold semiotic deflections and ocular displacements, although the principal form by which it is imaged is an anthropos, the primal Adam in whose image the lower Adam was created.[31] "It has been taught: When all the holy crowns of the king [*kitrin qaddishin de-malka*] are arrayed in their arrayments, they are called *adam*, the image [*diyoqna*] that contains everything."[32] The paradox that the hidden God appears to human beings in multiple forms, including, most significantly, that of an anthropos, is the enduring legacy of the revelatory tradition that has influenced and challenged Judaism throughout the ages. Ironically, the iconoclastic constraint against the use of images in worshiping God has fostered some of the most daring imaginative representations of the divine in the history of religions. Indeed, the role of the imaginal construct to serve as a symbolic intermediary allowing for the imaging of the imageless God is attested in prophetic, apocalyptic, aggadic, and poetic texts, although it is developed and articulated most fully in medieval mystical literature, including, the esoteric works of the Rhineland Jewish Pietists, the theosophic kabbalah, exemplified by the various strata of zoharic literature, and in the prophetic kabbalah elaborated in the compositions of Abraham Abulafia and his disciples.

I shall illustrate the point from a passage in the mystical diary *Otsar Hayyim*, composed in the early part of the fourteenth century by Isaac of

Acre. Isaac reports that the method of contemplation that he received from the master of his generation[33] consisted of setting the image of the ten *sefirot* in one's mind, a process linked exegetically to the verse "I set YHWH before me always" (Ps 16:8). The psalmist's insistence that one have the letters YHWH in mind is interpreted kabbalistically as the necessity to conjure an image of the sefirotic potencies in the imagination, for the *sefirot* are contained within the name. The nature of that image is depicted, moreover, in anthropomorphic terms, for the presumption is that the name, which is the esoteric essence of Torah, may be configured as an anthropos, an idea anchored exegetically in the numerical equivalence of the word *adam* and the full spelling of the letters of the name, *yod-he-waw-he* (both equal 45). To be sure, as Isaac of Acre notes, the objective of the contemplative path is to be conjoined to Ein Sof, the infinite source of all that exists beyond all names, but the only way to attain that end is through the demarcated letters of the name. In Isaac's own words, "As long as I contemplate this ladder, which is the name of the holy One, blessed be he, I see my soul cleaving to Ein Sof."[34]

The name is the ladder that connects the kabbalist to that which is beyond the name, but there is no way to get beyond the name except through the name. This is the intent of Isaac's remark that he could visualize himself cleaving to Ein Sof, the otherwise-than-being that lies beyond all names, only as long as he was contemplating the four-letter name, which assumes the form of an anthropos in the imagination of one who contemplates. Consider as well Isaac's account of the meditational practice connected to vocalizing the names in the heart in his biblical commentary *Me'irat Einayim*: "After having intended their vocalization, one should intend in his heart that the ten *sefirot* are unified in him and all is unified in Ein Sof. . . . Moreover, I will include an intention regarding the unique name [*shem ha-meyuhad*] together with the intention of the vocalizations that were mentioned, and it is that I intend when I see in my heart the crown of the *yod* of the unique name, which is the tip of the *yod*, mentioned in the words of the rabbis, blessed be their memory, with respect to *Keter*, and the *yod* itself to *Hokhmah*, the *he* to *Teshuvah*, the *waw* to *Tif'eret* together with the six extremities, for it is their foundation, and the final *he* to *Atarah*, until Ein Sof."[35] Building on the contemplative visualization technique attested in earlier kabbalistic sources whereby the vocalization of the name, whose enunciation is prohibited, is envisioned in the heart, Isaac articulates the *kawwanah* associated with imagining the ten *sefirot* comprised in the letters of YHWH. However, the last words of the *Me'irat Einayim* passage concur with the aforecited remark in *Otsar Hayyim,* as in both texts the author asserts that the name, which is visualized in the imagination as an anthropos, is the way to the nameless, boundless, and imageless Ein-Sof. Since every human body is experienced in a particular gendered embodiment, the imaginal body of God will similarly display gender characteristics.

Impulse for Idolatry and Mystical Transgression

The enduring quest to attain a vision of the image of the imageless God in the mystical current of Judaism, Christianity, and Islam may be termed the impulse for idolatry that stubbornly lingers in the heart of monotheism, especially pertinent in the domain of liturgical practice. To be sure, this impulse is mitigated by the ultimate paradox that if the God seen is not the invisible God, then it is not God who has not been (un)seen. Nonetheless, from the mystical perspective well attested in the three faiths, the yearning to image what has no image lies deep in the poetic sensibility of the religious soul. Every image of God conjured in the imagination may be considered an "icon of the invisible God."

The ideal of mystical contemplation culminates in the imageless vision of God as inaccessible light, light beyond light, modes of discourse indebted to neoplatonic speculation. From this vantage point contemplation is best characterized in apophatic terms as unknowing, unseeing, unsaying, fostering, as it were, "imageless prayer" as the supreme form of worship, which supersedes the conventional, sanctioned mode of liturgy. Yet, Jewish, Christian, and Muslim mystics could not ignore the kataphatic legacy of their respective scriptural traditions and thus access to the formless is always mediated through the particular forms of the given cultural context. The blending of the apophatic and kataphatic has produced a unique approach that is still relevant in the human pursuit of ultimate reality. From the medieval mystical figures in all three religions we learn that there is no naked truth to be disrobed, for the truth can only be apprehended as it is garbed in imaginal forms reflective of the physical universe. The mystical ladder of contemplation culminates in the paradox of thought thinking what cannot be thought, darkness illumined as darkness, immeasurability measured as immeasurable. The cogency of this argument notwithstanding, mystics have repeatedly emphasized that there is no way to visualize the formless except by means of form just as the nameless cannot be pronounced except through the countless names by which it is evoked. The combination of the apophatic and kataphatic bestowed by the history of mysticism has the potential to foster the affirmation of the underlying unity of all faiths without minimizing the intense devotion of those committed to each particular path. In the mystical worldview, one walks the path to get beyond the path, but there is no getting beyond the path unless one constantly walks the path.

Discussion Questions

1. What is mysticism?

2. How do Judaic, Christian, and Muslim mysticism cover the same ground, and how are they to be differentiated from one another?

3. What does mysticism in Judaic Qabbalah owe to Muslim and Christian mystical concepts? What does it contribute?

PART FOUR

HISTORIC ENCOUNTERS

CHAPTER 8

LATIN CHRISTIANITY, THE CRUSADES, AND THE ISLAMIC RESPONSE

James A. Brundage

Expeditions of European Christian warriors, whom later generations would refer to as crusaders, began to invade the Holy Land toward the end of the eleventh century. These warriors, however, thought of themselves as pilgrims and their contemporaries long continued to describe them that way. They believed that their campaigns in the Eastern Mediterranean lands associated with the life of Jesus and his early followers were a sacred mission. The purpose of that mission was to secure control of sacred regions, and especially of the holy city of Jerusalem, whose sanctity had been sullied ever since they fell into the hands of Muslim conquerors. Jerusalem, one of them wrote,

> Is held to be holier and more notable than all the other cities and places throughout the world, not because it is holy in itself, or by itself, but because it has been glorified by the presence of God himself, and our Lord Jesus Christ and his holy mother, and by the dwelling there, the doctrine, the preaching, and the martyrdom of patriarchs, prophets, Apostles, and other holy people.[1]

Pilgrimages

Devout Europeans began to make pilgrimages to Jerusalem and to write accounts of their journeys as early as the fourth century C.E. Following the invasion of Syria and Palestine by Turkish tribes in the middle of the eleventh century, journeys to the Holy City became increasingly dangerous. For this reason pilgrims, who had previously traveled as individuals or in small groups, commenced to join together in larger bands in order to be able to ward off attacks by Muslim marauders who infested the countryside. As the pilgrim Saewulf testified:

> Saracens, who are continually plotting an ambush against Christians, were hiding in the caves of the hills and among rocky caverns. They were awake day and night, always keeping a look-out for someone to attack, whether because he had not enough people with him, or because he was fatigued enough to leave a space between himself and his party. Sometimes the Saracens could be seen everywhere in the neighborhood, and sometimes they disappeared. Anyone who has taken that road can see how many human bodies there are in the road and next to the road, and there are countless corpses which have been torn up by wild beasts.[2]

A pilgrimage was a religious quest, as indeed it still is. Saint Paul exhorted his congregation at Corinth to conduct themselves in this life as pilgrims traveling to God (2 Cor 5:6-8). Elsewhere he declared that Christians ought to comport themselves as pilgrims and strangers on earth (Heb 11:13). Medieval confessors and other church authorities often required persons guilty of serious sins to go on pilgrimage to the Holy Land as part of the penance they owed to God in order to atone for their sins. Because of its penitential character, pilgrims had traditionally made their journeys unarmed, bringing with them only a purse to carry their money and a few belongings, since it was regarded as unseemly for them to bring more than the barest necessities, and a staff to help them negotiate the rough roads they could expect to encounter.

The perils of travel in Syria and Palestine by the late eleventh century, however, made pilgrimages so hazardous that bands of pilgrims commenced to bring along horses in order to escape from perilous situations speedily and to carry weapons to fight off assailants. When Muslim bandits attacked participants in the great German pilgrimage of 1064–1065, for example,

> The pilgrims decided to take up arms and with weapons in hand they courageously fought back. The enemy, more indignant than ever, pressed the attack more vigorously, for they saw that the pilgrims, who they had thought would not attempt anything against them, were resisting manfully. For three whole days both sides fought with full force. Our men, though handicapped by hunger, thirst, and lack of sleep, were fighting for their salvation and their lives. The enemy gnashed their teeth like ravening

wolves, since it seemed that they were not to be allowed to swallow the prey which they had grasped in their jaws.[3]

At the same time that pilgrimages were starting to become militarized, a second element of the mixture that would later produce the crusades was also taking on increased prominence in Western Christian thought. This was the idea of holy war.

Holy War

Christian attitudes toward war and violence were ambivalent from the outset. Some passages in the Gospels portray Jesus as counseling his contemporaries to avoid wrath, anger, and bloodshed. He advised his followers to turn the other cheek, to forgive those who wronged them, and declared that those who lived by the sword would perish by it (Matt 5:39, 41, 7:1, and 26:52; Rom 12:19, 13:13). Yet he also maintained that he came to bring not peace but the sword (Matt 10:34).

The medieval church inherited both of these traditions. Eleventh-century church authorities enthusiastically organized efforts to limit warfare. These movements, known as the Peace and Truce of God, began in France toward the end of the tenth century. A series of church councils, commencing with the Synod of Charroux in 989, forbade Christians to engage in killing or wounding other people or destroying others' property, especially on the holy days of the church year. These serious sins, were punishable by the most severe sanctions the church could muster.

Soldiers returning from battle might be required to atone for their actions by doing penance for shedding blood, even if they fought in self-defense or to defend third parties. A synod of Norman bishops, for example, imposed these penances on soldiers in William the Conqueror's army after the Battle of Hastings in 1066:

> Anyone who knows that he killed a man in the great battle must do penance for one year for each man that he killed. Anyone who wounded a man, and does not know whether he killed him or not, must do penance for forty days for each man he thus struck (if he can remember the number), either continuously or at intervals. Anyone who does not know the number of those he wounded or killed must, at the discretion of his bishop, do penance for one day in each week for the remainder of his life; or, if he can, let him redeem his sin by a perpetual alms, either by building or by endowing a church.[4]

The conqueror himself founded and richly endowed a new monastery. He directed that Battle Abbey should be situated on the spot where the battle had taken place, so that its monks could pray in perpetuity for the souls of those killed at Hastings and thus relieve the conqueror of the guilt he had incurred through the conquest. Yet at the same time, the church blessed the swords and other weapons that Christian warriors employed and likewise gave its blessing to knights.

When Muslim armies began to invade Western Europe, beginning in the eighth century, popes reacted by recruiting armies to repel the invaders with force and arms. Although Christian armies succeeded in turning back Moorish advances north of the Pyrenees, Muslim forces occupied most of the Iberian peninsula. Recovery of this vast territory from Islamic control became a long-term goal of papal policy. Generation after generation successive popes continued to call upon Christian rulers to take up arms to expel the Muslims from Spain and Portugal and to establish Christian control of the region. They ultimately succeeded but only after seven hundred years of trying.

Religious authorities justified these calls to arms on the grounds that the struggle to eject the Muslims from Christian Europe was a matter of self-defense. Spain had, after all, been a Christian country for centuries before the Islamic invasions began and it was unseemly, they argued, to allow Muslims to exercise authority over a population that remained overwhelmingly Christian. Christian warriors, they asserted, would not sin by using violence in such a holy cause. Indeed, they had a sacred obligation to liberate Spanish Christians from the control of infidel rulers.

These arguments had a theological foundation. Venerable authorities, most particularly St. Augustine (d. 430), had long ago established the principle that Christians were entitled to use violence to defend themselves in a just war. According to the widely accepted definition of Saint Isidore of Seville (ca. 560–636), "A war is just when it is fought by command [of a lawful ruler] in order to recover property or to repel attackers."[5] Under the terms of this definition, it was argued that wars to recover territory previously held by Christians and to replace Muslim rulers with Christian princes were not sinful; indeed, they were praiseworthy.

Church authorities in the tenth and eleventh centuries began to go even further than this. Some of them commenced to assert that making war against enemies of the Christian religion was not only just, but also a pious act that merited spiritual rewards. Several popes sought to attract recruits to these armies by exempting participants from the penalties for homicide and assuring them that their sins would be forgiven.

Byzantium in Crisis

A new theater of conflict between Christian and Muslim forces began to open up in 1071, when the forces of the Seljuk Turks virtually annihilated the main army of the Byzantine Empire, the greatest Christian power in the Mediterranean world, at the Battle of Manzikert. The disaster at Manzikert practically eliminated the empire's defenses in Asia Minor. Taking advantage of the military anarchy and civil wars that subsequently broke out in Byzantium, bands of Turkish soldiers flooded into the region. To make matters worse, other Turkish peoples, the Pechenegs and the Uzes, hammered Byzantium's northern defenses in the Balkan peninsula, burned and plundered towns and villages, and reduced much of the countryside to ruin.

Desperate to fight off these multiple attacks, the emperor Alexis Comnenos (1081–1118) sought help from his fellow Christians in Western Europe. This was not entirely a novelty. Earlier emperors had long made it a practice to supplement their armies with mercenary soldiers recruited from various sources, including Western Europe. Faced with immanent peril from the Muslim Turks on two fronts, the emperor apparently concluded that the time had come to play the religious card. He dispatched ambassadors to seek out Pope Urban II (1088–1099). His emissaries caught up with the pope early in March 1095 at Piacenza in northern Italy, where Urban was presiding over a church council. There the emperor's representatives urgently appealed to the pope to use his influence to encourage Western Christian soldiers to enlist in the Byzantine army. The empire, they reported, was threatened with disaster. Immediate assistance was vital in order to save the empire's Christian population from subjection to Muslim control.

Although relationships between the Byzantine and Roman churches had been uneasy for many years, Pope Urban was evidently much impressed by the gravity of the situation, for he invited the emperor's ambassadors to address the prelates assembled at the council. The imperial envoys took the opportunity to paint for their audience a fearful picture of the likely consequences of a Muslim conquest of Eastern Christendom. There is some reason to believe that they may have stressed that Jerusalem and the Lord's sepulcher were already being defiled by infidel hands. Even more lamentable consequences, they maintained, were sure to follow if help was not forthcoming quickly. United Christian resistance was imperative, they told the assembled bishops, to ward off utter disaster for the Christian faith. Pope Urban himself reinforced the ambassadors' message by urging the members of the council to do their utmost when they returned home to encourage the faithful to respond to their pleas.

We can only infer what may have been passing through Pope Urban's mind during the next several months, but by the end of the summer of 1095 he had almost certainly decided to take further action in response to the message that he had heard at Piacenza. His own predecessors and the patriarchs of Constantinople had been at odds with one another ever since 1054, when a papal legate had excommunicated Patriarch Michael Keroularios (1043–1058). Although that quarrel had been more or less patched up, each side continued to be suspicious of the other. The claims of papal supremacy in the church advanced by Urban's immediate predecessors had alarmed Byzantine churchmen, who felt that Roman ambitions threatened their own rather different theological views and traditions. It may well be, although we cannot know for sure, that Pope Urban saw the Byzantine appeal for military assistance as an opportunity to assert papal control over the churches of the Eastern Empire.

Proclamation of the First Crusade

What we can be certain of is that during the summer of 1095 Urban crossed the Alps and returned to the Midi, the region in the south of France where he had been born and raised. On August 15, when he was at Le Puy, Urban summoned the French bishops and selected members of the French nobility to meet with him in council at Clermont on Sunday, November 18. When the council convened several hundred bishops, archbishops, abbots, and other ecclesiastical dignitaries were present. For ten days the prelates discussed mainly ecclesiastical business, much of it having to do with church discipline.

The pope then announced that on Tuesday, November 27, he would address a plenary session of the council, to which both clergy and laity were invited. We will never know exactly what Urban said in the sermon that he delivered on that occasion. A half dozen accounts of it survive, three of them by eyewitnesses, although they were not written down until some time after the event. Among the more reliable of them is the version provided by Robert the Monk:

When the ecclesiastical business of the gathering had been disposed of, the lord Pope went out to a wide and spacious field, since the crowds could not easily be accommodated in any building. There the pope addressed the whole gathering in these words:

"Frenchmen! You who come from across the Alps; you who have been singled out by God and who are loved by him as is shown by your many accomplishments; you who are set apart from all other peoples by the location of your country, by your Catholic faith, and by the honor of the holy church; we address these words, this sermon to you!

We want you to know the melancholy reasons that have brought us among you and the peril that threatens you and all the faithful. Distressing news has come to us (as has often happened) from the region of Jerusalem and from the city of Constantinople; news that the people of the Persian kingdom, an alien people, a race completely foreign to God, 'A generation of false aims, of a spirit that broke faith with God,'[6] has invaded Christian territory and has devastated this territory with pillage, fire, and the sword. The Persians have taken some of these Christians as captives into their own country; they have destroyed others with cruel tortures. They have completely destroyed some of God's churches and they have converted others to the uses of their own cult. They ruin the altars with filth and defilement. They circumcise Christians and smear the blood from the circumcision over the altars or throw it into the baptismal fonts. They are pleased to kill others by cutting open their bellies, extracting the end of their intestines, and tying it to a stake. Then, with flogging, they drive their victims around the stake until, when their viscera have spilled out, they fall dead to the ground. They tie others, again, to stakes and shoot arrows at them; they seize others, stretch out their necks, and try to see whether or not they can cut off their heads with a single blow of a naked sword. And what shall I say about the shocking rape of women? On this subject it would perhaps be worse to speak than to keep silent. These Persians have so dismembered the kingdom of the Greeks and have sequestered so much of it that it would be impossible to cross the conquered territory in a two-month journey.

Who is to revenge all this, who is to repair this damage, if you do not do it? You are the people upon whom God has bestowed glory in arms, greatness of spirit, bodily agility, and the courage to humble the "proud locks"[7] of those who resist you.

Rise up and remember the many deeds of your ancestors, the prowess and greatness of Charlemagne, of his son Louis, and of your other kings, who destroyed pagan kingdoms and planted the holy church in their territories. You should be especially aroused by the fact that the Holy Sepulcher of the Lord our Savior is in the hands of these unclean people, who shamefully mistreat and sacrilegiously defile the Holy Places with their filth. Oh, most valiant knights! Descendants of unconquered ancestors! Remember the courage of your forefathers and do not dishonor them. . . .

Jerusalem is the navel of the world, a land that is more fruitful than any other, a land that is like another paradise of delights. This is the land that the Redeemer of mankind illuminated by his coming, adorned by his life, consecrated by his passion, redeemed by his death, and sealed by his burial. This royal city, situated in the middle of the world, is now held captive by his enemies and is made a servant by those who know not God for the ceremonies of the heathen. It looks and hopes for freedom; it begs unceasingly that you will come to its aid. It looks for help from you especially because, as we have said, God has bestowed glory in arms upon you more than on any other nation. Undertake this journey, therefore, for the remission of your sins, with the assurance of 'glory that cannot fade'[8] in the kingdom of heaven." When Pope Urban had said these and many similar things in his urbane sermon, those who were present were so moved that, as one man, all of them together shouted: "God wills it! God wills it!"[9]

Once the shouting had died down, the pope gave instructions about the organization of the expedition he had called for. Participants were to sew a cross on their outer garments as a symbol of their mission. Urban set an official departure date on August 15, 1096, in order to allow time to recruit additional volunteers and to permit those who took part to make the necessary arrangements for their journey, which he expected them to finance out of their own resources. The pope also named a papal legate, Bishop Adhemar of Le Puy, to accompany the army as his personal representative.

Finally, the council adopted a canon that authorized a spiritual reward for those who joined the expedition that the pope had proclaimed: "Whoever shall undertake the journey to liberate the church of God at Jerusalem solely out of devotion and not for the sake of honor or wealth may count that expedition in place of all penance (Ps. 77:8)."[10] This was the modest beginning of what came to be known as the crusade indulgence that was greatly expanded and elaborated by later popes and church councils.

We know, both from the accounts of Urban's sermon at Clermont and from letters that he subsequently wrote to encourage recruitment for the crusade, that the pope expected the expedition to consist of primarily professional soldiers, noblemen, and knights who would fight on horseback, together with trained infantrymen who would fight on foot, although he doubtless anticipated that the soldiers would bring along servants, blacksmiths, armorers, and other auxiliary personnel. What he almost certainly did not anticipate was the wave of religious enthusiasm for the venture whipped up by unofficial preachers and demagogues who encouraged vast crowds of other people with little or no military experience or training to begin almost immediately to set out for Jerusalem long in advance of the expeditions of knights and nobles.

The Popular Crusades

The throngs who made up these "popular crusades," as modern historians usually call them, were drawn mainly from the urban lower classes and in smaller numbers from the rural peasantry of northern France and the Rhineland. The best known of these popular expeditions was led by a fiery preacher known as Peter the Hermit. Contemporary descriptions of Peter's appearance verge on the repulsive. He was short, with a swarthy complexion on his long, bony face that, like the rest of his person, he seldom washed. His habits were ascetic: he went barefoot and rode from one place to another on the back of a donkey. He limited his diet to fish and wine and he was known as "the Hermit" because he habitually wore the style of cloak usually associated with solitary holy men. Despite his unattractive appearance, Peter was clearly an eloquent and persuasive preacher who gathered a following that contemporaries estimated in the thousands.

Numerous as they were, Peter's followers were totally undisciplined and completely inept as a military force. Although they managed to reach Constantinople, after having lost most of the money and supplies they had brought with them to thieves in the Balkans, Alexis Comnenos hurriedly dispatched them out of his capital and had his forces set them down in camp in Asia Minor. When they attempted to raid Turkish outposts in the vicinity, a Turkish retaliatory force quickly wiped out all but a handful of them. Peter himself was among the few survivors and ultimately joined the main crusading forces.

Other bands of popular crusaders were even less successful than Peter the Hermit's followers. Ill-prepared, poorly equipped, and undisciplined, most of the participants faltered and turned back home before even reaching Byzantine territory, and none of them managed to confront, much less defeat, the Muslim foes they had hoped to conquer. Three of these groups instead attacked Jewish communities in the cities of the Moselle and Rhine Valleys.

The First Crusade

While these horrors transpired in the late spring and early summer of 1096, the main crusading armies were still getting organized. The knights and nobles who would form the core of the fighting force were for the most part men of high position and substantial property whose preparations for the journey were accordingly more complex than those of the popular crusaders had been.

Leading members of the expeditions that ultimately combined to form the crusading army required a great deal of time to enlist the followers, in some cases thousands of them, who would accompany them on the journey. This involved lengthy and complex negotiations, not only to persuade lesser knights and noblemen to join forces with them, but also to work out the complicated logistics that the enterprise entailed. They needed to agree on the equipment, horses, pack animals, infantrymen, and supporting staff that would accompany each of them. It was imperative to make detailed plans about where and when they would rendezvous to commence their journey, as well as routes they would follow from that point.

Beyond this, participants needed to raise enormous amounts of ready money to support themselves and their followers. Since most of their assets were tied up in land, they did this by selling, leasing, or mortgaging their lands in return for cash. They frequently made these arrangements with nearby religious communities, with which many of them had long-standing ties. Thus, for example, Bernard Morel pledged a farm to the convent of religious women at Marcigny in return for a loan:

> On condition that while he remains in Jerusalem, where he was wanting to go, the nuns of Marcigny should take half the fruits of the land as their own and should put the other half on one side and should keep an account of how much that half is worth so that, if he returns, he should receive his share.[11]

In order to make binding deals of this sort, an intending crusader needed to persuade his feudal lord, wife, children, in-laws, and other family members to consent to these and similar arrangements. These people after all also had an interest in the disposition of landed property and certainly did not wish to see it permanently alienated or themselves impoverished. Nor could close family members be left without protection and means of support for the indeterminate time that a crusader was going to be away, especially since he was departing on a dangerous expedition from which he might never return. All of this took tact, as well as time.

Then, too, crusaders needed to acquire or put in order all the weapons, armor, shields, saddles, clothing, tents, bedding, pots, pans, and other equipment they were bound to need on their journey. They likewise felt the need to make spiritual preparations, often quite elaborate ones, before they departed so that they could be assured that the prayers and blessings of those who remained behind would follow them and support them while they were away.

Nor should we underestimate the emotional toll that crusading exacted from participants and their loved ones. To leave home, wives, children, and lovers for an enterprise of unknown duration, about which the only certainty was that it would be difficult, expensive, hazardous, and quite possibly fatal can never have been an easy decision, as numerous vernacular poems make clear:

To have perfect joy in paradise
I must leave the land I love so much,
Where she lives whom I thank every day.
Her body is noble and spirited, her face fresh and lovely;
And my true heart surrenders all to her.
But my body must take its leave of her:
I am departing for the place where God suffered death
To ransom us on a Friday.
Sweet love, I have great sorrow in my heart Now that at last I must leave you, With whom I have found so much good, such tenderness, Joy and gaiety to charm me.
But fortune by her power has made me Exchange my joy for the sadness and sorrow
I will feel for you many nights and many days. Thus will I go to serve my creator. . . .

Good Lord God, if I for you
Leave the country where she is that I love so,
Grant us in heaven everlasting joy My love and me, through your mercy,
And grant her the strength to love me,

So that she will not forget me in my long absence,
For I love her more than anything in the world
And I feel so sad about her that my heart is breaking.[12]

Crusading, in short, was far from easy financially, politically, socially, or emotionally and demanded deep resources of time, energy, and resilience. It also required unyielding commitment and iron determination to face up to the prospect of a dangerous journey of unknowable duration into strange lands, surrounded by foreign peoples speaking incomprehensible tongues, in order to fight unknown enemies who had already proved their prowess by savaging the greatest power of the Mediterranean world. No sensible person undertook this lightly or on a whim. This is not to say that crusading armies were filled solely with God-fearing heroes and idealists, although there were plenty of those. Their ranks also contained a generous leavening of adventurers, fortune-seekers, and outright villains. Although many went voluntarily, others enlisted because they had no choice. Some went because judges or confessors ordered them to, others, because of social pressures from families, feudal lords, or their peers.

The five main expeditions that would comprise the army of the first crusade began to assemble for their journey in the late summer of 1096. Each of them traveled separately under its own leader and followed overland routes through the Balkans to Constantinople. The earliest contingent to depart, which was also the smallest, left in mid-August. It consisted principally of knights from the region around Paris and was led by Hugh of Vermandois (d. 1101), the brother of the excommunicated King Philip I of France. Shortly thereafter Godfrey of Bouillon (d. 1100), Duke of Lower Lorraine, followed with a considerably larger force. The third expedition, made up of Norman adventurers from southern Italy and Sicily, and led by Prince Bohemund of Taranto (d. 1111), did not leave until October 1096. The largest group of all was commanded by the rich and elderly Raymond of Toulouse (d. 1105), Count of Saint Gilles. His followers, recruited principally from the south of France and accompanied by the papal legate, Adhemar of Le Puy, also departed in October. The last group to leave was a Norman army recruited from Brittany, Flanders, and Normandy. They were jointly commanded by a princely trio, Duke Robert of Normandy, the eldest son of William the Conqueror; his brother-in-law, Count Stephen of Blois (d. 1102), who was the son-in-law of William the Conqueror, and Count Robert of Flanders, a cousin of the Norman duke.

As they arrived at Constantinople during the winter of 1096 and the spring of 1097, the emperor Alexis demanded that the leaders of each group swear an oath that during their expedition they would not endanger Byzantine interests and that they would hand back to Byzantine control any former Byzantine territories that they might capture. A few of them readily agreed to do this, but others resisted. They distrusted the motives behind this demand and feared that the oath would subject them to imperial control. All of them eventually consented, however reluctantly. Even so, relations between Byzantium and the crusading leaders were strained from this point forward.

Once the difficulties over the oath had been settled, Alexis had each group ferried across the straits to camp in Asia Minor until the remaining crusading armies appeared. Once the Norman princes finally arrived in May 1097, the military operations of the crusade began in earnest. They first attacked the city of Nicaea, which they were able to take only with Byzantine assistance in mid-June. From there they set out across the arid Anatolian plains, where a major Turkish force attempted to ambush them. The Turks, perhaps misled by their easy victory over Peter the Hermit's band the previous summer, sorely underestimated the size and the strength of the main crusading armies. By a combination of skillful leadership and good luck the crusaders were able to turn the attempted ambush into a rout of the principal Turkish field army at the beginning of July and from that point onward encountered little serious resistance until October 1097, when they arrived at the city of Antioch.

Antioch proved a formidable obstacle. Its defenders were able to fight off attempts at frontal assault. Its walls were redoubtable and the crusading armies lacked the siege machinery necessary to break them down. The size of the city was so vast that the crusaders could not surround it and starve it into submission. Yet they could not afford to bypass Antioch, for until this city was in friendly hands no Christian army campaigning along the coast of Syria and Palestine could count itself safe. The crusading army settled in to a prolonged siege that wore on for more than seven months. The impasse only ended when Bohemund succeeded in contacting an officer among the defenders. This man agreed for a price to see to it that on the night of June 3, 1098, no guards would be posted along one section of the city's walls where he was in command. Bohemund and a few of his men were then able to climb unopposed over the wall. Once they had dispatched the guards on the adjoining sectors of the wall, Bohemund's men opened the gates to the remainder of their forces, who poured into the city. The crusaders proceeded to slaughter the defenders and other inhabitants of the city indiscriminately, which was (and long remained) the customary fate of the population of besieged towns that had refused to surrender. One of Bohemund's men described the carnage: "All the squares of the city were filled with the bodies of the dead and no one could stay there because of the terrible stench. One could not walk through the city streets without treading upon the bodies of the slain."[13]

After fighting off a late-arriving relief force from Mosul, the crusaders conducted mopping-up operations in the region around Antioch and then settled down to enjoy the fruits of their victory. Their leaders enjoyed them so long in fact that after six months of relative idleness their soldiers became restless and demanded that they push on to Jerusalem.

The crusading armies finally departed at the end of November 1098, after more than a year at Antioch. They made slow progress through southern Syria and Lebanon and chose to bypass the strongly held cities along the coast. They reached the northern borders of Palestine on May 19, 1099, and on the evening of June 7 they camped within sight of their final goal.

Jerusalem was at this point under Egyptian control, and its capture presented formidable problems for the crusaders. The city was heavily fortified, and its defenders, who had ample warning of the crusaders' approach, had laid in abundant stocks of provisions. They had also scoured the nearby countryside, burning the crops in the fields, poisoning or blocking up wells, and destroying any food supplies that they could not use themselves. A prolonged siege, such as the one at Antioch, was simply impractical, especially since the extreme heat of summer was about to set in.

After an initial assault had failed to breach the city's walls, the army settled down to build the kinds of siege machines that they had lacked at Antioch. They were able to do this now because shortly after they arrived at Jerusalem a Genoese fleet had put in at the nearby port of Jaffa. The fleet provided them not only with food and extra manpower, but also with the timber they needed to construct catapults and siege towers that they could push on log rollers up to the city's walls. After a month of labor their new equipment was ready.

Before beginning their attack on Jerusalem the crusaders made their spiritual preparations for battle by a three-day fast, followed by a penitential procession around the city's walls, while the Muslim defenders jeered and spat at them. Spurred on by this, the crusaders rolled their siege towers toward the city's walls and began the final attack on the evening of July 13. Fighting continued through the night and the next day. The final breakthrough occurred late in the following morning:

> At dawn on Friday [July 15] we attacked the city from all sides without being able to make any headway. We were all trembling and stunned. At the approach of the hour at which our Lord Jesus Christ deigned to suffer on the cross for us, our knights in the tower, namely Duke Godfrey and his brother, Count Eustace, made a fierce attack. Then one of our knights named Lethold climbed over the city wall. As soon as he ascended all the city's defenders fled from the wall. Our men followed, killing and beheading them all the way to the Temple of Solomon. There was such slaughter there that our men waded in blood up to their ankles·. The enemy fought most vigorously for a whole day and their blood flowed through the Temple. Finally the pagans were overcome·. Soon our men were running all around the city, seizing gold and silver, horses and mules, and houses filled with all kinds of goods.
>
> Our men took counsel and decided that everyone should pray and give alms so that God might choose for them whomever He pleased to rule over the others and govern the city. They ordered that all the dead Saracens should be cast out of the city because of the great stench, since the city was filled with their corpses. The living Saracens dragged the dead outside the gates and made heaps of them as large as houses. No one ever saw or heard of such a slaughter of pagan peoples, for funeral pyres were formed of them like pyramids and no one knows their number save God alone.[14]

With Jerusalem in their control, the crusaders needed to create a government for the city. After a week of looting and rejoicing following Jerusalem's capture, the leaders of the crusading forces gathered to decide what to do. They rejected a proposal from the clergy who accompanied them that only a cleric could be an appropriate ruler for the Holy City. After some wrangling they chose instead one of their own number, Godfrey of Bouillon, to take charge as the first ruler of what would soon come to be known as the Latin Kingdom of Jerusalem. A few days later they chose Arnulf Malecorne (d. 1118) as patriarch of Jerusalem and put him in control of the Holy Sepulcher and the city's other churches. Arnulf straightaway took steps to establish Latin services throughout the city, to the dismay of the local Christian population, whose Greek, Armenian, and Syrian clergy were banished not only from the sepulcher but also from most of the city's other shrines and churches.

Immediately following his election, King Godfrey rallied the crusading forces to face one last military crisis. A formidable Egyptian army was already moving toward Jerusalem to try to regain control of the city and Godfrey was determined to intercept them on the road. He and the bulk of the crusading forces, accompanied by Patriarch Arnulf, set out on August 9 and soon learned that the main Egyptian force was camped further down the coast near the city of Ascalon. After a brief rest to regroup and plan their strategy, the crusaders made their way as unobtrusively as possible toward the enemy during the night of August 11. Before dawn on August 12 they took up positions in the hills above the Egyptian camp on al-Majdal plain. At daybreak they swooped down and took the Egyptian army totally by surprise. The enemy's resistance was scattered and ineffective and virtually the entire Egyptian force was slaughtered in their camp. One group managed to break out and took refuge in a nearby grove of Sycamore trees. The crusaders set this afire and the escapees all burned to death.

Probably even more gratifying than victory itself, at least from the individual crusader's point of view, the soldiers were able to divide among themselves an immense amount of booty, including huge stores of gold and jewels, as well as horses, weapons, tents, and a host of delicacies. On August 14 they returned to Jerusalem in a triumphal procession.

The Latin States in the Holy Land

Their work accomplished, the crusading army now began to break up. Most of the expedition's members were anxious to return home to the wives, children, families, and friends whom they had not seen for three years. They typically spent a few days visiting the various shrines and wonders of the Holy Land. Many made a point of bathing in the river Jordan. Those who could picked up relics (a few of which may even have been genuine) and other mementos. They collected palms to bring back home as symbols that they had successfully completed their mission. Pilgrims returning from the Holy Land had long been known as Palmers. By the end of August the departures had begun.

Only a few chose to settle in the East. Some joined with Raymond of Saint Gilles in attacks upon some of the coastal cities that they had

bypassed on their way to Jerusalem. These campaigns ultimately succeeded in creating a crusader state known as the County of Tripoli which
linked the Kingdom of Jerusalem with the principality that Bohemund
had created in the region around Antioch. Others joined Baldwin of
Boulogne, who carved out a principality for himself in the Tigris-
Euphrates Valley with its capital at Edessa. Most of the veterans of the
first crusade who remained in the East settled in the Latin Kingdom of
Jerusalem, which they gradually enlarged through a lengthy series of campaigns in the years following 1099.

The number of Latins resident in the crusading states fluctuated constantly. Each spring, once the uncertain winter weather and its attendant
hazards at sea had begun to disappear, fleets of ships set out from Europe
bound for the Latin East. These fleets brought pilgrims and merchants,
but they also regularly carried soldiers who came to help defend the Holy
Land. Many of them, too, hoped to scout out the possibilities of acquiring land and career opportunities where experienced military men were
constantly in short supply. Most stayed only for the fighting season from
May to October and then returned to the West. Some wintered over and
returned home the following year. A few settled permanently.

Those who stayed for the long term soon began to assimilate to their
new neighbors and their surroundings. They depended heavily on the
indigenous inhabitants, who mainly spoke Arabic, Greek, or Armenian,
for the labor force to work their fields, clean their houses and stables, sell
them food and other daily necessities, cook their meals, and tend to most
of the menial tasks of daily life. Permanent settlers consequently found it
necessary to learn the local languages and many of them adopted native
dress, as well as the dietary habits and social customs of the region. One
of these settlers, Fulcher of Chartres, a chaplain to two of the leaders of
the first crusade, described the process in these terms:

> I pray you, consider and reflect on how God has in our times changed West
> into East. For we, who were occidentals, have now become Orientals. The
> man who was a Roman or a Frank has, in this land, been turned into a
> Galilean or a Palestinian. He who was once a citizen of Reims or of
> Chartres has now become a citizen of Tyre or Antioch. We have already
> forgotten the places where we were born; many of us either do not know
> them or have never even heard of them. One among us now has his own
> houses and retainers, just as if he possessed them through hereditary or
> family right. Another takes as his wife, not a woman of his own stock, but
> rather a Syrian or Armenian, or even, occasionally, a Saracen who has

obtained the grace of baptism. One man may possess vineyards, while another has farms. Men address one another in turn in the speech and idiom of various languages. The several languages of various nations are common here and one joins faith with men whose forefathers were strangers. For it is written: "The lion and ox shall eat straw side by side." He who was a foreigner is now just like a native. The interloper has been made into a resident. We are followed here, from day to day, by our neighbors and parents, who abandon, though reluctantly, all their possessions. Those who were needy have here been enriched by God. Those who had a few pennies, here possess countless Bezants. He who had not a village, here possesses a God-given city. Why should one who has found the East to be like this return to the West? Nor does God wish to burden with poverty those who have vowed to follow (or rather pursue) Him with their crosses. You see, therefore, that this is a great miracle, most astonishing to the whole world. Who has ever heard of such a thing? For God wishes to make us all rich and to draw us to himself as the dearest of friends. Since He desires this, we also willingly desire it. We shall do what pleases Him with a humble and benign heart, so that we may reign happily with him forever.[15]

While permanent settlers in the Latin States were usually able to adjust over time to conditions in their new home, those who came for shorter periods, whether as members of a fresh crusading expedition or as temporary visitors, often found it difficult or even impossible to fit into the physical and cultural environment in which they found themselves. They found conditions of life in the Near East bewildering, and they were rarely prepared to accommodate themselves to the unfamiliar practices and folkways of the region. Their problems were particularly acute when they first encountered the religious observances of the Muslim population. An elderly Syrian gentleman Usamah ibn-Munqidh (1095–1188) tells us in his memoirs about an encounter with one newly arrived Westerner in Jerusalem:

Everyone who is a fresh emigrant from the Frankish lands is ruder in character than those who have become acclimatized and have held long association with the Moslems. Here is an illustration of their rude character.

Whenever I visited Jerusalem I always entered the Aqsa Mosque, beside which stood a small mosque which the Franks had converted into a church. When I used to enter the Aqsa Mosque, which was occupied by the Templars, who were my friends, the Templars would evacuate the little adjoining mosque so that I might pray in it. One day I entered this mosque, repeated the first formula, "Allah is great," and stood up in the act of praying, upon which one of the Franks rushed on me, got hold of me and turned my face eastward saying, "This is the way thou shouldst pray!" A group of Templars hastened to him, seized him and repelled him from me. I resumed my prayer. The same man, while the others were otherwise busy, rushed once more on me and turned my face eastward, saying, "This is the way thou shouldst pray!" The Templars again came in to him and expelled him. They apologized to me, saying "This is a stranger who has only recently arrived from the land of the Franks and he has never before seen anyone praying except eastward." Thereupon I said to myself, "I have had enough prayer." So I went out and have ever been surprised at the conduct of this devil of a man, at the change in the color of his face, his trembling and his sentiment at the sight of one praying towards the qiblah.[16]

Latin settlers in the newly founded crusader states were so few, however, that even the continuing infusion of short-term visitors plus the recruitment of mercenary troops from among local Christians left their forces perilously short of military manpower, particularly in times of crisis. Their survival over the long term required a dependable supply of skilled soldiers and substantial financial investments from Western Europe to finance the costs of their defense.

The Military Orders

They found both of these in the military religious orders that began to appear during the early decades of the twelfth centuries. The military orders were hybrid organizations. They resembled monasteries in that their members took religious vows, wore a distinguishing religious habit, lived in communities presided over by a superior, and followed rules that prescribed daily devotional exercises. Their communities differed from monastic houses, however, because the principal occupation of their members was fighting, not praying. They were, so to speak, monasteries composed of warriors.

The first of these organizations, the Knights Templar, appeared around 1118. Archbishop William of Tyre described the circumstances of their origin:

In this same year, certain noble men of knightly rank, religious men, devoted to God and fearing him, bound themselves to Christ's service in the hands of the Lord Patriarch. They promised to live in perpetuity as regular canons, without possessions, under vows of chastity and obedience. Their foremost leaders were the venerable Hugh of Payens and Geoffrey of Saint Omer. Since they had no church nor any fixed abode, the king [Baldwin II of Jerusalem, r. 1118–1131] gave them for a time a dwelling place in the south wing of the palace near the Lord's Temple. The canons of the Lord's Temple gave them, under certain conditions, a square near the palace which the canons possessed. This the knights used as a drill field. The Lord King and his noblemen and also the Lord Patriarch and the prelates of the church gave them benefices from their domains, some for a limited time and some in perpetuity. These were to provide the knights with food and clothing. Their primary duty, one which was enjoined upon them by the Lord Patriarch and the other bishops for the remission of sins, was that of protecting the roads and routes against the attacks of robbers and brigands. This they did especially in order to safeguard pilgrims. . . .

Although the knights had now [1127] been established for nine years, there were still only nine of them. From this time onward their numbers began to grow and their possessions began to multiply. . . . They have now grown so great that there are in this Order today [ca. 1170–1174] about three hundred knights who wear white mantles, in addition to the brothers, who are almost countless. They are said to have immense possessions both here and overseas, so that there is now not a province in the Christian world that has not bestowed upon the aforesaid brothers a portion of its goods. It is said today that their wealth is equal to the treasures of kings. Because they have a headquarters in the royal palace next to the Temple of the Lord, as we have said before, they are called the Brothers of the Militia of the Temple.[17]

About twenty years after the appearance of the Templars, an order of male nurses who worked in a hospital set up for pilgrims to the Holy Land also began to take on military functions as well. These were the Knights of Saint John, also known as the Hospitallers. The Hospitallers, like the Templars, soon began to prosper. By 1168 they were able to furnish the Latin Kingdom with some 500 knights and another 500 light cavalry to bolster its defenses. The Templars and Hospitallers were joined toward the end of the twelfth century by a third major military order, the Teutonic Knights who, like the Knights of Saint John, took their origin from an order attached to a hospital that cared specifically for German pilgrims to the Holy Land.

The military orders provided the crusader states with a much needed standing army, while their popularity, as William of Tyre related, induced donors to lavish numerous gifts of farms and other landholdings in

Western Europe upon them. The revenues from these sources helped the knights not only finance their continuing military operations, but also pay for the building of numerous castles and other strong points that guarded the frontiers of the Latin States against Muslim attacks. Without the manpower and fiscal resources that the military orders provided the crusader states could not have survived nearly as long as they did.

Astonished contemporaries in the West had viewed the results of the first crusade as nothing short of miraculous. The capture of Jerusalem, many believed, was an act of God performed by sinful men and women whose deeds would have been impossible without divine aid. Abbot Guibert of Nogent, writing a history of these events about ten years after they occurred, thought it proper to entitle his account of them "The Deeds of God through the Franks" because, as he explained:

> Kings, leaders, rulers and consuls, have collected vast armies from everywhere, and from among the so-called powerful of nations everywhere, have amassed hordes of people to fight. They, however, came together here out of fear of men. What shall I say of those who, without a master, without a leader, compelled only by God, have traveled not only beyond the borders of their native province, beyond even their own kingdom, but through the vast number of intervening nations and languages, from the distant borders of the Britannic Ocean, to set up their tents in the center of the earth? We are speaking about the recent and incomparable victory of the expedition to Jerusalem, whose glory for those who are not totally foolish is such that our times may rejoice in a fame that no previous times have ever merited. Our men were not driven to this accomplishment by desire for empty fame, or for money, or to widen our borders, motives which drove almost all others who take up or have taken up arms. . . . God ordained holy wars in our time, so that the knightly order and the erring mob, who, like their ancient pagan models, were engaged in mutual slaughter, might find a new way of earning salvation.[18]

Muslim Reaction to the First Crusade

No subsequent crusading venture ever equaled, or indeed even approached, the success of the expedition of 1095–1099. Modern historians generally agree that the First Crusade succeeded as it did mainly because the Muslim powers of the Middle East at the end of the eleventh century were divided among themselves. Their rulers kept their attention so closely focused on quarrels with rival Muslim rulers that not only were they unable to coordinate a defense against the crusading armies, but indeed they paid scarcely any attention to the appearance of these Western Christian forces in their midst. No Muslim writer of the period thought it necessary to write a history of the wars against the European invaders and scarcely any contemporary historian writing in Arabic gave the First Crusade much more than a cursory mention in passing.

A consolidation of the Muslim governments in the Levant only began to take shape with the rise to power of Imad ad-Din Zengi (d. 1146), the ruler of Mosul and Aleppo. In 1144, Zengi for the first time turned his unwelcome attention toward the most vulnerable of the Latin States, the County of Edessa. In a lightning campaign that year, Zengi succeeded in capturing Edessa itself and within a few months was able to seize many of the remaining strongholds of the County. Zengi was largely responsible for setting in motion a Muslim countercrusade against the Latins, whom Arabic writers usually referred to as the Franks. He vigorously promoted the popularity of the concept of jihad, which before his time had not usually featured very prominently in Islamic law or theology. Zengi clearly saw the potential of jihad as a propaganda tool not only to promote his own status as a champion of the faith, but also to convince Muslims throughout the Levant that they had a religious obligation to reconquer Jerusalem and the rest of the Latin States. Fortunately for the remaining Latin States, Zengi was murdered by one of his own slaves before he could muster the additional forces necessary to follow up on these victories.

The Second Crusade

News of Edessa's fall caused consternation when it reached the West in the autumn of 1145. The immediate reaction of Pope Eugene III was to call for a massive renewal of crusading efforts. He did so in a letter that he addressed to King Louis VII of France (r. 1137–1180), who greeted the pope's summons enthusiastically. The pope commissioned Saint Bernard (1090–1153), the abbot of Clairvaux, to organize the recruitment for the new expedition, a task that Bernard undertook with enormous vigor and considerable success:

Bernard not only raised armies from France, Germany, and England to attack the Muslims in the Holy Land, but he also recruited additional forces to push back the Muslim rulers who controlled much of Spain and Portugal. In addition he enrolled more troops to mount a crusade against Slavic pagans on Germany's eastern frontier. The mission of this latter expedition, Saint Bernard declared, was to wipe out either the Slavs or their religion. Despite the fact that both of these opponents managed to survive, the Slavic crusade of 1148 marked the beginning of a process of conquest and colonization that would ultimately lead to the christianization of Estonia, Latvia, Lithuania, Brandenburg, and Prussia. This crusade, like the expeditions in the Iberian peninsula, aimed at the conversion of native pagan or Muslim populations to Christianity, as well as at military and political conquest of the regions that they inhabited. The crusades in the Near East, by contrast, had conquest, not conversion, as their primary goal. Missionary activity played virtually no part either in the first crusade or in subsequent crusading expeditions during the twelfth century. Only in the thirteenth century would conversion become a prominent theme, especially among the mendicant friars, in the Holy Land crusades.

Two main crusading expeditions to the Holy Land in 1147–1149 began well but ended in bitter disappointment. The first of these was a huge German army led by the Emperor Conrad III (r. 1138–1152). The emperor and his troops, accompanied by numerous pilgrims and other noncombatants, arrived at Constantinople in September 1147. Rather than waiting for the French army under King Louis VII to join them, Conrad and the majority of his followers set out straightway to attack the Turks in Asia Minor, only to fall into an ambush in which a large part of the German expedition perished. Conrad and the other survivors made their way painfully back toward Constantinople and met up with the French expedition part way there. Conrad and a fraction of what was left of his army, after taking some time to recover from their ordeal, decided to continue on toward Jerusalem, but most of the surviving German troops gave up and made their way back home by sea.

The French and the much-reduced German armies made painfully slow progress overland through Asia Minor and by mid-January 1148 had only reached Adalia on the peninsula's southern coast. The French king decided at that point that he and a part of his army would make the rest of their journey by sea, leaving the rest of his forces to continue by land. Many of the troops he left behind were killed in combat along the way, so that both the French and German forces were still further reduced in numbers before they finally reached Jerusalem in 1148.

There the Latin princes in the Holy Land persuaded the newly arrived crusaders that they could best relieve the military pressures on the remaining crusader settlements by attacking the Syrian capital, Damascus. The campaign against Damascus quickly turned into a fiasco. After a difficult series of engagements in which they were able to take control of the northern and western approaches to the city, the leaders decided to change tactics and attack the city from the south and east instead. There they quickly discovered that the new positions to which they moved were barren, with insufficient food and water to be tenable for more than a few days. The only solution was to retreat back to Jerusalem. After this shattering experience, the crusading armies soon broke up. The two kings, together with the remnants of their exhausted armies, returned home by sea, disgruntled, disappointed, and impoverished by their experience.

Muslim Unification

The crusade of 1147–1149 did nothing to improve the ability of the Latin states to resist the growing unification of their Muslim foes. Not only was the County of Edessa irretrievably lost, but the Latin principality centered at Antioch was coming under relentless pressure from Zengi's son and successor, Nur ad-Din (r. 1146–1174), who greatly enlarged the realm that his father had built up. Six years after the crusading army retreated ignominiously from its failed siege of Damascus, Nur ad-Din capped a series of successful campaigns in Syria by adding that city to the territories that he already possessed. During the next year, 1154, he managed to bring the remaining cities of Muslim Syria under his control. In the following years, Nur ad-Din consolidated his empire with the result that his forces sealed off the northern and eastern frontiers of the Principality of Antioch and the County of Tripoli. Then in 1169 he dispatched an army commanded by Shirkuh, one of his generals, who waged a brief but successful campaign to take control of Egypt. Once his forces had the country firmly in their grasp, Shirkuh arranged for the murder of the previous ruler and his children and made himself ruler of Egypt, although he still retained his loyalty to Nur ad-Din. Shirkuh's victory left Nur ad-Din in control of the southern flank of the crusader states as well.

Nur ad-Din, like his father, shrewdly exploited the notion of jihad as a mechanism for unifying the Islamic world against the Franks. He became a generous patron of Muslim theologians, lawyers, and poets who celebrated the virtues jihad and lavishly supported the founding of schools and mosques to train up students in the study of Islamic law and theology. The great Arabic historian, Ibn al-Athir (1160–1223), a younger contemporary of Nur ad-Din described him in these terms:

> Nur ad-Din was a tall swarthy man with a beard but no mustache, a fine forehead and a pleasant appearance enhanced by beautiful, melting eyes.

His kingdom extended far and wide, and his power was acknowledged even in Medina and Mecca and the Yemen. . . .

Among his virtues were austerity, piety and a knowledge of theology. His food and clothing and all his personal expenditure came out of income from properties bought with his legal share of booty and money allocated for communal Muslim interests. His wife complained to him of his austerity, and so he allotted to her, from his private property, three shops in Hims that would bring her in about twenty dinars a year. When she objected that this was not much he said: "I have no more. Of all the wealth I have at my disposal, I am but the custodian for the Muslim community, and I do not intend to deceive them over this or to cast myself into hell-fire for your sake." He often got up to pray at night and his vigils and meditations inspired praise. He had a good knowledge of Muslim law of the Hanafite school, but he was not a fanatic. He set up "Houses of Justice" throughout his realm, and with his qadi [judge] sat to administer justice to the oppressed, Jew or Muslim, at the expense of the oppressor, even if it were his own son or his chief amir.

He built numerous Hanafite and Shafi'ite madrasas, the Great Mosque of Nur ad-Din at Mosul, hospitals and caravanserai along the great roads, Dervish monasteries in every town, and left generous endowments to each. I have heard that the monthly income of all his foundations amounted to 9,000 Tyrian dinars. He honored scholars and men of religion and had the deepest respect for them. He would rise to his feet in their presence and invite them to sit next to him. Many were his virtues, innumerable his merits; this book is not large enough to encompass them all.[19]

Saladin Conquers Jerusalem

By the time of his death in 1174 Nur ad-Din had succeeded in unifying the Muslim powers that bordered on the crusader states. He had brought all of the major regions of Syria under his direct control, and he had capped that achievement by securing dominion over Egypt into the bargain. He had failed, however, to establish a clear-cut line of succession, and his death brought a power struggle among his generals. The victor in the contest was Saladin, who had by this time succeeded his uncle, Shirkuh, as ruler of Egypt. Within a few months Saladin was able to occupy Damascus and from this base directed a lengthy series of campaigns to take over the remainder of Nur ad-Din's Syrian territories. These lasted until 1186 and it was only then that he began to turn his attention to the Latin settlements along the coast of the Mediterranean Sea.

During the years while Saladin was preoccupied with unifying Muslim power in Syria, a series of political crises was weakening the Latin States. These crises were closely tied to rivalries between two competing factions among the Frankish nobility, which led to numerous clashes over military and diplomatic policy. Under these circumstances unified action became at best difficult and at worst impossible. One faction consisted primarily of descendants of Europeans who had settled in the Levant immediately following the first crusade. These families comprised the established core of the Latin establishment. During the early expansion of the Kingdom of Jerusalem and the other Latin States they had been able to acquire the most valuable fiefs and the most productive landholdings. These "native" barons were naturally anxious to preserve what they had and hence strongly preferred prudent and defensive policies that seemed unlikely to put their possessions at risk. The other party among the Latin nobility were mainly recent immigrants, bent on acquiring lands of their own. This led the "newcomers" to favor aggressive expansionist policies that promised to open up the opportunities that they needed in order to prosper. To complicate matters further, the reigning monarch of the Latin Kingdom of Jerusalem, Baldwin IV (r. 1174–1185), had contracted leprosy as a child and recurrent periods of acute illness required the appointment of temporary regents (*baillis*) to take charge of affairs until he could recover. During the early years of Baldwin IV's reign the regency was held by Count Raymond III of Tripoli (1152–1187), the young king's closest male relative and leader of the "native" faction among the nobility. Then in 1180 Baldwin's sister, Sibyl, married a handsome but reckless young "newcomer," Guy of Lusignan (d. 1192). To the consternation of the "native" barons this turn of events gave Sibyl's new husband a strong claim on the regency and possibly even on succession to the throne. The result was a sharp increase in tension between the two groups, which made stable governance far more difficult than before.

So long as Baldwin IV remained in reasonably good health it was possible to hold these internal conflicts in check, but in 1183 the king's condition deteriorated sharply. Baldwin summoned all his barons, announced that he was appointing his brother-in-law as regent, and required them to swear fidelity to Guy.

Guy's regency polarized the divisions among the Latin nobility and the political situation deteriorated rapidly. The situation worsened still further because Saladin now commenced to attack positions along the frontiers of the Latin States. As Guy's incompetence became increasingly obvious, Baldwin finally removed him as regent and recalled Raymond III of Tripoli to replace him, to the consternation of the "newcomer" group. Then in March 1185, Baldwin IV died at the age of twenty-four.

Upon the death of the leper king the crown of the Latin Kingdom passed briefly to his eight-year-old nephew, Baldwin V, and Raymond of Tripoli continued as regent. The boy king died unexpectedly in the summer of 1186 while Raymond was away from Jerusalem. Sybil and Guy de Lusignan immediately took advantage of the situation. They snatched the crowns of the kingdom from the royal treasury and persuaded the patriarch of Jerusalem to use one of them to crown Sybil as queen. She then crowned her husband, Guy, as king.

These events not unnaturally infuriated Raymond and the "native" barons loyal to him, but there was little they could do to reverse what had been done. Open rebellion was not a serious option in view of the looming military crisis. With extreme reluctance most of the barons grudgingly swore allegiance to Guy as their king. Raymond however retired to Tripoli as quickly as he could and sent messengers to ask Saladin's help in case Guy should attempt to attack him there. Saladin, eager to take advantage of the discord in Jerusalem agreed to do so.

As it turned out even Guy was not so foolhardy as to risk a civil war and invite intervention by Saladin. An uneasy truce prevailed for the remainder of 1186. Then early in 1187 Reginald of Châtillon, one of Guy's most reckless allies among the "newcomer" faction, yielded to the temptation to attack and loot a rich merchant caravan that was traveling from Cairo to Damascus. Saladin, infuriated by Reginald's audacity, vowed to kill him with his own hands. He also proclaimed a jihad against Jerusalem and prepared to attack. He commenced to soften up the Latin resistance through a series of preliminary raids, beginning on May 1. Guy de Lusignan summoned every able-bodied man in the Latin States to assemble at the springs of Saffuriyah, where they had ready access to water and food supplies. They camped there to await the full-scale invasion, which began at the end of June.

After a series of maneuvers calculated to lure the Latins out of their encampment, Saladin moved his main forces on July 2 toward Tiberias, on the shores of the Sea of Galilee. When word reached the Latin army that Saladin's forces were about to besiege Tiberias, Guy de Lusignan made what proved to be a fatal decision: he would move his army out to intercept the enemy and save Tiberias. They set out at dawn on July 3. The terrain between Saffuriyah and Tiberias was arid and rocky.

Skirmishers from Saladin's forces, who had been awaiting their move, harassed them continuously along the way. Both men and horses soon began to falter in the heat of high summer. By late afternoon it became clear that they would be unable to reach Tiberias that day and would need to encamp en route overnight. Guy and his advisers decided to do so on the slopes of the Horns of Hattin. The decision was disastrous. After an enervating day's march under the sun they found that the Muslims had drained the cisterns, so that they had neither water for themselves nor forage for the horses. During the night Saladin moved up his main forces to surround them and had his men set fire to the dry brush, whose smoke combined with hunger and thirst to torment the Latin army through a sleepless night. When July 4 dawned, battle was joined. The exhausted Christian army was beaten from the start. Although they fought desperately, they were unable to push through the enemy lines. At the end the infantry broke ranks and the fight was over. The disorganized remnants of the Latin forces were soon cut to pieces. As Ibn al-Athir related:

> I was told that al-Malik al-Afdal, Saladin's son, said: "I was at my father Saladin's side during that battle, the first that I saw with my own eye. The Frankish king had retreated to the hill with his band, and from there he led a furious charge against the Muslims facing him, forcing them back upon my father. I saw that he was alarmed and distraught, and he tugged at his beard as he went forward crying: "Away with the Devil's lie!" The Muslims turned to counter-attack and drove the Franks back up the hill. When I saw the Franks retreating before the Muslim onslaught I cried out for joy: "We have conquered them!" But they returned to the charge with undiminished ardour and drove our army back toward my father. His response was the same as before, and the Muslims counter-attacked and drove the Franks back to the hill. Again I cried: "We have beaten them!" But my father turned to me and said: "Be quiet; we shall not have beaten them until that tent falls!" As he spoke the tent fell, and the Sultan dismounted and prostrated himself in thanks to God, weeping for joy. This was how the tent fell: the Franks had been suffering terribly from thirst during their charge, which they hoped would win them a way out of their distress, but the way of escape was blocked. They dismounted and sat on the ground and the Muslims fell upon them, pulled down the King's tent and captured every one of them, including the King, his brother, and Prince Arnat of Karak [Reginald of Châtillon], Islam's most hated enemy. They also took the ruler of Jubail, the son of Humphrey [of Toron], the Grand Master of the Templars, one of the Franks' greatest dignitaries, and a band of Templars and Hospitallers. The number of dead and captured

was so large that those who saw the slain could not believe that anyone could have been taken alive, and those who saw the prisoners could not believe that any had been killed. From the time of their first assault on Palestine in 491/1098 until now, the Franks had never suffered such a defeat.

When all the prisoners had been taken, Saladin went to his tent and sent for the King of the Franks and Prince Arnat of Karak. He had the King seated beside him and as he was half-dead with thirst gave him iced water to drink. The King drank and handed the rest to the Prince, who also drank. Saladin said: "This godless man did not have my permission to drink, and will not save his life that way." He turned on the Prince, casting his crimes in his teeth and enumerating his sins. Then he rose and with his own hand cut off the man's head.

A year later I crossed the battlefield, and saw the land all covered with their bones, which could be seen even from a distance, lying in heaps or scattered around. These were what was left after all the rest had been carried away by storms or by the wild beasts of these hills and valleys.[20]

The slaughter of the Christian forces at Hattin wiped out almost all the military forces available to defend the states that the First Crusade had created ninety years before. The few soldiers who escaped made their way to Tyre, which enabled that city to hold out, while Saladin proceeded in short order to sweep up the remaining strongholds of the Latin States. Jerusalem fell after only token resistance. So too did Beirut, Jaffa, Ascalon, and Sidon, as well as the inland towns and nearly all the crusaders' castles, save for a half-dozen that were so heavily fortified that even tiny garrisons could manage to resist Saladin's attacks. Tripoli and Antioch were also able to hold out, but lost control of nearly all of their surrounding territories. For most practical purposes by the beginning of 1188 Saladin had reduced the Latin States to a mere handful of isolated strong points. He and his army then retired from the field.

The Third Crusade

News of the catastrophe at Hattin and Saladin's capture of Jerusalem stunned Pope Gregory VIII (r. 1187–1188) when it finally reached him in the autumn of 1188. His immediate reaction was to assume that the disaster represented God's retribution for the sins of the settlers in the Latin State:

On hearing with what severe and terrible judgment the land of Jerusalem has been smitten by the divine hand, we and our brothers have been confounded by such great horror and affected by such great sorrow that we could not easily decide what to do or say.

We ought not to believe, however, that these things have happened through the injustice of a violent judge, but rather through the iniquity of a delinquent people. It is nothing new for this land to be struck by divine judgment, nor is it unusual for it, once whipped and chastised, to seek mercy. The Lord, indeed, could save it by his will alone, but it is not for us to ask him why he has acted thus. For perhaps the Lord has wished to find out and bring to the notice of others whether there is anyone who has knowledge of him or is seeking after him and might joyfully embrace the chance of penitence offered to him and, in laying down his life for his brothers, may be killed in a brief moment and gain eternal life.[21]

The pope went on to ordain that all the faithful should abstain from eating meat on Fridays in order to atone for the sins that had resulted in the recent disasters and appealed to Christian rulers to organize another expedition to the Holy Land.

The call for a new crusade began auspiciously as the three most powerful monarchs in Europe responded by taking the cross, although with varying degrees of enthusiasm. The German king and emperor Frederick Barbarossa (r. 1152–1190), the French king Philip Augustus (r. 1179–1223), and the English king Richard Lionheart (r. 1189–1199) all enrolled in the crusaders' ranks and began to raise larger, better financed, and more powerful armies than any previous crusading expedition had ever known. At the same time, however, rivalries between the three kings and their followers inevitably led to mistrust that hampered cooperation between them in the pursuit of a common goal.

Each of the three major armies involved in what historians conventionally call the Third Crusade set out to the Holy Land separately. Barbarossa and his German army were the first to depart. They set out from Regensburg at the beginning of May 1189 and took the same land route that so many earlier crusaders had traveled. They marched through Hungary and the Balkans to Constantinople with minimal difficulty. In Asia Minor they ran into sporadic resistance but had to fight just one pitched battle in May 1190, from which they emerged victorious with only minor losses. Then on June 10 disaster struck: the emperor Frederick drowned while attempting to swim across the Saleph River. Their leader's death crippled the German army. Some of its members headed for nearby port cities and returned home at once. The remainder split into three groups. One took ship and sailed directly to Tripoli, while a second group, led by Barbarossa's son, Duke Frederick of Swabia, sailed to Antioch. The third contingent chose to march to Antioch by land and suffered serious losses along the way. An epidemic at Antioch further reduced the size of the German army, which then met with still further losses as it battled its way down the coast to Acre, where Guy de Lusignan and a small contingent of knights had begun to lay siege to the city.

King Philip Augustus and the French army meanwhile rendezvoused with Richard Lionheart and the English army at Vézelay in July 1190. Philip and Richard with their armies marched south from there to take the sea route to Palestine, Philip from Genoa, Richard from Marseilles. The two forces met again in Sicily, where they arrived at Messina in mid-September. Winter storms routinely halted shipping across the Mediterranean from late September until the end of March and as a result the French and English armies spent the winter in Sicily. King Philip and the French army finally joined the remnants of the German army and Guy de Lusignan's troops at Acre on April 20, 1191. Richard and his forces, however, stopped along the way to conquer the island of Cyprus and consequently did not appear at Acre until the beginning of June.

Once they were all assembled the combined forces prosecuted the siege of Acre vigorously and took the city by frontal assault on July 12. Philip Augustus had never been as keen as Richard Lionheart was for the crusading enterprise and, to make matters worse, had been in poor health since his arrival at Acre. Once Acre was securely in the crusaders' hands, Philip decided that he had fulfilled his obligations and prepared to return to France, although a great many of his followers chose to remain in the Holy Land. Richard insisted that Philip promise before he departed that he would not make war against English possessions in France, which had long been a source of friction between the two. Philip grudgingly agreed, and Richard graciously loaned him two galleys to facilitate his trip and Philip departed on July 31.

Richard remained behind and began to recover control of many of the coastal cities taken by Saladin's armies in 1187/1188. He succeeded in doing so during a series of campaigns in 1191/1192 but eventually concluded that retaking Jerusalem, which had been his fondest dream, was not feasible. He was troubled by events in England, where his brother

John had become embroiled in quarrels with the royal officials whom Richard had appointed to govern the kingdom during his absence. Even more worrisome were the activities of Philip Augustus, who was threatening to invade Richard's duchy of Normandy and was reported to be carrying on secret negotiations with John. In view of these developments Richard commenced to negotiate a truce with Saladin, who had problems of his own to contend with. Saladin's army was restive. His men had been on campaign almost continuously for nearly five years and were threatening to mutiny if he extended their service much longer. Under the circumstances both sides were prepared to bargain and by the beginning of September they finally agreed on a three-year truce. Saladin agreed not to attack the narrow strip of land between Tyre and Jaffa that Christian armies now controlled, along with Tripoli and Antioch. Both Christians and Muslims were accorded the right to travel unmolested throughout Palestine, so that pilgrims could have access to Jerusalem and the other sacred shrines and Muslim merchants could trade in the port cities under Christian control. As soon as the truce was in place, Richard and most of the other crusaders took ship to return to their homes.

The Third Crusade was at least a partial success. It left behind a reconstituted, although much diminished, Latin Kingdom. Although Jerusalem itself remained in Muslim hands, the coastal cities that the crusaders had reconquered gave Latin forces a foothold in Syria and Palestine. The harbors and warehouses of those cities provided Western merchants with the commercial facilities they needed to carry on what became an increasingly active trade with Muslim suppliers. Merchants, mainly from Genoa, Pisa, and Venice, established their own colonies in these cities, where they observed their own laws and customs, built churches, and transplanted other institutions from their homes in the West. Tolls and taxes on this commercial activity provided the economic base for the cities' rulers and helped to finance their governments and armies. Pilgrims, too, continued to flood into the restored Latin States, and providing them with food and lodgings during their stay in the Holy Land became an important industry. All of this suited Saladin and his successors as well. It gave Muslim merchants easy access to Western markets, while the fees that pilgrims paid for the privilege of visiting the sacred shrines at Jerusalem and Bethlehem provided a welcome and relatively stable flow of cash. In this situation the well-being of the Latin States depended upon continued peace, not more war.

The Fourth Crusade

Despite this, the idea of crusading—the belief that Western Christians had not only a right but a moral obligation to continue to mount military expeditions in order to resume control over Jerusalem and other holy places in the Levant—remained strong, and thirteenth-century popes continued to press for new crusades.

In August 1198, just few months after his election, Pope Innocent III (1198–1216) dispatched letters to archbishops, bishops, and abbots of the Western church. In these letters Innocent touched on themes that had become so familiar since Urban II's sermon at Clermont. He deplored the sufferings of Jerusalem under Muslim rule, upbraided Christian princes for their devotion to vice and luxury, which had caused earlier crusades to fail, and summoned the Christian faithful to take the cross once more to rescue the holy places from the infidel yoke. He pledged that he would contribute money from the papal treasury to help finance the expedition, demanded that all bishops and other prelates either lead their own forces on the crusade or contribute substantial sums of money to defray the costs of participation by others, and promised that members of the crusading army would receive a plenary indulgence for their sins, as well as papal protection for the wives and families they would leave behind when they departed on their sacred mission.

The expedition, which is conventionally known as the Fourth Crusade, was slow to take shape. Innocent had originally hoped that it would depart in the spring of 1199, but springtime came and passed without significant progress toward this goal. Innocent wrote more and more urgent letters. He resorted to the extraordinary step of imposing a tax on the incomes of the clergy with the proceeds to be used to support would-be crusaders who lacked the means to undertake the journey to the Holy Land. In 1201 he approached the kings of France and England with a further request for contributions to speed up recruitment for the crusade.

All the while Innocent continued to urge crusade preachers to do their utmost to bring in more recruits. By the beginning of 1201 his efforts had begun to pay off and a strategic plan for the crusade had commenced to emerge. Innocent and his advisers had concluded that since Egypt was by now the principal center of Islamic power the crusaders should accordingly make an attack upon Egypt their primary goal. In order to do this they also determined that the army must travel by sea, since a land route to Egypt seemed impractical.

In order to implement this strategy a fleet was obviously essential and the leaders of the crusade approached Venice to propose that the Venetian government undertake to furnish the necessary ships and supplies to transport the crusaders, their horses, pack animals, supplies, and equipment. After some hard bargaining the Venetians agreed to do so in return for a payment of 94,000 silver marks. This sum was based on the leaders' projections of the size of the crusading force.

The army was to assemble in Venice at the end of April 1202, but when the time arrived it was immediately apparent that the force numbered only about two-thirds of the size that the leaders had projected. In the end they were able to put together only about 60,000 marks instead of the 94,000 they had promised. The Venetians, who had gone to great expense to build and outfit the crusading fleet, shortly offered to settle for the lesser amount provided that the crusading army would attack, conquer, and turn over to them the city of Zara on the east coast of the Adriatic Sea. After heated debate the majority of the crusaders decided to accept the deal, despite the fact that Zara was a Christian city. The crusaders set sail at the beginning of October, landed at Zara, and in due course captured the city.

It was by now November, too late in the year to undertake a voyage across the Mediterranean to Egypt. Meanwhile fresh complications had arisen. Some time previously a revolution had occurred at Constantinople and the reigning emperor had been deposed. The son of the deposed ruler now approached the Venetians to propose that they and the crusading army restore him to power, in return for which he would pay off the crusaders' debt to Venice, reward the crusaders handsomely, and raise a Byzantine army that would provide powerful reinforcements for the invasion of Egypt.

The Venetian leaders readily agreed, but opinion among the crusaders was sharply divided. After intense disputes among themselves the majority agreed to the proposed scheme, although a significant minority rejected it and returned home disillusioned. The remaining crusaders sailed for Constantinople in April 1203 and after a difficult siege succeeded in entering the city, which they turned over to Alexius IV, the pretender to the Byzantine throne. The crusaders then camped outside the city wall, awaiting the rewards they had been promised. Alexius IV, however, proved unable to keep any of his obligations to them. Instead, his efforts to do so provoked yet another revolution inside the city, during which he was strangled. The revolutionary government, headed by the new emperor, Alexius V, had no intention of making good on Alexius IV's promises, and the crusaders then attacked the city, which they took for the second time on April 13, 1204. This time they occupied the city, sacked it thoroughly, and installed their own government.

The conquest of Constantinople by the Fourth Crusade was of no assistance to the Latin States in the Levant. Indeed its long-term effect was to weaken their position. Although successive Byzantine governments had frequently seemed ambivalent about the whole crusading enterprise and occasionally quarreled with the leaders of crusading expeditions, Byzantium had often enough lent its support to the Latin States. The events of 1204, however, permanently ended any possibility that this might happen again.

The Later Crusades

Innocent III and his successors nonetheless continued to call for further crusades. The Fifth Crusade (1218–1221), unlike the Fourth Crusade, actually did attack Egypt and was able to seize the city of Damietta, which its army held for a short time but then had to abandon in 1221. The German king and emperor Frederick II (1197–1250) led the strangest crusade of all. Frederick had taken the cross in 1215 but postponed actually embarking on an expedition for thirteen years. By the time he finally did set out he had been excommunicated by Pope Gregory IX (r. 1227–1241) for his failure to fulfill his earlier crusade vow. When he arrived in the Holy Land, Frederick chose to prosecute his crusade by diplomacy rather than warfare. By a treaty that he concluded with the Sultan of Egypt, al-Kamil (r. 1218–1238), in February 1229, Frederick succeeded in securing control of Jerusalem once again. For his efforts he was spurned by the nobility of the rejuvenated Latin States, who on account of his status as an excommunicate refused to enter Jerusalem so long as he was present. The pope meanwhile took advantage of Frederick's absence on crusade to attack his domains in southern Italy and Sicily. On this account Frederick sailed back to Italy at the beginning of May 1229, while the townspeople of Acre threw garbage at his departing ship.

Another major crusading expedition was organized in 1248, by which time Frederick II's peace treaty with Egypt had expired and Muslim forces had reoccupied Jerusalem. The 1248 crusade was organized and led by the saintly King Louis IX of France (r. 1226–1270). Adopting the crusade strategy current since the beginning of the thirteenth century, Louis IX saw control of Egypt as essential to the conquest of Jerusalem and the remainder of Palestine. Louis's campaign was initially successful. His army, like the forces of the Fifth Crusade, took Damietta in 1249. They then began a march southward with the aim of besieging Cairo but made the fatal mistake of failing to guard their flanks. This allowed Egyptian forces to raise the sluice gates in the Nile River valley and flood their route of march. King Louis himself, together with those of his men who escaped drowning, were taken prisoner and held for ransom by the Egyptians.

In return for their release Louis agreed to withdraw his garrison from Damietta and to pay a substantial ransom, roughly equivalent to a full year's revenue from his French kingdom. Once the ransom had been paid, Louis and his remaining forces, now much diminished, sailed to Acre. He and his men stayed on in the Latin States for nearly four years. He spent this time bolstering the defenses of the Latin Kingdom, building new fortifications and refurbishing older ones that had fallen into disrepair. He returned to France in 1254.

Even his extended stay in Palestine did not satisfy Louis IX's commitment to the crusade. He took the cross again in 1267. Despite widespread opposition from many of his barons the king proceeded with preparations for his new expedition. Rather than strike directly at Egypt, Louis planned this time to make a preliminary attack on Tunisia. He apparently calculated that this would benefit the interests of his brother, Charles of Anjou, who controlled the Sicilian kingdom, and would also give him a foothold on the North African coast. From that base of operations he would then attack Egypt by land from the west and, if that were successful, push on eastward into Palestine and Syria.

In the event, this ambitious strategy came to naught. Louis and his forces sailed from Aigues-Mortes at the beginning of July 1270, then rendezvoused in Sardinia with other groups of crusaders who had set out from Genoa and Marseilles. From Sardinia they made a quick crossing to Tunisia, where they landed successfully and carved out a foothold. While they were regrouping for a further attack, King Louis fell ill, and on August 25, he died. The whole ambitious enterprise immediately began to crumble and the crusaders quickly withdrew to return home.

Louis IX's crusade of 1270 was the last major crusading expedition to challenge Muslim domination of the Holy Land. The remnants of the Latin States were left to defend themselves against increasingly ominous odds, especially after Baybars, the Mamluk sultan of Egypt and Syria (r. 1260–1277) commenced a series of systematic campaigns aimed at the elimination of the Latin presence in Palestine. One after another the coastal cities and the inland castles controlled by the Latins fell before his onslaught until only the city of Acre and a half-dozen other strong points remained in Christian hands. Finally, in May 1291, Acre fell to the Mamluk Sultan al-Ashraf Khalil (r. 1290–1293). Henry II of Lusignan, the titular King of Jerusalem (r. 1286–1291), fled with his court to Cyprus and the Latin States founded at the close of the First Crusade in 1099 were at an end.

The Legacy of the Crusades

The ghost of the crusades has lingered on in the Mediterranean world in the centuries since the fall of Acre. The rulers of Cyprus continued to affect the title of King of Jerusalem for generations. The Knights Hospitallers who ruled Rhodes until 1523 and Malta until 1798 thought of themselves and were seen by others as continuators of the crusading tradition. Even in the twenty-first century the terms *crusade* and *crusaders* still retain their power to inspire hatred, fear, and loathing in the Islamic world.

The crusades left their most lasting legacy, however, in the West itself. Their purposes, scope, and character underwent continuous change and enlargement throughout their history. Crusades, as we have seen, originated in the first place as campaigns that aimed at military conquest of the Holy Land and then later at the establishment and maintenance of Western Christian control over Jerusalem, Bethlehem, and other sites connected with the life of Jesus and his apostles. Early in the twelfth century popes had broadened the notion of what constituted a crusade to include campaigns against Muslims in Spain and Portugal. By the time of the Second Crusade in the mid-twelfth century the definition of a crusade expanded still further when military campaigns against Slavic pagans in eastern and central Europe were brought under the crusade umbrella. The thirteenth-century sequel of those campaigns was the conquest by German crusaders of Brandenburg, Prussia, and the Baltic states that are now known as Estonia, Latvia, and Lithuania.

During the early thirteenth century another fundamental transformation occurred when Pope Innocent III proclaimed a crusade against

Christian heretics known as the Cathars or Albigensians in the south of France. Innocent III also called for crusades against Christians, such as the imperial steward, Markward of Anweiler, who opposed papal policies. His successors later in the century would continue this process by proclaiming crusades, for example, against Frederick II's son, Manfred, governor of Sicily (r. 1250–1258), and Pedro III of Aragon (r. 1276–1285). Still later popes in the sixteenth and seventeenth centuries would designate the Spanish and Portuguese wars of conquest in the Americas, the Philippines, and other newly discovered regions as crusades.

Crusades thus evolved into an institution. Like many other institutions, this one, too, long outlived its original function. The crusade evolved into a mechanism that facilitated not only the religious policies of popes, but also the expansionist designs of European rulers.

Discussion Questions

1. The crusaders' conquest of the Holy Land lasted slightly less than two hundred years. What have been their long-term consequences?

2. A recent commentator concluded that the history of the crusades shows "the wretched consequences when people take religion too seriously." Do you agree? If so, why? If not, why not?

3. What relevance do the crusades have for present-day politics and religion in the Middle East?

JUDAISM, CHRISTIANITY, AND ISLAM IN SPAIN FROM THE EIGHTH TO THE FIFTEENTH CENTURIES

Olivia Remie Constable

Religious Coexistence in Medieval Spain

Jews, Christians, and Muslims all lived in medieval Spain, and this region has been described as both a brilliant model of tolerance and interfaith cooperation and a dismal example of intolerance and persecution of religious minorities. Both of these images reflect a reality of life in medieval Spain, yet each has also often been exaggerated. For many centuries (711–1492), the south of Spain was controlled by Muslim rulers, while the north was in Christian hands. Muslim emirs and Christian kings each ruled significant numbers of subjects belonging to the other two religious communities. As elsewhere in the Islamic Mediterranean world, the minority communities in Muslim Spain (called *al-Andalus* in Arabic) were Jews and Christians, while in the Christian kingdoms of Castile and Aragón, the minority populations were composed of Muslims and Jews. In both Muslim and Christian regions, it was possible to find not only examples of great tolerance for religious minorities, but also examples of religious persecution.

In order to understand this complex situation, we must keep in mind that modern understandings of tolerance and religious equality did not apply in the Middle Ages. In fact, medieval people would probably have found the modern notion that "all men are created equal" difficult to comprehend. Nobody in al-Andalus, Castile, or Aragón would have questioned the fact that members of the dominant religion had the upper hand—religiously, socially, economically, and politically—in the regions where they ruled. As we will see in the following texts, this hierarchy was reiterated not only in legal texts (indicating some degree of enforcement), but also in chronicles, poetry, art, and other sources. Nevertheless, minority communities were not always oppressed, and often thrived. This is particularly noteworthy in the case of the Iberian Jewish population, which had the status of a religious minority in both Muslim and Christian Spain. Jews could attain positions of economic, professional, intellectual, and political distinction, especially in court circles, yet their lives were always overshadowed by the precarious nature of religious inferiority in the eyes of the majority. As well as keeping in mind the very different understanding of tolerance during the Middle Ages, we should be aware that this was a period of many centuries and there were significant changes over time.

Historical Overview

The political and religious balance in Spain changed dramatically during the course of eight centuries. In the early Middle Ages, Spain was ruled by the Visigoths. This group of Arian Christians had taken the peninsula from Roman control in the fifth century, before their conversion to Catholicism in the sixth century. Under Visigothic administration, Spain had a mixed population of Hispano-Romans, Gothic peoples, and Jews.

Muslim Spain (*al-Andalus*)

In 711, Muslim armies from the Near East and North Africa entered the peninsula, overthrew the last Visigothic ruler, and captured the Visigothic capital city of Toledo. In many regions, Muslim rule was established by military force, but other areas capitulated by treaty, as seen in the section below titled "The Arrival of Islamic Rule in Spain." For the next four centuries, Muslim emirs and caliphs would control most of the peninsula, sometimes as one unified kingdom (with the capital at Córdoba), but more frequently as smaller city states. The latter was the case in the eleventh century, when the territory of Granada was ruled by a Berber dynasty known as the Zirids. We have good information on Muslim Granada in this period, and especially on the situation of Jews in this city. Two important Jewish administrators, Samuel ibn Naghrela and his son Joseph ibn Naghrela, particularly stand out in this period; the texts in the section titled "Samuel Ibn Naghrela and the Jewish Community of Granada" pertain to their careers. As can be seen in the texts, both men held positions of authority at the Zirid court in Granada, yet both were vulnerable and in danger of losing their positions (and their life, in the case of Joseph) if they fell from favor. Jews were also prominent in other Andalusi cities, and many sources, in both Hebrew and Arabic, survive to document their lives and activities. The same is not true for the Christian population living under Muslim rule in al-Andalus (these people are called *mozarabs*). Unlike the Jewish population in Muslim Spain, we have very little data on *mozarabs* to document their position in society. Virtually the only information concerns the so-called Cordoban Martyrs, a group of Andalusi Christians who provoked and achieved martyrdom at Muslim hands in ninth-century Córdoba. It is hard to know what to make of the Cordoban Martyrs. The account of their activities is important as one of our few bits of data on *mozarabs*, yet it was almost certainly a very unusual event, since Christians were generally protected under Muslim rule. The executions were recorded by a contemporary Christian author, who not only praised the faith of these few, but also deplored the tendency of many fellow *mozarabs* to learn Arabic and assimilate with Muslim society. After this period, the *mozarabs* virtually disappear from Andalusi records. We know they still existed as a religious minority, however, from fleeting references in Muslim texts such as the *hisba* manual of Ibn Abdûn (in the section titled "Regulations for Non-Muslims in Seville"), which describes regulations for Jews and Christians in twelfth-century Seville. Ibn Abdûn's text is important in that it gives us a glimpse of daily life and religious interaction in a medieval Andalusi city.

Christian Spain and the Reconquista

Starting in the ninth century, Christian kingdoms began to take shape in the northern peninsula, and the frontier was pushed southward as Christian armies conquered Muslim-held regions. In Christian eyes, this conquest was a "reconquest" (*reconquista*), since Visigothic Spain had been Christian before the Muslim arrival in the eighth century. The *reconquista* gained force in the later eleventh and twelfth centuries (at the same time as the Crusades to Jerusalem), especially after King Alfonso VI of Castile captured Toledo in 1086. The thirteenth century proved a major turning point. By 1250, Christian armies had gained much of the southern peninsula, including the important cities of Córdoba, Seville, and Valencia. Thereafter, only the kingdom of Granada remained in Muslim hands. It would hold out as the final bastion of Muslim rule in Spain until it was conquered in 1492 by the combined forces of King Ferdinand of Aragón and Queen Isabella of Castile.

Changes in the frontier created a continually shifting balance between Christians, Muslims, and Jews in Spain. As northern armies took over Muslim lands, local Muslim populations came under Christian adminis-tration. Some Muslims decided to emigrate to Granada or to North Africa rather than live under a Christian king, but many remained. The situation for Jews was slightly different, since large numbers of Jews had already left al-Andalus during the twelfth century in the wake of perse-cutions. Many of these refugees elected to settle in northern Christian kingdoms, usually joining established Jewish communities that had already existed for centuries in the Christian north. By the late thirteenth century, therefore, Christian kings in Castile and Aragón ruled over Muslims and Jews, as well as Christians, and this situation is reflected in the texts in the section titled "Muslims and Jews under Christian Rule in the Thirteenth Century." These texts show that Christian rulers had to make special arrangements, and to establish new laws, in order to regu-late religious coexistence in their kingdoms. For much of this period, the three religious communities lived together in a relatively peaceful, though carefully regulated, society. Historians have coined the Spanish term *convivencia* ("living together") to describe this situation; the term is also often used to describe earlier religious coexistence in al-Andalus. By the late fifteenth century, however, interfaith relations took a turn for the worse, eventually resulting in the Spanish Inquisition, the Christian con-quest of Granada, and the expulsion of both Jews and Muslims from Spain. These events are discussed and documented in the section titled "Inquisition and Expulsion."

The Arrival of Islamic Rule in Spain

The Treaty of Tudmîr (713)

No eyewitness chronicles survive to provide descriptions of the Muslim conquest of Spain in 711; the first account appears in a Latin chronicle written in the middle of the eighth century, and Arabic descriptions are even later. However, we do have a record of an Arabic document that appears to date from 713, two years after the Muslim arrival. This text records a peace treaty between ᶜAbd al-Azîz, the son of Mûsâ ibn Nus̱ air (the general who commanded Muslim armies at the time of the conquest) and Theodemir (called Tudmîr in Arabic), the local Christian ruler of Murcia, in southeastern Spain. In contrast to the accounts of the conquest provided in later chronicles, which describe a quick and violent military victory, this document suggests that the Muslim mastery of the peninsula may have been a more gradual and piecemeal endeavor. In fact, it is probable that two complementary processes—war and negotiation—worked together to bring the former Visigothic realm under Muslim rule. Some cities, including the Visigothic capital of Toledo, appear to have capitulated quickly in the face of military force. Other areas, however, may have been won by more peaceful means, using treaties such as this one to enlist the cooperation of local administrators and inhabitants. The terms of this treaty are not unlike roughly contemporary treaties known from other regions conquered by Muslim armies. The text establishes the local Christian population as a protected group under Muslim rule. As with any *dhimmî* group, Christians in Murcia were guaranteed personal safety and allowed to retain their religion in return for their loyalty to the Muslim regime and payment of an annual tax.

The Treaty of Tudmîr

In the name of God, the merciful and the compassionate.

This is a document [granted] by 'Abd al-'Azîz ibn Musa ibn Nuṣair to Tudmîr, son of Ghabdûsh, establishing a treaty of peace and the promise and protection of God and his Prophet (may God bless him and grant him peace). We ['Abd al-'Azîz] will not set special conditions for him or for any among his men, nor harass him, nor remove him from power. His followers will not be killed or taken prisoner, nor will they be separated from their women and children. They will not be coerced in matters of religion, their churches will not be burned, nor will sacred objects be taken from the realm, [so long as] he [Tudmîr] remains sincere and fulfills the [following] conditions that we have set for him. He has reached a settlement concerning seven towns: Orihuela, Valentilla, Alicante, Mula, Bigastro, Ello, and Lorca. He will not give shelter to fugitives,

> nor to our enemies, nor encourage any protected person to fear
> us, nor conceal news of our enemies. He and [each of] his men shall
> [also] pay one dinar every year, together with four measures of
> wheat, four measures of barley, four liquid measures of concentrated
> fruit juice, four liquid measures of vinegar, four of honey, and four
> of olive oil. Slaves must each pay half of this amount.

*Names of four witnesses follow, and the document is dated from the
Muslim month of Rajab, in the year 94 of the Hijra (April 713).*

Samuel Ibn Naghrela and the Jewish Community of Granada (Eleventh Century)

Samuel Ibn Naghrela (993–1056) was the first great poet of the
"Hebrew Golden Age," a period in which a number of Jewish poets in
Spain began to compose both secular and religious verse using the language of the Hebrew Bible. Samuel often used his poetry to describe the
events and passions of his day. Aside from his role as a poet, Samuel was
also a key figure in the Jewish community in Muslim Granada. He and
his son Joseph both served as viziers (high court officials) to the Zirids, a
Berber family who were rulers of Granada in the middle of the eleventh
century. Samuel, in particular, presents a brilliant example of the
"courtier-rabbi," a man who held prominent positions in both the
Muslim and Jewish communities of his day. Andalusi Muslim rulers often
employed Jewish administrators because they posed no threat to their
political position. The Jews, in their turn, benefited from the protection
of the ruler. Nevertheless, the relationship could be dangerously insecure,
since the perceived power of Jewish courtiers might rouse resentment in
the Muslim community, and in the absence of a strong royal patron, the
Jews were in danger. The precariousness of the Jewish position was
demonstrated in 1066, when the fall from power of Samuel's son, Joseph
ibn Naghrela, resulted in the massacre of thousands of Jews in Granada.

The following three selections concern the careers of Samuel and
Joseph ibn Naghrela, and the Jewish community in Granada during their
lifetimes. The texts show both the power of these men, as leaders in war

and politics, and their vulnerability to intrigue and hostility. The first text is a poem by Samuel, describing the Battle of Alfuente in 1038. The second is an incendiary verse denouncing these Jewish viziers. This was written by a Muslim courtier, Abu Isḥâq, a contemporary of Samuel and Joseph who apparently hated them because they held power over Muslims. The third text, an account of the situation in Granada in the middle of the eleventh century, was written by the Jewish chronicler Abraham ibn Daud nearly one hundred years after the events that it describes.

1. Samuel ibn Naghrela (d. 1056), "The Battle of Alfuente"

Samuel ibn Naghrela served as vizier to Bâdîs ibn Ḥabbûs, the Zirid king of Granada, from 1027 to 1056. This poem describes a battle that took place in 1038, when Zuhair, the Muslim ruler of Almería, marched against Bâdîs ibn Ḥabbûs, meeting at a place called Alfuente. Zuhair was killed in the battle, and his vizier, Ibn ᶜAbbâs (who had encouraged Zuhair to attack Granada) was taken prisoner and executed. Samuel ibn Naghrela was present at the battle, and later wrote this poem thanking God for the victory and for divine support of his own and the Jewish community's interests in Granada. Samuel's poetry is marked by its blend of two older literary traditions, the Hebrew voice of the psalmist and the voice of the Arabic tribal poet. The latter tradition comes out strongly in this selection, and many elements of the poem, especially descriptions of the battle, draw on Arabic precedents. The poet likewise employs biblical images and references in telling his tale.

> ### "The Battle of Alfuente"
>
> When Prince Zuhair, whose land was by the sea,
> and his vizier, one Ibn ᶜAbbâs, observed
> my status with my king, realized that all
> state counsels and affairs were in my hands,
> noticed that no decree was ever final
> but that the decree had my consent—
> they felt resentment over my high rank,
> resolved to see me overthrown at once;
> for how (they said) can aliens like these
> be privileged over Muslim folk
> and act like kings legitimate?

So this vizier spread awful things about me,
reckless slanders, brazen, wicked gossip,
had his heinous lies, and plenty of them,
artfully written up as open letters
(but God forbid that I should say a word
that might make anyone think ill of him!).
He circulated these among the towns
to put his slanders in the Muslims' mouths,
inciting them against me with foul words
as Moses' spies used words that caused much grief.
It was not only me he hoped to harm
by framing these malicious, lying words;
his purpose was to wipe out all the Jews,
old, young, men, women, children still unborn.
My master paid no heed to his foul words
(he could not take such nonsense seriously)
but not long after these events he died,
on a day fraught with calamity for me.
Now I was worried. "How," I said, "can I
survive with my protector gone? It's over now!
God has examined me, found out my sin,
and passed on me the sentence I deserve."

Delighted to see the trouble I was in,
my foe, gloating, sent word to all his friends:
"This is the day I have been waiting for;
the only obstacle has been removed.
With Ḥabbūs dead, this Samuel is finished,
and all his hopes are ended, done, and gone."
It angered me: it made God angry too,
made his nostrils rage with the ancient fire.
Then Bâdîs, lion of the nations, rose,
succeeded to his fathers' throne, and ruled.
Losing no time, my enemy now wrote
strong letters with peremptory demands:
"Are you aware that in our Muslim faith
it is a sin to spare this Samuel's life?
Never will I let you be in peace
as long as any breath is left inside this Jew.

Get rid of him, and that will put an end
to quarreling and strife; come, deal with me.
But if you won't, just know that all the kings
of Andalus have formed a league against you."
Bâdîs sent in reply: "If I should do
what you demand, damnation fall on me!
Before I yield my servant to his foes,
I'd see myself a bondsman to my own!"
At this my enemy became enraged,
and furiously increased hostilities,
nor did he rest until his troops were massed,
a league of Slavs and Christians and Arabians
at Alfuente. Here God, when He created
heaven and earth, had laid a trap for him.
He marched his troops at double time, rushing
to battle like a hawk that rides the breeze.
He had designs, but our God had His own;
the Lord's designs cannot be overthrown.
So Av, the month of ancient woes, went out,
And Elul entered, bringing quick relief.
He bivouacked on one side of the pass,
and we took our position facing them.
We chose to ignore his troops, regarding them
as just an ordinary caravan.
But he, on drawing up, harangued my men,
trying to turn them against me with his words.
But seeing that my men were all behind me,
supporting me as one in word and thought,
he tilted lance, drew sword, and leveled spear,
and, closing in, made ready to attack.
He rose to strike; to strike him, God arose –
can creature duel Creator and prevail?
The armies stood arrayed, rank facing rank,
the kind of men who think that death
in raging battle is a boon,
and each has only one desire: to buy renown
although the purchase cost their lives.[1]

2. Abû Isḥâq of Elvira (d. 1067), *Qaṣîda*

Although Samuel and Joseph Ibn Naghrela rose to the peak of power in Muslim society, their success made them unpopular in some circles. Many Muslims objected to the fact that Jews would have power over them. These hostile feelings created insecurity for any Jewish administrator in a position of authority in Muslim Spain, and they were only protected by the favor of the ruler. In Granada, hostility and intrigue eventually led to the downfall of Joseph ibn Naghrela. This poem is an example of the kind of hostility that he faced. Its author, Abu Isḥâq, was born of an Arab family, trained as a jurist, and worked as a scribe and teacher in Granada, the capital of the Zirid dynasty. He served as a secretary to the chief judge of Granada during the reign of Bâdîs ibn Ḥabbûs. At some point in his career, Abu Isḥâq appears to have fallen from grace, either through a conspiracy of other Muslim jurists (as his own writing implies) or through the slander of Jewish enemies (as has been claimed by others). Whatever the original cause, Abu Isḥâq was embittered by this event and later blamed the Jews for his fall. Before his death in 1067, he composed this poem attacking the Jews of Granada and targeting Joseph ibn Naghrela in particular. His efforts may have helped to incite the massacre of Jews in Granada in 1066.

Qaṣîda

Go, tell all the Ṣanhāja
The full moons of our time, the lions in their lair
The words of one who bears them love, and is concerned
And counts it a religious duty to give advice.
Your chief had made a mistake
Which delights malicious gloaters
He has chosen an infidel as his secretary
When he could, had he wished, have chosen a Believer.
Through him, the Jews have become great and proud
And arrogant—they, who were among the most abject
And have gained their desires and attained the utmost
And this happened suddenly, before they even realized it.
And how many a worthy Muslim humbly obeys
The vilest ape among these miscreants.
And this did not happen through their own efforts
But through one of our own people who rose as their accomplice.

Oh why did he not deal with them, following
The example set by worthy and pious leaders?
Put them back where they belong
And reduce them to the lowest of the low,
Roaming among us, with their little bags,
With contempt, degradation and scorn as their lot,
Scrabbling in the dunghills for colored rags
To shroud their dead for burial.
They did not make light of our great ones
Or presume against the righteous,
Those low-born people would not be seated in society
Or paraded along with the intimates of the ruler.
Bâdîs! You are a clever man
And your judgment is sure and accurate.
How can their misdeeds be hidden from you
When they are trumpeted all over the land?
How can you love this bastard brood
When they have made you hateful to all the world?
How can you complete your ascent to greatness
When they destroy as you build?
How have you been lulled to trust a villain
And made him your companion—though he is evil company?
God has vouchsafed in His revelations
A warning against the society of the wicked.
Do not choose a servant from among them
But leave them to the curse of the accurst!
For the earth cries out against their wickedness
And is about to heave and swallow all.
Turn your eyes to other countries
And you will find the Jews are outcast dogs.
Why should you alone be different and bring them near
When in all the land they are kept afar?
You, who are a well-beloved king,
scion of glorious kings,
And are the first among men
As your forebears were first in their time.
I came to live in Granada
And I saw them frolicking there.
They divided up the city and the provinces
With one of their accursed men everywhere.

They collect all the revenues,
They munch and they crunch.
They dress in the finest clothes
While you wear the meanest.
They are the trustees of your secrets
-yet how can traitors be trusted?
Others eat a dirham's worth, afar,
While they are near, and dine well.
They challenge you to your God
And they are not stopped or reproved.
They envelop you with their prayers
And you neither see nor hear.
They slaughter beasts in our markets
And you eat their *trefa*.
Their chief ape has marbled his house
And led the finest spring water to it.
Our affairs are now in his hands
And we stand at his door.
He laughs at us and at our religion
And we return to our God.
If I said that his wealth is as great
As yours, I would speak the truth.
Hasten to slaughter him as an offering,
Sacrifice him, for he is a fat ram
And do not spare his people
For they have amassed every precious thing.
Break loose their grip and take their money
For you have a better right to what they collect.
Do not consider it a breach of faith to kill them
-the breach of faith would be to let them carry on.
They have violated our covenant with them
So how can you be held guilty against violators?
How can they have any pact
When we are obscure and they are prominent?
Now we are the humble, beside them,
As if we had done wrong, and they right!
Do no tolerate their misdeeds against us
For you are surety for what they do.
God watches His own people
And the people of God will prevail.[2]

3. Abraham ibn Daud (d. 1181), *The Book of Tradition*

Stories of Samuel ibn Naghrela and Joseph ibn Naghrela lived on in Jewish memory and historical writing for many centuries. The brilliant career of Samuel and the dramatic downfall of Joseph would provide an object lesson for both the opportunities and the dangers of Jewish life in Muslim Spain. In this passage from the *Sefer ha-Qabbalah* (Book of Tradition), written in 1161, the Jewish chronicler Abraham ibn Daud recounts events that took place in Granada a century earlier. He provides details on the career of Samuel ibn Naghrela, his rise to power at the Zirid court, and his status in the Jewish communities of Córdoba and Granada. He likewise describes the career of Joseph ibn Naghrela and his downfall. The dates used in this passage are cited according to the Jewish calendar.

The Book of Tradition

One of his outstanding disciples was R. Samuel ha-Levi the Nagid b. R. Joseph, surnamed Ibn Naghrela, of the community of Córdoba. Besides being a great scholar and highly cultured person, R. Samuel was highly versed in Arabic literature and style and was, indeed, competent to serve in the king's palace. Nevertheless, he maintained himself in very modest circumstances as a spice-merchant until the time when war broke out in Spain. With the termination of the rule of the house of Ibn Abi 'Amir and the seizure of power by the Berber chiefs, the city of Córdoba dwindled and its inhabitants were compelled to flee. Some went off to Saragossa, where their descendants have remained down to the present, while others went to Toledo, where their descendants have retained their identity down to the present.

This R. Samuel, however, fled to Málaga, where he occupied a shop as a spice-merchant. Since his shop happened to adjoin the courtyard of Ibn al-'Arif—who was the *Kâtib* of King Ḥabbûs b. Mâksan, the Berber king of Granada—the *Kâtib's* maidservant would ask him to write letters for her to her master, the Vizier Abu al-Qâsim ibn al-'Arif. When the latter received the letters, he was astounded at the learning they reflected. Consequently, when, after a while, this Vizier, Ibn al-ᶜArif, was given leave by his King Ḥabbâs to return to his home in Málaga, he inquired among the people of his household: "Who wrote the letters which I received from you?" They replied: "A certain Jew of the community of Córdoba, who lives next door to your courtyard, used to do the writing for us." The *Kâtib* thereupon ordered that R. Samuel ha-Levi be brought to him at once, and he said to him: "It does not become you to spend your time in a shop. Henceforth you are to stay at my side." He thus became the scribe and counselor of the counselor to the King. Now the counsel which he gave was as if one consulted the oracle of God, and thanks to his counsel King Ḥabbûs achieved successes and became exceedingly great.

Subsequently, when the *Kâtib* Ibn al-'Arif took ill and felt his death approaching, King Ḥabbûs paid him a visit and said to him: "What am I going to do? Who will counsel me in the wars which encompass me on every side?" He replied: "I never counseled you out of my own mind, but out of the mind of this Jew, my scribe. Look after him well, and let him be a father and a priest to you. Do whatever he says and God will help you."

Accordingly, after the death of the *Kâtib,* King Ḥabbûs brought R. Samuel ha-Levi to his palace and made him *Kātib* and counselor. Thus, he entered the King's palace in 4780.

Now the King had two sons, Bâdîs the elder and Buluggîn the younger. Although the Berber princes supported the election of the younger, Buluggîn, as king, the people at large supported Bâdîs. The Jews also took sides, with three of them, R. Joseph b. Megash, R. Isaac b. Leon and R. Nehemiah surnamed Ishkafa, who were among the leading citizens of Granada supporting Buluggîn. R. Samuel ha-Levi, on the other hand, supported Bâdîs. On the day of King Ḥabbûs's death, the Berber princes and nobles formed a line to proclaim his son Buluggîn as king. Thereupon, Buluggîn went and kissed the hand of his older brother Bâdîs, thus acknowledging the latter as king. This happened in the year 4787. Buluggîn's supporters turned livid with embarrassment, but in spite of themselves they acknowledged Bâdîs as king. Subsequently, his brother Buluggîn regretted his earlier action and tried to lord it over with his brother Bâdîs. There was nothing, however trivial, that the King would do that Buluggîn would not frustrate. When, after a while, his brother took ill, the King told the physician to withhold medications from his brother, and the physician did just that. Buluggîn then died, and the kingdom was established in the hand of

Bâdîs. Thereupon, the three leading Jewish citizens mentioned above fled to the city of Seville.

Now R. Samuel was appointed as nagid in [4]787. He achieved great good for Israel in Spain, the Maghreb, Ifriqiya, Egypt, Sicily, indeed as far as the academy in Babylonia and the Holy City. He provided material benefits out of his own pocket for students of the Torah in all these countries. He also purchased many books— [copies] of the Holy Scriptures as well as of the Mishna and Talmud, which are also among the holy writings. Throughout Spain and the countries just mentioned, whoever wished to devote full time to the study of the Torah found in him a patron. Moreover, he retained scribes who would make copies of the Mishna and Talmud, which he would present to students who were unable to purchase copies themselves, both in the academies of Spain as well as of the other countries we mentioned. These gifts were coupled with annual contributions of olive oil for the synagogues of Jerusalem, which he would dispatch from his own home. He spread Torah abroad and died at a ripe old age after having earned four crowns: the crown of Torah, the crown of power, the crown of a Levite, and towering over them all, by dint of good deeds in each of these domains, the crown of a good name. He passed away in 4815.

His son, R. Joseph ha-Levi the Nagid, succeeded to his post. Of all the fine qualities which his father possessed he lacked but one. Having been reared in wealth and never having had to bear a burden [of responsibility] in his youth, he lacked his father's humility. Indeed, he grew haughty—to his destruction. The Berber princes became so jealous of him that he was killed on the Sabbath day, the ninth of Tebet [4]827, along with the community of Granada and all those who had come from distant lands to see his learning and power. He was mourned in every city and in every town. (Indeed, a fast had been decreed for the ninth of Tebet as far back as the days of our ancient rabbis, who composed *Megillat Ta͗anit*; but the reason had not been known. From this [incident] we see that they had pointed prophetically to this very day.) After his death, his books and treasures were scattered all over the world. So, too, the disciples he raised became the rabbis of Spain and the leaders of the following generation.[3]

Regulations for Non-Muslims in Seville

Ibn ᶜAbdûn, Selections from *Ḥisba* Manual
(Early Twelfth Century)

The proper relations between people of different religions were also described in Muslim legal writings. This text is a classic example of the genre of Muslim legal text known as *ḥisba*. It is a guide for a market inspector (*muḥtasib* in Arabic) that lays out the proper economic and moral administration of a Muslim city—in this case Seville. Technically, a *muḥtasib*'s duty was "to promote good and prevent evil." In practice this task encompassed a wide range of powers. One aspect of the job was to enforce the proper relationship between Muslims, Christians, and Jews in the city. The market inspector was likewise responsible for the moral conduct of the city's inhabitants, public decency, and segregation of the sexes. Because the instructions presented in *ḥisba* manuals are prescriptive, it is difficult to know to what extent they reflect actual practice. Nevertheless, there is sufficient incidental detail in Ibn ᶜAbdûn's text to indicate that his description of Seville's markets was accurate and specific. If nothing else, this text shows that some Muslims desired to enforce a hierarchical structure in which Christians and Jews were socially and economically inferior to Muslims, and in which Muslim women were protected from contact with non-Muslim men. Little is known about the author, but it appears that Ibn ᶜAbdûn was either a Muslim judge (*qâḍî*) or a market inspector (*muḥtasib*) in Seville during the late eleventh and early twelfth centuries.

from *Ḥisba* Manual

A Muslim must not massage a Jew or a Christian nor throw away his refuse nor clean his latrines. The Jew and the Christian are better fitted for such trades, since they are the trades of those who are vile. A Muslim should not attend to the animal of a Jew or of a Christian nor serve him as a muleteer, nor hold his stirrup. If any Muslim is known to do this, he should be denounced.

Muslim women shall be prevented from entering their abominable churches, for the priests are evil-doers, fornicators, and sodomites. Frankish women must be forbidden to enter the church except on days of religious services or festivals, for it is their habit to eat and drink and fornicate with priests, among whom there is not one who has not two or more women with whom he sleeps. This has become a custom among them, for they have permitted what is forbidden and forbidden what is permitted. The priests should be ordered to marry, as they do in the eastern lands. If they wanted to, they would.

No women may be allowed in the house of a priest, neither an old woman nor any other, if he refuses marriage. They should be compelled to submit to circumcision, as was done to them by al-Muᶜtadid ᶜAbbād. They claim to follow the rules of Jesus, may God bless and save him. Now Jesus was circumcised, and they celebrate the day of his circumcision as a festival, yet they themselves do not practice this.

* * *

A garment belonging to a sick man, a Jew, or a Christian must not be sold without indicating its origin; likewise, the garment of a debauchee. Dough must not be taken from a sick man for baking his bread. Neither eggs nor chickens nor milk nor any other foodstuff should be bought from him. They should only buy and sell among themselves.

The sewer men must be forbidden to dig holes in the streets, as this harms them and causes injury to people, except when they are cleaning the entire street.

Itinerant fortune-tellers must be forbidden to go from house to house, as they are thieves and fornicators.

A drunkard must not be flogged until he is sober again.

Prostitutes must be forbidden to stand bareheaded outside the houses. Decent women must not bedeck themselves to resemble them. They must be stopped from coquetry and party making among themselves, even if they have been permitted to do this [by their husbands]. Dancing girls must be forbidden to bare their heads.

No contractor, policeman, Jew, nor Christian may be allowed to dress in the costume of people of position, of a jurist, or of a worthy man. They must on the contrary be abhorred and shunned and should not be greeted with the formula "Peace be with you," for the devil has gained mastery over them and has made them forget the name of God. They are the devil's party, "and indeed the devil's party are the losers" (Qur'an 57:22). They must have a distinguishing sign by which they are recognized to their shame.

Catamites must be driven out of the city and punished wherever any one of them is found. They should not be allowed to move around among the Muslims nor to participate in festivities, for they are debauchees accursed by God and man alike.[4]

Muslims and Jews under Christian Rule in the Thirteenth Century

The first half of the thirteenth century was marked by a dramatic increase in Christian-held territory as armies from Castile and Aragón pushed southward and captured one Andalusi city after another. In 1236, King Ferdinand III of Castile captured Córdoba, and in 1248, he took Seville. In the eastern peninsula, King James I of Aragón conquered Mallorca in 1229, then the city and region of Valencia in 1238. By the middle of the century, only the small southern kingdom of Granada, ruled by the Naṣrid dynasty, remained in Muslim hands. Many Muslims from conquered regions took refuge in Naṣrid Granada, while others emigrated to North Africa or the Middle East. Nevertheless, a certain number of Muslims in Seville, Valencia, and elsewhere elected to remain behind, now living under Christian rule, either because they could not leave or did not wish to. The life of Muslims remaining in newly Christian lands was difficult, but not impossible, though in some cases, they were removed from their homes and resettled, either in rural areas or in special areas of the city (called *morerías*) designated for Muslim inhabitants. Over time, Muslims living in Christian Spain came to be called *mudejars*. The situation for Jews living in Christian Spain was in some ways similar in this period, yet also quite different. There had been Jewish communities in Christian Spanish cities since the Visigothic period, and many Jews had immigrated into Christian Spain from al-Andalus during periods of persecution in the thirteenth century. For this reason, Jews were already a well-established presence in northern cities during the thirteenth century, although—like Muslims—they often lived in their own separate part of the city (called *judería* or *calle*). Because Jews were more familiar with life under Christian rule and often knew Catalan or Castilian, they had more opportunities for employment and economic advancement than did the Muslim population. Many Jews were engaged in professional activities (such as medicine) or commerce that brought them into frequent contact with Christians. As under Muslim rule, a number of Jews were also employed in various capacities at Christian courts. This was never the case for *mudejars*, who tended to find employment in agrarian or menial occupations and often remained more segregated from Christians. As a conquered population, and a possible fifth column, the *mudejars* were never well integrated into Christian society.

Muslims and Jews were always considered to be second-class citizens in Christian society. Their lives and property were generally protected by the king, and they were allowed to practice their own religion, but their social opportunities and ability to interact with Christians were strictly circumscribed. An uneasy balance would be preserved until the later fourteenth century, but Jewish massacres in 1391 and the renewal of the *reconquista* in the fifteenth century opened a new phase in the interfaith relationship that would eventually lead to the expulsion of Jews and Muslims from the peninsula.

The three selections below demonstrate various aspects of Christian attitudes towards Muslims and Jews in thirteenth-century Spain. The first is a peace treaty describing the terms for the surrender of Muslim Valencia to James I of Aragón in 1238. The second lays out the legal status of Muslims and Jews in Castile under Alfonso X (r. 1252–1284), while the third consists of two poems written at the court of Alfonso X and describing miracles resulting in the conversion of Jewish and Muslim women.

1. The Surrender of Valencia City and Its Region

The first text is a brief treaty laying out the terms for the surrender of the city of Valencia in 1238. This town had held out against King James's armies for so long that hardly any chance remained for a negotiated surrender. As the text outlines, the Muslims were allowed to keep only their lives and movable property; they must abandon the city itself and could remain on their farms only as renters. The severity here contrasts with most other surrender agreements in the region of Valencia, which allowed Muslims to remain in their homes. The second text is a more typical example of a surrender document. Dated 1242, it establishes the Muslims of six small places as a protected community (*aljama*) with special rights under the rule of King James. Originally, there would have been both an Arabic and a Latin version, but the Arabic text has been lost.

Charter to Valencia City (1238)

We Juame by the grace of God king of the Aragonese and of the kingdom of the Mallorcas [Balearic Islands], and count of Barcelona and Urgell and lord of Montpellier, promise to you King Zayyân, grandson of King Lūb and son of Mudāfic, that you and all the Moors, both men and women, who wish to go away from Valencia, may travel and leave safe and secure with their weapons and all their movable belongings that they wish to take and carry with them, under Our protection and safeguard from this present day when they are outside the city, up through twenty following consecutive days.

We wish and concede besides that all those Moors who wish to stay in the district of Valencia city may remain under Our protection safe and secure, and that they may make [rental] agreements with the [Christian] landlords who will own the properties.

Besides, We give security and solid truce, for Us and all Our vassals, that henceforth for seven years We shall not do any damage, harm, or war by land or sea, nor shall We permit any to be done in Denia or Cullera or their districts. And if perhaps any of Our vassals and men shall do so, we shall make amends fully according to the amount of the said damage.

The more firmly to attend, fulfill, and observe these conditions, we in Our own person swear, and cause [the following] to swear . . . [the names of two princes and eighteen barons are here]. Besides, We Pere by the grace of God [bishop] of Barcelona, Bernardo bishop of Zaragoza, Vidal bishop of Huesca, García bishop of Tarazona, Ximèn bishop of Segorbe, Ponç biship of Tortosa, and Bernat bishop of Vic, promise to observe all the aforesaid and to have it observed as far as in Us lies or as We shall in good faith be able.

And I Zayyân, the aforesaid king, promise you Jaume, by the grace of God king of the Aragonese, that I shall hand over and surrender to you all the castles and towns that are and that I hold above the Júcar River, within the aforesaid twenty days, keeping out and retaining for myself those two castles, namely Denia and Cullera.

Given in Ruzafa, in the siege of Valencia, on the fourth kalends of October, in the [Aragonese] era 1276 [1238].

The [notarial] sign of Guillem Escrivá who wrote this charter by order of the lord king for the lord Berenguer bishop of Barcelona his chancellor, in the place, date, and era placed above.

Charter to the Muslims of Eslida and Five Other Villages (1242)

This is a charter of favor and protection that Jaume, by the grace of God king of the Aragonese, the Mallorcas, and Valencia, count of Barcelona and Urgell, and lord of Montpellier, makes to the entire community *[aljama]* of Saracens who are in Eslida and in Ahín, in Veo, in Senquier, in Pelmes and Sueras, who placed themselves in his power and became his vassals.

Therefore he granted them that they may keep their homes and possessions in all their villages with all their districts, income and profits, in [both] dry-farming and irrigated lands, cultivated and unworked, and all their farms and plantings.

And they may make use of waters just as was the custom in the time of the Saracens, and may divide the water as was customary among them.

And they may pasture their stock in all their districts as was customary in the time of the pagans [Muslims].

And Christians or anyone of another Law [religio-ethnic group] are not to be sent to settle in their districts without their permission.

Nor may anyone bother their pasturage or stock. And they are to be safe and secure in their persons and things. And they can travel over all their districts, for tending to their affairs, without Christian [interference].

And the castellans of the castles, or the bailiffs, may not demand castle provisioning *[azofres]* of wood and pack animals and water or any service for the castles. Nor are [Christians] to bother them in their houses or vineyards and trees and produce.

Nor may they forbid preaching in the mosques or prayer being made on Fridays and on their feasts and other days; but they [the Muslims] are to carry on according to their religion. And they can teach students the Quran and all the books of the *hadith* [Muḥammad's authenticated example]; and the mosque endowments are to belong to the mosques.

And they are to judge legal cases under the control of their *qâḍî* for those Saracens who are in Eslida, about marriages, and inheritance shares, and purchases and all other cases, according to their Law.

And Saracens who are now outside the villages of the said castles, whenever they come back, can recover their properties forever. And Saracens who want to go away from there can sell their properties and other things to Saracens living there, and the bailiffs cannot stop them; nor are they to pay any fee for that purpose to the castellan of the castle.

And they are to be secure in going about by land or sea, in person and possessions and family and children. And they are not to pay any military-exemption fee, or army substitute, or tally upon their properties except the [civil or rental] tenth on wheat, barley, panic-grass, millet, flax, and vegetables; and the tenth is to be paid on the threshing floor. And they are to give from mills, public ovens, shops, merchants' inns, [and] baths that portion which they used to give in the time of the pagans.

And when they wish, they can go visit relatives, wherever they may be.

And the dead may be buried in the cemeteries, without interference or fee. And fines are to be given according to their Law.

And they are not to pay on any produce, such as onions, cucumbers or other fruits of the land except the aforesaid. On trees and their fruits and on climbing vines they are not to give a tenth, but they give a tenth on vineyards and they give the *zakāt* [Islamic alms tax] on livestock according as they are accustomed.

And Christians may not be housed in their homes and properties unless the Saracens wish. And Christians are not to bring charges against Saracens except with a proper Saracen witness.

And the Saracens of the said castle are to recover their properties, wherever they may be [in the kingdom] except in Valencia city and Burriana.

And on beehives and domestic animals they are not to have anything except what has been said.

And if a Saracen dies, his heirs are to inherit the property. And Saracens who want to marry [*contrahere*] outside their village may do so, without opposition from the castellan or a fee.

And those of Eslida, Ahín, Veo, Pelmes, and Senquier are tax-free on all things from the day on which the lord king granted this charter up through one year. And when that year is finished, they are to discharge the services as above. And the lord king receives them and theirs under his protection and safeguard.

Done at Artana, on the fourth kalends of June, in the year of our Lord 1242.

Witnesses to this matter are the Master of the Templars; the Master of the Hospitallers; Guillem d'Entença; Ximèn de Foces; Lladró; Ximèn Periç; the commander of Alcañiz; Fray Garcés.

The sign of Jaume, by the grace of God king of the Aragonese, of the Mallorcas, and of Valencia, count of Barcelona and Urgell, and lord of Montpellier, who approves and grants the aforesaid as contained above.

I, Guillemó, scribe of the lord king, by his mandate transcribed this in the place, day, and year affixed.[5]

2. The Legal Status of Muslims and Jews in Castile (from the *Siete Partidas*)

Visigothic law codes had regularly included legislation relating to Jews, and such regulations continued to concern Christian rulers and jurists in the later Middle Ages. By the thirteenth century, however, Jews were not the only religious minority living under Christian rule, and law codes also began to include laws pertaining to Muslim subjects. This selection is taken from the *Siete Partidas*, a massive law code commissioned by King Alfonso X of Castile (r. 1252–1284). As its name implies, the *Siete Partidas* is composed of seven sections detailing a vast corpus of medieval legal thought and heavily influenced by Roman law. Although the project was begun at the instigation of Alfonso X, it was not completed until the early fourteenth century. The *Siete Partidas* was formally adopted as law by Alfonso XI in 1348. These passages demonstrate that conversion was of particular concern in interfaith relations, as was sexual contact between Christians and non-Christians. Both Muslims and Jews were entitled to certain protections under law, and both were closely regulated, but legislation indicates that the two groups were not viewed equally. In particular, regulations on conversion and places of worship suggest a greater fear and antipathy on the part of Christians toward the *mudejars*.

In What Way Jews Should Pass Their Lives Among Christians; What Things They Should Not Make Use of or Practice, According to Our Religion; and What Penalty Those Deserve Who Act Contrary to Its Ordinances

Jews should pass their lives among Christians quietly and without disorder, practicing their own religious rites, and not speaking ill of the faith of Our Lord Jesus Christ, which Christians acknowledge. Moreover, a Jew should be very careful to avoid preaching to, or converting any Christian, to the end that he may become a Jew, by exalting his own belief and disparaging ours. Whoever violates this law shall be put to death and lose all his property. And because we have heard it said that in some places Jews celebrated, and still celebrate Good Friday, which commemorates the Passion of Our Lord Jesus Christ, by way of contempt; stealing children and fastening them to crosses, and making images of wax and crucifying them, when they cannot obtain children; we order that, hereafter, if in any part of our dominions anything like this is done, and can be proved, all persons who were present when the act was committed shall be seized, arrested, and brought before the king; and after the king ascertains that they are guilty, he shall cause them to be put to death in a disgraceful manner, no matter how many there may be.

We also forbid any Jew to dare to leave his house on his quarter on Good Friday, but they must all remain shut up until Saturday morning; and if they violate this regulation, we decree that they shall not be entitled to reparation for any injury or dishonor inflicted upon them by Christians.

* * *

How Jews Can Have a Synagogue Among Christians

A synagogue is a place where the Jews pray, and a new building of this kind cannot be erected in any part of our dominions, except by our order. Where, however, those which formerly existed there are torn down, they can be built in the same spot where they originally stood; but they cannot be made any larger or raised to any greater height, or be painted. A synagogue constructed in any other manner shall be lost by the Jews, and shall belong to the principal church of the locality where it is built. And for the reason that a synagogue is a place where the name of God is praised, we forbid any Christian to deface it, or remove anything from it, or take anything out of it by force; except where some malefactor takes refuge there; for they have a right to remove him by force in order to bring him before the judge. Moreover, we forbid Christians to put any animal into a synagogue, or loiter in it, or place any hindrance in the way of the Jews while they are there performing their devotions according to their religion.

No Compulsion Shall Be Brought to Bear upon the Jews on Saturday, and What Jews Can be Subject to Compulsion

Saturday is the day on which Jews perform their devotions and remain quiet in their lodgings, and do not make contracts or transact any business; and for the reason that they are obliged by their religion, to keep it, no one should on that day summon them or bring them into court. Wherefore we order that no judge shall employ force or any constraint upon Jews on Saturday, in order to bring them into court on account of their debts; or arrest them; or cause them any other annoyance; for the remaining days of the week are sufficient for the purpose of employing compulsion against them and for making demands for things which can be demanded of them, according to law. Jews are not bound to obey a summons served upon them on that day; and moreover, we decree that any decision rendered against them on Saturday shall not be valid; but if a Jew should wound, kill, rob, steal, or commit any other offense like these for which he can be punished in person and property, then the judge can arrest him on Saturday.

We also decree that all claims that Christians have against Jews, and Jews against Christians, shall be decided and determined by our judges in the district where they reside and not by their old men. And as we forbid Christians to bring Jews into court or annoy them on Saturday; so we also decree that Jews, neither in person, nor by their attorneys, shall have the right to bring Christians into court, or annoy them on this day. And in addition to this, we forbid any Christian, on his own responsibility, to arrest or wrong any Jew either in his person or property, but where he has any complaint against him he must bring it before our judges; and if anyone should be so bold as to use violence against the Jews, or rob them of anything, he shall return them double the value of the same.

Jews Who Become Christians Shall Not Be Subject to Compulsion; What Advantage a Jew Has Who Becomes a Christian; and What Penalty Other Jews Deserve Who Do Him Harm

No force or compulsion shall be employed in any way against a Jew to induce him to become a Christian; but Christians should convert him to the faith of Our Lord Jesus Christ by means of the texts of the Holy Scriptures, and by kind words, for no one can love or appreciate a service which is done him by compulsion. We also decree that if any Jew or Jewess should voluntarily desire to become a Christian, the other Jews shall not interfere with this in any way, and if they stone, wound, or kill any such person, because they wish to become Christians, or after they have been baptized, and this can be proved; we order that all the murderers, or the abettors of said murder or attack, shall be burned. But where the party was not killed, but wounded, or dishonored; we order that the judges of the neighborhood where this took place shall compel those guilty of the attack, or who caused the dishonor, to make amends to him for the same; and also that they be punished for the offence which they committed, as they think they deserve; and we also order that, after any Jews become Christians, all persons in our dominions shall honor them; and that no one shall dare to reproach them or their descendants, by way of insult, with having been Jews; and that they shall possess all their property, sharing the same with their brothers, and inheriting it from their fathers and mothers and other relatives, just as if they were Jews; and that they can hold all offices and dignities which other Christians can do.

What Penalty a Christian Deserves Who Becomes a Jew

Where a Christian is so unfortunate as to become a Jew, we order that he shall be put to death just as if he had become a heretic; and we decree that his property shall be disposed of in the same way that we stated should be done with that of heretics.

No Christian, Man or Woman, Shall Live with a Jew

We forbid any Jew to keep Christian men or women in his house, to be served by them, although he may have them to cultivate and take care of his lands, or protect him on the way then he is compelled to go to some dangerous place. Moreover, we forbid any Christian man or woman to invite a Jew or a Jewess, or to accept an invitation from them, to eat or drink together, or to drink any wine made by their hands. We also order that no Jews shall dare to bathe in company with Christians and that no Christian shall take any medicine or cathartic made by a Jew; but he can take it by the advice of some intelligent person, only where it is made by a Christian, who knows and is familiar with its ingredients.

What Penalty a Jew Deserves Who Has Intercourse with a Christian Woman

Jews who live with Christian women are guilty of great insolence and boldness, for which reason we decree that all Jews who, hereafter, may be convicted of having done such a thing shall be put to death. For if

Christians who commit adultery with married women deserve death on that account, much more do Jews who have sexual intercourse with Christian women, who are spiritually the wives of Our Lord Jesus Christ because of the faith and the baptism which they receive in His name; nor do we consider it proper that a Christian woman who commits an offense of this kind shall escape without punishment. Wherefore we order that, whether she be a virgin, a married woman, a widow, or a common prostitute who gives herself to all men, she shall suffer the same penalty which we mentioned in the last law in the Title concerning the Moors, to which a Christian woman is liable who has carnal intercourse with a Moor.

* * *

Jews Shall Bear Certain Marks in Order That They May Be Known

Many crimes and outrageous things occur between Christians and Jews because they live together in cities, and dress alike, and in order to avoid the offenses and evils which take place for this reason, we deem it proper, and we order that all Jews male and female living in our dominions shall bear some distinguishing mark upon their heads so that people may plainly recognize a Jew, or a Jewess; and any Jew who does not bear such mark, shall pay for each time his is found without it ten *maravedis* of gold; and if he has not the means to do this he shall publicly receive ten lashes for his offence.

* * *

Concerning the Moors

We decree that Moors shall live among Christians in the same way that we mentioned in the preceding Title that Jews shall do, by observing their own law and not insulting ours. Moors, however, shall not have mosques in Christian towns, or make their sacrifices publicly in the presence of men. The mosques which they formerly possessed shall belong to the king; and he can give them to whomsoever he wishes. Although the Moors do not acknowledge a good religion, so long as they live among Christians with their assurance of security, their property shall not be stolen from them or taken by force; and we order that whoever violates this law shall pay a sum equal to double the value of what he took.

Christians Should Convert the Moors by Kind Words, and Not by Compulsion

Christians should endeavor to convert the Moors by causing them to believe in our religion, and bring them into it by kind words and suitable discourses, and not by violence or compulsion; for if it should be the will of Our Lord to bring them into it and to make them believe by force, He can use compulsion against them if He so desires, since He has full power to do so; but He is not pleased with the service which men perform through fear, but with that which they do voluntarily and without coercion, and as He does not wish to restrain them or employ violence, we forbid anyone to do so for this purpose; and if the wish to become Christians should arise among them, we forbid anyone to refuse assent to it, or oppose it in any way whatsoever. Whoever violates this law shall receive the penalty we mentioned in the preceding Title, which treats of how Jews who interfere with, or kill those belonging to their religion who afterwards become Christians, shall be punished.

What Punishment Those Deserve Who Insult Converts

Many men live and die in strange beliefs, who would love to be Christians if it were not for the villification and dishonor which they see others who become converted endure by being called turncoats, and calumniated and insulted in many evil ways; and we hold that those who do this wickedly offend, and that they should honor persons of this kind for many reasons, and not show them disrespect. One of these is because they renounce the religion in which they and their families were born; and another is because, after they have understanding, they acknowledge the superiority of our religion and accept it, separating from their parents and their relatives, and abandoning the life which they have been accustomed to live, and all other things from which they derive pleasure. There are some of them who, on account of the dishonor inflicted upon them after they have adopted our Faith, and become Christians, repent and desert it, closing their hearts against it on account of the insults and reproaches to which they are subjected; and for this reason we order all Christians, of both sexes, in our dominions to show honor and kindness, in every way they can, to persons of other strange beliefs, who embrace our religion; just as they would do to any of their own parents or grandparents, who had embraced the faith or become Christians; and we forbid anyone to dishonor them by word or deed, or do them any wrong, injury, or harm in any way whatever. If anyone violates this law we order that he be punished for it, as seems best to the judges of the district; and that the punishment be more severe than if the injury had been committed against another man or woman whose entire line of ancestors had been Christians.

What Punishment a Christian Deserves Who Becomes a Moor

Men sometimes become insane and lose their prudence and understanding, as, for instance, where unfortunate persons, and those who despair of everything, renounce the faith of Our Lord Jesus Christ, and become Moors; and there are some of them who are induced to do this through the desire to live according to their customs, or on account of the loss of relatives who have been killed or died; or because they have lost their property and become poor; or because of unlawful acts which they commit, dreading the punishment which they deserve on account of them; and when they are induced to do a thing of this kind for any of the reasons aforesaid, or others similar to them, they are guilty of very great wickedness and treason, for on account of no loss or affliction which may come upon them, nor for any profit, riches, good fortune, or pleasure which they may expect to obtain in this world, should they renounce the faith of Our Lord Jesus Christ by which they will be saved and have everlasting life.

Wherefore, we order that all those who are guilty of this wickedness shall lose all their possessions, and have no right to any portion of them, but that all shall belong to their children (if they have any) who remain steadfast in our Faith and do not renounce it; and if they have no children, their property shall belong to their nearest relatives within the tenth degree, who remain steadfast in the belief of the Christians; and if they have neither children nor relatives, all their possessions shall be forfeited to the royal treasury; and, in addition to this, we order that if any person who has committed such an offence shall be found in any part of our dominions he shall be put to death.

* * *

What Penalty a Moor and a Christian Woman Deserve Who Have Intercourse with One Another

If a Moor has sexual intercourse with a Christian virgin, we order that he shall be stoned, and that she, for the first offense, shall lose half of her property, and that her father, mother, or grandfather shall have it, and if she has no such relatives, that it shall belong to the king. For the second offense, she shall lose all her property, and the heirs aforesaid, if she has any, shall obtain it, and if she has none, the king shall be entitled to it, and she shall be put to death. We decree and order that the same rule shall apply to a widow who commits this crime. If a Moor has sexual intercourse with a Christian married woman, he shall be stoned to death, and she shall be placed in the power of her husband who may burn her to death, or release her, or do what he pleases with her. If a Moor has intercourse with a common woman who abandons herself to everyone, for the first offense, they shall be scourged together through the town, and for the second, they shall be put to death.[6]

3. The Cantigas de Santa María

Alfonso X of Castile is often known as "Alfonso the Wise" (or Alfonso el Sabio) because of the intellectual productivity of his court. As well as the *Siete Partidas*, Alfonso commissioned a number of other important works, including scientific treatises, poetry, and a manual on the game of chess. The two poems below are taken from a collection of over four hundred songs written in praise of the Virgin Mary (thus entitled the *Cantigas de Santa María*). The songs describe miracles attributed to the Virgin, and many of them tell stories of the conversion of Muslims or Jews. There are many indications that Christians in thirteenth-century Spain hoped for the conversion of non-Christians, and these stories are just one example of the role that this wish played in the Christian imagination. Some of the poems may have been composed by King Alfonso himself, and most are lavishly illustrated and set to music (the notation is included in the manuscript). The images of Muslims and Jews in the *Cantiga* manuscripts often reflect stereotypical features, yet they also provide precious clues as to the dress and appearance of religious minorities in Christian Spain.

107

How Holy Mary saved from death the Jewess who was thrown over a cliff in Segovia. Because she commended herself to Holy Mary, she did not die nor suffer harm.

The Holy Virgin will aid those in distress if they believe in Her.

Concerning this, the Mother of Mercy performed a miracle, in all truth, in the city of Segovia, as this song will relate.

It was for a Jewess who was caught in a crime and arrested and taken to be hurled from a high and rugged cliff in that place.

She said: "Oh, woe is me, how can anyone who falls from here remain alive unless it be by God's will?

"But you, Queen Mary, in whom Christians believe, if it is true, as I have heard, "that you succor the unfortunate women who are commended to you, among all the other guilty women, come to my aid, for I have great need.

"If I remain alive and well, I will, without fail, become a Christian at once, before another day dawns."

The Jews who led her, dressed only in her shift, let go of her and pushed her over the cliff, shouting: "There she goes!"

But when she fell from there, the Virgin came to her aid. Therefore, she did not perish but fell clear of the rocks

Right at the foot of a fig tree. She sprang up nimbly and went on her way, saying: "May the Glorious One, Precious Mother of God, who was so merciful to me, be ever praised. Who will not serve Her?"

She arrived at the church of Her who should always be blessed, where she saw a great crowd of people, and she said:

"Come at once and baptize me, then you will hear a miracle which will astound you and all who hear it."

Those people baptized her without delay, and she was henceforth always a devoted believer in the One who prays

To Her glorious Son for us, that He have mercy on us the fearful day when He will come to judge us.

205

How Holy Mary saved a Mooress who was holding her son in her arms while she sat on a tower between two merlons. The tower, fell, but neither she nor her son were killed nor hurt in the slightest. This was because of the prayer of the Christians.

The Virgin gladly hears a pious prayer and because of it will protect the one who is commended to Her.

For these two things more surely win Her love and blessing, if they are done devoutly, as they should be, and thus Her power is freely shown to everyone in need.

Concerning this, I beg you to hear a miracle which Holy Mary performed, and if you listen well, you will hear a great marvel and may be certain that it was performed in the presence of many honorable men because of prayer.

On the frontier there was a very strong Moorish castle besieged by Christians who were attacking from Uclés and Calatrava. Don Alfonso Téllez, a worthy nobleman, was there and brought with him a large company of excellent knights, brave and strong and, moreover, good warriors, and also many raiders, foot soldiers, and crossbowmen, by whom the castle was speedily invaded.

The castle was fiercely attacked on all sides, and the walls knocked down, which greatly alarmed the people who were inside. When they saw that they were defeated, they took refuge in a very strong tower. In each side of the tower, the attackers made great holes and set fire to it. The Moors who were inside, in order to escape from the fire, began to thrown themselves from the battlements, and thus many of those ill-fated folk died.

With this great affliction of the smoke which blinded them and also of the fire which fiercely burned them, a Mooress carrying her son, whom she loved more than herself, climbed up to the top with him so that he might not be suffocated.

The poor woman sat down between two merlons with her little son clasped in her arms. Although a great fire raged on all sides, the Mooress was not burned nor her baby touched by the fire.

Master don Gonzalo Eanes of Calatrava, who diligently waged war on the Moors in God's service, and also don Alfonso Téllez, of whom I spoke, ordered all-out attack upon the tower, and when they saw that the tower was completely destroyed and noticed that Mooress seated between the merlons, she looked to them like the statue of the Holy Virgin Mary depicted with Her Son held in Her arms.

They and all the other Christians who saw her felt pity and imploringly raised their hands to God to save the two from death, even though they were pagans. Because of this, God performed a great miracle.

> The side of the tower where they were slid down to earth on a great open plain, so gently that neither mother nor child was killed, harmed or shaken.
>
> The Holy Virgin Mary, to whom the Christians prayed for the Mooress' sake, set them down in a meadow. Therefore, all were filled with wonder and gave great praise to Her and Her Son. The Mooress became a Christian and her son was baptized.[7]

Inquisition and Expulsion

The late fifteenth century witnessed striking new developments in Spain, especially in terms of interfaith relations. The conversion of many Iberian Jews in the wake of massacres in 1391 had created a growing community of "new Christians," sometimes called *conversos*, by the fifteenth century. At first, it appears that these new Christians were accepted and integrated within the Christian community, but over time suspicions arose as to the sincerity of their belief. Many converts and descendants of converts were accused of retaining—or returning to—Jewish practices (this was known as "Judaizing"). In order to determine whether these suspicions were accurate, inquisitorial trials were held and suspects were interrogated concerning their beliefs and customs. The first text below records part of the trial of a *converso* woman called Inés López, who was suspected of Judaizing and came before the Inquisition in the late fifteenth century. The process of inquisition was not an innovation, since it had been established elsewhere in Europe in the thirteenth century to handle cases of Christian heresy, but its evolution in late medieval Spain took new and more terrifying forms. Suspects were urged to confess their heresy and repent; those found guilty were punished or executed. The Inquisition was aimed at *conversos*, not at Jews, but the latter were seen as an aggravating influence. Christians feared that as long as there were Jews in the peninsula, they would provide a model to corrupt the proper Christian belief of converts. This fear was one of the reasons behind the expulsion of all Jews from Castile and Aragón in 1492, and from other Iberian kingdoms soon after. The second text below is the Edict of Expulsion, ordered by King Ferdinand and Queen Isabella in 1492.

1. The Inquisitorial Trials of Inés López (1495–1496, 1511–1512)

Inés López was born in 1464 or 1466, the daughter of a shoemaker and his wife. She was married in 1494, when she was about twenty-nine, but was already a widow by the time of her first trial the following year. She came twice before the Inquisition, once in 1495–1496 and again in 1511–1512. After the first trial, Inés was convicted of Judaizing and sentenced to participate in an *auto de fe*, a humiliating public spectacle during which those accused of heresy were marched through the streets and urged to abjure their errors. Those who confessed and repented were received back into the Church; unrepentant heretics would be executed by secular authorities. After surviving the *auto de fe*, Inés lived for the next fifteen years under house arrest, though she retained a certain degree of freedom. In 1511, however, she was again found guilty of Judaizing, and this time she was imprisoned and all her property was confiscated. Inés was not the only member of her family to suffer in this way. Both of her parents were tried by the Inquisition (though her father's trial was posthumous), as were three of her sisters. Her sister Leonor was accused of Judaizing and condemned to life imprisonment, and her sister Violante was burned at the stake in 1494, a year before Inés's own trial.

Inquisitorial trials consisted of a series of interrogations, and the accused was never told the reasons for his or her imprisonment. Instead, he or she was given three warnings, over a period of weeks, to confess. This was a strategy intended to elicit spontaneous confessions of heresy and Judaizing. In her confessions, Inés López admitted to observing some Jewish precepts, many of which had less to do with beliefs than with social and culinary customs. As in many cases, inquisitors also collected testimony about Inés from neighbors and family members.

Confession of 22 October 1495

Most reverend Lords:

I, Inés López, a resident of Ciudad Real, wife of the late Alonso de Aguilera, appear before Your Reverences with the greatest contrition and repentance for my sins of which I am capable, and I beg Our Lord Jesus Christ for His pardon and mercy, and I beg of Your Reverences a saving penance for my soul, and for those [sins] that I have committed by which I have offended My Lord Jesus Christ and His Holy Catholic Faith, which are the following in this manner:

I declare, My Lords, that I did not do servile work on some Saturdays, and on Saturdays I put on clean clothes. And sometimes I ate food that was prepared on Friday for Saturday, and I lit candles on Friday evening in accordance with Jewish ritual.

Likewise, I observed some of the Jewish fasts, [fasting] until nightfall. Moreover, I sometimes observed Jewish holidays, when I found out about them from a cousin of mine named Isabel de Lobón, when I was [staying] with her, for she was a widow. And she told me to do so for the benefit of my soul, especially [to observe] Passover, for the aforementioned Isabel de Lobón every so often gave me [unleavened bread], warning me not to tell anyone. The aforementioned Isabel de Lobón has left Villareal [Ciudad Real]; for where, no one knows.

Likewise, I removed the fat from meat whenever I could.

Likewise, My Lords, I declare that I ate on low tables at funeral banquets. . . .

Additional Confession of 14 January 1496

My most reverend Lords:

I, Inés López, daughter of Diego López, a resident of Ciudad Real, appear before Your Reverences to say that, because I made a confession of the sins I had committed against Our Lord in which I said that if any further sin came to mind I would declare and reveal it, I now declare, My Lords, that what I further remember is the following:

I declare and confess to Your Reverences that on some Friday nights my sister [Violante], the [wife] of [Pedro de] San Román, and I tidied up the house and cooked Saturday's food on those nights. We did this sometimes, and other times we didn't, so that we wouldn't be found out, etc.

Moreover, My Lords, I had little desire to eat pork, and when I could, I didn't eat it, and neither did my aforementioned sister, who told me that I shouldn't eat [it] nor anything cooked with it because I was younger than she.

Moreover, My Lords, sometimes when I went to Mass it was my custom and habit to chatter and not to pray . . .

Moreover, My Lords, on Sundays and holidays I sometimes sewed things I needed and also performed other tasks . . .

Moreover, My Lords, on days of abstinence in Lent and the vigils of other holidays and on ember days, I often prepared and ate food, and I saw that my aforementioned sisters ate meat and other [forbidden] delicacies.

Moreover, My Lords, I declare that when my father died, I saw Diego Díez's wife and Sezilla, the wife of Martín González, put a pot of water in the parlor where [his body] was. I don't know why, except that I heard it said that it was to bathe my aforementioned father, who was dirty. And I placed a basin of water and a cloth in said parlor—I don't remember who told me to do so, except that I believe that it was Mayor Alvarez, my sister, who was there.

Moreover, I often lit candles on Friday nights in San Román's house, because I usually lived with San Román and his wife, my sister, for I was twelve or fifteen years old.

Moreover, my Lords, I saw that my mother did not spin on Saturdays, and I saw this during the whole time that I live [with her] . . .

Additional Confession of 19 January 1496

My most reverend Lords:

I, Inés López, a resident of Ciudad Real, appear before Your Reverences and declare that, in addition to what I have declared and confessed to you, I often porged meat and removed the tendons from legs of lamb.

Arraignment: 16 September 1511

I. First, that the aforementioned Inés López, after her aforementioned false reconciliation and abjuration, often and at many times and in many places disclaimed the confession that she had spontaneously made, declaring and affirming that she had never perpetrated or committed the crimes of heresy that she had confessed to and for which she was reconciled, and [declaring] that false witnesses had imputed [such crimes] to her and to others, and that she had never done or committed such things, saying: "See how my life hangs on the words of a drunken man or a drunken woman" and that the Lord should preserve her from false witnesses, always declaring and affirming that she had never done any of those things for which she had been reconciled, and that she had only been reconciled so that they wouldn't burn her at the stake . . .

II. Moreover, that the aforementioned Inés López, after her reconciliation and abjuration, defended and continued to defend many condemned heretics, declaring and affirming that they had been unjustly condemned, that they were no heretics, except that they had been falsely accused and condemned without their deserving it; in particular, she said that her mother and her sisters, who had been condemned and had not committed any crime of heresy whatsoever that would justify their being burned at the stake. . . .

[III. Inés is also accused of defending certain deceased "heretics" whose bodies were discovered to be shrouded in the Jewish manner and buried without any crosses.]

IV. Moreover, that the aforementioned Inés López, often speaking after her reconciliation about the Inquisition and about heretics, said that everything had been fabricated by false witnesses and that the Inquisition had been set up for the sole purpose of extracting money and robbing them. . . .

V. Moreover, that the aforementioned Inés López did not know how to cross herself nor did she ever cross herself, until such time eight or ten months ago when they said that the Inquisition was coming to Ciudad Real. And afterwards, if she ever did make the sign of the cross, it was not done as a Christian, crossing herself and saying "In the name of the Father and of the Son, etc." And if ever they got her to say "In the name of the Father", she was reluctant and even refused to say "and of the Son" or "of the Holy Spirit".

VI. Moreover, that the aforementioned Inés López, an unbeliever and a mocker of our holy Catholic Christian faith and of the things of the Church and the Eucharist, sometimes when she returned from hearing mass, which she only attended in order to look good in the eyes of her neighbors, would make jokes, saying that she had come from such and such a church and that she had heard a smoked mass, which she said because they had used incense. . . . [8]

2. The Expulsion of the Jews (1492)

King Ferdinand of Aragón and Queen Isabella of Castille have often been called the "Catholic Monarchs," since husband and wife were united in their ambitions to conquer the last Muslim kingdom of Granada and to remove the Jews from Spain. In many other respects, however, their kingdoms remained separate entities. The year 1492 was critical for Ferdinand and Isabella since they not only finally captured Naṣrid Granada, but also expelled the Jews from their realms and funded the first voyage of Christopher Columbus to the New World.

This charter begins by explaining the rationale for requiring that all unconverted Jews leave the kingdoms of Castile and Aragón, and it goes on to set the terms for their expulsion. Although the text was dated March 31, 1492, it was not actually issued until a month later, thereby giving the Jews only three months, instead of the original four, in which to prepare for departure. The delay may have been caused by attempts to persuade the monarchs to rescind the order, an effort for which there is substantial contemporary evidence. In the end, these attempts failed. Many Castilian and Aragonese Jews departed for Italy, North Africa, and Turkey, while others sought refuge in Portugal and Navarre, where this order of expulsion was not in effect. These havens proved transitory, however, since Jews would also be expelled from these peninsular kingdoms in 1496 and 1498.

31 March 1492. Granada

[1] Lord Ferdinand and Lady Isabella, by the grace of God king and queen of Castile, León, Aragon, Sicily, Granada, Toledo, Valencia, Galicia, the Balearic Islands, Seville, Sardinia, Córdoba, Corsica, Murcia, Jaén, of the Algarve, Algeciras, Gibralter, and of the Canary Islands, count and countess of Barcelona and lords of Biscay and Molina, dukes of Athens and Neopatria, counts of Rousillon and Cerdana, marquises of Oristan and of Gociano, to the prince Lord Juan, our very dear and much loved son, and to the [other] royal children, prelates, dukes marqueses, counts, masters of [military] orders, priors, grandees, knight commanders, governors of castles and fortified places of our kingdoms and lordships, and to councils, magistrates, mayors, constables, district judges, knights, official squires, and all good men of the noble and loyal city of Burgos and other cities, towns, villages of its bishopric and of other archbishoprics, bishoprics, dioceses of our kingdoms and lordships, and to the residential quarters of the Jews of the said city of Burgos and of all the aforesaid cities, towns, and villages of its bishopric and of the other cities, towns, and villages of our aforementioned kingdoms and lordships, and to all Jews and to all individual Jews of those places, and to barons and women of whatever age they may be, and to all other persons of whatever law, estate, dignity, preeminence, and condition they may be, and to all to whom the matter contained in this charter pertains or may pertain. Salutations and grace.

[2] You know well, or ought to know, that whereas we have been informed that in these our kingdoms, there were some wicked Christians who Judaized and apostatized from our holy Catholic faith, the great cause of which was interaction between the Jews and these Christians, in the cortes which we held in the city of Toledo in the

past year of one thousand, four hundred and eighty, we ordered the separation of the said Jews in all the cities, towns, and villages of our kingdoms and lordships and [commanded] that they be given Jewish quarters and separated places where they should live, hoping that by their separation the situation would remedy itself. Furthermore, we procured and gave orders that inquisition should be made in our afore-mentioned kingdoms and lordships, which as you know has for twelve years been made and is being made, and by it many guilty persons have been discovered, as is very well known, and accordingly we are informed by the inquisitors and by other devout persons, ecclesiastical and secular, that great injury has resulted and still results, since the Christians have engaged in and continue to engage in social interaction and communication they have had and continue to have with Jews, who, it seems, seek always and by whatever means and ways they can to subvert and to steal faithful Christians from our holy Catholic faith and to separate them from it, and to draw them to themselves and subvert them to their own wicked belief and conviction, instructing them in the ceremonies and observances of their law, holding meetings at which they read and teach that which people must hold and believe according to their law, achieving that the Christians and their children be circumcised, and giving them books from which they may read their prayers and declaring to them the fasts that they must keep, and joining with them to read and teach them the history of their law, indicating to them the festivals before they occur, advising them of what in them they are to hold and observe, carrying to them and giving to them from their houses unleavened bread and meats ritually slaughtered, instructing them about the things from which they must refrain, as much in eating as in other things in order to observe their law, and persuading them as much as they can to hold and observe the law of Moses, convincing them that there is no other law or truth except for that one. This proved by many statements and confessions, both from these same Jews and from those who have been perverted and enticed by them, which has redounded to the great injury, detriment, and opprobrium of our holy Catholic faith.

[3] Notwithstanding that we were informed of the great part of this before now and we knew that the true remedy for all these injuries and inconveniences was to prohibit all interaction between the said Jews and Christians and banish them from all our kingdoms, we desired to content ourselves by commanding them to leave all cities,

towns, and villages of Andalusia where it appears that they have done the greatest injury, believing that that would be sufficient so that those of other cities, towns, and villages of our kingdoms and lordships would cease to do and commit the aforesaid acts. And since we are informed that neither that step nor the passing of sentence [of condemnation] against the said Jews who have been most guilty of the said crimes and delicts against our holy Catholic faith have been sufficient as a complete remedy to obviate and correct so great an opprobrium and offense to the faith and the Christian religion, because every day it is found and appears that the said Jews increase in continuing their evil and wicked purpose wherever they live and congregate, and so that there will not be any place where they further offend our holy faith, and corrupt those whom God has until now most desired to preserve, as well as those who had fallen but amended and returned to Holy Mother Church, the which according to the weakness of our humanity and by diabolical astuteness and suggestion that continually wages war against us may easily occur unless the principal cause of it be removed, which is to banish the said Jews from our kingdoms. Because whenever any grave and detestable crime is committed by members of any organization or corporation, it is reasonable that such an organization or corporation should be dissolved and annihilated and that the lesser members as well as the greater and everyone for the others be punished, and that those who perturb the good and honest life of cities and towns and by contagion can injure others should be expelled from those places and even if for lighter causes that may be injurious to the Republic, how much more for those greater and most dangerous and most contagious crimes such as this.

[4] Therefore, we, with the counsel and advice of prelates, great noblemen of our kingdoms, and other persons of learning and wisdom of our council, having taken deliberation about this matter, resolve to order the said Jews and Jewesses of our kingdoms to depart and never to return or come back to them or to any of them. And concerning this we command this our charter to be given, by which we order all Jews and Jewesses of whatever age they may be, who live, reside, and exist in our said kingdoms and lordships, as much those who are natives as those who are not, who by whatever manner or whatever cause have come to live and reside therein, that by the end of the month of July next of the present year, they depart from all of these

our said realms and lordships, along with their sons and daughters, manservants and maidservants, Jewish familiars, those who are great as well as the lesser folk, of whatever age they may be, and they shall not dare to return to those places, nor to reside in them, nor to live in any part of them, neither temporarily on the way to somewhere else nor in any other manner, under pain that if they do not perform and comply with this command and should be found in our said kingdom and lordships and should in any manner live in them, they incur the penalty of death and the confiscation of all their possessions by our Chamber of Finance, incurring these penalties by the act itself, without further trial, sentence, or declaration. And we command and forbid that any person or persons of the said kingdoms, of whatever estate, condition or dignity that they may be, shall dare to receive, protect, defend, nor hold publicly or secretly any Jew or Jewess beyond the date of the end of July and from henceforth forever, in their lands, houses, or in other parts of any of our said kingdoms and lordships, under pain of losing all their possessions, vassals, fortified places, and other inheritances, and beyond this of losing whatever financial grants they hold from us by our Chamber of Finance.

[5] And so that the said Jews and Jewesses during the stated period of time until the end of the said month of July may be better able to dispose of themselves, and their possessions, and their estates, for the present we take and receive them under our security, protection, and royal safeguard, and we secure to them and to their possessions that for the duration of the said time until the said last day of the said month of July they may travel and be safe, they may enter, sell, trade, and alienate all their movable and rooted possessions and dispose of them freely and at their will, and that during the said time, no one shall harm them, nor injure them, no wrong shall be done to them against justice, in their persons or in their possessions, under the penalty which falls on and is incurred by those who violate the royal safeguard. And we likewise give license and faculty to those said Jews and Jewesses that they be able to export their goods and estates out of these our said kingdoms and lordships by sea or land as long as they do not export gold or silver or coined money or other things prohibited by the laws of our kingdoms, excepting merchandise and things that are not prohibited.

[6] And we command all councils, justices, magistrates, knights, squires, officials, and all good men of the said city of Burgos and of the

other cities, towns, and villages of our said kingdoms and lordships and all our new vassals, subjects, and natives that they preserve and comply with and cause to be preserved and complied with this our charter and all that is contained in it, and to give and to cause to be given all assistance and favor in its application under penalty of [being at] our mercy and the confiscation of all their possessions and offices by our Chamber of Finance. And because this must be brought to the notice of all, so that no one may pretend ignorance, we command that this our charter be posted in the customary plazas and places of the said city and of the principal cities, towns, and villages of its bishopric as an announcement and as a public document. And no one shall do any damage to it in any manner under penalty of being at our mercy and the deprivation of their offices and the confiscation of their possessions, which will happen to each one who might do this. Moreover, we command the [man] who shows them this our charter that he summon [those who act against the charter] to appear before us at our court wherever we may be, on the day that they are summoned during the fifteen days following the crime under the said penalty, under which we command whichever public scribe who would be called for the purpose of reading this our charter that the signed charter with its seal should be shown to you all so that we may know that our command is carried out.

[7] Given in our city of Granada, the XXXI day of the month of March, the year of the birth of our lord Jesus Christ one thousand four hundred and ninety-two years. I, the king, I the queen, I, Juan de Coloma, secretary of the king and queen our lords, have caused this to be written at their command. Registered by Cabrera, Almacan chancellor.[9]

Conclusion

During the centuries under consideration, from the beginning of the eighth century when Muslim armies arrived in Spain until the end of the fifteenth century when Ferdinand and Isabella united the region under Christian rule, the Iberian Peninsula was home to a population that included Christians, Muslims, and Jews. Yet this diversity came at a price. Although there were long periods of relative tolerance, during which minority populations flourished, there were also periods of intolerance and persecution. Because of the nature of historical writing, which tends to record and preserve moments of difficulty, discontent, and drama, texts from medieval Spain (including those collected here) often show intolerance more clearly than tolerance. The reader should keep this in mind.

Also important to note is that, starting in the fifteenth century, there were significant changes in the relationship among Christians, Muslims, and Jews in Spain. During the reign of Ferdinand and Isabella, the dual processes of inquisition and expulsion made life intolerable for Jews in the kingdoms of Castile and Aragón. Although the Inquisition initially had little to do with Muslims, in part because *mudejars* (Muslims living under Christian rule) remained quite segregated from Christian society, this would soon change. In 1525, the Muslims of Aragón (the only region where a significant Islamic population remained) were ordered to convert or leave the kingdom, and in 1609, even those who had converted (called *moriscos*) were expelled. By the early seventeenth century, the Iberian Peninsula had become a region entirely populated by Christians.

Note: *All of the texts in this chapter, except for the selections from the* Cantigas de Santa María, *have been reprinted from* Medieval Iberia: Readings from Christian, Muslim, and Jewish Sources, *ed. Olivia R. Constable (Philadelphia: University of Pennsylvania Press, 1997).*

Discussion Questions

1. Discuss the meaning of *convivencia*. What did it mean to "live together" in medieval Spain, and how did this change over time?

2. Do you think that the *reconquista* ("reconquest") was more about religion, or more about politics and territory?

3. Compare the position of Jews in Spain under Muslim and Christian rule.

CHRISTIANITY AND ISLAM IN THE BALKANS FROM THE FIFTEENTH TO THE TWENTIETH CENTURIES

Amila Buturovic

The Balkans: What Is in the Name?

At the turn of the twentieth century, the word *Balkan* became a ubiquitous metaphor for political fragmentations, reversion to chaos and disorder, and absence of civilized behavior. Originally a Turkish word that means "mountain chain" and refers to the term *Balkan* and its derivatives, such as *Balkanization*, *Balkan ghosts*, and *Balkan hatreds*, have all gained strong currency in political, popular, and academic discourse alike to refer to violent political processes. Yet the Balkans is also a historical reality composed of rich and complex experiences of religious and ethnic diversity and centuries-long interaction and coexistence among Christians, Muslims, and Jews. In light of this double association, it seems necessary to begin the analysis of the Balkan religious and ethnic mosaic in general and the relations between Christianity and Islam in particular with a discussion of what lies in the name *the Balkans* itself: where it came from, how it evolved, and what associations it has evoked. This overview should not only help us understand better the ways in which a specific geographic term or location can be transformed into a seemingly timeless symbol, but also make us aware of the historical factors that can disturb the otherwise stable balance of interfaith relations in any given place, and even lead to outbursts of violence and fragmentation in which religion can be assigned a crucial role. In the book *The Balkans: A Short*

History, author Mark Mazower draws attention to this perilous intersection between history and ideology by looking at the example of the
Balkans. He cautions against uncritical acceptance of the term *balkanization* as an immutable fact of life and advocates that the Balkans be looked
at as a product of specific historical circumstances that enveloped the
region in the early twentieth century, by and large through Western
European political orchestration. In analyzing the history behind the
term, Mazower concisely and astutely examines the complexity of Balkan
demography and draws important links among religion, culture, and
political conditions. Here is a summary of his introduction:[1]

> At the end of the twentieth century, people referred to the Balkans as if it
> had existed forever, yet two hundred years earlier, it had not yet come into
> being. "Balkan" was originally applied only to the mountain range that
> stretches between the Alps and that in the ancient times had been known
> as Haemus. In the Ottoman period that starts in the Balkans roughly on
> the eve of the 15th century and ends at the turn of the 20th century, the
> region was never referred to as "the Balkans" but rather as "Rumeli," that
> is, the lands of Orthodox Romans/Byzantines from whom the Ottomans
> seized the control over the region. Until the 19th century, Europeans spoke
> of the region as "European Turkey" or "Turkey in Europe" and made hardly
> any ethnic distinction, if any, between its Orthodox Greek and Slav pop-
> ulations. Nor before the 1880s were there many references to "Balkan"
> peoples either. The world of the Orthodoxy was by and large considered
> unified so it took time for ethnographic and political distinctions to
> emerge. It was therefore only with the rise of Slav nationalism in the late
> 19th and early 20th centuries that the regional complexity became a more
> pressing issue in the European political affairs, especially as the post-
> Ottoman future of the region was debated in its diplomatic circles. Since
> hardly anyone had expected a complete collapse of the regional unity,
> there was a sense that the Balkan people were heading toward relatively
> easy solutions for their political future: "Even in our days," wrote a
> Frenchman in 1864, "how often have I heard people as who the Christian
> population of Turkey belonged to—Russia, Austria, France? And when
> some dreamers replied: These populations belong to themselves—what
> amusement, what pity at such utopianism."[2]
>
> With the advent of nationalism, however, and the creation of successor
> states—Greece, Bulgaria, Serbia, Romania, Montenegro, and later
> Albania—the region became a great point of interest to travelers, journal-
> ists and propagandists who popularized the new, broader use of the term
> "Balkans" to replace the now outdated "Turkey in Europe." By the time of
> the First Balkan War in 1912, the term has become common currency so

much so that by 1917, a standard history of the Eastern Question regularly used "Balkan Peninsula" or simply "the Balkans" as the new name that encapsulated the changing political makeup of the region.

From the beginning, then, the Balkans was more than a geographical concept. The term, unlike it predecessors, was loaded with negative con-notations—of violence, savagery, primitivism—to an extent for which it is hard to find a parallel. "Why 'savage Europe'?" asked the journalist Harry de Windt in his 1907 book. "Because . . . the term accurately describes the wild and lawless countries between the Adriatic and the Black Seas." A series of revolts, political incidents, and assassinations came to associate the region with violence and bloodshed. Most liberal thinkers and advo-cates of self-determination found it hard to reconcile their ideals with the realities of a fragmented and destabilized world.

If the intellectual history of Western stereotypes of the Balkans were no more than one century old, it would be hard to explain the grip they still have on us. But the term, though recent, rests upon a foundation of other associations which reach more deeply into Western thought. One of those is the tension between Orthodox and Catholic Christianity that was crys-tallized by the Crusaders' sacking of Constantinople in 1204. But more important still is surely the deep rift of incomprehension that lies between the worlds of Christianity and Islam, which for more than a millennium were locked in a complex struggle for territory and minds of Europe. This relation went through different stages, from an earlier one of the 16th and 17th centuries when Europeans both feared and admired the Ottomans to the 18th century and onwards when the tables turned and the Ottoman army was reaching its limits. With the rise of science and the Enlightenment that unified European elite culture, the Ottoman world became regarded as despotic, sensual, and slow-moving.

Within that image making, the geography of the Balkans had always evoked a sense of marginality, unpredictability, and impenetrability. The high mountains, the often-harsh climate, and inaccessible villages ensconced in hidden valleys and passages made the Balkans into a source of wonder. The Balkans was at once the periphery of the Ottoman Empire and the periphery of Europe. Many 19th century travelers who flocked to discover the Balkans commented on the unexpected colors, smells, mix-tures of peoples: "Entering these regions, the scene is suddenly shifted, and you have before your eyes a new species of beings, with all those gaudy appendages of oriental character and scenery which have so long delighted the imagination in the tales of the East." The disconcerting interpenetra-tion of Europe and Asia, East and West, looms over all descriptions of the Balkans. Signs of Europe, which was seen as a civilizing force, were looked for in local life, but this was usually followed by the expectation that behind a European façade lay an Oriental reality full of colors, smells, filth, and chaos. That Oriental reality, with its power of religion, agrarian lifestyle, traditional impulse, and poverty, was assumed to be the permanent state of affairs which European modernization could never change. Indeed, at least in diplomatic circles, the Balkans was never to be accepted as part of Europe, especially because of its Muslim population. In the increasingly racialized vocabulary of 19th century Europe, the Muslims were considered by definition more backward and cruel than Christians and, through their mere presence, sore reminders of Balkan unsuitability to be considered real Europe. Edith Durham, a well-known Victorian traveler who critically observed European attitudes towards the Balkan people in general and the Muslims in particular, summed up the general attitudes as follows: "When a Moselm kills a Moslem, it does not count. When a Christian kills a Moslem, it is a righteous act; when a Christian kills a Christian it is an error of judgment better not talked about; it is only when a Moslem kills a Christian that we arrive at a full blown atrocity."[3] It is no wonder, then, that Christian Europe was blind to Muslim victims in the wake of the Balkan wars. Expelling Muslims from their ancestral homes in order to turn the Balkans into a uniquely Christian zone was a political imperative of the new nation-states, one that likened, by some critical observers at least, to "a decree as inhumane as the expulsion of the Jews from Spain or Protestants from France."[4] Yet that expulsion did happen: according to some estimates, some 5 million Muslims were driven out from the Balkans and the Black Sea region between 1821 and 1922. In the 1990s, the ethnic cleaning and the dynamiting of mosques in Bosnia-Herzegovina [and Kosovo] was thus a continuation in an extreme form of the same process of de-Islamization that had begun at the turn of the 20th century.

As the Ottoman empire collapsed and the West commemorated the final expulsion of a Muslim power from Europe as the triumph of Christendom and modernity, expectations were high that the new Balkan states would sooner or later make their way back to European civilization: "The Turk is a Moslem, and the soul of the true Moslem is indifferent to progress." Indeed, this was the attitude that fueled new nation-states in the Balkans as they try to reclaim their Christian roots and assert their allegiance to European powers. However, it was soon clear that this was a problematic attitude and as such hard to implement in real life. A French traveler to Greece remarked the following: "The Greeks as slaves of the Turks were to be pitied. The Greeks once free merely horrify. Their life is a sequence of thefts and assaults, fires and assassinations are their pastime."[5] When the Serbian nationalist student Gavrilo Princip assassinated the Austro-Hungarian Archduke Franz Ferdinand in Sarajevo in 1914 in order to free South Slavs from foreign domination, he triggered the First World War and, as a domino effect, another Balkan war, finally destroying

Europe's old order. For this, if nothing else, the Balkans remained cursed in the European consciousness.

This attitude, it must be emphasized, had nothing to do with the assumed propensity of the Balkan people to be vile. Rather, it rested on the logic that to be European meant nothing less than denying the legitimacy of the Ottoman past and the links with Islam. Nationalist passions and struggles were, in the eyes of the emerging Balkan states, necessary for membership to the European club, and the struggle against the national [and collective] enemy—the Turk—necessitated getting rid of, or at least suppressing, the reality of religious diversity in one's midst. It is only recently that some historians have tried to bring forth that aspect of the Balkan life as its virtue rather than its curse. The questions remain: since the religious and ethnic mosaic of the Balkans was long embedded in the region and has, remarkably, survived the waves of brutality and violence in the past century or so, why is it only in the most recent history that this mosaic became a negative issue? Is it possible that the Balkan history of religious and ethnic diversity does not so much affirm as undermine Europe's sense of superiority? For just as Europe gave the Balkans the categories with which its peoples defined themselves, it also gave them the ideological weapons—in the shape of nationalism—with which to destroy themselves.

The Balkans Before the Ottoman Rule: Religion, Culture, Politics

Before the advent of the Ottoman Empire, the Balkans had been part of what some scholars refer to as the "Byzantine commonwealth." Although the Roman Catholic church had gained some followers in the region—in Western Balkans especially but also in other pockets of the rest of the peninsula—the Balkan population was mainly christianized through the missionaries of the Eastern Orthodox Church. The Eastern Orthodox Church has its basis in the Greek-speaking church of the Byzantine Empire whose spiritual and ecumenical leadership (patriarchate) had been based at Constantinople since the fourth century. The two churches, Roman Catholic and Eastern Orthodox, share a long history of tension and rivalry that date back to the very establishment of Constantinople as the capital of the Roman Empire ("new Rome") that deepened the rift between Latin and Greek speaking realms. More consequential for this gap, however, were early medieval doctrinal discussions on the nature of the Trinity as well as the debates on the extent of papal authority. Regarding the former, the patriarchs of the Eastern Orthodox

Church found it unacceptable that the Western Church single-handedly changed certain premises on the nature of Trinity that had been ecumenically accepted at the council of Nicaea in 381 (the Nicene Creed). Regarding the issue of papal authority, the Eastern Orthodox Church rejected the claim that the pope could have full power over both secular and ecumenical matters. They considered the pope to be senior to other church fathers but not absolute in his power. Finally, in contrast to the Catholic Church, the Eastern Orthodox Church was decentralized among five patriarchates that shared equal spiritual authority. The debates over these issues culminated in 1054, the year of the Orthodox-Catholic schism that led to mutual excommunication. However, it was the fourth crusade of 1204 when the Catholic armies sacked and pillaged Constantinople that a more permanent damage was inflicted from which the relations between the two churches have never fully recovered.

But what is the nature of the Eastern Orthodox religion and culture that has left such a lasting and important effect on the Balkans since the missionary activities that began in the ninth century? The most important element of those activities was the translation of the Bible into local Slavonic dialects by two brothers and monks of Thessalonika, Cyril and Methodius. This not only turned the Slavic-speaking lands of the Balkans into the main stronghold of Eastern Orthodox Christianity, but also created distinctive national orthodoxies among the Slavs. In Bulgaria, an independent patriarchate was created by 927; Serbia was converted between 867 and 874. Romania, which had been predominantly Latin, was incorporated around the fourteenth century. All revealed local variations as well as a sense of unity. One eminent scholar of the Byzantine Empire, Dimitri Obolensky, argues that the diffusion of Eastern Orthodox values in the region implied a full acceptance of many common patterns in belief and worship. In his view, local variances are far less important than the relatively high level of religious uniformity. They are more an expression of different cultural emphases placed on the common features of the Byzantine tradition rather than arbitrary modifications of that tradition or introductions of new elements. In his study *The Byzantine Commonwealth: Eastern Europe 500–1453*, which is perhaps the single most influential work on the political, religious, and social life in the Byzantine Empire, Obolensky discusses the complex orbit of the Byzantine civilization, laying out a detailed account of its dissemination and consolidation in the Balkans. Although ethnically diverse, the Balkans had been, by the eleventh century, almost fully incorporated into the Byzantine Empire. Despite minor movements in and out of the Byzantine orbit and occasional resistance to political centralization, Orthodox Christianity prevailed in the region. In the fourteenth century, Hungary and Croatia turned to Rome for spiritual support, but the rest of the peninsula remained loyal to Constantinople as its spiritual mentor and cultural matrix. Here is, then, what Obolensky says about the diffusion of Eastern Orthodox values in the Balkans and their homogenizing tendencies. The following is a summary of a chapter dealing with religion, law and literature in the Byzantine commonwealth:[6]

In matters of religion, Byzantine Christianity permitted few local variations and promoted a sense of sacred and indivisible unity of its teachings. For example, a prominent Orthodox monk, John of Damascus, wrote that even a small change in the structure of the church could threaten the stability of the entire edifice, reflecting the sense of indivisibility of the tradition. Because of that homogenizing tendency, it is difficult to assess the presence of pre-Christian pagan elements, including Slavic customary law, in local traditions. While at the popular level religious cultures did develop distinct flavors, the Church demanded uniformity. One of the most pervasive features of that uniformity in this region was monasticism, strengthened especially after the defeat of Iconoclasm in 843, which had marked the triumph of the Orthodox Church's teaching that the icons were to be freely venerated not just in the church but in the liturgical activities at home and monastery as well.

Monastic lifestyle took on different forms. First, there was a tradition of individual asceticism ("eremetical tradition"), which, despite its relative decline in the East, flourished in the Balkans. The second form was an organized community system known as *lavra* associated with monks who lived separately but whose ritual life was directed by a single abbot with whom they congregated every Sunday for the common celebration of Eucharist. The third form was most widespread. It consisted of a centralized monastic life where monks, having no personal property, were subject to identical discipline and ritual under the authority of an abbot. Otherwise secluded, the monks performed charity work in the community and ran schools. Many of these monasteries became the leading centers of religious activities and teachings. In addition to Greek Mount Athos, important were the Bulgarian monastery of Zographou, the monasteries of Ohrid and Preslav [present day Macedonia], the Serbian monastery of Chilindar, and a number of others where Byzantine writings were copied, often translated into Slavic languages, and disseminated around the region.

Later on, a fourth form of monasticism took shape when a great Byzantine ascetic, St. Gregory of Sinai, founded a community in the remote region southern Bulgaria in about 1330 that gradually attracted disciples from around the region. This form of monasticism emphasized silent forms of meditations and contemplation. It became known as Hesycham (form Greek *hesychia*, quietude), a term used to describe the state of recollection and inner silence that leads a monk, through "the prayer of the heart" to the knowledge of God. As of the second half of the 14th century the Hesychast movement became also important for intellectual and interactive movements among the monks. Most monks were acquainted with one another and took active part in the religious and political affairs, both locally and internationally. Perhaps because of that level of interactivity, the monasteries, that were so central to the preservation and dissemination of Orthodox values, managed to preserve the essential features of the spiritual tradition of this Church. Most monastic practices derived from common sources, above all Mount Athos, Constantinople, and to a lesser degree, Thessalonika. Despite differences in their formal structures, the unity of the religious experience reflects the achievements of the Byzantine ethos. Given this spiritual uniformity of Orthodox life, one must look for issues of inter-communal differences in another field, and that field is the cult of national leaders that developed in several countries in the region.

To be sure, the Byzanitines typically endowed their emperors with sacred attributes that linked their earthly rule with God's kingdom in heaven. The office of the monarch was thus raised above the level of the ordinary. The epithets given to the *basileus* carried divine connotation—e.g., hagios ("holy"), theios ("divine")—as well as liturgical mention and the anointing at the coronation ceremony (as of 12th century in particular), all implied the holy nature of the emperor. However, for all his exalted titles, the Byzantine emperor never served as the axis of the Byzantine world. There are a number of reasons for it including that of racial diversity, for example, which forestalled any sense of absolute unity. More important perhaps was the fact that the Byzantines had more veneration for the office itself than individual sovereigns—a fact exemplified by the frequency of forced abdications and overthrows in the history of the empire.

At the same time, however, especially among Balkan Slavs, native pre-Christian traditions of kinship assigned to the local ruler both the military role and some of the divine attributes blessed by the church. The cult of the national ruler had another important feature found in the posthumous veneration of the princes who were victims of political murder and whose death was interpreted as conscious imitation of Christ's sacrificial death. They were thus treated as martyrs in popular lore, by the state authorities and recipients of the saints' posthumous favors. In medieval Balkans, the cult of ruler was most prominent among the Serbs, especially during the

12th and 13th century when they were ruled by a single native dynasty, the house of Stjepan Nemanja. As attested by both folklore and hagiographical literature that depicts the lives of saints, the Nemanja family was hailed for great achievements in both political and religious realms. Among them, St. Sava was most celebrated for his church patronage, the foundations of monasteries, friendships with the Byzantine emperor, and his territorial gains. His achievements provided the model for future rulers as well as writers of royal biographies. These biographies may have been influenced by Constantinople but their narrative style reveals local tradition of family chronicles as well as local monastic and hagiographical influences. The best of such biographies date to late 13th and early 14th centuries, and are considered as the best contribution made by the Serbs to medieval European literature.

In terms of **literary activities,** one of the most important issues that concerned the dissemination of Byzantine culture in the Balkans and beyond was the role of Old Church Slavonic language. The rise of this language owes much to the missionary activities of Cyril, a monk who was, along with his collaborators, engaged in the translation of the Greek New Testament into the spoken languages of the Slav people, leading to the liturgical and scriptural empowering of the Old Church Slavonic language. In the earliest phases, an attempt was made to translate into Old Slavonic a variety of Byzantine Greek literature. The task proved to be difficult because of the traditions of classical rhetoric was absent from the target language and its newly assigned Glagolitic script. Old Slavonic was gradually enriched with loan words, syntax, and semantic devices borrowed from Greek. By the 11th century, the growing number of translations made this language both richer and more complex, but this emphasis on Old Slavonic, ironically, diverted people from learning Greek and reading the rich ecclesiastical literature that was continuously produced in Greek. Only limited genres of production, such as Byzantine patristic works and the Christian hymnography, were made available.

In terms of the quality of its output, the summit of literary achievements is associated with the earliest phase of literary history of Old Church Slavonic, notably, the late 9th and early 10th centuries. This was partly due to the status which Old Church Slavonic acquired and which prompted the medieval writers to regard this language employed by Cyril and Methodius as a divine legacy that had no equivalent. Until the 11th century this language was relatively uniform. In later works, however, neither the original works nor translations produced in Church Slavonic were as meticulous, so the unity of the language gradually began to disintegrate under the pressure of vernacular variants. However, it must be added that the vernacular variants in fact testified to the presence of a supranational Byzantine literature of which Slavonic material is but a recension. The variants thus appear because of the migration of the common body of literature through different cultural spaces, none of which could override the feeling of belonging to a larger community and its values. The question of "originality" is therefore relative since all literary conventions lay in the Byzantine Greek model. A few examples, however, testify to a certain degree of adaptability exhibited by the more gifted Slavonic writers. They include the biographies of Cyril and Methodius written in the 9th century that capture very vividly the life of the period in lay and spiritual matters and reflected commitment to the Slavonic language. Most importantly, this and similar works that come out of the literary style, all seem to indicate the idea that the Slavonic version of the Scriptures and the liturgy is the manifestation of the Divine Word, which has made it possible for the Slavs to be elevated to the status of the peoples of God and the universal Christian family. Although the unity of the language gradually broke apart, this ethnic self-conceptualization allowed different Slav groups to maintain that feeling of belonging to God's providence. So while on the one hand in the early middle ages the emphasis was placed on the commonalities of the Old Salvonic in diffusing the divine word among the Slavs, in the later medieval period the Old Slavonic as a literary language depended on elaborate and floral syntax familiar only to the highly educated monks. As a consequence, another, more elitist form of unity was established, while common masses still enjoyed the vernacular and vestiges of the Cyril and Methodius in giving Slavs a new language and feeling of belonging.

After the Ottoman conquest of the Balkans, and in some respects because of the Turkish rule, the Byzantine influence over the region survived longer than elsewhere. To begin with, several Byzantine institutions, such as the fiscal system for example, survived and were taken over by the Ottomans. The early Ottoman sultans presented themselves to their Christian subjects as the heirs of the Byzantine Emperors. Sultan Mehmet II had many Greek subjects from the Empire moved to the depopulated city of Constantinople, now renamed Istanbul. The Orthodox Christians of the Empire, though accorded a lower status, were allowed to retain their customs as a separate *millet*, or nation. All the Orthodox subjects, with the exception of the Serbs who were granted religious autonomy between 1557 and 1766, were placed under the ecclesiastical jurisdiction of the patriarch in Constantinople, who was now treated as a high Ottoman official with all the Byzantine vestment. This dignitary was not only granted the privileges and immunities enjoyed by his Byzantine predecessors; he was also recognized by the sultan as the secular as well as the spiritual head of all his Christian subjects. Far more than in the late Byzantine period, the patriarch of Constantinople were thus able, under Turkish rule, to vindicate their ancient title of "oecumenical" [universal].

The Balkans Under the Ottoman Rule: Change and Challenge

The fall of the medieval Balkan states under the Ottomans was a gradual process with the region succumbing to the Ottoman jurisdiction in several waves between the late fourteenth and fifteenth centuries. The effect of the Ottoman occupation was profound, as it concerned all aspects of life. In the matters of religion, the patterns of change can be traced through the conversion process on the one hand, and the grouping of population according to their religious belonging on the other. It has to be noted, however, that conversion was neither linear nor uniform. For example, studies show that, at least in some parts of the Balkans, conversion was a multifaceted process that involved not only conversion to Islam but also intra-Christian conversions as well. For example, in Bosnia-Herzegovina where the Catholic and Orthodox Church coexisted with a local "Bosnian Church" (Bosanska crkva) that is often, albeit problematically, associated with Bogomil dualism, conversion was large scale and multidirectional, whereby members of the Bosnian Church were converting to Islam, Orthodoxy, and Catholicism and eventually disappearing. Likewise, the number of Catholics was in steady decline, while Orthodoxy was gaining in numbers though still losing membership mainly to Islam but also to Catholicism.[7] The Catholics were treated with more suspicion for fear that the Ottomans' fierce enemy from the West, the Austro-Hungarian Empire, was Catholic. In turn, the Orthodox Church was more privileged, as is clear from the court cases and the sheer demographic increase of the Orthodox population and the number of their churches in many regions.[8] Finally, in the late fifteenth century the Ottoman sultan welcomed the Ladino Jews fleeing the Spanish Reconquista and settled them in many towns across Asia Minor and the Balkans. One of the most profound consequence of this historical period was the increased diversity of the religious profile of the Balkan people.

In administering their new subject, the Ottomans relied on some of the existing structures and practices, but most important, they introduced the so-called millet system of grouping the population according to their religion. Although scholarly opinion varies regarding the origins and institutional makeup of the millet system, it is by and large agreed that, as far as the Ottoman court was concerned, the millet was the main form of identification of people outside their nuclear contexts. The heads of each millet were state functionaries appointed by the sultan, and they were given full ecclesiastical, fiscal, and legal control over the members of their millet. Despite this centralized authority, there did exist internal variances. For example, while the Orthodox millet, which was the largest of all, was placed under the jurisdiction of the Greek patriarchate in Istanbul, the Serbs were granted independent patriarchate in 1557 and thus escaped threats of Greek assimilations that their fellow Slavs, the Bulgarians, who had no such status, faced.[9] In the Jewish case, the Sultan appointed chief rabbi in Istanbul, although it is certain that not all Jews recognized him as the sole religious authority. Moreover, many sources from the period, including material culture such as books, tombstones, artifacts, and architecture, as well as immaterial culture such as folk poetry and popular legends and stories, indicate that the millet boundaries were quite porous and cultural exchange happened at many different levels, so that local sensibilities were never completely abandoned in favor of the larger imperial structures. That local atmosphere also affected the parameters of religious and cultural belongings and allowed the population to form alliances in a more immediate way.

An interesting analysis of the changing religious life in the Ottoman Balkans can be found in the work by the Greek historian Speros Vryonis whose interests lie in the transition from Byzantine to Islamic administration of the region and the cultural and religious challenges that that transition engendered. In the following article that traces the patterns of change, Vryonis especially emphasizes popular religious life rather than the official policies of the Ottoman government. After all, he argues, most of the people in the Balkans were exposed to religious practices of their communities as they evolved over time rather than as they were imposed from the ruler, whosoever he may be. Looking at folk religion emphasizes the issues of continuity and change in both historical and regional terms. Here is a summary of his argument:[10]

When the Byzantine and Turkish world came into contact in the 14th century, and until the former was subdued and the latter crystallized in the 16th century, there were two basic formal religio-political systems in the Balkans: The Orthodox Basileia and the Muslim Sultanate. However, it would be a serious failure were one to consider the religious changes that occurred after that encounter only in terms of the formal culture of the ruling classes. The latter usually formed less than 10% of the total population and most frequently the divergences between folk and formal cultures were extensive. Consequently the evolution and change which took place in the Balkans during the late medieval period occurred not only on the formal level of culture and society but also on the folk level.

To understand these changes, one must, temporarily, dispense with the conceptualization of the Balkans as divided between the Patriarch of Constantinople and the Sheyh-ul-Islam of Istanbul. For neither one nor the other was ever completely successful in imposing an absolute harmony and obedience upon his respective flock. In each following were to be found heretical, heterodox, and even pagan elements. There was tension (among the various elements), therefore, within each of these two major religions, as well as tensions between two religions themselves. The scheme of such religious variety becomes more complex if we include the categories of Catholics, Armenians, and Jews, who constituted the religious minorities of the region.

A discussion on these issues can best be conducted through three components: first, by listing and describing the various types of religiosity in the Balkans in this period; second, by examining the basic transition from Christianity to Islam; and third, by discussing examples and patterns of this change and thus illustrating the variety of combinations and forms of Islam.

1. Various Types of Religiosity

Christianity—When they invaded the area, the Turks found a population which was, at least formally, almost completely Christian, and of which the major portion was Orthodox. This Orthodoxy had a uniform dogma and a set of canons which had emerged from seven ecumenical councils and which had been expanded by its commentators. The formal religious apparatus was closely intertwined with the political life. As the Byzantine Empire declined, three Orthodox Balkan states emerged—Byzantium, Serbia, and Bulgaria—which came to constitute the precursors of their modern counterparts. In spite of this splintering of the Orthodox body at the political level, however, formal dogma and cult were identical. It needs to be noted that within this Orthodox enclave there were small groups of Latin Christians as well, concentrated especially in the Ionian and Aegean isles, in Galata and Constantinople, coastal Albania, Dalmatia, Croatia, Slovenia, and Bosnia. Also, Jewish merchants and craftsmen had been present for centuries, but their number would become substantial only after the Ottoman conquests and the flight of the Jews from Spain.

Although the states were predominantly Orthodox when the Ottomans invaded, folk religious life resided on a foundation which was heavily influenced by their pagan roots. In fact, the popular religion of the Balkan peoples, even in modern times, displays many pronounced archaic features that predate both Christianity and Islam. This is perhaps not so surprising given the late appearance of Christianity in the region (9th century), which makes Balkan Christianity replete with cults and practices that date back to the pagan past of both the Greeks and the Slavs, including many that related to the life cycle of the human being.

Furthermore, the peasant's way of life changed remarkable little so that religious and superstitious practices were all geared to promote fertility. The practices of animal sacrifice, mimes, celebratory dances, and others, testify to this preoccupation with the land. The calendar is full of seasonal festivals intimately associated with agrarian, pastoral, and maritime life. Similarly, there was concern with health, expressed, for example, in the practice of dedicating silver or gold likeness of parts of the body to the saint's icon. Of cult practices, however, the most widespread and deeply rooted were hagiolatry and iconolatry [veneration of saints and icons], both of which had strong connections with the pagan past and bore strong resemblances to the cult of the ancient hero and to polytheism.

In that sense, Balkan folk Christianity in this period represented a syn-cretism of magic, animism, monotheistic dogma, polytheistic practices, monism, and dualism. Christianity succeeded in destroying or effacing the major gods and in replacing them with a triune surface. But underneath this surface the old spirits and forces retained their grip on the masses, so the folk religion displays many common but also divergent elements in a way that one can refer to these phenomena as "religious Balkanisms."

Islam—Because of their adoption of Sunni Islam, the formal structures of the Ottoman sultans adhered to the typical Sunni practices, including an elaborate system of religious schools, legal institutions, and religious endowments, through which Islam was spread and cemented in the region. But the Turks were also rather open to religious heterodoxy that stemmed out of their long-term exposure to and fascination with mystical practices, popular superstitions, and folk religion. In that sense, Turkish Islam, when it appeared in the Balkans, represented a bewildering array of variations, perhaps more so than Balkan Christianity. After all, they had traveled through many lands of central Asia, Iran, Iraq, Azerbaijan, Syria, and Anatolia, before reaching the Balkans, representing an ethnic group that was in constant state of ethnogenesis by virtue of assimilation and absorp-tion of other tribal and cultural groups.

2. The Basic Religious Transition from Christianity to Islam

On the eve of the Ottoman invasions the number of Muslims to be found in the Balkans was practically non-existent. Two centuries later, the census shows that 18.8% of the population was Muslim, 80.7% was Christian and 0.5% Jewish. The Muslim element was most numerous in

Thrace, Macedonia, Thessaly, Bosnia, Herzegovina, and Silistria. The most marked presence was in towns, rather than countryside. By way of example, the town of Sofia had a Muslim majority of 66.4% whereas the larger district of Sofia was only 6% Muslim. The nascent Muslim population had a double origin: the colonization of Muslims from outside of the peninsula, and more significantly, the conversion of Christian and Jews within the peninsula. There are both general and specific indications that conversion happened throughout the centuries of the Ottoman rule. Though the Muslim rulers and religious men tolerated Christianity formally, and allowed the patriarchate to be resurrected after its temporary demise in 1453, the Ottoman administration welcomed Islamization, and indeed contemporary observers describe the celebrations and joy with which conversions occasioned. The proselytizing spirit was perhaps most pronounced among the dervish orders, of whom Bektashis and Mevlevis already displayed remarkable success among the Orthodox Christians in Anatolia. Also, the administrative and military apparatus was an important channel of conversion as well. Intermarriage, primarily between Muslim males and Christian females had a long and fascinating history. Finally, there were instances of conversion under duress and the related phenomenon of Crypto-Christianity.

The reasons for conversion may be reduced to three basic phenomena: first, there were real or material advantages, including the fact that Muslims paid a lighter tax burden; second was the successful appeal of religious preaching and spiritual attraction; finally, there was the element of fear, particularly in stressful times, that predisposed some Christian individuals or groups to convert. Whatever the case, the fact remains that, unlike in Asia Minor where Islamization had happened on a much larger scale and over a much longer period of time, in the Balkans, Muslims remained a great minority. In some areas, such as Bosnia, Islam found a very fertile ground and became the religion of the majority, but overall, one can observe a mass survival of Christianity in the Ottoman Balkans that in many respects indicates a clear continuity.

3. Examples and Patterns of This Religious Change

The statistical approach, useful as it is to the historian, tells us nothing of the everyday details or quality of religious life among the converts. Franz Babinger, a famous historian of Balkan Islam, contends that two religious phenomena gave Balkan Islam its real content: hagiolatry and the dervish brotherhoods.[11] These two elements, the one Christian and the other Islamic, were essentially popular religion that appealed to both Muslims and Christians. In addition, the Ottoman conquests of the Balkans brought no overall disruption and change to the rural population's attachment to the seasonal-religio-magical calendar or to its concerns for health and fertility. These elements were primarily passed on through the mass conversions of Albanians, Bosnians, Bulgar Pomaks, and Greeks. Also, wherever large-scale intermarriages of Muslim men and Christian women took place, the women were the vehicle by which popular Christianity was passed into Islam. Institutionally, the syncretism of the dervish orders allowed many Christian practices to be adopted. The vitality of Christian folk culture and the importance of Christians in Ottoman commercial life meant that the old forces and elements of Christian folk religion enjoyed a considerable continuity. Among such practices were baptism that represents a specifically and uniquely Christian form but was practiced by Muslim converts in some Balkan areas to allegedly secure good health; animal sacrifice that is done in a particularly pagan form; and hagiolatry, whereby both Christians and Muslims frequently appealed to one or another of the saints. Some saints were both Muslim and Christian, and were associated through common attributes, and often were interchangeable with one another.

Conclusions

This brief survey of the Balkan religious configuration leads to the following conclusions: first, on the eve of the Ottoman invasion, paganism was a marked characteristic of Balkan folk Christianity and shamanism of nomadic Islam. Second, although the Anatolian Christians largely converted to Islam, Islamization in the Balkans as a whole remained a peripheral phenomenon. The difference in the fate of Christianity and Islam in the two peninsulas has to do with the nature of conquest in the two areas. Third, although Islam which emerged in the Balkans was "orthodox" on the formal level, on the popular level it was heavily influenced by the ancient pagan and Christain elements even after conversion. The majority of the Balkanites did not convert, and many of those who did retained a number of common practices. Thus, in spite of the religious change which accompanied the Ottoman rule, continuity was the dominant feature of the Balkans religious life in the early period at least.

Religion, Culture, and Politics in the Balkans Nowadays

The modern-day Balkans is a mosaic of religions, ethnicities, and cultures. We have seen how its mixture has served both as a political powder keg and as a source of fascination, especially for Western Europeans used to more homogenous demographic environments in their home countries. In the Balkans, even the Muslims themselves do not represent a homogenous group, ethnically, linguistically, or ritually. In Albania, Muslims form the overwhelming majority (ca. 70 percent). In Bosnia-Herzegovina, they constitute around 40 percent of the population. In Turkey, over 90 percent. In Bulgaria, about 13 percent. Muslim Albanians form 90 percent of the population of Kosovo, and Slavic Muslims some 53 percent of the Serbian Sandzak region. About 30 percent of Macedonia is Muslim. In Greece, some 120,000 Muslims live in the Thrace region, constituting just over 1.2 percent of the overall population of Greece. The ethno-linguistic diversity of Balkan Islam and its variances in religious worship and spiritual edification testify to its ongoing exposure to different political orders and non-Islamic influences. Most Balkan Muslims are Sunni, and there is a significant presence of Sufi orders. Important, albeit not numerically, is the presence of Bektashis, a community formed at the intersection of Shi^{c}i, Sufi, and Turkic folk practices. Despite this rich mosaic—or perhaps because of it—the Muslims of the Balkans have been poorly studied as regards their minority status in many Balkan states, and even more important, as regards their regional interconnectedness.[12] In the past decade, however, the "Muslim question" of the Balkans has been given a new prominence because of the political upheavals enveloping the region. The upheavals indicate that the Muslim-Christian relations in modern times have been driven by political goals that often clash with the historical reality of close coexistence. To discuss the situation of Islam and Muslims in today's Balkans, and through that, the issue of Muslim-Christian relations, we turn to the work by Hugh Poulton who focuses on minority questions in the Balkans but also the modes of grouping of Balkan population along ethnic and religious lines. In the following article he looks at the way in which the modern Balkan states that rest on the principle of single nationhood that ties ethnicity and religion have addressed, or not, the minority question. And because Muslims have by and large been excluded from the concept of nation because of their religion, the minority status is intrinsically tied to the question of religious rights and relations. The following section summarizes Hugh Poulton's argument:[13]

Muslim communities in the Balkans derive from those who had arrived with the Ottomans after their establishment in the course of the late 14th and 15th century and those who had converted to Islam. Except for Albania, these communities formed minorities within the new successor states following the fall of the Ottoman empire.

Recent history shows that the tensions were primarily manifest between the Orthodox Christians and Muslim minorities who were perceived by the former as undesirable relics from the Ottoman past. The disintegration of Yugoslavia in 1991 and the tragedies of Bosnia-Herzegovina [and Kosovo] underline the potential for acute conflicts. It is therefore important to understand the minority status of Muslims who, despite tensions, remain the integral part of the present day Balkans.

All Balkans states are new, despite their claim to continuity with ancient or medieval polities. In fact, the oldest state appears in the 1830s. Nationalist ideology that underpins the self-definition of all these states was imported from Western Europe and has been primarily secular. However, there is a close connection between religion and identity all over the Balkans, which can be seen as the legacy of the Ottoman *millet* system of grouping population according to their religion. This is especially so with Orthodox Christianity, as it is obvious from the case of Greece where religion, ethnicity, and citizenship are often confused.

Muslims in the Balkans are predominantly Sunni but there is an important presence of Shi'a Bektashis in Albania who trace their origins to an Anatolian Sufi order that combines popular practices with Christian and Shi'a teachings. On the whole, there are three main linguistic branches of Balkan Islam: Serbo-Croat, Albanian, and Turkish.

Although after the Ottoman invasion many locals converted to Islam, Ottoman rule in the region was non-assimilative and multireligious. Consequently, Balkan peoples managed to maintain separate identities and cultures. Many also deeply nurtured the memory of their pre-Ottoman past. During the 19th century national awakening, such claims were revived, often at the expense of the historical changes that happened and at the expense of neighbors who made different claims over the same territory. The Republic of Macedonia is a good case in point.

The gradual loss of Ottoman control in the Balkans in the 19th century gave rise to small Orthodox Christian national states, especially in the Empire's periphery. Serbia and Greece broke away first, followed by Rumania, Bulgaria, and Montenegro. They all pursued policies of territorial expansion, initially at the expense of the withdrawing Ottoman empire but later over the same territory, notably Macedonia.

After the establishment of new Bulgaria in the aftermath of the 1877 war, large numbers of Muslims emigrated to the rump Ottoman empire. Later on, Slavic and Albanian Muslims as well as Turks from other regions followed. After 1953, Yugoslavia's leadership permitted extensive emigration of Turkey to "Turks," though the definition of who constituted the

"Turks" was as much religious as it was ethnic. Emigration has happened from Greece as well.

Despite such emigrations, Muslims continued to constitute sizeable population in their states of origin. However, because the successor states were essentially ethnic based on one dominant nation, the question of minority rights has remained problematic.

In fact, the legacy of the Ottoman millet system has persisted, and religion continues to be an important factor of differentiation. In most cases, if a minority group is Orthodox Christian—like the Vlachs or the Roma—they tended to be more easily assimilated into the dominant nation. In contrast, Muslim and Jewish minorities have been much harder to assimilate, though smaller Muslim groups were more readily assimilated by larger ones. This is clearly the legacy of the *millet* system that gave smaller groups a sense of security in the face of definition of the nation, as well as the concept of Islam as a trans-national community of believers.

In the countries that were not conceived as the Orthodox Christian national states, such as Yugoslavia, the fate of Muslims was different. In the 19th century Muslims of Bosnia-Herzegovina were the target of Serb nationalist statesmen who considered them as Serbian co-nationals. However, when the Austro-Hungarian government took over the possession over Bosnia-Herzegovina in 1878, its Muslim population understood quickly that it needed to cooperate with the central government to guarantee its own survival and continued this strategy after the Austro-Hungarian collapse and the formation of royalist Yugoslavia in 1918. While the Serbs of the state considered Muslims to be ethnic Serbs of Islamic faith and the Croats thought of them as ethnically Croat, there was no sense of alienation from the state, even though other ethnic Muslims certainly felt it. The same survival strategy continues in the post-Second World War era when communists came to power. In order to end competition between Serbs and Croats over their ethnic ownership of Bosnian Muslims, Tito created a new ethno-national category in the 1971 census, notably "Muslims," to be used at par with Serb [Orthodox] and Croatian [Catholic].

The 1992 war in Bosnia-Herzegovina created its own breed of nationalistic sentiments among its Muslim population that had until then nurtured a rather weak sense of national distinctiveness. This new feeling mirrored the form of nationalism embraced by Serbs and Croat nationalists, which led to widespread slaughter and atrocities in which the Muslims were the main victims.

In contrast, Albania, where the Muslims form a large majority, followed a different route of national awakening that stemmed from the realization that, unless the Albanians formed their own state, they were in danger of being divided among the Greeks from the south, and the Serbs and the Montenegrins from the north. The first Albanian state formed in 1913 was politically very week, so much so that it came increasingly under Italian control. After World War Two and the establishment of communist rule under Enver Hoxha, all religious activity was severely punished. Since the end of this period of persecution during which all religious groups equally suffered, Albania nowadays enjoys a significant level of religious tolerance, which seems rarity in the Balkan context. Also, Albania's late arrival as a state resulted in the fact that as many Albanians live in neighboring states as within Albania. In Greece, they tend to be more assimilated by the Orthodox. The Albanians in the former Yugoslavia's province of Kosovo formed a majority and under Tito enjoyed relative autonomy and protection. Both were destroyed after the Milosevic regime came to power in Serbia, which embarked on an acute repression of the Kosovo Albanians with the intent of recovering Kosovo for Serbs as it had purportedly been in pre-Ottoman past. Finally, the Albanians in Macedonia make up compact regional majorities.

But the fact that the classic state emerging from the Ottoman empire was essentially ethnic based on one dominant nationality, and all but Albania were dominantly Christian, placed Muslim minorities in a problematic position. This situation has been made worse by the ideology that the state is the natural territory of one dominant national group that has resulted in the accumulation of political power in the hands of that dominant group, with little concern from religious minorities. While Yugoslavia under Tito presented a bit of an exception, instances of centralization were equated with dominant Serb Orthodox nationalism. The break-up of Yugoslavia in 1991 can indeed be seen as a reaction to such form of centralization, led this time by Slobodan Milosevic. However, the new post-Yugoslav states [with the exception of Bosnia-Herzegovina and Macedonia], have generally tended to revert to the classic Balkan model of centralization, leading to the inevitable question of minority rights.

In that sense, Balkan nation-states appear to follow a model explicated by Ernest Gellner, according to which the official "high" culture of the state and its rulers is imposed on the "low" culture of the general population. This method, according to Gellner, stresses the role of culture and education in disseminating national ideals, which is why the school system tends to be monolithic and geared to produce an intelligentsia that safeguards the state ideology. Ironically, however, nationalists usually claim the reverse, namely, that they are acting in the name of a folk culture that is imagined or presumed, rather than real. (In contrast to this kind of allegiances, in the Ottoman context the real was the tie forged within a community of villagers of city dwellers, while the imaginary was the "millet" system that united people of one religion across the Empire.) Accordingly, the entire period after the collapse of the Ottoman empire in the Balkans has been one of the state imposing a sense of nationhood, but since so many of the states intertwine nationhood with religion, the sense of modern national community has been confused with the pre-modern Ottoman one of religious cohesion.

However, in recent times the situation has been changing due to the impact of the "'communications revolution'" to both gain and disseminate information within and outside the borders of any given nation state and thus both preserve and strengthen cultural differences. Furthermore, the increasing awareness of the minority problems in this and other parts of the world is likely to bring forth any country's record under international scrutiny, so that the abuse of or denial of minorities rights in many places, from Turkey to Greece and others, will likely subject the offenders to international censure.

This does not mean that nationalism is a diminishing force in the Balkans. On the contrary, the break-up of Yugoslavia has occasioned an intensification of various nationalisms throughout the region, although Bosnia-Herzegovina has avoided going through the classic Balkan route. However, total assimilation—except by mass expulsion and genocide—is a thing of the past as the state is in no position any more to monopolize or propagate national culture.

In light of these developments, Islam appears destined to remain a major component in the regional politics and culture, despite the dissatisfaction by nationalist forces of both Catholic and Orthodox kind. The question remains, however, how these communities will develop politically. The events in Bosnia-Herzegovina [and Kosovo] show that faced with a continuation of the traditional Balkan state model of intolerance to minorities and attempts at assimilation, Muslims will need to revert or continue the policies of education and cultural unification that are secular in nature.

Conclusion

The Balkans has been a meeting ground of different religions since early medieval times. Until the fourteenth century, it was different Christian churches that had collided and coexisted in the region, although the dominant one remained the spiritually decentralized but theologically unified Eastern Orthodox Church. However, the establishment of the Ottoman rule in much of the Balkans between the fifteenth and twentieth centuries considerably complicated the religious composition of the region: although Orthodox Christianity maintained its dominant status, many Balkan people converted to Islam so much so that some areas, such as present-day Bosnia-Herzegovina and Albania, acquired a Muslim majority. Furthermore, after the Spanish Reconquista of 1492, the Ottoman Sultan granted the Jews of Spain protection throughout the Ottoman lands. Many settled in the Balkans, especially Balkan cities, adding more texture to the existing religious mosaic.

Although each religious group maintained its distinctiveness and loyalty to its spiritual center, historical sources show that the population actively coexisted and interacted with members of other religious groups. This can be partly explained by the mountainous Balkan geography, in which communities are tightly knit and have to share resources by relying on one another for sustenance and well-being. In addition, religious institutions have never held a tight grip on the Balkan population so that the religious teachings were mainly passed on through local cultural practices and communal involvement. Many of these practices predate Christianity, Islam, and Judaism and permeate the rituals of each, which testifies to a great level of cultural syncretism across the region.

In the nineteenth and twentieth centuries, with the collapse of the Ottoman and Austro-Hungarian empires, the Balkans underwent a tumultuous fragmentation into nation states, modeled after Western European states. That process, more often than not, implied associating the dominant nation with a particular religious teaching at the exclusion of religious minorities within (for example, the Greek constitution explicitly places Orthodox Christianity at the heart of Greek citizenship). Such political processes disturbed the historical balance in the Balkan religious mosaic and gave rise to tensions among different communities and frequent harassments of religious minorities. At times, these tensions have been expressed in violent ways, creating the image of the Balkans as a zone of perpetual strife among religions. But it is important to keep in mind that all religious coexistence—which, in the Balkans, is a centuries-long reality—can generate both creative and destructive energy and lead to the practices of inclusion as much as the polices of exclusion. Therefore, the future of religious pluralism in the Balkans, and elsewhere, is intricately linked with the politics of the nation states and their willingness to acknowledge and accommodate the religious diversity within.

Discussion Questions

1. What does *balkanize* mean, and why is it an appropriate title for the region? Why is it inappropriate?

2. How do Christianity and Islam interact in the Balkans? Why is that region relevant to today's politics and religion?

3. In what ways does the Balkans history signal the larger situation of Western civilization in the twenty-first century? What are we to learn from the Balkans, and how are we to benefit from the experience of their people?

ZIONISM, IMPERIALISM, AND NATIONALISM

Judaism, Christianity, and Islam met not only in medieval Spain and in early modern Balkans. They also encountered one another in modern times. Any picture of the religious foundations of Western civilization must take account of that ongoing engagement, which is destined to continue through the twenty-first century. This chapter forms the transition between the study of the West as Christianity, Judaism, and Islam defined matters and our concentration, on the history of Christianity in the West, the dominant religious factor in modern times.

We see continuities between medieval and modern times. In all three cases we take up movements of renewal and restoration of an ideal past. Zionism in the setting of Judaism proposed to restore the Jewish people to the land of Israel. Christian imperialism undertook to bring Christianity to distant countries and continents. The Islamic movement proposed to recover the purity of Islam at the time of the prophet Muhammad and beyond.

Zionism, Imperialism, and Nationalism: Zionism

Jacob Neusner

What Is Zionism?

Zionism is the Jewish nationalist movement that was founded in 1897 in Basel, Switzerland, by Theodor Herzl, and created the State of Israel in 1948. Zionism defined its task as solving the Jewish problem, which it defined as political anti-Semitism. This would be done by attaining political sovereignty for the Jewish people in the Jewish state. The word *anti-Semitism* referred to the political platform that blamed the Jews for everything troubling the social order. Political anti-Semitism, as distinct from religious anti-Judaism characteristic of Christianity from its beginnings, culminated in the Holocaust, the murder of nearly six million European Jews by the Germans and their allies between 1933 and 1945, an event in Western civilization that continues to produce effects.

Theodor Herzl and the Beginning of Zionism

Herzl, a Viennese journalist, responded to the recrudescence of anti-Semitism he witnessed in covering the Dreyfus trial in Paris. Dreyfus was a Jewish officer in the French Army accused of handing over military secrets to the Germans. Herzl noticed that the crowds roared not "down with the traitor" but "down with the Jew." In the anti-Jewish demonstrations of the day he discovered what people then called "the Jewish problem"—defined in political terms—and proposed the Zionist solution to it. That was to build a state enjoying international recognition and create a sovereign nation able to defend its citizens and provide a refuge for all who needed one.

Herzl contributed the notion that the Jews everywhere lived in a single situation, which is anti-Semitism. They should then live in a single country and in their own state (wherever it might be located). He proposed evacuating the Jews from the European nations altogether to that safe haven. Anti-Semitism, accordingly, formed the antithesis of Zionism, and anti-Semites, growing in strength in European politics, would assist the Jews in building their state and thereby solve what they deemed to be their "Jewish problem." In Herzl's vision the Jews were now to become a political entity, something that they had not been for that two thousand years, since 70 C.E. when the Roman Empire destroyed the temple of Jerusalem and suspended the Jewish autonomous government of that time.

Herzl assumed the role of prophet. In Basel in 1897, when Herzl founded the Zionist Organization, he said that he had founded the Jewish state and that, in a half century, the world would know it. The prophecy came true practically to the day. Fifty years later, in November, 1947, the United Nations General Assembly approved the creation—in Palestine and the land of Israel—of two states: the Jewish state, called into existence on May 15, 1948, as the State of Israel, and the Arab state of Palestine. Zionism proposed political means to solve a political problem and in fifty years achieved its goal. A political movement built on religious foundations, Zionism is the single most important component of Western civilization that derives from contemporary Judaism.

Judaism the Religion and Zionism the Political Movement

Zionism was not accepted by all Jews, and in the beginning, a majority of Jews in the Western democracies rejected it. They regarded themselves as citizens of the countries where they lived, Germany, France, Britain, the United States, for example. They did not concur that the Jews constituted a nation in search of its own sovereign state.

Not only so, but the religion, normative Rabbinic Judaism, which we met in chapter 3, had made no provision for a this-worldly politics. It regarded the Jewish people as holy and separate, not participating in the secular politics of the nations. Jews should wait for the Messiah, who will restore the Jewish state and bring the people back to the Holy Land. Until God sent the Messiah, many believed, nothing was to be done. Reform and Orthodox Judaism therefore maintained that Zionism represented a secularization of that Messianic hope. That was because Zionism proposed that the Jewish people save itself and accomplish the return to Zion on its own. The Reform rabbis of Germany rejected the Zionist system and program. So too did much, though not all, of Orthodoxy in central and eastern Europe. Each community of Judaism saw Zionism as a political definition of what it held to be the holy people that God had called into being for sacred tasks.

Why Does Zionism Fit into This Account of Religious Foundations of Western Civilization?

Clearly, Zionism was a secular movement nourished by a religious narrative. Zionism also cannot be divorced from Judaism, because it defined its political goals in terms of the stories of the Hebrew Scriptures (a.k.a., *Old Testament*). It took up the story of the people that possessed but lost the promised land—the story told in the biblical books of Genesis through Kings—and promised to continue that story to a happy ending by restoring the people to the land and the land to the people. That is how Zionism formed a political movement based on a religious myth, by retelling in nineteenth- and twentieth-century terms the biblical story of the Jewish people, which possessed and lost its land and aspired to return to it.

Defining Zionism as a Secular, Political Movement

Herzl stressed that the Jewish state would come into existence with the approval and recognition of the great powers. The instruments of state—

a political forum, a bank, a mode of national allegiance, a press, a central body and leader—came into being in the aftermath of the first Zionist congress in Basel. Herzl spent the rest of his life after 1897—he died in 1904, less than a decade later—seeking an international charter and recognition of the Jews' state. The British government offered land in Africa, which Herzl favored accepting. For him the goal was totally secular. Scripture's narrative did not shape his policies. However, the Zionist congress to which he proposed a state in East Africa rejected the proposal. Only the land of Israel, then a part of the Syrian province of the Ottoman Empire based in Istanbul, would serve. Migration would be directed to the Holy Land alone. That stress on the Holy Land as the goal of Zionism represents a Judaic religious response to what was framed as the Jewish ethnic dilemma of political anti-Semitism.

By World War I Zionist progress in European Jewry proved considerable. Land was purchased for agricultural projects, and the settlements in the land were beginning to take shape. Still, Zionism represented a minority-position among the Judaisms of Europe and the United States. A political event changed the status of Zionism: the Allies, led by the British, in World War I, affirmed the Zionist goal of building Jewish settlement in the land of Israel. When the British and their Arab allies conquered Palestine from the Ottoman Turks, in the midst of World War I, the Imperial government in London issued a statement on November 2, 1917, called the Balfour Declaration. This approved the development of a Jewish homeland in Palestine. The Allies thus supplied that charter that Herzl had sought in his lifetime. The Balfour Declaration further provided that the civil and religious rights of non-Jews in the country were protected and the status of the Jews living elsewhere than in the Jewish homeland was left unaffected. That same declaration won the endorsement of other countries and the League of Nations, and Zionism began to move from the realm of theory to the work of nation-building.

Zionism and European Ethnic Nationalism

Over the fifty years in which it did its principal work, from 1897 to 1947, Zionism participated in European history and politics and won considerable support in the United States as well. Zionism arose "within the milieu of European nationalism."[1] Most of Europe was then organized in polyglot, multicultural and diverse empires, Russia, Austria-Hungary, and Germany (not to mention Britain, an eighteenth-century construction of Scotland, England, Wales, and Ireland, and France, equally regional in language and culture but centralized in Napoleon's times). But peoples—linguistic-cultural-religious-ethnic entities—within those empires had wanted their own nation-states instead. Just as the Finns, Latvians, Lithuanians, Estonians, and Poles ruled by Russia, and Czechs, Serbs, and other Poles, ruled by Austria-Hungary, aspired to form nation-states such as Finland, Latvia, Lithuania, Estonia, Serbia, the Czech Republic, and Poland, so the Zionists held the Jewish people aspired to form the Jewish state.

In addition to qualities held in common with other peoples, Zionism bears traits all its own, as the great historian of Zionist thought, Arthur Hertzberg, points out in his classic account: "All of the other nineteenth-century nationalisms based their struggle for political sovereignty on an already existing national land or language. . . . Zionism alone proposed to acquire both of these usual preconditions of national identity by the élan of its nationalist will."[2]

The Zionists thus had to match the territory with the people. And since the Jews of Europe spoke the languages of the places in which they lived, Zionism had also to find a language that all of the Jews would adopt. Zionism thus recognized not only a political but a cultural task. Zionism furthermore rejected the Jews' traditional economic role, which made them middlemen, and wanted to turn the Jews into productive farmers and industrial workers.

The Three Streams of Zionism: Political, Cultural, and Socialist

In the beginning Zionism quickly divided into three streams, each with its own theory of the tasks of the movement. One stream emphasized issues of Jewish culture, language, and literature. The second stressed the political task of gaining recognition for the Jews as a political entity. The third, dominant before the State of Israel came into being and for a generation afterward, through the 1970s, wanted the Jewish state to be socialist, to create an economy based on public ownership of the means of production, as we shall see.

Political Zionism, formed by Herzl, maintained that the Jews should provide for the emigration of the masses of their nation from Eastern Europe. The goal of political Zionism was to evacuate the Jews from the lands they had occupied for a thousand years and create a national home for them in their own land. The masses of Jews lived in the German, Russian, and Austro-Hungarian empires, as well as Romania. Russia and Austria-Hungary were then entering a protracted state of political disintegration and already long suffering from economic dislocation. All effort and energy should be directed at removing those masses, in danger for their very lives, to a secure refuge. Zionism was the only movement of modern Judaism that foresaw the Holocaust and tried to save lives. Herzl in particular placed the requirement for legal recognition of a Jewish state over the location of the state, and, in doing so, he set forth the policy that the practical salvation of the Jews through political means would form the definition of Zionism.

Cultural Zionism, represented by the social philosopher resident in Odessa, in Russia, Asher Ginzberg, who took the pen name Ahad HaAm ("One of the People"). Cultural Zionism stressed Zion as a spiritual center, to unite all parts of the Jewish people. He emphasized the importance of spiritual preparation and ideological and cultural activities. It addressed not immediate projects but the long-term intellectual issues. It wanted to persuade the Jews of the Zionist premises concerning the Jews as a secular people aiming at building a nation-state. Cultural Zionism opted for the use of not Yiddish, the Jewish language that most Jews spoke, but Hebrew, an ancient language, lacking adequate vocabulary for the contemporary task. Hebrew therefore was resurrected and turned into a language of literature and technology alike. Jewish writers were encouraged by Zionism to write in the Hebrew language, and a literature took shape, including poetry and fiction.

Cultural Zionism's Doctrine of Jewish History

The earliest initiatives of Zionism in resettling Jews in the land of Israel stimulated a great flowering of scholarship on Judaism and the history of the Jews. Zionism provoked thought on the meaning of events, the pattern to be discerned when historians looked back upon the Jews' past from the perspective of the Zionist revolution in Jewish politics and culture. One of cultural Zionism's earliest public projects after the end of World War I and the promulgation of the Balfour Declaration was the founding of the Hebrew University of Jerusalem, intended as a center of

Jewish culture. Among its earliest departments were Mathematics and Jewish Studies, with emphasis on Jewish history and literature.

Zionism explained how the Jews formed "a people, one people." To support its claims Zionism turned to the study of "Jewish history," that is, a continuous narrative of a single, coherent group, a narrative read as a single and unitary story. According to that story the Jews all came from some one place, traveled together, and were going back to that same one place: one people. Zionist theory therefore derived strength from the study of history. The sort of history that emerged took the form of factual and descriptive narrative. Its selection of facts, its recognition of problems requiring explanation, its choice of what mattered and what did not—all of these definitive questions found answers in the larger program of nationalist ideology.

At the same time Zionist theory explicitly rejected the precedent formed by that Torah, selecting as its history not the history of the faith, of the Torah, but the history of the nation, Israel construed as a secular entity. Zionism defined episodes as history, linear history, Jewish History, and appealed to those strung-together events, all of a given classification to be sure, as vindication for its program of action.

Socialist Zionism wanted the Jewish state to be a Socialist society and economy. In fact for its first three decades of independence the State of Israel was socialist. Socialism in general, not under Jewish auspices, posited a class struggle between the working class and the middle class for control of the instruments of production. These Socialists regarded the Jews as a nation not a class, and their theory dismissed nationalism as bourgeois. The Jews as such had no role to play in the class struggle, and the triumph of the proletariat would solve the Jewish problem. But the Zionist Socialists saw matters differently.

They held that the class struggle would be fought in the Jewish state, and the Jews would turn themselves into working class by building the economy of the Jewish state. Ber Borochov, ideologist for this Zionism, explained:

> Jewish immigration is slowly tending to divert itself to a country where petty Jewish capital and labor may be utilized in such forms of production as will serve as a transition from an urban to an agricultural economy and from the production of consumers' goods to more basic forms of industry. . . . This land will be the only one available to the Jews. . . . It will be a country of low cultural and political development. Big capital will hardly find use for itself there, while Jewish petty and middle capital will find a

market for its products. . . . The land of spontaneously concentrated Jewish immigration will be Palestine. . . . Political territorial autonomy in Palestine is the ultimate aim of Zionism. For proletarian Zionists, this is also a step toward socialism.[3]

The Socialist Zionists enjoyed much support among the East European Jews and predominated in the Jewish settlement of the land of Israel and controlled the political institutions for three quarters of a century, to 1975. They founded the labor unions, the large-scale industries, the health and welfare and educational institutions and organizations. They controlled the national institutions that were taking shape. They created the press, the nascent army—the nation. No wonder that from the beginnings of political Zionism through the first quarter-century after independence in 1948, the Socialist Zionists made all the decisions and controlled everything. Government, university, and army positions went to the Socialists, and others could scarcely make their way in the State of Israel.

Creating in the Land of Israel a New Society of Jewish Collectives

Socialist Zionists formed a Zionist-Socialist way of life, finding their ideal in collective settlements in farming. These settlements, called Kibbutzim, were mainly agricultural. They operated in theory, from each according to one's ability, to each according to one's needs. They built collectively owned industrial enterprises, a powerful national workers union, and a political party of workers and farmers. So settling on the Land was not sufficient. Doing so in a certain way was required. This way of life expressed a worldview particular to Socialist Zionism, but treated as essential to Zionism: the building of an ideal society by Israel, the Jewish nation, on its own land, in agriculture.

Socialist Zionists accepted the Socialist critique of the Jews as a people made up of parasites, not productive workers. That was because they were shopkeepers, not farmworkers, small traders, not factory workers. The Socialist Zionists held that the Jews should create a productive society of their own, so that they could enter the arena of the class struggle, which would result in due course in the creation of a class-less society. Socialist Zionism maintained that the Jews had first to constitute an appropriately divided society of classes. This they would accomplish only when they formed their own nation. They had further to enter productive economies and build an economy of their own. Then the Jews would work out the class struggle in terms appropriate to their nation and produce the classless society. As a result the creation of a Jewish national economy took on importance as the mode of establishing a healthy class struggle, and above all, physical labor and the development of rootedness in the soil would accomplish the Socialists' goal. That thesis then carried within itself the prescription of the way of life that would lead to the founding of collective farms and the building of a Jewish agricultural life in the land of Israel.

Zionism Versus Judaism

Political, cultural, and socialist Zionism had in common a sense of competition with Judaism. Each dismissed the religion for its own reasons. The political Zionists had a secular state in mind. The Socialist Zionists, in the main, affirmed a secular definition of the Jews. The cultural Zionists saw Judaism as competition for Zionism. Haam, the philosopher of Zionism as a cultural movement, not a political one, made the explicit claim that Zionism would succeed Judaism, so states Arthur Hertzberg:

> The function that revealed religion had performed in talmudic and medieval Judaism, that of guaranteeing the survival of the Jews as a separate entity because of their belief in the divinely ordained importance of the Jewish religion and people, it was no longer performing and could not be expected to perform. The crucial task facing Jews in the modern era was to devise new structures to contain the separate individual of the Jews and to keep them loyal to their own tradition. This analysis of the situation implied . . . a view of Jewish history which Ahad HaAm produced as undoubted . . . , that the Jews in all ages were essentially a nation and that all other factors profoundly important to the life of this people, even religion, were mainly instrumental values.[4]

Hertzberg contrasts that statement with one made a thousand years earlier by the first great philosopher of Judaism, Saadiah, in tenth-century Baghdad: "The Jewish people is a people only for the sake of its Torah." That statement of the position of the Rabbinic Judaism contrasts with the view of Zionism that the Jews form a nation like any other and that the practice of Judaism is not essential to the life of that nation. The theological definition of the Jewish people thus competed with the nationalist definition.

Accordingly, the Zionist worldview competed with the religious one(s). The formidable statement of Jacob Klatzkin (1882–1948), a historian of the Jews, provides the solid basis for comparison:

> In the past there have been two criteria of Judaism: the criterion of religion, according to which Judaism is a system of positive and negative commandments, and the criterion of the spirit, which saw Judaism as a complex of ideas, like monotheism, Messianism, absolute justice, etc. According to both these criteria, therefore, Judaism rests on a subjective basis, on the acceptance of a creed . . . a religious denomination . . . or a community of individuals who share in a Weltanschauung. . . . In opposition to these two criteria, which make of Judaism a matter of creed, a third has now arisen, the criterion of a consistent nationalism. According to it, Judaism rests on an objective basis: to be a Jew means the acceptance of neither a religious nor an ethical creed. We are neither a denomination or a school of thought, but members of one family, bearers of a common history. . . . The national definition too requires an act of will. It defines our nationalism by two criteria: partnership in the past and the conscious desire to continue such partnership in the future. There are, therefore, two bases for Jewish nationalism—the compulsion of history and a will expressed in that history.[5]

Klatzkin's stress on "a will expressed in . . . history"—"one family, bearers of a common history"—is the key. Zionists would find it necessary to reread the whole of the histories of Jews and compose a single, unitary, continuous, harmonious "Jewish History," a linear system leading inexorably to the formation of the Jewish state on the other end of time. Klatzkin defined being a Jew not as something subjective, but as something objective: "on land and language. These are the basic categories of national being."

That definition would lead directly to calling the Jewish state, "the State of Israel." The doctrine formed by Zionism of what is Israel would then clearly state, "Israel" is a place, a nation. In contributing, as Klatzkin said, "the territorial-political definition of Jewish nationalism," Zionism offered a genuinely fresh worldview: "Either the Jewish people shall redeem the land and thereby continue to live, even if the spiritual content of Judaism changes radically, or we shall remain in exile and rot away, even if the spiritual tradition continues to exist."

In this way Zionism clearly stated the intention of providing a worldview to replace that of the received Rabbinic Judaism and in competition with all efforts of the continuators of that Judaism, so Klatzkin argued: "Zionism stands opposed to all this. Its real beginning is *The Jewish State* [referring to Herzl's manifesto in founding the Zionist Congress], and its basic intention, whether consciously or unconsciously, is to deny any conception of Jewish identity based on spiritual criteria." Obviously, Klatzkin's was not the only voice. But in his appeal to history, in his initiative in positing a linear course of events of a single kind leading to one goal, the Jewish state, Klatzkin expressed that theory of history that would supply Zionism with a principal plank in its platform. And the theory proved familiar, for it adapted the pattern of exile and return, which had defined Judaism from the very beginning.

Zionism and the Bible: Digging for Roots in the Land

In its eagerness to appropriate a usable past, Zionism, and its successor, Israeli nationalism, identified archaeology as a principal cultural activity. Zionism dug for roots in history, finding in archaeology links to the past between the Jewish people and the land of Israel. So in pre-State times and after the creation of the State of Israel in 1948, Zionist scholars and institutions devoted great effort to digging up the ancient monuments of the land of Israel. Archaeology became a principal instrument of national expression, much as, for contemporary believers in Scripture, archaeology would prove the truths of the biblical narrative. It was not surprising, therefore, that in the Israeli War of Independence, 1948–1949, and in later times as well, Israeli generals explained to the world that by following the biblical record of the nation in times past, they had found hidden roads, appropriate strategies—in all, the key to victory.

Zionism and the Holocaust

The Holocaust is the point at which Judaism and the Jewish people took center stage in the life of Western civilization. The mass murder by the Germans and their allies of nearly six million people by reason of their originating in Jewish families came about as a direct result of the German exterminationist anti-Semitism. Zionism alone responded to the threats of mass murder and then to the events of the Holocaust with its theory of Jewish history and its meaning. It had begun with a warning of such a calamity and had proposed a final solution to the problem of Gentile anti-Semitism. So Zionism and the State of Israel that it created captured the imagination of nearly all Jews throughout the world, many of whom defined their ethnic identity in relationship to the Holocaust from then on.

Specifically, Zionism explained the Holocaust as the result of the Jews living in exile, and it portrayed the Jewish state as the return to Zion that the prophets foresaw thousands of years ago. Within that pattern of exile and return Zionism could explain what happened and provide hope for what must follow. History was seen to validate the ideology of Zionism. When the surviving Jews of Europe straggled out of the death camps in 1945, Zionism came forth with an explanation of what had happened and a program to provide for the survivors.

Zionism turns out to have selected the right problem and given the right solution to that problem. Others did not. Reform Judaism had adopted the belief in progress characteristic of nineteenth-century religious thinkers and affirmed the essential goodness of humanity. That conviction lost credibility. Jews who became Socialists and Communists shared the expectation of world-brotherhood, in the realization of the rule of the working class. The Communists' prohibition of the teaching and practice of Judaism deprived that expectation of plausibility. The cheerful prognostications of a solution of "the Jewish problem" through the end of history, characteristic both of Reform Judaism and of Socialism, perished in the death factories built by Germany in Auschwitz, Treblinka, and elsewhere in Poland. The Zionists correctly understood the meaning of events. They furthermore had a program to respond to them. It was to create the Jewish state and to resettle the survivors of the Holocaust there.

Even as early as 1940 Zionists foresaw what Hitler's Germany was going to do. At a meeting in December 1940, Berl Katznelson, an architect of Socialist Zionism in the Jewish community of Palestine before the creation of the State of Israel, announced that European Jewry was finished:

> The essence of Zionist awareness must be that what existed in Vienna will never return, what existed in Berlin will never return, nor in Prague, and what we had in Warsaw and Lodz is finished, and we must realize this! . . . Why don't we understand that what Hitler has done, and this war is a kind of Rubicon, an outer limit, and what existed before will never exist again. . . . And I declare that the fate of European Jewry is sealed.[6]

Even before the systematic mass murder got underway, Zionism grasped that, after World War II, Jews would not wish to return to Europe, certainly not to those places in which they had flourished for a thousand years. Zionism offered the alternative: the building, outside of Europe, of the Jewish state.

So Zionism took a position of prophecy and found its prophecy fulfilled. It held that the Jews were living in exile. That view found verification in the destruction of European Jewry, the end of a thousand years of Jewish life in many parts of Europe. And Zionism's further claim to point the way forward proved to be Israel's salvation in the formation of the State of Israel on the other side of the Holocaust. So Katznelson maintained: "If Zionism wanted to be the future force of the Jewish people, it must prepare to solve the Jewish question in all its scope." The secret of the power of Zionism lay in its ability to make sense of the world and to propose a program to solve the problems of the age.

Zionist Theory and Jewish Ethnic Reality

Zionism conflicted with the facts of the Jews' existence. The Jews did not form a nation. They did not live in a common territory, speak a common language, participate in a common culture. But Zionism insisted that the Jews constitute a people and should form a state of their own. And, as we have seen, Zionism accomplished its goals. How to account for the success of Zionism in transforming into a people and a nation what was in fact a polyglot, diverse, divided, group of people, with little in common except the fate of anti-Semitism imposed on them all from the outside? Zionism afforded pride and dignity to a people despised and demeaned in everyday life throughout Europe. Amos Elon, describing the opening days of the first Zionist congress in Basel in 1897, contrasts the ideal of "a people, one people," and the reality of the Jews, diverse and divided as they were:

> The narrow streets of Basel were alive with a strange assortment of people. Students from Kiev, Stockholm, Montpellier, and Berlin, with proud duel slashes across their cheeks. Pious, bearded rabbinical scholars with earlocks mingled with scions of long-assimilated or even baptized families of the West and publishers of obscure little newspapers appearing in Warsaw and Odessa. Neurotic Hebrew poets, who wrote for audiences of a few hundred readers, or spent their lives translating Shakespeare, Goethe, and Homer

into Hebrew, came in the hope of reviving their ancient national tongue. There were Romanian and Hungarian businessmen, university professors from Heidelberg and Sofia, a Kiev oculist, doctors, engineers, a small sallow Polish shopkeeper, a yellow-bearded Swede, a bespectacled French intellectual, a stiff Dutch banker, a courtly Viennese lawyer, and many journalists from all over the Jewish world, for whom Zionism was the great and sacred work of their lives. . . . All were wearing small blue, seven-cornered shields embossed with twelve red and gold stars and bearing the legend, in German, "The only solution to the Jewish question is the establishment of a Jewish state."[7]

To see these diverse people as "a people, one people" required a vision not of what was, but of what in order to be believed had to be self-evident. The power of Zionism was to take that vision and transform it into fact. What gave the whole urgency? It was the emphasis on the reality of anti-Semitism. So, as Elon says, Zionism came into being through a "congress [that] was the first authoritative assembly of the Jewish people since their dispersion under the Roman Empire." The power of Zionism as a system of thought and a program of action lay in its capacity to explain events that cried out for explanation. History proved Zionism right. Things that really happened made all the difference.

Western civilization produced Zionism in two ways. First, the anti-Semitism of the West framed the urgent question the entire Jewish group had to answer. Western anti-Semitism, whether racist or religious or cultural or political or social, made the Jews overlook their differences and recognize what all had in common, the experience of being hated.

Second, in its modern age of nationalism the West defined for many Jews the self-evidently valid answer to their dilemma. It did this by its invention of the nation-state, which was meant to solve problems of cultural, ethnic and religious difference. In the nation-state all who belonged were equal as citizens, sharing a common culture, nationality, and (in many instances) religion. So the Jews would form a nation-state and solve their Gentile problem.

The pathos of Zionism emerged from its power; the refuge it built for the Jewish people in the land of Israel competed for the same territory with another people and its claims. Much of the history of the West from World War II to the present would be written in the conflict between Zionism and the State of Israel and Arab nationalism and the state of Palestine. There is no more probative evidence of the importance of religion in Western civilization in modern times as much as in the past than that fact.

Discussion Questions

1. How does Zionism relate to Judaism: what are the connections between the ancient religion and its narrative and the modern political movement and its program? Why did Reform and much of Orthodox Judaism originally oppose Zionism?

2. What marks Zionism as a secular political movement? How is it congruent with a religious one? Do the Jews form a religious group or an ethnic community? What difference does the answer to that question make in making sense of Zionism? History plays a role in the modernization of Judaism. How did, and do, history and archaeology form a medium of expression of Zionist convictions?

3. What are the three streams of Zionism, and how does each form part of the modern State of Israel? In what way does cultural Zionism compete with Judaism? What defines Socialist Zionism? Does political Zionism speak to the Jews who live outside of the State of Israel?

ZIONISM, IMPERIALISM, AND NATIONALISM: CHRISTIAN IMPERIALISM

Bruce Chilton

Introduction

Constantine's settlement handed Christianity an influential position within the Roman Empire; theologians of the church became key advisers and also exercised juridical functions as magistrates. That arrangement did not give the church direct political control over government, but a profound effect upon imperial policies was involved. The development of views of history and society as part of a theological perspective by Eusebius and Augustine enabled Christians to exercise an influential role in public life. All the while, however, earlier and different attitudes toward government had already been embedded in Christian teaching, starting with its Scriptures.

The interaction of those attitudes explains the volatility of Christian teaching in regard to politics and government. In teachings cited below, Christians are mandated by Jesus to reject human government, by Saint Paul to support duly constituted authority, by Origen and Augustine not to confuse this world's power with God's power, and by Eusebius and Constantine himself to see the emperor as Christ's representative on earth. By examining the types of attitudes Christians have developed toward government, the course of political history in the West can be more readily understood. Their interactions have produced the model of an empire founded on trade rather than on conquest, and this commercial model has succeeded many times in the modern period.

Four Christian Views of Government

Although the Gospel according to Matthew in the New Testament was published as we know it in 80 C.E., it accurately portrays Jesus' teaching around 24 C.E. "No one can serve two lords, because either he will hate the one and love the other, or adhere to one and disdain the other: you cannot serve God and mammon" (Matt 6:24, in the author's translation). *Mammon* exactly transcribes the Aramaic term Jesus used; it means money such as you might offer to bribe someone. To Jesus, currency was emblematic of the Roman occupation of rural Galilee, where power was concentrated in the hands of military garrisons and a client-king (Herod Antipas) who served at Rome's pleasure. That had nothing to do with his passionate concern, "the kingdom of God," also an Aramaic conception. For Jesus and his movement, the institutions of this world simply offered no interest; they diverted attention to the only rule that mattered, which was God's. Jesus had no philosophy of government. He proclaimed a political anti-philosophy, rooted in his eschatological vision.

Paul's position was similar, and yet distinctive. Writing to Christians in Rome around 57 C.E., he said: "Render to all what is owed: to whom tribute, tribute; to whom tax, tax; to whom fear, fear; to whom honor, honor. Owe no one anything, except to love one another" (Rom 13:7-8, in the author's translation). Paul mandated the acceptance and support of human authority on the grounds that it had been put in place by structures of power and justice that God had ultimately sanctioned. This is a provisional imperative where it concerns government. Paul goes on to cite the command to love one another (Rom 13:8-10, a summary rooted in Jesus' teaching) and explicitly states that this command conditions all the other mandates.

In addition to Jesus' authority, what makes mandates regarding government provisional within Paul's thought is his conviction that "the form of this world is passing away" (1 Cor 7:31, written around 55 C.E.). Those words articulate the same eschatological perspective from which Jesus taught, but Paul's teaching relates eschatology to the conduct of every individual:

> Every person remain in the calling one was called in. Were you a slave when you were called? What does that matter? (Yet if you are able to become free, take the opportunity.) For the slave called is the Lord's freed person; likewise a free person called is Christ's slave. (1 Cor 7: 20-21)

Paul's endorsement of the current social structure of the Roman Empire and his endorsement of the emperor's authority have been compared to the thought of the Stoic philosopher Seneca, who in 55 C.E. described the emperor himself as "chosen and thought worthy to do the work of the gods upon the earth" (*De Clementia* 1). Yet Paul's loyalty to Jesus' teaching clearly made him a more qualified supporter of the Roman Empire than Seneca was.

Paul modified his teaching after his arrest by the Romans and his own direct experience of unjust accusation. He then declared that "our citizens' status belongs in heaven" (Phil 3:20, words written in 60 C.E., and published at a later time by Timothy). Loyalty to God replaced the obedience Paul had earlier said Christians owed to their rulers (Rom 13:1-7). Paul's own death in 64 C.E. during Nero's anti-Christian pogrom opened a period of sporadic, sometimes vicious persecution of Christians by Roman officials at various levels.

By the third century Origen pursued Paul's later thinking and conceived of God and of divine reward as completely beyond this world and its misery. His discussion appears within his use of the imagery of light to understand God (*On First Principles* 1.1.5; 220 C.E.):[1]

> Having then refuted, to the best of our ability, every interpretation which suggests that we should attribute to God any material characteristics, we assert that he is in truth incomprehensible and immeasurable. For whatever may be the knowledge which we have been able to obtain about God, whether by perception or reflection, we must of necessity believe that he is far and away better than our thoughts about him. For if we see a man who can scarcely look at a glimmer of the light of the smallest lamp, and if we wish to teach such a one, whose eyesight is not strong enough to receive more light than we have said, about the brightness and splendor of the sun, shall we not have to tell him that the splendor of the sun is unspeakably and immeasurably better and more glorious than all this light he can see?

Hand in hand with this teaching, Origen urged a selective obedience to the rulers of this world, depending on whether their orders served the wisdom of God (*On First Principles* 3.2). No merely human institution could be assumed to accord with the light of the transcendent God, so that Origen urged believers to keep that light, rather than the claims of the world around them, at the center of their attention.

Augustine developed just this model, derived from Plato's philosophy, within his comprehensive, political philosophy of history (*City of God* 14.28; 426 C.E.):

> So two loves have constituted two cities—the earthly is formed by love of self even to contempt of God, the heavenly by love of God even to contempt of self. For the one glories in herself, the other in the Lord. The one seeks glory from man; for the other God, the witness of the conscience, is the greatest glory.

The place of God within the individual conscience made this philosophy a vitally important influence within the emergence of democratic institutions in the West. Once Augustine's interpretation elevated the conscience of the individual over loyalty to institutions, the way was open to argue that those institutions should be *shaped* by the convictions of the people, rather than by the reverse. Many centuries passed before that argument was mounted, but Augustine's thought proved pivotal during the Reformation of the sixteenth century and the political revolutions that followed.

Augustine's sober detachment from the demands of government, even Christian government, is at odds with Eusebius's enthusiasm a century before (*Praise of Constantine* 1.6; 337 C.E.): "Our Emperor, beloved of God, bearing a kind of image of the supreme rule as it were in imitation of the greater, directs the course of all things upon earth." From a communication short of ten years into his reign, Constantine makes it clear that he thought of his own authority along the lines that Eusebius articulated (Constantine to Elpidius; 3 July 321):[2]

> Just as we thought it most unfitting that the day of the Sun, with its venerable rites, should be given over to the swearing and counter-swearing of litigants and their unseemly brawls, so it is a pleasant and joyful thing to fulfill petitions of special urgency on that day. Therefore on that festal day let all be allowed to perform manumission and emancipation; and let nothing that concerns this be forbidden.

Here the powers of church and states are wielded with a single, sovereign authority, a far cry from Jesus' rejection of government, Paul's resignation to human authority, or the theological skepticism of secular power represented by Origen and Augustine.

Imperial Power and Its Fission

Imperial authority as defined by Constantine and Eusebius involved no recognizable division between church and state. One of Constantine's successors, Theodosius, makes this explicit in his influential legal conventions (Theodosian Code, 395 C.E.):

> It is our desire that all the various nations which are subject to our Clemency and Moderation should continue in the profession of that religion that was delivered to the Romans by the divine Apostle Peter, as it has been preserved by faithful tradition; and which is now professed by the Pontif Damascus and by Peter, Bishop of Alexandria, a man of apostolic holiness. According to the apostolic teaching and the doctrine of the Gospel, let us believe the one deity of the Father, the Son and the Holy Spirit, in equal majesty and in a holy Trinity. We authorize the followers of this law to assume the title of Catholic Christians; but as for the others, since, in our judgment, they are foolish madmen, we decree that they shall be branded with the ignominious name of heretics, and shall not presume to give to their conventicles the name of churches.

Trinitarian orthodoxy was a policy of state, no mere theology, and heresy emerged as a proper concern for the emperor, to be addressed with all his power.

Prominent Christian leaders not only embraced this model of state-sanctioned religion, but also pressed to extend its reach to permit orthodox Christians to attack their competitors. In a letter to Emperor Theodosius, Bishop Ambrose of Milan most clearly expresses the emergent attitude toward Judaism and Jews, whom he wants treated as if they were heretics. Far to the east of Ambrose, in Callinicum on the Euphrates, the local bishop had encouraged the plunder and arson of a synagogue. Concerned by such behavior as a breach of public order, Theodosius directed that the bishop rebuild the synagogue at his own expense. Ambrose's response, in a letter of December 388 C.E., is infamous, but its argument is worth more than the general characterization it usually receives (*Epistle* 40.8):

> This, I ask, Emperor: that you turn your vengeance upon me, and, if you consider this act a crime, that you impute it to me. Why order the absent to be punished? I am present here before you, and confess my guilt. I proclaim that I set the synagogue on fire, or at least ordered others to do so, that there might not be left a building in which Christ is denied. If you ask me why I have not burned the synagogue in my neighborhood, I answer that its destruction has already been begun by the judgment of God, and my work was at an end.

F. Homes Dudden, a sympathetic biographer, goes on to describe the "really astounding perversity" of Ambrose's argument, where he goes on to say that since similar actions had been taken against churches under the emperor Julian, the burning of a synagogue could also be overlooked. To Dudden's mind, the whole incident is an example of "how religious prejudice could so warp the judgment of a good and wise man as to cause him to condone the crimes of robbery and arson, and actually plead the unpunished outrages of brutal mobs and heathen persecutors as precedents for pardoning fanatical Christian criminals."[3]

Dudden wrote during a time that brought all too salient examples of the atrocities that Ambrose's argument and attitude warranted. He explains that "unbalanced zeal" on the part of Ambrose "induced him to step outside his proper province, and inflict an undeserved humiliation on a monarch who was doing his best." To Dudden's mind, the whole business was "surprising."[4] Undue enthusiasm has been the diagnosis of many religious ills since the eighteenth century, but "zeal" as such has been considered a virtue during most of the history of Christianity. It only becomes a problem when its purpose turns destructive, and religious arson is without question a good example of that. The real culprit in this argument is not Ambrose's zeal or some defect of his temperament, a momentary loss of self-control, or a lapse in his sense of propriety or law. Ambrose clearly believes that setting fire to synagogues is not a bad thing to do.

What shapes Ambrose's attitude is his sense of history, his conviction that the judgment of God—unfolding historically since the conversion of Constantine, as Eusebius taught—was against all those who heard the Scriptures of Israel read every week and yet did not turn to Christ. Behavior such as that of the mob at Callinicum, from Ambrose's point of view, simply helps God's will along. By his own testimony, he would have done the same thing in Milan, except the synagogue there was already on the way out.[5]

For Ambrose, Theodosius is emperor for the service of true religion, to which the maintenance of civil law is secondary (*Epistle* 40.11). That general point of view permitted him to make an argument on behalf of the Christian arson when he preached in Theodosius's presence on this subject. "In plain words, honor the least of Christ's disciples and pardon their faults, that the angels may rejoice, that the apostles may exult, that the prophets may be glad."[6] The means chosen for removing the synagogue were imperfect, but that did not make it any less the outcome of divine will in history.

In Ambrose's case, as in Eusebius's, the union of the Roman Empire and the Catholic Church signals a fundamental change in the order of social experience and conduct. Judaism is now treated as a peculiar, passing problem, which history is in the process of resolving on behalf of the church. That shows how powerful and how political the Christian conception of history could be. Within this context, we can understand Lee McDonald's observation that "Some of the most intense Christian writers against the Jews (Aphrahat, Ephraem, Chrysostom, Cyril of Alexandria, and even Augustine of Hippo) are from the fourth and fifth centuries, when the Jews were still active in proselytizing Gentiles and having significant successes among the Christian population."[7] The issue, however, is not merely competition with a perceived "heresy" in itself, which had been the perennial environment of the primitive church and the early church. For the Orthodox and Catholic Church, the very existence of Judaism, whether conceived of as offering heretical options within Christianity or as a social entity outside the church, was at best to be tolerated only until the work of history was done.

Yet the Christian empire experienced a steady loss of control, not only at its borders, but also over Rome itself in 410, when Alaric sacked the ancient capital. The successes of "barbarians" who were also often "heretics" (that is, non-orthodox Christian believers, who had not embraced the creed of Nicaea) threatened the Imperial mentality at a fundamental level. The emperor had to cede power, and the Eusebian belief in the inexorable triumph of Christ through the empire had to be changed. Even Augustine taught that God is represented on earth in the power of the Catholic Church and that the present Christian epoch (*Christiana tempora*) corresponds to the millennium promised in Revelation 20 (*City of God* 20.9). Against this model, a powerful opposition had emerged. As Augustine says in *Sermon* 62, "Heretics, Jews and pagans—they have come to form a unity over against our Unity." In order to account for the slippage of the triumphal victory of Christ in government, Augustine conceived of all the opposing forces as motivated by Satan, the rebellious angel who had beset the world with sin and evil.

During the Middle Ages and the Reformation, Christianity in the West saw an increased belief in the power of Satan as compared to the ancient period, in order to account for the many contradictions that Christians experienced to the faith that God in Christ ruled the world. To some extent, that was a function of the belief that the golden age of the single empire had been lost, undermined by Satan's legions. Charlemagne attempted to revive the classic Imperial settlement, as in his "General Admonition" of 789 C.E.:

Correct carefully the Psalms, the signs in writing, the songs, the calendar, the grammar, in each monastery or diocese, and the Catholic books; because often men desire to pray to God properly, but they pray badly because of incorrect books. And do not permit mere boys to corrupt them in reading or writing. If the Gospel, Psalter, and Missal have to be copied let men of mature age do the copying, with the greatest care.

Charlemagne's policies were in line with his ambition to claim the power of Constantine in the West; and on Christmas day in the year 800, Pope Leo III crowned him Emperor of the Romans.

This attempt at a Holy Roman Empire survived for centuries (in one form or another, until the rise of Napoleon),[8] but it never approached the Constantinian settlement in power, influence, or territory. To begin with, Constantine's heirs still ruled in the east of the empire in Constantinople, which only fell to the Ottomans in 1453.[9] Moreover, the classic model of Constantine was ill suited to the dynasties of European warlords. Charlemagne's territory was eventually divided up among his grandsons:[10] under the emerging feudal settlement (frequently called a "system," but far from systematic), marriages joined territories, and births split them apart again. It was a recipe for ceaseless armed conflict, which the Viking raids and invasions only exacerbated.

In any case, during the eighth century, while Charlemagne was approaching a Constantinian model, the papacy was assuring it could never emerge again, because it sought to establish its power as superior to that of any emperor. At this time, in all probability, "The Donation of Constantine" was fabricated. In this document, the dying Emperor is alleged to have handed his power over to the Church of Rome:

We convey to the oft-mentioned and most blessed Silvester, universal pope, both our palace, as preferment, and likewise all provinces, palaces and districts of the city of Rome and Italy and of the regions of the West; and, bequeathing them to the power and sway of him and the pontiffs, his successors, we do (by means of fixed imperial decision through this our divine, sacred and authoritative sanction) determine and decree that the same be placed at his disposal, and do lawfully grant it as a permanent possession to the holy Roman Church.

In effect, the "West" is defined as a political unit under the authority of the bishop of Rome, who here goes by his Latin form of address (once applied to many senior clergy), "Papa," or "pope." From that perspective, there could never be another Constantine again because he had given his power away to the pope.

Claiming secular power for the pope and exercising it were two different things. In various regions of Europe local rulers (kings and lords) struggled with the pope and ecclesiastical authorities over the authority to appoint bishops. Pope Gregory VII's letter to the Bishop of Metz (1081) sets out a line of argument:

> Every Christian king, when he comes to die, seeks as a pitiful suppliant the aid of a priest, that he may escape hell's prison, may pass from the darkness into the light, and at the judgment of God may appear absolved from the bondage of his sins. Who, in his last hour (what layman, not to speak of priests), has ever implored the aid of an earthly king for the salvation of his soul? And what king or emperor is able, by reason of the office he holds, to rescue a Christian from the power of the devil through holy baptism, to number him among the sons of God, and to fortify him with the divine unction? Who of them can by his own words make the body and blood of our Lord—the greatest act in the Christian religion? Or who of them possesses the power of binding and loosing in heaven and on earth? From all these considerations it is clear how greatly the priestly office excels in power.

Precisely as this argument comes to its resounding close, it betrays its commitment more to Augustine's ideas than to those of Eusebius: the power of the church is in the end not of this world. Although the papacy had acquired large tracts of land by Gregory's time, and would consolidate its power in canon law, its attempt to control secular rulers often failed precisely because it conceived of its power in spiritual, Augustinian terms.

A brilliant attempt to rectify that was made by Pope Urban II, who called Europe to the Crusades in 1095. His explicit purpose, among other things, was to stop kings and knights fighting among themselves and get them to make war on a common enemy—the "infidel" Muslims—under the united banner of Christ and the papacy:

> Remission of sins will be granted for going there, if they end a shackled life either on land in crossing the sea, or in struggling against the heathen. I, being vested with that gift from God, grant this to those who go. Let those who are accustomed to wage private wars wastefully even against believers, go forth against the infidels in a battle worthy to undertaken now and to be finished in victory.

After some initial success and colonization, setbacks and sporadic campaigns became the rule, and by 1270 the Crusaders had manifestly failed to hold on to the territory they had conquered. But they had greatly expanded trade, commerce, and intellectual contact with Muslim nations that at the time were far in advance of the West in all those domains.

With the expansion of trade, commerce, and intellectual contact came the increasing predominance of the great cities of Europe, and the centralization of power along national lines in the hands of kings. As a hegemony of monarchs emerged, religious leaders came to accept that "the world" was no longer under their sway. The Monastic Rule of Saint Francis (3.394; 1223) makes this explicit:

> The clerical brothers shall perform the divine service according to the order of the Holy Roman Church, excepting the Psalter, of which they may have extracts. But the lay brothers shall say twenty-four Paternosters at Matins, five at Lauds, seven each at Prime, Terce, Sect and None, twelve at Vespers, seven at the Completorium; and they shall pray for the dead. And they shall fast from the feast of All Saints to the nativity of the Lord; but as to the season of Lent, which begins after the Epiphany of the Lord and continues forty days, a season the Lord consecrated by his holy fast— those who fast during this time shall be blessed of the Lord, and those who do not wish to fast shall not be bound to do so; but otherwise they shall fast until the Resurrection of the Lord. At other times the brothers shall not be bound to fast save on the sixth day; but when there is a compelling reason the brothers shall not be bound to observe a physical fast. But I advise, warn and exhort my brothers in the Lord Jesus Christ, that, when they go into the world, they shall not quarrel, nor contend with words, nor judge others. But let them be gentle, peaceable, modest, merciful and humble, with honorable conversation towards all, as is fitting. They ought not to ride, save when necessity or infirmity clearly compels them so to do.

Of course, not all Catholic leaders were monastics, and the attempt of the Roman Church to extend its power through the Holy Roman Emperor and the papacy by no means came to end with the Middle Ages.

The power of kings had to be factored into any political theology, and taxation as well as the selection of bishops became a preoccupation (Pope Boniface VIII, *Clericis Laicos*, 1296):

> That laymen have been very hostile to the clergy antiquity relates; and it is clearly proved by the experiences of the present time. For not content with what is their own the laity strive for what is forbidden and loose the reins for things unlawful. Nor do they prudently realize that power of clerks or ecclesiastical persons or goods is forbidden them: they impose heavy

burdens on the prelates of the churches and ecclesiastical persons regular and secular, and tax them, and impose collections: they exact and demand from the same the half, tithe, or twentieth, or any other portion or proportion of their revenues or goods; and in many ways they try to bring them into slavery, and subject them to their authority.

Despite these arguments, King Philip IV of France had Pope Boniface kidnapped and his treasury plundered. This kind of royal autonomy, including kings who used their alliance with Rome to extend their influence, was only the prelude to extensions of power beyond the ken or complaint of any king or pope.

National States and Their Imperial Extensions

Pope Boniface's complaint about the growing hegemony of rulers who superseded the power of the church was but the prelude to the secular dominance in politics that characterizes the West since the Middle Ages. That shift was encouraged by the wars of religion that the Reformation brought: it has been estimated that the Thirty Years' War left four million dead in Germany (out of a population of fifteen million in 1600). But after the Peace of Westphalia in 1648 that ended that war, it would be difficult to argue that international conflicts were principally religious in origin.[11]

Two factors in postmedieval Europe totally changed the equations of power. The first was the rise of commerce, and the second was the role of individual conscience as an important consideration in governance. Although the Crusades proved a fiasco from the perspective of the initial aims involved, they did provide an enormous incentive to trade, and offered the West the ideas and culture of the more developed civilizations to the east. Those contacts provoked an unprecedented age of exploration by sea, whose aim was primarily to improve trade.

The explosive effect of that development can be gauged by the emergence of Portugal (under Prince Henry the Navigator, 1394–1460) and Spain (whose queen, Isabella of Castille, underwrote an adventurer named Christopher Columbus) as leading European powers. The Netherlands became the greatest trading empire by the seventeenth century, followed by England and France by the end of that century after a series of mercantile wars.

Trade brought wealth, commerce, and manufacture to Europe in ways these nations had never known. Because these opportunities arose as the continent had already nationalized along linguistic and cultural lines, the royal heads of Europe reaped the rewards. These monarchs' settlements regarding the question of religion, whether as Catholics or Protestants, involved a drastic reduction of ecclesiastical power and wealth as compared to the settlement of the Middle Ages.

Yet at the same time kings and queens insisted on their identities as Christians; the concept of a separation between church and state emerged as a viable option only at the end of the eighteenth century, and even then it by no means prevailed universally. As European states made their commercial and territorial conquests in "the new world," Africa, India, and the "East," each assumed an imperial stature and claimed the warrant of religion for its extension. So, for example, Britain shouldered "the White Man's burden" in India,[12] while America pursued its "manifest destiny" to the Pacific Ocean.[13]

Those conquests were more and more commercial, and less military, over the course of time. Well-established trade proved a better, more wealth-producing mode of occupation than the dispatch of armies. Yet the force of arms backed trade, and wars over land, commerce, trade routes, and ports have been as much a feature of the modern period as jousting was during the Middle Ages. Each national empire produced its own patriotism, involving the claim best to represent the Christian faith among the other options of the time. Yet conversion played a relatively minor role in imperial extension. After all, it was more difficult to enslave or take the land of baptized fellow believers than of strangers whose civilization could be dismissed as savagery.

Concurrent with commercial imperialism, the West during the same period, as a result of the Reformation and the Enlightenment, elevated the role of individual conscience and insight in political thought. The mix of that principle with the absolutist claims of many monarchs in Europe proved revolutionary. But the underlying tension reflected the old difference between the positions of Origen and Augustine on the one hand, and of Eusebius and Constantine on the other. The English Civil War (1642), the American Revolution (1776), the French Revolution (1789), and the Paris Commune (1871) represent the resurgence of the former position. But the latter position made itself felt in the restoration of Charles II (1660), the repression of freedom of the press under John Adams (in the Alien and Sedition Acts, 1798)[14] and Napoleon (who took the Roman title of "consul" in 1799, and "emperor" in 1804), and Bismarck's proclamation of the Second Reich (at Versailles in 1871).

War has marked the modern period to an extent unknown before. To a considerable degree, that is because these different models of government run up against people who have means at their disposal to defend themselves. Napoleon and Hitler tried to achieve Constantine's success, and their imperial models—clearly inspired by the Romans—fell apart despite spectacular military successes.

In contrast to experiments in absolute power, successful empires in the modern period have harnessed military force to the extension of trade. The British used an advantage at sea over a long period to construct bases of power and alliances that ultimately defeated Napoleon. Similarly the United States resorted to dominance in sea and air together with carefully constructed alliances in their conflict with the Third Reich and the Soviet Union. The trading empire, a mix of Augustinian conscience with the categorical imperative of trade and profit, has emerged as an ideal type of government in the modern period, and is frequently embraced by economists and politicians who seem to have no idea of its complex theological origins when they claim that is a natural or inevitable model.

One key to the success of the model of a trading empire is that this amalgamation of Augustinian and Eusebian models tolerates the other Christian attitudes toward government, based on Jesus' and Paul's teaching. So, for example, churches today routinely boast of how much power they have given up and should give up, rejecting what they call the "Constantinian triumphalism" of earlier times.[15] Whether or not that position is as noble as it may seem, the irony is that pragmatic empires have come more "triumphal" as the church has ceded ground in public discourse.

Because these empires are ambient in secular governments, with barely a corner of life free of the claims of politics and commerce, Christians who espouse an eschatological rejection of human governance have often become militant in the modern period. Even those who adopt a more Pauline position, supporting government in a provisional sense, frequently insist that its role be limited. Using a phrase initial developed in art history, Herbert N. Schneidau has written of the "sacred discontent" of the West when it comes to all forms of intellectual endeavor, driving it to invent new forms.[16] Nowhere is that truer than in the field of politics, in which four sacred models constantly vie with one another for dominance, and may yet subvert the model of a trading empire that they have produced.

Discussion Questions

1. Compare Jesus and Paul in their attitudes toward the Roman Empire.

2. What role did Eusebius play in the development of a Christian theology of government?

3. How would you characterize Augustine and Origen in their differing political theologies?

Zionism, Imperialism, and Nationalism: Political Islam

Th. Emil Homerin

Revival and Reform

By the middle of the seventeenth century, the Ottoman, Safavid, and Mughal empires had reached their territorial limits. Due to a combination of geographic factors and the presence of rival empires on their frontiers, further expansion was not possible. All of the imperial powers of the time depended on the expansion of their territory to provide the new lands and revenues necessary to maintain their economies. Yet the Muslim empires could no longer grow, and their military campaigns, whether against enemies without or dissidents within, were increasingly futile and costly. The large armies and bureaucracies maintained by the three Muslim empires required substantial expenditures, and so rulers took extraordinary measures in an attempt to raise needed cash. Sultans allowed wealthy men in search of prestige and power to purchase the rights to hold various government or religious offices for which they were not qualified. Further, government officials also sold the rights to collect taxes for a fixed cash sum paid in advance. Those collecting taxes, in turn, taxed the people at increasingly higher rates so as to make huge profits, but at the taxpayers expense. These practices led to political and economic oppression and an overall decline in agricultural and industrial productivity. This was accompanied by frequent military and territorial losses due, in part, to poor and corrupt leadership.

While some Ottoman, Safavid, and Mughal rulers set about to reform and restore their political and military power, religious leaders hoped to rejuvenate Muslim society by calling Muslims to renew their faith in Islam. In many places, Muslims combined a firm commitment to Islamic law with devotional aspects of the Sufi orders to nurture a religious life of personal piety and public charity. In India, Shah Wali Allah of Delhi (d. 1762), called for renewed study of the Qur'an and hadith in a more historic and systematic fashion. A prominent religious thinker, teacher, and prolific writer, Shah Wali Allah called for reduced taxes and economic justice on behalf of peasants, artisans, and merchants. Further, he hoped to unify and revitalize the legal system by reconciling the various recognized law schools, which in turn, would serve as the basis for social and moral reform. Shiite religious scholars in former Safavid domains were also active in reform during the eighteenth century. A number of Shiᶜi ᶜulama' known for their learning and rational legal analysis (*ijtihad*) rose to prominence and acquired a large following and great influence among the populace. Their schools and shrines became centers for study and points of autonomous stability in the midst of political turmoil.

Movements of Islamic revival and reform were also potent forces on the peripheries of the empires. In central Arabia, a conservative Hanbali theologian, Muhammad ibn ᶜAbd al-Wahhab (1703–1791) believed that Muslims had strayed from their true faith. In the tradition of the Hanbali activist Ibn Taymiyah, Ibn ᶜAbd al-Wahhab denounced the veneration of the saints and Sufi masters, Shiᶜism, and any belief or practice that he believed compromised God's oneness (*tawhid*). Particularly abhorrent to him was the veneration of the saints, which Ibn ᶜAbd al-Wahhab regarded as idol worship compromising Islam's monotheism. His opinion was opposed to the inclusive nature of much of medieval Sunni Islam, which viewed the cult of the saints and some other traditional practices involving personal piety as acceptable innovations. Ibn ᶜAbd al-Wahhab, however, rejected religious innovation of any sort, even including celebration of the prophet Muhammad's birthday. Rather than rely upon what he regarded as untrustworthy sources, Ibn ᶜAbd al-Wahhab called for a return to a largely literal interpretation of the Qur'an. He too advocated the use of independent legal reasoning (*ijtihad*), albeit restricted by hadith, the custom of the pious ancestors (*salaf*), and Hanbali law, in what came to be known as the Wahhabi movement.

A defining feature of the Wahhabi and similar reform movements of the eighteen and early nineteenth centuries was an overtly political and often militant agenda. Ibn ᶜAbd al-Wahhab and his supporters spread his teachings throughout central Arabia, winning over several local tribal chiefs, including Muhammad ibn Saᶜud (d. 1765), who, with Ibn ᶜAbd al-Wahhab, created a state based on the purification of Islam. Their vision was carried on by their descendants who razed shrines and cemeteries to prevent saint veneration, and suppressed religious innovation, on occasion massacring other Muslims who they regarded as infidel pagans. Many Muslims condemned the Wahhabis as extremists, yet the new Saudi state was able to unite a number of tribes and bring security to the holy land of Mecca and Medina. This, together with Ibn ᶜAbd al-Wahhab's call for radical reform, impressed some pilgrims to Mecca, who returned to their lands committed to militant reform and jihad, if necessary.[1]

Among these reformers was Sayyid Ahmad Barelwi (1786–1831). Sayyid Ahmad was from a scholarly Indian family; he had studied with Shah ᶜAbd al-Qadir, a son of Shah Wali Allah of Delhi. Like Ibn ᶜAbd al-Wahhab, Sayyid Ahmad opposed saint veneration, much Sufi practice, and Shiᶜism. Faced with the decline of the Mughal Empire, Sayyid Ahmad hoped to establish an Islamic state that would oppose religious innovation, which, in Northern India, included Sikhism. The Sikh religion arose from the creative and synthetic religious currents in Mughal India, including devotional elements of both Hinduism and mystical Islam. Guru Nanak (c. 1470) is regarded as the founder of this movement, which preached a doctrine of loving devotion to the one true God, while rejecting asceticism, caste, and idolatry. Over time, his teachings solidified into a distinctive religious tradition of teacher (*guru*) and disciple (*sikh*), known as Sikhism. The hymns and writings of venerated gurus were collected in the *Adi Granth*, the Sikh's sacred scripture. Sikhism was initially pacifist; however, later, largely political disputes with the Mughals resulted in a series of skirmishes and uneasy relations between the Sikhs and Muslims. This persisted into the nineteenth century, when Sayyid Ahmad Barelwi preached jihad against the Sikhs. Unlike Ibn ᶜAbd al-Wahhab, however, Sayyid Ahmad was not successful in establishing a reformed Muslim state, as he died in battle against a Sikh army.

There were other similar movements of Islamic revival, expansion, and state-building undertaken throughout the nineteenth century, from Indonesia to West Africa, Chechnya to Somalia. Common to most of these movements was a desire to free Islam from local non-Muslim religious practices and the veneration of the saints and to establish a Muslim community based on Islamic law. However, in contrast to the Wahhabi, many of these movements drew inspiration from more recent Sufi orders (*tariqah*), including the Naqshbandiyah, the Tijaniyah, and the Ahmadiyah-Idrisiyah, which preached individual piety, social activism, and moral reform. Further, these movements frequently called for jihad, whether against non-Muslims or other Muslims, as a means to establish and spread what they viewed as their authentic Islamic community.

This was the case of the jihad of Usman dan Fodio (1755–1817). Usman was from a scholarly family of the Fulani tribe in what is present-day Nigeria. His religious education included the study of Maliki law and mysticism in a reformist Sufi order. Islam was relatively new to this region of Africa, and Usman aimed to establish Muslim religious practice there more firmly based on Maliki law and combined with a devotional spirit infused by mystical experience and personal piety. His popular preaching and poetry led many peasants and slaves to convert to Islam. These new converts then claimed exemption from onerous taxes imposed by Hausa Muslim rulers on non-Muslims. As a result, the Hausa sultans opposed Usman. He and his followers then formed armed communities for their own protection. The Hausa Sultans were angered by Usman, and they attacked him and his followers. Usman then declared jihad against them and other Muslim rulers who would not accept his reforms. After a series of victories, Usman, together with his brother and a son, established what would come to be known as the Sokoto caliphate in 1806, the largest independent state in Africa at the time, and the basis for the modern state of Nigeria. Nearly a hundred years later, in 1904, the British would occupy their capital of Sokoto.

Muslim Responses to Threats from a New Europe

The presence of the British in West Africa at the beginning of the twentieth century was indicative of changing political fortunes. While the great Muslim empires slowly contracted in the eighteenth and nineteenth centuries, European nations grew in wealth and power. The age of exploration begun in the fifteenth century provided European nations with colonies in the New World whose natural and human resources fed imperial ambitions. Further, the industrial revolution led to technological advances, which quickly gave European powers a further edge in the quest for global hegemony. Searching for resources, markets, strategic locations, and glory, European nations began to colonize the ancient world, as well. By the end of the nineteenth century, the Netherlands ruled much of Indonesia, while England controlled Burma, India, southern Arabia, Palestine, Egypt, and various parts of Africa. France occupied Indo-China, Lebanon, Algeria, and most of northwest Africa. Italy ruled Somalia and would soon take Libya, and Russia continued to expand east, absorbing Muslim populations in Chechnya, Turkmenistan, and Uzbekistan.

Muslims met this new threat in a variety of ways. The remnants of the Mughal Empire revolted against the British in 1857 and were crushed. Other groups of Muslims declared jihads. Muslim revivalists fought the Dutch in the Padri War of 1821–1838, ᶜAbd al-Qadir (1808–1883) led Muslims against the French in North Africa, and Imam Shamil (1798–1871) rallied Muslims in Chechnya and Dagestan against the Russians. Yet in the end, resistance seemed futile as, one by one, Muslim territories fell to the European powers with their superior military strength and technology. One exception occurred in the Sudan in which a Sufi shaykh, Muhammad Ahmad ibn ᶜAbd Allah (1844–1885) declared himself to be the long-awaited *mahdi*, the divinely guided one who would initiate an era of truth and justice for Muslims. He was able to unite various Arab tribes of the region into a large army and to declare jihad against the oppressive Egyptian rule. Though Muhammad Ahmad ibn ᶜAbd Allah died in 1885, his successors defeated an Anglo-Egyptian army in 1889. However, a new railroad system organized by the British in Egypt provided excellent logistical support to the better armed Anglo-Egyptian army, which defeated the remnants of Ibn ᶜAdb Allah's army and took control of much of the Sudan in 1898. Subsequently, the British would be involved in governing the Sudan, but descendants of the Mahdi are still active in Sudanese politics today.

Several other messianic movements arose at this time, though they were not militant. In India's Punjab region, Mirza Ghulam Ahmad (1839–1908) claimed to have been sent by God to renew the faith of Islam, and he declared himself to be an avatar, or incarnation of the Hindu deity Krishna, as well as the messiah and the mahdi. He viewed the colonialism by the Christian West and its domination of Muslim lands as signs of the end of time. However, he did not preach a jihad, rather he emphasized the need to return to the error-free Qur'an in order to revitalize Islam and free it from foreign rule, violence, and false traditions. Ahmad's followers broke into two groups shortly after his death in 1908. Some claimed that Ghulam Ahmad was a new prophet and founder of a new religion, the Ahmadiyah, while others maintained that Ghulam Ahmad was not sent to supersede Muhammad's revelation, but only to reform Islam, much in the same way that Jesus was sent to revive Moses' original message. Ghulam Ahmad continues to have thousands of followers today, especially in Africa and Asia, but most Muslims have rejected his religious claims and teachings as inauthentic. As a result, Ahmadis have sometimes faced persecution by Muslims, and a 1974 law in Pakistan declared both groups of his followers to be non-Muslims.

While Ghulam Ahmad spread his message in India, another prophet came to light in Iran. The unstable political and social environment there had led many Shiꞌi Muslims to look for the return of the twelfth Hidden Imam, who would inaugurate a glorious age of peace and prosperity. Some claimed that the Hidden Imam spoke through a chosen follower known as the *Bab*, or "door," who would prepare the way for him. A direct descendant of the prophet Muhammad, Mirza ꞌAli Muhammad (1819–1850) announced in 1844 that he was this spokesperson, and he soon drew a large following for his militant messianic movement. Preaching a message of religious and social reform, the Bab and his followers seceded from Islam in 1848, and this led to uprisings against the government. To put an end to the crisis, the Qajar ruler Nasir al-Din Shah (1848–1896) captured and executed Mirza ꞌAli Muhammad and killed or exiled many of the Bab's disciples. Among the exiles was Mirza Husayn ꞌAli (1817–1892), who took the title *Baha' Allah* (Splendor of God). In 1863, he declared himself to be the one foretold by the Bab, a new prophet with a new universal religion for humanity, which today is known as the Baha'i faith. Baha' Allah asserted that God sends a new prophet with a divine dispensation appropriate to the times, and that God had sent him to declare the unity of humanity, which should strive to create a nonviolent world of peace and happiness with equal rights for all. Though the Baha'i faith is a worldwide religion today, most Muslims have denied Baha' Allah's claims, and many Baha'is in Iran were persecuted as apostates in Iran after the 1978 revolution.

Unlike the messianic movements of the nineteenth century, a number of individual Muslim thinkers made efforts to forge modern interpretations of Islam. These "Islamic modernists" stressed that the Qur'an, sunnah, and the original pristine religion of Islam were fully compatible with reason and rationality, modern society and its institutions. An early and influential figure in this movement was the Indian scholar Sayyid Ahmad Khan (d. 1898), who actively promoted modern education, founding what would later be the Aligarh Muslim University. His Egyptian contemporary, Muhammad ꞌAbduh (d. 1905) also believed that educational reform could free Muslims from blindly following tradition. A legal scholar and theologian, ᶜAbduh taught that reason and scientific analysis had been given to humanity by God as a means to understand revelation. The use of independent human reasoning *(ijtihad)*, then, was requisite for religious and social reform. ᶜAbduh also shared with Sayyid Ahmad Khan the concern for Muslim political independence from a largely Christian Europe, and he was an advocate of the Pan-Islamic movement actively promoted by his teacher Jamal al-Din al-Afghani (d. 1897). Al-Afghani was born and educated in Iran and traveled widely throughout the Islamic world, calling for Muslim religious and social reform and, especially, political solidarity in the face of European imperialism and colonialism. Al-Afghani dreamed of a new Islamic empire that would unite Muslims under the rule of a new universal caliph, perhaps the Ottoman sultan. Al-Afghani's Pan-Islamism was thwarted, however, by British opposition to him and by another very popular and competing ideology, nationalism.

Islam and Nationalism

In an effort to stop the European expansion into Muslim lands, the Ottomans sought to westernize their army and administration, just as Muhammad ᶜAli (r. 1804–1848) in Egypt, and the Qajar dynasty (r. 1779–1925) in Iran had done. Muslim students were sent abroad to study the latest in medicine and military technology, but they returned with other knowledge as well. Students learned about patriotism and nationalism, which emphasized ideas of one's homeland, nationality, and native language as essential features of political organization. These ideas soon took root among the Western-educated elite who desired to be independent of foreign rule. Nationalist movements arose in India, Iran, Egypt, and other Arab lands. Turkish nationalism also became popular after World War I, with the demise of the Ottoman Empire and the Pan-Islamic movement, and Turkey became an independent, secular republic in the early 1920s. Nevertheless, England, France, Russia, and other European nations resisted these nationalist movements as they sought to hold onto their colonies either directly or through unofficial spheres of influence. However, in the aftermath of World War II, the exhausted European powers granted independence to most of their former Muslim countries. Still, some colonial aspirations lingered, and Algeria was forced to fight a bloody war of independence against the French from

1954–1962, which left over one million Algerians dead and another two million homeless.

Many Muslim clerics supported twentieth-century independence movements in India, Egypt, and elsewhere, in order to free Muslims from European imperialism and colonialism, but they have been more wary of nationalism. Today, the Muslim community is divided into nearly fifty different countries based on numerous geographic, ethnic, and linguistic differences. As a result, some Muslim thinkers have regarded nationalism as a divisive foreign ideology undermining Islamic unity and promoting secularism. The Indian Muslim Abu al-ʿAla Maududi (d. 1979) went so far as to denounce nationalism as a form of idolatry, of worshiping the nation not God, and secularism as godlessness. He founded the revivalist party Jamaat-i Islami ("Islamic Society") in 1941 with the aim of placing Islam at the center of all aspects of life and society, and especially to unite the Muslim minority of India amidst the Hindu majority. Because Maududi rejected nationalism, he opposed the concept of Pakistan, a separate state for India's Muslims. But after Pakistan was created in 1947, he worked to ensure that it would be an Islamic state, not a secular one.

By contrast, many westernized civilian and military leaders within Muslim countries have embraced nation building and development as the mission of the state, while recognizing that Islam should play some role. The relationship between Islam and the state varies from country to country but usually falls into one of three general types. The secular state is one that declares the clear separation between religious institutions and government, especially in matters of politics, law, and education. The only Muslim majority countries avowedly secular have been Albania and Turkey. Opposite the secular state is the Islamic state, which professes to base its government and society on the Qur'an and Islamic law. Wahhabi Saudi Arabia, the Islamic Republic of Iran, and Pakistan are prominent examples of Islamic states. Falling somewhere between these two types is the vast majority of Muslim countries, often termed Muslim states. In these countries, Islam is recognized as an essential part of the national heritage and as the religion of state, yet their leaders often follow modern, more secular models of government.[2]

Though many of Muslim political leaders have sought economic development and social reform, particularly in law and education, they have generally been unwilling to share power through political reform, preferring, instead, to replace colonial self-interest with their own. This has done little to alleviate the poverty that is often exacerbated by overpopulation, an economic dependence on the West, and continued Western political interference. Therefore, the quality of life and society continues to deteriorate throughout most countries with Muslim majority populations. For example, the African nation of Mali has a population of about 12,000,000 people, nearly 50 percent of who are under the age of fifteen. The average life expectancy is around forty-seven, with a per capita income of $820; literacy stands at 31 percent. The literacy of Pakistan is slightly better at 38 percent out of a population of over 147,000,000. Pakistan's per capita income is $2,000, and life expectancy is sixty-one years of age; currently, 40 percent of Pakistanis are under the age of fifteen. These numbers improve somewhat for Muslims in other countries such as Egypt, Saudi Arabia, and Indonesia, with literacy rates of 51 percent, 63 percent, 84 percent, respectively, but a very large and growing number of Muslims are poor, illiterate, and face a short and dismal future.[3]

"Islam Is the Solution"

The failure of most governments over the last fifty years in Muslim-majority nations to ameliorate this dire situation has led some Muslims to search for a solution within Islam. One such movement arose within a Muslim minority among poor and oppressed African Americans. During the twentieth century, a number of African Americans converted to Islam in search of a meaningful identity within a racist American society. For some, this was a return to their religious roots since many slaves had originally been Muslims. Islam, then, became an authentic religious alternative to Christianity, which they regarded as the slave masters' faith. Islam spread steadily among African Americans in the 1930s and 1940s along with ideas of black nationalism and separatism, as some African Americans sought to live free of white control in their own state or nation, or by returning to Africa, as was the case with the creation of Liberia.

Elijah Muhammad's Nation of Islam was prominent among American Muslim movements. Born into a poor southern family, Elijah Poole was attracted to the teachings of a Muslim immigrant, W. D. Fard, who claimed that all African Americans were originally Muslims. Fard established a temple in Detroit and preached among African Americans, calling them back to the "Lost-Found Nation of Islam in the Wilderness of North America." His movement was later called the Nation of Islam.

Poole converted to Islam and changed his last name to Muhammad. When Fard disappeared in 1934, Elijah Muhammad assumed leadership of the movement and moved its headquarters to Chicago. He declared that Fard was the mahdi and an incarnation of God and that he, Elijah Muhammad, was a new prophet. Together with his disciples, including Malcolm X (d. 1965) and Louis Farrakhan (b. 1933), Elijah Muhammad vociferously denounced whites for their racial oppression and genetic inferiority, and he urged all African Americans to unite in an independent black nation separate from white America. Sunni and Shiʿi Muslims rejected Elijah Muhammad's claims regarding his own prophecy and the divine nature of W. D. Fard, since Muhammad of seventh-century Arabia was the last prophet, while God, alone, is divine. However, Malcolm X responded:

> You must remember: The condition of America's twenty million ex-slaves is uniquely pitiful. But just as the old religious leaders in the days of Moses and Jesus refused to accept Moses and Jesus as religious reformers, many of the religious leaders in the old Muslim world today may also refute the teachings of Mr. Elijah Muhammad, neither realizing the unique condition of these twenty million ex-slaves nor understanding that Mr. Elijah Muhammad's teachings are divinely prescribed to rectify the miserable condition of the oppressed people here. . . .
>
> The Christian world has failed to give the black man justice. The [American] Christian government has failed to give her twenty million ex-slaves [just compensation] for three hundred years of free slave labor. Even despite this, we have been better Christians than those who taught us Christianity. We have been America's most faithful servants during peace time, and her bravest soldiers during war time. But still, white Christians have been unwilling to recognize us and to accept us as fellow human beings. Today we can see that the Christian religion of the Caucasian race has failed us. Thus the black masses are turning away from the Church and toward the religion of Islam. . . . Therefore, Mr. Muhammad has demanded that you and your government let us separate ourselves from you right here, into a separate territory that we can call our own and on which we can do something for ourselves and our own kind.[4]

The Nation of Islam became a powerful voice for disenfranchised African Americans in the 1960s and continues today under the leadership of Louis Farrakhan. The Nation's call for Muslim unity and independence, equality and social justice, resonates with a larger Muslim critique of Western colonialism and contemporary society, both in the

West and in Muslim nations as well. Often termed Islamist, many Muslim activists today belong to a range of Islamic political parties and organizations that are highly critical of current governments, and call for political and social reform and the implementation of Islamic law. Some Islamist movements have had substantial political influence, such as Maududi's Jamaat-i Islami in Pakistan, or the Shi'i-led 1978 revolution in Iran. The Iranian revolution overthrew the tyrannical Muhammad Reza Shah (d. 1980), who was supported by the United States. In place of his monarchy, an Islamic republic arose led by the senior cleric Ayatollah Khomeini (d. 1989). Other influential Islamist groups include the Muslim Brotherhood *(al-Ikhwan al-Muslimun)* of Egypt founded in 1928 by Hasan al-Banna' (d. 1949). He opposed Arab nationalism and secularism and called for a united Muslim community based on social justice and Islamic law. Further, he asserted that Muslims had the obligation, collectively and individually, to undertake jihad against those who stood in their way, and the Brotherhood took up arms against British colonialism and Zionism in the 1940s and 1950s.

One of the Brotherhood's most articulate and influential thinkers was Sayyid Qutb (d. 1966). He sanctioned the use of violence not only against non-Muslims, but also against Muslims who failed to promote an Islamic revolution to overthrow godless nations and replace them with an authentic Muslim society. In fact, Qutb and the militant wing of the Brotherhood became the targets of Egyptian authorities after members of the Brotherhood were accused of attempting to assassinate the Egyptian president Gamal Abdel Nasser (d. 1971). Since then many members of the Brotherhood have disavowed militancy and have taken part in the Egyptian parliamentary process, while the Brotherhood continues to serve as a political party and a fraternal society to help Muslims in need.

Other nonmilitant Islamist parties have risen to power in several Muslim countries, including Turkey and Indonesia. Still, many governments in Muslim-majority nations have eliminated any type of political opposition in the name of national unity and development, and, ironically, they have banned popular Islamic political parties as a threat to democracy. While it is true that some Islamists are suspicious of democracy and Western institutions, Islamist parties may well support forms of representative government and notions of human progress. The Muslim activist Rashid al-Ghannoushi (b. 1941), for instance, believes that there can be an Islamic democracy with a moral imperative based on the Shari'ah. In 1981, he was one of the founders of Tunisia's Renaissance

Party (*al-Nahdah*), which was barred from local elections in 1989 by Tunisian president Ben ᶜAli who wanted no opposition to his rule. Ghannoushi is in exile in Europe where he continues to advocate representative government based on Islam. But there are great obstacles to a Muslim democracy including despotic rulers, reactionary Muslims, and ironically, Western governments that claim to support democracy.

> Regrettably, [the current political situation] is also accentuated by the ignorance and reactionary actions of Muslims who express antagonism towards the accomplishments of humanity in areas such as civil liberties, human rights, and so on. The Islamic image has also suffered considerably at the hands of despots who, seeking to legitimate the injustices perpetuated under their authoritarian rule, invoke religion to whitewash their crimes.
>
> Nevertheless, the West remains guilty of hypocrisy at the very least. . . . The justification proffered [by the West for supporting these despots] is the threat of extremism—a tide emphatically rejected by the mainstream of political Islam. Thus, what becomes evident to us is that the West is not motivated by the desire for democracy, modernism, human rights, international legitimacy, or even the spread of Christianity. The overwhelming evidence points towards the preservation of interests, which necessitate the domination of the world by controlling its resources and hampering its growth. Islam and its people, territory, culture, and civilization have traditionally been deemed obstacles to the colonial tendencies of the West— erstwhile physical masters and currently ideological expansionists, aided by force when necessary.[5]

Ghannoushi has pointed to the Bosnian crisis in the early 1990s as an example of the West's reluctance to act on behalf of Muslims. It took several years and the slaughter of thousands of Bosnian Muslims by the Serb army before the United States and the nations of Western Europe acted to stop the genocide and civil war in what had once been Yugoslavia. Many others single out the unresolved dispute between Pakistan and India over Kashmir and the ongoing Israeli-Palestinian conflict as blatant examples of Western hypocrisy. Indeed, the vast majority of Muslims and Arabs viewed the creation of the State of Israel in 1948 as a disastrous humiliation by the West, which ignored Arab and Muslim claims and aspirations in the region. As a result, Palestinians have waged a war of independence for their own state. The subsequent Arab-Israeli wars in 1967 and 1973, Israel's occupation of Jerusalem, and the continued expansion of Jewish settlers into the West Bank and Gaza are increasingly seen by many Muslims as further aggression not only against Arabs but also against Islam. In fact, U.S. support for Israel has been likened to a new crusade to push Muslims from their homeland. Muslims point to the second Gulf War beginning in 2003 and the U.S. invasion and occupation of Iraq as further proof of America's crusader mentality.

As a result, Qutb's militant theology has been taken up by other Islamist movements. These include the Palestinian Islamist organization Hamas ("zeal"). Hamas rejected the political and nationalist program of the Palestinian Liberation Organization, and instead declared a jihad against Israel in 1987, calling for suicide bombings to protect Muslim holy land. Other groups influenced by Qutb's ideology include Egypt's Islamic Jihad, which assassinated President Sadat in 1980. Islamic Jihad's spiritual leader ʿUmar ʿAbd al-Rahman (b. 1938) is currently in a U.S. prison for his alleged part in the 1993 bombing of the World Trade Center. Similarly, Qutb's influence is evident in the global Muslim militant organization al-Qaeda (Arabic: *al-qaʿidah*, "The Base").

The founder of al-Qaeda, Osama bin Laden (b. 1957) encountered Qutb's ideas as a young man growing up in a wealthy and religiously conservative family in Saudi Arabia. After the Soviet Union invaded Afghanistan in 1979, Bin Laden used his considerable financial resources to support the *mujahidin*, or Muslim "holy warriors" fighting the Soviets. In time, he established his own organization, al-Qaeda, to recruit and train foreign fighters for the Afghan resistance. This resistance movement was supported by a number of governments, including those of Saudi Arabia, Pakistan, and the United States. Yet after the Afghan's victory and Soviet withdrawal in 1989, these countries did little to rebuild war-ravaged Afghanistan. Several years of ethnic and sectarian violence ensued, until the Wahhabi-inspired Taliban movement arose and took control, enforcing a puritanical religious code on individuals and society. Music and televisions were banned as evil influences, men were told to grow their beards long and to attend mosque regularly, while women were required to wear a veil and stay at home whenever possible.

Meanwhile, Bin Laden returned a hero to Saudi Arabia, where he sought to organize Arab fighters against Iraq after it invaded Kuwait in 1990. Much to his horror, the Saudi government ignored his efforts and, instead, allowed U.S. and other non-Muslim troops on Saudi soil to fight Iraq. Bin Laden denounced this as an egregious breech of Islamic law. As a result, the Saudi government began to view him with suspicion. Bin Laden left Saudi Arabia and continued to finance and oversee his al-Qaeda organization, which was dedicated to driving all foreign troops from Saudi Arabia and other Muslim countries and to overthrowing the Saudi government. In 1996, he declared a jihad against the United States, its allies, and their citizens for the humiliation and atrocities that they had committed and continue to inflict upon Muslims, especially the Palestinians, who are frequent victims of Israeli aggression. The result has been a series of attacks against Western, largely American, targets, including New York's World Trade Center on September 11, 2001.

But why would anyone support such violence and the sacrifice of life to kill others? Some in the West claim that Islam is inherently violent, yet suicide attacks are a recent phenomena of the last twenty years. There are deeper causes than religion at work in the nations of the Middle East and in poor non-Muslim nations, including Sri Lanka and Peru, where communist movements have also resorted to suicide attacks as part of their revolutionary campaigns. What is often ignored by many in the West is that at least two-thirds of the world's population faces severely limited political freedoms, crushing poverty, and the absence of significant opportunities for improvement on a daily basis. In such an environment, many people may fear annihilation. When people believe that they have nothing to live for, they have nothing to lose, and it takes very little to push them to desperate actions. Militant Islamist groups, including Hamas, al-Qaeda, and the Taliban, have drawn on this despair and sense of humiliation shared by many Muslims to recruit new members. These extremist groups teach that the sacrifice of life and property will lead to a triumphal Islam that will defeat the satanic Zionist-Christian West. But, despite their rhetoric, the real enemies of the Islamists are not the Christians, Jews, and infidels of old, but secular democracy. Religious fundamentalists of all sorts, Muslim, Hindu, Christian, or Jewish, struggle with the concepts of individual equality and autonomy, government by the people for the people, and the freedom of religion. All of these propositions imply the possibility of experimentation and change and thus pose a direct challenge to fundamentalists who claim to hold absolute religious truth. Thus, the doubts that freedom brings must be driven out by the eradication of freedom itself through the forceful imposition of God's commandments. For Islamist militants, then, jihad is no longer a defensive action, as many Muslims have believed, but an ever-expanding aggressive mission to destroy the enemy and to rule by Muslim law. In the view of these militants, those people who died on September 11, 2001, are necessary casualties in their holy war of good against evil.

Many Muslims have strongly condemned the atrocities of September 11 and other acts of religious violence. Nevertheless, as world leaders have called for unity and justice in their "war on terrorism," many Muslims may rightfully ask where was America and the West when thousands of innocent Arabs and Muslims have faced terrorism over the years whether in Lebanon, Israel, Palestine, Bosnia, Kashmir, or elsewhere. How can the United States and some European countries call for democracy throughout the world, yet still continue to support despotic regimes that deny rights to their citizens? Now add to this, wars in Afghanistan and Iraq, with thousands of casualties, many of whom are women and children. President George W. Bush claimed that the United States went to Iraq to liberate its citizens from tyranny. Yet, when Iraqis and Muslims in other countries saw the graphic pictures or heard reports of U.S. troops abusing Iraqi prisoners, they had reason to think otherwise. It is no wonder many people hate America and the West. This is the hate that neglect produced.[6]

The events of September 11, 2001, and its aftermath have brought into dramatic perspective the need for change on the part of both Muslims and non-Muslims. Pervez Hoodbhoy, a dedicated Muslim peace activist, reflects on this urgent need in the following essay written shortly after September 11, 2001. Dr. Hoodbhoy is a professor of nuclear and high-energy physics at Quaid-e-Azam University in Islamabad, Pakistan, and author of *Islam and Science*.[7]

Muslims and the West After September 11[8]

Pervez Hoodbhoy

America has exacted blood revenge for the twin towers. A million Afghans have fled U.S. bombs into the cold wastelands and face starvation. B-52s have blown the Taliban to bits and changed Mullah Omar's roar of defiance into a pitiful squeak for surrender. Usama bin Laden is on the run (he may be dead by the time this article reaches the reader). But even as the champagne pops in the White House, America remains fearful—for good reason.

Subsequent to September 11 we have all begun to live in a different, more dangerous world. Now is the time to ask why. Like clinical pathologists, we need to scientifically examine the sickness of human behavior that impelled terrorists to fly airliners filled with passengers into skyscrapers. We also need to understand why millions celebrated as others died. In the absence of such an understanding there remains only the medieval therapy of exorcism: for the strong to literally beat the devil out of the weak. Indeed, the Grand Exorcist, disdainful of international law and the growing nervousness of even its close allies, prepares a new hit list of other Muslim countries in need of therapy: Iraq, Somalia, and Libya. We shall kill at will is the message.

This will not work. Terrorism does not have a military solution. Soon—I fear perhaps very soon—there will be still stronger, more dramatic proof. In the modern age, technological possibilities to wreak enormous destruction are limitless. Anger, when intense enough, makes small stateless groups and even individuals extremely dangerous.

Anger is ubiquitous in the Islamic world today. Allow me to share a small personal experience. On September 12, 2001, I had a seminar scheduled at the department of physics in my university in Islamabad, part of a weekly seminar for physics students on topics outside of physics. Though traumatized by events, I could not cancel the seminar because sixty people had already arrived, so I said, "We will have our seminar today on a new subject: on yesterday's terrorist attacks." The response was negative. Some students mindlessly rejoiced in the attacks. One said, "You can't call this terrorism." Another said, "Are you only worried because it is Americans who have died?" It took two hours of sustained, impassioned, argumentation for me to convince my students that the brutal killing of ordinary people who had nothing to do with the policies of the United States was an atrocity. I suppose that millions of Muslim students the world over felt as mine did, but heard no counter arguments.

If the world is to be spared what future historians may call the "Century of Terror," we must chart a perilous course between the Scylla of American imperial arrogance and the Charybdis of Islamic religious fanaticism. Through these waters we must steer by a distant star towards a careful, reasoned, democratic, humanistic, and secular future. Else, shipwreck is certain.

Injured Innocence

"Why do they hate us?" asked George W. Bush. This rhetorical question betrays the pathetic ignorance of most Americans about the world around them. Moreover, its claim to injured innocence cannot withstand even the most cursory examination of U.S. history. For almost forty years, this "naiveté and self-righteousness" has been challenged most determinedly by Noam Chomsky. As early as 1967, he pointed that the idea that "our" motives are pure and "our" actions benign is "nothing new in American intellectual history—or, for that matter, in the general history of imperialist apologia."

Muslim leaders have mirrored America's claim and have asked the same question of the West. They have had little to say about September 11 that makes sense to people outside their communities. Although they speak endlessly on rules of personal hygiene and halal or haram, they cannot even tell us whether or not the suicide bombers violated Islamic laws. According to Dr. Taha Jabir Alalwani, chair of the Virginia-based (and largely Saudi-funded) Fiqh Council, "This kind of question needs a lot of research and we don't have that in our budget."

Fearful of backlash, most leaders of Muslim communities in the United States, Canada, and Europe have responded in predictable ways to the Twin Towers atrocity. They have proclaimed first that Islam is a religion of peace and second that Islam was hijacked by fanatics on the September 11. They are wrong on both counts.

First, Islam—like Christianity, Judaism, Hinduism, or any other religion—is not about peace. Nor is it about war. Every religion is about absolute belief in its own superiority and its divine right to impose itself upon others. In medieval times, both the Crusades and the jihads were soaked in blood. Today, Christian fundamentalists attack abortion clinics in the United States and kill doctors; Muslim fundamentalists wage their sectarian wars against each other; Jewish settlers holding the Old Testament in one hand and Uzis in the other burn olive orchards and drive Palestinians off their ancestral land; Hindus in India demolish ancient mosques and burn down churches; Sri Lankan Buddhists slaughter Tamil separatists.

The second assertion is even further off the mark: even if Islam had in some metaphorical sense been hijacked, that event did not occur on September 11, 2001. It happened around the thirteenth century. Indeed, Islam has yet to recover from the trauma of those times.

A Dismal Present

Where do *Muslims* stand today? Note that I do not ask about *Islam*; Islam is an abstraction. Moulana Abdus Sattar Edhi and Mullah Omar are both followers of Islam, but the former is overdue for a Nobel Peace Prize while the other is a medieval, ignorant, cruel fiend.

Edward Said, among others, has insistently pointed out that Islam carries very different meanings to different people. It is as heterogeneous as those who believe and practice it. There is no "true Islam." Therefore it only makes sense to speak of people who *claim* that faith.

Today Muslims number one billion, spread over forty-eight Muslim countries. None of these nations has yet evolved a stable democratic political system. In fact, all Muslim countries are dominated by self-serving corrupt elites who cynically advance their personal interests and steal resources from their people. No Muslim country has a viable educational system or a university of international stature.

Reason too has been waylaid. To take some examples from my own experience: You will seldom encounter a Muslim name as you flip through scientific journals, and, if you do, chances are that this person lives in the West. There are a few exceptions: Abdus Salam, together with Steven Weinberg and Sheldon Glashow, won the Nobel Prize for Physics in 1979 for the unification of the weak and electromagnetic forces. I got to know Salam reasonably well—we even wrote a book preface together. He was a remarkable man, terribly in love with his country and his religion. And yet he died deeply unhappy, scorned by his country and excommunicated from Islam by an act of the Pakistani parliament in 1974. Today the Ahmadi sect, to which Salam belonged, is considered heretical and harshly persecuted. (My next-door neighbor, also an Ahmadi, was shot in the neck and heart and died in my car as I drove him to the hospital. His only fault was to have been born in the wrong sect.)

Though genuine scientific achievement is rare in the contemporary Muslim world, pseudoscience is in generous supply. A former chairman of my department has calculated the speed of heaven: it is receding from the earth at one centimeter per second less than the speed of light. His ingenious method relies upon a verse in the Qur'an that says that worship on the night on which the Qur'an was revealed is worth a 1,000 nights of ordinary worship. He states that this amounts to a time-dilation factor of 1,000, which he plugs into a formula belonging to Einstein's theory of special relativity.

A more public example: one of two Pakistani nuclear engineers recently arrested on suspicion of passing nuclear secrets to the Taliban had earlier proposed to solve Pakistan's energy problems by harnessing the power of genies. The Qur'an says that God created man from clay, and angels and genies from fire; so this highly placed engineer proposed to capture the genies and extract their energy. (The reader may wish to read the rather acrimonious public correspondence between Sultan Bashiruddin Mahmood and myself in 1988 on this subject, reproduced in my book *Islam and Science—Religious Orthodoxy and the Battle for Rationality*, published in 1991.)

A Brilliant Past That Vanished

Today's sorry situation contrasts starkly with the Islam of yesteryear. Between the ninth and the thirteenth centuries—the Golden Age of Islam—the only people doing decent science, philosophy, or medicine were Muslims. For five straight centuries they alone kept the light of learning ablaze. Muslims not only preserved ancient learning, they also made substantial innovations and extensions. The loss of this tradition has proved tragic for Muslim peoples.

Science flourished in the Golden Age of Islam because there was within Islam a strong rationalist tradition, carried on by a group of Muslim thinkers known as the Mutazilites. This tradition stressed human free will, strongly opposing the predestinarians who taught that everything was foreordained and that humans have no option but to surrender everything to Allah. While the Mutazilites held political power, knowledge grew.

But in the twelfth century Muslim orthodoxy reawakened, spearheaded by the cleric Imam al-Ghazali. Al-Ghazali championed revelation over reason, predestination over free will. He refuted the possibility of relating cause to effect, teaching that man cannot know or predict what will happen; God alone can. He damned mathematics as against Islam, an intoxicant of the mind that weakened faith.

Islam choked in the vice-like grip of orthodoxy. No longer, as during the reign of the dynamic caliph al-Mamum and the great Harun al-Rashid, would Muslim, Christian, and Jewish scholars gather and work together in the royal courts. It was the end of tolerance, intellect, and science in the Muslim world. The last great Muslim thinker, Abd-al Rahman Ibn Khaldun, belonged to the fourteenth century.

Islam Under Imperialism

Meanwhile, the rest of the world moved on. The Renaissance brought an explosion of scientific inquiry in the West. This owed much to Arab translations and other Muslim contributions, but that fact would matter little. Mercantile capitalism and technological progress drove Western countries rapidly to colonize the Muslim world from Indonesia to Morocco. Always brutal, at times genocidal, it made clear, at least to a part of the Muslim elites, that they were paying a heavy price for not possessing the analytical tools of modern science and the social and political values of modern culture—their colonizers' real source of power.

Despite widespread resistance from the orthodox, the logic of modernity found nineteenth-century Muslim adherents. Modernizers such as Muhammad Abduh and Rashid Rida of Egypt, Sayyed Ahmad Khan of India, and Jamaluddin Afghani (who belonged everywhere) wished to adapt Islam to the times, to interpret the Qur'an in ways consistent with modern science, and to discard the *Hadith* (the traditions, or ways of the Prophet) in favor of the Qur'an. Others seized on the modern idea of the nation-state. It is crucial to note that not a single twentieth-century Muslim nationalist leader was a fundamentalist. Turkey's Kemal Ataturk, Algeria's Ahmed Ben Bella, Indonesia's Sukarno, Pakistan's Muhammad Ali Jinnah, Egypt's Gamal Abdel Nasser, and Iran's Muhammad Mosaddeq all sought to organize their societies on the basis of secular values.

However, like other anti-colonial nationalist currents across the third world, Muslim and Arab nationalism included the desire to control and use national resources for domestic benefit. Conflict with Western greed was inevitable. Imperial interests in Britain and later the United States feared independent nationalism. Anyone willing to collaborate was preferred, even ultraconservative Islamic regimes like that of Saudi Arabia. In time, as Cold War pressures rose, nationalism became intolerable. In 1953, Mosaddeq of Iran was overthrown in a Central Intelligence Agency (CIA) coup and replaced by Reza Shah Pahlavi. Britain targeted Nasser. Indonesia's Sukarno was replaced by Suharto after a bloody coup that left a million dead.

Pressed from without, corrupt and incompetent from within, secular governments proved unable to defend national interests or to deliver social justice. As they failed they left a vacuum which Islamic religious movements grew to fill. After the fall of the Shah, Iran underwent a bloody revolution under Ayatollah Khomeini. General Muhammad Zia-ul-Haq ruled Pakistan for eleven hideous years [1977-88] and strove to Islamize both state and society. In

Sudan, an Islamic state arose under Ja'far al-Numayri [r. 1969–89]; amputation of hands and limbs became common. Decades ago the Palestinian Liberation Organization (PLO) was the most powerful Palestinian organization, and largely secular; after its defeat in 1982 in Beirut, it was largely eclipsed by Hamas, a fundamentalist Muslim movement.

The lack of scruple and the pursuit of power by the United States combined fatally with this tide in the Muslim world in 1979 when the Soviet Union invaded Afghanistan. With Pakistan's Zia-ul-Haq as America's foremost ally, the CIA openly recruited Islamic holy warriors from Egypt, Saudi Arabia, Sudan, and Algeria. Radical Islam went into overdrive as its superpower ally and mentor funneled support to the *mujahideen*, whom Ronald Reagan feted on the lawn of White House, lavishly praising them as "brave freedom fighters challenging the Evil Empire."

After the Soviet Union collapsed, the United States walked away from an Afghanistan in shambles, its own mission accomplished. The Taliban emerged; Usama bin Laden and his al-Qaeda made Afghanistan their base. Other groups of holy warriors learned from the Afghan example and took up arms in their own countries.

At least until September 11, U.S. policymakers were unrepentant. A few years ago Zbigniew Brzezinski, Carter's U.S. national security adviser, was asked by the Paris weekly *Nouvel Observateur* whether in retrospect, given that "Islamic fundamentalism represents a world menace today," U.S. policy might have been mistaken. Brzezinski retorted: "What is most important to the history of the world? The Taliban or the collapse of the Soviet empire? Some stirred-up Muslims or the liberation of Central Europe and the end of the Cold War?"

But Brzezinski's "stirred up Muslims" wanted to change the world; and in this they were destined to succeed. With this we conclude our history primer for the seven hundred years until September 11, 2001.

Facing the Future

What should thoughtful people infer from this whole narrative? I think the inferences are several—and different for different protagonists. For Muslims, it is time to stop wallowing in self-pity: Muslims are not helpless victims of conspiracies hatched by an all-powerful, malicious West. The fact is that the decline of Islamic greatness took place long before the age of mercantile imperialism. The causes were essentially internal. Therefore, Muslims must introspect and ask what went wrong.

Muslims must recognize that their societies are far larger, more diverse and complex than the small homogenous tribal culture that existed in Arabia 1,400 years ago. It is therefore time to renounce the idea that Islam can survive and prosper only in an Islamic state run according to Islamic *Sharia* law. Muslims need a secular and democratic state that respects religious freedom and human dignity, founded on the principle that power belongs to the people. This means confronting and rejecting the claim by orthodox Islamic scholars that in an Islamic state sovereignty does not belong to the people but, instead, to the vice-regents of Allah *(Khilafat-al-Allah)* or Islamic jurists *(Vilayat-e-Faqih)*.

Muslims must not look towards the likes of Bin Laden; such people have no real answer and can offer no real positive alternative. To glorify their terrorism is a hideous mistake—the unremitting slaughter of Shias, Christians, and Ahmadis in their places of worship in Pakistan, and of other minorities in other Muslim countries, is proof that all terrorism is not about the revolt of the dispossessed.

The United States, too, must confront bitter truths. It is a fact that the messages of George W. Bush and his ally Tony Blair fall flat, while those of Usama bin Laden, whether he lives or dies, resonate strongly across the Muslim world. Bin Laden's religious extremism turns off many Muslims, but they find his political message easy to relate to— stop the dispossession of the Palestinians, stop propping up corrupt and despotic regimes across the world just because they serve U.S. interests.

Americans will also have to accept that the United States is past the peak of its imperial power; the 1950s and '60s are gone for good. U.S. triumphalism and disdain for international law are creating enemies everywhere, not just among Muslims. Therefore, Americans must become less arrogant and more like other peoples of this world. While the United States will remain a superpower for some time to come, inevitably it will become less and less "super." There are compelling economic and military reasons for this. For example, China's economy is growing at 7 percent per year while the U.S. economy is in recession. India, too, is coming up very rapidly. In military terms, superiority in the air or in space is no longer enough to ensure security; in how many countries can U.S. citizens safely walk the streets today?

Our collective survival lies in recognizing that religion is not the solution; neither is nationalism. Both are divisive, embedding within us false notions of superiority and arrogant pride that are difficult to erase. We have but one choice: the path of secular humanism, based upon the principles of logic and reason. This alone offers the hope of providing everybody on this globe with the right to life, liberty, and the pursuit of happiness.

Discussion Questions

1. Name the Ottoman, Safavid, and Mughal empires. What were the geographic areas of their respective empires? What were their capitals? What were the high points and major features of each one? What major factors led to their decline?

2. What was the Wahhabi reform movement? Who started it, when, where, and why? What has been its effect on Muslim life, society, and politics?

3. What is colonialism and why is it important to the history of Islam? In what ways have Muslims reacted to Western colonialism? What are some of the colonial legacies facing Muslim peoples today?

4. Discuss some of the current examples of Muslim militancy. What economic, political, and/or social situations foster militancy? How does religious ideology color militancy, and how do militants interpret the concept of jihad? What do militants hope to achieve through violence?

PART FIVE

MODERNITY AND RELIGION IN THE WEST: NEGOTIATING CHANGE

CHAPTER 12

THE MODERNIZATION OF CHRISTIANITY

Bruce Chilton

Renaissance and Reformation

Introduction

The Renaissance and the Reformation were cultural movements that took their bearings from the past. The Renaissance looked to ancient classical culture, and the Reformation looked to the Scriptures, both in an effort to fashion their worlds afresh. Both of them succeeded so well that they made civilization in Europe into the dynamic, dominant power that emerged in the modern period. Yet neither movement achieved its aims of conservative reform. The greatest artists of the Renaissance quickly changed the classical ideals that inspired it, and the Reformation thrashed out issues and debates unknown to the world of the Bible. Together, these two efforts at conservative reform unleashed the most innovative forces the West has ever known, ultimately subjecting Europe to its worst self-inflicted violence until the twentieth century.

The Renaissance

With the end of the last crusade under Louis IX of France in 1270, the medieval dream of the conquering the "infidels" in the east effectively came to an end. Yet by that time, the crusader program had helped transform Europe itself. Trade, currency, and commerce with Islamic and

Asian lands had spurred the growth and influence of cities together with the financial institutions required to support them. Universities arose—first in Bologna in the eleventh century, and then in Paris during the twelfth century—challenging what had been the monopoly of learning in monasteries. Peasant life in the countryside also changed. Land was cleared, techniques of farming improved, and the population almost doubled between 1000 and 1300 as landed gentry turned more to hiring than to serfdom for their labor. Knights increasingly allied themselves with national monarchs so that states emerged to challenge the dominance of the papacy and the Holy Roman Empire.

In the midst of all this change, two factors stand out that largely occasioned the Renaissance. First, intellectual contact with the Muslim world, for example in Toledo and Salerno, brought to the West some texts of Aristotle it had not known during the Middle Ages. That opened up new dimensions in natural philosophy, ethics, and metaphysics. Coping with that learning occupied the universities, especially in Paris with the work of Peter Abelard (1079–1142) and Thomas Aquinas (1225–1274). Second, 1300 saw the height of Europe's population until the seventeenth century; plague, famine, and wars among the emerging nation-states had fearful consequences. Between 1347 and 1352, it has been estimated that the epidemic called "the Black Death" took between one-third to one-half of human life in Europe.[1]

"The Ancient Path" of New Learning

In the midst of turmoil, revolution, and war, the Renaissance was born. By 1370, Giovanni Boccaccio could already look back with pride on the achievements of revived literary accomplishment in Italy ("Letter to Jacob Pizzinghe"):

> Then after Dante, his fellow citizen of Florence, that illustrious man, Francesco Petrarca, my teacher, rejecting the principles of writers who, as has already been said, had hardly touched the threshold of poetry, began to follow the ancient path, with such fortitude of heart, such ardor of spirit, and such acuteness of talent that no hindrances could stop him, and no obstacles on the way could frighten him.[2]

The "ancient path"—the newly opened world of classical learning—was no mere repetition of ancient forms, because studying the classics released the creativity of the masters of the Renaissance.

The way of antiquity in Boccaccio's estimation changed Petrarch from a student to an unstoppable poet. This was also Petrarch's ideal (in his letter to Tommasco da Messina):

> The fact remains that where the mind has been cultivated, speech cannot be disregarded, just as, on the other hand, there can be no merit to speech unless a certain dignity is present in the mind. What good will it do if you immerse yourself wholly in the Ciceronian springs and know well the writings either of the Greeks or of the Romans? You will indeed be able to speak ornately, charmingly, sweetly and sublimely; you certainly will not be able to speak seriously, austerely, judiciously and, most importantly, uniformly. The reason for this is that unless our desires first order themselves (and you must know that no one can achieve this except a wise man) it is inevitable that such disorder will be reflected in our conduct and in our words. The well-ordered mind is the image of an undisturbed serenity and is always quiet and peaceful. It knows what it wants, and does not cease wanting what it desires.[3]

Petrach was a model of the method of the Renaissance, polishing his own Latin style and searching out ancient manuscripts in universities, papal archives, and royal archives. But his philosophical orientation was eclectic rather than methodical. In the passage just cited, he cites the Stoic Cicero as a model, yet he praises a life of holy passion in the manner of Saint Augustine, another of his heroes.

The Power of Patronage

Learning throughout the Renaissance celebrated the liberating properties of Greek and Latin that Petrarch represented, but that only encouraged the emergence of poetry and prose in the vernacular. Italian, likewise English, French, and other European languages, became the vehicles of artistic expression. Even as Europe's population shrank, the relative size and influence of cities grew, and vernacular poetry found an eager audience among the increasing numbers of displaced peasants and townspeople, as well as among wealthy patrons.

Patronage, support of the burgeoning arts of the period, became one of the great civic virtues of the age, and its practitioners included Pope Nicholas V, as described in 1460 by Bartolommeo Platina:

> Pope Nicholas built magnificently and splendidly, moreover, both in the city and on the Vatican. In Rome itself he reconstructed the papal palace adjoining Santa Maria Maggiore. He restored also the church of San

Stefano Rotondo on the Caelian hill; and from its very foundation he rebuilt the church of San Teodoro, which is situated on the plain between the Palatine and the Capitoline hills. The Pantheon, which is a very ancient temple, built by M. Agrippa and lying in the center of the city, was rebuilt with a leaden roof. . . . He also began the great vault for the apse of St. Peter's, popularly called a tribune, by which the church itself is made more splendid and capable of holding more people. He restored the Milvian bridge and erected a princely palace to house the baths of Viterbo.[4]

This great project of architectural revival and reconstruction, paving the way for Michelangelo to move to Rome in 1496, expresses the inclusive genius of the Renaissance. Here was a pope willing to build afresh as well as to restore, constructing a bathhouse and restoring a pantheon that had once housed the gods of Rome as well as a suitable edifice of Saint Peter.

The exuberance of this movement was not that of artists against clergy or academic learning against poets. People of learning generally were humanists, dedicated to the revival of classical learning and the extension of its goals. Such was the nature of humanism. Thomas Aquinas made Aristotle a saint of the church. In Thomas's teaching, intellectual reflection was not against revelation; rather, the disclosure of grace completed the findings of reason. In the Eucharist, for example, the "accidents," or physical composition, of bread and wine did not change, but their "substance"—their intellectual, immaterial reality—became the body and blood of Christ.[5] This was Thomas Aquinas's teaching of "transubstantiation," a philosophical doctrine emblematic of his capacity to link empirical observation in the classical tradition with the Platonist teachings of the church that conceived of "substance" in ideal terms.

Thomas's achievement in the thirteenth century encouraged the revival of the classical tradition alongside rigorous insistence on the Christian faith. More specifically, inventive investigations of nature during the Renaissance, together with an active recourse to philosophy, nurtured the beginnings of modern science. One of Petrarch's friends was Giovanni Dondi dall'Orologio (d. 1388), a professor of medicine, connoisseur of the classics and theology, and inventor of an astronomical clock, which showed the positions of the planets as then known on seven dials.

Given Orologio's accomplishment, his own estimate of the science of his time is telling ("Letter to Fra Guglielmo Centueri da Cremona," a Franscican friar):

For it is absurd to ask what sciences are now found out from scratch, they are so meager or non-existent. It is enough and plenty for moderns if they can just touch the surface of what those ancients treated in greatest depth. So that if by chance some modern should have the confidence in himself to try to invent something or presume to change what has been handed down before (as in our days some dialecticians have done, as you know), it is sufficiently clear how much their results are worth, and how much has endured. They have scarcely lasted past the age in which they were produced, and have perished along with their authors.[6]

This sense of dependency upon ancient attainments and of explicit inferiority to them may help explain why science made its way during the Renaissance with a conventional devotion to the idea of an immovable earth until Copernicus wrote his treatise *On the Revolutions of the Heavenly Spheres* (1543).

In the sphere of linguistic analysis, the savants of the Renaissance were less respectful. Lorenzo Valla (1407–1457), in the service of the king of Naples, gave his patron an indispensable weapon in the midst of disputes with the Papal States. The pope had used his supposed authority, under the Donation of Constantine, to recognize a monarch's legitimacy or not. But Valla proved on linguistic grounds that the Donation was a fraud, written in eighth-century Latin and not at all in the idiom of Constantine during the fourth century. Scholars were also courtiers and made common cause with royal patrons all over Europe. They were entrepreneurs as well as intellectuals.

Philosophy and Art

The revival of philosophy was exuberant and eclectic. The rediscovery of Aristotle by no means excluded an interest in other philosophers. Plato's works enjoyed a spectacular revival, and a fresh interest in the esoteric arts flourished. Marsilio Ficino was a principal exponent of this Renaissance enthusiasm and has drawn followers to this day:

> Man is really the vicar of God, since he inhabits and cultivates all elements and is present on earth without being absent from the ether. He uses not only the elements, but also all the animals which belong to the elements, the animals of the earth, of the water, and of the air, for food, convenience, and pleasure, and the higher, celestial beings for knowledge and the miracles of magic.[7]

Much as Thomas Aquinas made Aristotle compatible with a platonic view of ineffable substances, so Marsilio Ficino insisted on a Plato whose

435

views would embrace the physical elements of the earth. The revival of ancient tradition largely proceeded on the unspoken assumption that classical authors agreed with one another to a greater degree than would be claimed by scholars today.

Leonardo da Vinci

Ficino established a platonic academy in Florence, a city whose wealth and culture made it a hub of the Renaissance. In this city, the handsome but illegitimate son of a notary, Leonardo da Vinci, was apprenticed to a painter and sculptor named Andrea del Verrocchio. Leonardo remains to this day the most famous product of the Renaissance.[8] From the outset of his career, he was exposed to the practical necessities of artistic production, including the study of anatomy and of architecture.

Leonardo's sympathies, both philosophical and temperamental, were more with Aristotle than with Plato. He did not sympathize with Ficino's ethereal orientation, and he articulated a skepticism that sounds modern: "If we entertain doubts about the certainty of each thing that passes through the senses, how much more ought we to doubt things hostile to the senses, such as the essence of God and of the soul and similar things about which people are always arguing and fighting."[9] His doubts about his own senses could also make him a slow craftsman, and his delays sometimes resulted in his losing commissions. Perhaps even less to his credit, he was not in the platonic fashion of the city under Lorenzo de' Medici.

As V. P. Zubov points out, Ficino struck a very different attitude in dedicating his translation of Plato to Lorenzo de' Medici, called "the Magnificent":

> In the gardens of the Academy, beneath the laurels, poets will hear the singing Apollo, orators on the threshold will catch sight of Mercury declaiming poetry, jurists and rulers of governments on the portico and in the hall will hear Jupiter himself giving laws, defining rights, ruling states. Finally, philosophers within the building will recognize their Saturn, the contemplator of heavenly mysteries. And everywhere priests and clergy will find weapons with which to defend piety steadfastly against the profane.[10]

Leonardo complained about those who dismissed him as a man without learning, a mere painter, but he also knew that Lorenzo's power could not be thwarted. Leonardo vividly drew the hanging of Bernardo Bandini de Baronncelli, who conspired to kill Lorenzo and establish a republic in 1479.

In 1481, Leonardo made bold a strategic move to enhance his career. He wrote to Lodovico Sforza, the ruler of Milan, offering his services as an engineer and an artist—in that order. Lodovico had to deal with increasing military threats from Venice, the papal armies, and the French. In Leonardo's letter of twelve paragraphs, only one is devoted to his artistic capacity, and then the modesty of the statement is almost comic:

> In times of peace, I believe that I can give you as complete satisfaction as anyone else in architecture, in the construction of buildings both public and private, and in conducting water from one place to another. Also I can execute sculpture in marble, bronze, or clay, and also painting, in which my work will stand in comparison with that of anyone else, whoever he may be.[11]

This comes on the heels of a detailed description of how he could make bridges and tunnels for war, siege works, artillery, catapults, armored vehicles, and the like. Not a prince himself, Leonardo nevertheless knew how to get a prince's attention.

His letter of application proved successful, and Leonardo undertook a variety of projects in Milan, most of them never completed. But on the commission of Lodovico and the Dominicans, he painted *The Last Supper* for the refectory of the Church of Santa Maria della Grazie between 1495 and 1498. He invented a new technique of fresco, which enabled him to return to paint on a dry surface instead of having to paint while the plaster was wet. The material proved unstable, however, and decay was apparent within decades. But the combination of mathematical angles, psychological as well as physical observation, and the mastery of traditional forms, makes this an undoubted masterpiece of the Renaissance.[12]

Leonardo wrote in the "Treatise on Painting": "Painting is born of nature—or to speak more correctly, we will say it is the grandchild of nature; for all visible things are produced by nature, and these her children have given birth to painting. Hence we may justly call it the grandchild of nature and related to God." Painting was the science of the Renaissance, and Leonardo was its Einstein.

In recent years, attempts have been made to portray Leonardo as a purveyor of esoteric knowledge. In his *Last Supper*, for example, the beloved disciple John is said to be a woman—Mary Magdalene in particular.[13] But Leonardo's own studies for the piece show that his John, like his Philip and like his John the Baptist in other works, looks effeminate by modern standards. Such conventions are hardly remarkable, although they have been grist for the analysis of Leonardo as a homosexual.

Psychoanalysis has also been productive in treating *Mona Lisa*, which Leonardo painted after his return to Florence following the capture of Milan by Louis XII of France in 1499.[14] In his own mind, the work was never finished, and it was with him in the French city Amboise when he died in 1519. There can be no doubt of his deep affinity with his subject, but the mystery surrounding the piece is less striking than its complete mastery of light and composition, hallmarks of the Renaissance.

Leonardo's final years in France were spent in honor and comfort. He came to Amboise at the invitation of King François I, and Benvenuto Cellini reported the high esteem in which François held him:

> I feel that I must not neglect to repeat the exact words which I heard from the King's own lips about him, which he told me in the presence of the Cardinal of Ferrara, the Cardinal of Lorraine, and the King of Navarre. He said that he did not believe that there had ever been another man born into the world who had known as much as Leonardo, and this not only in matters concerning sculpture, painting, and architecture, but because he was a great philosopher.[15]

The veneration of Leonardo's genius began before his death, even among those who knew very well of his trouble finishing commissions.

Adulation of the geniuses of the Renaissance went hand in hand with admiration for Renaissance rulers. Francois I assured himself a reputation for his wise patronage in making claims about Leonardo's brilliance. The alliance between power and knowledge, both in alleged accordance with nature, emerged as a characteristic ideal of the period. The ideal was so influential, it could overwhelm the memory of setbacks. In 1509, for example, Francesco Guicciadrini described Florence in a way that papers over the tumult of the civil wars that had torn the city apart:

> The city was in a state of perfect peace, the citizens of the state united and bound together, and the government so powerful that no one dared to oppose it. Every day the populace delighted in spectacles, feasts, and novel diversions. The city was sustained both by its abundant supplies and its flourishing and well-established business enterprises; men of talent and ability were rewarded through the recognition of support given to all letters, all arts, all gifts.[16]

A natural state of peace could be extolled, even as wars and plague took their toll, because the Renaissance was as much about perception, and the glory of perceiving, as it was a time of undoubted progress. The *Mona Lisa* smiles perfectly against a landscape that Leonardo painted in a way that deliberately distorted any possible natural perspective. Perhaps the sign of his true genius was that he understood the times he lived in.

Oral histories describe Leonardo as acquainting himself more fully with Catholicism when he realized he was dying.[17] His pragmatism extended to the next world as well as to the physical senses. But just as belief in nature's coherence led to progress in science and unprecedented advances in the arts, the Renaissance was bound eventually to turn to issues of belief and religious practice with its optimistic reliance on human insight. That process had already begun with promising results during Leonardo's life.

Erasmus of Rotterdam

Intellectuals such as Ficino, the lettered men who looked down on the likes of Leonardo da Vinci, pursued the study of Christianity's foundations. One of them, the most prominent intellectual of the sixteenth century, long enjoyed the fame and prosperity that eluded Leonardo until the end of his life. But like his older contemporary from Italy, Desiderius Erasmus of Rotterdam was born illegitimate, probably in 1469.[18] His rise to a position of unrivaled influence in the world of letters and the church marks the high water mark of the Renaissance in reshaping the very conception of the Christian faith.

Eramus's life was influenced by the distinctive piety of the Low Countries (the Netherlands), where lay movements of asceticism flourished. Men and women joined to undertake disciplines of prayer, meditation, and good works, but without accepting monastic vows. The most prominent of these associations were the Sisters and Brothers of the Common Life, founded by Gerard Groote during the fourteenth century. These communities focused on a teaching of practical mysticism called the *devotio moderna*, expressed most influentially in *The Imitation of Christ*, compiled by Thomas à Kempis after Groote's death.[19] Women and men lived in separate communities, but each community included both laypeople and priests together. By Erasmus's time many houses of the movement were composed mostly of priests and accepted the Augustinian rule of monasticism. That proved to be crucial to Erasmus's development.

His father became a priest, probably after the birth of his two illegitimate sons, but when Erasmus's parents died, guardians enrolled him and his brother in a hostel for the poor run by Brothers of the Common Life. That decision virtually obliged him to join an Augustinian monastery at the age of sixteen. From the outset of his career as a monastic and a priest, an extraordinary facility in Latin was apparent, and it was put to good use by his house. He wrote a treatise called "On Contempt of the World," in which he wrote:

> I am ready to swear that there is no duty here which is not filled with happiness. There is nothing more lucrative than our poverty, nothing more free than our servitude, nothing more carefree than our labors, nothing more filled than our emptiness, nothing more broad than our narrowness, nothing more joyful than our sorrow.[20]

Later in his life, as he distanced himself from monasticism, Erasmus tried to argue he hadn't really meant to say that. But from the beginning of his career to its end, his hero was Saint Jerome, who for Erasmus combined classical learning and true devotion within a single Christian philosophy of life.

That synthesis became the goal of his life, and Erasmus quickly became a passionate enthusiast for the humane letters that all humanists revered (*Against Barbarians*):

> There are those who want the Republic of Letters to be destroyed root and branch. Others are doing their best to get its power not exactly extinguished, but restricted within narrower limits. Lastly there are those who want to see the republic preserved but utterly ruined, by themselves becoming tyrants, abrogating the laws of our fathers, and introducing foreign magistrates and behaviour. The first named of these, as I see it, are those quite uncouth people who detest the whole of literature (which they call poetry) on some vague religious pretext, whether from jealousy or stupidity I cannot say. The second lot I understand to be the educated who are really uneducated, the people who somehow find other studies acceptable (that is, their own), but as for the humanities, without which all learning is blind, they hate them worse than a snake. Then there are the last, and who else are they but the people who admire and approve of every kind of literature, especially poetry and rhetoric, but on condition that they themselves are considered the finest poets and orators—which is far from the case.[21]

This intellectual confidence, expressed in free, elegant Latin, suited Erasmus better to appreciative patrons and fellow authors than to monasteries. In fact, by the time he wrote his attack on behavior he no doubt

had experienced firsthand, he had left the cloister to serve as Latin secretary to a prominent bishop.[22] His extraordinary productiveness and his
genius for making connections eventually won Erasmus many readers all
over Europe.

He made those connections in Paris and in England, and English
scholars first convinced him of the importance of learning Greek. He did
that, despite having turned thirty, and went on to read Origen, one of the
most challenging of patristic writers. This influence is evident in
Eramasus's *Handbook of the Christian Soldier*, published in 1503:

> Let us imagine, therefore, two worlds, the one only intelligible, the other
> visible. The intelligible, which may also be called the angelic, is the one in
> which God dwells with the blessed spirits, while the visible world com-
> prises the celestial spheres and all that is contained therein. Then there is
> man, who contributes, as it were, a third world, participating in the other
> two, in the visible world through the body, and in the invisible through the
> soul. Since we are but pilgrims in the visible world, we should never make
> it our fixed abode, but should relate by a fitting comparison everything that
> occurs to the sense either to the angelic world or, in more practical terms,
> to morals and to that part of man that corresponds to the angelic. What
> the visible sun is here in the visible world the divine mind is in the intel-
> ligible world and in that part of you related to it, namely, the spirit. What
> the moon is here is in that world the assembly of angels and blessed spirits,
> which they call the church triumphant, and in you it is the spirit.
> Whatever influence the upper world has over the earth, which lies beneath
> it, God exercises this same influence over your soul.[23]

The *devotio moderna* had long insisted on the way of what it already called
"our reformation," aimed at kindling "the fires of religious fervor in the
cold hearts of men."[24] Desiderius Erasmus alloyed that fervor so completely with humanistic learning in a platonic key that he made the two
virtually indistinguishable.

The *Handbook* pressed its theme without compromise. Some baptized
people were "more pagan than the pagans": "what does it matter if the
body has been washed when the soul remains defiled?" Erasmus derided
those who "worship the bones of Paul preserved in a relic casket, but do
not worship the mind of Paul hidden away in his writings," and trade in
the "true cross" brought out his invective:

> You think it an immense privilege to have a tiny particle of the cross in
> your home. But that is nothing compared to carrying about in your heart

the mystery of the cross. If such things constitute religion, who could be more religious than the Jews? Even the most impious among them saw Jesus living in the flesh with their own eyes, heard him with their own ears and touched him with their own hands. Who is more fortunate than Judas, who pressed his lips upon the divine mouth?[25]

Humanists gave Erasmus an enthusiastic hearing, and as he benefited more from patronage, he grew bolder.

In Praise of Folly remains Erasmus's most famous work, a biting indictment of the posturing of the powerful in his own time. His attack on theologians, not just popular superstition, became instantly controversial when it was published in 1511:

> In addition, they interpret hidden mysteries to suit themselves: how the world was created and designed; through what channel the stain of sin filtered down to posterity; by what means, in what measure, and how long Christ was formed in the Virgin's womb; how, in the Eucharist, accidents can subsist without a domicile. But this sort of question has been discussed threadbare. There are others more worthy of great and enlightened theologians (as they call themselves) which really can rouse them to action if they come their way. What was the exact moment of divine generation? Are there several filiations in Christ? Is it a possible proposition that God the Father could hate his Son? Could God have taken on the form of a woman, a devil, a donkey, a gourd, or a flint stone? If so, how could a gourd have preached sermons, performed miracles, and been nailed to the cross? And what would Peter have consecrated if he had consecrated when the body of Christ still hung on the cross?[26]

Erasmus targeted not only abuses of piety, but also the scholastic method of those who attempted to parse Christian doctrine with the philosophy and method of Aristotle. For him, that represented a confusion of the intelligible world with the visible world.

Against the scholastics, Erasmus proposed the *philosophia Christi* or *doctrina Evangelica*—the transformative power of truth shining into emotions as well as into minds.[27] His dedication to this principle came to fruition in *Novum Instrumentum*, his edition of the New Testament in Greek with his own Latin translation and explanatory notes. He referred to the text as an *instrumentum*, as Tertullian had during the second century, because for him the New Testament was an "instrument" of change, not just words to be studied.[28] And change through the ages, in crucial questions such as the theology of the Eucharist, the discipline of divorce, the marriage of clergy, and the power of popes, was a simple fact of history and experience.

The Building of Saint Peter's

Erasmus conceived a particular disdain for Pope Julius II (1503–1513), a pontiff who went to war against fellow Christians to extend papal lands and who sold church offices in order to finance his patronage of the arts. But while Erasmus went to the extent of penning *Julius Excluded from Heaven*,[29] events were to prove that the conduct of popes was not merely a matter of their individual characters. Julius's excesses, as Erasmus judged them, included engaging Michelangelo to decorate the Sistine Chapel, adjacent to a new papal residence. That was part of a program of building that extended over several papacies, a projection of faith's character in stone and paint that embodied the values of the Renaissance.

The restoration and extension of Saint Peter's Basilica in Rome has been more or less constantly undertaken since its construction in the fourth century. But Julius II and his architect, Donato Bramante, effectively wanted to see a cathedral worthy of the Renaissance to house the bones of Saint Peter. The new Saint Peter's was only dedicated in 1626, more than a century after Julius's death. Even Michelangelo's legendary powers (who took over as chief of works between 1546 until his death in 1564) did not see it through to anything like completion.[30]

The achievement was as expensive as it was heroic, and during much of the earlier period of construction, the papacy had a greater ambition for patronage than it could meet from its own resources. Julius II's successor, Giovanni de' Medici of Florence, took the name of Leo X. He unsuccessfully called for a new crusade, but proved a highly effective patron of St. Peter's. In order to finance his huge campaign, Leo authorized the sale of indulgences; that marketing device was to prove the pivot on which the Renaissance became the Reformation.

The theology of the indulgence turned on exactly the kind of Aristotelian logic that Erasmus and other Christian humanists despised.[31] The whole enterprise was predicated on the scholastic method. Indulgences had been introduced at the time of the Crusades, as a promise that the crusaders' sacrifice would bring them remission of their sins. But as time went on, popes claimed that activities well short of martyrdom—such as making pilgrimages and giving money—could release a departed soul from some of its punishment in purgatory. The idea was that, although hell was outside the pope's jurisdiction, one's sentence to purgatory—a temporal punishment, for a set period of time after death in view of sins committed during life—could be shortened by papal authority. Pope Clement VI, forced by French power and turmoil in Italy to reside at Avignon rather than Rome, articulated this theology in the bull *Unigenitus* in 1343. Sales of indulgences made the construction of the papal palace in Avignon possible and formed a key aspect of the growing financial network of the papacy.

Leo X readily embraced this method for the extension of St. Peter's on a scale worthy of the Medicis. He promulgated an indulgence for this purpose, and at the same time entered into a lucrative arrangement with Archbishop Albert of Mainz. Albert, at twenty-seven, was already Archbishop of Magdeburg, and he needed Rome's permission (called a dispensation) to combine ecclesiastical offices. He paid for this dispensation by taking a loan from the Fugger banking house in Augsburg, and brought in Johann Tetzel, a Dominican friar, to sell indulgences, splitting the revenue to pay for Leo's building project and his own loan.

By 1517 Tetzel had a well-established and well-deserved reputation for the sale of indulgences. His big claim to fame was the assertion that, armed with his indulgences, one could help not only oneself, but also departed relatives out of purgatory. He paraded into town with bells literally ringing, banners of the papal arms, huge red crosses, preaching, it was claimed, "Once you hear the money ring, the soul from purgatory is free to spring."

By the largely unwritten rules of the Renaissance, this kind of excess was unfortunate and worthy of scorn, but only in appropriate company— and preferably in Latin.[32] As late as 1529 Erasmus complained about indulgences, "Monks and commissaries filled the world with them to line their own pockets," although he also acknowledged that they were "tolerable within limits."[33] But what would happen if the whole system the sale of indulgences represented were attacked directly, and in a way that engaged the popular imagination as well as learned opinion? It did not take long after Tetzel's arrival in Brandenburg for that question to be answered.

The Reformation

Near Brandenburg lay Wittenberg, but Tetzel was prohibited from going there. Frederick, called "the Wise," the Elector of Saxony, had his own fine collection of relics—bits of bone and other holy remains—that assured him revenues that he had no wish to see diluted.[34] People paid fees to see and reverence relics, acquiring indulgences for themselves and providing Frederick with an income. Contemplating his collection of 5,005 items could in theory bring 1,443 years of exemption from purgatory.[35]

But an Augustinian priest had been stirring up controversy over the question whether indulgences were really permissible at all. In fact, Martin Luther annoyed Frederick by preaching against the practice.[36] That, however, was the most minor of skirmishes, compared to the controversy Luther stirred up over the papal indulgences that Tetzel sold. In retrospect, the passion of the two sides may seem difficult to understand, especially in the light of all the debates that the Christian humanists had long pursued. But his personal character and his position in German society made Martin Luther into the most prominent teacher of the Reformation.

Martin Luther

By 1517, Luther had passed through two fateful conversions, each of which proved crucial to subsequent events. The son of a copper miner whose family managed to support him through studies in the liberal arts and law at Erfurt University, he broke with his father's wishes by entering an Augustinian monastery and living as a recluse. Although he had been known during his course of study as formidable in argument, Richard Friedenthal has plausibly suggested that Luther had already grown weary of the speculative character of legal disputation in the scholastic tradition.[37] A near miss of lightning prompted Luther's decision to enter a monastery to come when it did in 1505 (when he was just shy of twenty years old), but its roots lie deeper in his temperament.

As much as Erasmus read Saint Augustine for his Platonism, Luther read him for guidance in the experience of conversion. He developed a passion for the study of the Scriptures, learning Hebrew and Greek in the course of his teaching, which focused especially on the Psalms and Paul's Letter to the Romans. The key to Paul's theology and to human experience, he believed, was "The just shall live by faith" (Rom 1:17, citing Hab 2:4). Direct trust in God, apart from reliance on the conventions of earthly authorities, was the only path of justice, the single means to salvation.

He lectured on Romans in 1515, and by the time of Tetzel's campaign, he had found a big local audience. He wrote to a friend in May of 1517:

My theology—which is St. Augustine's—is getting on, and is dominant in the university. God has done it. Aristotle is going downhill and perhaps he will go all the way down to hell. It amazes me that so few people want lectures on the Sentences of Peter Lombard. Nobody will go to hear a lecture unless the lecturer is teaching my theology—which is the theology of the Bible, of St. Augustine, and of all true theologians of the Church. I am quite sure that the Church will never be reformed unless we get rid of canon law, scholastic theology, philosophy and logic as they are studied today, and put something else in their place.

Although he was simply a parish priest and a professor at a provincial university, Martin Luther at the age of thirty-three was thinking on the grandest of scales.

Johann Tetzel's activities came to Luther's attention through the people of his parish. He reacted to what they told them as their priest and took up the academic cudgels as a proud professor. He wrote first, in suitably deferential terms, to Archbishop Albert and, in the absence of a response, proposed certain theses for discussion and debate by posting them on the door of the Schlosskirche in Wittenberg on the Feast of All Saints in 1517. He entitled his proposal "Disputation on the Power and Efficacy of Indulgences," which ran to ninety-five theses, the popular name of his notice.

The first ten propositions set the tone for the whole and demonstrated the depth of Luther's challenge to the whole system of papal indulgence:[38]

1. When our Lord and Master, Jesus Christ, said "Repent," He called for the entire life of believers to be one of penitence.
2. The word cannot properly be understood as referring to the sacrament of penance, i.e., confession and satisfaction, as administered by the clergy.
3. Yet its meaning is not restricted to penitence in one's heart; for such penitence is null unless it produces outward signs in various mortifications of the flesh.
4. As long as hatred of self abides (i.e., true inward penitence) the penalty of sin abides, viz., until we enter the kingdom of heaven.
5. The pope has neither the will nor the power to remit any penalty beyond those imposed either at this own discretion or by canon law.
6. The pope himself cannot remit guilt, but only declare and confirm that it has been remitted by God; or, at most, he can remit it in cases reserved to his discretion. Except for these cases, the guilt remains untouched.

7. God never remits guilt to anyone without, at the same time, making him humbly submissive to the priest, his representative.
8. The penitential canons apply only to men who are still alive, and, according to the canons themselves, none applies to the dead.
9. Accordingly, the Holy Spirit, acting in the person of the pope, manifests grace to us, by the fact that the papal regulations always cease to apply at death, or in any hard case.
10. It is a wrongful act, due to ignorance, when priest, retain the canonical penalties on the dead in purgatory.

Luther deployed all his considerable forensic skill to probe into discovering how God can forgive and—equally mysterious—how human beings can move beyond their self-loathing without usurping the power of God.

The vehemence of Luther's theses reflects his passionate commitment to the principle of what has accurately but a bit aridly been called "justification by faith alone." A peerless interpreter of Paul, Luther frequently spoke of Satan as a genuine force, but a force not to be taken too seriously:

> When the devil comes at night to worry me, this is what I say to him: "Devil, I have to sleep now. That is God's commandment, for us to work by day and sleep at night." If he keeps on nagging me and trots out my sins, then I answer: "Sweet devil, I know the whole list. Also write on it that I have shit on my breeches. Then hang that around your neck and wipe your mouth on it."[39]

In his experience, complete and personal trust to God cut through doubt in oneself and inner torment. His sense of the power of this faith was as vivid as his expression of it could be crude.

Even Luther, however, was unprepared for the level of controversy that erupted over his theses. He famously complained that "the song was pitched in too high a key for my voice."[40] His character was only one dimension of the controversy; the other was where the dispute had broken out. Frederick of Saxony was not a supporter of Luther's theology on indulgences, but he was a proud local ruler suspicious of incursions into his territory. That Luther had annoyed his ecclesiastical superiors did not disturb Frederick, and he supported this "impertinent monk," as Archbishop Albert called Luther.[41]

Pope Leo sent Cardinal Cajetan as his legate to deal with the case. As a Dominican, also Tetzel's order, there was no doubt about the side Cajetan would come down on. But because the theology of indulgences (especially as preached by Tetzel) was questionable, Cajetan pitched the dispute in terms of papal authority. In this regard, he colluded with Luther in framing the debate in terms of the limits of the Pope's power in relation to God.

Luther's demand for the recognition of those limits struck a deep chord in Germany. When Cajetan came to the meeting of local rulers in Augsburg in 1518, he had to listen to a long series of complaints about Rome's interference. Cajetan demanded Luther's retraction of his theses, and Luther refused.

The exchange transpired in an atmosphere of violence. Luther's theses had been translated into German, and he enjoyed enormous popular support. Over the years, his direct, passionate prose became a benchmark of Reformation preaching and the pride of German nationalism. Tetzel, although honored by Rome, was afraid to appear in public. Incipient unrest, however, invited countermeasures. Cajetan came armed to Augsburg, and Luther escaped under cover of darkness. The fear of heresy went hand in hand with the fear of revolt. Jan Huss had been burned at the stake in 1415 for his combined program of Bible translation and local revolution, and Czech nationalism remained a problem a century later. The Inquisition, the burning of witches, pogroms against Jews, the expulsion of Muslims and Jews from Spain in 1492 all represent Catholic Europe's violent fear of apostasy and insurrection. Luther's public constituted a greater threat to the Pope than Luther himself posed.

Leo attempted to resolve the issue by diplomacy, while Luther called for a General Council of the Church, whose authority he said exceeded that of the Pope. Meanwhile, writing *To the Christian Nobility of the German Nation* in 1520, Luther called on kings and princes to resist papal incursions, including indulgences. All Christians are priests according to the teaching of the New Testament, so it was right for rulers to use their civic power to uphold the authority of the Bible:

> The Romanists have very cleverly surrounded themselves with three walls, which have protected them till now in such a way that no one could reform them. As a result, the whole of Christendom has suffered woeful corruption. In the first place, when under the threat of secular force, they have stood firm and declared that secular force had no jurisdiction over them; rather the opposite was the case, and the spiritual was superior to the secular. In the second place, when the Holy Scriptures have been used to reprove them, they have responded that no one except the pope was competent to

expound Scripture. In the third place, when threatened with a council, they have pretended that no one but the pope could summon a council. In this way, they have adroitly nullified these three means of correction, and avoided punishment. Thus they still remain in secure possession of these three walls, and practise all the villainy and wickedness we see today. . . . May God now help us, and give us one of those trumpets with which the walls of Jericho were overthrown; that we may blow away these walls of paper and straw, and set free the Christian, corrective measures to punish sin, and bring the devil's deceits and wiles to the light of day. In this way, may we be reformed through suffering and again receive God's blessing.

In his own mind and for his followers, Martin Luther's majestic invective became that trumpet.

On June 15, 1520, Leo issued *Exsurge Domine*, excommunicating Luther unless he recanted and ordering his books burned. That bull was as inevitable as Luther's reaction: he burned the Pope's edict in public, along with copies of canon law and other papal decrees. That act and the raucous popular violence he attracted required some action by Charles V, the young and newly chosen Holy Roman Emperor (and therefore the titular ruler of Germany). Luther had appealed to him in his call *To the Christian Nobility of the German Nation*, but the Emperor was also the king of Spain, newly emerged as a dominant Catholic power, and he could only see the events swirling around Luther as threats to the unity and stability of his domains as a whole. He convened a Diet at Worms in 1521.

Luther attended under an imperial safe-conduct. The Emperor asked him to recant on April 18. Luther replied: "Unless I am proved wrong by Scriptures or by evident reason, then I am a prisoner in conscience to the Word of God. I cannot retract and I will not retract. To go against the conscience is neither safe nor right. God help me. Amen."[42] Later that same year, despite suffering depression and having to live concealed in Wartberg, Luther began his translation of the Bible into German, a pillar of the Reformation, as important to this movement's intellectual life as his hymns were to its liturgical life.

Revolution

Reformation meant revolution in several ways. Basic worship was reformed, beginning with the practice of permitting laypeople to receive both bread and wine during Eucharist, rather than reserving the wine for priests alone. Priestly vestments were simplified, priests were permitted to marry, and zealots for change began to demolish altars they considered too ornate. On a more systematic level, civic authorities confiscated ecclesiastical funds and began to administer them for social services. When Luther returned to Wittenberg in 1522, it was as much to contain the Reformation as to spread it.

A series of peasant revolts broke out in the south of Germany in 1524–1525, and Luther responded with his characteristic passion *Against the Murdering, Thieving Hordes of Peasants*: "These times are so extraordinary that a prince can more easily win heaven by bloodshed than by prayer."[43] To his mind, the priesthood of all believers, which made Christians of every station individually accountable before God and jointly responsible for the church, needed to be exercised within the natural authorities of this world.

In this realm of theological politics, Luther—himself no politician—set out a position that also became emblematic of the Reformation as a whole. He had already written *Secular Authority* in 1523:

> All who are not Christian belong to the kingdom of the world and are under the law. Since few believe and still fewer live a Christian life, do not resist the evil, and themselves do no evil, God has provided for non-Christians a different government outside the Christian estate and God's kingdom, and has subjected them to the sword, so that, even though they would do so, they cannot practise their wickedness, and that, if they do, they may not do it without fear or in peace and prosperity. Even so a wild, savage beast is fastened with chains and bands, so that it cannot bite and tear as is its wont, although it gladly would do so; whereas a tame and gentle beast does not require this, but without chains and bands is nevertheless harmless. If it were not so, seeing that the whole world is evil and that among thousands there is scarcely one true Christian, men would devour one another, and no one would preserve wife and child, support himself and serve God; and thus the world would be reduced to chaos. For this reason, God has ordained the two governments; the spiritual, which by the Holy Spirit under Christ makes Christians and pious people, and the secular, which restrains the unchristian and wicked so that they must needs keep the peace outwardly, even against their will.[44]

A wily monarch could easily press such a teaching to his own advantage. That was exactly the case with Christian II of Denmark, who invited Lutheran preachers from Wittenberg. His attempt to extend his power over Sweden led to revolt there under Gustavus Vasa, and Sweden established a national church along the lines of the Reformation in 1527, guided by Olaus Petri, who had personally studied with Luther. The settlements in Norway and Finland were comparable in religious terms.[45]

The Reformation fomented a brisk nationalism that could decay into civil war, the division of traditional hegemonies, and uprisings of popular heretics, while it also offered rulers such as Gustavus and Christian undoubted opportunities. Charles V, as we have already seen, sided with the papacy, despite Luther's hopes. François I of France, the same king who had brought Leonardo da Vinci to Amboise, permitted bishops such as Guillaume Briçonnet of Meaux to pursue some of the aims of the Reformation, within the polity of the Catholic Church. In England, the papacy found a staunch defender in Henry VIII, who—prompted by Thomas More, Erasmus's friend—in 1521 wrote *The Defense of the Seven Sacraments against Martin Luther*, dedicating the work to Leo X. The grateful pontiff bestowed the title "Defender of the Faith" on Henry, which is borne by British monarchs to this day. In contrast to these national sovereigns, all committed in varying degrees to papal authority, the German princes joined in a "protest" against the emperor and his allies at the Diet of Speyer in 1529, and they linked up in 1531 into an alliance called the Schmalkadic League.

Henry VIII

With the exception of Scandinavia, the prospects of the Protestants in Europe looked precarious. Both in Rome and in England, however, events took a surprising course, which put Henry and the pope of the time, Clement VII, at loggerheads. Henry's wife had delivered only one child that survived, a girl. Five children had been stillborn. Henry desperately wanted a male heir to inherit his throne in order to avoid wars of succession. He claimed that his plight was divine punishment for his having married his brother's wife, against the teaching of Leviticus (18:16; 20:21). It was within the pope's power, as defended by Henry, to declare the marriage invalid, and there were many precedents for such declarations for reasons of state.

But after 1527, there were excellent reasons of state for Clement to deny the request. In that year, the troops of Charles V had sacked Rome, as part of his extension of imperial power, capturing the pope at the same time. Catherine of Aragon, Henry's wife, was also Charles's aunt.[46] By the summer of 1529 the papal legates commissioned by Clement still had reached no decision about invalidating Henry's marriage, and Cardinal Compeggio adjourned the case, on the improbable grounds that the British summer was too hot.

Henry acted in that same year to pressure Clement to act on his behalf, chipping away at papal power through acts of Parliament. This required no great statesmanship; Parliament was always ready to go much further in the direction of Reformation teaching than Henry was. But what was called "the king's matter" opened the way to change.

By 1531, Parliament insisted that clergy could not administer canon law independently of the crown. "As far as the law of Christ allows," they declared, the king was "especial Protector," "even supreme Head of the Church." In 1533, appeals from England to Rome were prohibited, and in the same year, Thomas Cranmer—as Archbishop of Canterbury—annulled Henry's marriage to Catherine, and Henry married Anne Boleyn. The settlement was sealed by violence: Bishop Fisher of Rochester and Sir Thomas More were beheaded in 1535 for refusing to swear their agreement to the royal supremacy in the church. From that year, the crown increasingly took over the properties and revenues of monasteries. In effect, Henry's dispute with Clement brought to England the Reformation according to the Scandinavian model.

The Reformed Movement

Events in England corresponded to new outbreaks of much less orderly demands for change on mainland Europe. In Münster (Westphalia), Bernard Rothman, an Anabaptist leader, took control of the city council in 1533 and followed the teaching of a self-styled prophet named John of Leyden. Anabaptists insisted correctly that, according to the New Testament, baptism is a spiritual rebirth that only believers committed to Christ can enjoy. John went beyond that program, however, declaring himself King of Zion and sanctioning polygamy as it was practiced among the patriarchs of Israel.[47] His revolution encouraged outbreaks in other cities until the local bishop's army killed him in 1535.

François I of France had by this time already executed people on the charge of heresy, but after 18 October 1534, his policy became more vigorous. That morning, placards were found in Paris, Orléans, and Blois denouncing him and his régime.[48] Blaming Protestant elements in his country, François had thirty-five Lutherans burned after he made a procession to the cathedral of Notre Dame in Paris, and Protestant leaders made an exodus from France, especially to Switzerland.

The Swiss Reformation already had a more coordinated aspect than Luther's movement by this time. Ulrich Zwingli of Zürich embraced Luther's writings from 1519, but he adhered to a program of Reform that was more biblical and more militant than Luther's program. (In fact, the "Reformed" churches defined themselves in distinction to Lutheran churches as well as to Roman churches.) In his view, not only were Christians to correct their practices with reference to the Scriptures, but also the Scriptures ought actually to sanction their practices. He opposed Luther's teaching on the Lord's Supper or Eucharist, for example, because he refused to believe in any substantial change in bread and wine or in Jesus being present in them. The body and blood of Christ were apprehended spiritually, more in the manner of the Christian humanism of Erasmus. Zwingli and Luther never reconciled after a public dispute in 1529.

Supported by the civic council in Zürich, Zwingli engaged in a program of reforming the city itself, in a manner that came to typify Reformed churches. The militancy of Zwingli was such that he took to the field in helmet and sword against his Catholic opponents. He was captured in 1531 and was drawn and quartered; his ashes were scattered after his corpse was burned.[49]

But the Reform prospered in Strasbourg under Martin Bucer, and was introduced to Geneva by Guillaume Farel, who had left France and arrived in Geneva under the protection of the Berne city council. By 1535, Geneva was an independent city, no longer obliged to the authority of the local bishop. The following year Farel invited a fellow French reformer, Jean Calvin, to remain in Geneva.

Calvin had to struggle to work out his theological and organizational principles at the same time that he implemented them in a contentious political environment. But his two major works, *The Institutes of the Christian Religion* and the *Ecclesiastical Ordinances* that he had the council pass, constitute an enduring contribution to Christian faith and polity.[50] The first of these works was published in 1536, and the *Ordinances* took recognizable shape in 1541. But they were lifeworks to which Calvin devoted himself until his death in 1564.

Calvin conceived a scheme in which pastors appointed teachers in consultation with the city government. The civic council, in turn, appointed elders in consultation with the pastors. The purpose of the elders was to survey the morals of the city—public and private—and act against such dangers as heresy and popery as well as dancing and prostitution. The Scottish advocate of the Reform, John Knox, called Geneva "the most perfect school of Christ that ever was on earth since the days of the Apostles."

Calvin's genius was theological as well as organizational. He stated the principle of justification by faith lucidly:

> To declare that by him alone we are accounted righteous, what else is this but to lodge our righteousness in Christ's obedience, because the obedience of Christ is reckoned to us as if it were our own? For this reason, it seems to me that Ambrose beautifully stated an example of this righteousness in the blessing of Jacob: noting that, as he did not of himself deserve the right of the first-born, concealed in his brother's clothing and wearing his brother's coat, which gave out an agreeable odor (Gen. 27:27), he ingratiated himself with his father, so that to his own benefit he received the benefit while impersonating another. And we in like manner hide under the precious purity of our first-born brother, Christ, so that we may be attested righteous in God's sight. Here are the words of Ambrose: "That Isaac smelled the odor of the garments perhaps means that we are justified not by works but by faith, of the weakness of the flesh is a hindrance to works, but the brightness of faith, which merits the pardon of sons, overshadows the error of deeds." And this is indeed the truth, for in order that we may appear before God's face unto salvation we must smell sweetly with his odor, and our vices must be covered and buried by his perfection.[51]

The logic, elegance, and feeling of this explanation help account for Calvin's deep influence on the people of Geneva and for the seamless combination of emotion and thought in the best Reformed theology.

But Calvin understood, and knew all too well from practical experience, that people can wear faith as a mask, concealing the truth of themselves even from themselves. An even more careful reader of Augustine than of Ambrose, Calvin investigated the consequences of this hard truth:

> Yet what Augustine writes is nonetheless true: that all who are estranged from the religion of the one God, however admirable they may be regarded on account of their reputation for virtue, not only deserve no reward but rather punishment, because by the pollution of their hearts they defile God's good works. For even though they are God's instruments for the preservation of human society in righteousness, continence, friendship, temperance, fortitude, and prudence, yet they carry out the good works of God very badly. For they are restrained from evil-doing not by genuine zeal for good but either by mere ambition or by self-love, or some other perverse motive. Therefore, since by the very impurity of men's hearts these good works have been corrupted as from their source, they ought no more to be reckoned among the virtues than the vices that commonly deceive on account of their affinity and likeness to virtue. In short, when we remem-

ber the constant end of that which is right—namely, to serve God—whatever strives to another end already deservedly loses the name "right." Therefore, because they do not look to the goal that God's wisdom prescribes, what they do, though it seems good in the doing, yet by its perverse intention is sin. He therefore concludes that the Fabriciuses, Scipios, and Catos in their excellent deeds have sinned in that, since they lacked the light of faith, they did not apply their deeds to the end to which they ought to have applied them. Therefore, true righteousness was not in them, because duties are weighed not by deeds but by ends.[52]

This rigorous focus on the end of life gives Calvin's thought its characteristically teleological character because the end of any human being could only truly be known by God.

God alone knew the outcome of all choices any human being might make. On that Augustine and Calvin were agreed. Predestination, to salvation or damnation, was a matter of God being God: "It is a question of the secret judgments of God whose brightness not only dazzles the minds of men when they presume to approach them too closely, but destroys and consumes them utterly."[53] A modern scholar, Bernard Cottret, has called predestination "the werewolf of Reformed theology," and there is no doubt that it became a principle mark of division between Catholic and Protestant thought and piety.

Erasmus had already parted company with Luther over this issue in 1524:

> For when I hear that the merit of man is so utterly worthless that all things, even the works of godly men, are sins, when I hear that our will does nothing more than clay in the hand of a potter, when I hear all that we do or will referred to absolute necessity, my mind encounters many a stumbling block.[54]

Calvin's theology offered him only more obstacles, in spelling out this worthlessness in ever-greater detail. Erasmus died in the Reformed city of Basel in 1536, having declined the offer to become a cardinal the previous year. Neither side of the Reformation was congenial to his moderate Platonism.

The End of United Christendom in the West

The offer of a cardinalship to Erasmus, however, signaled an attempt at reconciliation with at least some of the principles of the Reformation by

Paul III, who became pope in 1534.[55] Under his authorization, a discussion with Protestant theologians at Regensburg in 1541 reached a remarkable agreement on the theology of justification. But transubstantiation and papal supremacy still remained sticking points, and Luther himself repudiated what he saw as an unacceptable compromise of the doctrine of justification by faith alone.

By this time, Protestantism and Roman Catholicism, both products of the Catholic Church of the Middle Ages, had emerged with different structures of belief. Obviously, they shared many beliefs in detail, but their definition of the central tenet that gave faith coherence differed. Justification by faith alone and papal supremacy in the order of the church had become mutually exclusive principles.

Those issues put other elements of faith in the background. In England, for example, Henry VIII issued his Act of Six Articles in 1539, which set out punishment for denying transubstantiation and the need for clerical celibacy. Thomas Cranmer himself opposed the act during debate in the House of Lords; hardly surprising, when you consider he himself was married to the niece of the Lutheran theologian Osiander.[56] But Henry and Cranmer were more bound together by their mutual denial of any papal control over England than they were divided by doctrinal disagreement.

In any case, the accession of Edward VI in 1547 opened the floodgates of reform in England. The Six Articles were repealed, and protestant ministers were free to remove images from their churches, to give wine at Communion as well as bread, and to live openly with their wives. Cranmer was responsible primarily for the *Book of Common Prayer* in 1549 and again in 1552. One difference between the two books is instructive. While the 1549 Communion has the minister say, "The Body of our Lord Jesus Christ which was given for thee, preserve they body and soul unto everlasting life," from 1552 he was to say, "Take and eat this in remembrance that Christ died for thee, and feed on him in thy heart by faith, with thanksgiving." The growing influence of Reformed rather than Lutheran teaching is evident. In Scotland, John Knox even managed to force Cranmer to agree in writing that kneeling to receive the sacrament did not imply "any real and essential presence there being of Christ's natural body and blood."[57] The trenchantly Reformed character of the Anglican Church was now undeniable, although far less complete than Calvin's Geneva.

From 1542, papal policy also took a trenchant form. Paul's bull, *Licit ab initio*, established an inquisition in Italy (on the Spanish model) in order to root out heresy. The Inquisition authorized the by now traditional methods of confiscating property, imprisonment, torture, and execution. Cardinal Caraffa, who had initiated the plan, guided the Inquisition in its attack on Protestants, Anabaptists, and those whose orthodoxy was suspect. His decrees were explicit: "No man is to lower himself by showing toleration towards any sort of heretic, least of all a Calvinist." Caraffa became Pope Paul IV in 1555; he began the *Index of Prohibited Books*—including all of Erasmus and the *Decameron* of Boccaccio—that resulted in the burning of tens of thousands of volumes, and the rule that Jews were to live in ghettos and wear yellow hats.[58] Paul IV's conduct was extreme, and public demonstrations greeted his death in 1559. But even toward the end of Paul III's reign as pope, the consolidation of papal power in the realm of doctrine became the chief characteristic of Roman Catholic theology.

From 1545, successive popes convened councils of the Church at Trent (south of the Alps) in a series of three sessions until 1563. From the outset, the bishops who attended (only twenty-eight at first, more than two hundred by the close of proceedings) denied Protestant doctrine and went on to canonize the Latin Vulgate and the Latin Mass together with transubstantiation. In reaction to Calvin's *Institutes*, they made Thomas Aquinas the premier theologian of systematic doctrine. But at the same time, these meetings also achieved genuine reform and represent what is called the Catholic Reformation or the Counter-Reformation. The bishops addressed the problem of absentee clergy and immorality in the church hierarchy, provided for a new emphasis on preaching and on education at all levels, and abolished arrangements for the sale of indulgences such as Johann Tetzel had proferred.

The Jesuits, as members of the Society of Jesus came to be called, played a key role in these developments. In 1521, a Spanish soldier named Ignatius Loyola was wounded in the French siege of Pamplona. His smashed leg meant the end of his military career, but he determined to continue as a soldier of Christ, writing in his *Spiritual Exercises* of how a person might take Jesus' sufferings on oneself, in order to heal one's soul and submit it in obedience to the Church as the Bride of Christ.[59] In 1540, Paul III authorized the Society of Jesus, and it proved an ideal instrument of the Catholic Reformation.

Loyola appealed to "all those who want to fight under the banner of God in our Society, which we wish to designate with the name of Jesus, and who are willing to serve solely God and his vicar on earth."[60] In his

Spiritual Exercises, he adapted the *devotio moderna* (and particularly *The Imitation of Christ* by Thomas à Kempis) to a new aim: complete obedience to the pope as the divinely appointed "vicar on earth."

After 1542, religion divided Europe between Roman Catholic and Protestant Christianity; sometimes the fault line ran between nation-states, and sometimes within them. In every case, however, the emerging theologies called on the force—if necessary, the violent force—of secular power in order to protect the truth of their positions. In the Protestant view, the very purpose of any state was, as Luther said, to "set free the Christian, corrective measures to punish sin, and bring the devil's deceits and wiles to the light of day" (quoted earlier from *To the Christian Nobility of the German Nation*). In the Roman Catholic view of Ignatius Loyola, only obedience to the pope, God's "vicar on earth," could transcend the violent factionalism and warfare of suffering Europe.

Neither of these programs promoted the values of the Renaissance, although both of them took their roots in that rebirth of culture. If Geoffrey Elton's claim that the Roman inquisition "put an end to the Italian Renaissance"[61] imperils a good insight with exaggeration, it is true that books and paintings were as suspect in Rome as they were in Geneva. Paul IV actually commissioned Daniel of Volterra to cover up some of the indecency of the images in the Sistine Chapel.[62] Both Roman Catholic and Protestant theology had become deductive systems with results logically related to basic premises. The pressure of debate and the practicalities of public policy inclined both sides to a scholastic style of argument, rather than to the methods of Aristotle or Plato.

Beyond the harm done to the values of the Renaissance and philosophical discourse, however, the Reformation posed a greater danger to Europe. Two mutually exclusive theologies—in effect, different religions—stood armed at approximate parity, and neither side saw pacifism as a virtue. War was inevitable, although it came with a ferocity few observers could have predicted.

The Enlightenment

Prelude to War

By the time the Council of Trent ceased meeting in 1563, the nation-states of Europe had chosen sides over the issue of religion, or were in the process of doing so. Religious dedication translated into armed violence; the Enlightenment emerged as a movement dedicated to the rule of Reason (regularly capitalized during this whole period) in a time when Europe might have drowned in pessimism. Although the Renaissance and the Enlightenment were quite different periods, the optimism inherited from the Renaissance enable the Enlightenment to take place.

Spain and eventually France were as committed to Roman Catholicism as England and Scandinavia were to the Protestant cause. Italy's city-states continued to vie with the Vatican for prominence, but their devotion to their traditional faith was secure. Germany was deeply divided among Catholic and Protestant counties; present-day Belgium was split down the middle.

In terms of theological adherence, the map of Europe would not change greatly over the century. But each side of the divide, Protestant and Catholic, was convinced that its version of Christianity was alone valid, and that no government could legitimately rule without the endorsement of God. As a result, nation-states, city-states, counties, and regions purged their own populations so as to become as purely Catholic or Protestant as they could. They also fought one another, advancing their religious and political agendas with implacable and often murderous force.

In France both Protestants and Catholics—each represented in the aristocracy, and even the royal line—armed themselves for war against each other. In 1563, the assassination of the Catholic duc de Guise brought on a civil war with many atrocities. The most famous of them was the Saint Bartholomew's Day Massacre (which in fact lasted for weeks), when Protestant leaders were invited to Paris in 1572 to celebrate a marriage between the daughter of Catherine de Médici, of the Catholic royal house, and Henry of Navarre, a Protestant. Their massacre at what should have been a reconciling marriage only inflamed the war, which was finally stopped when the same Henry prevailed on the field of battle. He announced his conversion to Roman Catholicism in order to reign as Henry IV from 1594. Four years later, he issued the Edict of Nantes, which offered toleration to Protestant practice.

Spanish power under the Catholic Philip II (1556–1598) reached its height. He became king of Portugal as well as of Spain in 1580, commanded an empire in the New World, and ruled territories in the Netherlands and in Italy. The range of Spanish power proved fateful in the unfolding pattern of war in Europe. In 1571, Philip's navy proved the decisive force in the battle with the Ottoman fleet. Married to Mary I of England (1553–1558), he aspired to put down the Reformation there with her active cooperation. When Mary died, Philip proposed marriage to Elizabeth I (1558–1603), but the daughter of Ann Boleyn predictably rejected him. His response was to prepare an invasion of England in 1588. His armada foundered amidst the unpredictable English Channel and the smaller English merchant vessels converted for battle.

The armada had been on the way to the Netherlands, part of Philip's realm and—he hoped—a bridgehead for assaulting England. But the increasing Protestant Netherlands themselves revolted and achieved independence from Spain by the beginning of the seventeenth century. In addition, Sweden establish virtual control of the Baltic during this period, and its king, Gustavus Adolphus (1611–1632) was one of the preeminent Protestant leaders of Europe, in alliance with both England and the Netherlands. Power at sea therefore became a Protestant trademark.

Sweden's attractiveness to the English and Dutch also lay in its counterweight to Denmark, although Denmark was itself a Protestant nation. As Europe geared up for war, it became plain that religion alone would not determine who was an ally, who was an enemy, and when battle would be engaged. Although the battles, atrocities, and intellectual combat of this period are commonly called "The Wars of Religion," this period saw secular concerns masquerading under the cover of religion in ways that had not been the case earlier. In addition to the extreme violence of these wars, they marked the emergence of considerations of state predominating over matters of faith.

The Thirty Years' War and the Monopoly of Violence in Nation-States

The election of Ferdinand Habsburg as king of Bohemia precipitated Protestant rebellion, when Ferdinand did not deliver the toleration he promised. In 1618, two of his advisers were thrown out the window of the royal palace in Prague, and for thirty years violence spiraled out of anyone's control.

At first Ferdinand seemed invincible; he had Prague sacked in 1620. His victory emboldened Spain under Philip III to seize its territory in the Netherlands. The intervention of the Danish king, Christian IV, on behalf of the Protestants only resulted in Christian's defeat in 1629. The following year, however, Gustavus Adolphus of Sweden entered the fray, supported with aid from Catholic France (designed to resist the power of Spain, despite its being a Catholic nation). In a brilliant campaign—that also exacted sacking in revenge for sacking—Gustavus conquered most of central and northern Germany by the time of his own death in battle in 1632.

Gustavus's victories signaled the erosion of Habsburg power. Even France actually declared war on Catholic Spain in 1635, and fighting see-sawed in the Netherlands. Meanwhile, the Dutch fleet destroyed much of Spain's navy, and Portugal seceded from its union with Spain in 1640. The Spanish empire disintegrated in the attempt to extend its power beyond its capacity to control events, territories, or the loyalties of those it sought to conquer—a lesson in the fragility of empire.

By 1648 an exhausted Europe settled its war in the Peace of Westphalia, which was signed at Münster. The Netherlands gained state-hood, and Switzerland achieved independence. Both France and Sweden acquired territory. Most important, however, each nation gained autonomous sovereignty, the power of each nation-state to reach a reli-gious settlement, based on Catholicism, Protestantism, or the toleration of the two. That was a real gain from a war that cost millions of lives, Europe's last great war of religion.

The Thirty Years' War therefore gave Europe what has been called the royal state, an unprecedented concentration of power in the hands of the sovereign ruler, conceived to reign by the divine right of kings. James VI of Scotland, who later became James I of England, wrote a tract in 1598 called "The True Law of Free Monarchies," in which he set out a theol-ogy of divine right:

> As there is not a thing so necessary to be known by the people of any land, next the knowledge of their God, as the right knowledge of their alle-giance, according to the form of government established among them, especially in a Monarchy (which form of government, as resembling the Divinity, approaches nearest to perfection, as all the learned and wise men from the beginning have agree upon; Unity being the perfection of all things). So has ignorance, and (which is worse) the seduced opinion of the multitude blinded by them who think themselves able to teach and instruct the ignorant, procured the rack and overthrow of sundry flourish-ing Commonwealths; and heaped heavy calamities, threatening utter destruction upon others. And the smiling success, that unlawful rebellions have oftentimes had against Princes in ages past (such has been the misery, and iniquity of the time) has by way of practice strengthened many in their

error . . . as hereafter shall be proved at more length. And among others, no Commonwealth, that ever has been since the beginning, has had greater need of the true knowledge of this ground, then this our so long disordered, and distracted Commonwealth has: the misknowledge hereof being the only spring, from whence have flowed so many endless calamities, miseries, and confusions, as is better felt by many, then the cause thereof well known, and deeply considered. The natural zeal therefore that I bear to this my native country, with the great pity I have to see the so-long disturbance there for lack of the true knowledge of this ground (as I have said before) has compelled me at last to break silence, to discharge my conscience to you my dear countrymen herein, that knowing the ground from whence these your many endless troubles have proceeded, as we as you have already too-long tasted the bitter fruits thereof, you may by knowledge, and eschewing of the cause escape, and divert the lamentable effects that ever necessarily follow thereupon. I have chosen then only to set down in this short Treatise, the true ground of the mutual duty, and allegiance between a free and absolute Monarch and his people; not to trouble your patience with answering the contrary propositions, which some have not been ashamed to set down in writ, to the poisoning of the infinite number of simple souls, and their own perpetual, and well deserved infamie.[63]

In James's mind, ruling was what kings were for, not for answering pesky arguments that contradicted his assertion of sovereign power. Freedom in his mind, and in the absolutist ideology, involved the unconstrained exertion of power by the monarch, not rights attributed to his subjects.

James's belief that kings were free of constraint from their subjects was not at all unique. In 1614, the Estates General in France agreed that "the king is sovereign in France and holds his crown from God only."[64] Bureaucracy, tax, and military expenditure all grew at a rapid pace as a result of the acceptance of royal and national absolutism, upsetting the old, decentralized web of obligations that Europe had evolved during the Middle Ages. Europe's religions also took on distinctively national characteristics during this period, as sovereigns were believed to embody the faith as well as the power of their people.

National Purges

Europe's political and religious character changed under the force of arms. In France, popular frustrations led to the uprising called the *Fronde* (a name for a slingshot) in the same year the Peace of Westphalia was signed. The *Fronde* successfully occupied Paris, but deteriorating conditions there made it easy for Louis XIV, only thirteen years old and hastily declared to be mature enough to rule, to order the capture of the city. His welcome there was an indication that monarchy was the agreed paradigm of rule, even among those who rebelled against particular rulers.

By the time of the *Fronde*, England had already been submerged in a civil war for six years. Charles I and a Parliament dominated by Puritans (as partisans of Reformed Christianity were called) could not settle their argument over whether Reformation principles should govern the Church strictly. The Puritan program of replacing the hierarchy of bishops and archbishops with elected presbyters was never wholly agreed, and the result was relentless fighting. Under General Oliver Cromwell's coup, Charles was executed in 1649, and England became a commonwealth of citizens instead of a monarchy of subjects.

One of Cromwell's most effective propagandists was John Milton, who in that same year published "The Tenure of Kings and Magistrates," arguing that society was constituted by a covenant between ruler and ruled which was greater than any party. Despite the brevity of Cromwell's experiment, the conception that Milton developed proved over the long term an effective counterweight to the divine right of kings.

The displacement of divine right by a covenantal principle of governance became emblematic of the Enlightenment, and Milton stated it with elegant brutality:

No man who knows ought, can be so stupid to deny that all men were naturally born free, being the image and resemblance of God himself, and were by privilege above all the creatures, born to command and not to obey: and that they lived so. Till from the root of Adam's transgression, falling among themselves to do wrong and violence, and foreseeing that such courses must needs tend to destruction of them all, they agreed by common league to bind each other from mutual injury, and jointly defend themselves against any that gave disturbance or opposition to such agreement. Hence came Cities, Towns and Commonwealths. And because no faith in all was found sufficiently binding, they saw it needful to ordain some authority, that might restrain by force and punishment what was violated against peace and common right. This authority and power of self-defense and preservation being originally and naturally in every one of them, and unitedly in them all, for ease, for order, and lest each man should be his own partial Judge, they communicated and derived either to one, whom for the eminence of his wisdom and integrity they chose above the rest, or to more than one whom they thought of equal deserving: the first was called a King; the other Magistrates. Not to be their Lords and Masters (though afterward those names in some places were given voluntarily to such as had been authors of inestimable good to the people) but, to be their Deputies and Commissions, to execute, by virtue of their entrusted power, that justice which else every man by the bond of nature and of Covenant must have executed for himself, and for one another.[65]

Here is the Puritan myth of power in its political application: a demolition of the divine right of kings by means of the prior authority of divine creation and covenant, from the pen of the author of that greatest of all re-writers of the Genesis myth. Posterity knows John Milton as the poet of *Paradise Lost*, but his political influence is as epochal as that of Eusebius of Caesarea. Where Eusebius was the author of the divine right of the ruler to govern as the image of Christ on earth, Milton articulated the logic that the image of God in every human being provides a primordial precedent deeper than any king's authority for power on earth as well as redemption in heaven.

Cromwell's Commonwealth did not last long beyond his death, and Charles II, son of Charles I, was recalled from exile in 1660. Even so, England was not done with revolutions. James II (1685–1688) attempted to impose a Catholic settlement, and leaders of Parliament negotiated with William, Prince of Orange, to take over the throne. He did that so bloodlessly his achievement is called the Glorious Revolution, and the Toleration Act of 1689 at last accorded British subjects the sort of religious freedom enjoyed in the Netherlands.

The Enlightenment's Celebration of Reason

The British model of a constitutional monarchy checked by the rights and interests of its subjects spawned the Enlightenment's political theory. John Locke, in his "Two Treatises on Government" (1698), opposed any arbitrary construction of power and insisted upon the natural rights of individuals to life, liberty, and property.[66] His argument shows a debt to John Milton but also a growing reliance on the conception that "the people" in aggregate might be capable of exercising reason better than monarchs.

The Miltonian aspect of Locke's argument is evident in his citation from the opening chapters of Genesis (*First Treatise* §145):

The Scripture says not a word of their Rulers or Forms of Government, but only gives an account, how Mankind came to be divided into distinct

Languages and Nations; and therefore 'tis not to argue from the Authority of Scripture, to tell us positively, *Fathers* were their *Rulers,* when the Scripture says no such thing, but to set up Fancies of ones own Brain, when we confidently aver Matter of Fact, where Records are utterly silent.

Although Locke's argument is formally similar to Milton's, it results in a more sweeping claim for the capacity of people to determine their own form of government, as Locke's conclusion then makes clear (*Second Treatise* §§241-243):

But farther, this Question, (*Who shall Judge?*) cannot mean, that there is no Judge at all. For where there is no Judication on Earth, to decide Controversies amongst Men, *God* in Heaven is *Judge;* He alone, 'tis true, is Judge of the Right. But *every* Man is *Judge* for himself, as in all other Cases, so in this, whether another hath put himself into a State of War with him, and whether he should appeal to the Supreme Judge, as *Jephtha* did.

If a Controversie arise between a Prince and some of the People, in a matter where the Law is silent, or doubtful, and the thing be of great Consequence, I should think the proper *Umpire,* in such a Case, should be the Body of the *People.* For in Cases where the Prince hath a Trust reposed in him, and is dispensed from the common ordinary Rules of the Law; there, if any Men find themselves aggrieved, and think the Prince acts contrary to, or beyond that Trust, who so proper to *Judge* as the Body of the *People* (who, at first, lodg'd that Trust in him) how far they meant it should extend? But if the Prince, or whoever they be in the Administration, decline that way of Determination, the Appeal then lies no where but to Heaven. Force between either Persons, who have no known Superiour on Earth, or which permits no Appeal to a Judge on Earth, being properly a state of War, wherein the Appeal lies only to Heaven, and in that State the *injured Part must judge* for himself, when he will think fit to make use of that Appeal, and put himself upon it.

To conclude, The *Power that every individual gave the Society,* when he entered into it, can never revert to the Individuals again, as long as the Society lasts, but will always remain in the Community; because without this, there can be no Community, no Common-wealth, which is contrary to the original Agreement: So also when the Society hath placed the Legislative in any Assembly of Men, to continue in them and in their Successors, *the Legislative can never revert to the People* whilst that Government lasts: Because having provided a Legislative with Power to continue forever, they have given up their Political Power to the Legislative, and cannot resume it. But if they have set Limits to the Duration of their Legislative, and made this Supreme Power in any Person, or Assembly, only temporary: Or else when by the Miscarriages of those in Authority, it is forfeited; upon the Forfeiture of their Rulers, or at the Determination of the Time set, *it reverts to the Society,* and the People have a Right to act as Supreme, and continue the Legislative in themselves, or erect a new Form, or under the old form place it in new hands, as they think good.

Locke read the myth of Genesis as Milton did, framing a defense of conscience as the ground of government, but this conscience was defined in terms of Reason.

Locke did not hesitate to call for a new settlement in regard to religion in order to facilitate this process of opening government and public affairs to the sway of Reason (*Letters concerning Toleration* [1689–1693]):

> The toleration of those that differ from others in matters of religion, is so agreeable to the Gospel of Jesus Christ, and to the genuine reason of mankind. . . . I esteem it above all things necessary to distinguish exactly the business of civil government from that of religion, and to settle the just bound that lies between the one and the other. If this be not done, there can be no end put to the controversies that will be always arising. . . . The commonwealth seems to me to be a society of men constituted only for the procuring, preserving, and advancing of their own civil interests. Civil interests I call life, liberty, and indolency of body; and the possession of outward things, such as money, lands, houses, furniture, and the like. It is the duty of the civil magistrate, by the impartial execution of equal laws, to secure unto all the people in general, and to every one of his subjects in particular, the just possession of these things belonging to this life. . . . Now the whole jurisdiction of the magistrate reaches only to these civil concernments, and all civil power, right, and dominion, is bounded and confined to the only care of promoting these things; and it neither can nor ought in any manner to be extended to the salvation of souls.[67]

In a few lines, Locke establishes the foundation for both the distinction between church and state and the inherent liberties of individuals, both keystones of the Enlightenment and of the modern age. At the same time, Locke assumes that the interests of all concerned, church, state, and individual, cohere within their mutual consent to the adjudication of reason.

A natural corollary of Locke's perspective was that the violent zeal for religion, as in the past, should be cured by rational and wise leadership. That is just the position of the Earl of Shaftsbury in his treatise "On

Enthusiasm" (1699), which made the word *enthusiasm* synonymous with fanaticism throughout the Enlightenment:

Thus, my lord, there are many panics in mankind besides merely that of fear. And thus is religion also panic; when enthusiasm of any kind gets up, as oft, on melancholy occasions, it will. For vapors naturally rise; and in bad times especially, when the spirits of men are low, as either in public calamities, or during the unwholesomeness of air or diet, or when convulsions happen in nature, storms, earthquakes, or other amazing prodigies: at this season the panic must needs run high, and the magistrate of necessity give way to it. For to apply a serious remedy, and bring the sword, or *fasces*, as a cure, must make the case more melancholy, and increase the very cause of the distemper. To forbid men's natural fears, and to endeavor the overpowering them by other fears, must needs be a most unnatural method. The magistrate, if he be any artist, should have a gentler hand; and instead of caustics, incisions, and amputations, should be using the softest balms; and with a kind sympathy entering into the concern of the people; and taking, as it were, their passion upon him should, when he has soothed and satisfied it, endeavor, by cheerful ways, to divert and heal it.

This was ancient policy: and hence (as a notable author of our nation expresses it) 'tis necessary a people should have a *public leading* in religion. For to deny the magistrate a worship, or take away a national church, is as mere enthusiasm as the notion which sets up persecution. For why should there not be public walks as well as private gardens? Why not public libraries as well as private education and home-tutors? But to prescribe bounds to fancy and speculation, to regulate men's apprehensions and religious beliefs and fears, to suppress by violence the natural passion of enthusiasm, or to endeavor to ascertain it, or reduce it to one species, or bring it under any one modification, is in truth no better sense, nor deserves a better character, than what the comedian declares of the like project in the affair of love.

Not only the visionaries and enthusiasts of all kinds were tolerated, your lordship knows, by the ancients; but, on the other side, philosophy had as free a course, and was permitted as a balance against superstition. And whilst some sects, such as the Pythagorean and later Platonic, joined in with the superstition and enthusiasm of the times; the Epicurean, the Academic, and others, were allowed to use all the force of wit and raillery against it. And thus matters were happily balanced; reason had fair play; learning and science flourished. Wonderful was the harmony and temper which arose from all these contrarieties. Thus superstition and enthusiasm were mildly treated, and being let alone they never raged to that degree as to occasion bloodshed, wars, persecutions, and devastation in the world.

But a new sort of policy, which extends itself to another world and considers the future lives and happiness of men rather than the present, has made us leap the bounds of natural humanity; and out of a supernatural charity has taught us the way of plaguing one another most devoutly. It has raised an antipathy which no temporal interest could ever do; and entailed upon us a mutual hatred to all eternity. And no uniformity in opinion (a hopeful project!) is looked on as the only expedient of this evil. The saving of souls is now the heroic passion of exalted spirits; and is become in a manner the chief care of the magistrate, and the very end of government itself.[68]

Shaftsbury's strictures on religion impose a constraint on the religious policies of the state as well as on individual persons. Just as no individual or group should fall victim to "enthusiasm," so no state should stray from the duty to seek out a national religious consensus on the basis of reason. In effect, the divine right of kings was distributed within the rule of reason, to include all aspects of human social life.

But although constitutional monarchy prospered in England, Holland, and Sweden, the absolute model of monarchy remained viable, especially in France under Louis XIII and Louis XIV. In fact, Thomas Hobbes in his *Leviathan* (1651) championed absolutism against the predations of the civil war back in his native England:

And because I find by diverse English books lately printed, that the civil wars have not yet sufficiently taught men, in what point of time it is that a Subject becomes obliged to a Conqueror; nor what is Conquest; nor how it comes about, that it obliges men to obey his laws: Therefore for farther satisfaction of men therein, I say, the point of time, wherein a man becomes subject to a Conqueror, is that point, wherein having liberty to submit to him, he consents, whether by express words, or by other sufficient sign, to be his Subject.[69]

Hobbes subtitled his book "The Matter, Form and Power of a Commonwealth, Ecclesiastical and Civil." It was (among many other things) an effective answer to Milton and has attracted admiration and controversy for its rigorous pragmatism since its first appearance. Hobbes's concentration on the issue of power is a harbinger of the intellectual climate at the close of the Enlightenment.

Louis XIV's example of absolutism was followed by Frederick William, the Great Elector of Brandenburg-Prussia (1640–1688), and Peter I of Russia (1682–1725). Louis's grandeur is still illustrated by his palace at

Versailles, just as the blighting effect of his power was demonstrated by his revocation of the Edict of Nantes in 1685. Some 200,000 Huguenots fled France, thousands died in pogroms authorized or tolerated by the king, and to this day only remnant communities have survived. Absolute monarchy had shown its taste for genocide. Reason showed itself as ineffective at preventing that in the eighteenth century as it did during the twentieth century. Politically, the Enlightenment proved unable finally to adjudicate the dispute between those who saw the agency of Reason and power as the province of rulers and those who looked rather to the inherent conscience of the people.

The Reign of Science and the Rule of Reason

Within conditions of war and struggle, the discoveries of science seemed to offer some prospect of rational order. The great powers of the sixteenth and seventeenth centuries continued to support scientists, in the tradition of François I and Leonardo da Vinci. Pope Gregory XIII gave his name to the calendrical reform in 1582, which slightly shortened the year as counted out in days, to accord with the solar cycle better. Protestant England was loath to accept this papal improvement, but since it was a more accurate calendar, Queen Anne at last promulgated it in 1704. Russia did not make the change until the Soviet Revolution, and the Orthodox Easter is still computed on the Julian calendar rather than on the present Gregorian calendar. Although the Catholic Reformation is not usually associated with the Enlightenment, the simple fact of the matter is that the method of counting our days, taken increasingly as a matter of course, came from the Vatican's efforts to reassert its authority on rational grounds.

Although the papacy had been a vital force in the encouragement of science, Galileo famously proved too much of a challenge. His embrace of the Copernican theory that the earth moved around the sun seemed to contradict the dogma that humanity was the purpose and height of God's creation. Galileo was forced to recant and kept under house arrest by the inquisition in 1634, just one year after publishing "A Dialogue Between the Two Great Systems of the World." Nonetheless, Galileo inspired René Descartes in his "Discourse on Method" (1637) to craft his method of doubting one's thoughts and perceptions:

> And as a multitude of laws often furnishes excuses for vice, so that a state is much better governed when it has but few, and those few strictly

observed, so in place of the great number of precepts of which logic is composed, I believed that I should find the following four sufficient, provided that I made a firm and constant resolve not once to omit to observe them.

The first was, never to accept anything as true when I did not recognize it clearly to be so, that is to say, to carefully avoid precipitation and prejudice, and to include in my opinions nothing beyond that which should present itself so clearly and so distinctly to my mind that I might have no occasion to doubt it.

The second was, to divide each of the difficulties which I should examine into as many portions as were possible, and as should be required for its better solution.

The third was, to conduct my thoughts in order, by beginning with the simplest objects, and those most easy to know, so as to mount little by little, as if by steps, to the most complex knowledge, and even assuming an order among those which do not naturally precede one another.

And last was, to make everywhere enumerations so complete, and surveys so wide, that I should be sure of omitting nothing.[70]

Only the fact of thought could be proved to exist; after that, Descartes held that matter followed laws of mathematics, while the mind brought one to the Spirit of God. Descartes lived in the Netherlands rather than in his native France, to some extent wary of the kind of response Galileo had received at the hands of Catholic theologians. But Descartes's example should long ago have put to rest the frequently repeated claim that Catholic Europe was inimical to the Enlightenment and to science. Catholicism was ambivalent toward pursuits guided by Reason rather than by faith, but that ambivalence should not be caricatured as rejection.

With its claim that the methods of science can be applied to human affairs in all their range, the Enlightenment became a dominant cultural force in Europe. It was more than an intellectual fashion; it was a transnational cause. Descartes's program of explaining the material world mathematically was taken up by Sir Isaac Newton in *Mathematical Principles of Natural Philosophy* (1687). His laws of motion revolutionized the physical understanding of the universe and dominated the imagination of Europe.

Newton's rules for reasoning (in which Descartes's are axiomatic) are economical and now recognized almost universally. These are worth considering as Newton composed them, because they became self-evident for the Enlightenment:

Rule I: We are to admit of no more causes of natural things than such as are both true and sufficient to explain their appearances.

To this purpose the philosophers say that Nature does nothing in vain when less will serve; for Nature is pleased with simplicity, and affects not the pomp of superfluous causes.

Rule II: Therefore to the same natural effects we must, as far as possible, assign the same causes.

As to respiration in a man and in a beast; the descent of stones in Europe and in America; the light of our culinary fire and of the sun; the reflection of light in the earth, and in the planets.

Rule III: The qualities of bodies, which admit neither intensification nor remission of degrees, and which are found to belong to all bodies within the reach of our experiments, are to be esteemed the universal qualities of all bodies whatsoever.

For since the qualities of bodies are only known to us by experiments, we are to hold for universal all such as universally agree with experiments; and such as are not liable to diminution can never be quite taken away. We are certainly not to relinquish the evidence of experiments for the sake of dreams and vain fictions of our own devising; nor are we to recede from the analogy of Nature, which is wont to be simple, and always consonant with itself. We no other way know the extension of bodies than by our senses, nor do these reach it in all bodies; but because we perceive extension in all that are sensible, therefore we ascribe it universally to all others also. That abundance of bodies are hard, we learn by experience; and because the hardness of the whole arises from the hardness of the parts, we therefore justly infer the hardness of the undivided particles not only of the bodies we feel but of all others. That all bodies are impenetrable, we gather not from reason but from sensation. The bodies which he handle we find impenetrable, and thence conclude impenetrability to be a universal property of all bodies whatsoever. That all bodies are movable, and endowed with certain power (which we call the inertia) of persevering in their motion, or in their rest, we only infer from the like properties observed in the bodies which we have seen. The extension, hardness, impenetrability, mobility, and inertia of the whole, result from the extension, hardness, impenetrability, mobility, and inertia of the parts; and hence we conclude the least particles of all bodies to be also all extended, and hard and impenetrable, and movable, and endowed with their proper inertia. And this is the foundation of all philosophy. Moreover, that the divided but contiguous particles of bodies may be separated from one another, is matter of observation; and, in the participles that remain undivided, our minds are able to distinguish yet lesser parts, as is mathematically demonstrated. But whether the parts so distinguished, and not yet divided, may, by the powers of Nature, be actually divided and separated from one another, we cannot certainly determine. Yet, had we the proof of but one experiment that any undivided particle, in breaking a hard and solid body, suffered a division, we might by virtue of this rule conclude that the undivided as well as the divided particles may be divided and actually separated to infinity.

Lastly, if it universally appears, by experiments and astronomical observations, that all bodies about the earth gravitate towards the earth, and that in proportion to the quantity of matter which they severally contain; that the moon likewise, according to the quantity of its matter, gravitates towards the earth; that, on the other hand, our sea gravitates towards the moon; and all the planets one towards another; and the comets in like manner towards the sun; we must, in consequence of this rule, universally allow that all bodies whatsoever are endowed with a principle of mutual gravitation. For the arguments from the appearances concludes with more force for the universal gravitation of all bodies than for their impenetrability; of which, among those in the celestial regions, we have no experiments, nor any manner of observations. Not that I affirm gravity to be essential to bodies: by their vis insita I mean nothing but their inertia. This is immutable. Their gravity is diminished as they recede from the earth.

Rule IV: In experimental philosophy we are to look upon propositions inferred by general induction from phenomena as accurately or very nearly true, notwithstanding any contrary hypothesis that may be imagined, till such time as other phenemona occur, by which they may either be made more accurate, or liable to exceptions.

This rule we must follow, that the argument of induction may not be evaded by hypotheses.[71]

These conceptions of an ordered world, accessible by observation and reason, became self-evident truths in Enlightenment Europe. Although Newton himself was actively engaged in other forms of philosophical thinking, including hermeticism and Platonism, and at the end of his life described all his efforts in comparison to a child playing at the seaside, without cognizance of the vast ocean beyond, his Aristotelian and mechanical account of the cosmos was embraced throughout Europe.

With the influence of Newton's approach, the principle of reasoning from induction and inference on the basis of observation and experiment, rather than deductively from a priori principles, became standard in every field of human endeavor, including religion. Although the twentieth century saw the eclipse of Newton's views of particles (with Heisenberg's Uncertainty Principle) and of gravitation (with Einstein's General Theory of Relativity), his insistence upon induction rather than deduction in critical thinking remains dominant. "*The analogy of Nature, which is wont to be simple, and always consonant with itself"* indeed became "the foundation of all philosophy." It appeared that Nature (conceived of as a cosmic, anthropomorphic teacher) had herself healed the breach between matter and mind that Descartes had identified.

Newton gave logical rigor to an almost poetic veneration of Nature, an inheritance from the Renaissance that is characteristic of the Enlightenment. In 1620, Francis Bacon had written in his *Novum Organum* (1620): "Man, being the servant and interpreter of Nature, can do and understand so much and so much only as he has observed in fact or in thought of the course of nature: beyond this he neither knows anything nor can do anything."

Reason now came to the service of revelation, illuminating the mind of God insofar as it influenced Nature. In 1712, Joseph Addison in England wrote a paraphrase of Psalm 19, which was subsequently set to music written by Franz Josef Haydn, and the hymn is still used in many churches:

> The spacious firmament on high,
> With all the blue ethereal sky,
> And spangled heavens, a shining frame,
> Their great Original proclaim.
> The unwearied sun from day to day
> Does his Creator's power display;
> And publishes to every land
> The work of an almighty hand.

Addison's paraphrase is typical of the English Enlightenment in its stress upon the regular pattern of creation in its relation to the recognition of God.

In fact, the final stanza of Addison's paraphrase makes it clear beyond a doubt that, for him, the existence of God is an inference of reason:

> What though in solemn silence all
> Move round the dark terrestrial ball?
> What though no real voice nor sound
> Amid their radiant orbs be found?
> In reason's ear they all rejoice,
> And utter forth a glorious voice;
> For every singing as they shine,
> "The hand that made us is divine."

Writing in a period in which the angels in heaven were being steadily replaced by laws of nature, Addison paraphrased the psalm along the lines of Paul's insight in Romans (1:19-20): the natural world attests the invisible power and transcendence of God.

Alexander Pope wrote with considerably less reverence than Addison of Newton's achievement in his "An Essay on Man" (1733), but his puckish humor attests the range of Newton's influence:

> Superior beings, when of late they saw
> A influential mortal man unfold all Nature's law,
> Admired such wisdom in an earthly shape,
> And show'd a NEWTON as we show an ape.
> Could he, whose rules the rapid comet bind,
> Describe or fix one movement of his mind?

The very angels Newton supplanted are made to show him off in admiration. He seemed to have plumbed the mind of God.

Reason itself came to be used to frame political settlements that were more just and durable than the monarchies of the Middle Ages, the Renaissance, and the Reformation. The divine right of kings was replaced by the balance of powers among interested citizens and their inclusion in a social covenant or compact. Jean-Jacques Rousseau and Montesquieu were especially influential as theorists who built upon the insights of John Locke. The effect of their ideas in France and in Britain's American colonies was literally revolutionary.

Rousseau confidently brought the insight of reason together with the sensibilities of religion, as he has a priest articulate in his 1762 novel, *Emile*:

> I believe, therefore, that the world is governed by a wise and powerful *Will*. I see it, or rather I feel it; and this is of importance for me to know. But is the world eternal, or is it created? Are things derived from one self-existent principle, or are there two or more, and what is their essence? Of all this I know nothing, nor do I see that it is necessary I should. In proportion as such knowledge may become interesting I will endeavor to acquire it: but further than this I give up all such idle disquisitions, which serve only to make me discontented with myself, which are useless in practice, and are above my understanding.
>
> You will remember, however, that I am not dictating my sentiments to you, but only explaining what they are. Whether matter be eternal or only

created, whether it have a passive principle or not, certain it is that the whole universe is one design, and sufficiently displays one intelligent agent: for I see no part of this system what is not under regulation, or that does not concur to one and the same end; viz., that of preserving the present and established order of things. That Being, whose will is his deed, whose principle of action is in himself—that Being, in a word, whatever it be, that gives motion to all parts of the universe, and governs all things, I call GOD.

To this term I affix the ideas of intelligence, power, and will, which I have collected from the order of things; and to these I add that of goodness, which is a necessary consequence of their union. But I am not at all the wiser concerning the essence of the Being to which I give these attributes. He remains at an equal distance from my senses and my understanding. The more I think of him, the more I am confounded. I know of a certainty that he exists, and that this existence is independent of any of his creatures. I know also that my existence is dependent on his, and that every being I know is in the same situation as myself. I perceive the deity in all his works, I feel him within me, and behold him in every object around me: but I no sooner endeavor to contemplate what he is in himself—I no sooner enquire where he is, and what is his substance, than he eludes the strongest efforts of my imagination; and my bewildered understanding is convinced of its own weakness.

Rousseau combined Locke's understanding of a social contract among human beings and between human beings and their God with Milton's numinous sense of the primordial covenant that bound all living things together.

Yet the power of this unitive bond was such that some thinkers represented the thought that the balance of interests that produced justice was a more compelling truth than even the existence of God. One of this emerging strand of intellectuals was the Baron de Montesquieu, here speaking in a letter written in 1721:

Justice is a true relation between two things: this relation is always the same, no matter who examines it, whether it be God, or an angel, or lastly, man himself.

It is true that men do not always perceive these relations; often even when they do perceive them, they turn away from them, and their self-interest is what they perceive most clearly. Justice cries aloud, but her voice can hardly be heard among the tumult of the passions.

Men can commit unjust acts because it is to their advantage to do so and because they prefer their own contentment to that of others. They always act from selfish motives: no man is evil gratuitously: there must be a deter-mining cause, and that cause is always selfishness.

But God cannot possibly commit an unjust act: once we assume that he perceives what is just he must of necessity act accordingly, for since he is self-sufficient and in need of nothing, he would otherwise be the most wicked of beings, since he has no selfish interests.

Thus if there were no God, we would still be obliged to venerate justice, that is, we should do everything possible to resemble that being of whom we have such an exalted notion and who, if he exits, would necessarily be just. Free though we might be from the yoke of religion, we should never be free from the bonds of equity.

Despite such skeptical voices, in the conviction and the experience of this period, the apogee of the Enlightenment, religion and reason went hand in hand. In Catholic France, Blaise Pascal, a brilliant mathemati-cian who died in 1662, expressed the poetic conviction that rigorous logic and the revelation of the God of Abraham, Isaac, and Jacob were complementary. To him, in his posthumously published "Thoughts," the truth of Christ was demonstrable in nature and history (*Pensées* 617):

Let us consider that, since the beginning of the world, the expectation or worship of the Messiah has subsisted without interruption; that there have been men who said that God had revealed to them that a Redeemer who would save His people would be born; that Abraham came afterwards to say that it had been revealed to him that He would be born of him by a son that he would have; that Jacob declared that among his twelve children He would be born of Judah; that Moses and the prophets came afterwards to announce the time and manner of His coming; that they said that the law which they had was valid only until the coming of the Messiah's; that until then it would be perpetual, but that the other would endure forever; that thus their law, or that of the Messiah of which it was a promise, would always be on earth; that in fact it has always lasted; that finally Jesus Christ came in all the foretold circumstances. That is admirable.[72]

Secular thinkers seem never to tire of remarking on the paradox of Pascal's faithful rationality and rational faith, but Pascal here expresses widespread convictions of the Enlightenment. Reason and revelation both derived from the mind of God.

With no less vehemence, Jonathan Edwards of Connecticut insisted in his *Treatise Concerning Religious Affections* (1746) that emotions have their role in divine revelation:

Holy affections are not heat without light; but evermore arise from some information of the understanding, some spiritual instruction that the mind receives, some light or actual knowledge. The child of God is graciously affected, because he sees and understands something more of divine things than he did before, more of God or Christ and of the glorious things exhibited in the gospel; he has some clearer and better view than he had before, when he was not affected; either he receives some understanding of divine things that is new to him; or has his former knowledge renewed after the view was decayed. . . .

Now there are many affections which don't arise from any light in the understanding. And when it is thus, it is a sure evidence that those affections are not spiritual, let them be ever so high. Indeed they have some new apprehensions which they had not before. Such is the nature of man, that it is impossible his mind should be affected, unless it be by something that he apprehends, or that his mind conceives of. But in many persons those apprehensions or conceptions that they have, wherewith they are affected, have nothing of the nature of knowledge or instruction in them. As for instance; when a person is affected with a lively idea, suddenly excited in his mind, of some shape, or very beautiful pleasant form of countenance, or some shining light, or other glorious outward appearance: here is something apprehended or conceived by the mind; but there is nothing of the nature of instruction in it: persons become never the wiser by such things, or more knowing about God, or a mediator between God and man, or the way of salvation by Christ, or anything contained in any of the doctrines of the gospel. Persons by these external ideas have no further acquaintance with God, as to any of the attributes or perfections of his nature; nor have they any further understanding of his word, or any of his ways or works. Truly spiritual and gracious affections are not raised after this manner: they arise from the enlightening of the understanding to understand the things that are taught of God and Christ, in a new manner, the coming to a new understanding of the excellent nature of God, and his wonderful perfections, some new view of Christ in his spiritual excellencies and fullness, or things opened to him in a new manner, that appertain to the way of salvation by Christ, whereby he now sees how it is, and understands those divine and spiritual doctrines which once were foolishness to him.[73]

Edwards understood that Reason was not merely empirical, but reached into the realm of emotions, so that a human being could stand before his creator with integrity. Enlightenment was not a matter of arid deduction, but of a complete transformation of the thinking and believing person.

The Unraveling of Reason

Edwards and Pascal represent the Enlightenment at its most confident. After them, events and inquiry turned against confidence in the harmony of reason and revelation, as reason, empirical phenomena, and emotions all seemed to go their separate ways. Descartes had already observed that matter and mind were on different planes, and this divide reached within reason itself with the thought of Immanuel Kant. He believed that pure reason, reflection on phenomena, and the practical reason that leads to ethical judgments are different kinds of cognition.

Kant also argued that the exercise of reason was actually inhibited by religion, in a way that has influenced philosophers to this day. In his essay, "What Is Enlightenment?" (1784), Kant wrote:

> If we are asked, "Do we now live in an *enlightened age?*" the answer is, "No," but we do live in an *age of enlightenment*. As things now stand, much is lacking which prevents men from being, or easily becoming, capable of correctly using their own reason in religious matters with assurance and free from outside direction. But, on the other hand, we have clear indications that the field has now been opened wherein men may freely deal with these things and that the obstacles to general enlightenment or the release from self-imposed tutelage are gradually being reduced. In this respect, this is the age of enlightenment, or the century of Frederick.
>
> A prince who does not find it unworthy of himself to say that he holds it to be his duty to prescribe nothing to men in religious matters but to give them complete freedom while renouncing the haughty name of *tolerance*, is himself enlightened and deserves to be esteemed by the grateful world and posterity as the first, at least from the side of government, who divested the human race of its tutelage and left each man free to make use of his reason in matters of conscience.[74]

Kant's confidence in the sufficiency of reason to determine the policy of the state in regard to religion is surprising in two ways. First, the role of intuition in Kant's analysis of reason, especially practical reason, might have made for a less confident assertion of reason's public capacity to correct religion.[75] Second, Kant's praise of Frederick shows the extent to which his own program of Enlightenment was tied to a distinctly pro-imperial conception of authority, rather than to the ideals that guided the American Revolution and were about to unleash the French Revolution five years after Kant wrote. That kind of power was necessary, in his mind, to free people from the tyranny of religion:

For this enlightenment, however, nothing is required but freedom, and indeed the most harmless among all the things to which this term can properly be applied. It is the freedom to make public use of one's reason at every point. But I hear on all sides, "Do not argue!" The officer says: "Do not argue but drill!" The tax collector: "Do not argue but pay!" The cleric: "Do not argue but believe!"

In Kant's essay, the shift from freedom of religion to freedom from religion is achieved as if it were without effort.

Confident children of the Enlightenment such as Thomas Jefferson could likewise conceive of God as requiring no miracles to support faith in his providence. His famous colleague, Benjamin Franklin, in popular terms a more influential thinker, put this Enlightenment piety in plain language in a letter to the president of Yale College, and he articulated a view of theology and of Jesus that characterizes liberal Christianity to this day (Letter to Ezra Stiles, 1790):

> Here is my creed. I believe in one God, Creator of the universe. That he governs it by his Providence. That he ought to be worshipped. That the most acceptable service we render to him is doing good to his other children. That the soul of Man is immortal, and will be treated with justice in another life respecting its conduct in this. These I take to be the fundamental principles of all sound religion, and I regard them as you do in whatever sect I meet with them.
>
> As to Jesus of Nazareth, my opinion of whom you particularly desire, I think the system of morals and his religion, as he left them to us, the best the world ever saw or is likely to see; but I apprehend it has received various corrupting changes, and I have, with most of the present dissenters in England, some doubts as to his divinity; tho' it is a question I do not dogmatize upon, having never studied it, and think it needless to busy myself with it now, when I expect soon an opportunity of know the truth with less trouble.[76]

Believers who insisted on the rational order of the universe without miraculous intervention, such as Jefferson and Franklin, were called *Deists*. David Hume pressed the logic of Deism to it inevitable conclusion in his "Essay on Miracles" (1768), a classic of the Enlightenment during a period that saw rational order and revelation go their separate ways: "A miracle is a violation of the laws of nature; and as a firm and unalterable experience has established these laws, the proof against a miracle, from the nature of the fact, is as entire as any argument from experience can possibly be imagined."[77]

The growing divide between philosophy and religion was reinforced by political turmoil. Ironically, the French Revolution unleashed its Reign of Terror against political enemies in the name of Reason, with Catholic priests required to convert to the Cult of Pure Reason, or face death (Records of Chalons-sur-Marne, 1794):

> A detachment of cavalry, national constabulary, and hussars mingled together, to strengthen the bonds of fraternity, led the march, and on their pennant there were these words: "Reason guides us and enlightens us." It was followed by the company of cannoneers of Chalons, preceded by a banner with this inscription: "Death to the Tyrants." This company was followed by a cart loaded with broken chains, on which were six prisoners of war and a few wounded being cared for by a surgeon; this cart carried two banners, front and back, with these two inscriptions, "Humanity is a Republican virtue" and "They were very mistaken in fighting for tyrants."

As the French Revolution degraded itself with tactics of violence and humiliation, political theories of the Enlightenment seemed to be called into question by experience, and Napoleon Bonaparte's rise and astounding conquests pulled all of Europe into a reactionary posture of supporting the old monarchies and traditional settlements with new fervor.

The nineteenth century saw a reaction against the Enlightenment in religion as well as in politics. Churches attempted to shore up their claims of authority intellectually and legally, and professing religion became a formal requirement of attending universities in Europe. Increasingly, philosophers took refuge in the insistence that reason is worked out in the mind rather than in the world. F. D. E. Schleiermacher in Germany pioneered an idea cherished by the Romantic movement, that insight is a matter of intuition and sensibility, not deduction from observation. He wrote to his future wife in 1807, to console her on her first husband's death:

> What would, or what ought to satisfy you in a future life, you cannot know; for you cannot know the order that prevails there. But when you are removed thither you will know it, and then there, as little as here, you will desire what would be opposed to it, and most assuredly it will afford you as full and rapturous satisfaction. But if your imagination suggests to you a merging in the great All, do not let this fill you with bitter anguish. Do not conceive of it as a lifeless, but as a living commingling—as the highest life. Is not the ideal toward which we are all striving even in the world, though we never reach it, the merging of the life of each in the life of all, and the

putting away from us of every semblance of a separate existence? If then he lives in God, and you love him eternally in God, as you knew God and loved God in him, can you conceive of anything more glorious or more delightful? Is it not the highest goal which love can reach, compared with which every feeling which clings to the personal life, and springs from that alone, is as nothing?[78]

More influential than Schleiermacher over the long term, G. W. F. Hegel developed a dialectical argument to the effect that, even with its setbacks (some of which he was undoubtedly living through), the progress of history was a matter of interactions of conflicting ideas and their synthesis with what he called spirit. Indeed, Hegel described the interactions of the state and religion as crucial within this process, and culminating in a single uniting power. He even argued that the end of freedom would ultimately reveal that the state and religion are not separate after all ("The Relationship of Religion to the State," 1831):

The state is the true mode of actuality; in it, the true ethical will attains actuality and the spirit lives in its true form. Religion is divine knowledge, the knowledge which human beings have of God and of themselves in God. This is divine wisdom and the field of absolute truth. But there is a second wisdom, the wisdom of the world, and the question arises as to its relationship to the former, divine wisdom.

In general, religion and the foundation of the state are one and the same thing—they are *identical in and for themselves*. In the patriarchal condition and the Jewish theocracy, the two are not yet distinct and are still outwardly identical. Nevertheless, the two are also different, and in due course, they become strictly separated from one another; but then they are once more posited as genuinely identical. That the two have then attained that unity which has being in and for itself follows from what has been said; religion is knowledge of the highest truth, and this truth, defined more precisely, is *free spirit*. In religion, human beings are free before God. In making their will conform to the divine will, they are not opposed to the divine will but have themselves within it; they are free inasmuch as they have succeeded, in the religious cult, in overcoming the division. The state is merely *freedom in the world,* in actuality. The essential concept here is that concept of freedom which a people carries in its self-consciousness, for the concept of freedom is realized in the state, and an essential aspect of this realization is the consciousness of freedom with being in and for itself. Peoples who do not know that human beings are free in and for themselves live in a benighted state both with regard to their constitution and to their religion.—There is *one* concept of freedom in both religion and the state.

This *one* concept is the highest thing which human beings have, and it is realized by them. A people which has a bad concept of God also has a bad state, a bad government, and bad laws.[79]

Karl Marx attempted to work out Hegel's system in political and economic terms. Marx's own orientation was not totalitarian, but his development of Hegel's idealism would contribute to the command and control states of the twentieth century. That was not because Marx or Hegel favored a return to divine right as a model of authority, but because they saw the powers of human community flowing into a union of power. (In fact, Hegel's dialectical approach to the emergence of spirit has recently been revived in the interests of an antiauthoritarian perspective.[80]) Marx wrote in 1842 on the plight of peasants in the Moselle region:

Therefore, to resolve the difficulty, the administration and the people administered both equally need a *third* element, which is *political* without being official and hence does not proceed from bureaucratic premises, an element which is likewise civil without being directly involved in private interests and their needs. This supplementary element which *bears the mind of a citizen concerned with the state* and *the heart of one concerned with civil society* is the free press.[81]

The European revolutions of 1848, partially encouraged by Marx's thought but pushed forward by famine and fierce pressures for democracy,[82] exacerbated the sense that a dedication to reason was unleashing forces of chaos, and the American Civil War confirmed that impression. Finally, however, two intellectual developments insured that reason and revelation would no longer be seen as complementary, despite Hegel's attempt to finesse a hybrid with his conception of freedom ensconced in power.

With the publication of Charles Darwin's *On the Origin of Species* in 1859, evolution seemed to provide an elegant account of the taxonomy of living beings, without reference to God. Darwin's theory has recently been restated in terms perhaps more accessible than his own:

The fact, as we have seen, that all past and present organic beings constitute one grand natural system, with group subordinate to group, and with extinct groups often falling in between recent groups, is intelligible on the theory of natural selection with its contingencies of extinction and divergence of character. On these same principles we see how it is, that the mutual affinities of the species and genera within each class are so complex and circuitous. We see why certain characters are far more serviceable than others for classification;—why adaptive characters, though of paramount importance to the being, are of hardly any importance in classification; why characters derived from rudimentary parts, though of no service to the being, are often of high classificatory value; and why embryological characters are the most valuable of all. The real affinities of all organic beings are due to inheritance or community of descent. The natural system is a genealogical arrangement, in which we have to discover the lines of descent by the most permanent characters, however slight their vital importance may be.[83]

In 1863, the publication of Ernst Renan's *La vie de Jésus* revolutionized the study of Jesus and marks the moment when the Enlightenment's compromise between faith and rationality came permanently unstuck. Renan believed that Jesus could be appreciated—and could only be appreciated—in historical terms, apart from dogma:

Jesus, it is seen, never in his action went out of the Jewish circle. Although his sympathy for all the despised of orthodoxy led him to admit the heathen into the kingdom of God, although he had more than once resided in a pagan country, and once or twice he is found in kindly relations with unbelievers, it may be said that his life was passed entirely in the little world, close and narrow as it was, in which he was born. The Greek and Roman countries heard nothing of him; his name does not figure in profane authors until a hundred years later, and then only indirectly, in connection with seditious movements provoked by his doctrine, or persecutions of which his disciples were the object. Within the heart even of Judaism, Jesus did not make any durable impression. Philo, who died about the year 50, has no glimpse of him. Josephus, born in the year 37, and writing in the last years of the century, mentions his execution in a few lines, as an event of secondary importance; and in the enumeration of the sects of his time, he omits the Christians. The *Mischna*, again, presents no trace of the new school; the passages in the two Gemaras in which the founder of Christianity is named, do not carry us back beyond the fourth or fifth century. The essential work of Jesus was the creation around him of a circle of disciples in whom he inspired a boundless attachment, and in whose breast he implanted the germ of his doctrine. To have made himself beloved, so much that after his death they did not cease to love him, this was the crowning work of Jesus, and that which most impressed his contemporaries. His doctrine was so little dogmatical, that he never thought of writing it or having it written. A man became his disciple, not by believing this or that, but by following and loving him. A few sentences treasured up in the memory, and above all, his moral type, and the impression which he had produced, were all that remained of him. Jesus is not a founder of dogmas, a maker of symbols; he is the world's initiator of a new spirit.[84]

Darwin's science refuted the picture of creation in the book of Genesis, and Renan's history refuted any deification of Jesus. When science and history asserted they could overthrow religion, religion reacted, and the post-Enlightenment age (today called postmodernism)[85] was born.

Discussion Questions

1. Why did Europe enter the Renaissance when it did?

2. Which elements of Renaissance thinking most influenced the Reformation?

3. In what ways were Luther and Calvin similar and different in their approach to reforming the theology of their time?

4. How did the theology of the Roman Catholic Church emerge as a result of the Reformation?

5. Describe how different readings of the book of Genesis influenced the political theory of the Enlightenment.

6. Who would you say best represents the ideals of the Enlightenment?

CHAPTER 13

THE MODERNIZATION OF JUDAISM

Jacob Neusner

For Judaism, modern times begin with political change in the status of the Jews. The American Constitution (1787) and the French Revolution (1789) turned the Jews into undifferentiated citizens before the law. They had formed a community separate from the politics and culture of the lands where they lived, and now they had to rethink their definition of the community of holy Israel (not to be confused with the contemporary State of Israel). The result was the development of Reform Judaism, which defined the Jews as a religious community, Jews by religion, Germans or French or British or Americans by nationality. The changes brought about by Reform Judaism provoked a negative reaction on the part of Orthodox Judaism. A centrist group, Conservative Judaism, mediated. All three Judaic communities dealt with the same issues that the modern situation raised, a new set of questions without precedent in prior times.

"Israel" as the Holy People: Answering the Question Raised by Christianity and Islam

From ancient times to the nineteenth century, the Jews in Western civilization formed islands in an ocean of Gentiles, Christian in most of Europe, Muslim in the Near and Middle East. They were always and only "Israel," meaning, the holy people of God, subject to a single sovereignty, that of the Torah. They spoke their own language (in Europe, Yiddish), just as other ethnic and religious groups spoke their respective languages.

They wore distinctive clothing. They ate only their own food. They controlled their own sector of the larger economy and ventured outside of it only seldom; and, in all, they formed a distinct and distinctive group. What this meant is simple. Not only in theology but also in social reality Jews were always that holy people of Israel and only Israel. They did not aspire to be anything else but what they believed God had made them. The received rabbinic system that we met in chapter 3 explained their social condition. They had no difficulty identifying themselves in the stories they read in Scripture, their way of life in the laws set forth in the Mishnah and its commentaries, their view of matters in the exegeses of Scripture laid out in the interpretation of the ancient sages. So the Jews for a long time formed a caste, a distinct and clearly defined group—but within the hierarchy ordered by the castes of the society at hand.

The normative system could explain how and why Jews should be solely "Israel." But that system could not explain how they could be both "Israel" and something else. No one until the nineteenth century had ever imagined that a Jew belonged to any community other than the community of Judaism, "Israel." A secular definition of "Israel" lay beyond the community's imagining. But with the rise of the nation-state the urgent question emerged: how and why be *both* Jewish *and* American or Jewish and German or Jewish and French or Jewish and British? Indeed, in 1807, Emperor Napoleon convened in Paris a Sanhedrin of French rabbis to ask exactly that question: are you members of the Jewish nation or the French nation?

For reasons having little to do with the Jews, beginning in the late eighteenth century, political change in Christian Europe aimed at breaking down the differences that distinguished one religio-ethnic group from another. The new, totalitarian politics of the nation-state meant to form of them all a single nation, a body of citizens equal before the law and uniform in culture as well. That meant the Jews had to redefine the very character of the "Israel" of which the Torah spoke. In chapter 12 we met one consequence, Zionism. Now we address the two most important Judaic religious systems, Reform Judaism and integrationist Orthodox Judaism (terms defined presently), that responded to the new political order of the West. We take note also of a third Judaic religious system, Conservative Judaism, formed in response to the two primary systems and proposing to mediate between them. But among the three, as we shall see, Reform defined the issues in the modernization of Judaism.

The modern period in the history of Judaism in the West began with wrenching political changes: the American Constitution in 1787, and the French Revolution in 1789. The U.S. Constitution accorded equality before the law. The French Revolution treated as citizens all people, whatever their culture or religion. This policy was expressed in the promise, "To the Jews as a distinct nation, nothing, to the Jews as individual citizens, everything." The nation-state demanded conformity of all citizens to a common nationalism. The Jews in both countries and elsewhere in the West had to define for themselves a way of being Jewish and practicing Judaism that took account of the change in their status. They had formerly been identified only as Jews, part of the holy people, Israel. Now they had to define themselves as both Jewish and American or Jewish and German or Jewish and French. They no longer formed a distinct group separate from the larger society but were supposed to be like everybody else.

In France, Germany, Britain, and America the solution was found in freedom of religion. This meant that people could differ from their neighbors by reason of their religious convictions, but not by reason of national loyalty. The mark of the political shift for Jewry was the definition of Jews as "Germans of the Mosaic persuasion" or as "Americans by nationality, Jews by religion." The nation-state, with its concept of the citizen equal before the law and its rejection of mediating powers vested in autonomous communities, thus promised political emancipation, but demanded national conformity.

Emancipation

A process called "emancipation"—part of a larger movement to afford equal rights of citizenship before the law to serfs, women, slaves, and Catholics (in Protestant countries, for instance, England and Ireland)—encompassed the Jews. The historian Benzion Dinur defines this process of emancipation as follows:

> Jewish emancipation denotes the abolition of disabilities and inequities applied specially to Jews, the recognition of Jews as equal to other citizens, and the formal granting of the rights and duties of citizenship. Essentially the legal act of emancipation should have been simply the expression of the diminution of social hostility and psychological aversion toward Jews in the host nation . . . but the antipathy was not obliterated and constantly hampered the realization of equality even after it had been proclaimed by the state and included in the law.[1]

The political changes that fall into the process of the Jews' emancipation—the acceptance of the Jews as citizens—began in the eighteenth century and in a half-century affected the long-term stability that had characterized the Jews' social and political life from Christian Rome onward. These political changes raised questions that the Jews had not previously found urgent and, it follows, also precipitated reflection on problems formerly neglected.

Dinur traces three periods in the history of the Jews' emancipation, from 1740 to 1789, ending with the French Revolution, to which we have already made reference; then from 1789 to 1878, from the French Revolution to the Congress of Berlin, when in many countries Jews and others were politically emancipated; and from 1878 to 1933, from the Congress of Berlin to the rise of the Nazis to power in Germany. The first period marks the point during the French Enlightenment when the emancipation of the Jews first came under discussion. The second marked the period in which as the nation-states emerged in Western and Central Europe, the new governments accorded to the Jews the rights of citizens. The third brought to the fore a period of a racism, including the secular, political anti-Semitism that in the end annihilated the Jews of Europe.

1740–1789: In the first period advocates of the Jews' emancipation maintained that religious intolerance accounted for the low caste status assigned to the Jews. Liberating the Jews would mark another stage in overcoming religious intolerance. In the second period, in the West but not in Russia, the Jews were accorded the rights and duties of citizenship. Dinur explains: "It was stressed that keeping the Jews in a politically limited and socially inferior status was incompatible with the principle of civic equality . . . 'it is the objective of every political organization to protect the natural rights of man,' hence, 'all citizens have the right to all the liberties and advantages of citizens, without exception.'" At that time Jews entered the political and cultural life of the Western nations, including that of their overseas empires (hence Moroccan and Algerian Jews received French citizenship, but evacuated their homelands when the French left Morocco and Algeria in the 1960s).

1789–1878: During this second period, Reform Judaism reached its first stage of development, beginning in Germany. Jews were able to hold together the two things they deemed inseparable—their desire to remain Jewish, and their wish also to be one with their "fellow citizens." By the middle of the nineteenth century, Reform had reached full expression and had won the support of a sizable part of German Jewry. In reaction against Reform, Orthodoxy came into existence. Affirming the received heritage of law and theology, Orthodoxy in the Western democracies also asked how Judaism could coexist with German-ness, meaning, how Jews could have citizenship in a republic of undifferentiated citizens.

1878–1933: In the third period, anti-Semitism as a political ideology and social movement attained power. Jews began to realize that, in Dinur's words, "the state's legal recognition of Jewish civic and political equality does not automatically bring social recognition of this equality." The Jews continued to form a separate group; they were racially "inferior." The effect of the new racism would be felt in the twentieth century. The Judaisms of the twentieth century raised the questions of political repression and economic dislocation, as Judaisms faced the Jews of Eastern Europe and America.

The Jews of Western Europe and the United States, preoccupied with change in their political position, formed only a small minority of the Jews of the world—the Western frontier of the Jewish people. But their confrontation with political change defined the pattern. They were the ones to invent the Judaisms of the nineteenth century, and these Judaisms have persisted through the twentieth and into the twenty-first centuries.

The Principal Judaisms of Modernity: The Reform and Orthodox Judaic Religious Systems

Between 1800 and 1850 two main systems took shape. Reform Judaism was the first Western Judaism, coming to expression in Germany in the early part of the nineteenth century. Reform Judaism made important changes first in liturgy, when it accepted use of the organ on the Sabbath and encouraged rabbis to give sermons, then in doctrine, regarding the Jews not as a holy people but as a religious community, and finally in the way of life of the received Rabbinic Judaism that we met in chapter 3. In this third aspect, Reform Judaism gave up dietary restrictions (not eating pork) and other practices that separated Jews from their Gentile neighbors. Reform Judaism recognized the legitimacy of making changes and regarded change as reform. It did this as part of a project to define Judaism as a religion in the Western model, a matter of religious belief and behavior, not an encompassing tradition permeating culture and politics as well. That would leave space for Jews to participate also in German culture and nationality.

The second system was Orthodox Judaism. It reacted to Reform and reaffirmed the received law and theology, but held that one could participate both in Judaism and in Western culture. Orthodox Judaism reached its first expression in the middle of the nineteenth century. Orthodox Judaism addressed the issue of change and held that Judaism lies beyond history; it is the work of God; it constitutes a set of facts of the same order as the facts of nature. Hence change is not reform, and Reform Judaism is not Judaism. But, at the same time, in principle no different from Reform Judaism, Orthodox Judaism affirmed that one could devote time to science, and not only to Torah study; that affirmation stood for an accommodation with modern politics and culture, different only in degree from the Reform compromise.

The Judaic systems had three traits in common. First, each of these Judaic systems asked how one could be both Jewish and something else, that is, also a citizen, a member of a nation in addition to, or instead of, the holy nation of Israel. Second, it defined *Judaism* (that is, its system) as a religion viewed as belief and ethics, so leaving ample space for that something else, namely, nationality, whether German ("*Deutschtum und Judentum,*" German-ness and Jewish-ness) or British or French or American. Third, both Judaisms appealed to history to prove the continuity between its system and the received Rabbinic Judaism.

Defining Reform Judaism: The Pittsburgh Platform of 1885

For Reform Judaism in the nineteenth century, the full and authoritative statement of the system—its worldview, with profound implications on its way of life, and its theory of what is Israel and who is an Israelite—came to expression not in Europe, but in America. An assembly in Pittsburgh in 1885 of Reform rabbis took up the issues facing Reform Judaism and made an authoritative statement on them.

What is decisive in the Pittsburgh platform is its formulation of the issue of Israel as political circumstances defined it. The view of Israel as God's people, a supernatural polity, living out its social existence under God's Torah, had been critical to Rabbinic Judaism. The way of life—one of sanctification—and the worldview—one of persistent reference to the Torah for rules of conduct, on the one side, and of the explanation of conduct, on the other—began in the basic conception of who is Israel:

> We recognize in the Mosaic legislation a system of training the Jewish peo-
> ple for its mission during its national life in Palestine, and today we accept
> as binding only its moral laws and maintain only such ceremonies as ele-
> vate and sanctify our lives, but reject all such as are not adapted to the
> views and habits of modern civilization. . . . We hold that all such Mosaic
> and Rabbinical laws as regular diet, priestly purity, and dress originated in
> ages and under the influence of ideas entirely foreign to our present men-
> tal and spiritual state. . . . Their observance in our days is apt rather to
> obstruct than to further modern spiritual elevation. . . . We recognize in
> the modern era of universal culture of heart and intellect the approaching
> of the realization of Israel's great messianic hope for the establishment of
> the kingdom of truth, justice, and peace among all men. We consider our-
> selves no longer a nation but a religious community and therefore expect
> neither a return to Palestine nor a sacrificial worship under the sons of
> Aaron.

The Pittsburgh Platform takes up each critical question in turn. Who is Israel? What is its way of life? How does it account for its existence as a distinct and distinctive group? Israel once was a nation ("during its national life") but today is not a nation. It once had a set of laws that reg-ulated diet, clothing, and the like. These no longer apply, because Israel now is not what it was then. Israel forms an integral part of Western civ-ilization. The reason to persist as a distinctive group was that the group has its work to do, namely, to realize the messianic hope for the estab-lishment of a kingdom of truth, justice, and peace. For that purpose Israel no longer constitutes a nation. It now forms a religious community. So individual Jews live as citizens in their respective nations.

Accordingly, it is all right to be different by religion, but not by nation-ality. That position accords fully with the definition of citizenship of the Western democracies, which accorded freedom of religion but no choice as to nationality to their citizens and ignored ethnic groups altogether. The way of life of Reform Judaism admits to no important traits that dis-tinguish Jews from others, since morality, in the nature of things, forms a universal category, applicable in the same way to everyone. Jews do not eat or dress in distinctive ways. They are to seek a place within "modern spiritual elevation . . . universal culture of heart and intellect." The Reform rabbis impute to that culture the realization of "the messianic hope"—a considerable stake.

The Program of Reform Judaism

Reform Judaism dates its beginnings to the late eighteenth and early nineteenth centuries with changes, called reforms and regarded as the antecedents of Reform, in trivial aspects of public worship in the synagogue.[2] The motive for these changes derived from the simple fact that many Jews rejected the received system. People were defecting from the synagogue. Reform addressed two issues at one time: (1) making the synagogue more attractive so that (2) defectors would return and others would not leave.

To begin with, the theological issue involved not politics but merely justification for changing anything at all. But that issue asked the wrong question in the wrong way. The Reformers maintained that change was all right because historical precedent proved that change was all right. Change had long defined the constant in the ongoing life of rabbinic Judaism. Change had marked the vitality of the system. Rabbinic Judaism endured, never intact but always unimpaired, because of its power to absorb and make its own the diverse happenings of culture and society. So long as the structure of politics remained the same, the system answered the paramount question. The trivial questions could work their way through and become part of the consensus. A catalogue of changes that had taken place over fifteen hundred years, from the birth of Judaism to the age in which it met competition, therefore will list many more dramatic and decisive sorts of change than those matters of minor revision of liturgy (e.g., sermons in the vernacular, which attracted attention at the dawn of the age of change become Reform).

Justifying Reform: Historical Study as an Instrument of Reform

Why was this movement of modernization in Judaism called *Reform*? The reason is, it was organized in Germany, the home of the Reformation of Christianity. The model of the Protestant Reformation defined the context for change in Judaism, too, and the Reform theologians found it natural to appeal to the Reformation-Protestant model. The Reformation in Germany appealed to questions of historical fact, settled by scriptural evidence. As opposed to church tradition, Martin Luther had demanded proof only from Scripture. What could be shown to form the original heritage of Christ defined authentic Christianity—which sacraments, for example, and which doctrines—and what could not be validated historically should be excised. So history was invoked to settle questions of faith, and facts of history answered theological questions.

So, too, history formed the court of appeal to validate as Reform what were clearly changes in Judaism. What formed the justification for these changes was the theory of the incremental history of a single, linear Judaism as it played a powerful role in the creative age of Reform Judaism. The ones who made changes to begin with rested their case on an appeal to the authoritative texts. They claimed that change is legitimate, and these changes in particular are wholly consonant with the law. They were represented as justifiable within the tradition. They emerged out of the inner dynamics of the faith. They obeyed the dictates of history. Reform claimed to restore, to continue, to persist in the received pattern.

The justification of change always invokes precedent. People who made changes had to show that the principle that guided what they did was not new, even though the specific things they did were innovations. The appeal to history, a common mode of justification in the politics and theology of the nineteenth century, therefore defined the principal justification for the new Judaism: it was new because it renewed the old and enduring, the golden Judaism of a mythic age of perfection. Arguments on precedent drew the Reformers to the work of critical scholarship as they settled all questions by appeal to the facts of history.

We cannot find surprising, therefore, the theory that Reform Judaism stood in a direct line with the prior history of Judaism. Judaism is a single unitary tradition—not a set of kindred religious systems, all invoking the same revelation. Judaism has a history, that history is single, and it was always leading to its present outcome: Reform Judaism. Orthodox Judaism would deny that Judaism has a history at all. Positive-Historical Judaism, called Conservative Judaism in the United States, would discover a different goal for history from that embodied by Reform Judaism. But the mode of argument—appealing to issues of an historical and factual character—and the premises of argument—insisting that history proved, or disproved, matters of theological conviction—characterized all the Judaisms of the nineteenth century.

Abraham Geiger: The original changes, in the first decades of the nineteenth century, produced a new generation of rabbis. Some forty years into the century, these rabbis gave to the process of change the name *Reform* and created those institutions of Reform Judaism that would endow the nascent movement with a politics of its own. In the mid-1840s a number of rabbinical conferences brought together the new generation of rabbis. Trained in universities, rabbis who came to these gatherings turned backward, justifying the changes in prayer rites long in place, effecting some further, mostly cosmetic changes in the observance of the Sabbath and in the laws covering personal status through marriage and divorce. The Reformers appealed for their apologia to the received writings, insisting that they formed a natural continuation of the processes of the "tradition." Indeed, that point of insistence—that Judaism formed, in Jakob J. Petuchowski's words in regard to Geiger, "a constantly evolving organism"[3]—formed the centerpiece of the nascent Judaism at hand. Reform forms the natural and necessary outcome of history.

Abraham Geiger, Principal Theologian of Reform Judaism in the Beginning

Abraham Geiger presented in clearest form the argument that Reform carried forward the historical processes of Judaism, hence position both a single, linear Judaism and a Judaism affected by history, that is, by change. He appealed to the facts of history, beginning with the critical study of the Bible. The Reform theologian Jakob J. Petuchowski summarizes his view as follows:

> Judaism is a constantly evolving organism. Biblical Judaism was not identical with classical Rabbinic Judaism. Similarly, the modern age calls for further evolution in consonance with the changed circumstances. . . . The modern rabbis are entitled to adapt medieval Judaism, as the early rabbis had the right to adapt biblical Judaism. . . . He found traces of evolution within the Bible itself. Yet for Geiger changes in Judaism had always been organic. . . . The modern changes must develop out of the past, and not represent a revolutionary break with it.[4]

Geiger therefore recognized change as "traditional," meaning that change represents the way things always were and so legitimately go forward. The Jews change, having moved from constituting a nation to a different classification of social entity. The Messiah idea now addresses the whole of humanity, not only speaking of national restoration. Revelation then turns out to form a progressive, not a static fact. In these diverse ways Geiger—and with him, Reform Judaism through its history—appealed to history to verify its allegations and validate its positions. So facts turn into the evidence for faith.

Geiger was born in 1810 and died in 1874.[5] Growing up in Frankfurt, he undertook university studies at nearby Heidelberg, then to the Rhine in Bonn, with special interest in philosophy and Semitics. Jews rarely undertook university study. But among the intellectual leaders in Geiger's day, not only he, but his archopponent, Samson Raphael Hirsch, founder of integrationist Orthodox Judaism also acquired a university education.

Then despite the established bias against secular education, how were the Jews to harmonize that education and its values with the education in the Judaic science? Earlier generations had not sent their sons to universities (and their daughters would have to wait until nearly our own day for a similar right). So before Geiger and Hirsch could reach the academy, their parents had to affirm the value of such an education. But prior to that generation, most parents did not send their sons to universities. Knowledge of a secular sort, under other auspices, bore no value. So before the advent of the reformer, whether the great intellect of Reform Judaism or the leader of integrationist Orthodoxy, change had already taken place.

Once he had completed his university studies, Geiger followed the conventional path and served in synagogue pulpits. The congregants did not always appreciate his flawless German and his questioning of routine.[6] What he did with most of his time, however, concerned not the local synagogue community, but the constituency of Judaic learning. He produced a periodical, the *Scientific Journal for Jewish Theology*, from 1835 onward. *Science* meant critical, systematic learning, propositions tested against evidence and established through rational argument. Geiger's biographer defines the purpose of scientific knowledge: "They were convinced that, given the historical facts, it would be possible to draw the correct practical conclusions with regard to the means by which their religion could best be served and elevated to the level of contemporary culture."[7]

That is to say, through systematic learning Judaism would undergo reform. Reform Judaism rested on deep foundations of scholarship of a certain sort, specifically, of a historical character.

What Geiger had in mind was to analyze the sources of Judaism and the evolution of Judaism. If science (once more used in its German sense, systematic learning) could uncover the sources of the Jewish "spirit," then, in Wiener's words, "the genius of his people and . . . its vocation" would serve "as a guide to the construction of a living present and future." Geiger's principle of Reform remained fixed. Reform had to emerge from scientific learning, the German word for which was *Wissenschaft*, "a term which he equated with the concept of the understanding of historical evolution."[8] To him "Judaism in its ideal for was religion per se, nothing but an expression of religious consciousness. Its outer shell was subject to change from one generation to another."[9] All things emerge out of time and of change. But when it comes to trace the history of time and change, contemporary categories assuredly defined the inquiry. Thus Geiger produced, out of ancient times, portraits suspiciously congruent to the issues of his own day.

A New Judaism or Renewed Judaism?

Geiger represents the answer of Reform Judaism: it renews, it does not invent. There was, and is, only a single Judaism. On what basis? Reform lays its foundations on the basis of history, which is to say, tradition. Propositions of a theological character—for example, concerning the dual Torah revealed at Sinai, the sanctified and therefore supernatural character of Israel, the holy people, and the coming Messiah sage at the end of times—take their place in the line of truths to be investigated through historical method and in historical sources.

We cannot ask whether the claim of Reform Judaism finds justification in "the facts." The question proves beside the point. The facts are what people make of them, whether discovered in history or imputed in revealed and holy writings, in a canon of truth. We can scarcely say that the position of Reform Judaism, as outlined by a brief sketch of Geiger's thought, even intersects or connects with what had gone before. Once the Judaism at hand had come into being, people knew what they wanted to find out from history, and that was whether or not things change. Geiger followed a far more sophisticated program, since, knowing that things do change (to whom would the proposition have brought surprise?), he asked exactly how, in Judaism, change takes place and in what direction.

Jacob Marcus's Introduction to Cronbach's *Reform Movements in Judaism*: The Appeal to Historical Precedent

Clearly, Reform Judaism, once well under way, would have to situate itself in relationship to the past. Geiger's powerful appeal to precedent left no choice. As learning rolled forward, the question emerged: Precisely what, in history, serves as a precedent for change to become Reform?

The answer came down to the appeal to continuing traits of change, the search for constants about change. Specifically, in his preface to Abraham Cronbach's *Reform Movements in Judaism*,[10] Jacob Rader Marcus, a principal voice in Reform Judaism in the twentieth century, provides a powerful statement of the Reform view of its place in history. Marcus recognizes that diverse Judaisms have flourished in the history of the Jews. What characterizes them all is that each began as a reform movement but then underwent a process we might characterize as "traditionalization." That is to say, change becomes not merely reform but tradition, and the only constant in the histories of Judaisms is that process of transformation of the new to the conventional, or, in theological language, the traditional. This process Marcus describes as follows: "All [Judaisms] began as rebellions, as great reformations, but after receiving widespread acceptance, developed vested 'priestly' interests, failed their people, and were forced to retreat before the onslaught of new rebellions, new philosophies, new challenges."

Nothing in Marcus's picture can have presented a surprise to Geiger. So the fundamental theological method of Reform Judaism in its initial phase, the appeal to facts of history for the validation of theological propositions, endures. But the claim that everything always changes yields a challenge, which Marcus forthrightly raises:

> Is there then nothing but change? Is change the end of all our history and all our striving? No, there is something else, the desire to be free. . . . In the end [the Jew] has always understood that changelessness is spiritual death. The Jew who would *live* must never completely surrender himself to one truth, but . . . must reach out for the farther and faint horizons of an ever Greater God. . . . This is the meaning of Reform.

Marcus thus treats Reform as self-evident—obvious because it is a fact of history. He affirms the simple point that change sets the norm. The appeal to the facts of history fails at the point at which a constructive position demands articulation. "The desire to be free" bears a predicate: free of what? Free to do and to be what? If Marcus fails to accomplish the whole of the theological task, however, he surely conveys the profoundly constructive vision that Reform Judaism afforded to its Israel.

For his part, Cronbach sets forth as the five precedents for the present movement the Deuteronomic Reformation, the Pentateuchal Reformation, the Pharisaic Reformation, the Karaite Reformation, and the Hasidic Reformation. He looks forward to a further reformation, one that appeals to social psychology and aims at tolerance:

> Felicitous human relationships can be the goal of social welfare and of economic improvement. . . . Our Judaism of maturity would be dedicated to the ideal of freedom. Corollary of that ideal is what we have just observed about courtesy toward the people whose beliefs and practices we do not share.[11]

The Reform Challenge to the Received Tradition

The Reform theologians rejected the claim that the oral part of the Torah came from God. It was the work of men, time-bound, contingent, possessed of a mere advisory authority. Whatever precedents and antecedents Reform historians and theologians sought, they would not look in the rabbinic writings that, all together, fall under the name *the Talmud*, because there their orthodox critics found their principal ammunition. The Judaism from which Reform took its leave—the one that required the changes become reforms yielding Reform—that Judaism found its definition in the dual Torah of Sinai, as written down from the Mishnah onward. So, quite naturally, when the Reformers addressed the issue of continuity, they leapt over the immediate past, represented by Rabbinic Judaism, and sought their antecedents in the processes of change instead. The Protestant Reformation once more supplied the model, but the urgent questions facing the "Israel" represented by Reform Judaism dictated the result.

Orthodox Judaism

Many people reasonably identify all "traditional" or "observant" Judaism with Orthodoxy—a word made up of the Greek roots that yield "right doctrine"—and they furthermore take for granted that all traditional Judaisms are pretty much the same. But a wide variety of competing Judaisms all affirm the Torah, Oral and Written, and abide by its laws, as interpreted by their authorities. But these masters radically differ from one another on many important points. In chapter 3 we have already noticed the differences between Hasidic Judaism and its opposition, all parties concurring on the definition of the law and lore of the Torah. We also distinguished integrationist from self-segregationist Orthodox Judaisms. Self-segregationist Judaisms maintain that the holy people should maintain high walls of separation between themselves and the Gentiles, interacting only in carefully limited transactions, but in no way participating in a common culture or society.

Orthodox Judaism (a.k.a. "modern" or "Western" Orthodoxy or neo-Orthodoxy) embodies the opposite, the integrationist ideal. Within the large camp of the Torah, Oral and Written, modern or Western Orthodoxy is the one that affirms the divine revelation and eternal authority of the Torah, *but* that favors the integration of the Jews ("holy Israel") into the national life of the countries of their birth. This Judaism holds that Israelites may study philosophy, not only the Torah, and they may integrate themselves into the culture and the social order of the nations in which they live. Other Judaisms adhering to the received system of rabbinic Judaism and regarded as Orthodox affirm the Torah but favor the segregation of the holy Israel from other people in the countries in which they live, including the State of Israel. Indicators such as clothing, language, and, above all, education differentiate integrationist from self-segregationist Orthodox Judaisms. But when the adjective *orthodox* was first used with the noun *Judaism*, it referred to the integrationist Orthodoxy that took shape in response to the formation of Reform Judaism in nineteenth-century Germany.

The Origins of Integrationist Orthodoxy

Exactly where and when did integrationist Orthodox Judaism come into being? It was predictably in Germany. Integrationist Orthodox took shape in the middle of the nineteenth century in response to Reform. Integrationist Orthodox Judaism reached articulated expression among Jews who rejected Reform and made a self-conscious decision to remain within the way of life and worldview that they had known and cherished all their lives. They framed the religious issues in terms of change and history. The Reformers had held that Judaism could change and that Judaism was a product of history. True to the received system, the integrationist Orthodox opponents denied that Judaism could change and insisted that Judaism derived from God's will at Sinai and was eternal and supernatural, not historical and man-made. In these two convictions the integrationist Orthodox recapitulated the convictions of the received system. But when they maintained that Judaism formed a religion to be seen as distinct and autonomous of politics, society, "the rest of life," they entered that same world of self-conscious believing that the Reformers also explored.

Integrationist Orthodox Judaism dealt with the same urgent questions as did Reform Judaism. These were questions raised by political emancipation, such as whether and how Jews could integrate themselves into the politics and culture of their countries. But integrationists gave answers different from those of Reform Judaism's followers. Integrationist Orthodoxy maintains the worldview of the received dual Torah, constantly citing its sayings and adhering with only trivial variations to the bulk of its norms for the everyday life. At the same time integrationist Orthodoxy holds that Jews should adhere to the dual Torah yet may wear clothing that non-Jews wear and do not have to wear distinctively Jewish clothing; they may live within a common economy and not practice distinctively Jewish professions (however, in a given setting, these professions may be defined).

Many hold that integrationist Orthodoxy stands for how things always were, for all time. But in the context of the history of Judaism the term *Orthodoxy* takes on meaning only in the contrast to Reform. So in a simple sense, integrationist Orthodoxy owes its life to Reform Judaism.

The term *Orthodox* first surfaced in 1795,[12] and includes all Jews—not just integrationist Orthodox Jews—who believe that God revealed the dual Torah at Sinai, and that Jews must carry out the requirements of Jewish law contained in the Torah as interpreted by the sages through time. So long as Rabbinic Judaism enjoys recognition as a set of self-evident truths, those truths add up not to something so distinct and special as "religion," but to a general statement of how things *are*: all of life explained and harmonized in one whole account.

The former of the two events—the view that the received system was "traditional"—came first. The matter of the self-aware recognition of "Judaism" as "religion" comes later. Calling "tradition" what former generations deemed obvious truth came about when the received system met the challenge of competing Judaisms. Then, on behalf of the received way of life and worldview addressed to supernatural Israel, people said that Rabbinic Judaism was established of old, was the right and only way of seeing and doing things. It was how things have been and should be naturally and normally—in short: tradition. But that is a category that contains within itself an alternative, namely, change, as in "tradition and change."

When does established truth turn into "tradition"? When the system has lost its power of self-evidence, then it enters the classification "the tradition." And in the formation of Judaisms in modern times that came about when integrationist Orthodoxy met head-on the challenge of change become Reform. We understand why the category of tradition, the received way of doing things, became critical to the framers of integrationist Orthodoxy when we examine the counterclaim. That is to say, just as the Reformers justified change, the integrationist Orthodox theologians denied that change was ever possible, so Walter Wurzburger, historian and theologian of orthodox Judaism, wrote in the *Encyclopaedia Judaica*: "Orthodoxy looks upon attempts to adjust Judaism to the 'spirit of the time' as utterly incompatible with the entire thrust of normative Judaism which holds that the revealed will of God rather than the values of any given age are the ultimate standard."[13]

The spirit of the times involved responding to political rights assigned to the Jews, among other citizens, by the nation-states of Western Europe. But Orthodoxy had a different view from Reform Judaism of the primacy of political emancipation. To begin with the issue important to the Reformers, the value of what was called *emancipation*, meaning, the provision to Jews of civil rights, defined the debate. The debate, however, between Reform and Orthodoxy followed the agenda of Reform Judaism, since the Reformers insisted that making changes was historically legitimate. Orthodoxy then maintained changes were never legitimate.

The issues then were drawn in humble matters but referred to transcendent concerns. If the Reform made minor changes in liturgy and its conduct, the Orthodox rejected even those that, when the tradition was not threatened, might have found acceptance under other circumstances. Saying prayers in the vernacular, for example, provoked strong opposition. But everyone knew that some of the prayers, said in Aramaic, in fact were in the vernacular of the earlier age. The Orthodox thought that these changes, not reforms at all, represented only the first step of a process leading Jews out of the Judaic world altogether, so, as Wurzburger says, "the slightest tampering with tradition was condemned."

If we ask where self-segregationist Orthodox Judaism or, by contrast, integrationist Orthodoxy prevailed, we would best follow the spreading-out of railway lines. That is, reform, the affirmation of change, responded to economic and political change. For example, the growth of new industry, the shifts in political status accorded to, among other citizens, Jews, changes in the educational system, all raised questions about the Jews that the age of Christianity and Islam did not address. In all, the entire process of political change, economic and social, demographic and cultural shifts of a radical and fundamental nature were bound up in the reform of Judaism. Where the changes came first, Reform Judaism responded, and integrationist Orthodox answered back. Where change came later in the century, as in the case of Russian Poland, the eastern provinces of the Austro-Hungarian Empire, and Russia itself, there, in villages contentedly following the old ways, the received system endured for another century.

Then self-segregationist Orthodoxy was challenged by mass migration of traditionalist Jews to the United States and other Western countries. In an age of mass migration from Eastern Europe those who experienced the upheaval of leaving home and country met the challenge of change either by accepting new ways of seeing things or articulately and in full self-awareness reaffirming the familiar ones, once more, Reform or integrationist Orthodoxy. We may, therefore, characterize the received system as a way of life and worldview wedded to an ancient peoples' homelands, the villages, and small towns of central and eastern Europe, and integrationist Orthodoxy as the heir of that received system as it came to expression in the towns and cities of central and Western Europe and America. That allows us to distinguish between the piety of a milieu and the theological conviction of a self-conscious community. Or we may accept the familiar distinction between tradition and articulate Orthodoxy, a distinction with its own freight of apologetics to be sure.

When, therefore, we refer to political and economic change in the beginnings of Reform Judaism, we also understand the point of origin of integrationist Orthodoxy. Clearly, the beginnings of integrationist Orthodoxy took place in the areas where Reform made its way, hence in Germany and in Hungary. In Germany, where Reform attracted the majority of many Jewish communities, the integrationist Orthodox faced a challenge indeed. Critical to their conviction was the notion that

"Israel," all of the Jews, bore responsibility to carry out the law of the Torah. But the community's institutions in the hands of the Reform did not obey the law of the Torah as the integrationist Orthodox understood it. So, in the end, integrationist Orthodoxy took that step that marked it as a self-conscious Judaism. Integrationist Orthodoxy separated from the established community altogether. The integrationist Orthodox set up their own organization and seceded from the community at large. They even prohibited integrationist Orthodox from participating in non-Orthodox organizations altogether. Isaac Breuer, a leading theologian of integrationist Orthodoxy, would ultimately take the position that "refusal to espouse the cause of separation was interpreted as being equivalent to the rejection of the absolute sovereignty of God."[14]

The matter of accommodating to the world at large did not allow for so easy an answer as mere separation. The specific issue—integration or segregation—concerned preparation for life in the large politics and economic life of the country, and that meant secular education involving not only language and science, but also history and literature, matters of values. Orthodoxy proved diverse, with two wings as we have said. The self-segregated one rejected secular learning as well as all dealing with non-Orthodox Jews. The one that favored cultural integration also cooperated with non-Orthodox and secular Jews and accepted the value of secular education. That position in no way affected loyalty to the law of Judaism (e.g., belief in God's revelation of the one whole torah at Sinai).

The point at which the received system and integrationist Orthodox split then requires specification. In concrete terms we know the one from the other by the evaluation of secular education. Proponents of the received system never accommodated themselves to secular education, while the integrationist Orthodox in Germany and Hungary persistently affirmed it. That represents a remarkable shift, since central to the received system of the dual Torah is study of Torah—Torah, not philosophy. Explaining where we find the one and the other, Katzburg works with the distinction we have already made, between an unbroken system and one that has undergone a serious caesura with the familiar condition of the past. He states:

> In Eastern Europe until World War I, Orthodoxy preserved without a break in its traditional ways of life and the time-honored educational framework. In general, the mainstream of Jewish life was identified with Orthodoxy, while Haskalah [Jewish Enlightenment, which applied to the Judaic setting the skeptical attitudes of the French Enlightenment] and secularization

were regarded as deviations. Hence there was no ground wherein a Western type of Orthodoxy could take root. . . . European Orthodoxy in the 19th and the beginning of the 20th centuries was significantly influenced by the move from small settlements to urban centers . . . as well as by emigration. Within the small German communities there was a kind of popular Orthodoxy, deeply attached to tradition and to local customs, and when it moved to the large cities this element brought with it a vitality and rootedness to Jewish tradition.[15]

Katzburg's observations provide important guidance. He authoritatively defines the difference between integrationist Orthodoxy and what he calls "tradition" and what we call "the received system."

Old and New in Integrationist Orthodoxy

Orthodox Jews of both types of Orthodoxy in Germany's cities experienced change. They daily encountered Jews unlike themselves, and no longer lived in that stable Judaic society in which the received Torah formed the given of life. They could not pretend that Jews had no choices to make. Nor did the generality of the Jews propose, in the West, to preserve a separate language or to renounce political rights. So integrationist Orthodoxy made its peace with change, no less than did Reform. The educational program that led Jews out of the received culture of the dual Torah, the use of the vernacular, the acceptance of political rights, the renunciation of Jewish garments, education for women, abolition of the power of the community to coerce the individual—these and many other originally Reform positions characterized the integrationist Orthodoxy that emerged.

It is clear that Orthodoxy made changes. Then, we ask, how new was the integrationist Orthodox system? We find ambiguous answers. In conviction, in way of life, in worldview, we may hardly call it new at all. For the bulk of its substantive positions found ample precedent in the received dual Torah. From its affirmation of God's revelation of a dual Torah to its acceptance of the detailed authority of the law and customs, from its strict observance of the law to its unwillingness to change a detail of public worship, integrationist Orthodoxy rightly pointed to its strong links with the chain of tradition.

But integrationist Orthodoxy constituted a distinct component within Jewry. Its definition of the "Israel" to whom it wished to speak and the definition characteristic of the dual Torah hardly coincide. Rabbinic Judaism addressed all Jews, and integrationist Orthodoxy recognized that it could not do so. So integrationist Orthodoxy acquiesced in a situation that lay beyond the imagination of the framers of Rabbinic Judaism. True, the integrationist Orthodox had no choice. Their seceding from the organized, state-recognized Jewish community and forming their own institutions ratified the simple fact that they could not work with the Reformers. Orthodoxy found it necessary to rethink the meaning of "Israel" as much as did the Reformers. In Germany that meant separating from the community of the Jews and forming a community of Judaism— a religious community. That represented a formidable change, as we shall now see.

Judaism Enters the Category: Religion

The single most significant trait of integrationist Orthodoxy is its power to see the "Torah" as "Judaism." That defines the category shift that changed everything else (or, that ratified all other changes). And close in line, the second remarkable trait of that same Orthodoxy was its classification of "Judaism" as a religion.

The category *religion,* with its counterpart *secular,* recognizes matters having to do with the church, the life of faith, as distinct from "all of life." Those distinctions were lost on the received system of the dual Torah, which legislated for matters we should regard today as entirely secular or neutral, for example, the institutions of state (e.g., king, priest, army). We have already noted that as the received system took shape in Eastern and Central Europe, Jews wore garments regarded as distinctively Jewish, and some important traits of these garments indeed derived from the Torah. They pursued sciences that only Jews studied, for instance, the Talmud and its commentaries. In these and other ways, the Torah encompassed all of the life of Israel, the holy people. The recognition that Jews were like others, that the Torah fell into a category into which other and comparable matters fell was long in coming.

For Christians, it had become commonplace in Germany and other Western countries to see "religion" as distinct from other components of the social and political system. While the Christian Orthodox Church in Russia identified with the Tsarist state, and the Roman Catholic Church in Poland with the national aspirations of the Polish people, for example, in Germany two churches, Catholic and Protestant, competed. The terrible wars of the Reformation in the sixteenth and seventeenth centuries, particularly 1618–1648, which ruined Germany, had led to the uneasy compromise that the prince might choose the religion of his principality, and people understood that "the way of life and worldview" in fact constituted a religion, and that one religion might be compared with some other. By the nineteenth century, moreover, the separation of church and state in the United States' Bill of Rights ratified the important distinction between religion, in which difference would be tolerated, and the secular, in which citizens were pretty much the same.

Integrationist Orthodox Judaism held that one could observe the rules of the Judaic system of the ages and not only keep the laws of the state—Rabbinic Judaism had affirmed the validity of state law from the third century C.E. forward—but also conform to its neutral culture. More important, integrationist Orthodox Judaism took full account of the duties of citizenship, so far as being a good citizen imposed the expectation of conformity in certain aspects of everyday life. So a category, "religion," could contain the Torah, and another category, "the secular," could allow Jews a place in the accepted civic life of the country. The importance of the category shift therefore lies in its power to accommodate the political change so important to Reform Judaism. The Jews' differences from others would fit into categories in which difference was (in Jews' minds, at any rate) acceptable and would not violate those lines to which all citizens had to adhere.

How different then was the thought process of integrationist Orthodoxy from that of Reform Judaism? The two systems disagreed on detail, but their basic reasoning coincided. Clothing, language, and education now fell into the category of the secular, while other equally important aspects of everyday life remained in the category of the sacred. Integrationist Orthodox Judaism, as it came into existence in Germany and other Western countries, therefore found integration possible by recognizing the category of the secular to accept the language, clothing, and learning of those countries. And these matters serve openly to exemplify a larger acceptance of Gentile ways, not all ways but enough to lessen the differences between the holy people and the nations.

Integrationist Orthodox Jews maintained those distinctive beliefs of a political character in the future coming of the Messiah and the reconstitution of the Jewish nation in its own land, which Reform Jews rejected. But placing these convictions in the distant future, the integrationist

Orthodox Jews nonetheless prepared for a protracted interim of life within the nation at hand, and not in nationality as represented by citizenship. What follows for our inquiry is that integrationist Orthodoxy, as much as Reform, signals remarkable changes in the Jews' political situation and—more important—aspiration. They did want to be different, but not so different as the received system without much modification would have made them.

Was Integrationist Orthodoxy Traditional?

Still, integrationist Orthodoxy in its nineteenth-century formulation laid claim to carry forward "the tradition." That claim demands a serious hearing, for the things that integrationist Orthodoxy taught, the way of life it required, the Israel to whom it spoke, and the doctrines it deemed revealed by God to Moses at Sinai. All of these conformed more or less to the system of the received Rabbinic Judaism as people then knew it. Therefore any consideration of the issue of a linear and incremental history of Judaism has to take at face value the character, and not merely the claim, of nascent integrationist Orthodoxy.

But we do not have to concede that claim. Each Judaism, after all, demands study not in categories defined by its claims of continuity, but in those defined by its own distinctive and characteristic choices, for a system takes shape and then makes choices in that order. But the issue facing us in Orthodoxy is whether or not Orthodoxy can be said to make choices at all. Is it not what it says it is, "just Judaism"? Indeed so, but the dual Torah of the received tradition hardly generated the base category "Judaism." And "Judaism," Orthodox or otherwise, is not "Torah."

That is the point at which making self-conscious choices enters discourse. For the integrationist Orthodoxy of the nineteenth century—that is, the Judaism that named itself "Orthodox"—exhibited certain traits of mind that marked its framers as distinctive, that is, as separate from the received Rabbinic Judaism as the founders of Reform Judaism. By adopting for themselves the category "religion," and by recognizing a distinction between religion and the secular, the holy, and other categories of existence, the founders of integrationist Orthodoxy performed an act of choice and selectivity. The Torah found itself transformed into an object, a thing out there, a matter of choice, a deliberation, an affirmation. In that sense integrationist Orthodoxy recognized a break in the line of the received "tradition" and proposed to repair the break. It was a self-conscious, modernizing decision. Rabbinic Judaism had a native category, "Torah," that expressed what we mean by "Judaism," but it had no word for "Judaism." Integrationist Orthodoxy did.

From "Torah" to "Judaism"

Let us dwell on the matter of the category "Judaism," a species of the genus religion. The fact is, those Jews for whom the received Judaism retained the standing of self-evident truth in no way recognized the distinctions implicit in the category, a religion. Those distinctions separated one dimension of existence from others, specifically, the matter of faith and religious action from all other matters, such as politics, economic life, incidental aspects of everyday life such as clothing, vocation, and avocation, and the like. Rabbinic Judaism, for its part, encompasses every dimension of human existence, both personal and public, both private and political. The "Jews" constitute "Israel," a supernatural people. Their politics form the public dimension of their holiness. Their personal lives match the most visible and blatant rules of public policy. The whole forms a single system of the social order, an indivisible and totally coherent entity, at once cultural, economic, and political and in all parts and dimensions, holy. The recognition, therefore, that we may distinguish the religious from the political, or concede as distinct any dimension of a person's life or of the life of the community of Judaism, forms powerful evidence that a fresh system has come into existence.

For nineteenth-century Reform and integrationist Orthodox theologians alike, the category "Judaism" defined what people said when they wished all together and all at once to describe what the Jews believe, or the Jewish religion, or similar matters covering religious ideas viewed as a system and as a whole. It therefore constituted a philosophical category, instructing thinkers to seek the system and order and structure of ideas: the doctrine of this, the doctrine of that, in Juda-*ism*. The nineteenth-century Judaic religious thinkers invoked the category, Judaism, when they proposed to speak of the whole of Judaic religious existence. Available to Rabbinic Judaism are other categories, other words, to tell how to select and organize and order data—all together, all at once to speak of the whole.

To the Jews who abided within the received Rabbinic Judaism, the discovery of Orthodoxy therefore represented an innovation, a shift from the perceivedly self-evident truths of the Torah. For their word for Judaism was Torah, and when they spoke of the whole all at once, they used the word *Torah*. But in using that word, they also spoke of different things from the things encompassed by Judaism. For example, the received Rabbinic Judaism did not use the word the nineteenth-century theologians used when speaking of the things of which they spoke when they said Juda-*ism*.

Judaism falls into the classification of a philosophical or ideological or theological word, while *Torah* fell into the classification of a symbol, that is, a symbol that in itself encompassed the whole of the system that the category at hand was meant to describe. The *-ism* category does not invoke an encompassing symbol but a system of thought. Judaism is an "it," an object, a classification, an action. Torah, for its part, is an "every-thing in one thing," a symbol. Even though both encompassed the same way of life and worldview and addressed the same social group, they are separate categories. So Torah as a category serves as a symbol, everywhere present in detail and holding all the details together. Judaism as a cate-gory serves as a statement of the main points. The conception of Judaism as an organized body of doctrine, as in the sentence, *Judaism teaches*, or *Judaism says*, derives from an age in which people had determined that Judaism belonged to the category of religion, and, of still more definitive importance, a religion was something that *teaches* or *says*. This thought results from the conception that Judaism is a religion, and a religion to begin with is a composition of beliefs.

The Protestant Premises of Integrationist Orthodoxy

We noted earlier in this chapter that in calling change "reform" and its Judaism, "Reform," the founding theologians of Reform Judaism invoked the precedent of the Protestant Reformation, which had split Western Christianity in two and yielded a schism that has lasted to this day. But the integrationist Orthodox theologians also evinced evidence of the Protestant givens of their circumstance and their thought. For the cate-gory of religion as a distinct entity emerges from Protestant theological thought. Everything depended on what one believed, hence the self-evidence that religion formed a system of beliefs above all else.

In Protestant theological terms, the individual is saved by faith. But the very components of that sentence prove incomprehensible in the categories constructed by Torah. What marked not only Reform but integrationist Orthodoxy as a work of the German culture? It was not only the stress on right doctrine as source of salvation but the insistence that one can speak of religion apart from such matters as clothing and education. For the Orthodox of Germany who dressed like other Germans and studied in universities, these evidences of cultural integration testify to the same fact. Both Reform and integrationist Orthodoxy marked the end of self-evidence. Each ratified in its way the same fact, namely, the substitution of the distinction between religion and secularity, the creation of *Judaism* as the definitive category.

Samson Raphael Hirsch

Just as Reform Judaism owed much to a single towering intellect, Abraham Geiger, integrationist Orthodoxy was associated with the name of a single founding theologian, Samson Raphael Hirsch. The importance of Hirsch (1808–1888), the first great intellect of integrationist Orthodoxy, derives from his philosophy of joining Torah with secular education, which produced a synthesis of Torah and modern culture. He represents the strikingly new Judaism at hand, exhibiting both its strong tie to the received system but also its innovative and essentially new character.

Sometimes called "neo-Orthodox,"[16] Hirsch's position stressed the possibility of living in the secular world and sustaining a fully Orthodox life. This rallied the Jews to begin a counterreformation. But Hirsch and his followers took over one principal position of Reform, the possibility of integrating Jews into modern society. What made Hirsch significant was that he took an affirmative view of integration into the nation-state not only on utilitarian grounds, as Samet says, "but also through the acceptance of its scale of values, aiming at creating a symbiosis between traditional Orthodoxy and modern German-European culture; both in theory and in practice this meant abandonment of Torah study for its own sake and adopting instead an increased concentration on practical *halakhah* (law)."[17] On that basis we rightly identify integrationist Orthodoxy as a distinct Judaism from the system of the dual Torah. Hirsch himself studied at the University of Bonn, specializing in classical languages, history, and philosophy.[18] So he did not think one had to spend all his time studying Torah, and in going to a university he implicitly affirmed that he could not define, within Torah study, all modes of learning. But the self-segregationist continuators of Rabbinic Judaism thought whatever is worth knowing is in the Torah.

In his rabbinical posts, Hirsch published a number of works to appeal to the younger generation. His ideal for them was the formation of a personality that would be both enlightened and observant, that is to say, educated in Western knowledge and observant of the Judaic way of life. This ideal took shape through an educational program that encompassed Hebrew language and holy literature, and also German, mathematics, sciences, and the like. In this way he proposed to respond to the Reformers' view that Judaism in its received form constituted a barrier between Jews and German society. The Reformers saw the received way of life as an obstacle to the sort of integration they thought wholesome and good. Hirsch concurred in the ideal and differed on detail.

For example, in Hirsch's view, distinctive Jewish clothing, enjoyed a low priority. To the contrary, he himself wore a ministerial gown at public worship, which did not win the approbation of the traditionalists. When Hirsch preached, he encompassed not only the law of the Torah but also other biblical matters, equally an innovation. Hirsch argued that Judaism and secular education could form a union. This would require the recognition of externals, which could be set aside, and the emphasis on the principles, which would not change.

In his selections Hirsch included changes in the conduct of the liturgy, involving a choir, congregational singing, sermons in the vernacular. A generation earlier, sermons in German signified a Reform temple, not a traditional synagogue. He required prayers to be said only in Hebrew and Jewish subjects to be taught in that language. He opposed all changes in the Prayer Book. At the same time he sustained organizational relationships with the Reformers and tried to avoid schism. By mid-career, however, toward the middle of the century, Hirsch could not tolerate the Reformers' abrogation of the dietary laws and their eating forbidden foods such as pork and shellfish. He also found unacceptable their dismissal of the laws affecting marital relationships, such as those that forbade sexual relations with a woman during her menstrual period. Therefore he made his break, accusing the Reformers of disrupting Israel's unity. In the following decades he encouraged Orthodox Jews to leave the congregations dominated by Reform, even though, in the locale, such was the only synagogue. Separationist synagogues formed in the larger community.

We come now to Hirsch's framing of issues of doctrine. He constructed an affirmative system, not a negative one. His principal argument stressed that the teachings of the Torah constitute facts beyond all doubt, as much as the facts of nature do not allow for doubt. This view of the essential facticity—the absolute givenness—of the Torah led to the further conviction that human beings may not deny the Torah's teachings even when they do not grasp the Torah's meaning. Wisdom is contained within the Torah, God's will is to be found there. Just as the physical laws of nature are not conditioned by human search, so the rules of God's wisdom are unaffected by human search. The Torah constitutes an objective reality, and, in Katz's words, its laws form "an objective disposition of an established order that is not dependent on the will of the individual or society, and hence not even on historical processes."[19] Humanity nonetheless may gain religious truth through time.

What makes Israel different is that the holy people gain access to the truth not through experience but through direct revelation. Gentile truth is truth, but it derives from observation and experience. What Israel knows through the Torah comes through a different medium. That people then stands outside of history and does not have to learn religious truth through the passage of history and changes over time. Israel then forms a supernatural entity, a view certainly in accord with Rabbinic Judaism. But when it came to explaining the way of life at hand, Hirsch went his own way. Hirsch pursued a theory of the practice of the religious life through concrete deeds—the commandments—in a highly speculative and philosophical way. What he maintained was that each of the deeds of the way of life represented something beyond itself, served as a symbol, not as an end in itself. So when a Jew carries out a holy deed, the deed serves to make concrete a revealed truth. This mode of thought transforms the way of life into an exercise in applied theology and practical, practiced belief.

Specifically, in Katz's words,

> the performance of a commandment is not determined by simple devotion but by attachment to the religious thought represented in symbolic form by the commandment. Symbolic meanings must be attributed . . . particularly to commandments which are described by the Torah itself as signs . . . and commandments which are established as pointing to historical events . . . and commandments whose entire content testifies to their symbolic character.[20]

The diverse commandments altogether stand for three principles: justice, love, and "the education of ourselves and others."

Hirsch's theory of who is Israel stood at the opposite pole from that of Geiger and the Reformers. To them Israel fell into the classification of a religious community, that alone. They afforded recognition, moreover, to other religious communities, with which Judaism bore much in common. To Hirsch Israel constituted a people, not a religious congregation, and Hirsch spoke of "national Jewish consciousness," "the Jewish people, though it carries the Torah with it in all the lands of its dispersion, will never find its table and lamp except in the Holy Land." Israel performs a mission among the nations, to teach "that God is the source of blessing." Israel then falls between, forming its own category, because it has a state system, in the land, but also a life outside.[21] In outlining this position, Hirsch reaffirmed the theory of the supernatural Israel laid forth in the dual Torah.

What was the value of the doctrine of Israel as a supernatural people? The power of the national ideal for Hirsch lay in its polemical force against the assimilationists. These were Jews who wanted the Jews gradually to disappear as a distinct social group. He also invoked the ideal of Israel as holy people against the Reformers:

> The contempt with which the assimilationists treat David's [fallen] tabernacle and the prayer for the sacrificial service clearly reveals the extent of their rebellion against Torah and their complete disavowal of the entire realm of Judaism. They gather the ignorant about them to whom the Book of Books, the Divine national document of their Jewish past and future, is closed with seven seals. With a conceit engendered by stupidity and a perfidy born from hatred they point to God's Temple and the Divine Service in Zion as the unholy center of the "bloody cult of sacrifices." Consequently, they make certain to eliminate any reference to the restoration of the Temple service from our prayers. . . . The "cultured, refined" sons and daughters of our time must turn away with utter disgust from their "prehistoric, crude" ancestors who worship their god with bloody sacrifices.

Hirsch reviews the long line of exalted leaders who affirmed sacrifice and who were not crude, such as Moses, Isaiah, Jeremiah, and so on. Then he concludes:

> The Jewish sacrifice expresses the highest ideal of man's and the nation's moral challenge Blood and kidney, head and limbs symbolize our service of God with every drop of blood, every emotion, every particle of our being. By performing the act of sacrifice at the place chosen by God as the site of His Law, we proclaim our determination to fulfill our lofty moral and

ethical tasks to enable God to bless the site of the national vow with the presence of this glory and with the fullness of this love and grace.[22]

Hirsch framed doctrines in response to Reform's challenges, and that explains his defense of the sacrifices. That is why he entered into argument about the worth of animal sacrifices in the restored temple that the Messiah would reconstruct in the same terms as did the Reformers.

What's New in Orthodoxy

That Hirsch's integrationist Orthodoxy flows directly out of the received system no one doubts. But—as we have already seen in theory, so too in fact—it also takes a position separate from that system in both doctrine and method. Hirsch spent much energy defending the practice of the religious duties called commandments, such as circumcision; the wearing of fringes on garments; the use, in morning worship, of *Tefillin* (commonly translated phylacteries); and the sacrificial cult and temple. He did not consider these as givens of the holy life. Rather, he transforms them into symbols of a meaning beyond. And that exercise, in his context, testifies to the utter self-consciousness of the Judaism at hand, hence to the formation of a new Judaism out of received materials, no less than Reform Judaism constituted a new Judaism out of those same received materials. For the sole necessity for making up such symbolic explanations derived from decision: defend these explanations, at all costs. Equivalent explanations and a counterpart process of articulated defense of the holy way of life hardly struck Hirsch's contemporaries living in the villages of the East as equivalently urgent.

When, therefore, Hirsch invoked the parallel, to which we have already alluded, between the study of nature and the study of the Torah, he expressed the freshness, the inventiveness of his own system, thereby testifying to the self-consciousness at hand. A sizable abstract provides a good view of Hirsch's excellent mode of thought and argument:

One word here concerning the proper method of Torah investigation. Two revelations are open before us, that is, nature and the Torah. In nature all phenomena stand before us as indisputable facts, and we can only endeavor a posteriori to ascertain the law of each and the connection of all. Abstract demonstration of the truth, or rather, the probability of theoretical explanations of the acts of nature, is an unnatural proceeding. The right method is to verify our assumptions by the known facts, and the highest attainable degree of certainty is to be able to say: "The facts agree with our assumption"—that is, all the phenomena observed can be explained according to our theory. A single contradictory phenomenon will make our theory untenable. We must, therefore, acquire all the knowledge possible concerning the object of our investigation and know it, if possible, in its totality. If, however, all efforts should fail in disclosing the inner law and connection of phenomena revealed to us as facts in nature, the facts remain, nevertheless, undeniable and cannot be reasoned away.

The same principles must be applied to the investigation of the Torah. In the Torah, even as in nature, God is the ultimate cause. In the Torah, even as in nature, no fact may be denied, even though the reason and the connection may not be understood. What is true in nature is true also in the Torah: the traces of divine wisdom must ever be sought. Its ordinances must be accepted in their entirety as undeniable phenomena and must be studied in accordance with their connection to each other, and the subject to which they relate. Our conjectures must be tested by their precepts, and our highest certainty here also can only be that everything stands in harmony with our theory.

In nature the phenomena are recognized as facts, though their cause and relationship to each other may not be understood and are independent of our investigation. So too the ordinances of the Torah must be law for us, even if we do not comprehend the reason and the purpose of a single one. Our fulfillment of the commandments must not depend on our investigations.[23]

Here we have the counterpart to Hirsch's theory of Torah and worldly learning. Just as Hirsch maintained the union of the two, so he worked out that same union in his thought. Natural science dictated rules of inquiry, specifically, the requirement that we explain phenomena through a theory that we can test. The phenomenon is the given. Then, for the Torah, the requirements of the Torah constitute the givens, which demand explanation, but which must be accepted as facts even when explanation fails. Clearly, Hirsch addressed an audience that had come to doubt the facticity of the facts of the Torah in a way in which none doubted the facticity of the facts of nature.

Once we compare the Torah to nature, the Torah no longer defines the worldview and the way of life at hand. Rather, the Torah takes its place as part of a larger worldview and way of life, one in which the Israelite human being has to accommodate both the received of the Torah and the given of nature. In this worldview the Torah demands explanation, its rules find themselves reduced to the lesser dimensions of an apologia of symbolism, so that they form not givens in an enduring and eternal way of life, but objects of analysis, defense, and reasoned decision. True, Hirsch insisted, "our fulfillment of the commandments must not depend on our investigations." But the investigations must go forward, and that, in and of itself, tells us we deal with a new Judaism.

Restoration and Renewal

Integrationist Orthodoxy never claimed to mark the natural next step in the history of Judaism. For it never conceived of an unfolding history of Judaism. What began at Sinai was fully perfected at Sinai. Integrationist Orthodoxy, along with the entire Torah camp saw itself as nothing other than Judaism pure and simple. In its near-total symmetry with the received system, integrationist Orthodoxy surely made a powerful case for that claim. What is striking is that integrationist Orthodoxy defends propositions that, in the received system, scarcely reached a level of articulate discourse. One striking instance suffices: the absolute necessity to conform to the holy way of life of the Torah. The necessity for making such an argument testifies to the fact that people, within Orthodoxy, thought they confronted the need to choose and they did choose.

Integrationist Orthodoxy formed a deliberate act of restoration and renewal, therefore an act of innovation. The modes of Hirsch's argument, representative as they are of the mentality of the integrationist Orthodoxy he defined, call into question the linear descent of integrationist Orthodoxy from what people called "tradition"—incremental progress, perhaps, but a lineal and unbroken journey, no. Just as the Reformers of the nineteenth century laid emphasis on the points of continuity they located between themselves and the past, so did the integrationist Orthodox. Just as the integrationist Orthodoxy of the nineteenth century specify what mattered more than something else, so did the Reformers (and from their perspective, with greater relevance to the situation at hand).

"The Historical School" or Conservative Judaism: Between Reform and Integrationist Orthodoxy

The story of the modernization of Judaism does not end with integrationist Orthodoxy. The Historical School, a group of a nineteenth-century

German scholars of Judaism, and Conservative Judaism, in America, took the middle position between Orthodoxy and Reform.[24] Conservative Judaism stressed moderation in making change, accommodation between "the tradition" and the requirements of modern life, and above all, adaptation to circumstance. In 1886–1887 rabbis of this same centrist persuasion organized the Jewish Theological Seminary of America, and the Conservative Movement developed as a result. The order of the formation of the several Judaisms of the nineteenth century therefore is, first, Reform, then Orthodoxy, and finally, Conservatism—the two extremes, then the middle. The Historical School shaped the worldview, and Conservative Judaism later brought that view into full realization as a way of life characteristic of a large group of Jews. For a time nearly half, and now at least a third, of all American Jews who practice a Judaism identify themselves with Conservative Judaism.

"Eat Kosher and Think *Traif* [unkosher]"

Conservative Judaism set forth a system of orthopraxy—right deeds without attention to matters of dogma—instead of orthodoxy—right doctrine. Orthopraxy is contained in the odd and cynical slogan of its intellectuals and scholars: "Eat kosher and think *traif*." *Traif* refers to meat that is not acceptable under Judaic law, and the slogan announced: "Do the right thing and it doesn't matter what you believe." That statement meant people should keep the rules of the holy way of life but ignore the convictions that made sense of them. Some would then classify Conservative Judaism in America as an orthoprax Judaism defined through works, not doctrine. Some of its leading voices even denied Judaism set forth doctrine at all in what is called "the dogma of dogmaless Judaism." That dogma would have amazed the framers of Rabbinic Judaism, whose ethical monotheist theology we surveyed in chapter 3.

The Middle of the Road

The middle position then derived in equal measure from the two extremes. The way of life was congruent in most aspects with that of integrationist Orthodoxy, and the worldview was parallel with that of Reform. The two held together in the doctrine of "Israel" that covered everyone. Conservative Judaism laid enormous stress on what the people were doing, on the consensus of what one of its founders called "catholic Israel," meaning, the ethnic-religious group whole. Conservative Judaism saw the Jews as a(nother) people, not merely a(nother) religious community, as Reform did, nor as a unique and holy people, as Orthodoxy did. Orthodoxy took a separatist and segregationist position, leaving the organized Jewish community in Germany as that community fell into the hands of Reform Jews. Reform Judaism, for its part, rejected the position that the Jews constitute a people, not merely a religious community. Conservative Judaism emphasized the importance of the unity of the community as a whole and took a stand in favor of Zionism as soon as that movement got under way.

What separated Conservative Judaism from Reform was the matter of observance. Fundamental loyalty to the received way of life distinguished the Historical School in Germany and Conservative Judaism in America from Reform Judaism in both countries. When considering the continued validity of a traditional religious practice, the Reformers asked why, while the Conservatives asked why not. The Orthodox would ask no questions to begin with. The fundamental principle, that the worldview of the Judaism under construction would rest upon (mere) historical facts, came from Reform Judaism. Orthodoxy could never have concurred. The contrast to the powerful faith despite the world, exhibited by integrationist Orthodoxy's stress on the utter facticity of the Torah, presents in a clear light the positivism of the Conservatives, who, indeed, adopted the name "the *positive* Historical School."

The emphasis on research as the route to historical fact, and on historical fact as the foundation for both theological change and, also, the definition of what was truly authentic in the theological tradition, further tells us that the Historical School was made up of intellectuals. In America, too, a pattern developed in which congregations of essentially nonobservant Jews called upon rabbis whom they expected to be pious and observant of the rules of the religion. As a result many of the intellectual problems that occupied public debate concerned rabbis more than laypeople. That is because the rabbis bore responsibility—so the community maintained—for not only teaching the faith, but also, on their own, embodying it. An observer described this Judaism as "Orthodox rabbis serving Conservative synagogues made up of Reform Jews."

But in a more traditional liturgy, in an emphasis upon observance of the dietary taboos and the Sabbath and festivals—which did, and still does, characterize homes of Conservative more than of Reform Jews—Conservative Judaism did establish an essentially mediating position between Orthodoxy and Reform Judaisms. And the conception that Conservative Judaism is a Judaism for Conservative rabbis in no way accords with the truth. For a long time Conservative Judaism enjoyed the loyalty of fully half of the Jews in America and today, while down to a third of the Jewish community still retains the center and the influential position of Judaism in America. The viewpoint of the center predominates even in the more traditional circles of Reform and the more modernist sectors of Orthodoxy.

Responding to Reform Judaism

Adoption, according to the Reform rabbis, of the Pittsburgh Platform of 1885, cited above, triggered the founding of another school for the education of rabbis besides Hebrew Union College. That marked the beginning of Conservative Judaism. At that point a number of European rabbis now settled in America determined to break from Reform and establish what they hoped would be simply "traditional" Judaism in America. In 1886 they founded the Jewish Theological Seminary of America. The actual event was simple. The final break between the more traditional and the more radical rabbis among the non-Orthodox camp and produced the formation of a group to sponsor a new rabbinical school for "the knowledge and practice of historical Judaism."[25]

The power of Reform Judaism to create and define the character of its own opposition—Orthodoxy in Germany, Conservative Judaism in America—tells us how accurately Reform had outlined the urgent questions of the age. Just as Reform had created Orthodoxy, it created Conservative Judaism. Reform, after all, had treated as compelling the issue of citizenship ("Emancipation") and raised the heart of the matter, how could Jews aspire to return to the Holy Land and form a nation and at the same time take up citizenship in the lands of their birth and loyalty? Jews lived a way of life different from that of their neighbors, with whom they wished to associate. Judaism had to explain that difference.

Both in Germany, in the middle of the century, and in America, at the end, the emphasis lay on "knowledge and practice of historical Judaism as ordained in the law of Moses expounded by the prophets and sages in Israel in Biblical and Talmudic writings," so the articles of Incorporation of the Jewish Theological Seminary of America Association stated in 1887. Calling themselves "traditionalists" rather than "Orthodox," the Conservative adherents accepted the principles of modern critical scholarship for most Judaic subjects. Conservative Judaism therefore exhibited traits that linked it to Reform but also to Orthodoxy, a movement very much in the middle. Precisely how the historical school related to the other systems of its day during the mid- and later-nineteenth century requires attention to that scholarship that, apologists insisted, marked the Historical School off from Orthodoxy.

History and Religion:
The Power of Historicism

Once again we find ourselves squarely in the center of German Reformation theology, with its stress on historical fact as a medium for validating change as Reform. The principle argument in validation of the approach of the Historical School and Conservative Judaism derived from these same facts of history. Change now would restore the way things had been during that golden age that had set the norm and defined the standard. So by changing, Jews would regain that true Judaism that, in the passage of time, had been lost. Reform, then, added up to more than mere change to accommodate the new age, as the Reformers claimed. This kind of reform would conserve, recover, and restore accounting for the basic claim that the centrists discovered how things had always been. By finding out how things had been done, and what had been found essential as faith, in that original and generative time, scholarship would dictate the character of the Judaic system. It would say what it was and therefore what it should again become; and it followed, Conservative Judaism then would be Judaism and not a distinct system thereof. For a long time the leadership of Conservative Judaism refused to frame its message as other than that of "Judaism pure and simple."

Reform identified its Judaic system as the linear and incremental next step in the unfolding of the Torah. The Historical School and Conservative Judaism in the United States later regarded its Judaism as the reversion to the authentic Judaism that had been lost through time. Change was legitimate, as the Reform said, but only that kind of change that restored things to the condition of the original and correct Judaism. This position formed a powerful apologetic because it addressed the Orthodox view that Orthodoxy constituted the linear and incremental outgrowth of "the Torah" or "the tradition," hence, the sole legitimate Judaism. It also addressed the Reform view that change was all right. Conservative Judaism established a firm criterion for which change was all right—the kind that was, really, no change at all. For the premise of the Conservative position was that things should become the way they had always been.

Here we come to the strikingly secular character of the reformist Judaisms. They insisted that religious belief could be established upon a foundation of historical fact. The category of faith, belief in transcendent things (matters not seen or tangible but nonetheless deeply felt and vigorously affirmed) hardly played a role. Rather, fact, ascertained by secular media of learning, would define truth. And truth corresponded to here-and-now reality: how things are. Scholarship would tell how things had always been and dictate those changes that would restore the correct way of life, the true worldview, for the Israel composed of pretty much all the Jews—the center. Historical research therefore provided a powerful apologetic against both sides.

History was the ultimate weapon in the nineteenth century in the struggle among the Judaisms of the age. We therefore understand how much authority was carried by the name "the Historical School" in Germany of the mid-nineteenth century. The claim to replicate how things always had been and should remain thus defined as the ultimate weapon historical research, of a sort. That was, specifically, a critical scholarship that did not accept at face value as history the stories of holy books, but asked whether and how they were true, and in what detail they were not true. That characteristically critical approach to historical study would then serve as the instrument for the definition of Conservative Judaism, the Judaism that would conserve the true faith, but also omit those elements, accretions of later times, that marred that true faith.

Not Revealed Truth but Historical Facts

At issue in historical research into secular facts, out of which the correct way of life and worldview would be defined, was the study of the talmudic literature, that is, the Oral Torah. The Hebrew Scriptures enjoyed immunity. Both the Reformers and the Historical School theologians stipulated that the Written Torah was God given. The Conservatives and Reformers concurred that God gave the Written Torah, and that man made the Oral Torah. So the two parties of change, Reformers and Historical School alike, chose the field of battle, declaring the Hebrew Scriptures to be sacred and outside the war. They insisted that what was to be reformed was the shape of Judaism imparted by the Talmud, specifically, and preserved in their own day by the rabbis whose qualification consisted in learning in the Talmud and approval by those knowledgeable therein.

The Reform and Historical School (Conservative) theologians revered Scripture. Wanting to justify parting company from Orthodox and the received tradition of the Oral Torah, they focused on the Talmud because the Talmud formed the sole and complete statement of the one whole Torah of Moses our rabbi, to which Orthodoxy and the traditionalists of the East, appealed. Hence in bringing critical and skeptical questions to the Talmud, but not to the Hebrew Scriptures, the Conservatives and Reformers addressed scholarship where they wished and preserved as revealed truth what they affirmed as God's will. Therefore the intellectual program of the Historical School in Germany and Conservative Judaism in America consisted of turning the Talmud, studied historically, into a weapon turned against two sides: against the excessive credulity of the Orthodox, but also against the specific proposals and conceptions of the Reformers.

Since the role of scholarship was critical, Conservative Judaism looked to history to show which changes could be made in the light of biblical and rabbinic precedent, "for they viewed the entire history of Judaism as such a succession of changes," Arthur Hertzberg explains.[26] The continuity in history derives from the ongoing people. The basic policy from the beginning, however, dictated considerable reluctance at making changes in the received forms and teachings of the Judaism of the dual Torah. The basic commitments to the Hebrew language in worship, the dietary laws, and the keeping of the Sabbath and festivals, distinguished the Historical School in Europe and Conservative Judaism in America from Reform Judaism. The willingness to accept change and to affirm the political emancipation of the Jews as a positive step marked the group as different from the Orthodox. So far as Orthodoxy claimed to oppose all changes of all kinds, Conservative Judaism took a position in the middle of the three.

Explaining Orthopraxy

The claim of Reform Judaism to constitute an increment of Judaism, we recall, rested on the position that the only constant in "Judaism" is change. The counterpart for Conservative Judaism comes to expression in the writings of Robert Gordis, since his writings set the standard and defined the position of the center of the religion. Specifically, we seek Gordis's picture of the Judaism that came before and how he proposes to relate Conservative Judaism to that prior system. We find a forthright account of "the basic characteristics of Jewish tradition" as follows:

> The principle of development in all areas of culture and society is a funda-
> mental element of the modern outlook. It is all the more noteworthy that
> the Talmud . . . clearly recognized the vast extent to which Rabbinic
> Judaism had grown beyond the Bible, as well as the organic character of
> this process of growth. . . . For the Talmud, tradition is not static—nor does
> this dynamic quality contravene either its *divine origin* or its *organic conti-
> nuity* [all italics his]. . . . Our concern here is with the historical fact, intu-
> itively grasped by the Talmud, that *tradition grows.*[27]

Gordis's appeal is to historical precedent. Without the slightest concern for anachronism, the Conservative theologians found in the tradition ample proof for precisely what they proposed to do. For Gordis's genera-tion the argument directed itself against both Orthodoxy and Reform. In the confrontation with Orthodoxy, Gordis points to new values, institu-tions, and laws "created as a result of new experiences and new felt needs." But to Reform Gordis points out "instances of accretion and of reinterpre-tation, which . . . constitute the major modes of development in Jewish tradition." That is to say, change comes about historically and gradually, over time, and change does not take place by the decree of rabbinical con-vocations. The emphasis of the positive Historical School upon the pro-bative value of historical events, we now recognize, serves the polemic against Reform as much as against Orthodoxy. To the latter, history proves change, and to the former, history dictates modes of appropriate change.

Gordis thus argues that change deserves ratification after the fact, not deliberation beforehand: "Advancing religious and ethical ideals were inner processes, often imperceptible except after the passage of cen-turies." Gordis explicitly claims, on behalf of Conservative Judaism, ori-gin in an incremental and continuous, linear history of Judaism. He does so in an appeal to analogy:

If tradition means development and change . . . how can we speak of the continuity or the spirit of Jewish tradition? An analogy may help supply the answer. Biologists have discovered that in any living organism, cells are constantly dying and being replaced by new ones. . . . If that be true, why is a person the same individual after the passage of . . . years? The answer is twofold. In the first instance, the process of change is gradual. . . . In the second instance, the growth follows the laws of his being. At no point do the changes violate the basic personality pattern. The organic character and unit of the personality reside in this continuity of the individual and in the development of the physical and spiritual traits inherent in him, which persist in spite of the modifications introduced by time. This recognition of the organic character of growth highlights the importance of maintaining the method by which Jewish tradition . . . continued to develop.[28]

The incremental theory follows the modes of thought of Reform, with their stress on the continuity of process. Here too, just as Marcus saw the permanence of change as the sole continuity, Gordis sees the ongoing process of change as permanent. The substance of the issues, however, accords with the stress of Orthodoxy on the persistence of a fundamental character to Judaism. The method of Reform then produces the result of Orthodoxy, at least so far as practice of the way of life would go forward. The differences between Conservative and Reform Judaisms mattered mostly to the rabbis, but to ordinary folk the two Judaisms said mostly the same things to the same people, and that sufficed.

The Middle of the Road Is Never Crowded

The middle did not hold. Aiming at the best of all worlds, Conservative Judaism got the worst. In the mid-1950s, Conservative Judaism was the largest Judaism in the United States and Canada, encompassing one half of the entire Judaic population of North America. At the end of the twentieth century, it had fallen to second place, behind Reform Judaism, and held scarcely a third. The center had collapsed. The elite of Conservative Judaism found its way to Orthodoxy, and the masses began to flow to Reform Judaism.

The most recent scholarship on Conservative Judaism sees the movement at a turning point:

All those who were part of its founding or were educated by the founders have passed away or retired. The new generation taking the lead . . . is a produce of the postwar flowering and was influenced by the institutions created in that flowering. . . .The defection of the most traditional wing to the Union for Traditional Judaism, developments affecting the Masorti Movement in Israel . . . the decision of the University of Judaism to found its own rabbinical school . . . challenge Seminary and United Synagogue leadership to rethink the structure of the Movement.[29]

Conservative Judaism is in decline, but has hope: "Even as its overall membership is declining, there seems to be emerging a generation of Conservative Jews who take Conservative Judaism seriously."[30] Most significant, after a century of development, at this time "no more than 40,000 to 50,000 members . . . live up to the standards of Conservative Judaism as defined by its leadership," out of an estimated million and a half Jews affiliated with that Judaism. Although the center did not hold, in the encounter with modern times, that was the norm for religions.

Discussion Questions

1. How did the change in the status of Christianity (and later on, Islam) affect the questions Judaism had to answer for the Jewish people? What was the effect of political emancipation on the Jews? Did all Jews want to be emancipated, and why not?

2. What made the Reformers call change "reform"? How did the model of the Lutheran Reformation shape the thinking of the founders of Reform Judaism? What was the role of critical history in the theology of the Reformers of Judaism?

3. What is integrationist Orthodoxy, and what is segregationist Orthodoxy? What issue raised by Reform Judaism was addressed by Western Orthodox Judaism? Why did the issue of cultural assimilation demand attention in Germany but not in Poland or Ukraine? How did Reform Judaism define the opposition represented by Orthodox Judaism? Is Orthodox Judaism uniform, or are there types of Orthodox Judaisms to be distinguished from one another?

4. Why does critical history define the method of Conservative Judaism in America, called "the historical school" in Europe? How

does history define legitimate change, and how does historical study lead to valid theological and legal change?

5. What do Conservative theologians mean when they say, "the tradition grows"? How does that affirmation sort out issues of tradition and change?

CHAPTER 14

THE MODERNIZATION OF ISLAM

Th. Emil Homerin

The Problem of Change

Over the centuries, Muslims have experienced periods of religious revival and reform, which have produced diverse interpretations of faith and practice within the Islamic community. Prior to the nineteenth century, movements for religious reform were generally more moral than theological in nature. Activist members of the ʿulama', including al-Ghazali (d. 1111), Ibn Taymiyah (d. 1328), Shah Wali Allah of Delhi (d. 1762), and Ibn ʿAbd al-Wahhab (d. 1791) aimed to cleanse Muslim society of foreign accretions and immoral practices. They also attempted to return the community of believers to the teachings of the Qur'an and the exemplary life of the prophet Muhammad as codified in the shariʿah. However, political dimensions and the urgency of reform became pronounced in the nineteenth and twentieth centuries. Western colonialism, political hegemony, and missionary activity challenged centuries-old notions of Muslim dominance and superiority.[1]

Yet more than political independence was at stake, as western and, later, global cultures have raised a host of new issues and concerns regarding nationalism and secularism, revelation and reason, science, medicine, and technology, modernization and humanism, education and human rights, to name a few. Similar to Jews, Christians, Hindus, and Buddhists, Muslims have responded in various ways to these issues, from the reassertion of traditional beliefs and ritual, to messianic and militant movements for religious sovereignty. Beginning in the mid-nineteenth century, Islamic modernism also arose as a number of Muslims, often liberal intellectuals, tried to forge positive links between the moral and social dimensions of the Qur'an and sunnah, and modern society and institutions in an attempt to reinvigorate Muslim societies.

Islamic modernism has stressed the role of independent human reasoning *(ijtihad)* and the good of the public interest *(maslahah)* as important tools for the reform of religious tradition and society. Of particular importance to Islamic modernists has been the reform of the political process, law, education, and women's rights. The early Egyptian reformist Muhammad Abduh (d. 1905) asserted that the Qur'anic revelation and modern science were compatible, and that modern scientific education was requisite for social, religious, and legal reform. Further, Abduh and other modernists claimed that modern science was, in fact, the product of classical Islam, a part of its heritage to be reappropriated by Muslims. Abduh's views spread throughout the Islamic world and reached as far as Indonesia, while similar ideas were championed among Indian Muslims, especially by Sayyid Ahmad Khan (d. 1898), who inspired the creation of the All-India Muslim League in order to promote Indian nationalism and modern education.

Pakistan's Modernist Experiment

Unlike Muslims in Egypt, Indonesia, Turkey, and Iran, the Muslims of India were a minority. Therefore, some modernists such as Muhammad Iqbal (d. 1938) called for a separate Muslim state there. His dream was realized in 1948 with the creation of Pakistan. In the decades that followed, Pakistan struggled to write a constitution and create a society that would embody Islamic ideals, although these ideals differed among the various political and religious leaders. To help resolve differences of opinion and establish Pakistani law and society on valid Islamic principles, the 1956 and 1961 constitutions mandated the creation of an Advisory Council of Islamic Ideology. The Council was to advise the government regarding proposed legislation and its compatibility with Islam. Similarly the constitutions created the Central Institute of Islamic Research in order to define Islam's fundamental principles "in a 'rational and liberal manner' so as to 'bring out the dynamic character in the context of the intellectual and scientific progress of the modern world.'"[2]

In 1962, Dr. Fazlur Rahman was appointed director of the Institute in addition to serving as a member of the Advisory Council. Rahman seemed ideally suited for these positions; he had received a traditional Muslim education in Pakistan and a Ph.D. in philosophy at Oxford. However, his modernist and scholarly approach to the study of Islam often led him to question contemporary belief and practice, and this angered traditionalists and other conservative religious leaders. Frequently led by the religious activist Abu al-ᶜAla Maududi (d. 1979), mass demonstrations were held against Rahman. He and his family received death threats, and Rahman was forced to resign his positions in 1968 and immigrate to Canada.

In the decades that followed, Pakistan rapidly moved away from its earlier modernist ideals, while appealing to more traditional and Islamist views. Succeeding governments have invoked these traditional and Islamist views to garner the support of the largely illiterate masses. President Muhammad Zia-ul-Haq (d. 1988), for example, openly embraced the "Islamization" of the government and society and went so far as to impose the traditional penalties of lashing, amputation, and stoning for breaking Muslim laws. Subsequent presidents have denounced Zia-ul-Haq's regime as repressive, though much of his program remains in place. As for Rahman, he accepted a position as professor of Islamic studies at the University of Chicago where he continued to teach and study Islam and modernity until his death in 1988.

Among his many publications is the following article from 1970 in which he reflects on Islamic modernism in light of his own experience. Rahman notes that in the late nineteenth and early twentieth centuries, some Muslim thinkers hoped to reform Islamic institutions based on new developments in science, education, economics, and political and social life. Many of their efforts, however, were opposed by conservative religious officials who resisted change and by politicians who wanted to avoid religious controversies and possible social unrest. For these politicians national unity and solidarity against colonialism were to be maintained at all costs. Further, in the 1950s and 1960s, governments in Muslim nations stressed economic development, but not expanded education or a more democratic political system. The result, Rahman maintains, is that Muslim nations today continue to languish in poverty with high rates of illiteracy within their populations. Conservative clerics maintain a strong hold on the largely traditional masses in rural and urban areas, and so governments hesitate to undertake reforms that might offend the religious establishment. This has led to what Rahman terms "the moral underdevelopment" of people who require more education, political rights, and economic justice.

As for progressive Muslim thinkers, they must struggle to carry on their mission in the face of government inaction, hostile religious conservatives, and threats against them by Muslim militants. Some intellectuals choose to remain silent while others seek compromise with tradition, or give up altogether and opt for secularism. Yet Rahman believes that the only honest solution is to rethink Islamic doctrine and practice, especially law, through an historical approach to the Qur'an and its systematic reinterpretation, which must be based on the Qur'an's moral objectives, not on medieval tradition. As we shall see, Rahman's appraisal of efforts toward Muslim reform still holds true more than three decades later.

Islamic Modernism: Its Scope, Method, and Alternatives[3]

Fazlur Rahman

I. Intellectual Modernism

The classical Muslim modernists of the nineteenth century envisaged Islamic Reform as a comprehensive venture: it took in its purview law, society, politics and intellectual, moral and spiritual issues. It dealt with questions of the law of evidence, the status of women, modern education, constitutional reforms, the right of a Muslim to think for himself, God and the nature of the universe and man and man's freedom. A tremendous intellectual fervour and ferment were generated. The liberals and the conservatives battled; the intellectual innovators were opposed and supported, penalized and honored, exiled and enthusiastically followed. Although the modernist movement dealt with all the facets of life, nevertheless, in my view, what gave it point and significance was its basically intellectual *élan* and the specifically intellectual and spiritual issues with which it dealt. This awakening struck a new and powerful chord in the Muslim mind because intellectual issues had remained for centuries under a state of self-imposed dormancy and stagnation at the insistence of conservative orthodoxy. The nineteenth century was also the great age of the battle of ideas in the West, ideas and battles whose strong injections into Muslim society found a ready response. The character of this movement was then primarily intellectual and spiritual.

Intellectual and spiritual issues were given this primacy because the mind of man was thought to be the crucial locus of reform and

530

progress. Whether or not man was a mere plaything in the hands of economic forces and urges, whether he was the grandchild of the ape or a chance product of matter or the immediate cream of creation of an omnipotent and good God, whether or not he was a mere victim of his direct and camouflaged sexual urges—these questions were important because they touched the valuation and destiny of man. Progress was, therefore, essentially *human progress* and its real locus the mind of man—which affected his attitudes and behaviour towards fellow humans and the forces of nature. Gradually but surely, however, this position gave way (under the impact of the ideologies of behavioristic and economic determinism) through new sociological doctrines and new concepts of economic progress—to the view of man as an essentially economic unit and of human progress as essentially economic progress. It would not be perhaps too much to say that Karl Marx remains the genuine father of the present human generation all the world over.

In the case of the Muslim countries, the emphasis on and zeal for pure economic development can be understood, at least on the surface. Like all underdeveloped nations of the East, the Muslims, since their independence, began to exert themselves to catch up with the developed nations and in the process construed their "backwardness" in purely economic terms. They pursued what seemed to them obvious, viz. to try to fill the tremendous economic gap between them and the developed countries. In this conception they were encouraged by their advisors from the developed countries, which also had come to regard development as being essentially economic. These advisors were probably also afraid that their advocacy of changing people, even if for the sake of economic development, might lead to suspicions on the part of the advisees and irreparable frictions. Above all, the concept of purely economic development seemed easy of implementation, for to count inputs and outputs in purely financial terms was easy and allegedly tangible and objective. It is only the failures of such plans to achieve their economic targets that has led sociologists and economists—generally Western—to an awareness that the "intangible" human element with its moral factors may be all-important, although they are still not prepared to do much about it.

But it would be wrong to think that the policies of contemporary Muslim governments are alone responsible for the demise of Islamic intellectual modernism, although they are doing whatever they can to perpetuate its demise by not doing anything to revive it. We have already alluded to the anti-intellectualist posture of Islamic orthodoxy throughout the later medieval centuries of Islam and to the fact that the intellectual ferment was a relatively brief interregnum from the nineteenth to the earlier part of the twentieth century.[4] But even while this intellectual modernism was in progress, the idea that the Muslims must not allow their "unity" and "solidarity" to be endangered in their encounter with the West was strongly asserted and acclaimed. Jamal al-Din al-Afghani, the real father of this modernism, himself called patently both for internal reforms at all levels and presenting a solid unified front against the West. The plea for unity and solidarity was at the outward-looking political level, while the reforms were inward-looking at the socio-intellectual level. As time went on and the conservative forces reacted to this modernizing trend, however, they did not fail to effectively turn the face of the solidarity appeal from outward to inward by pointing out that the forces of modernist reform were creating friction and disunity inside the community, which is the inescapable consequence of any reform. Questions were also raised about the wisdom of the reformists in shaking the confidence of Muslims in themselves—i.e. in their age-old institutions and values—and making them dependent on an alien and inimical civilization. As time went on, undesirable changes in the Western social system—such as the threat to the family institution—were picked up as targets, and a vindication of unqualified pride in the traditional Muslim social institutions was vigorously undertaken.

Under the impact of these and similar factors, the modernist gave in and even joined the reactionary chorus. In the absence of desirability of any kind of change, exercise in intellectual modernism was not only futile but even impossible. The Muslims reverted to stability-in-rigidity, the status of inertia.

II. The Dilemma of the Ruling Modernist

Upon the assumption or reassumption of effective sovereignty, the rulers of the Muslim states were, generally speaking, direct heirs to the pre-independence legacy of inhibitions to socio-moral change, for which theoretical defenses had been produced by the apologetic and revivalist intellectuals. Whereas they saw the imperative necessity of economic development, they generally did not admit the desirability of change in institutions in the socio-moral sphere. Since the Muslim community was sound spiritually, morally and socially and was weak only economically, it must borrow from the West only its economic techniques and must guard itself generally from the socio-moral evil of the modern West, with the exception of modern education—more particularly technological education—and the West's attitude to work. Education and a positive attitude to work, however, were in themselves fundamental social changes, and the direct path of social change being barred, the only hope to bring them about was economic incentive and stimulation. The mass attitude to education has rapidly changed over the years, but the attitude to work has not appreciably altered, particularly in the rural areas, under economic stimuli which, however, have been weak. But the thesis, that many Asians (i.e. Easterners in general) are inherently "backward slopers" does not appear correct to me.[5] Islamic society's attitude to work is a result of depression caused by centuries of exploitation by the upper classes, which can be changed by suitable moral and economic stimuli over a period of time. If this were an inherent feature, why should the upper classes show thrift and "forward sloping"?

This was undoubtedly the initial attitude of most Muslim rulers after independence. But when the thrust for economic progress did not bring satisfactory results and in some cases was almost frustrated because the whole complex of socio-moral institutions was pulling in the opposite direction, the realization began to dawn that it was necessary to change these institutions simultaneously and disturb the status quo. Injustices and exploitation on the farm, in the family, in the factory and the market had to be eliminated or minimized to raise production and, above all, capital formation had to be undertaken through banking institutions. But here the Muslim governments were faced with a new and formidable inhibition, the creation of the post-independence era—popular appeal.

In those sectors within the cultural pattern where reform has required hitting at particular vested groups—powerful though these groups were and entrenched in their vested interest—the rulers have generally carried out total or partial reforms by assuming requisite dictatorial powers. This was the case, for example, with agrarian reforms. In cases, however, where reform—however direly required—was likely to injure the feelings of the masses in general or on a large scale—as, for example, in the family law sphere or in applying direct methods to secure mass mobilization for work—the requisite measures were either not taken or were half-hearted. Outside Turkey, it was in Tunisia alone that polygamy was banned, for instance, and this was facilitated by, among other factors, the relatively small size of its population. The influence of the conservative ʿUlamaʾ is usually feared to be so strong that no authoritarian ruler has been able to face them squarely.

An interesting and revealing feature of the situation has been that the reformist regimes, while they appealed to Islam in their reform bids against the conservatives in the sphere of personal law, ignored Islam altogether when carrying out, for example, sorely needed agrarian and commercial reforms. One reason for this is that the conservative ʿUlamaʾ themselves have been treating subjects like family law as though they were in a specific sense "Islamic," while economic and financial and even political life in general has been relegated by them to a secular or quasi-secular sphere, where the political authority could take independent decisions.[6] This shows how far-reaching the sweep of the secularization of life had become during recent centuries. The point, however, is that whereas the new reformist regimes, in presenting their agrarian or financial reforms as pieces of Islamic social justice, could have enhanced their Islamic *bona fides* and Islamic good will capital, as it were, which would have helped them win mass-support in their struggle against the ʿUlamaʾ they did not do so.[7] In Pakistan, for example, where certain powerful conservatives, including Maududi, attacked the government's land reform measures as being un-Islamic because they involved expropriation of private property—the government did not make a single gesture to prove that these reforms were a requirement of Islamic social justice, and merely relied on the general popularity of these measures for acceptance by the public. In Egypt, the wholesale nationalization of wealth has been presented by Gamal Abdul-Nasser as "Arab socialism," although he allowed and doubtlessly encouraged certain ʿUlamaʾ of al-Azhar to style these very measures as "Islamic socialism." But on the question of mobilization of the masses for work, both Arab and Islamic socialism are silent because this step might not be popular with the masses, however urgently needed and however logical a complement it might be for the nationalization of wealth.

In fact, the feebleness of the modern regimes in the East and their inability to carry out adequate social reforms in the name of popularity, even though most of these regimes are authoritarian, is a very fundamental feature of the present situation. Myrdal has incisively remarked that the modern Western democratic governments have, in fact, been able to apply pressure for effecting their socioeconomic reform programs in the recent past to a much greater extent than these Eastern governments.[8] "Force" here primarily means the force of law, i.e. the ability to make the law effective. In Western countries this has been obviously made possible by a more developed socio-economic consciousness of the public and a more mature moral sense in the socio-political sphere. However, certain governments have mobilized troops at certain points; for instance, the United States of America has had to do so to enforce civil rights.[9] This reveals the real dilemma of the Eastern regimes, viz. the *moral underdevelopment* of the people *for* whom and *in* whose name development programs are undertaken without any role being taken by them. This is the dilemma of democracy in an underdeveloped— primarily *morally* underdeveloped—society. This is what gives meaning to the concept of "authoritarian democracy," a regime through which one hopes real democracy will develop.

Yet, the authoritarian ruler has the best existential chance of succeeding in carrying out large-scale socio-moral reforms if only he shows boldness and courage. He not only possesses sufficient actual power for enforcement but also controls the media of mass communication—the press, radio and television—which can be effectively used for suitable inducement of public opinion if tactfully operated. In such a situation, if *he* does not implement such reforms, it is difficult to see how else reform will come about at all. By his faint-heartedness and lack of determination, he lets slip his most valuable opportunity in the name of the unity and solidarity of the society. He thus inadvertently plays into the hands of and strengthens the conservative extremists who killed the earlier modernist reform trends precisely on the same platform. A state of true stability and solidarity does not consist of merely static internal cohesion of the various factors and elements of society; it consists of an adjustment to the total social organism to movement and change. The concept of partial reform cannot work, for it reverts to negative stability.

It is not, however, the authoritarian ruler alone who acts as a drag on reform in the Islamic world. Besides the alleged pressure of the masses, the greatest limitation of today's dictator is his own advisors and particularly the bureaucratic machinery of the government. Even though the governments in these countries are and, indeed, have to be the main agency of change, many bureaucrats, for a number of reasons, are themselves averse to change and very often thwart the policies and even the specific orders of the top rulers.[10] One can still find officials who, for example, think mass literacy to be an eventual threat to the bureaucratic authority itself. If one works with these governments closely and for a long enough period, one is astonished to see to what extent lack of reform may be attributed not to the masses directly but to the drag-effect of government officialdom.

III. Intellectuals' Methods of Reform

If the governments' minimal-action policies were restrictable to government circles alone, the field would be left free for intellectuals to conduct free discussion, and such uninhibited public debate could produce the necessary milieu for the governments to act in turn. In the Muslim countries, however, the governments' attitudes—explicit, but even implicit, ones—tend to affect and inhibit the intellectuals as well in various ways. All-powerful and mostly authoritarian as these governments are, most intellectuals—and, indeed, everybody—in these countries tend to "look up" to the center of power; it takes nothing short of a "rebel" to speak out without taking government policies into consideration. This, combined with the massive power of the conservative ᶜUlama' tends to crush intellectualism out of existence. Under the circumstances, the intellectuals toy with, advocate, and sometimes practice various approaches to Islamic modernism. These approaches can be broadly classified as follows:

(1) Silence

One may question the permissibility of categorizing as intellectuals people who are simply mute. But if being educated and having a capacity to think are any criteria for being an intellectual, this mute class is very large indeed. Nor would it be true to say that they are "indifferent." Occasionally when they talk in private, they may exhibit a high degree of sensibility and intelligence, but in the general atmosphere prevailing they either lose the propensity to be intellectuals or think it "inadvisable" to be so. Sometimes their intellectualism may be channeled into different directions. This class includes a large number of government officials, lawyers and other educated persons.[11] This category should be extended to include those small groups that meet at a friend's residence and informally discuss questions, either haphazardly or regularly. This group, although it is not vocal is, at least, not equivocal either and does not possess the duplicity we find in the following group.

(2) Double-speaking and double-writing

All over the modern world there is to be found not infrequently a phenomenon of janus-faced attitudes. When a society is in change, people—not excluding intellectuals—exhibit attitudes and also express views at least partially under the impact of and in response to the new forces of change, with part being a relic of or hang-over from the traditions of the past. This feature is particularly accentuated when the changing society is wedded to a strong tradition especially backed by powerful institutions. Often this attitude is not crass duplicity or hypocrisy, but there is a genuine contradiction within the person's mind and he gives his loyalty to both terms of the contradiction. This is a form of doublemindedness and is a function of the transition period.[12]

There is, however, a different type of attitude which is the result of systematic and cultivated double-mindedness, and this is duplicity or hypocrisy *par excellence*. This happens when people hold different views and beliefs from those of the masses in a highly traditional society which has strong social institutions for penalizing change. Often this is a function of a very limited "elite" in a sea of traditionalism. The intellectual in this case tries to ease his conscience from the inner strains of double mindedness and justifies for himself and, by implication for others, the entertainment, or at least expression of loyalty to contradictory beliefs "at different levels." Sometimes a grandiose principle is erected to the effect that the masses may hold beliefs which are contrary to truth but which may have pragmatic effects. Certain late Greek philosophers, particularly the Stoics, defended their popular religion on this principle from the onslaughts of Christianity. Certain Hindu intellectuals of today hold similar views about the cults of their popular religion. When these people are with the masses they identify themselves with mass religion, when they are in the company of the elite, they express contrary views.

In Islam, the tradition of such cultivated duplicity runs quite strong and deep. Not only do the *Shiʿa* traditionally believe in *Taqiya*, or cultivated dissimulation of beliefs, but the Sunnis also have powerful strands of this attitude. Often the apparently sound principle: "You should talk to people at the level of their understanding"—which is essentially a principle of diplomacy—is invoked to justify duplicity. The Muslim philosopher Avicenna, while accepting the doctrine of the resurrection of the body in all his major philosophical works, wrote a special treatise for his inner circle seeking to prove that physical resurrection was impossible and was intended only as a measure of "inducement and warning" for the masses so that they would be virtuous. In general, the Muslim philosophers believed with the Greeks—that all religious movements were purely pragmatic (but untrue) measures meant for the masses. Al-Ghazali, while he bitterly attacked the philosophers, nevertheless wrote certain esoteric works incorporating much of the same philosophy. Esotericism has, indeed, infected Sunni Islam quite strongly via Sufism. There are other important examples. Muhammad Iqbal, for instance, wrote his *Reconstruction of Religious Thought in Islam*, which contained sweeping reform proposals in English—a language not understood by the masses or the ͨ*Ulama*', and kept his powerful and moving poetry—meant for the common man—mainly free of such reforms.[13]

If Muslim tradition offers many cases of such duplicity, it has hit the modern educated Muslim intelligentsia on the scale of a plague. This phenomenon obviously has a tendency to generate extremists—by pushing otherwise moderate people of integrity to rebellion and therefore producing pure secularists of various types against Islam.

(3) Reform through tradition

Most modern reformists who are genuine espouse the principle of reform through tradition. Its use reaches back into the heart of Islamic modernism in the nineteenth and the early twentieth centuries. Since the motivation for adopting this principle is to ensure the all-important purpose of continuity-in-change, it is basically sound provided it is wielded with care and honesty. There are certain questions which may particularly lend themselves to such a treatment by appeal to a traditional authority. Several Muslims have, for example, sought to support their advocacy of family-limitation programmes, opposed by most traditionalists, quoting al-Shafiͨi's interpretation of the Qur'an[14] or the *Khutba* of ͨAmr ibn al-ͨAs to the Muslim camps in Egypt. The value of this procedure lies in the fact that one is able to meet the traditionalists by their own weapons in using tradition.

But it is obvious that this approach suffers from serious limitations and a fundamental drawback. Its fundamental shortcoming consists in the fact that by an appeal to tradition (rather than to a rational interpretation of tradition), one is strengthening traditionalism itself and doing fundamental harm to modernism. If tradition were rationally interpreted and then conclusions drawn from it for the present Muslim situation, this would be the proper procedure. But usually a simple mechanical appeal to tradition is made. When, in such a context, a tradition is quoted, the traditionalist is often in the strong position of quoting a much larger number of traditions, appealing to the centuries-long practice on his side and dismissing the modernist's tradition as "weak" and inconsequential even if he cannot claim *Ijma*[15] for himself thanks to the modernist's tradition. There is, therefore, no real substitute for a genuinely rational and honest interpretation of traditions. By so interpreting tradition, the same purpose of continuity can be served, while at the same time vindicating the modernist's advocacy of reform.

A classic case of this type is the new inheritance law in Egypt, which seeks to give benefit to an orphaned grandchild from the inheritance of his deceased grandfather through the principle of a mandatory will on the part of the grandfather. Since the framers of this law were afraid that they could not find support in tradition for granting a direct share to the orphaned grandchild, they had recourse to the "mandatory will" concept. But this idea is also against tradition, and the mention of the will—not mandatory will—in the Qur'an cannot give it putative traditional support. Further, by measuring the grandchild's portion as being equivalent to "his father's share if the latter were alive," the law clearly reveals that what is really being given is a share in inheritance and not the benefit of any will.

A more formalized procedure of reform through tradition is the principle known as *Talfiq*. According to this principle, if on a given issue serious hardship is likely to be experienced by the opinion of a particular school of traditional law, recourse may be had to the opinion of another school of traditional law, which may be more accommodating or expedient. This procedure is a legacy of premodernist liberalizing trends in Islam. To a limited extent, this principle may be still applied on certain questions without injuring the fundamentals of modernist reform, provided the demands of inner consistency are not violated. But a wholesale application of it would obviously sacrifice modernism at the altar of traditionalism. In a sense, the acceptance of this procedure as a *principle* is a retrogression even from the position of the Wahhabism of the eighteenth century. For, whereas the Wahhabis had limited traditional authority, besides the Qur'an and the Sunna, to the earliest generations, this principle allows appeal to anything in the past as though the past as such had authority. And, of course, it makes *Ijtihad*[16] utterly redundant—because this principle looks backward, not forward.

But often even the demands of consistency are sacrificed by the operations of *Talfiq*. Since, for example, Hanafi law concerning the prolonged absence of a husband whose whereabouts are not known creates difficulties by demanding that the wife wait ninety years before she can remarry, modern legislation in various Muslim countries has adopted the Maliki law which requires a waiting period of four years only. The bases of the two laws are, however, quite different. Whereas Hanafi law contends that the woman should wait until the natural (maximum) life-term expires, and only then can she presume her husband dead, the Maliki law, instead of requiring a life-term waiting, requires that the woman wait till the natural maximum gestation period expires, which according to Malik is four years. In fact, this was a perfect case for *Ijtihad* if only the modernists had chosen to perform it. Of the three bases for waiting, i.e. the Hanafi basis of a life-term, the Maliki idea of a maximum period of gestation (according to Malik) and the time it takes to find out, through the modern developed media of communication, the possible whereabouts of the husband, the new legislation could have chosen a lesser period by rejecting the Hanafi basis altogether and modifying the Maliki view about the duration of gestation in favour of a lesser period established by gynecology. Indeed, the Laws of Evidence of these countries, do, in fact, fix the period of gestation in conformity with the general findings of modern gynecology, thus contradicting Islamic law on the matter.

Sometimes a curious simple reversion to traditionalism takes place under the stress of exceptional circumstances. The presidential election of Pakistan of 1964-5 is an instance in point. During the heat-period of the campaign, Ayub Khan was persuaded by his advisors to condemn the candidacy of his opponent, Miss Fatima Jinnah, on the traditionalist ground that Islam does not permit a woman to be head of state. Miss Jinnah herself was, of course, primarily exploiting the image of her dead brother (besides whatever resentment existed against Ayub Khan), rather than standing on her personal merit. Ayub Khan may well have achieved the same object by stressing the question of the relative merits, capacities, and performance of the two candidates; instead, he created a serious dent in his otherwise admirably consistent and steadfast modernist position by appealing to traditionalist forces. Incidentally, Maududi, the authentic and effective voice of organized conservatism in Pakistan, who in an earlier book had tried to prove that in Islam a woman could not only not be head of a state but could hold no public office at all, supported Miss Jinnah publicly with a severe resultant loss of his clientele on such a blatant *volte face!*

(4) The partialist and link approach

Another attitude, rather vague in its substance but very strong in its motivation, is what may be termed the partialist and/or the link method. This approach contends that Islamic modernism must not be undertaken simultaneously on all levels or so many fronts but must be piecemeal and "gradual," avoiding swift and large-scale change. This position seems attractive enough on its face, but when one pauses to inquire into its content, extraordinary confusion and vagueness are revealed. Very often it means simply that one must not discuss the problems of modernization intellectually, explicating the issues involved, but that modern institutions should be set up and worked "silently" and independently as separate units without any reference to Islam.[17] Banks should be established and multiplied for capital formation and should be allowed to work "successfully" without raising and solving the issue of the almost unanimous traditionalist position that bank-interest is illegal in Islam. Certain modern Western practitioners of economic development in the Middle East hold similar views. Max Thornburg, in his otherwise admirably sober work *People and Policy in the Middle East*, states:

> If values reflect a long gone past that cannot be changed now, how can these values themselves be changed? . . . But, the practitioner asks, does the process of growth require that existing values be changed? Or only that new values—values upon innovations—be created that are more compelling in their effect than the old ones?[18]

That this path is the path of gradual but sure secularism—the total displacement in time of not only traditional Islam but Islam itself—is obvious, for it seeks to create modern institutions divorced from, not in integration of, Islamic values. This is also what is often meant by "gradual" reform. It is obvious that whereas the proponents of this view often describe it as "link-approach", it is in reality just the opposite—discarding even the very need for links with the Islamic sources. When a Muslim propounds this view, he only authenticates the intellectual demise of Islamic modernism. While admitting that Islamic reform is a process and not a coup, one may be permitted to ask how this process is to be made possible at all on the basis of such an approach. There is simply no substitute for a conscious formulation of the problem, however irksome and painful this procedure may be. And given time, it will not remain as painful.

A slightly different but fundamentally the same intellectual approach is illustrated by the question of *Zakat*, the only tax imposed by the Qur'an. Its expenditure items are so multifarious—including defense, communications, education (according to Qur'an commentators) and even diplomatic expenditure—that all the social needs of the Prophet's society were thought to be covered by it, although it is generally misunderstood today to be only a "poor-tax." Since the economy in which it was conceived and to which it was applied was a predevelopment economy, it was conceived as a wealth-tax leviable on the surplus and hoarded wealth of a person (not on the yearly revenue as some writers think). Particularly in the modern period, *Zakat* became a purely voluntary charity when its place was taken by the secular taxation of the modern state.

There is, however, a general demand by the Muslim public to restore *Zakat* as a tax—it was enshrined in the two late constitutions of Pakistan, and several Middle Eastern countries have, in fact, set up offices to collect voluntary payments of *Zakat*. In the new developing economy, however, large industrialists can usually escape it as it was conceived in medieval times since they usually have heavy overdrafts from the banks (and are thus "debtors") and little cash surplus. A more invidious phenomenon is that many people—including industrialists— evade government and "secular" taxes and ease their consciences by paying a pittance of *Zakat*, the primary beneficiaries of which are the traditional schools, or *Madrasas* run and controlled by the *Ulama'*. In 1966 when I suggested in Pakistan that Muslims might rationalize and streamline the taxation structure by reintroducing *Zakat*, refixing its rates in view of the colossal rise in government spending, extending it to the sector of the invested wealth from merely hoarded wealth and thus restoring to the tax-payer his proper Islamic motivation and minimizing tax-evasion, the amount of opposition it provoked from the ranks of the *Ulama'* was astonishing. There was a controversy on a national scale.

The advice which came forth from most modernists in the aftermath of this controversy was that I was seeking too abrupt a change in the established practice of current Islam, that at first the government might collect *Zakat* on a voluntary basis, later it could turn it into a formal tax, and after that all taxation could be brought under the aegis of *Zakat* by introducing changes into its structure similar to those I had suggested. The point to note here is that these modernists were as much shocked as were the conservatives by my *intellectual formulation* of the problem for, so far as the practical side is concerned, I was not advocating an overnight change in the taxation system since this would be possible only under an extraordinary dictatorial modernist regime. What is important is that the modernist not only wants piecemeal and gradual implementation but also piecemeal *thinking* and is shocked by an intellectual formulation which attempts to identify the various aspects of the matter and seeks to produce a coherent view of it. It is this attempt at keeping intellectual activity either at zero point or at the minimal possible level and to excogitate fundamental issues that is the bane of Islamic modernism. How is any reform to come about?

(5) The systematic interpretation method

If the Muslims' loud and persistent talk about the viability of Islam as a system of doctrine and practice in the world of today is genuine (a question the answer to which is not easy to determine), then it seems clear that they must once again start at the intellectual level. They must candidly and without inhibitions discuss what Islam wants them to do today. The entire body of the *Shari'a* must be subjected to fresh examination in the light of the Qur'anic evidence. A systematic and bold interpretation of the Qur'an must be undertaken. The greatest peril in this undertaking would be, no doubt, the projection of subjective ideas into the Qur'an, making it the object of arbitrary treatment. But although this may be a very grave danger it is not all as inevitable as it has been made out to be, and it can certainly be largely minimized. A strict methodology for understanding and interpreting the Qur'an should be adopted.

(a) A sober and honest historical approach must be used for finding the meaning of the Qur'anic text. The metaphysical aspect of Qur'anic teaching may not lend itself very easily to historical treatment, but the sociological part certainly will. First of all, the Qur'an must be studied in chronological order. An examination of the earliest revelations to begin with will bestow an accurate enough perception of the basic impulse of the Islamic movement as distinguished from measures and institutions established later. And so one must follow the unfolding of the Qur'an through the career and struggle of Muhammad. This historical method will save us much of the extravagance and artificiality of modernist interpretations of the Qur'an. Apart from fixing the meaning of details, this method will also bring out the overall import of the Qur'anic message in a systematic and coherent manner.

(b) Then one is ready to distinguish between Qur'anic legal dicta and the *objectives* and *ends* these laws were expected to serve. Here one is again exposed to the danger of subjectivity, but this can again be reduced to the minimum by using the Qur'an itself. It has been all too often overlooked by non-Muslims and Muslims alike that the Qur'an normally gives reasons for its specific legal pronouncements. Two women's evidence in lieu of one man's, why?—"so that one woman should remind the other in case the other forgets":[19] This is a clear commentary on the sociological setting of the Prophet's Arabia and an insistence that correct evidence must be produced as far as possible. Is this imperative so difficult of implementation that the Muslim should feel peculiarly embarrassed today?

(c) The objectives of the Qur'an must be understood and fixed, keeping in full view its sociological setting, i.e. the environment in which the Prophet moved and worked. This will put an end to subjective interpretations of the Qur'an, be they medieval or modern— even if these interpretations appear to be coherent within themselves. A person like Mr. G.A. Parvez, for example, may systematically produce from the Qur'an a communist type of doctrine and use all the tools at his disposal to do so, but the historic-sociological approach will belie him. If one is determined not to carry one's own obsessions into the Qur'an, this approach will be most rewarding and, we believe, the only real hope for a successful interpretation of it today. In a macroscopic sense (as opposed to distinctions of detail), however, all interpretations and approaches to truth are subjective, and this cannot be eliminated. All views have a point of view, and there is no harm in this provided the angle of vision does not distort the object of vision and is also exposed to other viewers' visions. Indeed, the difference of opinion thus generated is healthy provided only the opinions are not unreasonable.

Difficulties and differences of interpretation will undoubtedly arise also on this sociological approach, but it is the only approach that can also lead to satisfactory solutions. Take, for example, the case of punishment for theft stated in the Qur'an, viz. the cutting off of a hand. The classical jurists tried to find a "way out" by making the definition of theft very narrow and by applying the principle of "benefit of doubt" with extraordinary generosity to all cases of what they call *hudud*.[20] This, of course, meant that even people who were really guilty received no punishment at all, for no other punishment, in their view, could be substituted for a *hadd* punishment. When there exists a law—and divine law at that—which is hardly ever applied, the moral evil wrought by such a situation is obvious. In modern times there have been other attempts at interpreting this verse. The phrase "the cutting of a hand" (*qat͑ al-yad*), it has been argued, may be taken metaphorically, i.e. making it impossible for people to commit theft or putting it "beyond their reach" through economic sufficiency. Historically, however, it is certain that the cutting off of a hand of a thief was literally meant and practiced. On what basis, then, can we turn from the literal to the metaphorical? Sociologically, it appears that this practice already existed among certain tribes before Muhammad and that it was adopted by the Qur'an. In the concept of theft there are two main elements, the wrongful taking away of an *economic* entity and the violation of the right of *private* possession. In a tribal setting the right of possession is strongly associated with an accentuated sense of personal honor and theft is primarily regarded, not as an economic crime, but as a crime against values of personal honor and its inviolable sanctity. In advanced urbanized societies, however, there is a visible shift in values, and theft comes to be looked upon more in economic terms as wrongful depriving of the owner by the thief of the former's right to use a certain economic asset or facility. Already ͑Izz al-Din ibn ͑Abd al-Salam has noted that "many people have a tendency in our day to forgive the thief out of sympathy for him."[21] This genuine shift in values requires a change in punishment.

This sociological approach does raise serious questions of a theological nature about the eternity of the Word of God and Divine Law.

But theological questions can be and, indeed, must be tackled at the proper plane of theology. The eternity of the Word of God can be substantially admitted. As for the eternity of the letter of the Law, it may be justifiably contended that in questions which touch social regulations, the Divine Ordinance has a moral plane and a specifically legal plane, the latter being a transaction between the eternity of the Word and the actual ecological situation of seventh-century Arabia. The ecological aspect is obviously liable to change. We know that ʿUmar ibn al-Khattab, [the second caliph], had to introduce certain drastic changes in social regulations, sometimes bitterly opposed by eminent Companions of the Prophet.

Although this method of interpretation of the Qur'an and the Sunna seems to be the most satisfactory and perhaps the only possible one—it is honest, true and practical—there is no reason to believe that Muslims are ready to accept it. The backwash on conservatism since the second decade of this century has been so strong that it has virtually killed intellectualism, of whose revival there are no signs at present for reasons briefly outlined in the earlier part of this paper. Certainly in Pakistan, where it was mooted, this approach met with an almost total negative response—largely without being even studied properly. It has been accused of being too total and abrupt, of sacrificing too much of traditional, i.e. "historic," Islam at a single stroke, and of suspected "West-oriented" motivation. However, all other methods, as our analysis has shown, are essentially farcical devices of marking time. Under the circumstances, secularism alone would seem to have the best chance of eventual success.

(6) Secularism

The pressures of a moribund conservatism and the imbecilities of Islamic modernism directly generate secularism. Secularism in Islam, properly speaking, is the acceptance of laws and other social and political institutions *without reference to Islam*, i.e. without their being derived from, or organically linked with, the principles of the Qur'an and the Sunna. In the West, however, there is a pervasive confusion with regard to the concept of secularism in Islamic society. Despite the work of H. A. R. Gibb (and partly W. C. Smith) many Western writers, particularly sociologists, tend to think, along with Muslim conservatives, that changes induced into the content of the *Shariʿa* constitute secularism. But if Islamic modernism means anything, it means precisely the induction of change into the content of the *Shariᶜa*—large-scale and multilateral change indeed. And once the principle of change has been admitted on the line enunciated in this paper, it cannot stop anywhere—not even short of touching the specifically legal dicta of the Qur'an. Its only limit and necessary framework is the spiritual and ethical foundational principles and social objectives of the Qur'an.

At the bottom of this confusion, both among Muslim conservatives and Western writers, lies the stated or implicit identification of the *Shariᶜa* with the Muslim past, rather than with the truth of Islam. Thus, when Maududi says, "Islam is not our property for us to *offer it to others*, with alterations suitable to the requirements of the market," it is in substance what Manfred Halpern says, "The *Shariᶜa* has by now ceased to be the primary source of ethics, and insofar as its rules survive in modern laws, it has ceased to be either divine or final. . . . Once everyone was free to make judgments, it was clear that the *Shariᶜa* would have to give way. There was no longer a single highway into the future. The Turks did not bother to retain any part of the *Shariᶜa*."[22] The author of this quotation obviously thinks that Muslims should change bits of the *Shariᶜa* content here and there and still have the consolation that they have not tampered too much with "God's will" after all!—a less logical position than Maududi's. If the test of the distinction between secular law and religious law is that the former is man-made while the latter is God-made, then classical Muslim law is already largely secular for it is clearly the work of Muslim legists.

Secular attitudes and procedures are an important fact of reality in the Muslim world. The actual workings of the governmental institutions in all Muslim countries are secular, whether in the declared Islamic Republic of Pakistan or the declared Secular Republic of Turkey or the silent Republic of Egypt. The most important fact about this phenomenon, however, is that, as we said earlier, this secularism is forced by, and a natural reaction to, the conservative forces in Islam which did not and still do not allow a consistent and large-scale rethinking of the content of the *Shariᶜa* at an ethico-legal plane. Not even Turkey, where secularism has been espoused expressly and as a principle, is an exception to this for, in fact, Turkish secularism was historically induced, not on any philosophic basis, but as the stark alternative to conservatism. In the West too secularism came as a relief from the encroachments of the Church on the State but it found its philosophic basis, not only in reason, but in the earlier Christian formula of a division of labor between Caesar and God.

Muslim secularism could, therefore, be possibly conceived as an alternative form of, or as a phase of, Islamic modernism. It could also, of course, become genuine secularism in the course of time if either the forces of conservatism did not weaken or become enlightened or if, by the time the conservative forces weakened, the will to return to Islam did not remain strong enough on the part of the modernized classes. This is a very strong possibility, and certain current trends in the rising Muslim middle class support this alternative. But should the attachment to Islam remain undiminished (and it is a remarkable fact how strong this attachment is even in the younger generation in Turkey), the possibility remains vivid that the entire content of modern secularism, as imbibed by Muslim societies, would be organically integrated into the truth-sources of Islam—the Qur'an and the Sunna. That this is theoretically feasible cannot be denied, even in the initial phase of the legal development of Islam both processes took place, viz. to attempt to derive law directly from the Qur'an (the task we have assigned to Islamic modernism) and to Islamize the legal and institutional materials that were simply adopted from outside Islam (the task of Islamization of secular modernism).

Time alone will tell what choice the Muslims will make. For the time being, there exists only a total vacuum of Islamic intellectualism and a proliferation of modern secular institutions, which are ill at ease and largely sterile and unproductive due to a lack of integration with the conservative milieu. The new forces being generated on a gigantic scale by education, industry and development have clustered around the issues not so much of law but of the methods of generations of wealth, the nature of the means of production and, above all, of social justice. The earlier legal terms have been completely overshadowed. Ideologically, therefore, the Muslim countries are desperately ill-prepared with an Islamic framework to direct and channel these new forces and to control change.

Women

Until his death in 1988, Fazlur Rahman pursued his proposed systematic study of the Qur'an and Islam, most notably in *Major Themes of the Qur'an* (1980) and "The Status of Women in Islam: A Modernist

Interpretation" (1982). In the latter article, he carefully reviewed the Qur'an's many statements regarding the religious and social status of women and the related issues of veiling, polygamy, inheritance, and other matters. Rahman found that the Qur'an promoted religious and social equality and justice between men and women and that "what the Qur'an basically aimed at was the removal of certain abuses to which women were subjected."[23] Thus Rahman concluded that many of the Qur'an's legal rules applied only in specific social-historical conditions, which may no longer apply today. What is eternal within the laws is the social objectives and moral principles, and so reform or further legislation should be carried out in light of these explicit objectives and principles, not outdated rules and regulations.[24]

Rahman's modernist position in support of women and their individual dignity and human rights has been shared by other Muslim modernist men and women who hold that the liberation of Muslim women from patriarchy is essential to religious and social reform. Since the mid-1970s, scores of publications have appeared on various aspects of the lives and rights of Muslim women, though few scholars have had Rahman's mastery of the scriptural sources and theological positions involved. A notable exception, however, is Riffat Hassan, professor of religious studies and the humanities at the University of Louisville in Kentucky. Actively involved with human rights today, Dr. Hassan is an outspoken advocate for Muslim women as well as a feminist scholar of Islam. In the following article, Dr. Hassan draws on both her experience as a Muslim woman and her insightful research as a scholar of Islam.

The Issue of Woman-Man Equality in the Islamic Tradition[25]

Riffat Hassan

Background of My Work in the Area of Theology of Women in Islam

Experientially I have always known what it means to be a Muslim woman since I was born female in a Saiyyad[26] Muslim family living in Lahore, a historic Muslim city in Pakistan, a country created in the name of Islam. However, it was not until the fall of 1974 that I began my career as a "feminist" theologian almost by accident and rather reluctantly. I was, at that time, faculty adviser to the Muslim Students' Association (MSA) chapter at Oklahoma State University in Stillwater, Oklahoma. This "honor" had been conferred upon me solely by virtue of the fact that each student association was required to have a faculty adviser, and I happened to be the only Muslim faculty member on campus that year. The office bearers of the MSA chapter at Stillwater had established the tradition of having an annual seminar at which one of the principal addresses was given by the faculty adviser. In keeping with tradition I was asked—albeit not with overwhelming enthusiasm—if I would read a paper on women in Islam at the seminar that was to be held later that year. I was aware of the fact that, in general, faculty advisers were not assigned specific subjects. I was asked to speak about women in Islam at the seminar— in which, incidentally, Muslim women were not going to participate—because in the opinion of most of the chapter members it would have been totally inappropriate to expect a Muslim woman, even one who taught them Islamic Studies, to be competent to speak on any other subject pertaining to Islam. I resented what the assigning of a subject meant. Furthermore, I was not much interested in the subject of women in Islam until that time. Nevertheless, I accepted the invitation for two reasons. First, I knew that being invited to address an all-male, largely Arab Muslim group that prided itself on its patriarchalism, was itself a breakthrough. Second, I was so tired of hearing Muslim men pontificate upon the position, status, or role of women in Islam, while it was totally inconceivable that any woman could presume to speak about the position, status, or role of men in Islam. I thought that it might be worthwhile for a Muslim woman to present her viewpoint on a subject whose immense popularity with Muslim men, scholars and non-scholars alike, could easily be gauged by the ever-increasing number of books, booklets, brochures, and articles they published on it. Having accepted the invitation I began my research more out of a sense of duty (knowing that willing the end involves willing the means to the end) than out of any deep awareness that I had set out on perhaps the most important journey of my life.

I do not know exactly at what time my "academic" study of women in Islam became a passionate quest for truth and justice on behalf of Muslim women—perhaps it was when I realized the impact on my own life of the so-called Islamic ideas and attitudes regarding women.

What began as a scholarly exercise became simultaneously an Odyssean venture in self-understanding. But "enlightenment" does not always lead to "endless bliss." The more I saw the justice and compassion of God reflected in the Qur'anic teachings regarding women, the more anguished and angry I became, seeing the injustice and inhumanity to which Muslim women, in general, are subjected in actual life. I began to feel strongly that it was my duty—as a part of the microscopic minority of educated Muslim women—to do as much consciousness-raising regarding the situation of Muslim women as I could. The journey that began in Stillwater has been an arduous one. It has taken me far and wide in pursuit of my quest. When I remember the stormy seas and rocky roads I have traversed, it seems like the journey has been a long one. But when I think of my sisters who, despite being the largest "minority" in the world—more than half of the one-billion-strong Muslim *ummah*[27]—remain for the most part nameless, faceless, and voiceless, I know that there is no end to the journey in sight.

Despite the fact that women such as Khadijah and 'A'ishah (wives of the Prophet Muhammad) and Rabi'a al-Basri (the outstanding woman Sufi) figure significantly in early Islam, the Islamic tradition has, by and large, remained rigidly patriarchal until the present time, prohibiting the growth of scholarship among women particularly in the realm of religious thought. This means that the sources on which the Islamic tradition is mainly based, namely, the Qur'an, the Sunnah,[28] the Hadith literature,[29] and Fiqh,[30] have been interpreted only by Muslim men who have arrogated to themselves the task of defining the ontological, theological, sociological, and eschatological status of Muslim women. It is hardly surprising that until now the majority of Muslim women have accepted this situation passively, almost unaware of the extent to which their human (also Islamic, in an ideal sense) rights have been violated by their male-dominated and male-centered societies, which have continued to assert, glibly and tirelessly, that Islam has given women more rights than any other religious tradition. Kept for centuries in physical, mental, and emotional bondage, and deprived of the opportunity to actualize their human potential, even the exercise of analyzing their personal experiences as Muslim women is, perhaps, overwhelming for these women. (Here it needs to be mentioned that while the rate of literacy is low in many Muslim countries, the rate of literacy of

Muslim women, especially those who live in rural areas, where most of the population lives, is among the lowest in the world.)

In recent times, largely due to the pressure of anti-women laws that are being promulgated under the cover of "Islamization" in some parts of the Muslim world, women with some degree of education and awareness are beginning to realize that religion is being used as an instrument of oppression rather than as a means of liberation. To understand the strong impetus to "Islamize" Muslim societies, especially with regard to women-related norms and values, it is necessary to know that of all the challenges confronting the Muslim world, perhaps the greatest is that of modernity. The caretakers of Muslim traditionalism are aware of the fact that viability in the modern technological age requires the adoption of the scientific or rational outlook that inevitably brings about major changes in modes of thinking and behavior. Women, both educated and uneducated, who are participating in the national work force and contributing toward national development, think and behave differently from women who have no sense of their individual identity or autonomy as active agents in a history-making process and regard themselves merely as instruments designed to minister to and reinforce a patriarchal system that they believe to be divinely instituted. Not too long ago, many women in Pakistan were jolted out of their "dogmatic slumber" by the enactment of laws (such as those pertaining to women's rape or women's testimony in financial and other matters) and by "threatened" legislation (such as proposals pertaining to "blood-money" for women's murder) that aimed to reduce them systematically, virtually mathematically, to less than men. It was not long before they realized that forces of religious conservatism were determined to cut women down to one-half or less of men and that this attitude stemmed from a deep-rooted desire to keep women "in their place," which means secondary, subordinate, and inferior to men.

In the face of both military dictatorship and religious autocracy, valiant efforts have been made by women's groups in Pakistan to protest against the instituting of manifestly anti-women laws and to highlight cases of gross injustice and brutality toward women. However, it is still not clearly and fully understood, even by many women activists in Pakistan and other Muslim countries, that the negative ideas and attitudes pertaining to women that prevail in Muslim societies, are in general rooted in theology—and that unless, or until, the theological foundations of the misogynistic and androcentric tendencies in the Islamic tradition are demolished, Muslim women will continue to be brutalized and discriminated against, despite improvements in statistics such as those on female education, employment, and social and political rights. No matter how many sociopolitical rights are granted to women, as long as they are conditioned to accept the myths used by theologians or religious hierarchs to shackle their bodies, hearts, minds, and souls, they will never become fully developed or whole human beings, free of fear and guilt, able to stand equal to men in the sight of God. In my judgment, the importance of developing what the West calls "feminist theology" in the context of Islam is paramount today with a view to liberating not only Muslim women but also Muslim men from unjust structures and laws that make a peer relationship between men and women impossible. It is good to know that in the last hundred years there have been at least two significant Muslim men scholars and activists—Qasim Amin from Egypt and Mumtaz 'Ali from India—who have been staunch advocates of women's rights, though knowing this hardly lessens the pain of also knowing that even in this age that is characterized by the explosion of knowledge, all but a handful of Muslim women lack any knowledge of Islamic theology. It is profoundly discouraging to contemplate how few Muslim women there are in the world today who possess the competence, even if they have the courage and commitment, to engage in a scholarly study of Islam's primary sources in order to participate in the theological discussions on women-related issues that are taking place in much of the contemporary Muslim world.

Returning to the time when I began my career as a "feminist" theologian, I remember how stricken I felt when I first began to see the glaring discrepancy between Islamic ideals and Muslim practice insofar as women are concerned. Convinced of the importance of underscoring this discrepancy and believing that most Muslim women (even those who were all too well aware of the reality of their own life-situation) were largely unaware of it, I set out to articulate what I considered to be the normative Islamic view of women. This view is rooted largely in what all Muslims accept as *the* primary source, or highest authority, in Islam—the Qur'an, which Muslims believe to be the Word of Allah conveyed through the agency of the angel Gabriel to the Prophet Muhammad, who transmitted it without change or error to those who heard him.

In 1979, while I participated in an ongoing "trialogue" of Jewish, Christian, and Muslim scholars (under the sponsorship of the Kennedy Institute of Ethics in Washington, D.C.) who were exploring women-related issues in the three "Abrahamic" faith-traditions, I wrote the draft of a monograph entitled *Women in the Qur'an*. In this study I gave a detailed exposition of those passages of the Qur'an that related to women in various contexts (e.g., women vis-à-vis God; women in the context of human creation and the story of the "Fall"; women as daughters, wives, and mothers; women in the context of marriage, divorce, inheritance, segregation, veiling, witnessing to contracts, economic rights, afterlife, etc.). In particular, I focused attention upon those passages that were regarded as definitive in the context of woman-man relationships and upon which the alleged superiority of men to women largely rested. It was this study that I hoped to finalize when in the spring of 1983 I went to Pakistan and spent almost two years there, doing research but also watching, with increasing anxiety, the enactment of anti-women laws in the name of Islam and the deluge of antiwomen actions and literature that swept across the country in the wake of the "Islamization" of Pakistani society and its legal system.

As I reflected upon the scene I witnessed, and asked myself how it was possible for laws that were archaic if not absurd to be implemented in a society that professed a passionate commitment to modernity, the importance of something that I had always known dawned on me with stunning clarity. Pakistani society (or any other Muslim society for that matter) could enact or accept laws that specified that women were less than men in fundamental ways because Muslims, in general, consider it a self-evident truth that women are not equal to men. Anyone who states that in the present-day world it is accepted in many religious as well as secular communities that men and women are equal, or that evidence can be found in the Qur'an and the Islamic tradition for affirming man-woman equality, is likely to be confronted, immediately and with force, by a mass of what is described as "irrefutable evidence" taken from the Qur'an, Hadith, and Sunnah to "prove" that men are "above" women. Among the arguments used to overwhelm any proponent of man-woman equality, the following are perhaps the most popular: according to the Qur'an, men are *qawwamun* (generally translated as "rulers," or "managers") in relation to women;[31] according to the Qur'an, a man's share in inheritance is twice that of a woman;[32] according to the Qur'an, the witness of one man is equal to that of two women;[33] according to the Prophet, women are deficient both in prayer (due to menstruation) and in intellect (due to their witness counting for less than a man's).[34]

Since I was (in all probability) the only Muslim woman in the country who was attempting to interpret the Qur'an systematically from a nonpatriarchal perspective, I was approached numerous times by women leaders (including the members of the Pakistan Commission on the Status of Women, before whom I gave my testimony in May 1984) to state what my findings were and if they could be used to improve the situation of women in Pakistani society. I was urged by those spirited women who were mobilizing and leading women's protests in the streets to help them refute the arguments that were being used to make them less than fully human on a case-by-case or point-by-point basis. I must admit that I was tempted to join the foray in support of my beleaguered sisters who were being deprived of their human rights in the name of Islam. But I knew through my long and continuing struggle with the forces of Muslim traditionalism (which were now being gravely threatened by what they described as "the onslaught of Westernization under the guise of modernization") that the arguments that were being broadcast to "keep women in their place" of subordination and submissiveness were only the front line of attack. Behind and below these arguments were others, and no sooner would one line of attack be eliminated than another one would be set up in its place. What had to be done, first and foremost, in my opinion, was to examine the theological ground in which all the anti-women arguments were rooted to see if, indeed, a case could be made for asserting that from the point of view of normative Islam, men and women were *essentially* equal, despite biological and other differences.

My inquiry into the theological roots of the problem of man-woman inequality in the Islamic tradition led to the expansion of my field of study in at least two significant areas. First, realizing the profound impact upon Muslim consciousness of Hadith literature, particularly the two collections *Sahih al-Bukhari* and *Sahih Muslim* (collectively known as the *Sahihan*, which the Sunni Muslims regard as the most authoritative books in Islam next to the Qur'an), I examined with care the women-related ahadith in these collections. Second, I studied several important writings by Jewish and Christian feminist theologians who were attempting to trace the theological origins of the antifeminist ideas and attitudes found in their respective traditions.

As a result of my study and deliberation I came to perceive that not only in the Islamic, but also in the Jewish and Christian traditions, there are three theological assumptions on which the superstructure of men's alleged superiority to women (which implies the inequality of women and men) has been erected. These three assumptions are: (1) that God's primary creation is man, not woman, since woman is believed to have been created from man's rib, hence is derivative and secondary ontologically; (2) that woman, not man, was the primary agent of what is customarily described as the "Fall," or man's expulsion from the Garden of Eden, hence all "daughters of Eve" are to be regarded with hatred, suspicion, and contempt; and (3) that woman was created not only from man but also for man, which makes her existence merely instrumental and not of fundamental importance. The three theological questions to which the above assumptions may appropriately be regarded as answers, are: How was woman created? Was woman responsible for the "Fall" of man? Why was woman created?

Given the profound significance—both theoretical and practical—of these three questions in the history of ideas and attitudes pertaining to women in the Islamic (as well as the Jewish and Christian) tradition, I hope to write a full-scale book in response to each. However, at this time I would like to focus on the first question, which deals with the issue of woman's creation. I consider this issue to be more basic and important, philosophically and theologically, than any other in the context of woman-man equality, because if man and woman have been created equal by Allah who is the ultimate arbiter of value, then they cannot become unequal, essentially, at a subsequent time. On the other hand, if man and woman have been created unequal by Allah, then they cannot become equal, essentially, at a subsequent time.

Made from Adam's Rib?
The Issue of Woman's Creation

The ordinary Muslim believes, as seriously as the ordinary Jew or Christian, that Adam was God's primary creation and that Eve was made from Adam's rib. If confronted with the fact that this firmly entrenched belief is derived mainly from the Bible and is not only extra-Qur'anic but also in contradiction to the Qur'an, this Muslim is almost certain to be shocked. The rather curious and tragic truth is that even Western-educated Muslims seldom have any notion of the extent to which the Muslim psyche bears the imprint of the collective body of Jewish and Christian ideas and attitudes pertaining to women.

The Biblical account of the creation of the first human pair consists of two different sources, the Yahwist and the Priestly, from which arise two different traditions, subject of much Jewish and Christian scholarly controversy. There are four references to woman's creation in Genesis: (1) Gen. 1:26-27, 5th century B.C.E., Priestly tradition; (2) Gen. 2:7, 10th century B.C.E., Yahwist tradition; (3) Gen. 2:18-24, 10th century B.C.E., Yahwist tradition; (4) Gen. 5:1-2, 5th century B.C.E., Priestly tradition. A study of these texts shows that the Hebrew term "Adam" (literally, "of the soil," from *adamah*: "the soil") functions mostly as a generic term for humanity. Pointing out that the correct translation of this term is "the human," Leonard Swidler observes: "It is a mistake to translate it ["ha Adam"] in Genesis 1 to 2:22 either as man in the male sense or as a proper name, Adam (until Genesis 4:25 the definite article "ha" is almost always used with "Adam," precluding the possibility of its being a proper name: in 4:25 it becomes a proper name, "Adam" without the "ha"). Moreover, it is clearly a collective noun in Genesis 1 to 2:22, as can be seen in the plural 'let *them* be masters' (Genesis 1:26)."[35] Of the four texts referring to creation, undoubtedly the most influential has been Genesis 2:18-24, which states that woman *(ishshah)* was taken from man *(ish)*. From this text it has generally been inferred that: (1) Adam was God's primary creation from whom Eve, a secondary "creation, was derived," hence Eve is inferior and subordinate to Adam; and (2) Eve was created simply and solely to be the helpmate of Adam.

While in Genesis specific reference is made to the creation of Adam and Eve, there is no corresponding reference in the Qur'an. In fact, there is no mention of Eve *(Hawwa')* at all in the Qur'an. The term *Adam* occurs twenty-five times in the Qur'an, but there is only one verse (Surah 3: *Al-'Imran*: 59) that refers to the creation of Adam: "Certainly with Allah the likeness of 'Isa [Jesus] is as the likeness of Adam. Allah created him from the earth, then said to him, 'Be,' and he was." Here it needs to be mentioned that the term "Adam" is not an Arabic term but a Hebrew term, and the description of Adam as a creature of earth in the verse cited above is no more than an explication of the meaning of the term. There are three other verses (Surah 3: Al-'Imran: 33; Surah 19: Maryam: 58; Surah 5: Al-Ma'idah: 27) in which the term "Adam" is used as a proper name for an individual who was probably a prophet. Since Arabic has no capital letters, it is often not possible to tell whether a term is used as a proper name or as a common noun without looking at the context in which it occurs. However, there is no categorical statement in the Qur'an to the effect that Adam was the first human being created by Allah. The term is used most frequently in reference to more than one or two human beings. That the term "Adam" functions as a collective noun and stands for humankind is substantiated by an analysis of several verses in which this term occurs. It is also corroborated by the fact that all human beings are assimilatively addressed as "Children of Adam" (*Bani Adam*) in Surah 7: Al-'Araf: 26, 27, 31, 35, 172, Surah 17: *Bani Isra'il*: 70, and Surah 36: *Ya-Sin*: 60, and also by the fact that the Qur'an sometimes replaces the term "Adam" by *al-insan* or *bashar*, which are both generic terms for humanity. Here it is important to note that though the term "Adam" mostly does not refer to a particular human being, it does refer to human beings in a particular way. As pointed out by Muhammad Iqbal:

Indeed, in the verses which deal with the origin of man as a living being, the Qur'an uses the word "Bashar" or "Insan," not "Adam," which it reserves for man in his capacity of God's vicegerent on earth. The purpose of the Qur'an is further secured by the omission of proper names mentioned in the Biblical narration—Adam and Eve. The word "Adam" is retained and used more as a concept than as the name of a concrete human individual. This use of the word is not without authority in the Qur'an itself."[36]

It is noteworthy that the Qur'an uses the terms bashar, al-insan, and an-nas while describing the process of the physical creation of human beings. It uses the term "Adam" more selectively to refer to human beings only when they become representative of a self-conscious, knowledgeable, and morally autonomous humanity.

Instead of "Adam and *Hawwa'*," the Qur'an speaks of "Adam and *zauj*" in Surah 2: Al-Baqarah: 35, Surah 7: Al-'Araf 19, and Surah 20: Ta-Ha: 117. Muslims, almost without exception, assume that "Adam" was the first human being created by Allah and that he was a man. If "Adam" was a man, it follows that "Adam's *zauj*" would be a woman.

Hence the *zauj* mentioned in the Qur'an becomes equated with *Hawwa'*. Neither the initial assumption nor the inferences drawn from it are, however, supported in a clear or conclusive way by the Qur'anic text. The Qur'an states neither that Adam was the first human being nor that he was a man. The term "Adam" is a masculine noun, but linguistic gender is not sex. If "Adam" is not necessarily a man, then "Adam's *zauj*" is not necessarily a woman. In fact, the term zauj is also a masculine noun and, unlike the term "Adam," has a feminine counterpart, *zaujatun*. (Here, it may be noted that the most accurate English equivalent of *zauj* is not "wife" or "husband," or even "spouse," but the term "mate." The Qur'an uses the term *zauj* with reference not only to human beings but to every kind of creation, including animals, plants, and fruits.) However, neither the term *zaujatun* nor the plural form *zaujâtun* is used anywhere in the Qur'an, which consistently uses the masculine forms *zauj* and *azwaj*. It has been pointed out by the authoritative Arabic lexicon *Taj al-'Arus* that only the people of Al-Hijaz (Hejaz) used the term *zauj* in reference to women, and elsewhere the usage was *zaujatun*. Also, Arabic legal terminology always uses the term zaujâtun in reference to women. Why, then, does the Qur'an, which surely was not addressed only to the people of Al-Hijaz, use the term *zauj* and not *zaujatun* if the reference is indeed to woman? In my opinion, the reason why the Qur'an leaves the terms "Adam" and *zauj* deliberately unclear, not only as regards sex but also as regards number, is because its purpose is not to narrate certain events in the life of a man and a woman (i.e., the Adam and Eve of popular imagination), but to refer to some life experiences of all human beings, men and women together.

The Qur'an describes human creation in thirty or so passages that are found in various chapters. Generally speaking, it refers to the creation of humanity (and nature) in two ways: as an evolutionary process whose diverse stages or phases are mentioned sometimes together and sometimes separately, and as an accomplished fact or in its totality. In the passages described "concretely" or "analytically," we find that no mention is made of the separate or distinct creation of either man or woman, as may be seen, for instance, from the following: Surah 15: *Al-Hijr*: 26, 28, 29; Surah 16: *An-Nahl*: 4; Surah 22: *Al-Hajj*: 5; Surah 23: *Al-Mo'minun*: 12-14; Surah 25: *Al-Furqan*: 54; Surah 32: *Al-Sajdah*: 7-9; Surah 39: *Ya-Sin*: 77; Surah 38: *Sad*: 71-72; Surah 39: *Az-Zumar*: 6; Surah 40: *al-Mo'min*: 67; Surah 55: *Ar-*

Rahman:3, 4, 14; Surah 71: *Nuh*: 14, 17; Surah 76: *Ad-Dahr*: 2; Surah 77: *Al-Mursalat*: 20-22; Surah 82: *Al-Infitar*: 6-8; Surah 86: *At-Tariq*: 5-7; Surah 95: *At-Tin*: 4; and Surah 96: *Al-'Alaq*: 1-2. In some passages (e.g., Surah 49: *Al-Hujurat*: 13; Surah 53: *An-Najm*: 45; Surah 78: *An-Naba*: 8), though reference is made to Allah's creation of human beings as sexually differentiated "mates," no priority or superiority is accorded to either man or woman.

There are, however, some verses in the Qur'an that are understood in such a way that they appear to endorse a version of the *Genesis 2* story of woman's creation from man. These verses can be grouped into two categories. The most important verses in the first group are: Surah 16: *An-Nahl*: 72; Surah 30: *Ar-Rum*: 20-21; and Surah 35: *Al-Fatir*: 11. Muslim arguments that women were created from and for men are supported as follows: (1) Surah 30: *Ar-Rum*: 21 uses the term *ilaihâ* to refer to "mates" created from, and for, the original creation. Since *hâ* is a feminine attached pronoun, the "mates" it refers to must be female (thus making the original creation male); (2) all three verses cited use *kum* as a form of address. Hence these verses are addressed not to humanity collectively, but only to men, since the term used is a masculine attached pronoun (second person plural). Men are, therefore, the primary creation from and for whom the "mates" were created. Regarding (1), *ilaihâ* literally means "in her" and not "in them" and refers not to women (who are not mentioned here) but to *azwaj* (masculine plural used in the Qur'an for both men and women). If the "mates" were clearly designated as women, the term used would be *hunna*, not *hâ*. The use of *hâ* here is consistent with the Arabic rule that permits the use of feminine singular terms for a class or collectivity. The fact that the creatures to who this passage is addressed are referred to as *bashar* further supports the argument that the "mates" created by Allah are not only women (for men) since *bashar* obviously has a bisexual reference. Regarding (2), Arabic usage permits the use of *kum* in reference to men and women together. When women alone are concerned, *kunna* is used. Here it is of interest to note that in his book *Haquq-e-Niswan* (The Rights of Women, 1898), Mumtaz 'Ali pointed out that the Qur'an uses the masculine form of address to prescribe fundamental duties (e.g., salat, zakat, fasting) to Muslim men and women. If masculine terms of address are understood by the entire Muslim *ummah* to apply to both men and women in highly significant contexts, such as the prescription of basic religious duties, then it cannot consistently be argued that these terms apply to men invariably and exclusively.

Regarding the second group of verses that are cited to prove man's ontological priority and superiority to woman, the following are of exceptional importance: Surah 4: *An-Nisa'*: 1; Surah 7: *Al-'Araf*: 189; and Surah 39: *Az-Zumar*: 6. In these verses (as also in Surah 6: *Al-An'am*: 98 and Surah 31: *Luqman*: 28) reference is made to the creation from one source or being *(nafsin wahidatin)* of all human beings. Muslims, with hardly any exceptions, believe that the one original source or being referred to in these verses is a man named Adam. This belief has led many translators of the Qur'an to obviously incorrect translations of simple Qur'anic passages. For instance, Surah 4: *An-Nisa'*: 1, if correctly translated, reads as follows: "O *an-nas* be circumspect in keeping your duty to your Sustainer who created you [plural] from one being *[nafsin wahidatin]* and spread from *her* [*minhâ*] *her* mate [*zaujahâ*] and spread from these two beings many men and women." However, most translators (e.g., Hashim Amir-'Ali, Muhammad Ali, A. J. Arberry, A. K. Azad, A. M. Daryabadi, N. J. Dawood, S. A. Latif, A. A. Maududi, M. M. Pickthall, George Sale, and M. Y. Zayid) translate the feminine attached pronoun *hâ* in *minhâ* and *zaujahâ* as "his" instead of "her". How is such a mistake possible? Could it be the case that given their preconceptions and psychological orientation, these interpreters of the Qur'an (who all happen to be men) are totally unable to imagine that the first creation could have been other than male? Or are they afraid that a correct translation of *hâ* might suggest the idea—even for an instant—that woman, not man, was the prior creation (and therefore superior if priority connotes superiority) and that man was created from woman and not the other way around (which, in a reversal of the Eve from Adam's rib story would give Eve the primacy traditionally accorded to Adam)? Certainly no Qur'anic exegete to date has suggested the possibility that *nafsin wahidatin* might refer to woman rather than man.

Summing up the Qur'anic descriptions of human creation, it needs to be emphasized that the Qur'an evenhandedly used both feminine and masculine terms and imagery to describe the creation of humanity from a single source. That Allah's original creation was undifferentiated humanity and not either man or woman (who appeared simultaneously at a subsequent time) is implicit in a number of Qur'anic passages, in particular Surah 75: *Al-Qiyamah*: 36-39, which reads:

Does *al-insan* think that he will be left aimless? Was not a drop of semen emitted then he became something which clings; then He [Allah] created and shaped and made of him [*minhu*] two mates [*zaujain*] the male and the female.

If the Qur'an makes no distinction between the creation of man and woman, as it clearly does not, why do Muslims believe that Hawwa' was created from the rib of Adam? Although the Genesis 2 account of woman's creation is accepted by virtually all Muslims, it is difficult to believe that it entered the Islamic tradition directly, for very few Muslims ever read the Bible. It is much more likely that it became a part of Muslim heritage through its assimilation in Hadith literature, which has been, in many ways, the lens through which the Qur'an has been seen since the early centuries of Islam.

Hadith literature, which modernist Muslims tend to regard with a certain skepticism, is surrounded by controversies, centering particularly around the question of the authenticity of individual ahadith as well as the body of the literature as a whole. These controversies have occupied the attention of many Muslim scholars since the time of Ash-Shafi'i (d. A.H. 204/A.D. 809). Fazlur Rahman has pointed out that "a very large portion of the Hadiths were judged to be spurious and forged by classical Muslim scholars themselves," but goes on to add that "if the Hadith as a whole is cast away, the basis for the whole historicity of the Qur'an is removed with one stroke."[37] Noted Islamicists such as Alfred Guillaume,[38] H. A. R. Gibb,[39] and M. G. S. Hodgson[40] have underscored the importance of the Hadith literature, which not only has its own autonomous character in point of law and even of doctrine, but also has an emotive aspect, hard to overstate, relating to the conscious and subconscious thought and feeling of Muslims, both individually and as a group. That the story of Eve's creation from Adam's rib had become part of the Hadith literature is evident from the following Hadith related from Ibn 'Abbas and Ibn Mas'ud, which is referred to by authoritative commentators on the Qur'an, including Fakhr ud-Din ar-Razi, Isma'il ibn 'Umar Ibn Kathir, and al-Fadl ibn al-Hasan al-Tabarsi:

When God sent Iblis out of the Garden and placed Adam in it, he dwelt in it alone and had no one to socialize with. God sent sleep on him and then He took a rib from his left side and placed flesh in its place and created Hawwa' from it. When he awoke he found a woman seated near his head. He asked her, "Who are you?" She answered, "Woman." He said, "Why were you created?" She said, "That you might find rest in me." The angels said, "What is her name?" and he said, "Hawwa'." They said, "Why was she called Hawwa'?" He said, "Because she was created from a living thing." [41]

Another Hadith, related from Ibn 'Abbas and cited by Ibn Kathir in his *Tafsir*, which also refers to the creation of Hawwa' from Adam's rib, reads as follows:

After Iblis had been chastised and Adam's knowledge had been exhibited, Adam was put to sleep and Hawwa' was created from his left rib. When Adam awoke he saw her and felt affection and love for her since she was made from his flesh and blood. Then Allah gave Hawwa' in wedlock to Adam and told them to live in al-jannah. [42]

Both of the above ahadith clash sharply with the Qur'anic accounts of human creation, while they have an obvious correspondence to Genesis 2:18-33 and Genesis 3:20. Some changes, however, are to be noted in the story of woman's creation as it is retold in the above ahadith. Both mention "the left rib" as the source of woman. In Arab culture great significance is attached to "right" and "left," the former being associated with everything auspicious and the latter with the opposite. In Genesis, woman is named "Eve" after the Fall, but in the above ahadith she is called Hawwa' from the time of her creation. In Genesis, woman is named Eve because "she is the mother of all who live" (thus a primary source of life), but in the first of the aforementioned ahadith, she is named Hawwa' because "she was created from a living thing" (hence a derivative creature). These variations are not to be ignored. Biblical and other materials are seldom incorporated without alteration into ahadith. The above examples illustrate how in respect of woman, Arab biases were added to the adopted text.

The citing of the above ahadith by significant Muslim exegetes and historians shows the extent to which authoritative works both of Qur'anic exegesis and Islamic history had become colored by the Hadith literature. In course of time, many ahadith became "invisible," the later commentators referring not to them but to the authority of earlier commentators who had cited them, to support their views. This made it very hard to curtail their influence since they became diffused throughout the body of Muslim culture. A typical example of how the Qur'anic account of human creation is distorted by means of inauthentic ahadith (which identify *nafsin wahidatin* from which all human beings, including Hawwa', originated, with Adam the man), even when these ahadith are not mentioned or affirmed directly, is provided by A. A. Maududi, author of a well-known modem commentary on the Qur'an[43] and one of contemporary Islam's most influential scholars. In commenting on Surah *An-Nisa'* 1, Maududi observes:

"He created you of a single soul." At first one human being was created and then from him the human race spread over the earth. . . . We learn from another part of the Qur'an that Adam was that "single soul." *He was the first man from whom the whole of mankind sprang up* and spread over the earth. "And of the same created his mate": we have no definite detailed knowledge of how his mate was created of him. *The Commentators generally say that Eve was created from the rib of Adam and the Bible also contains the same story. The Talmud adds to it that she was created from the thirteenth rib of Adam. But the Qur'an is silent about it, and the Tradition of the Holy Prophet that is cited in support of this has a different meaning from what has been understood.* The best thing, therefore, is to leave it undefined as it has been left in the Qur'an, and not to waste time in determining its details.[44]

In the above passage, Maududi has no difficulty in affirming what has traditionally been made the basis of asserting woman's inferiority and subordination to man, namely that woman was created from man. Having made the deadly affirmation, however, he is reluctant to explicate further, nor does he reveal what he considers to be the "true" meaning of the Hadith pertaining to Eve's creation from Adam's rib. His justification for not discussing the issue of woman's creation is that the Qur'an has deliberately left it undefined. But this is simply not the case. The creation of woman is as clearly defined in the Qur'an as the creation of man, and the Qur'anic statements about human creation, diverse as they are, leave no doubt as to one point: both man and woman were made in the same manner, of the same substance, at the same time. Maududi (like the majority of Muslim exegetes, who happen to be all men) does not want to face this fact, so he declares that the discussion of the issue of woman's creation is a waste of time. If the issue in question was not worthy of serious theological reflection, or one that had no significant effect on the lives of human beings, particularly of women, one would, perhaps, be less critical of a scholar who has had massive impact on the minds of the Muslim masses, for dereliction of scholarly duty. But theologically the issue of creation of woman is of such import that it cannot be allowed to be dismissed in the manner in which Maududi has done.

Perhaps no better proof can be given of how totally ahadith such as the ones cited above have penetrated Muslim culture than the fact that the myth of the creation of Hawwa' from Adam's rib was accepted uncritically even by Qasim Amin (1863–1906), the Egyptian judge and feminist whose books *Tahrir al-Mara'* (*The Emancipation of Women*, 1899) and *Al-Mara' al-Jadida* (*The Modern Woman*, 1900) were epoch-making in the history of Muslim feminism. Amin's romantic interpretation of the myth, reminiscent of Milton's, shows that he did not realize how fundamentally the issue that concerned him most deeply, namely, woman's social equality with man in a strongly male-centered and male-dominated Muslim society, hinged upon the acceptance or rejection of a creation story that asserted woman's derivative status and had been interpreted traditionally to affirm her inferiority and subordination to man. It is unfortunate that many present-day Muslim advocates of women's rights also do not realize the profound implications of this myth that undergirds the anti-women attitudes and structures they seek to change.

Anti-women ahadith are found not only in the significant secondary sources of Islam but also in *Sahih al-Bukhari* (compiled by Muhammad ibn Isma'il al-Bukhari, A.H. 194–256/A.D. 810–870) and *Sahih Muslim* (compiled by Muslim bin al-Hajjaj, A.H. 202 or 206–261/A.D. 817 or 821–875), the two most influential Hadith collections in Sunni Islam. Cited below are six ahadith, the first three from *Sahih al-Bukhari* and the last three from *Sahih Muslim*, that have had a formative influence upon the Muslim mind:

1. Abu Karaith and Musa bin Hazam related to us: Husain bin 'Ali told us that he was reporting on the authority of Zai'dah who was reporting on the authority of Maisarah al-Ashja'i who was reporting on the authority of Abu Hazim who was reporting on the authority Abu Hurairah (with whom may Allah be pleased) who said: Allah's Rasul[45] (may peace be upon him) said:

Treat women nicely, for a woman is created from a rib, and the most curved portion of the rib is its upper portion, so if you should straighten it, it will break, but if you leave it as it is, it will remain crooked. So treat women nicely.[46]

2. 'Abd al-'Aziz related to us that he was reporting on the authority of 'Abd Allah who said: Malik had told us that he was reporting on the authority of Abu Zinad who was reporting on the authority of al-A'raj who was reporting on the authority of Abu Hurairah (with whom may Allah be pleased) who said: Allah's Rasul (may peace be upon him) said:[47]

The woman is like a rib, if you try to straighten her, she will break. So if you want to get benefit from her, do so while she still has some crookedness.[48]

3. Ishaq bin Nasr related to us: Husain al-Jo'fi related to us that he was reporting on the authority of Za'idah who was reporting on the authority of Maisarah who was reporting on the authority of Abu Hazim who was reporting on the authority of Abu Hurairah (with whom may Allah be pleased) who said: The Holy Prophet (may peace be upon him) said:[49]

Whoever believes in Allah and the Last Day should not hurt (trouble) his neighbor. And I advise you to take care of the women, for they are created from a rib and the most crooked part of the rib is its upper part; if you try to straighten it, it will break, and if you leave it, it will remain crooked, so I urge you to take care of woman.[50]

4. Harmalah bin Yahya related to me: Ibn Wahb informed us: Yunus informed me that he was reporting on the authority of Ibn Shihab who said: Ibn al-Musayyab told me that he was reporting on the authority of Abu Hurairah (with whom may Allah be pleased) who said: Allah's Rasul (may peace be upon him) said:[51]

Woman is like a rib. When you attempt to straighten it, you would break it. And if you leave her alone you would benefit by her, and crookedness will remain in her.[52]

5. 'Amr an-Naqid and Ibn 'Umar related to us saying: Sufyan related to us that he was reporting on the authority of Abu Zinad who was reporting on the authority of al-A'raj who was reporting on the authority of Abu Hurairah (with whom may Allah be pleased) who said: Allah's Rasul (may peace by upon him) said:[53]

Woman has been created from a rib and will in no way be straightened for you; so if you wish to benefit by her, benefit by her while crookedness remains in her. And if you attempt to straighten her, you will break her, and breaking her is divorcing her.[54]

6. Abu Bakr bin Abu Shaibah told us: Husain bin 'Ali told us that he was reporting on the authority of Za'idah who was reporting on the authority of Maisarah who was reporting on the authority of Abu Hazim who was reporting on the authority of Abu Hurairah (with whom may Allah be pleased) who said: The Holy Prophet (may peace be upon him) said:[55]

He who believes in Allah and the Hereafter, if he witnesses any matter he should talk in good terms about it or keep quiet. Act kindly towards women, for woman is created from a rib, and the most crooked part of the rib is its top. If you attempt to straighten it, you will break it, and if you leave it, its crookedness will remain there so act kindly towards women.[56]

While it is not possible, within the scope of this chapter, to give a detailed critical analysis of either the *isnad* (list of transmitters) or *matn* (content) of the above ahadith, a few comments on both may be useful. With regards to the *isnad* the following points may be noted: (1) All these ahadith are cited on the authority of Abu Hurairah, a Companion who was regarded as controversial by many early Muslim scholars, including Imam Abu Hanifah (A.D. 700–767),[57] founder of the largest Sunni school of law. Here it is pertinent to point out that though a more critical attitude toward Hadith and Hadith-transmitters prevailed during the earliest phase of Islam, later, as stated by Goldziher,[58] it became "a capital crime" to be critical of any Companion; (2) All six of the above ahadith are *gharib* (the lowest grade of Hadith classification) because they contain a number of transmitters who were single reporters. (Al-Hazim Abu 'Abd Allah al-Naysaburi and Ibn Hajar al-'Asqalani, who were eminent scholars of Hadith, defined a *sahih* or sound Hadith as one that is related in the first place by a well-known Companion, in the second place by at least two Followers, and thereafter by many narrators.);[59] (3) All of the above ahadith are *da'if* (weak) because they have a number of unreliable transmitters (e.g., Maisarah al-Ashja'i, Harmalah bin Yahya, Zaidah, and Abu Zinad).[60]

Analysis of the *matn* of the above ahadith leads to the following statements: (1) Woman is created from a rib or is like a rib; (2) The most curved and crooked part of the rib is its top; (3) The crooked-ness of the rib (and of the woman) is irremediable—any effort to remove it will result in breakage; and (4) In view of the above, an atti-tude of kindness is recommended and those who wish to benefit from women are advised to do so "while crookedness remains in her." Concerning these statements the following observations arc made: (a) The rib story obviously originates in Genesis 2, but no mention is made in any of these ahadith of Adam. This eliminates the Yahwist's androcentrism but also depersonalizes the source of woman's creation (i.e., the "rib" could, theoretically, be nonhuman); (b) The misogynist elements of the ahadith, absent from Genesis, clash with the teach-ings of the Qur'an which describes all human beings as having been created *fi ahsan-i taqwim* (most justly proportioned and with the high-est capabilities); (c) I cannot understand the relevance of making the statement that the most crooked part to the rib is the top; (d) The exhortation to be kind to women would make sense if women were, in fact, born with a natural handicap and needed compassion. Is "irre-mediable crookedness" such a handicap? (e) The advice to benefit from women without making any effort to help women deal with their "crookedness" (in case it is a natural handicap) smacks of hedonism or opportunism and is hard to appreciate even if women were indeed "irremediably crooked."

The theology of woman implicit in the above ahadith is based upon generalizations about her ontology, biology, and psychology that are contrary to the letter and spirit of the Qur'an. These ahadith ought to be rejected on the basis of their content alone. However, "*matn*-analy-sis" (which was strongly urged by Ibn Khaldun, A.D. 1332–1406)[61] has received scant attention in the work of many Muslim scholars, who insist that a Hadith is to be judged primarily on the basis of its *isnad*. It is not difficult to see why *isnad*-criticism—particularly if it excludes a scholarly scrutiny of initial reports of a Hadith—is not a sufficient methodological tool for establishing the reliability of a Hadith. Not all initial reporters of ahadith were the Prophet's close Companions whose word would be difficult to question. (The word "Companion" has come to be applied rather loosely to a variety of persons, some of whom spent only a limited amount of time with the Prophet and cannot necessarily be presumed to have known him well.) Furthermore, it is not always possible to say in the case of a Hadith whether its *isnad* (including the name of the Companion initially narrating the Hadith) is authentic and not fabricated. In such cases references to the *matn* of other ahadith ascribed to the same initial narrator, or to other ahadith with similar content, become critically important in determining the degree of reliability of both the narrator and the Hadith in question.

Conclusion

To sum up the foregoing discussion on the issue of woman's creation, I would like to reiterate that according to the Qur'an, Allah created woman and man equal. They were created simultaneously, of like substance, and in like manner. The fact that almost all Muslims believe that the first woman (Hawwa') was created from Adam's rib shows that, in practice, the Hadith literature has displaced the teaching of the Qur'an at least insofar as the issue of woman's creation is concerned.

While all Muslims agree that whenever a Hadith attributed to the Prophet conflicts with the Qur'an it must be rejected, the ahadith discussed in this chapter have not only not been rejected, they have in fact remained overwhelmingly popular with Muslims through the ages, in spite of being clearly contradictory to the Qur'anic statements pertaining to human creation. While being included in the *Sahihan* gives the ahadith in question much weight among Muslims who know about the science of Hadith, their continuing popularity among Muslims in general indicates that they articulate something deeply embedded in Muslim culture-namely, the belief that women are derivative creatures who can never be considered equal to men.

Even the courageous Muslim women presently leading women's movements in oppressively conservative Muslim societies, which in the name of "Islamization" are systematically legitimizing the reduction of women to less than fully human status, are not aware of the far-reaching implications of the ahadith that make them derivative or devious creatures. It is imperative for the Muslim daughters of Hawwa' to realize that the history of their subjection and humiliation at the hands of sons of Adam began with the story of Hawwa's creation, and that their future will be no different from their past unless they return to the point of origin and challenge the authenticity of ahadith that make them ontologically inferior, subordinate, and crooked. While it is not a little discouraging to know that these ahadith (like many other anti-woman ones) represent not only the ideas and attitudes regarding woman of the early generations of Muslims (whose views were reflected in the Hadith literature), but also of successive generations of Muslims until today, it is gratifying to know that they cannot be the words of the Prophet of Islam, who upheld the rights of women (as of other disadvantaged persons) throughout his life. Furthermore, regardless of how many Muslim men project their own androcentrism and misogyny upon the Prophet of Islam, it is valid to question how, being the recipient of the Qur'an, which states that all human beings were made from a single source (i.e., *al-insan, bashar,* or *nafsin wahidatin*), the Prophet of Allah could say that woman was created from a crooked rib or from Adam's rib.

Islamic Modernism at Home and Abroad

It is probably not a coincidence that Riffat Hassan, Fazlur Rahman, and other Muslim modernist scholars have spent a large part of their professional careers teaching and writing in Western Europe or North America. Though anti-Muslim and anti-Arab sentiments are frequently heard there, Muslims, and especially Muslim scholars, have greater individual and intellectual freedoms in secular societies to carry out research and voice their opinions on aspects of Islam and Muslim societies.

Over the last decade in Muslim nations, Islamic militants have targeted politicians, reporters, writers, and scholars who they deem to be apostates. Sadly, Rahman's forced exile from his homeland due to his religious views has been the fate of other Muslims, and recently that of the Egyptian scholar Nasr Hamed Abu Zeid. Author of a dozen books on Islam and a professor at the University of Cairo, Dr. Abu Zeid riled Egyptian Islamists in 1993 with his scholarship on the Qur'an and his assertion that the Qur'an should be read and understood in terms of its historical context in seventh-century Arabia. As a result, in 1995, the militant group *al-Jihad* publicly declared him as apostate and called for the annulment of his marriage and his execution. Islamist lawyers pursued the annulment and won their case in the Egyptian courts in 1996. As a result, Dr. Abu Zeid and his wife, Dr. Ibtihal Younis, went into exile in the Netherlands where Dr. Abu Zeid currently teaches at Leiden University. In 2002, he was interviewed by Daniel del Castillo, the Middle East correspondent for the *Chronicle of Higher Education*.

An Exiled Scholar of Islam[62]

Daniel del Castillo

Nasr Abu Zeid does a passable job of hiding his bitterness behind a warm smile. But after six years here, a continent away from his homeland, he cannot conceal his anger.

Mr. Abu Zeid's story is the stuff of nightmares. A professor and eminent Egyptian scholar of Islamic studies at Cairo University, he was propelled to notoriety in 1993 when a colleague who is an Islamist—an advocate of fundamentalist Islamic political rule—accused him of apostasy and of blaspheming Islam in his scholarship on Koranic exegesis.

His alleged crime was the reconciliation of Islam with modernity. He argued in his writings that Islam, like all religions, must be seen in its historical context and that its holy book, the Koran, should be given the same scrutiny as other texts. He applied techniques of literary criticism to the Koran and insisted that religious interpretation is and has been dependent on social, political, and historical currents; that, in effect, reason and rationalism go hand in hand with faith.

Because of the fundamental belief that the Koran is an eternal sacred text, no solid tradition of exegesis or textual criticism emerged outside a brief two-decade period in the ninth century.

So Mr. Abu Zeid's rationalist writings cost him his country, his career as an Egyptian professor, and, in a strictly technical sense, his marriage. Under an arcane loophole in Egyptian law, he was ordered forcibly divorced from his wife—it was the only punishment the Islamists could levy against him, since Egypt is governed by secular rather than Islamic law. Under Islamic law, though, he would have been executed for apostasy, and after a series of death threats, the most serious one issued as a fatwa by Osama bin Laden's associate Ayman al-Zawahiri, Mr. Abu Zeid and his wife fled to the Netherlands, where he now teaches Islamic history at Leiden University.

Q: Why didn't you just leave early on, before things got ugly?

A: I am a 58-year-old Egyptian professor. Teaching was like a mission for me. Teaching Egyptian students about Islam, how not to be deceived by this manipulation of Islam, was something more than a position. If I had decided to go to Saudi Arabia for five years, I could have become wealthy as a scholar of Islam, but I made my choice, and I have no regrets. This is what is keeping me alive, that I am not on the wrong track. I have my students here, and I am still working and traveling.

Q: Was it difficult to make the decision to leave Egypt?

A: The first time I went to the university after the verdict, the security procedure was like the president was going to the university. The university wasn't just a place I worked, it was a dream. A dream that turned into a nightmare very much like the dream of Egypt that turned into a nightmare. Under this protection, my wife and I exchanged one word in our bulletproof car on the way home from the university: "No!"

Q: Forced divorce had to have been a fairly traumatic experience— couldn't you have spun your ideas to be more palatable to the Islamists?

A: I don't believe soft discourse can possibly bring about change. Maybe a challenging discourse can create reaction and draw the attention of the silent majority. We have a problem in the Arab world of intellectuals only talking to intellectuals. Not compromising your critical approach as a scholar might provoke, and this provocation would create a sphere of discussion.

Q: Many Arab academics and intellectuals contend that universities in Egypt have been taken over by Islamists. True?

A: I would put it in a rather different way. Their power, in my opinion, is based on the weakness of others. The whole weakness at that time wasn't only the university. It was the state of Egypt, which was [trying] to deal with terrorism without addressing the basic issue behind terrorism—the absence of any public sphere for exchanging ideas, the failure of development not only in villages but in the outskirts of Cairo. Development and enlightenment have not at any moment in the history of Egypt reached any area beyond the big cities of Cairo and Alexandria.

Q: So that lack of academic freedom means there is no real scholarship on Islam?

A: Right. In universities all over the Muslim world, there is no scholarship about Islam. There is preaching of Islam, so Islamic study is the preaching of Islam. There is no comparative study.

Q: What is it about Islam that tends to encourage rigidity?

A: The concept of the Koran as the literal utterance of God is a historical concept. Muslims from very early on have different opinions about this, and we have to bring to the attention of Muslims, not only scholars, that this is a dogma that was created and protected as a political decision. And we don't have to swallow it as the Islamic doctrine, it's a dogma, a human understanding.

Q: So how do you convince Muslims that this is a dogma and that it is not *haram*—religiously forbidden—for them to question things about their religion, just as people with other religious traditions do?

A: This is my work, this is my life. It's not impossible. What is needed in the Muslim world is more reformation. It is possible, if we have a free sphere of discussion in universities and the public sphere. I have been saying what I'm saying now in different contexts. For people who are open and willing to listen and who don't rush to say, "This is against something," the possibility is there. I have a feeling that so many Muslims—I am talking about the young generation now, those about to turn 30, are tired of the traditional answer, that the word of God is divine and human. As humans, we are entitled to bring our understanding and to bring history to the word of God to try to deduce answers to our questions. The problem in the Muslim world at large now is the absence of any theological discussion. Islamic theology has been frozen since the 12th century. To reopen questions of theology concerning God, man, the world, is essential and should be done outside the religious institutions. Universities should have done this.

Q: Is an Islamic revolution in Egypt likely?

A: To tell you the truth, all of the convictions I've had have become illusions after September 11. I was sure that even if Egypt had a very open system with free elections, a utopia of democracy, that religious groups might gain a few seats but never reach a majority. Because the Egyptian people are very religious, but mixing religion with politics—they have become aware of its danger. Now I am not sure. The new situation has given more power to the very traditional Islamic trend.

Q: Why haven't more Muslim intellectuals used September 11 as an opportunity to define what Islam is and what it is not?

A: We have to look at September 11 and the success of Osama bin Laden as the protector of Palestinian rights. Because what is Islam? is my question, and now, what is the West? Can I equate the United States with Europe? Now it seems, in the political arena, there is no difference between them, but to analyze the situation and explain differences, it would be very easily taken against me as a Westernized Muslim, and I'm already discredited. So the difficulty is how to produce an honest discourse to convey what you think is the truth and at the same time, not to let language use you. Now if you confront Islamists it will be easily understood that you are backing Westernism.

Q: Will you ever return to Egypt?

A: [I told my wife,] if I die any place in the world, don't take my body back to Egypt. Six years now, and I still feel the same way. I said this before, and it was published in Arabic and many Egyptians were angered by my statement. Deep inside I feel like a deserted child whose mother didn't like him. Egypt means more than people think it means to me, it's something that's in my blood. I am still very angry. What did I do? I was trying to teach the Egyptian people how to think. Maybe I was wrong—it's always possible for me to be wrong—but do you have to kill me because I was wrong?[63]

Discussion Questions

1. What is Islamic modernism? Historically, what major issues have been central to Islamic modernists and the focus of their efforts toward reform?

2. What are the six "methods of reform" described by Fazlur Rahman? What are the advantages and disadvantages of each?

3. Riffat Hassan states: "[T]he Islamic tradition has, by and large, remained rigidly patriarchal until the present time, prohibiting the

growth of scholarship among women particularly in the realm of religious thought." In light of her essay, what has been the major effect of this situation on the relationships of women and men?

4. How does Nasr Abu Zaid's exile to Europe reflect on current efforts to reform Islam?

PART SIX

RELIGION AND WESTERN CIVILIZATION IN THE TWENTY-FIRST CENTURY

CHAPTER 15

JUDAISM, CHRISTIANITY, AND ISLAM IN THEIR CONTEMPORARY ENCOUNTERS

Judaism, Christianity, and Islam in Their Contemporary Encounters: Judaism Addresses Christianity

Jon D. Levenson

Introduction

As we have seen, the encounter of Judaism and Christianity dates to the very beginnings of the church, for Christianity began as a Jewish sect, and the only Bible the earliest Christians recognized was the Jewish Bible.[1] Today, this is often seen as a basis for good relations between Jews and Christians, and not without some justice. Historically, however, the common foundation of the two religions in the same set of scriptures did not generate a sense of kinship and commonality, but rather suspicion and sometimes outright persecution. The reason is that Christianity has not, for the most part, viewed itself as a valid faith alongside Judaism. It has, instead, viewed itself as the fulfillment of Judaism, the true and enduring Judaism, as it were. Traditionally, it presented its gospel as surpassing the Jewish Torah and saw its own social body, the church, as the new Israel or the true Israel, replacing the Jewish people in that role. Furthermore, the church historically viewed the Jewish belief that Jesus was not the expectced messiah as a sign that the Jews were no longer the chosen people of the Hebrew Bible ("Israel") and that God had, to one degree or another, rejected them and condemned them to exile and similar miseries. The Jewish view of Christianity was not more favorable. It presented the Christian church as founded on false prophecies, a new home for the old anti-Jewish persecution, and a danger to the truths of the Torah and to the people charged with living the life of Torah.

In modern times, these traditional views have eroded substantially, although, as we shall see, some of them still survive, and the question of how to maintain the integrity of one's own religious convictions without subscribing to the old stereotypes is a large one. One of the most important new features of the encounter of Judaism and Christianity over the past half-century, at least in the West, has been the emergence of inter-religious dialogue. Of course, Jews and Christians had spoken to one another from the birth of Christianity on and sometimes even spoken to one another about religion. But the goal of the premodern conversations was usually to persuade the other community of the truth of one's own convictions (Christianity) or to defend one's endangered community from the attacks of the other (Judaism). The encounters, in other words, were often hostile, and neither community was interested in a patient and respectful hearing of the other's positions. In genuine interreligious dialogue, by contrast, the tone and the goal are different. Today, members of many religious communities that had long avoided courteous communication with one another on principle are now in regular discussions characterized by mutual respect, and the conversations not infrequently involve precisely the points of theological difference that had so long precluded dialogue. These conversations are, of course, symptomatic of a new understanding of religious identity characteristic of modernity, at least in democratic lands. But they have also played a major role in bringing that new relationship into existence and strengthening it, as the participating bodies have spread the new insights and revised images to their memberships through liturgical reform, preaching, and teaching.

Interreligious dialogue, needless to say, has its own inner tensions. The most important of these concerns is the very goal of the enterprise. Given the history of religiously inspired animosity and contempt to be overcome if dialogue is to develop and continue—a history that includes unspeakable acts of violence from some parties—it is tempting to adopt a model of conflict resolution or diplomatic negotiation as the basis for the conversations. The goal in that case is to come to agreement, rather in the manner of two countries seeking to bury the hatchet or of a couple going into marriage counseling in hopes of replacing a contentious relationship with one characterized by empathy and mutual support. The commonalities will be stressed and the differences minimized, neglected, or denied altogether. For the latter are correctly seen as sources of division, and division is then viewed as dangerous. The easiest way to avoid the hostility to which such division can (but does not have to) give rise is to assume that the communities in dialogue are really both just saying the same thing, only in different words. The assumption that all the religions are at base teaching the same thing looks tolerant and open-minded; in fact, it represents a refusal to deal responsibly with the fact of diversity in religion.

When this assumption is made, the dialogue may seem to have reached its goal, but the expense is deceptively great, so great that the whole enterprise is, in fact, imperiled. For dialogue on these terms quickly turns into a monologue, as each side simply phrases in its distinctive idiom what is, in fact, the common belief of all involved. Religious difference, once a matter of the deepest beliefs about the most important and universal truths, is thus rapidly downgraded to a matter of mere vocabulary. In this way, conflicting truths can all be held to be valid, only for different communities, so that everybody is right, no mutual critique is possible, and good relations will obtain—at the expense, of course, of the theological core of each community. And, in fact, it sometimes happens that the people engaging in the dialogue have a deeply conflicted relationship to the core affirmations and practices of the tradition they are representing and thus especially enjoy the encounter with individuals from other communities who experience the same conflict from their side.

Fortunately, there is an alternative to the self-defeating model based on conflict resolution or diplomatic negotiation.[2] This model, too, seeks good relations and requires each community to confront its misunderstandings of the other and the often-grievous results that these have had. It, too, is determined to confront and destroy prejudice and misunderstanding. At the same time, however, this other model also insists on the importance of the theological core of each tradition and requires both dialogue partners to reckon with the full import of the other's theology, even when it not only contradicts but also critiques one's own. In this model, in other words, the differences, no less than the commonalities, must be brought to the fore, for without them the full truth of the individual religious traditions and the relationship between them will remain concealed. In this more traditional and more theological understanding of dialogue, failure to come to an agreement need not mean the dialogue has failed. It may mean that it has succeeded.

Interreligious Dialogue

Most Christians and nearly all Jews accept that one of the most positive consequences of interreligious dialogue has been a dramatic reversal in Christian teaching about Judaism and the Jews over the past several decades. The classical view, as we have seen, portrayed Judaism as, at best, a preparation for the full and final truth that is the Christian gospel. In rejecting the gospel, the Jews proved unable to recognize the import of their own scripture and took upon themselves the role of enemies of the God who authored it. The ultimate example of this enmity was the Jews' unjust killing of their own messiah, a crime for which they must pay throughout their generations. "His blood be upon us and upon our children," cries the Jewish crowd to Pontius Pilate, the Roman prefect, in the Gospel according to Matthew (27:25). Their punishment entailed not only the loss of God's favor (and their corollary replacement by the new chosen people, the church), but also the destruction of the temple in Jerusalem (held to have been prophesied by Jesus himself) and exile from the promised land into the realms of the Gentiles. Indeed, at least from the time of Saint Augustine (early fifth century C.E.), the continued existence of the Jews in a state of degradation served as a proof of Christianity. Pope Innocent III summarized the classical view well in 1208. "The Jews, against whom the blood of Jesus Christ calls out," he wrote, "although they ought not to be killed, lest the Christian people forget the Divine Law, yet as wanderers they ought to remain upon the earth, until their countenance be filled with shame."[3] The Jews, in other words, survive, but in a state of punishment that witnesses to the truth of Christianity.

And what of their religion, Judaism? As the classical Christian view would have it, it had become obsolete, superseded by the Christianity to which it had always pointed. Its adherents, missing the meaning of their own practices, concentrated fruitlessly upon external rituals that had lost whatever efficaciousness they had once had, at the expense of the genuine faith of their ancestors. Seeking salvation in their own works rather than in the mysterious grace of God, they became ever more deeply entangled in petty legalism and lacked the means to draw closer to the God who had sent his only begotten son, Jesus Christ, for their salvation—and for the salvation of the entire world. The Jews read their scripture according to its literal, that is, carnal sense and persistently failed even to glimpse the spiritual sense, the sense altogether fulfilled in Jesus and the church.

The relationship between the theological teachings only roughly sketched above and the treatment of the Jews in Christendom over the centuries is highly complex. On the one hand, the church generally took a dim view of violence against the Jews, as suggested by Pope Innocent III's remarks. On the other hand, persistent accusation, recrimination, and defamation took their toll, one that was sometimes paid in blood. The bridge between theology and violence is chillingly evident in the pamphlet *Of the Jews and Their Lies* (1543) by one of the great heroes of the Protestant Reformation, Martin Luther:

> First, their synagogues or Churches should be set on fire, and whatever does not burn up should be covered or spread over with dirt so that no one may ever be able to see a cinder or stone of it. And this ought to be done for the honor of God and of Christianity. . . . Secondly, their homes should likewise be broken down and destroyed. For they perpetrate the same things there that they do in their synagogue. For this reason they ought to be put under one roof or in a stable, like gypsies.[4]

The difference between what Luther here advocates and what his German compatriots put into action in the Holocaust four centuries later (with considerable success) must not be overlooked. Whereas traditional Christian theology inspired the Protestant Reformer's remarks, so that the hoped-for result was violent religious persecution, modern racism motivated the Nazis, who sought not the conversion of the Jews, but their unqualified annihilation. The intended victims' beliefs were irrelevant to the genocidal campaign, and it would be misleading in the extreme to refer to the Holocaust as religious persecution. But it would also strain the historical imagination to claim that nearly two millennia of Christian demonization of Jews and Judaism played no role in laying the groundwork for what the Nazis hoped would be the Final Solution.

In the wake of the Holocaust, many (but not all) Christian communions have engaged in a soul-searching reexamination of the teaching of contempt that was so long dominant in their thinking about the Jews. The result has been a series of statements that reverse, or at least severely limit the classic theology. In most cases, these statements affirm the family connection of Judaism and Christianity, graciously acknowledging both the church's indebtedness to Judaism (especially for the set of scriptures it received from the Jews) and the continuing validity of the older tradition even after Jesus. In some instances, apologies are proffered for the history of persecutions, including, explicitly or implicitly, the Holocaust. Especially moving was the image of Pope John Paul II—who stood in line of succession to Innocent III and a long line of ancient, medieval, and modern despisers of the Jews—respectfully visiting the Great Synagogue of Rome and, later, praying at the Western Wall in Jerusalem under Israeli sovereignty.

It was inevitable that the changes in Christian attitudes toward Judaism would alter the very fabric of relations between the two communities. To the extent that Jewish attitudes toward Christianity were premised upon Christian animosity, these attitudes could not but be affected by the new situation (except, of course, among those Jews who live in self-enclosed communities opposed to change as a point of religious principle). Furthermore, it is understandable that Christians, having undergone a painful critical reevaluation of their own traditions (including their scriptures and even the presentation of Jesus in them), would want to know the Jews' reactions to all this. Are the regrets accepted, or do the Jews still hold them responsible for past persecutions? Do Jews acknowledge that the two communities are members of the same larger spiritual grouping, or do they see Christians as a religiously alien group, no closer to them in belief and practice than Hindus and Buddhists?

Dabru Emet

In the early 1990s, the Institute for Christian and Jewish Studies in Baltimore assembled a group of professors of Jewish Studies to pursue the question of a Jewish understanding of Christianity (the same organization had already been involved in the reverse project, the reassessment of Judaism by Christian scholars). Out of these consultations there emerged in September 2000, "A Jewish Statement on Christians and Christianity," entitled *Dabru Emet* (Hebrew for "speak the truth," after the words of the prophet, "Speak the truth to one another").[5] Four able and highly regarded academics authored the statement, and hundreds of other scholars and rabbis have signed it. Published in the *New York Times* and numerous other venues, it has since attracted vast attention, most of it extremely positive.[6] Given its prominence, *Dabru Emet* serves as an excellent vehicle to explore the promises and pitfalls of a Jewish reevaluation of Christianity in our time.

The statement essentially consists of eight theses of one sentence apiece (each of which is then followed by a brief explanatory paragraph):

- Jews and Christians worship the same God.
- Jews and Christians seek authority from the same book—the Bible (what Jews call "Tanakh" and Christians call the "Old Testament").

- Christians can respect the claim of the Jewish people upon the land of Israel.
- Jews and Christians accept the moral principles of Torah.
- Nazism was not a Christian phenomenon.
- The humanly irreconcilable difference between Jews and Christians will not be settled until God redeems the entire world as promised in Scripture.
- A new relationship between Jews and Christians will not weaken Jewish practice.
- Jews and Christians must work together for justice and peace.[7]

Jews and Christians Worship the Same God

The first of these theses is more daring and more innovative than appears at first glance. Historically, it would not, to be sure, have met with much dissent among Christians. However much they have believed Jewish modes of worship to be literal, carnal, and obsolete, orthodox Christians early on rejected the belief that the Christian God was a higher (and thus different) God from that of the Jews and their scriptures. But here—as generally in Jewish-Christian relations—asymmetry reigns, and simple reciprocity is a dangerous course indeed. For historically, Jews have not always been convinced that Christians worship *their* God. Maimonides, for example, the great Sephardic legal authority and philosopher of the twelfth century, explicitly classifies Christianity as idolatry, thus forbidding contact with Christians of the sort permitted with practitioners of other, nonidolatrous religions.[8] Maimonides lived under Islam and, it could be argued, had only meager knowledge of Christian communities and what they actually practiced. But in the medieval Ashkenazic world as well (that is, the world of western and central Europe, where Christianity dominated), some Jewish authorities interpreted the monotheistic affirmation of the *Shema‘*, the mandatory daily declaration of Jewish faith, as an outright denial of the Christian doctrine of the Trinity.[9] To them, too, the idea that God was Father, Son, and Holy Spirit and that Jesus was God made flesh directly contradicted a basic Jewish belief about the nature of the one God of the world.

Here, the issue is even more basic than the familiar questions of whether Jesus was the messiah and of whether the Torah is still in effect or superseded by the gospel: it is a question of the identity of God. For orthodox Christianity sees Jesus not only as a spokesman for God, in the manner of a Jewish prophet, but also and more importantly as an incarnation—nay, the definitive and unsurpassable incarnation—of the God of Israel. In the words of the Nicene Creed (recited in Eastern Orthodox, Roman Catholic, and many Protestant churches to this day), Jesus is "true God from true God, begotten, not made, of one being with the Father. Through him all things were made." *Dabru Emet*, like most participants in Jewish-Christian dialogue, speaks as if Jews and Christians agree about God, but disagree about Jesus. This is to overlook the key fact that in one very real sense, orthodox Christians think Jesus *is* God. For in the traditional Christian theology, God was *always* trinitarian, three-personed from all eternity to all eternity, and did not become so when the Second Person (the Son) became incarnate in Jesus of Nazareth.

One would never guess this from *Dabru Emet*, which lacks any reference to the doctrines of Trinity and incarnation. In an essay in a supporting volume, however, one of its authors, Peter Ochs, does address the issue. In essence, he argues that Christianity overlaps with Judaism but adds elements to it that "belong to a religion other than Judaism and are incompatible with what it means for a Jew to live according to the dictates of Jewish tradition." These additions do not, in his judgment, have "behavioral consequences that would violate Jewish beliefs or the Noahide laws [that is, the basic norms that Judaism expects everyone, Jew and gentile alike, to obey]."[10]

Even if we concede Ochs's point, however, we still must ask about the ensuing implications for the unqualified claim that *Jews and Christians worship the same God*. Surely, if God is known from the biblical story, those who want to understand the God of Christians can never relegate the New Testament (which is also unmentioned in *Dabru Emet*) to the status of a set of harmless superfluities.[11] Rather, they must openly acknowledge that the additions that that testament makes to Jewish tradition are indispensable to the Christian concept of God, for, without them, God is less fully known—or so the logic of Christian belief dictates. To do that, however, *Dabru Emet* would have to reckon openly and honestly with the key doctrines of incarnation and Trinity. The easier course is the one the statement takes—to speak only of the commonalities (real or imagined) and leave the points of division and opposition unmentioned. This course can help in the enterprise of conflict resolution, but it does so at considerable cost to the core theological affirmations of the two traditions.

As it happens, it is precisely the traditional Christian theology that enabled some Jewish authorities already in the Middle Ages to exonerate Christians of the accusation of idolatry that others had preferred against them. Thus, twelfth-century French authorities ruled that a Jew could accept the validity of the oath of Christians because even though the latter mention Jesus, this is not the name of an idolatrous god:

> For they mean the Maker of Heaven, and although they associate the Name of Heaven [i.e., God] and something else, we do not find it is forbidden to Gentiles to make such an association.[12]

Like *Dabru Emet*, this position (which grew in influence over the centuries, generally eclipsing the view that Christianity is thoroughly idolatrous) acknowledges "Jews and Christians worship the same God." But unlike *Dabru Emet*, it takes seriously the important aspects of Christian theology that had led other authorities to classify Christianity as idolatry, and, what is more, it explains why, in the words of *Dabru Emet*, "Christian worship is not a viable religious choice for Jews." The explanation lies precisely in the nature of Jewish monotheism, which does not accept the notion that a Jew may call Jesus "God." The issue is not about a viable choice versus one that is less viable. It is about religious truth. It is about the nature of the God of Israel.[13]

The eminent Protestant theologian Wolfhart Pannenberg sees in the first thesis of *Dabru Emet* a repudiation of the traditional Jewish theology of the "association" (*shittuf*) and a welcome (to him) concession on the part of the Jews that "the trinitarian doctrine of God is no longer considered a violation of biblical monotheism."[14] Pannenberg correctly identifies the tendency, but gives the statement too much credit, since, as I have been at pains to point out, it nowhere mentions the doctrines that Pannenberg finds it to repudiate boldly. It simply ignores the whole Jewish theology of the "association" (*shittuf*) that exonerated Christians from the charge of idolatry. In my judgment, a statement that either faithfully upheld the traditional idea of the *shittuf* or explicitly opposed it would have been more defensible than the studied ambiguity of *Dabru Emet*. Either alternative would have taken Christianity more seriously, but acknowledging the theology of the other community also has its cost. It requires one to acknowledge that not all the divisions result from misunderstanding or prejudice. They may also result from conflicting truth-claims. As I see it, a successful interreligious dialogue seeks to correct misunderstandings and false stereotypes, on the one hand, and to identify the enduring and irresolvable differences, on the other. To neglect either goal is to fail in the other one as well.

Partial and misleading as *Dabru Emet* is on God/Jesus, it altogether neglects to mention the personage whom hundreds of millions of ortho-dox Christians (principally in the Eastern Orthodox and Roman Catholic churches) call the "Mother of God"—the Virgin Mary. Indeed, the divinity of the human Jesus was so important to the fathers of the Third Ecumenical Council (431 C.E.) that they placed an anathema (a kind of curse) on anyone who failed to confess that "the Holy Virgin is the Mother of God."[15] Given the strategy of *Dabru Emet* for dealing with divisive points in the relationship of Jews and Christians, it is not hard to see why it avoids Mary altogether. If "Jews and Christians worship the same God," then why do the Jews neglect his mother, while so many Christians venerate and serve her? And if the Jews are right that in no sense whatsoever does God have a mother, what does *that* say about the doctrines of Trinity, incarnation, and Mary that the early church councils were so careful to define and protect? Again, it will not do to say that Jews and orthodox Christians worship the same God but disagree about Mary. For, according to the orthodox Christian theology, what is special about Mary is precisely that she is the Mother of God.

What, then, are we to make of the fact that "A Jewish Statement on Christians and Christianity," as *Dabru Emet* is subtitled, takes no account of doctrines central to historic Christianity and very much alive among hundreds of millions of modern-day Christians as well? Whatever the intentions of those who authored or signed it, the statement leaves the clear impression that it is directed only at those Christians for whom (whatever their church affiliations) the classical credal statements about Jesus and Mary have lost their theological centrality, perhaps even their fundamental credibility. Christians for whom the ancient doctrines are not so important or are an outright embarrassment are hardly likely to protest their omission. Indeed, they are likely to be happy to see an exter-nal group, rabbis and Jewish scholars to boot, confirming that their ver-sion of Christianity really is authentic. As for Christians for whom the classic doctrines remain important, they, too, have some reason to be happy with *Dabru Emet*. For in it the Jews have, at long last and without the slightest hint of reservation, accepted a claim that orthodox Christians have made for millennia: *"Jews and Christians worship the same God."*

Jews and Christians Seek Authority from the Same Book—the Bible (what Jews Call *Tanakh* and Christians Call the *Old Testament*)

A similar partiality of vision, a similar tendency to neglect rather than reassess historic points of discord, informs this second thesis of *Dabru Emet*. The awkward parenthetical gloss already points to the problem. Jews do not consider the New Testament to be the "Bible," and Christians do not refer to the Old Testament alone as the "Bible."[16] In fact, the very equation the gloss makes between the Tanakh and the Old Testament is a half-truth. The Old Testament of the Roman Catholic and Eastern Orthodox churches is larger than the Tanakh or the Old Testament of Protestant churches; it includes Jewish books that never attained canonical status in Rabbinic Judaism (and, in one case, a book that the rabbis seemed to have removed from the canon). The order of books in the Tanakh and in the Old Testament is also different in revealing ways. The Tanakh in its current form (the order of some biblical books was notoriously unstable into talmudic times), ends, for example, with the Persian emperor Cyrus's decree in Chronicles that exiled Jews may return to their homeland, where God has charged him to rebuild the Jerusalem temple, destroyed two generations earlier by the Babylonians. This is an unmistakable anticipation of the passion for return to the Land of Israel that has characterized Jewish thought, a passion that long predates but also energizes modern Zionism. The Old Testament, in contrast, ends with the prophet Malachi's prediction that God will send the prophet Elijah "before the coming of the awesome, fearful day of the LORD" (3:23). The latter arrangement makes a nice bridge to John the Baptist's heralding of Jesus in the New Testament.[17] In each case, even if the endings came about for reasons that are not theological, they tell us something important about the different underlying theologies of the two religions.

We must also reckon with the different priorities with which Judaism and Christianity have traditionally interpreted those scriptures that they hold in common. From the onset, Christians have been especially attentive to two books in particular, Psalms and Isaiah, priorities that can still be detected to this day.[18] In traditional Jewish thought, however, almost everything after the Pentateuch is thought to result from a lower order of revelation and thus exercises a lesser authority, so that Leviticus, for example, commands more attention than Psalms and Isaiah combined. (Even when the rabbis direct their exegetical skills to the non-Pentateuchal books, they often interpret them as commenting on the Pentateuch). This, too, renders the claim that *Jews and Christians seek authority from the same book* highly problematic. For when the "same book" is looked at with a difference in focus or priority, it is no longer "the same book."

But even if we assume that Jews and Christians have "the same book," the second thesis of *Dabru Emet* still skirts over essential points. For the Tanakh and the Old Testament are, in major ways, subordinated to other elements in their respective traditions. In Christianity, there is, as we have noted, a tradition, extending back to the origins of the new faith itself, that the true meaning of the Jewish scriptures is revealed in and by Jesus, and the Jews thus misread their own Bible. The Apostle Paul, who is responsible for much of the New Testament, could not be more explicit:

> Therefore, since we have such hope, we act very boldly and not like Moses, who put a veil over his face so that the Israelites could not look intently at the cessation of what was fading. Rather, their thoughts were rendered dull, for to this present day the same veil remains unlifted when they read the old covenant, because through Christ it is taken away. To this day, in fact, whenever Moses is read, a veil lies over their hearts, but whenever a person turns to the Lord the veil is removed.[19]

Paul indeed casts his argument as an exegesis of the Jewish scriptures, but he does not simply "interpret the Bible differently," as *Dabru Emet* puts it. Rather, he delivers a harsh broadside against the very way the Jews (and perhaps their Christian sympathizers) read that Bible, that is, non-christologically. The supporting assertion of *Dabru Emet* that "we each take away similar lessons" from our Tanakh/Old Testament is not false. It simply fails to mention that on certain fundamental points, the lessons we take away are not only different, but also mutually exclusive. To be sure, it can be salutary to draw attention to the similarities between religious traditions, for this can help diminish misunderstandings, some of them potentially fatal. But it is the differences, indeed the mutually exclusive truth-claims, that constitute the true challenge for interreligious conversation, and it is the differences that *Dabru Emet* consistently neglects. Its respect for Christianity is directly proportional to the extent to which Christianity can be made to look like Judaism.

In the case of Judaism, too, the Hebrew Bible (or Tanakh) is not the sole authority and often yields to another element, the rabbinic tradition or Oral Torah.[20] Had the statement taken a different and more accurate tack, however, pointing to the importance of this element, it would have undermined its claim that the two communities have "the same book," from which they "take away similar lessons." For just as Judaism lacks the New Testament, so does Christianity lack the Mishnah and subsequent rabbinic literature that serve as the literary embodiment of the Torah that was once only oral. Going even farther, one might say that one of the commonalities between the two traditions is that they both tend to read their Tanakh/Old Testament through the lens of other literature peculiar to themselves and not shared by the other tradition. In fact, some Jewish affirmations of the importance of the Oral Torah parallel Christian claims for the greater importance of the gospel:

> When the Holy One (blessed be He) said to Moses, "Write down [these commandments, for in accordance with these commandments I make a covenant with you and Israel]," Moses asked that the Mishnah be put into writing. Since the Holy One (blessed be He) foresaw that the nations of the world would translate the Torah, read it in Greek, and say, "We are Israel," and up to this point the scales are equally balanced [between the Jewish and the Gentile claimants to the status of Israel], the Holy One (blessed be He) said to the nations, "You say that you are My children. What I know is that those who have My secret with them—They are My children. And what is it? It is the Mishnah [i.e., teaching] which was given orally."[21]

Here, the key element is not the common scripture, but the element that is *not* shared, God's "secret," the means, that is, for arbitrating between the different readings of the same text. In sum, much of what Judaism and Christianity share in the matter of their common scriptures is a rivalry over how they should be read and who is now the "Israel" that is central to the scriptures and bears the irrevocable promise they repeatedly make. Were it not for the commonality, the rivalry could not develop. But to speak only of commonalities, ignoring the rivalry or degrading it to the level of mere "differences,"[22] is to miss essential aspects of scriptural reading and interpretation in the two related traditions. Indeed, it is only because of the commonality that the two traditions are able to have a meaningful debate about the interpretation of the scriptures that they have in common. Commonality and difference are not simply opposites; their relationship is more complex than that dichotomy suggests.

Consider as an illustration one of the "similar lessons" that *Dabru Emet* thinks Jews and Christians derive from their common "Bible": "God established a covenant with the people Israel." That covenant is first announced to Abraham in Genesis 15, following a report that the childless future patriarch trusted in God's unlikely promise to grant him innumerable progeny. The key verse here reads, "And because he put his trust in the LORD, He reckoned it to his merit."[23] Two chapters later, God again announces the covenant with Abraham, only this time ordaining that it shall have a sign, the mandatory circumcision of the males of the covenant people. And only several generations afterward is a covenant made with Israel at Mount Sinai under the leadership of Moses.[24]

Early in his career, Paul, the "apostle to the Gentiles," who had never known Jesus personally, found himself confronted by Jewish adherents of the new religion who had, and who insisted that Gentile men entering it must undergo circumcision and carry out other commandments of the Torah—not an unreasonable demand, given the example of Jesus, a Torah-observant Jew himself. This being a position that Paul vigorously opposed, for him the chronology of covenants in the Torah was a godsend. He understood Genesis 15:6 to mean that God reckoned Abraham as righteous purely on the basis of his faith, even before he became circumcised. Faith, in other words, could substitute for the commandments of the Torah. Or, as Paul put it in his own words at the end of his career, "It was not through the Law that the promise was made to Abraham and his descendants that he would inherit the world, but through the righteousness that comes from faith."[25]

At first glance, this may look like an intramural Christian quarrel of only peripheral relevance to Judaism, since the immediate issue concerns circumcision and Torah observance, and, like Paul, Judaism does not require non-Jews to be circumcised or to observe other commandments of the Torah (except for the seven Noahide laws mentioned earlier). On this reading, we simply see two different religions, related, to be sure, and with a common origin—even "the same book"—but with no need to critique each other or to challenge the other's reading of the shared scriptures. And just so have some New Testament scholars interpreted the situation. The rub is that in Paul's theology, Abraham serves as a model not only for Gentiles or for Christians, but also for all who wish to belong to Israel:

> For not all who are of Israel are Israel, nor are they all children of Abraham because they are his descendants; but "It is through Isaac that descendants shall bear your name." This means that it is not the children of the flesh who are the children of God, but the children of the promise are counted as descendants.[26]

Just as it is faith rather than circumcision that enables a man to attain the lofty status of Abrahamic descent, so it is faith rather than birth that determines who truly belongs to Israel (Paul sometimes vacillates on this). And the faith of which Paul speaks is not some vague existential stance, but precisely the faith in Jesus, the very thing that his Jewish kinsmen, to his great disappointment and annoyance, have not accepted, preferring their Torah and its commandments instead:

> What then shall we say? That Gentiles, who did not pursue righteousness, have achieved it, that is, righteousness that comes from faith; but that Israel, who pursued the law of righteousness, did not attain to that law? Why not? Because they did it not by faith, but as if it could be done by works. They stumbled over the stone that causes stumbling, as it is written:
>
> > "Behold, I am laying a stone in Zion
> > that will make people stumble
> > and a rock that will make them fall,
> > and whoever believes in him shall not be put to shame."[27]

Here Abraham, today often called the common father of Jews, Christians, and Muslims, serves a key role in advancing the claim that the Gospels have replaced the Torah (which, properly interpreted, always pointed to it and partook of its nature) and that the church has replaced the Jewish people, the natural descendants of Abraham. This is, to be sure, a theology from which Paul backs away in a few places and one that Christians involved in dialogue with Jews are usually (but not always) exceedingly eager to disown. For to the extent that the main outlines of Paul's theology remain in force, Christianity and Judaism become not simply different members of the same family (as *Dabru Emet* would have it), but rather, in the words of the late historian Jacob Katz, "conflicting exponents of the same tradition"—a tradition correctly interpreted by the Christians and profoundly misinterpreted by the Jews.[28]

Not surprisingly, much of the traditional Jewish theology of Abraham moves in a very different direction, in fact, the opposite direction. Two centuries before the emergence of Christianity, the idea had already appeared that Abraham observed norms disclosed only later, in the time of Moses, thus practicing Sinaitic religion even before Sinai.[29] As an addendum to a tractate in the Mishnah (compiled about 200 C.E.) would later put it, "We find that Our Father Abraham carried out the whole Torah before it had been given."[30] Whether by design or not, this view undercuts the Pauline use of Abraham as an object lesson in the sufficiency of faith at the expense of the specific norms of the Torah (Paul was not opposed to good works in general or at all reluctant to chastise those he thought lacking in them). For in this interpretation of the first Jew, the very difference between the Abrahamic and Mosaic dispensations dissolves. Elsewhere in rabbinic literature, we find the idea that Abraham did not observe all 613 commandments that the rabbis found in the Torah, but only the seven basic norms known to Noah (and incumbent upon all humanity, Jewish and Gentile), as well as the commandment of circumcision enjoined upon him in Genesis.[31] In this case, however, the point is that the Mosaic is the highest dispensation, higher than the Noahide and higher than the Abrahamic upon which Paul (and other Christians and Muslims as well) built so much. In making this evaluation, Rabbinic thought inverts the Pauline model, giving fullest praise to the Mosaic or Sinaitic mode of spirituality and placing the observance of commandments (rather than faith, grace, spirit, or the like) first in importance. Thus, although "Torah and commandments" is an expression that is absolutely critical to understanding the Jewish tradition, it is also an expression that calls attention to a key difference with Christianity in most of its versions. Given the strategy of *Dabru Emet* for dealing with these irresolvable differences between the two religions, we should not be surprised to note the total absence there of the words *law* and *commandment*.

But what does all this say about the claim in *Dabru Emet* that among the "similar lessons" that Jews and Christians derive from their common "Bible" is the idea that "God established a covenant with the people Israel"? We have already seen that the classic christological pronouncements render the Christian concept of "God" problematic for Jews in ways of which *Dabru Emet* seems unaware. As for "covenant," the two traditions differ markedly even on so fundamental a question as to what commandments, if any, that relationship requires (this is a matter of some disagreement within Christianity itself). They also differ on the worth and viability of that covenant. For example, the New Testament Epistle to the Hebrews claims Jesus mediated a "new covenant" vastly superior to the old one, which was of only temporary duration anyway.[32] And what of that third term, "the people Israel"? Surely, we must note that for all their striking similarities, the two sets of ancient normative books, the New Testament and the Oral Torah, often present diametrically opposed understandings of that all-important term. For the church early on claimed (with very few exceptions) not to share the status of Israel with the Jews, but to have supplanted the Jews in the role of God's chosen people, and, until rather recently, Christian tradition was all but unanimous in seconding (and even hardening) that ominous judgment. Similarly, Rabbinic Judaism was adamant that whatever spiritual dignity the nations could achieve (and many rabbis thought they could achieve much spiritual dignity indeed), "Israel" was composed of only the Jews— an extended natural family whose males, whether born or converted into that people, are marked by the covenantal sign of circumcision. Gentiles who "have a place in the world-to-come," to use the rabbinic terminology (it is like a Christian saying that someone is "saved"), are still Gentiles and not "Israel." They need not convert to Judaism to have a place in the world-to-come, but, without conversion, even if they worship God and act in a properly moral manner, they remain Gentiles and not Jews. "Israel" in traditional Jewish thought does not include non-Jews, just as "Church" in traditional Christian thought does not include Jews. Neither term refers to all humanity or even to all monotheists who trace their origins back to the Hebrew Bible.

This dispute between Christianity and Judaism in antiquity could take place only because the two communities worked from common scriptures that reported that "God established a covenant with the people Israel," in the words of *Dabru Emet*. The commonality, as we have seen, served not to minimize opposition, but to make dispute possible, and it now serves—and appropriately serves—to make Jewish dialogue with Christians vastly more encompassing, productive, and interesting than dialogue with adherents of other religions with which Jews have less in common and therefore also less to challenge. Much of what is at stake theologically in a dialogue grounded in these ancient sources disappears when the two disputants are depicted as simply different and therefore safely out of each other's way. When *Dabru Emet* affirms in a later paragraph that "Christians know and serve God through Jesus Christ and the Christian tradition. Jews know and serve God through Torah and the Jewish tradition," it thus achieves the desired comity by a kind of demarcation of spheres of influence that is too easy: Jesus Christ for the Christians, Torah for the Jews. In the process, however, it has radically changed the meaning of both "Jesus Christ" and "Torah." For historically, both these terms refer to realities that are larger than the communities that testify to them, realities that are cosmic and eternal in scope and import.

In the decades since the Holocaust, partly as a result of Jewish-Christian dialogue, many Christians have been courageously reassessing and even altering their theology so as to give a positive evaluation to Judaism and Jewish survival. In some instances, the result has been a theology that speaks of two covenants of equal worth, one for Jews and one for Gentiles, and this seems to be the model for *Dabru Emet*'s bold affirmation of both "Jesus Christ" and "Torah" as ways to "know and serve God." The affirmation is, however, in serious tension with the prior affirmation of a common "Bible." For however else they may differ, the Tanakh and the Old Testament know of only one Israel, only one chosen people in covenant with God, or to put it in more biblical language, only one son with the status of the firstborn. Ironically, to the extent that the two traditions turn either to their putatively common Bible or to their distinctive post-biblical traditions, they raise problems for the dual covenant theology. So, for all the appeal to common roots, the paramount and regulative claim of *Dabru Emet* is on behalf of a modern theology that relativizes Judaism and Christianity in ways that those ancient sources do not accept. Given the willingness to do so, it is unclear why it makes much difference whether the two religions appeal to "the same book" or not.

Christians Can Respect the Claim of the Jewish People upon the Land of Israel

The third of the eight affirmations of *Dabru Emet* tells us that *"Christians can respect the claim of the Jewish people upon the land of Israel."* No surprise there: since many Christians do respect the Jewish claim (as the paragraph later states), who would deny they "can"? Rather, it looks as though the statement really wants to tell Christians that they *should* do so. Thus the supporting paragraph states that "[a]s members of a biblically based religion, Christians appreciate that Israel was promised—and given—to Jews," and it applauds those "who support the State of Israel for reasons more profound than mere politics." The alternative position— that the Jews forfeited the land by not accepting the church's claims about Jesus—is, as we have seen, the traditional one. It is also very much alive and well today, even in some evangelical quarters. Here is an excerpt from a recent statement issued by one evangelical seminary and signed by hundreds of evangelicals:

> The entitlement of any one ethnic or religious group to territory in the Middle East called the "Holy Land" cannot be supported by Scripture. In fact, the land promises specific to Israel were fulfilled under Joshua. The

New Testament speaks clearly and prophetically about the destruction of the second temple in A.D. 70. No New Testament writer foresees a regathering of ethnic Israel in the land, as did the prophets of the Old Testament after the destruction of the first temple in 586 B.C. Moreover the land promises of the Old Covenant are consistently and deliberately expanded in the New Testament to show the universal dominion of Jesus.[33]

As biblical exegesis, this contemporary restatement of the classic supersessionist theology is not without its problems. After all, the God of the Old Testament does repeatedly assign the land to the descendants of Abraham, Isaac, and Jacob/Israel "to possess forever," as Exodus 32:13 puts it, and not only until the time of Joshua or some still later dispensation. But so to argue is to miss the larger claim of the Christian theology underlying the statement, the claim that the New Testament supersedes the Old, fulfilling and reassigning its promises. It stands to reason that Jews would object to this move, and, in fact, much of Jewish-Christian dialogue has long consisted of Jews' trying to persuade their Christian partners to give more weight to the Old Testament and less to the New. And such an entry into an intramural argument among Christians is precisely what *Dabru Emet*, for all its rhetoric about "a dramatic and unprecedented shift in Jewish and Christian relations," is undertaking here: it is taking a stand in favor of one Christian theology over another. The favored theology is, to be sure, both much more congenial to Judaism and upheld by millions of Christians, evangelical and other. But is that sufficient reason for Christians who hold a supersessionist theology to scuttle it in favor of something that finds more favor with Jews? It is hard to see a good theoretical reason to say that it is. Does *Dabru Emet* really maintain that Religion A should always change its theology simply because members of Religion B find it unworthy of belief or even downright offensive? If so, what should Jews do with Hindu or Buddhist reservations about Jewish monotheism, to give only two of dozens of similar cases facing *them*? It is healthy to examine ourselves carefully and critically to discover why we are giving offense. But it is not healthy to assume that if we give offense, we must be wrong. If we carry on interreligious dialogue with that as our operative principle, the dialogue (as mentioned above) soon degenerates into a monologue or an occasion for the blandest form of mutual admiration.

It must not be missed that supersessionist theology is not necessarily incompatible with the belief that God's gift of the land of Israel to the Jews is still in effect (which the statement quoted above denies). In this connection, I think of those Christians (hardly few in number) who support the State of Israel because they see the ingathering of the Jewish exiles as a necessary prelude to the second coming of Jesus and the conversion of all Israel to Christianity. Should Jews applaud *these* Christians for "support[ing] the State of Israel for reasons far more profound than mere politics," to use the words of *Dabru Emet*, or is there something deeply problematic in their theology that Jews (and Christians as well) need to face? Most Jews would say that there is, but on this, *Dabru Emet* is silent. The silence fits with the tendency of the statement to disregard points of contention between the two traditions.

Jews and Christians
Accept the Moral Principles of Torah

Dabru Emet is on more secure ground when, in its next thesis, it affirms that *Jews and Christians accept the moral principles of Torah*. All one has to do is compare the traditional ethic of the two religions to the materialism and egocentrism, not to mention the narcissistic body culture, rampant in Western culture today, to see the degree of commonality of Jews and Christians in bold relief. Surely there are many moral issues on which Jews and Christians, finding themselves on the same side, can and should work together. But "the moral principles of Torah" is an odd phrase in this context, since Judaism does not maintain that Torah obligates non-Jews or that Torah (as opposed to wisdom) is found among them. The phrase is similarly problematic from the other side, for exceedingly few are the Christians who ask of themselves, "Are my morals in line with Torah?" Instead, they are more likely to ask, "What would Jesus do?" (hence "WWJD" on bracelets, pens, pencils, T-shirts, and so on). Indeed, a tradition of Christian thought that goes back nearly two thousand years regards Jesus' moral principles as higher and better than those of the Torah, an improvement or a radicalization and not just a restatement of them.[34] What this suggests is that there is a moral debate between Jews and Christians alongside the theological debate, and that historically Christians have usually seen Jesus as instituting a new ethic at odds to one degree or another with that of the Old Testament. In addition, they have not infrequently been critical of the very idea of commandments as the vehicles of moral imagination, preferring love or the Spirit in their stead, the laws written upon the heart, as the Epistle to the Hebrews puts it (reworking Jeremiah),[35] over those written in the Torah. And so, even when the substantive moral norms are the same, the principle by which they are derived often is not, and this again renders the last two words in the phrase "the moral principles of Torah" in *Dabru Emet* highly problematic.

A more appropriately worded thesis would have invoked the "seven commandments of the descendants of Noah," which, it will be recalled, are the basic norms that the talmudic rabbis thought incumbent upon Jews and Gentiles alike. The seven forbidden actions are blasphemy, idolatry, sexual misdeeds, murder, robbery, failing to set up a system of law, and eating meat cut from a living animal.[36] To the extent that Christianity promotes adherence to the Noahide commandments, an authoritative talmudic tradition maintains that it aids its believers in attaining a proper relationship with God.[37] Amazingly, "the seven commandments of the descendants of Noah" go unmentioned in *Dabru Emet* (unless the phrase "moral principles of Torah" is intended as an indirect reference to them). Had the statement chosen to reaffirm the theology of the seven commandments, it could have affirmed the spiritual and moral integrity of Christianity powerfully while simultaneously avoiding the (Jewishly) highly inappropriate affirmation of "Jesus Christ" as a way "to know and serve God" alongside Torah. In so doing, it could have built on a long history of medieval and early modern Jewish authorities who rendered positive evaluations of Christianity without subscribing to Christian beliefs, resorting to a two-covenant theology that has no basis in the classical Jewish sources, or falling into outright relativism.

Nazism Was Not a Christian Phenomenon

A similar refusal to face the full measure of difference between Jews and Christians appears even in the finely crafted and exquisitely balanced statement on the Holocaust, which merits quotation in full:

Nazism was not a Christian phenomenon. Without the long history of Christian anti-Judaism and Christian violence against Jews, Nazi ideology could not have taken hold nor could it have been carried out. Too many Christians participated in, or were sympathetic to, Nazi atrocities against Jews. Other Christians did not protest sufficiently against these atrocities. But Nazism itself was not an inevitable outcome of Christianity. If the Nazi extermination of the Jews had been fully successful, it would have turned its murderous rage more directly to Christians. We recognize with gratitude those Christians who risked or sacrificed their lives to save Jews during the Nazi regime. With that in mind, we encourage the continuation of recent efforts in Christian theology to repudiate unequivocally contempt of Judaism and the Jewish people. We applaud those Christians who reject this teaching of contempt, and we do not blame them for the sins committed by their ancestors.

On the one hand, we find here a forthright acknowledgment that not only individual Christians, but also Christianity itself played a role in making the Holocaust possible. On the other, we see an ungrudging recognition that some Christians resisted the Nazis at the time and many since then, both as individuals and as churches, have repudiated the traditional anti-Semitism out of which Nazism partly grew. So far, so good. The problem comes with the speculation (reported as something much more certain than that) that, "If the Nazi extermination of the Jews had been fully successful, it would have turned its murderous rage more directly to Christians." Here again, the statement assimilates Jews and Christians much too readily.

The intended "Nazi extermination of the Jews" was, as we have noted, based in racism. Whether the victims believed in Judaism in any sense was not pertinent to their murderers' plan. People of Jewish ancestry who were altogether secular or who had converted to Christianity were sent to their deaths alongside their more observant kinsmen. In the case of Christians without Jewish ancestors, no such motivation obtained, and it was possible to stay out of the Nazis' way and even (if one's convictions allowed) to support them in full vigor, as some Christians did.

Had *Dabru Emet* acknowledged this critical difference, it would have touched upon the subject of a major Christian critique of Judaism. Here, I refer to the fact that Judaism, though it accepts converts, is in the first instance the religion of a kin-group. According to traditional Jewish theology, the Jews are a natural family with a supernatural mission. They are not a church, that is, an association of unrelated persons who join together on the basis of shared religious belief (that is why a nonreligious Jew is still a Jew). Especially since the Enlightenment (eighteenth century), Christians have often thought of this difference as that between tribalism (Judaism) and universalism (Christianity) and have not been shy about citing Paul's words that "in Christ Jesus . . . [t]here is neither Jew nor Greek"[38] against Judaism. That this is a misreading of Paul, and of the whole question of universalism and particularism,[39] need not detain us here. The point is that by assimilating the nature of membership in the Jewish people to the nature of membership in the church, *Dabru Emet* once again purchases a false commonality at the expense of an honest and frank confrontation of the differences and what they mean.

Dabru Emet not only fails to acknowledge the racist character of the Nazi persecution of the Jews; it compounds the problem by imagining that the Nazis planned a Holocaust-like fate for Christians as well once they succeeded with the Jews. This would, of course, have entailed annihilating nearly the entire European population, something that the Nazis, in fact, never contemplated. It is also to miss the well-known fact that the Nazis had support aplenty in the churches, especially in theology departments, including a number of influential scholars.[40] The effect of *Dabru Emet*'s unsubstantiated claim is to make Christians, too, victims of the Holocaust. It presents the Nazi failure to sponsor anti-Christian violence (except in the case of those few believers who spoke out against the regime) as accidental. Given more time, the Christians would have found themselves in concentration camps and death camps alongside the Jews. Here the underlying claim is that the Nazis were not, in the first instance, anti-Semitic: they were *anti-religious*. In the face of the historical record, *Dabru Emet* once again conveniently puts Jews and Christians in the same boat—or, to be more precise, on the same train to Auschwitz.

The Humanly Irreconcilable Difference Between Jews and Christians Will Not Be Settled until God Redeems the Entire World as Promised in Scripture

A similar flaw can be seen in this thesis. In this case, the effect is to make Christianity a participant in the events of the last days, events that the two traditions have historically envisioned in ways that are not only different, but also incompatible. But why should Jews affirm that the church will survive until God initiates the final redemption? I am very far from suggesting that it will not or that the world would be better off without it. Rather, the question is, why should Jews affirm that God has a specific commitment to the church that shall endure until God "redeems the entire world"?

The reverse question is easy to answer—and provides a clue as to why the drafters of *Dabru Emet* have made the dubious assumption that underlies this thesis. The prologue of this Jewish statement notes that its recent Christian counterparts "have declared . . . that Christian teaching and preaching can and must be reformed so that they acknowledge God's enduring covenant with the Jewish people." The prime basis for this reform in the New Testament is Paul's insistence that God has not rejected the Jewish people, who remain, in fact, "beloved because of the patriarchs [i.e., Abraham, Isaac, and Jacob]. For the gifts and the call of God are irrevocable." This affirmation (by no means Paul's only position on this, as we have seen) is pro-Jewish but not pro-Judaism. Its point is that God bears with the Jews despite the failure of so many of them to become Christians. "A hardening has come upon Israel in part," the apostle writes, "until the full number of the Gentiles comes in, and thus all Israel will be saved."[41] In response to the recent concentration on these ideas on the part of some Christians and the efforts to make them the basis for a positive evaluation of Judaism, it is readily understandable that the Jews would feel the need to reciprocate. The problem is again the one we have been exploring throughout our discussion of *Dabru Emet*: the relationship is not symmetrical. Classical Judaism, for all its abundant capacity to evaluate Gentiles and Christianity positively, knows of no specific covenant with the church, no parallel, that is, to Paul's belief in the irrevocable call of the Israelite patriarchs. Without that, the Jewish claim that the church will survive until God finally redeems the world seems like a thin imitation of the Christian doctrine contrived for the purpose of the dialogue. In many areas of life, reciprocity is a wise policy. In the pursuit of theological truth, however, it represents a dangerous temptation because it presupposes a false symmetry—as does *Dabru Emet* in general.

A New Relationship Between Jews and Christians Will Not Weaken Jewish Practice

The penultimate paragraph of the statement, alone phrased in the negative, strikes a defensive note:

> *A new relationship between Jews and Christians will not weaken Jewish practice.* An improved relationship will not accelerate the cultural and religious assimilation that Jews rightly fear. It will not change traditional Jewish forms of worship, nor increase intermarriage between Jews and non-Jews, nor persuade more Jews to convert to Christianity, nor create a false blending of Judaism and Christianity. We respect Christianity as a faith that originated within Judaism and that still has significant contact with it. We do not see it as an extension of Judaism. Only if we cherish our own traditions can we pursue this relationship with integrity.

Given the position *Dabru Emet* has already articulated, however, the worries it here dismisses require a more convincing response. The risk of amalgamation—whether through blending of worship or intermarriage—is especially great if Jews and Christians really do stand in the relationship that *Dabru Emet* describes in its other paragraphs. For the thrust of the statement is to make Judaism and Christianity look very much alike, indeed like two peas in the same Judeo-Christian pod. They have, after all, "the same God"—"the God of Israel," "the same book—the Bible" (from which they "take away similar lessons"), and the same "moral principles"—in fact, "the moral principles of Torah." Moreover, both religions now appreciate God's gift of the land of Israel to the Jews—or at least "can" do so—and, in principle (though not in the deed), both were the targets of the Nazis' "murderous rage." Although the statement mentions differences a few times and asks that they be respected, overall it leaves the impression that Judaism and Christianity represent minor variations on a common theme. The truth is that it is hard to come away from *Dabru Emet* without the sense that nearly two thousand years of Jewish-Christian disputation have been based on little more than the narcissism of small differences. What other conclusion can we draw from a statement in which a Judaism without law and commandments affirms its unqualified approval of a Christianity without New Testament, incarnation, Trinity, or Mary?

If the commonalities really are so basic and encompassing, many Jews will rightly wonder why intermarriage, conversion to Christianity, and "a false blending of Judaism and Christianity" are (as their own tradition used to tell them) to be strenuously avoided and counteracted (what sort of "blending" is not "false," *Dabru Emet* does not tell us). Indeed, the same decades that have witnessed the remarkable rapprochement of Jews and Christians have witnessed a soaring intermarriage rate and a novel and striking acceptance of intermarriage on the part of many (but not all) Jewish organizations.[42] This is not in the least to imply that interreligious dialogue has caused the increase of intermarriage and assimilation. It is to say, however, that the strategy *Dabru Emet* takes—stressing (or inventing) commonalities at the expense of mutually exclusive structures and truth claims—makes syncretism and conversion seem much less dangerous. That need not have deterred the signatories of *Dabru Emet* from speaking the truth about the relationship of Jews and Christians as they see it. But it ought to have given them pause about this claim that doing so poses no risks to Jewish practice and identity. For one teaching common to Judaism and Christianity that *Dabru Emet* omits to mention is that truth-telling on profound issues is not risk-free.

Wolfhart Pannenberg, the Protestant theologian mentioned earlier, finds confirmation of the risk-free scenario that *Dabru Emet* puts forth in the "emergence of 'messianic Jews,'" that is, "Jews who confess their faith in Jesus the Messiah without leaving the Jewish community and a Jewish way of life." "Sooner or later Christian-Jewish dialogue will have to take notice of this fact," he writes, gently chiding the Jewish statement.[43] Why did *Dabru Emet* not do so? In fact, it did, but to make a point diametrically opposed to Pannenberg's. "Christian worship is not a viable religious choice for Jews," it remarks, in a subordinate clause in the paragraph about our worshiping the same God. In other words, those Jews who combine Judaism with Christianity have indeed abandoned the Jewish way of life, and what Pannenberg sees as proof that the new closeness really is risk-free, *Dabru Emet* sees as a regrettable defection from Jewish authenticity. What the Christian views as positive, the Jews view as negative. But, whereas he is willing to recognize it and has a theology that can reckon with it, they simply deny the problem exists.

Jews and Christians Must Work Together for Justice and Peace

The gutsy stand of this last of the eight theses of *Dabru Emet* has undoubtedly provoked unimaginable consternation in the camp that advocates that Jews and Christians work separately for injustice and war.

The Agenda of *Dabru Emet*

What then is the agenda of *Dabru Emet*? In its own formulation, it is "to reflect on what Judaism may now say about Christianity" in light of the fact that that "Christianity has changed dramatically." The change to which the statement refers is the new respect for Judaism and the discarding of supersessionist theology in a number of Christian communions, large and small. There is, however, another change in Christianity to which *Dabru Emet* responds, namely a reformulation of Christian faith that removes, or at least weakens, the elements that put it into conflict with Judaism. I hope to have now demonstrated that the Christianity that this Jewish statement presupposes is, in fact, a

Christianity amazingly like Judaism. It is a monotheistic faith based in the Hebrew Bible, respecting the Jewish claim on the land of Israel, adhering to the moral principles of Torah, giving inevitable offense to Nazi murderers, lasting until the final redemption, and in no way challenging Jewish identity and practice or threatening the survival and integrity of the Jewish people (as through intermarriage). What the Christianity of *Dabru Emet* lacks are certain theological notions on which the classical Christian tradition had insisted and to which millions of Christians still adhere. It lacks the belief in the God who is triune and not simply one and who was definitively incarnate in Jesus Christ. It lacks the belief that through Jesus, God gave a new and more complete revelation, including a basis for morality in some ways at odds with the Judaic focus on law and commandments. It lacks a belief that the mission of Jesus called into existence a new Israel, a community that, unlike the Jewish people, was neither based on genealogy (and therefore immune to genocide, though not to martyrdom) nor promised any particular real estate.

The agenda of *Dabru Emet* is, as the statement itself implies, to give a positive Jewish response to the new Christian thinking about Jews and Judaism. In the process, it also specifies the terms under which a positive Jewish response is possible. Those terms require Christians to distance themselves not only from the anti-Jewish prejudices and false images of Judaism prominent in premodern Christianity and still potent today, but also from traditional doctrines that go back in one degree or another to the New Testament itself. In this, *Dabru Emet* exemplifies well the common opinion that the purpose of interreligious dialogue is to cultivate commonalities and minimize differences. It cannot be denied that the common opinion has borne some good fruit and that there are dangers in the frank examination of differences. Sometimes, however, the perceived differences and the judgments that Judaism and Christianity render upon each other are attributable not to prejudice and misconception, but to the deepest truths that the two traditions have sought to uphold. For Jews who are integrated into the modern world, the challenge is to uphold those truths while striving to divest themselves and their Christian dialogue partners of the misconceptions whose results Jewish history abundantly demonstrates to be tragic. In light of the religious situation in the contemporary West, both the challenge and the opportunity of Jewish-Christian dialogue are great.

Discussion Questions

1. What was the classical Christian view of Judaism and the Jews?

2. Based on Judaism and Christianity, why might one say that all religions do not teach the same thing?

3. Give three reasons why it is misleading to say that Judaism and Christianity share the Bible.

4. Why does overemphasizing the commonalities and neglecting the differences in interreligious dialogue threaten the minority community more than the majority?

Judaism, Christianity, and Islam in Their Contemporary Encounters: Christianity Meets Other Religions

Bruce Chilton

From the end of the nineteenth century, when reason came to be doubted as a vehicle of revelation, Christianity increasingly relied upon the assertion of ideological axioms, not subject to negotiation, as guardians of the truth of faith. That change was exacerbated by the perceived threat to faith posed by rational inquiry, so that belief was seen more and more as a denial of reason. The rise of Fundamentalism and the doctrine of papal infallibility—the Catholic counterpart of Protestant Fundamentalism—illustrate this shift, and damage prospects for Christian dialogue with other systems of belief.

Fundamentalism

During discussions with my students, they once asked me to define *Fundamentalism* for them. I explained its five main tenets, held to be "essential and necessary" teachings by the Presbyterian General Assembly in 1910:[1]

- biblical "inerrancy" in historical truth
- Jesus' birth from a biological virgin
- Jesus' performance of miracles that defy natural law
- Jesus' atonement for the sins of others by shedding his blood on the cross

• Jesus' resurrection in the same body in which he died, and his return to earth in that body at the end of days.

The response of my students was direct and to the point: "But isn't that what all Christians believe?"

Their reaction was telling. It reflects how little influence academic theology, the inheritance of the Enlightenment, has had on popular awareness in the United States over the past two hundred years. Academic theology understands Christianity as something far more symbolic, collective, and varied in its history than the Fundamentalist insistence on the literal belief of the individual. My students' reaction confirms what survey after survey has suggested, that the take on Christianity in the United States is along Fundamentalist lines among believers and nonbelievers.[2]

Fundamentals came to be asserted in both Protestantism and Catholicism in response to two basic challenges. Both of those challenges were voiced during the nineteenth century and continue to be influential today.

The first challenge is best appreciated by considering the example of David Friedrich Strauss, whose work later inspired Ernst Renan. The year 1835 saw Strauss's influential book, *The Life of Jesus,* published. It was so controversial that it was immediately assured many printings in several languages, but its publication also meant that Strauss would be denied teaching positions in Germany and Switzerland. Strauss, under the influence of the philosophy of Hegel, believed that Jesus in the Gospels embodies the synthesis between divinity and humanity, so that the texts should be read as symbols, not as literal or miraculous history. The idea that the Gospels are symbolic has continued to exert a powerful influence, both among those who are sympathetic to this approach and among those who react against it.

The second major challenge was Darwin's *On the Origin of Species* (1859), as discussed in the chapter 13 of this book. The idea of evolution has since been applied in many different domains, including the study of religion. In the development of theology, it leads to the assertion that we in the present are in a better position to understand the significance of past events—including the life of Jesus—than those who were alive at the time. Taken together with the reading of the Gospels as symbols, the principle of evolution makes for a strong tendency to reinterpret the Scriptures.

Among both Catholics and Protestants, the reaction against these two principles insisted upon certain fundamentals as literally true. In 1870, the First Vatican Council promulgated the doctrine of papal infallibility, according to which the pope could not err when he pronounced on matters of doctrine. Among Protestants, the very name of Fundamentalism was embraced, in order to insist that the Scriptures themselves set the infallible standard of faith.

Through the nineteenth century and the first half of the twentieth century, resistance to the teaching of literal fundamentals was adamantly maintained among Catholics and Protestants. In France and England, those who used historical tools to assert a symbolic and evolutionary approach to interpretation were called Modernists. The most famous of them was Alfred Loisy, a French priest who found it perfectly natural to deny the infallibility of any human being, who doubted the Virgin birth of Jesus, who saw Jesus' miracles as symbols, did not believe God needed a payment in blood in order to love us, and who overtly denied resurrection in the same body. For him, the meaning of the Gospels resided in their capacity to transform the nature of our collective existence.[3]

The Protestant Walter Rauschenbusch espoused a similarly collective, but less academic, theology in New York City. He called his message "the social gospel," and by it he intended to insist that the purpose of the Gospels was to overturn the structures of capitalism and totally to change the nature of our social life in the interests of justice.[4]

These theologians were both praised and attacked for their symbolic, evolutionary brands of Christianity. The Vatican banned Loisy's books; he himself submitted to their banning, and agreed not to engage in publication. But he refused to say that his opinions were wrong, and was excommunicated from the Catholic Church by Pope Pius X in 1908. His isolation from the church provided him with a new opportunity: a position in the Collège de France. Rauschenbusch was a Baptist pastor in Brooklyn during the final years of the century, just as Fundamentalism was making itself felt; he found a warmer welcome at the Rochester Theological Seminary, where he taught from 1897. His claim that Christianity was a matter of programmatic social action, rather than individual belief, found more support among intellectuals than in the Baptist hierarchy.

Both these thinkers are influential today. Loisy's methods, and his claims that Moses did not write the Pentateuch and that the Apostle John did not author the Gospel named after him, for example, are now taught as standard in Catholic and Protestant seminaries. Similarly, part of the formation of any pastor—no matter what the faith involved—will routinely include training in what most people would call social work and what Rauschenbusch saw as part of the gospel: counseling, community organizing, mediation, and the like. In religious academies, Loisy and Rauschenbusch prevailed a long time ago.

But popular religion has evidenced a reaction against symbol and evolution as providing keys to assessing the Gospels. Overtly Fundamentalist forms of Protestantism, and papalist[5] forms of Catholicism, have enjoyed enormous growth in the United States since World War II. That is one reason for which those interested in religion in America have little choice but to deal with the claim of literal fundamentals in Christianity.

The symbolic and evolutionary approach of Loisy and Rauschenbusch has nonetheless persisted. It has prospered better in Europe than in America, even in popular culture. Catholic Europe has largely made its peace with papal infallibility by restricting its validity to what individuals might choose to believe or not. (That explains, for example, why France is an international leader in the field of birth control.) Insofar as Protestant Fundamentalism is there at all is largely a result of American influence, especially by cable television. Because American academics still tend to look to Europe as an example, it is perhaps not surprising that our academies (including our seminaries) espouse a theology that is rarely spoken to the public at large, but that would be at home in Europe.

From a European perspective, it is a fairly easy step to confuse Fundamentalism with a devotion to literal history. From the vantage point of an emphasis upon symbol and evolution, the assertion of basic categories of revelation looks remarkably like an unsophisticated literalism. But Fundamentalism and literalism are in fact quite different. Yet as Fundamentalism grew in popular religion, theologians began to deny history as a serviceable approach to the study of theology. In that denial, academics found themselves in a strange alliance with the very Fundamentalists they enjoyed condemning.

The Denial of History

By identifying a salvation-historical perspective with Fundamentalism, James Barr joined and encouraged a theological change, away from the axiom that the time marked out in the Bible is linear,[6] and for that reason expressive of a particular sequence of consequential events. To him that idea was a kind of Fundamentalism. Of course, what he really rejected was a view associated with Augustine,[7] not the Bible. The Bible, Barr showed, is not the property of salvation history. Or, in the language of our interest here: the Bible is not the property of progressive time, a neat sequence from beginning, through the middle, and to the end, which wraps the whole of human experience within a coherent package.

But then, Fundamentalists were also in the process of denying that salvation is subject to human criticism, in a way much more vehement and emphatic than Barr's. They held that the Fundamentals of faith are not contingent matters which history can confirm or deny, but absolute truths, axioms attested by the inspired Bible. The irony is that Barr and others of the liberal viewpoint he represented seemingly did not notice that they had joined with Fundamentalists in an assault on the primacy of history within theological discussion.[8]

Barr's blind spot in this regard is revealing. By confusing Fundamentalism with historicism, he did not observe that Fundamentalists are less committed to any particulars of history than they are to the theological account that is defined by what they themselves call Fundamentals. In aggregate, those Fundamentals assert that God by miraculous means of atonement is reclaiming and therefore transfiguring human nature in its flesh, and the Bible is read, not literally, but as the coherent witness to that absolute truth. Barr, by contrast, is committed in theological terms, not to precise linguistics or pristine history, but to his conception that the act of interpretation itself is redeeming for the interpreter. That is, both conservative Fundamentalists and the liberal Barr illustrate the retreat from salvation history that has been characteristic of American and British theology since 1960.[9]

The details of the argument concerning linguistics and interpretation do not concern us here, but the retreat from the concept of the overarching significance of progressive time *is* of immediate import. What was going on in theological discussion was mirrored in wider intellectual trends, and also in political developments.

Where in theology Fundamentalism squared off against liberal interpretation, both of them ideologically committed and increasingly ahistorical in their basic orientation, in literary discussion structuralism and deconstruction vied for influence. Structuralism posited that in the development of language and literature, certain essentials of discourse could be discerned, and that without such discernment, interpretation was impossible.[10] Deconstruction, in contrast, insisted that meaning only occurs in the mind of the interpreter, by means of engagement with the text (and sometimes without that benefit, in theoretical discussion which non-Deconstructionists often find difficult or impossible to follow).[11]

The politics of this period, the final ideological push of the Cold War, saw the emergence in America and (to a lesser extent) in Europe of a conservative agenda, which, for the first time in the history of

Conservatism, wedded itself first of all to economic principles (free markets protected and extended by a strong military establishment, low-tax monetarism, no deficit in government, rejection of the redistribution of wealth).[12] Several of these commitments (which approach to being fundamentals in some circles) were woven into the aspirations of Conservatives during the course of the nineteenth and twentieth centuries, but the common, international program—especially during the nineteen-eighties in Reagan's America, Thatcher's Britain, and Kohl's Germany—marked a stunning intellectual and ideological development in the global political and economic scene during the past fifty years. Of course, there are Conservatives who stand for more than the free market, just as there are Fundamentalists who stand for more than scriptural infallibility, but what is similar in both groups is agreement by consensus to a limited range of principles and objectives.

But the apparent triumph of Conservatism on "the right" is no more momentous than the equally startling implosion of Liberalism on "the left." American political discourse has even seen a move away from using the "L word," as if it held the place of the term Communism a generation ago.[13] But the absence of agreed terminology among Liberals is not only the result of the successful challenge from the right. Liberals themselves, as compared to the great advances before, during, and after World War II, by the Democratic Party in America, the Labour Party in England, the Socialists in France, and the Social Democrats in Germany, have lost at least as much specificity in program as the Conservatives have gained. That is a consequence, not simply of factionalism (of which there is plenty, on left and right), but of a pronounced Liberal proclivity to put principle after personal inclination, program after personal preference. That helps to explain the uncertainty of much Liberal policy subsequent to victory in elections. As Deconstruction marks the victory of the interpreter over the text, so Liberalism has come to stand for the ascendancy of personal proclivity over conceptual platform.

So not only in theology, but also in the more general discussion of meaning, as well as in politics, we find ourselves divided between a programmatic attachment to fundamentals on the one hand, and a programmatic attachment to individual propensity on the other hand. The opposition of the two stances within each field of conflict is impossible to resolve, and what passes for discourse for that reason is shrill when the opposing stances meet, and self-referential when they do not. What is widely decried, from right and left, as a loss of civility in public discourse (both intellectual and political) is in fact even more corrosive than a simple lack of manners.

In the struggle between fundamentals and propensities, there are no rules of engagement. So the right can attack any target on the left for lacking one of the fundamental elements of civilization: the behavior and character of liberals can be used against them in public discussion. And the left can counter that all such allegations from the right are projections of self-interest, and deny that any propensities should be subject to such hindrance. Recently, journalists on both sides of the Atlantic told us more than we ever wanted to know about President Clinton, a sometime intern in the White House, and Kenneth Starr. The posturing on both sides, the lurid reporting in virtually all public media, and the factional confusion of the United States Congress, are perhaps the only instructive parts of that story. The Independent Counsel managed to extend his brief from investigating a land fraud to asking a private citizen and her mother about conversations they had about sexual encounters. The President and his advisers, in a skilled deployment of the hermeneutics of the left, pursued the pursuers by turning discussion to the motivations and interests of the Independent Counsel and his team. A better parable (or caricature) for the state of public discussion in the United States could not have been invented.

The most obvious victim of the charade was the intern herself, who after all made no public or legal complaint. Her sexual history became an issue when a friend tape-recorded a conversation, which was relayed to the Independent Counsel, and the reaction of the White House was to impugn the reliability of what she might say. This invasion of her privacy was defended in much commentary by the probability she would write a book about her ordeal, which she in fact did. So the victim was not a victim, because she eventually profited from the privacy she was robbed of. Privacy itself, the right to be secure in one's person,[14] is defended neither by Conservatives, who suffer from amnesia in regard to that Constitutional fundamental, nor by Liberals, who have kept repeating since the 1960s that "the personal is political," without explaining what they might mean by that.

History Strikes Back

How can the sense of crucial distinctions in discourse—between private and public, between invective and argument, between programmatic agenda and analysis—have been eroded so quickly and seemingly permanently? With the close of the Cold War, Francis Fukuyama wrote a controversial article, and then a book, called *The End of History*. He argued that history in the modern understanding is driven by conflict among nation-states; historians measure the importance of events by the influence of those events on the story of national contentions. Once such contentions come to an end, so does history.[15] The thesis was easily picked apart, since the emergence of the United States as the only remaining state with genuinely global power was never likely to bring more stability to international relations than the confrontation of the two "superpowers" had ensured. Events since the publication of his work have only underscored that: the ideological freeze of two single ideas at loggerheads which the Cold War imposed has given way, not to the dominance of a single, surviving idea, but to a multiplicity of new contenders for consideration.

But Fukuyama has been telling us something profoundly important about the way we in the West have sought to deal with the new situation. (He has, in his own way, shown us in politics what James Barr showed us in theology.) We have, on the right and on the left, disinvented history. On the right, alleged fundamentals of the free market are constantly invoked, which were discredited during the nineteenth century. Only willful ignorance can forget the child labor, the black lung disease among miners, the inhuman conditions imposed on seamstresses, which only legislation (and certainly not the free market) ended, and which today are virtually unknown in the United States, even as they are tolerated by Americans in other countries that we trade with. On the left, the very history that might have been used to make a cogent case against such abuses has been dissolved into a series of allegedly multicultural vignettes, whose apparent moral is that all sorts of behavior can be legitimated. So William Bennett can say only he is really right because his principles are correct,[16] and Cornell West can say only he is really correct because his heart is in the right place.[17]

Although both Fundamentalism and the reaction against Fundamentalism by liberal theology have shied away from history, history has not retreated from them. The basic facts of the Holocaust, emerging out of Christianity's post-Enlightenment crisis, and of militant Islam, a direct consequence of Christian policies of war and oppression, have rooted Christian thought afresh in historical contingency. Dialogue with Judaism has proceeded vigorously, and the inclusion of Islam within comparative theology has clearly been signaled.

In the Catholic Church, an openness to new historical expressions of faith was shown by the pontificate of Angelo Roncalli, Pope John XXIII—the greatest reformer in the modern history of Roman Catholicism. Soon after his election in 1958, he called the Second Vatican Council, making it clear that he wished the work of renewal to be undertaken by the bishops assembled, rather than by the court of the Pope himself. Despite opposition, the Council opened in 1962, and when that first session closed John announced himself satisfied with the work of updating *(aggiornamento)*. He convened the second session for the following year, but he died of cancer on 3 June 1963, before that session convened.

Despite the brevity of his pontificate and continuing disputes concerning the meaning of Vatican II, in one regard there can be no question of the influence of John XXIII. The Council accepted that the Mass and other sacraments should be made available in the actual language of the people who participated, rather than in Latin. Moreover, the report on liturgy also allowed that local variation, rather than rigid uniformity, should be admitted and encouraged in the development of worship. Both those principles, associated with Protestantism since the sixteenth century, entered the Catholic tradition with John's endorsement.

In this case, the rule of faith, which had long been discussed by Catholic theologians and pastors and laypeople, was able to articulate itself afresh in new circumstances by means of papal encouragement. The purpose, of course, was not in any way to diminish "the divine Eucharistic sacrifice," but to make it even more vivid as "the outstanding means by which the faithful can express in their lives, and manifest to others, the mystery of Christ and the real nature of the true Church."[18] In this statement, the Council made it clear that it was not adopting a Protestant emphasis upon the individual's understanding of the faith, but rather was enhancing its dedication to a sacramental definition of the church.

The same period also saw a fresh historical engagement on the part of Protestant Christianity. In his "Letter from Birmingham Jail," the Reverend Dr. Martin Luther King, Jr. set out the principles behind his teaching of nonviolence: "One has not only a legal but a moral responsibility to obey just laws. Conversely, one has a moral responsibility to disobey unjust laws. I would agree with Saint Augustine that 'an unjust law is no law at all.'"[19] That brave and lucid policy is grounded in the teaching of Jesus, perhaps best expressed in the following advice (Matt 5:38-42):

You have heard that it was said, An eye for an eye and a tooth for a tooth. But I saw to you not to resist the evil one. But to someone who strikes you on the right cheek, turn also the other. And to one who wants to enter judgment with you to take your shirt, give your cloak, too! And with someone who compels a mile's journey from you, travel with him two. Give to the one who asks of you, and do not turn away from one who wants to borrow from you. [the author's translation]

Of all the teachings of Jesus, none is more straightforward, and none more challenging. Evil is to be overcome by means of what is usually called nonresistance.

What follows in Matthew states the principle of Jesus' teaching, that we are to love in the way that God does (Matt 5:43-48, see Luke 6:36). The fundamental status of that teaching within Christianity is unquestionable (see Matt 22:34-40; Mark 12:28-34; Luke 10:25-28; Rom 13:8-10). But in the teaching about turning the other cheek, giving the cloak, going the extra mile, offering the money, everything comes down to particular conditions that prevailed during the Roman occupation of the Near East. The fact that this formulation only appears in Matthew (written around 80 C.E.) has given rise to the legitimate question whether it should be attributed to Jesus in its present form. The imagery corresponds to the conditions of the Roman occupation in an urban area (rather than rural Galilee), where a soldier of the Empire might well demand provisions and service and money, and all with the threat of force. But even if we acknowledge (as seems only reasonable) that Matthew's Gospel has pitched Jesus' policy in the idiom of its own experience, the policy itself should be attributed to Jesus.

Why should what is usually called nonresistance to evil be recommended? It needs to be stressed that nonresistance is not the same as acquiescence. The injustice that is done is never accepted as if it were just. The acts of turning the other cheek, giving the cloak, going the additional mile, offering the money, are all designed to be excessive, so that the injustice of what is demanded is underlined. Indeed, it is not really accurate to call the behavior "nonresistance." The point is for the person who makes demands that are unjust to realize they are unjust. Just that policy served Christians and their faith well during the centuries of persecution under the Roman Empire. It was effective because it brought about an awareness within the Empire, even among the enemies of Christianity, that the policy of violent persecution was unjust (and, for that matter, ineffective). Rather than a teaching of nonresistance, this is a version of the advice of how to retaliate. Instead of an eye for an eye, it suggests a cheek after a cheek. This is not nonresistance; it is exemplary response. That is, it is a form of retaliation: not to harm, but to show another way.

Christianity, with its durable and protean theology, has proved a volatile faith for two millennia and shows no sign of converting from that character. The resources of its own tradition, and the influences of Islam and Judaism will probably continue to prove seminal. Equally important—and perhaps transformative for Christianity in the West—the revival of Orthodoxy in lands formerly controlled by the Soviet Union means that an entirely different view of theology, of at least equal authority and integrity, will challenge both Catholic and Protestant thinkers. Perhaps in that context, the Christian engagement with Islam and Judaism—which has for the most part been conducted within academic theology—will prove to be a source of growing faith.

Discussion Questions

1. Which Christian doctrines emerged as a result of controversies at the close of the Enlightenment?

2. Explain the effect of the Protestant social gospel and the Catholic Modernist movement.

3. What role have differing conceptions of history played in the development of postmodern Christianity?

Judaism, Christianity, and Islam in Their Contemporary Encounters: Islam and Pluralism

Th. Emil Homerin

When Muslim militants killed thousands of people on September 11, 2001, the world witnessed the darker side of Islam. Like other religious traditions throughout history, Islam has been used at times to promote and justify violence against others.[1] Yet, Islam also has the means to foster pluralism and to resolve differences peacefully. In fact, it was the pilgrimage to Mecca in 1964 that helped Malcolm X (d. 1965) to turn away from his belief that all white people were evil, and to arrive at a new color-blind vision of human equality and social justice. Writing of his pilgrimage, Malcolm X said:

> During the past eleven days here in the Muslim world, I have eaten from the same plate, drunk from the same glass, and slept in the same bed (or on the same rug)—while praying to the *same* God—with fellow Muslims, whose eyes were the bluest of blue, whose hair was the blondest of blond, and whose skin was the whitest of white. And in the *words* and in the *actions* and in the *deeds* of the "white" Muslims, I felt the same sincerity that I felt among the black African Muslims of Nigeria, Sudan, and Ghana. We were *truly* all the same (brothers)—because their belief in one God had removed the "white" from their *attitude*. I could see from this, that perhaps if white Americans could accept the Oneness of God, then perhaps, too, they could accept *in reality* the Oneness of Man—and cease to measure, and hinder, and harm others in terms of their "differences" in color.[2]

In a similar spirit, Malcolm X's friend and colleague, Warith Deen Muhammad (b. 1933) transformed the Nation of Islam of his father

Elijah Mohammed into the American Muslim Mission. Succeeding to the position of Supreme Minister after his father's death in 1975, Warith Deen spoke out against the NOI's doctrine of black superiority. He also recognized the prophet Muhammad as the final prophet, thereby denying his father's claim to prophecy as well as the divine status of NOI founder W. D. Fard. As a result, over the last twenty-five years, Warith Deen has guided the vast majority of African American Muslims into the beliefs and practices of Sunni Islam. Further, like Malcolm X, Warith Deen finds in the Qur'an and Islam, a spirit of peace and respect for others, no matter their color or creed:

> All of the precepts, formulas, prescriptions etcetera for Islamic life in the Holy Qur'an moves, most of all on the principle and in the line of peace. Therefore, there are no radical teachings on race. The Holy Qur'an comes to us with the sober truth, wherein it says, "You are all descended from one ancestor, and he was made from dust" (Holy Qur'an 3:59) . . .
>
> God obligates us to seek an acquaintance with all people because this earth was not made to separate man. This earth was made to unite man, and in time man's aspirations, investments and adventurous spirit will carry him all over the world. He will have to meet his fellow man overseas in the far lands, in Asia, Europe, Africa or wherever they are. And in time, he will find that he cannot progress further without their assistance, without their alliances, without their peace treaties, without a place of co-operation.
>
> God has shown us these things, and He has given us the Guidance to have this healthy respect for each other. The purpose of this proper regard is not only for us to respect each other's rights, but also for us to co-exist. In order to co-exist, we should get acquainted with each other because if we don't know each other, it will add to the problem whenever we have a need to deal with one another.[3]

Building on such Islamic precepts of mutual respect, many Muslims in South Africa joined in solidarity with others to demand the end of apartheid there. Among the leaders of this movement was Farid Esack, who read the Qur'an in the context of an ongoing struggle against religious intolerance and political oppression. Based on his experience in South Africa and elsewhere, Esack has become an outspoken, articulate advocate of an Islamic liberation theology grounded in his close reading and interpretation of the Qur'an. He stresses the fact that the Qur'an calls for social justice, particularly for the oppressed, and for Esack *jihad* is not to be an act of violence against others, but a struggle for truth and justice.

A theology of liberation, for me, is one that works toward freeing religion from social, political and religious structures and ideas based on uncritical obedience and the freedom of all people from the forms of injustice and exploitation including those of race, gender class, and religion. Liberation theology tries to achieve its objective through a process that is participatory and liberatory.[4]

Esack calls attention to many passages in the Qur'an recognizing the religious validity of other faiths:

Surely those who have faith and those who are Jews and the Christians and the Sabeans, whoever has faith in Allah and the Last Day and does good, they have their reward with their Lord, there is no fear for them, nor shall they grieve. (2:62)[5]

Esack clearly supports interfaith dialogue as a means of nurturing understanding and pluralism, but he goes further in calling on all religious traditions to work together in the struggle against all forms of injustice, for as the Qur'an declares: "And each one has a goal toward which he strives; so compete with one another in righteous deeds. Wherever you are Allah will bring you all together. Surely Allah is able to do all things" (2:148).[6]

Taking a similar stance is Tariq Ramadan, a Muslim of Egyptian descent who now lives in Europe. In a number of publications, Ramadan has sought to define what it means to be a Muslim in the West and in today's global society. Aware of both pluralism and poverty he writes:

To be a Muslim is to act according to the teachings of Islam, no matter what the surrounding environment. . . . This "acting," in whatever country or environment, is based on four important aspects of human life: developing and protecting the spiritual life in society, disseminating religious as well as secular education, acting for justice in every sphere of social, economic, and political life, and, finally, promoting solidarity with all groups of needy people who are forgotten or culpably neglected or marginalized. In the North as well as in the South, in the West as well as in the East, a Muslim is a Muslim when he or she understands this fundamental dimension of his or her presence on earth: to be with God is to be with human beings, not only with Muslims but, as the Prophet said, "with people," that is, the whole of humankind: "The best among you is the one who behaves best toward people."[7]

In a similar vein, other Muslim scholars have turned to the Qur'an for ways to resolve peacefully conflicts over difference. Particularly noteworthy have been several studies by Mohammed Abu-Nimer who has carefully examined the Qur'an's notions of the sacredness of human life, patience, and forgiveness as he seeks to establish and advance nonviolent strategies for conflict resolution and peace, particularly in the Middle East.[8]

In the forefront of efforts to promote understanding and pluralism in the wake of September 11, 2001, have been a number of American Muslims and scholars like Abu-Nimer, and Ali S. Asani, Professor of the Practice of Indo-Muslim Languages and Culture at Harvard University.[9] Together with the vast majority of Muslims, here and abroad, they condemned the attack on the World Trade Center towers, though their reactions were often lost in the aftermath. These events once again underscored the anguish many Muslims experience from their ambivalent position as U.S. citizens. Given America's strongly Judeo-Christian culture, Muslims in the United States often feel that they are a powerless minority. They have been demonized by the Christian Right as "the enemy faith" and too frequently ignored by the American news media, which has tended to focus on Muslims elsewhere in the world, especially if involved in conflict and chaos.[10] Faced with a rising Islamophobia, American Muslims including Dr. Asani continue to counsel patience, education, and understanding, as we read in the following article.

"So That You May Know One Another": A Muslim American Reflects on Pluralism and Islam[11]

Ali S. Asani

As a Muslim involved in teaching and scholarship on the Islamic tradition, I have received many invitations over the past several weeks to speak about the role that religion and religious ideas may or may not have played in the horrific events of September 11, 2001. Non-Muslim audiences have wanted to know how Islam, a religion whose very name signifies peace for many Muslims, could be used to promote violence and hatred for America and the West. Why, many wonder, are some Muslims and some governments in Muslim nations anti-American, antagonistic to America and the West, and willing to condone or even applaud the loss of innocent American lives? For their part, Muslims I have spoken to have similar concerns. Why, many of them wonder, are some Americans and Europeans and some American and Western policies anti-Islamic, antagonistic to Muslim interests, and heedless to the loss of innocent Muslim lives? Under the circumstances, they ask, is peaceful coexistence and harmony between Muslim and non-Muslim really possible?

Though this mode of analysis has been popular in some circles, I believe that it is flawed in its formulation, for it oversimplifies many complexities. What we are witnessing is not so much a clash of civilizations as it is a clash of ignorances. In this clash of ignorances, deepseated stereotypes and prejudices have resulted in the "other," whether the "other" is the West or Islam, being perceived as evil, barbaric, and uncivilized. Moreover, this has led to the dehumanizing of each side, the inability to accept the fundamental humanity of the other. Such stereotypical perceptions are the unfortunate result of centuries-old antagonisms originating not merely in religion but in the intricate web of political and economic factors, specifically the competition for hegemony and control, expressed in the rhetoric of conquest and reconquest, crusade and jihad, imperialism and nationalism, occupation and liberation.

Over the past year and a half, as I have been engaged in providing audiences with historical and religious perspectives on the complex factors that have created such deep and profound misunderstandings, I have thought to myself on a number of occasions, Where does the common ground lie? Is there a bound that can serve as a bridge promoting understanding and tolerance? I believe that there is. I have come to the conclusion that the reconciliation and peace that we all long for must begin with the nurturing and fostering of a genuine ethos of pluralism. It seems to me that one of the principle causes underlying many of the seemingly irresolvable wars and conflicts that riddle our world today is the failure to come to terms with the essential pluralism of human societies. Bosnia, Rwanda, Afghanistan, Sri Lanka, Ireland, India, Pakistan, and the Ivory Coast are examples of nations that have experienced conflict as a result of one religious, ethnic, or tribal group being unable to respect and value the essential equality and humanity of groups different from itself. As a result, dominant religious, ethnic, or tribal groups seek to control and homogenize society by eradicating or marginalizing those who are different from themselves.

My conviction that hope lies in cultivating pluralism stems from the fact that pluralism is an ideal whose value has come to be recognized by many societies. History shows us that there are some societies that have been more successful in promoting this ideal, while for others, this ideal has remained just that and has never been realized in practice. History also shows that in most societies, pluralism does not occur naturally; it must be deliberately and carefully nourished, for we have plenty of examples of societies that were once pluralist becoming exclusivist and antipluralistic. The difficulties in nurturing and maintaining pluralism should not, however, preclude us from promoting it more aggressively as a means to achieve reconciliation.

In the Islamic tradition, the pluralist nature of human societies is well recognized. Contrary to the misinformed comments usually made about it the Qur'an, the scripture of Islam, has much to say on respect and tolerance for differences as principles for human co-existence. In this article, I would like to outline some of the core ideas in the Qur'an regarding pluralism, ideas that form the seeds for a theology of pluralism within Islam. I believe that such a theology of pluralism, based on the teachings of the Qur'an, can provide an authentic and solid foundation on which we can encourage pluralism within the world's many different Muslim communities and nations.[12]

Let me begin by sharing with you a verse in the Qur'an, that for me, has come to best represent the pluralist ethos that lies at the heart of the text. When I was nine or ten years old and wondering about racial and religious diversity, I asked my father, a devout Muslim, "Why didn't Allah make human beings all the same? Why did Allah make us all different?" In response, my father quoted a verse from the Qur'an:

O humankind, We [God] have created you male and female, and made you into communities and tribes, so that you may know one another. Surely the noblest amongst you in the sight of God is the most god-fearing of you. God is All-knowing and All-Aware. (Qur'an 49:13)

This verse from the Qur'an formed the first teaching I received as a child on the subject of pluralism. Now, many years later, as I reflect on it and its meaning, I believe it is clear that from the perspective of the Qur'an, the divine purpose underlying human diversity is to foster knowledge and understanding, to promote harmony and cooperation among peoples. God did not create diversity as a source of tensions, divisions, and polarization in society. Indeed, whether we recognize it or not, our diversity is a sign of divine genius. These sentiments are, in fact, echoed in another verse, in which God addresses humankind and affirms the principle that human plurality is not an accident but, in fact, a result of divine will: "If Your Lord had willed, He would have made humankind into one nation, but they will not cease to be different . . . and for this God created them [humankind]" (Qur'an 11:118-19).

An important aspect of the pluralistic message of the Qur'an is its emphasis on the universality of God's message: God has revealed His message to *all* peoples and to *all* cultures; not a single people or nation has been forgotten (Qur'an 35:24). Although humans may have misinterpreted that message to suit their needs in creating conflicting traditions, all religions, at their core, have sprung from the same divine source and inspiration. The idea that God's message is universal, but its manifestations are plural, provides the basic underpinning of the manner in which the Qur'an relates itself and the faith it preaches to the religious traditions that preceded it in the Middle East, namely Judaism and Christianity. Far from denying the validity of these predecessor traditions, the Qur'an repeatedly affirms their essential truth, acknowledging that their message comes from one and the same God, and that the Qur'an is only the latest of God's revelations to affirm and confirm those that preceded it. Characteristic of this affirmative and pluralistic stance is this command to believers:

> Say: we believe in God and what has been revealed to us and what was revealed to Abraham, Ismail, Isaac, Jacob, and the tribes, and in what was given to Moses, Jesus, and the prophets from their Lord. We make no distinction between one and another among them and to Him [God] do we submit. (Qur'an 3:84)

Qur'anic beliefs in the truth of the Judaic and Christian traditions are also encapsulated in another term: the *ahl al-kitab*, or People of the Book. This is the umbrella term in the Qur'an to refer to communities, or peoples, who have received revelation in the form of scripture. It is commonly used to refer to Jews, Christians, and Muslims. The pluralistic nature of this term is evident in the use of the noun *book* in the singular rather than the plural, to emphasize that Jews, Christians, and Muslims follow one and the same book, not various conflicting scriptures. The Old and New Testaments and the Qur'an are seen as being plural, earthly manifestations of the one heavenly scripture in which God has inscribed the Divine word. Significantly, the Qur'an does not claim that it abrogates the scriptures revealed before it. On the contrary, it affirms their validity. Another verse addressed to the Muslim faithful states:

> And argue not with the People of the Book unless it be in a way that is better, save with such of them as do wrong; and say we believe in that which has been revealed to us and to you; our God and your God is one and unto Him we submit. (Qur'an 29:46)

While the concept of the People of the Book was originally coined to refer to the major monotheistic traditions in the Arabian milieu, there were attempts to expand the term theologically to include other groups, such as the Zoroastrians in Iran and Hindus and Buddhists in India, as the Islamic tradition spread beyond the Middle East. For instance, in seventeenth-century India, Dara Shikoh, a prince from the ruling Mughal dynasty who was strongly influenced by the pluralistic teachings within Islamic traditions of mysticism, considered the Hindu scriptures, the Upanishads, to be the "storehouse of monotheism" and claimed that they were the *kitab maknun*, or "hidden scripture," referred to in the Qur'an (56:77-80). Hence, he personally translated these Sanskrit texts into Persian and urged that it was the duty of every faithful Muslim to read them. Admittedly, not all Muslims were comfortable with the broadening of the term "People of the Book" to include religious scriptures and traditions not mentioned specifically by name in the Qur'an, but the fact remains that these types of interpretations were made possible by the pluralistic nature of the Qur'anic worldview.

With such a universalist perspective, it goes without saying that the Qur'an does not limit salvation exclusively to Muslims. Salvation, according to the Qur'an, will be granted to any person who submits to (i.e., is a submitter) to the one God and to Divine Will (the literal meaning of the word *Muslim* in Arabic is "submitter"). Indeed, Islamic scripture regards Abraham, the patriarch, and all the other prophets of the Judeo-Christian tradition, including Moses and Jesus, as being *Muslim* in the true sense of the word. Repeatedly, the Qur'an declares that on the Day of Judgment all human beings will be judged on their moral performance, irrespective of their formal religious affiliation (See Sachedina 2001, 28).

> Those who believe, those who follow Jewish scriptures, the Christians, the Sabians, and any who believe in God and the Last Day, and do good, all shall have their reward with their Lord and they will not come to fear or grief. (Qur'an 5:72)

One other aspect of the Qur'an's teaching on tolerance is worth mentioning here. The Islamic scripture, while acknowledging diversity of belief and interpretation, specifically upholds the right of individuals to hold different opinions by declaring that belief is a matter of choice. God has blessed humans with intellect so that they may apply it to all aspects of life, including faith. Just as they have the ability to choose between good and evil, right and wrong, they have the right to choose when it comes to matters of faith. One of the most often quoted verses of the Qur'an declares: "Let there be no compulsion in religion" (Qur'an 2:256), explicitly acknowledging that individuals can not be forced to profess beliefs contrary to their will. Even if individuals perversely choose disbelief, they nevertheless have the right to make that choice, too. A chapter of the Qur'an entitled, *The Unbelievers*, referring to those who rejected the message of monotheism preached by the prophet Muhammad, stresses that belief is a matter of personal conviction and that difference in faith should not be the cause for persecution or abuse.

Say: O you who disbelieve, I worship not that which you worship, nor will you worship that which I worship, and I will not worship that which you have worshipped, and you will not worship that which I worship, to you your path [religion] and to me mine. (Qur'an 111)

The Qur'an's endorsement of religiously and culturally plural societies and the recognition of the salvific value of other monotheistic religions greatly affected the treatment of religious minorities in Muslim lands throughout history. From the earliest periods of Muslim history, we have examples of respect for the rights of non-Muslims under Muslim rule. Typical of this tolerance was a treaty that the Prophet Muhammad signed with the Christians of Najran:

To the Christians of Najran and the neighboring territories the security of God and the pledge of His Prophet are extended for their lives, their religion, and their property—to the present as well as the absent and others besides; there shall be no interference with the practice of their faith, in their observances; nor any change in their rights and privileges; no bishop shall be removed from his office; nor any monk from his monastery, nor any priest from his priesthood, and they shall continue to enjoy everything great and small as heretofore; no image or cross shall be destroyed; they shall not oppress or be oppressed . . . no tithes shall be levied from them, nor shall they be required to furnish provision for troops. (Ameer Ali, *The Spirit of Islam*, London, 1946, 273)

Ali ibn Abi Talib (d. 661), one of the early caliphs to succeed the Prophet Muhammad, instructed his governor in Egypt to show mercy, love, and kindness to all subjects under his rule, including non-Muslims, whom he declared to be "your equals in creation." Such tolerance is later reflected in the policies of the Arab dynasties of Spain, the Fatimids in North Africa, and the Turkish Ottomans in the Middle East, all of which granted maximum individual and group autonomy to those adhering to a religious tradition other than Islam. We can also cite the example of the Mughal Emperor Akbar (d. 1605), who, much to the dismay of the religious right wing of his time, promoted tolerance among the various traditions that composed the Indian religious landscape. While there have been instances when religious minorities were grudgingly tolerated in Muslim societies, rather than being respected in the true spirit of pluralism, the Qur'anic endorsement of a pluralistic ethos explains why the violent forms of anti-Semitism generated by exclusivist Christian theology in medieval and modern Europe, and the associated harsh treatment of Jewish populations that eventually culminated in the Holocaust, never occurred in regions under Muslim rule.

Although the Qur'an, when properly understood, espouses an essentially pluralist worldview, one that promotes peace and harmony among nations and peoples, its message has been perverted over time by those who have sought to interpret it in antipluralist or exclusivist ways. Such exclusivist interpretations of the Qur'an, premised on the hegemony of Islam over non-Islam, first emerged in the eighth and ninth centuries, when Islam became the religion of the Arab empire. Muslim exegetes, seeking religious legitimation for political hegemony, began reinterpreting Qur'anic verses to justify essentially political goals. By promoting the idea that Muslims, as followers of the latest of the monotheistic revelations, were superior to Jews, Christians, and all previous religious communities, they were able to forge a social and political solidarity among various Arab tribes and clans. This solidarity became the backbone of the early Arab Muslim empire, providing "an effective basis for aggression against those who did not share this solidarity with the community of believers" (Sachedina, 2001, 29). It is within this context that political concepts such as *dar al-islam* (territories under Muslim suzerainty) and *dar al-harb* (territories under non-Muslim control) became prominent, although they have no real basis in the Qur'an. In the same vein, the notion of *jihad*, a term fraught with definitional ambiguities, was reinterpreted to justify imperial expansion. Under the influence of political realities of later centuries, which witnessed an expansion of Arab rule, what was clearly a reference in the Qur'an to a moral struggle, or an armed struggle in the face of provocation and aggression came to be interpreted as a general military offensive against nonbelievers and as a means of legitimizing political dominion.[13]

To be sure, the religious legitimation of hegemonic interests had to be sought in the Qur'an, the very text that forbade compulsion in religious matters and contained verses of an ecumenical nature recognizing not only the authenticity of other monotheistic traditions, but the essential equality of all prophets sent by God. For this purpose, as Abdulaziz Sachedina has so ably demonstrated in his book *The Islamic Roots of Democratic Pluralism* (2001), some Muslim exegetes devised terminological and methodological strategies to mold the exegesis of the sacred text to provide a convincing prop for absolutist ends. The principal means by which the exclusivists were able to promote their view was through the declaration that the many verses calling for pluralism, commanding Muslims to build bridges of understanding with non-Muslims, had been abrogated by other verses that called for fighting the infidel. It is only by decontextualizing the exegesis of such verses, by disregarding their original historical context of revelation and by using them to engage in a large-scale abrogation of contradictory verses, that the exclusivist Muslim exegetes have been able to counteract the pluralist ethos that so thoroughly pervades the Qur'an.

From a historical perspective, exclusivist interpretations of the Qur'an have been used to justify political hegemony over not only non-Muslims but also over fellow Muslims whose interpretation and religious practices were perceived as deviating from the norms espoused by exclusivists. For instance, during the seventeenth and eighteenth centuries, several areas of the Muslim world witnessed the rise of movements that, in response to what was perceived as a general moral laxity and decline, attempted to "purify" Islam. The leaders of these movements targeted a whole range of practices and beliefs among fellow Muslims that, in their eyes, constituted evidence of religious backsliding. In certain cases, the attacks took on a military character; that is, a "jihad" was launched against fellow Muslims. Not surprisingly, such exclusivist groups, which were harsh on fellow Muslims, came to consider Jews and Christians to be infidels.

In recent times, the exclusivist view has been heavily promoted by the so-called fundamentalist groups in the Muslim world. The reasons for the rise of such groups are complex. Broadly speaking, these movements are a reaction against modernity, Westernization, global domination by Western powers (particularly the United States), and support of such powers for repressive regimes in predominantly Muslim lands. The failure of borrowed ideologies, such as capitalism, communism, or socialism, to deliver economic and social justice in many Muslim countries has created exclusivist groups looking for a "pure" and "authentic" language in which to criticize the failed modern Muslim state, a state that has marginalized, or displaced, traditional religious authorities in a bid to maximize political hegemony. The search for a solution to the myriad political, social, and economic problems confronting Muslims has led these exclusivist groups to use Islam as a political ideology for the state: "Islam is the solution." The commitment of such groups to understand Islam in a "pure" monolithic form, to engage in revisionist history, and to read religious texts in an exclusivist manner that denies any plurality of interpretations has unleashed a struggle in the Muslim world between the exclusivists and those who uphold the pluralist teachings of the Qur'an. An important dimension of the struggle between the exclusivists and the pluralists is the debate over the role and status of women in Muslim societies, for exclusivists tend to be antiegalitarian in their interpretations of gender roles. It is worth noting that groups such as the Taliban and al-Qaida, which attack Western targets, are at the same time attacking a centuries-old multivocal tradition of pluralism within Islam.

For Muslims to participate in the multireligious and multicultural world of the twenty-first century, it is essential that they fully embrace Qur'anic teachings on "religious and cultural pluralism as a divinely ordained principle of co-existence among human societies" (Sachedina, 2001, 13).

The implications of the Qur'anic sanctioning of diversity and its injunction to create harmony in diverse societies through the promotion of mutual knowledge needs to be more seriously explored by Muslim theologians and interpreters of the Islamic holy scripture.[14] Exclusivist interpretations of the Qur'an that are premised on the hegemony of Islam over non-Islam and promote the use of a rhetoric of hate and violence to attain such goals are outdated in a global society in which relations between different peoples are best fostered on the basis of equality and mutual respect—a basic principle underlying the Qur'anic worldview.

Since in several key Muslim nations the exclusivist message has been propagated by *madrasas*, or religious schools, sponsored by exclusivist groups or by the state itself, a key to the outcome of the struggle between pluralism and exclusivism in the Islamic tradition lies in the re-education of Muslim peoples concerning the pluralism that lies at the heart of the Qur'an. Without this pluralist education, they will continue to rely on the monolithic interpretations of scholars and demagogues to access the Qur'an. Alongside promoting religious literacy, it is equally essential to promote programs to eradicate poverty. As His Highness the Aga Khan, the leader of the Ismaili Muslim community, correctly pointed out in a recent speech, "Left alone, poverty will provide a context for special interests to pursue their goals in aggressive terms."[15] Indeed, recent history is replete with examples of well-financed exclusivist groups recruiting support for their cause in poverty-stricken Muslim communities by virtue of being the sole providers of educational and medical services.

As a pluralist Muslim who is American, I am struck by the resonance between the pluralism espoused in the Qur'an and that in the constitution and civic culture of the United States. Contrary to what some may claim, one can be fully American and fully Muslim simultaneously. In this regard, I was pleased recently to see a series of advertisements in major American newspapers that had chosen to stress the compatibility between being a Muslim and an American, presenting a Muslim American face of Islam. The underlying message of this campaign is laudable: Muslims are not the "other." However, even well-intentioned efforts to affirm the compatibility of Muslim and American identities may sometimes presuppose an unduly narrow and exclusionary vision of Islam. For instance, a recent ad in the *New York Times*, intending to explain the significance of the head covering, showed a Muslim woman in *hijab*. Unfortunately, the ad also implied that all "good" Muslim women cover their heads, not recognizing that there is a great deal of diversity in this practice among Muslim women both here in the United States and in other parts of the world. Not all Muslim women choose to define and express their religious identity through the headscarf. It is a matter of choice.

Muslim Americans are a remarkably diverse group, belonging to more than fifty different ethnicities and nationalities, mirroring, in fact, the diverse face of America itself. They come from many parts of the world and represent many different interpretations of Islam. Indeed, no other country in the world has a Muslim population that is as diverse as that of America. It is, therefore, crucial that this plurality is recognized in our understanding of what it means to be Muslim in America today. We should guard against presupposing unduly narrow and exclusionary visions of Islam as being representative of the whole. The plurality of cultures and interpretations within Islam in America presents a unique set of challenges. As Muslim Americans come to terms with the challenges posed by this internal pluralism, as well as the pluralism of America, I hope they will, God willing, have the unique opportunity to become champions of pluralism in the larger international Muslim world. My call for the enhancement of pluralism within Muslim societies as a means of reconciling Muslim with non-Muslim and Muslim with Muslim, however, must also be coupled with my challenging a phenomenon that threatens the pluralistic fabric of my adopted country.

Post 9/11, America has witnessed an alarming rise of Islamophobia—expressions of hatred for Muslims, for Islam and everything Islamic. Islam has been equated with Nazism. The Qur'an has been compared to Hitler's *Mein Kampf*, with the suggestion that reading it in the current context is an act of treason. Muslims have been likened to creatures who separate "like protozoa into cells from two to infinity." The Prophet Muhammad has been declared to be a terrorist on a prominent national TV show. American Muslims have been declared to be Trojan horses and a danger to national security and should, therefore, all be deported, while the holy city of Mecca should be nuked to send a message to all Muslims. A magazine with a national circulation even printed an article calling for Muslims to be buried in pigskins and lard! Two members of the Washington state legislature walked out of prayers led by a Muslim imam at the beginning of legislative sessions because they considered their participation in the prayers to be un-American and unpatriotic. Such actions and remarks may be too quickly dismissed "as understandable under the circumstances" or as being the rantings, ravings, and uninformed acts of individuals and not representative of national sentiments. Yet these are individuals with national stature, often belonging to the vocal

Christian Right. As their opinions are expressed in national media, there is a tendency to manipulate maliciously and exploit the profound ignorance and stereotypes about Islamic matters prevalent in the general American population. As I write, however, and over recent months, it seems that anything can be said about Islam and Muslims no matter how distasteful and demeaning. Muslims of America, themselves reeling from the impact of 9/11 on their communities and the resulting insecurities, find themselves besieged on almost a daily basis by vicious hate speech emanating from various media targeted at them or their religious beliefs. Hate crimes against Muslims have risen by a dramatic 600 percent. In addition, several mosques have been vandalized, the most recent incident occurring on 12 March 2003, when projectiles were hurled through the windows of one of the largest mosques and schools in America. The FBI predicts that as a result of the war in Iraq, there will be a further rise of violence against Muslims.

Incredibly, many of the public explanations of Islamophobia have been the direct result of certain government policies introduced in recent months in the interests of promoting national security. While it is debatable whether such policies are, in fact, effective in promoting security by apprehending potential terrorists, theses policies are clearly Islamophobic in effect if not intent. They have contributed to the escalation of fear in America about Islam and Muslims. As a result, they have also created fear and anxiety among many of America's Muslims, many of whom are afraid to attend mosques lest they be profiled. Some Muslim women are afraid to wear their headscarves in public, and some have even resorted to changing their names so that they cannot be identified as Muslim. A prominent Muslim civil rights advocate has described the situation as a "virtual internment."[16] In the fall of last year, the Canadian government issued a travel advisory for Canadian citizens of Muslim faith traveling to, or through, the United States in response to the discriminatory profiling and violation of fundamental liberties experienced by Muslim Canadians. Ironically, this advisory, from our neighbor and strong ally, was issued about the same time as the State Department began airing ads in Indonesia and other Muslim countries with the intention of promoting the image that Muslims in America practice their faith freely.

Today, I fear that pluralism, tolerance, freedom to practice one's faith openly without fear of being stigmatized, and respect for difference—these fundamental American values—are all under attack. There has been an ominously deafening silence from the leadership at all levels of society concerning the rise of Islamophobia. This silence itself is complicit in creating an atmosphere of fear and anxiety among American Muslims. We can no longer afford to remain silent when we encounter such bigotry; the consequences of silence are too dangerous for our nation and for the world. Certainly, such silence is not very helpful in nurturing much-needed understanding, goodwill, and respect between America and the nations of the Muslim world. We must not surrender the public arena to the forces that seek to promote hatred and polarization amongst the various communities in our nation. Islamophobia must be actively resisted and responded to so that such hate speech becomes totally unacceptable in our national vocabulary and in our national conscience. If unchallenged and unchecked, hate speech can erode and destroy the traditions of pluralism and respect for these differences that have made America the great nation that it is today. Every Islamophobic statement or action, no matter how ridiculous, is a deliberate attack on the pluralistic fabric of our society and on our shared values that demand justice, respect, tolerance, and compassion for all who live in our nation. We can best cultivate these values by paying heed to the Qur'an's call for "knowing one another" and struggling (jihad) against the most dangerous type of ignorance—the ignorance that dehumanizes. I close with a verse from Sadi (d. 1292), one of the great Muslim humanist poets of Iran:

> Human beings, created from the same essence, are limbs of
>   one another
> When one limb aches, the other limbs are restless, too
> O you who are indifferent to the pains of others
> You do not deserve to be called human.

Discussion Questions

1. Discuss the history of Islam in the North America, both in its various African American manifestations and as an immigrant phenomena. What are some of the problems facing American Muslims—immigrant and nonimmigrant—today?

2. What are the scriptural foundations for recent nonviolent Muslim liberation movements? How do they interpret *jihad*? What are their attitudes toward non-Muslims and other faiths?

3. According to Ali S. Asani, what is pluralism? What does the Qur'an say about it, and does the Qur'an have a pluralist worldview? Why does Asani think that pluralism is essential to the future of human society?

TIMELINE

Compiled by Cory Berry-Whitlock

ca. 1300 B.C.E.	The Exodus.
1010–970 B.C.E.	King David.
970–922 B.C.E.	King Solomon, followed by the division of his kingdom into Israel in the north and Judah in the south by 922 B.C.E.
753 B.C.E.	Founding of Rome.
722–721 B.C.E.	Assyrian Empire subjects the Northern Kingdom of Israel to a program of exile.
609 B.C.E.	King Josiah killed.
587–586 B.C.E.	The Babylonian invasion of the Southern Kingdom, Judea. Fall of Jerusalem.
539 B.C.E.	The Babylonian Empire falls to Cyrus the Persian who permits a return to Judea.
ca. 515 B.C.E.	Temple rebuilt, with completion of the Pentateuch thereafter.

427–347 B.C.E.	Plato lives.
323 B.C.E.	Death of Alexander the Great.
167 B.C.E.	Antiochus IV captures Jerusalem.
164 B.C.E.	Restoration of covenantal worship in the Temple.
63 B.C.E.	Pompey claims Jerusalem for Rome.
ca. 2 C.E.	Birth of Jesus.
31–32 C.E.	Jesus' last year in Jerusalem, aged 30.
ca. 35 C.E.	The meeting of Peter and James and Paul in Jerusalem, and the availability of the earliest sources of the Gospels: Peter's instruction for apostles such as Paul, and the mishnah of Jesus' teaching known to modern scholarship as "Q."
37 C.E.	The removal of Pontius Pilate and Caiaphas from power.
ca. 40 C.E.	The adaptation of Peter's Gospel by James, the brother of Jesus, in Jerusalem.
ca. 45 C.E.	In Antioch, outside of Palestine, followers of Jesus are for the first time called "Christians."
ca. 53–57 C.E.	Paul writes his major letters, Galatians, Corinthians, and Romans.
62 C.E.	The death of James by stoning in Jerusalem, at the instigation of the high priest.
64 C.E.	The death of Paul and Peter in Rome.
70-73 C.E.	The revolt against Rome by Titus; the composition of Mark's Gospel in Rome; the end of the revolt against Rome in Palestine (73 C.E.).

70 C.E.	Jerusalem taken. Temple burned.
75 C.E.	Josephus publishes his *Jewish* War.
80 C.E.	The composition of Matthew's Gospel, in Damascus.
90 C.E.	The composition of Luke's Gospel, in Antioch.
93 C.E.	Josephus publishes his *Antiquities of the Jews*.
100 C.E.	The composition of John's Gospel, in Ephesus.
111 C.E.	Writing to Pliny, the Emperor Trajan requires those denounced as Christians to recognize the gods of Rome.
132–135 C.E.	Second great Jewish revolt against Rome.
185–254 C.E.	Origen of Alexandria.
ca. 200 C.E.	The Mishnah came to closure under the sponsorship of Judah the Patriarch, ethnic ruler of the Jews of the Land of Israel.
202 C.E.	Emperor Severus forbids conversion to Christianity and Judaism.
250 C.E.	Emperor Decius's decree that all citizens were to take part in sacrifice to the gods.
ca. 300 C.E.	The Tosefta came to closure as a complement to the Mishnah's laws
303 C.E.	Emperor Diocletian persecutes Christianity.
312 C.E.	Constantine sees vision at Milvian Bridge.
354–430 C.E.	Augustine of Hippo.

ca. 400 C.E.	Talmud of the Land of Israel, commentary to the Mishnah and the Tosefta, reached conclusion.
410 C.E.	Alaric sacks Rome.
ca. 600 C.E.	Talmud of Babylonia, commentary on the Mishnah and the Tosefta, joined legal and theological expositions in a single systematic exposition of Judaism.
570 C.E.	Birth of Muhammad.
610 C.E.	First revelation of the Qur'an to Muhammad.
622 C.E.	Muhammad leaves Mecca for Yathrib (Medina).
632 C.E.	Muhammad dies.
632–661 C.E.	Rightly Guided Caliphs.
661–750 C.E.	Umayyad Caliphate.
711 C.E.	Muslim armies begin conquest of the Iberian peninsula.
750–1258 C.E.	Abbasid Caliphate.
800 C.E.	Charlemagne crowned as Emperor of the Romans on Christmas Day.
989 C.E.	Synod of Charroux.
1055 C.E.	Toghril Beg captures Baghdad, establishes the Saljuq sultanate.
1066 C.E.	Massacre of Jews in Granada.
1071 C.E.	Saljuq Turks destroy main army of Byzantine Empire at Manzikert.

1081 C.E.	Pope Gregory VII's letter to the Bishop of Metz.
1085 C.E.	King Alfonso VI captures Toledo.
1095 C.E.	Pope Urban II calls Europe to Crusade.
1000–1200 C.E.	Universities begin in Europe and the Middle East.
1147–1149 C.E.	Second Crusade.
1187 C.E.	Saladin captures Jerusalem.
1189–1192 C.E.	Third Crusade.
1202 C.E.	Fourth Crusade.
1204 C.E.	Constantinople sacked in the Fourth Crusade.
1218–1221 C.E.	Fifth Crusade.
1250 C.E.	Christian leaders capture most of Iberian peninsula.
1254 C.E.	King Louis IX's (St. Louis) first Crusade, Egypt; Louis is captured and ransomed.
1258 C.E.	Mongols sack Baghdad.
1260 C.E.	Mongols defeated, Mamluk sultanate begins in Egypt and Syria.
1270 C.E.	King Louis IX's (St. Louis) second Crusade, Tunis.
1347–1352 C.E.	"The Black Death".
1389 C.E.	Battle of Kosovo; Serbian king Lazar killed by Ottomans.

1396 C.E.	Crusaders defeated by Ottomans at Nicopolis.
1444 C.E.	Crusaders defeated by Ottomans at Varna.
1453 C.E.	Ottoman sultan Mehmed the Conqueror captures Constantinople.
1463 C.E.	Ottoman conquest of Bosnia.
1469–1536 C.E.	Erasmus of Rotterdam.
1476 C.E.	Wallachia becomes Ottoman vassal state.
1492 C.E.	Ferdinand and Isabella expel all Jews from Castile and Aragon.
1512 C.E.	Moldavia becomes an Ottoman vassal state.
1514 C.E.	Ottomans defeat Safavids at Chaldiran.
1516 C.E.	Ottomans defeat Mamluks at Marj Dabiq, and incorporate Syria, Egypt, Mecca and Medina into their domains.
1517 C.E.	Martin Luther's "Disputation on the Power and Efficacy of Indulgences".
1526 C.E.	Battle of Mohac; Ottomans seize Buda. Timurid/ Mughul dynasty begins in India.
1531 C.E.	The Schmalkadic League.
1545–1563 C.E.	Council of Trent.
1588 C.E.	Sinking of the Spanish Armada.
1618–1648 C.E.	Thirty Years' War.
1648 C.E.	Peace of Westphalia.
1683 C.E.	The unsuccessful Ottoman assault on Vienna.

1689 C.E.	Toleration Act passed in England.
1774 C.E.	Treaty of Kuchuk Kaynarja, where Ottomans cede Black Sea territory to Russia.
1775–1783 C.E.	American Revolution.
1787 C.E.	Adoption of the Constitution of the United States.
1789 C.E	French Revolution.
1792 C.E.	Bill of Rights adopted, assuring freedom of speech and religion in United States.
1798 C.E.	French forces under Napoleon occupy Egypt.
1800–1850 C.E.	Reform Judaism begins in Germany and America.
1804 C.E.	Napoleon Bonaparte takes the title of "Emperor." First Serbian Uprising against Ottomans.
1815 C.E.	Second Serbian Uprising.
1821 C.E.	Greek Wars of Independence.
1830 C.E.	Greek independence.
1835 C.E.	David Friedrich Strauss, *The Life of Jesus*.
1839 C.E.	Reforms in Ottoman Empire.
1848 C.E.	European Revolutions.
1857 C.E.	Muslims in India revolt against British rule.
1859 C.E.	Charles Darwin, *On the Origin of Species*.
1863 C.E.	Ernst Renan publishes *La vie de Jesus*.
1870 C.E.	The First Vatican Council.

1878 C.E.	Treaty of San Stefano; followed by Treaty of Berlin: independence for Bulgaria; Serbia; Montenegro; Romania; British occupation of Cyprus; Habsburg occupation of Bosnia-Herzegovina.
1886–1887 C.E.	Jewish Theological Seminary of America organized in New York City by rabbis and lay leaders of Conservative Judaism.
1885 C.E.	Pittsburgh Platform of Reform Judaism affirms the universalism of Judaism.
1897 C.E.	First Zionist Congress in Basel founded the Zionist Movement, to establish a Jewish state in Palestine, the historical homeland of the Jewish people.
1908 C.E.	Annexation of Bosnia-Herzegovina by Habsburgs; Young Turk revolt.
1912 C.E.	First Balkan War; Albania declared an independent state.
1913 C.E.	Second Balkan War.
1914–1918 C.E.	World War I.
1918 C.E.	Establishment of Kingdom of Serbs, Croats, and Slovenes ("First" Yugoslavia).
1917 C.E.	Balfour Declaration states that the British government looks with favor on the establishment of a Jewish national homeland in Palestine, giving political recognition to Zionism.
1924 C.E.	Ataturk replaces the remnants of the Ottoman Empire with the Republic of Turkey.
1933–1945 C.E.	Holocaust: culminating in the murder of nearly six million Jews in Germany and then German-

	occupied Europe for the sole crime of having been born to a Jewish grandparent.
1939–1945 C.E.	World War II.
1947 C.E.	Creation of Pakistan.
1947–1948 C.E.	State of Israel created by the United Nations, realizing the goal of Zionism.
1956 C.E.	Israel, Britain, and France invade Egypt over the Suez Canal, later withdraw.
1962 C.E.	The Second Vatican Council.
1967 C.E.	The "Six Day War".
1973 C.E.	The "Yom Kippur War"—Operation Badr.
1979 C.E.	Iranian Revolution; Soviets invade Afghanistan.
1989 C.E.	Downfall of Communism in Eastern Europe.
1990–1991 C.E.	The "Gulf War".
1991 C.E.	The breakup of Yugoslavia: war in Slovenia and Croatia.
1992–1995 C.E.	War in Bosnia-Herzegovina.
1999 C.E.	War in Kosovo; NATO bombing of Serbia.
2000 C.E.	Dabru Emet ("Speak truth"). A Jewish Statement on Christians and Christianity issued by a group of rabbis and Jewish scholars in the United States and Canada.
2001 C.E.	September 11 terrorist attack in the United States by Al-Qaeda and the beginning of the American war in Afghanistan.
2003 C.E.	American invasion of Iraq.

NOTES

Chapter 1: What Do We Mean by "Religion" and "Western Civilization"?

1. Robert Stone, "The Villain," *New York Times Magazine* (23 Sept. 2001): 22.

2. Samuel P. Huntington, *The Clash of Civilizations and the Remaking of World Order* (New York: Simon & Schuster, 1996).

3. Ibid.

4. Ibid.

5. Harold J. Berman, *Law and Revolution: The Formation of the Western Legal Tradition* (Cambridge: Harvard University Press, 1983), 2-4.

6. Samuel P. Huntington, *The Clash of Civilizations and the Remaking of World Order* (New York: Simon & Schuster, 1996), 53-54.

7. The Eighty Years' War for Dutch independence from Spain and the Thirty Years' War waged in the Holy Roman Empire (western and central Europe) between Protestants and Catholics.

8. Melford E. Spiro, "Religion, Problems of Definition and Explanation," in *Culture and Human Nature: Theoretical Papers of Melford E. Spiro*, ed. Benjamin Kilbourne and L. L. Langness (Chicago: University of Chicago Press, 1987), 187-222.

9. These paragraphs draw on my introduction to *God*, ed. Jacob Neusner (Cleveland: Pilgrim Press, 1997), xxiii-xxvii.

10. Apparently there are some views in Islam that include only the Torah, the Pentateuch, in *Tawrat*; others claim that the term encompasses the Jewish scriptures.

11. Joshua, Judges, 1 and 2 Samuel, 1 and 2 Kings, 1 and 2 Chronicles.

12. Isaiah, Jeremiah, Ezekiel, Hosea, Joel, Amos, Obadiah, Jonah, Micah, Nahum, Habakkuk, Zephaniah, Haggai, Zechariah, Malachi.

13. Psalms, Proverbs, Job, The Song of Songs, Ruth, Lamentations, Ecclesiastes, Esther, Daniel, Ezra, Nehemiah.

14. For example, although the Pentateuch contains ancient material, it was organized and edited into its final form by Jews during the Persian period in response to the demands of exile.

15. In Christianity, the Hebrew Bible is known as the "Old Testament," and some Christian denominations include other writings in the Old Testament that other Christians and Judaism exclude.

16. Daniel Elazar, *Covenant and Polity in Biblical Israel: Biblical Foundations and Jewish Expressions* (New Brunswick, N.J.: Translation Publishers, 1995), 1-2.

17. Other factors may play a role here as well. In the ancient Mediterranean, Judaism and Christianity emerged and operated in an imperialist context, in which religion could not constitute a government and there was considerable risk in claiming to do so. See W. S. Green, "Religion and

Politics: A Volatile Mix," in *God's Rule: The Politics of World Religions*, ed. J. Neusner (Georgetown: Georgetown University Press, 2003), 1-9, from which this paragraph derives.

18. Bernard Lewis, *What Went Wrong? Western Impact and Middle Eastern Response* (New York: Oxford University Press, 2002), 96-98.

19. Ibid., 100.

20. Brown, "Society and the Supernatural," 134.

21. Harold J. Berman, *Law and Revolution: The Formation of the Western Legal Tradition* (Cambridge, Mass.: Harvard University Press, 1983), 85-89.

22. *Encyclopedia Britannica*, 1969 ed., s.v. "myth."

23. Berman, *Law and Revolution*, 165-66, 194-98.

24. Rudolph Sohm, *Weltliches und geistliches Recht* (Munich and Leipzig, 1914), 69. (All translations are my own unless otherwise indicated. H. J. B.)

25. See Gerrard Winstanley, *Platform of the Law of Freedom* (quoted in Rosenstock-Huessy, *Out of Revolution*, 291): "The spirit of the whole creation was about the reformation of the world." See also Thomas Case, sermon preached before the House of Commons in 1641: "Reformation must be universal. Reform all places, all persons and callings; reform the benches of judgment, the inferior magistrates . . . Reform the universities, reform the cities, reform the countries, reform inferior schools of learning, reform the Sabbath, reform the ordinances, the worship of God. Every plant which my heavenly father hath not planted shall be rooted up." Quoted in Michael Walzer, *The Revolution of the Saints: A Study in the Origins of Radical Politics* (Cambridge, Mass.: Harvard University Press, 1965), 10-11. The sixteenth-century Reformation was conceived as a reformation of the church; a century later the Puritans were seeking, in Milton's words, "the reforming of reformation itself," which meant, as Walzer shows (p. 12), radical political activity, that is, political activity, that is, political progress as a religious goal.

26. See A. D. Lindsay, *The Modern Democratic State* (New York: Oxford University Press, 1962), 117-18; David Little, *Religion, Order, and Law: A Study in Pre-Revolutionary England* (New York: Harper & Row, 1969), 230.

27. Each of these four men was charged with civil disobediance. Each defended himself on the basis of a higher law of conscience as well as on grounds of fundamental legal principles derived from medieval English law (e.g., Magna Carta). The trials of Penn and Hampden are reported in 6 *State Trials* 951 (1670) and 3 *State Trials* 1 (1627) (the Five Knights' Case). An extract of the trial of Udall, together with background information, may be found in Daniel Neal, *The History of the Puritans* (Newburyport, Mass.: William B. Allen and Co., 1816), 492-501. The trial of Lilburne is discussed in Joseph Frank, *The Levellers: A History of the Writings of Three Seventeenth Century Social Democrats: John Lilburne, Richard Overton, and William Walwyn* (Cambridge: Harvard University Press, 1965), 16-18.

28. The theory of social contract is generally traced to seventeenth-century philosophers such as John Locke and Thomas Hobbes. But a century earlier, Calvin had asked the entire people of Geneva to accept the confession of faith and to take an oath to obey the Ten Commandments, as well as to sear loyalty to the city. People were summoned in groups by the police to participate in the covenant. See J. T. McNeill, *The History and Character of Calvinism* (New York: Oxford University Press, 1957), 142. See also Chapters 2 and 12 of this study, in which the theory of social contract is traced to the Papal Revolution and the formation of cities as sworn communes.

29. See Roscoe Pound, *Jurisprudence* (St. Paul, Minn.: West Publishing Co., 1959), III, 8-15.

30. The Moral Code of the Builder of Communism is part of the Program of the Community Party of the Soviet Union adopted by the twenty-second Party Congress in 1961. It may be found in Dan N, Jacobs, ed., *The New Communist Manifesto and Related Documents*, 3rd rev. ed. (New York: Harper & Row, 1965), 35.

31. See The Laws and Liberties of Massachusetts (Cambridge, Mass., 1929).

32. Berman, *Law and Revolution*, 29-33.

Chapter 2: Judaism

1. *Judaic* pertains to the religion, Judaism. *Jewish* speaks of the ethnic group, the Jews; hence here: *Judaic* not *Jewish*. This is a key problem in the study of the Jews and the religion, Judaism, and we shall return to it in due course.

2. And continuing through the Five Books of Moses (Genesis, Exodus, Leviticus, Numbers, and Deuteronomy) and on into the Prophets (Joshua, Judges, Samuel, Kings, Isaiah, Jeremiah, Ezekiel, and the Twelve Minor Prophets), and the Writings (Psalms, Proverbs, Chronicles, Job, Ecclesiastes, Esther, Ruth, Lamentations, and Song of Songs). The Five Books of Moses, called "the Pentateuch," the Prophets, and the Writings in Christianity are known as the Old Testament, completed and fulfilled by the New Testament; and by "the Bible," Christianity means "the Old Testament and the New Testament." Judaism knows the "Old Testament" as the Written Torah, in contrast to the Oral Torah, which we shall meet presently. Neutral terms for the same collection of writings include "the Hebrew Scriptures" or "the ancient Israelite Scriptures."

3. And, as we shall see in a moment, Judaism also defines itself by appeal to narratives of Scripture. Its worldview way of life and definition of the social group formed by the faithful take shape in constant dialogue with the Old Testament stories, laws, and prophecies.

4. We must be careful not to confuse the Israel of which Judaism speaks—namely, a holy family and community formed to realize God's instruction—with the modern, secular state of Israel, founded in 1948.

5. Following the usage of the pre-Copernican calendar of Judaism.

6. Yerushalmi-tractate Taanit 1:1 II:5

7. Bernard Lewis, *The Jews of Islam* (Princeton, N.J.: Princeton University Press, 1984), 8.

8. Cited by Louis Jacobs, "Basic Ideas of Hasidism," *Encyclopaedia Judaica* 7:1404

Chapter 3:
Christianity: What It Is and How It Defines Western Civilization

1. He was attempting to block the alliance between Pharaoh Neco and the Assyrians at a place called Megiddo. The impact of his death may be gauged by the impact of that name upon the apocalyptic tradition (Rev 16:16, see also Zech 12:11), in the form *Armageddon*.

2. See 1 Macc 1:20-64; Josephus, *Antiquities* 12 §§ 248-256).

3. His dynasty was named after Hasmoneus, Mattathias's ancestor (see 1 Macc 2:1–9:18, and Josephus, *Antiquities* 12 §§ 265-67; 16 § 187; 20 § 238). After Judas's death, his brother, Jonathan, was named high priest (10:20); and from that time until the period of Roman rule, the high priesthood was a Hasmonean prerogative.

4. Their insistence upon a doctrine of two messiahs, one of Israel and one of Aaron, suggests that it was particularly the Hasmoneans' arrogation of priestly and royal powers that alienated the Essenes. See James VanderKam, *The Dead Sea Scrolls Today* (Grand Rapids: Eerdmans, 1994).

5. King Alenxander's wife later came to an accommodation with the Pharisees that guaranteed them considerable influence (*Jewish War* 1 §§ 96-114). It appears clear that within the Hasmonean period, purity was a political issue and to some extent a symbol: the acquiescence of one of the dynasty to any Pharisaic stricture implicitly acknowledged that the Hasmonean priesthood was provisional, and the Pharisaic movement probably found its original, political expression in opposition to that priesthood (cf. *Antiquities* 13 §§ 288-98).

6. See Bruce Chilton and Jacob Neusner, *Judaism in the New Testament: Practices and Beliefs* (New York: Routledge, 1995).

7. See, for example, Eugene Ulrich, "Origen's Old Testament Text: The Transmission History of the Septuagint to the Third Century C.E.," *The Dead Sea Scrolls and the Origins of the Bible* (Grand Rapids, Mich.: Eerdmans, 1999), 202-23; and (more generally) Julio Trebolle Barrera, *The Jewish Bible and the Christian Bible* (Grand Rapids, Mich.: Eerdmans, 1998), 301-23.

8. See Henry Barclay Swete, *An Introduction to the Old Testament in Greek* (Cambridge: Cambridge University Press, 1902), 197-230, see especially pp. 201, 217-19.

9. See Philip Carrington, *The Early Christian Church*, II, *The Second Christian Century* (Cambridge: Cambridge University Press, 1957), 330-31; Francis Xavier Murphy, "Creed," *New Catholic Encyclopedia* (New York: McGraw-Hill, 1967), 432-38; Joseph Cullen Ayer, *A Source Book for Ancient Church History, from the Apostolic Age to the Close of the Conciliar period* (New York: C. Scribner's Sons, 1913), 123-26; Roger E. Olson, *The Story of Christian Theology: Twenty Centuries of Tradition & Reform* (Downers Grove, Ill.: InterVarsity Press, 1999), 128-31.

Chapter 4:
Islam: What It Is and How It Has Interacted with
Western Civilization

1. Abu Tammam, *Sharh Diwan al-Hamasah*, ed. A. A. Amin and A. Harun (Cairo: Matbaᶜah al-Ta'lif wa-al-Tarjamah wa-al-Nashr, 1951), 1:32-38, my translation.

2. For more on the pre-Islamic Arabs, see: Robert G. Hoyland, *Arabia and the Arabs* (London: Routledge, 2001); Gordon D. Newby, *A History of the Jews of Arabia* (Columbia: University of South Carolina Press, 1988); Patricia Crone, *Meccan Trade and the Rise of Islam* (Princeton: Princeton University Press, 1987); and Th. Emil Homerin, "Echoes of a Thirsty Owl: Death and Afterlife in Pre-Islamic Arabic Poetry," *Journal of Near Eastern Studies* 44:2 (1985): 165-84.

3. All translations are my own, unless otherwise noted. For a complete English translation of the Qur'an, see Ahmed Ali, *Al-Qur'an, a Contemporary Translation* (Princeton: Princeton University Press, 1984). For a fine translation of a selection of the earliest revelations with an audio of Qur'anic recitations, see Michael Sells, *Approaching the Qur'an* (Ashland, Oreg.: White Cloud Press, 1999).

4. For more on the Prophet Muhammad, see: F. E. Peters, *Muhammad and the Origins of Islam* (Albany: State University of New York Press, 1994); Michael Cook, *Muhammad* (Oxford: Oxford University Press, 1983); and A. Guillaume, *The Life of Muhammad* (Oxford: Oxford University Press, 1955).

5. For more on the Qur'an, see: Fazlur Rahman, *Major Themes of the Qur'an* (Chicago: Bibliotheca Islamica, 1980); and Michael Cook, *The Koran: A Very Short Introduction* (Oxford: Oxford University Press, 2000).

6. Al-Bukhari, *Sahih al-Bukhari*, ed. Muhammad Muhsin Khan (Cairo: Dar al-Fikr, n.d.), 4:502, #779, my translation.

7. Hadith are found in many collections including the popular one by Yahya al-Nawawi (d. 1277), *al-Arbaᶜin al-Nawawiyah*, ed. Ibrahim ibn Muhammad (Tanta, Egypt, 1986), 18, 47, 78, 95 (= #2, 13, 40); my translation. For a complete translation of al-Nawawi's collection, see: *An-Nawawi's Forty Hadith*, trans. Ezzedin Ibrahim and Denys Johnson-Davies (n.p., n.d.).

8. Al-Nawawi, *Al-Arbaᶜin al-Nawawiyah*, 93-94, #38. Also see William A. Graham, *Divine Word and Prophetic Word in Islam* (The Hague: Mouton, 1977), esp. 173-74.

9. For more on Islamic law, see chapter 6.

10. For a detailed analysis of Islamic history and civilization, see Marshal G. S. Hodgson, *The Venture of Islam*, 3 vols. (Chicago: University of Chicago Press, 1974).

11. For more on Islamic theology and philosophy, see Majid Fakhry, *A History of Islamic Philosophy*, 2nd ed. (New York: Columbia University Press, 1983).

12. Th. Emil Homerin, *ᶜUmar Ibn al-Fârid: Sufi Verse, Saintly Life* (New York: Paulist Press, 2001), 197-201.

13. See ibid., 269-75, for a fuller version.

14. For a detailed introduction to Islamic mysticism, see Carl W. Ernst, *The Shambala Guide to Sufism* (Boston: Shambala, 1997).

15. Norman Daniel, *Islam, Europe, and Empire* (Edinburgh: Edinburgh University Press, 1966), 9. Also see his *Islam and the West, the Making of an Image*, rev. ed. (Oxford: One World, 1993); and W. Montgomery Watt, *Muhammad: Prophet and Statesman* (Oxford: Oxford University Press, 1961), 231-36.

16. Ma'mun Jarrar, *Al-Ghazw al-Maghuli* (Amman: Dar al-Bashir, 1984), 38-40, vv. 20-22.

17. See William A. Graham, *Divine Word and Prophetic Word in Early Islam: A Reconsidertion of the Sources, with Special Reference to the Divine Saying or Hadith Qudsi* (The Hague: Mouton, 1977), 173-74.

18. See chapter 12 for more details.

19. My translation is based on *Selected Poems from the Divani Shamsi Tabriz*, ed. R. A. Nicholson (Cambridge: Cambridge University Press, 1977), 124-27. For more on Rumi, see Franklin D. Lewis, *Rumi: Past and Present, East and West* (Oxford: One World, 2000).

20. Daniel, *Islam, Europe, and Empire*, 37.

21. Quoted by Gerald M. Ackerman in *Jean-Leon Gerome* (New York, 1986), 24-25.

22. Edward Said, *Orientalism* (New York: Vintage Books, 1978), 108.

23. Ibid.

24. University of Rochester/Zogby, *International Global Religion Survey*, 2003.

25. For more on political Islam and militancy, see chapter 12 below.

26. See Malcolm X and Alex Haley, *The Autobiography of Malcolm X* (New York: Ballentine Books, 1973), esp. 364-82; and see chapter 17 below.

27. Farid Esack, *Qur'an, Liberation & Pluralism: An Islamic Perspective of Interreligious Solidarity Against Oppression* (Oxford: One World, 1997), 144; and see chapter 17 below.

Chapter 5: Religion, Politics, Culture, Law, and Society: Judaism

1. Translation: Jacob Neusner, *Torah from Our Sages: Pirke Avot* (Dallas: Rossel Books, 1984), 41-44.

2. On this point, see Jacob Neusner, *Foundations of Judaism* (Philadelphia: Fortress Press, 1989), 17.

3. If vegetable farmers routinely grew more produce than they could sell, they naturally would alter their behavior so as to grow less food. This would curtail the oversupply and would have the secondary effect, beneficial to the growers, of keeping prices high. Huna worried that such behavior would result in an inadequate food supply, high cost, and communal hunger. By buying the excess produce, he relieved farmers of the concern about oversupply (and the low prices that would result). As a result of Huna's actions, the food supply (and the prices the farmers could charge) remained appropriate.

4. Translation: Tzvee Zahavy, in Jacob Neusner, *The Tosefta. Translated from the Hebrew. First Division. Zeraim* (Hoboken: Ktav, 1986), 42-43.

5. On this passage, see David R. Carr in *The Blackwell Reader in Judaism*, ed. Jacob Neusner and Alan Avery-Peck (Oxford: Blackwell, 2000), 119-20.

6. Franz Kobler, *Letters of Jews Through the Ages* (New York: East and West Library, 1978), 156-65. Cited from Neusner and Avery-Peck, *Blackwell Companion*, 119-20.

Religion, Politics, Culture, Law, and Society: Christianity

1. Henry Chadwick, *The Early Church* (London: Penguin, 1993), 80.

2. See Jacob Neusner and Bruce Chilton, *The Intellectual Foundations of Christian and Jewish Discourse. The Philosophy of Religious Argument* (London: Routledge, 1997), 75-86.

Religion, Politics, Culture, Law, and Society: Islam

1. Frederick M. Denny, "The Great Indonesian Qur'an Chanting Tournament," *The World & I*, 6 (1986): 216-23.

2. See Carl W. Ernst, *The Shambala Guide to Sufism* (Boston: Shambala, 1997), 179-98.

3. See Th. Emil Homerin, "Living Love: The Mystical Writings of ʿA'ishah al-Baʿuniyah (d. 922/1516)," *Mamluk Studies Review* 7 (2003): 211-34.

4. ʿA'ishah al-Baʿuniyah, *Al-Mawrid al-Ahna*, ed. Faris al-ʿAlawi in his *ʿA'ishah al-Baʿuniyah* (Damascus: Dar Muʿadd lil-Tibaʿah wa-al-Nashr wa-al-Tawziʿ, 1994), 143, my translation. For more information on Islamic spirituality, see John Renard, *Seven Doors to Islam: Spirituality and the Religious Life of Muslims* (Berkeley: University of California Press, 1996), and his edited volume, *Windows on the House of Islam: Muslim Sources on Spirituality and Religious Life* (Berkeley: University of California Press, 1998).

5. Translated by B. W. Andrzejwski and Sheila Andrzejewski, *An Anthology of Somali Poetry* (Bloomington: University of Indiana Press, 1993), 67-68.

6. Abridged from Seyyed Hossein Nasr, *Ideals and Realities of Islam*, rev. ed. (Chicago: ABC International Group, 2000), 85-113.

Chapter 6: Philosophy: Averroes, Maimonides, and Aquinas

1. Averroes, *The Book of the Decisive Treatise Determining the Connection Between the Law and Wisdom*, trans. Charles Butterworth (Provo, Utah: Brighem University Press, 2001).

2. "Peripatetic sages" are the followers of Aristotle.

3. The dominant school of Medieval Muslim theology.

4. Moses Maimonides, *The Guide of the Perplexed*, trans. Shlomo Pines (Chicago: University of Chicago Press, 1963).

5. Aristotle, *Physics*, 8.1, 251b17ff.

6. Plato, *Timaeus*, 41B.

7. Alexander of Aphrodisias, a late second-century C.E. Greek commentator.

8. Mutakallimum are the dialectical theologians of Islam.

9. Aquinas, *Basic Writings of St. Thomas Aquinas*, ed. A. Pegis (Indianapolis: Hackett Publishing Co., 1997).

10. Augustine, *On the Trinity*, Book 14.

11. Boethius, *Commentary on Cicero's Topics*, Book 1.

12. Augustine, *The City of God*, Book 11, chap. 4.

13. Boethius, *The Consolation of Philosophy*, Book 5.

14. Aristotle, *Physics*, 6.6, 237b10.

Chapter 7: Mysticism as a Meeting Ground: Seeing the Unseen

1. Geoffrey S. Kirk and John E. Raven, *The Presocratic Philosophers: A Critical History with a Selection of Texts* (Cambridge: Cambridge University Press, 1979), 344.

2. All citations from Plotinus are taken from the Armstrong translation in the Loeb Classical Library series. The passage may be viewed as an interpretation of Plato's *Symposium*, 218E-219A. In the context of discussing the distinction between the "semblance of beauty" and the "thing itself," Plato remarks that the "mind's eye begins to see clearly when the outer eyes grow dim."

3. Peter Kingsley, *In the Dark Places of Wisdom* (Inverness, Calif.: Golden Sufi Center, 1999), 6. This locution calls to mind the *hadith* often cited by Sufi masters, "die before you die." See Annemarie Schimmel, *Mystical Dimensions of Islam* (Chapel Hill: University of North Carolina Press, 1975), 70, 135; *Death Before Dying: The Sufi Poems of Sultan Bahu*, trans. Jamal J. Elias (Berkeley: University of California Press, 1998). The Sufic maxim can be traced to older Jewish sources, such as the dictum in the rabbinic tractate *Derekh Erets, mut ad shelo tamut,* "die before you die." The passage from *Derekh Erets* is cited by Jonah Gerondi, *Sha'arei Teshuvah* 2:17, as noted by Michael Fishbane, *The Kiss of God: Spiritual and Mystical Death in Judaism* (Seattle: University of Washington Press, 1994), 22

4. Gregory of Nyssa, *The Life of Moses*, trans. by Abraham J. Malherbe and Everett Ferguson, in *Light from Light: An Anthology of Christian Mysticism*, 2d ed., ed. Louis Dupré and James A. Wiseman, O.S.B. (New York and Mahwah: Paulist Press, 2001), 48.

5. Ibid., 47.

6. Ibid., 49-50.

7. Ibid., 51-52.

8. *Pseudo-Dionysius: The Complete Works*, trans. Colm Luibheid (New York and Mahwah: Paulist Press, 1987), 49-50.

9. Ibid., 53.

10. Ibid., 108-9.

11. Ibid., 54.

12. Ibid., 109.

13. Ibid., 137.

14. Ibid., 109.

15. Ibid., 263.

16. Michael Sells, trans., ed., *Early Islamic Mysticism: Sufi, Qur'an, Mi`raj, Poetic and Theological Writings* (New York: Paulist Press, 1996), 84.

17. Ibid., 80.

18. *The Niche of Lights: A Parallel English-Arabic Text*, trans. David Buchman (Provo, Utah: Brigham Young University Press, 1998), 52.

19. Sells, *Early Islamic Mysticism*, 284.

20. *The Kashf al-Mahjûb: The Oldest Persian Treatise on Sufism*, trans. Reynold A. Nicholson (London: E. J. W. Gibb Memorial, 1936), 250.

21. Ibid., 274.

22. Ibid., 22.

23. Ibid., 374; see also 414.

24. Sells, *Early Islamic Mysticism*, 291.

25. William C. Chittick, *The Sufi Path of Knowledge: Ibn al-Arabi's Metaphysics of Imagination* (Albany: State University of New York Press, 1989), 230.

26. William C. Chittick, *The Self-Disclosure of God: Principles of Ibn al-'Arabi's Cosmology* (Albany: State University of New York Press, 1998), 110.

27. Ibid., 129.

28. Ibid., 156.

29. *Zohar* 3:120a.

30. *Zohar* 3:291b *(Idra Zuta)*. For an alternative translation and explication of this passage, see Isaiah Tishby, *The Wisdom of the Zohar,* trans. David Goldstein (Oxford: Oxford University Press, 1989), 246.

31. Tishby, *Wisdom of the Zohar,* 295-98.

32. *Zohar* 3:139b *(Idra Rabba)*.

33. Ephraim Gottlieb, *Studies in the Kabbala Literature,* ed. Joseph Hacker (Tel-Aviv: Tel-Aviv University Press, 1976), 236 (in Hebrew), identifies this as R. David Kohen.

34. The passage is cited in Gottlieb, *Studies in the Kabbala Literature,* 236. On the Abulafian background for this image, see Moshe Idel, *The Mystical Experience in Abraham Abulafia,* trans. Jonathan Chipman (Albany: State University of New York Press, 1988), 116. For recent discussion of visualization techniques and contemplation of the divine name in Isaac of Acre, see Eitan P. Fishbane, "Contemplative Practice and the Transmission of Kabbalah: A Study of Isaac of Acre's Me'irat 'Einayim," Ph.D. thesis, Brandeis University, 2003, 271-99.

35. Amos Goldreich, *Sefer Me'irat Einayim by R. Isaac of Acre: A Critical Edition* (Jerusalem: Akadamon, 1981), 91 (in Hebrew).

Chapter 8: Latin Christianity, the Crusades, and the Islamic Response

1. *Theoderich's Description of the Holy Places,* trans. Aubrey Stewart (London: Palestine Pilgrims' Text Society, 1896), 1.

2. Saewulf, "A Reliable Account of the Situation of Jerusalem," in *Jerusalem Pilgrimage 1099–1185,* trans. John Wilkinson et al. (London: Hakluyt Society, 1988), 100.

3. My translation of *Annales Altahenses maiores,* ed. W. von Giesebrecht, in *Monumenta Germaniae Historica, Scriptores,* vol. 20 (Hannover: Hahn, 1869), 820.

4. *De penitentia in bello homines occidentium,* trans. Bernard J. Verkamp, in *The Moral Treatment of Returning Warriors in Early Medieval and Modern Times* (Scranton, Pa.: University of Scranton Press, 1993), 21-22.

5. My translation of Isidore of Seville, *Etymologiae sive originum libri XX* 18.2, ed. W. M. Lindsay (Oxford: Clarendon Press, 1911).

6. Ps. 77:8.

7. Ps. 77:22.

8. 1 Pet 5:3.

9. My translation of Robert the Monk, *Historia Hierosolimitana* 1.1-3 from *Recueil des historiens des croisades, Historiens occidentaux,* vol. 3 (Paris: Académie des Inscriptions et Belles-Lettres, 1869), 727-30.

10. My translation of *Decreta Claromontensia,* canon 2, ed. Robert Somerville (Amsterdam: Adolf M. Hakkert, 1972), 74.

11. Translated from *Le cartulaire de Marcigny-sur-Loire* by Jonathan Riley-Smith, in *The First Crusaders, 1095–1131* (Cambridge: Cambridge University Press, 1997), 116.

12. "Por joie avoir perfite en paradis," ed. and trans. Louise and Jonathan Riley-Smith, in *The Crusades: Ideal and Reality, 1095–1274* (London: Edward Arnold, 1981), 157-58.

13. My translation from the *Gesta Francorum et aliorum Hierosolimitanorum,* ed. Louis Bréhier (Paris: Henri Champion, 1924), 110.

14. My translation from ibid., 202-6.

15. My translation of Fulcher of Chartres, *Historia Hierosolymitana,* ed. Heinrich Hagenmeyer (Heidelberg: Carl Winter, 1913), 748-49.

16. *An Arab-Syrian Gentleman and Warrior in the Period of the Crusades: Memoirs of Usāma ibn-Munqidh,* trans. Philip K. Hitti (New York: Columbia University Press, 2000), 163-64. A *qiblah* is a marker pointing in the direction of the Ka'bah in Mecca, toward which Muslims traditionally direct their prayers.

17. My translation of William of Tyre, *Chronicon* 12.7, ed. R. B. C. Huygens, 2 vols., Corpus Christianorum, Continuatio Mediaeualis, vols. 63-63A (Turnhout: Brepols, 1986), 1:553-54.

18. Guibert of Nogent, *The Deeds of God Through the Franks*, trans. Robert Levine (Woodbridge: Boydell Press, 1997), 27-28.

19. *Arab Historians of the Crusades*, trans. E. J. Costello (Berkeley: University of California Press, 1969), 70-72.

20. Ibid., 122-25.

21. Gregory VIII, *Audita tremendi*, trans. Louise and Jonathan Riley-Smith, in *The Crusades: Ideal and Reality*, 64-66.

Chapter 9: Judaism, Christianity, and Islam in Spain from the Eighth to the Fifteenth Centuries

1. Raymond P. Scheindlin, trans., *Eloah 'oz ve'el ayom venora*, from *Diwan shemuel hanagid*, ed. Dov Jarden (Jerusalem, 1966), 4-14; H. Schrimann, *Hashira ha'ivrit bisefarad uveprovans*, 2nd ed. (Jerusalem and Tel Aviv, 1960), 85-92.

2. Bernard Lewis, trans., *Islam in History: Ideas, Men, and Events in the Middle East* London: Alcove Press, 1973), 159-61.

3. Gerson D. Cohen, trans. *The Book of Tradition (Sefer ha-Qabbalah)* (Philadelphia: Jewish Publication Society, 1967), 71-76.

4. Bernard Lewis, trans., *Islam from the Prophet Muhammad to the Capture of Constantinople* (New York: Harper & Row, 1974), II, 157-65.

5. Translated from Latin by Robert I. Burns: First text translated from the Archive of the Crown of Aragón, Barcelona, Cancellería Real, Pergaminos de Jaime I, 734 (28 September 1238). Second text translated from the Archive of the Kingdom of Valencia, Bailiff General, Real Patrimonio, fol. 238 (29 May 1242).

6. Samuel P. Scott, trans., *Las Siete Partidas* (Chicago, 1931; reprinted Philadelphia, 2001), 1433-442.

7. Kathleen Kulp-Hill, trans., *The Songs of Holy Mary of Alfonso X, the Wise. A Translation of the Cantigas de Santa María* (Tempe, Ariz.: Arizona Center for Medieval and Renaissance Studies, 2000), 133-34, 246-47.

8. Ibid.

9. Edward Peters, trans., "Jewish History and Gentile Memory: The Expulsion of 1492," *Jewish History* 9 (1995): 23-28.

Chapter 10: Christianity and Islam in the Balkans from the Fifteenth to the Twentieth Centuries

1. The following is taken from Mark Mazower, "Introduction," *Balkans: A Short History* (London: Weidenfeld & Nicolson, 2000), 1-16.

2. Saint-Marc Girardin, cited in T. G. Djuvara, *Cent projets de partage de la Turquie* (Paris, 1914), 496.

3. M. E. Durham, *The Burden of the Balkans* (London: E. Arnold, 1905), 104.

4. Ami Boué, *Recueil d'itineraires*, vol. 2, 331.

5. J. V. de Roiere, *Voyage en Orient* (Paris, 1936), 23.

6. The following is taken from Dimitri Obolensky, "Religion, Law, Literature," in *The Byzantine Commonwealth, 500–1453* (Crestwood, N.Y.: St. Vladimir's Seminary Press, 1974), 381-477.

7. J. Fine, "Medieval and Ottoman Roots of Modern Bosnia," in *The Muslims of Bosnia-Herzegovina*, ed. M. Pinson (Cambridge, Mass.: Harvard University Press, 1994), 15-16.

8. Ibid., 14-15.

9. For a thorough study of this issue, see a collection of articles by B. Braude and B. Lewis, *Christians and Jews in the Ottoman Empire* (New York: Holmes and Meier, 1982).

10. The following is taken from Speros Vryonis Jr., "Religious Changes and Patterns in the Balkans, 14th-16th Centuries," in *Aspects of the Balkans: Continuity and Change*, ed. H. Birnbaum and S. Vryonis (The Hague: Mouton, 1972), 151-76.

11. F. Babinger, "Der Islam in Südosteuropa," in *Völker und Kulturen Südosteuropas* (Munich, 1959), 206-7.

12. Harry Norris, *Islam in the Balkans* (Columbia, S.C. University of South Carolina Press, 1994).

13. The following is taken from Hugh Poulton, "Islam, Ethnicity, and State in the Contemporary Balkans," in *Muslim Identity and the Balkan State*, ed. Hugh Poulton and Suha Taji-Farouki (Washington Square, N.Y.: New York University Press, 1997), 13-32.

Chapter 11:
Zionism, Imperialism, and Nationalism: Zionism

1. Walter Laqueur, *A History of Zionism* (New York: Holt, Rinehart and Winston, 1972), xiii.

2. Arthur Hertzberg, *The Zionist Idea. A Historical Analysis and Reader* (New York: Doubleday, 1959), 15.

3. Cited in ibid., 365-66.

4. Arthur Hertzberg, "Ideological Evolution," in "Zionism," *Encyclopaedia Judaica* 16:1044-1045.

5. Klatzkin, cited in Hertzberg, *Zionist Idea*, 319.

6. Anita Shapira, *Berl: The Biography of a Socialist Zionist. Berl Katznelson 1887–1944* (Cambridge: Cambridge University Press, 1974), 137.

7. Amos Elon, *Herzl* (New York: Holt, Rinehart and Winston, 1975), 235.

Zionism, Imperialism, and Nationalism: Christian Imperialism

1. For further discussion, see John Dillon, "Looking on the Light: Some Remarks on the Imagery of Light in the First Chapter of the *Peri Archon*," *The Golden Chain. Studies in the Development of Platonism and Christianity* (Aldershot: Variorum, 1990), 215-30 (essay XXII).

2. In this regard, Lactantius was also an important influence; see Elizabeth DePalma Digeser, *The Making of a Christian Empire. Lactantius and Rome* (Ithaca and London: Cornell University Press, 2000).

3. F. Homes Dudden, *The Life and Times of St. Ambrose* II (Oxford: Clarendon Press, 1935), 371-79, 378.

4. Ibid., 379.

5. Commentators frequently surmise that the synagogue had been struck by lightning, but it was more the victim of history, with or without natural collaboration.

6. He recounts this sermon in a letter to his sister Marcellina (*Epistle* 41.26), which was also written in December of 388 C.E.

7. See Lee Martin McDonald, "Anti-Judaism in the Early Church Fathers," *Anti-Semitism and Early Christianity. Issues of Polemic and Faith*, eds C. A. Evans and D. A. Hagner (Minneapolis: Fortress Press, 1993), 215-52, 217; and Leonard Rutgers, *The Hidden Heritage of Diaspora Judaism* (Leuven: Peters, 1998).

8. See Pierre Miquel, *Histoire de la France. De Vercingétorix à Charles de Gaulle* (Paris: Fayard, 1976), 308-10.

9. For a good, brief description, see Mark Kishlansky, Patrick Geary, and Patricia O'Brien, *Civilization in the West* (New York: Longman, 2003), 224-28.

10. That would have happened sooner, but only one son survived him, Louis the Pious. See *Civilization in the West*, 246-51.

11. See ibid., 458-65.

12. In the words of Rudyard Kipling, although the same argument was often used, see *Civilization in the West*, 818, 831

13. See Ray Allen Billington and Martin Ridge, *Western Expansion: A History of the American Frontier* (New York: Macmillan, 1982).

14. See Stanley Elkins and Eric McKitrick, *The Age of Federalism* (New York: Oxford University Press, 1993), 590-93.

15. See James Carroll, *Constantine's Sword. The Church and the Jews, A History* (Boston: Houghton Mifflin, 2001).

16. See Herbert N. Schneidau, *Sacred Discontent: The Bible and Western Tradition* (Berkeley: University of California Press, 1976); and especially his citation of the work of E. H. Gombeich on p. 265.

Zionism, Imperialism, and Nationalism: Political Islam

1. For more on the Wahhabis and other Muslim movements discussed in this chapter, see John O. Voll, "Foundations for Reform and Renewal," in *The Oxford History of Islam*, ed. John L. Esposito (Oxford: Oxford University Press, 1999), 509-47.

2. For further discussion, see S. V. R. Nasr, "European Colonialism and the Emergence of the Modern Muslim States," in *Oxford History of Islam*, 549-99; John L. Esposito, *The Islamic Threat: Myth or Reality*, 2nd ed. (Oxford: Oxford University Press, 1995), esp. 77-118.

3. *World Almanac 2003* (New York, 2003).

4. Malcolm X, "The Harvard Law School Forum of March 24, 1961," in *The Speeches of Malcolm X at Harvard*, ed. Archie Epps (New York: W. Marrow, 1968), 119-23. Also see, Jane I. Smith, *Islam in America* (New York: Columbia University Press, 1999); and Richard Brent Turner, *Islam in the African-American Experience* (Bloomington: Indiana University Press, 1997).

5. Rachid Gannouchi, "Islamic Civilization Need Not Clash with the West," trans. Ahmad Abul Jobain, in *Islam: Opposing Viewpoints*, ed. Paul A. Winters (San Diego: Greenhaven Press, 1995), 215-18.

6. For a fuller and insightful analysis of Islamist trends and movements discussed above, see John L. Esposito, *Unholy War: Terror in the Name of Islam* (Oxford: Oxford University Press, 2002). Also see Richard T. Antoun, *Understanding Fundamentalism: Christian, Islamic, and Jewish Movements* (New York: AltaMira, 2001); and Youssef M. Choueiri, *Islamic Fundamentalism*, rev. ed. (London: Pinter, 1997).

7. Pervez Hoodbhoy, *Islam and Science: Religious Orthodoxy and the Battle for Rationality* (Atlantic Highlands, N.J.: Zed Books, 1991).

8. Pervez Hoodbhoy, "Muslims and the West After September 11," *Free Inquiry Magazine*, 22:2.

Chapter 12: The Modernization of Christianity

1. See Mark Kishlansky, Patrick Geary, and Patricia O'Brien, *Civilization in the West* (New York: Longman, 2003), 314-17.

2. Giovanni Boccaccio, "Letter to Jacob Pizzinghe," in *The Portable Renaissance Reader*, ed. James Bruce Ross and Mary Martin McLaughlin (New York: Viking, 1953), 123-26; see also M. L. McLaughlin, "Humanism and Italian Literature," *The Cambridge Companion to Renaissance Humanism*, ed. Jill Kraye (Cambridge: Cambridge University Press, 2003), 224-45.

3. See *The Renaissance*, University of Chicago Readings in Western Civilization 5, ed. Eric Cochrane and Julius Kirshner (Chicago: University of Chicago Press, 1986), 32-33

4. Bartolommeo Platina, *The Life of Pope Nicholas V*, in *Portable Renaissance Reader*, 385-87.

5. See Anthony Kenny, *Aquinas*, Past Masters (Oxford: Oxford University Press, 1980), 33-49. As Kenny points out, the meaning of *accidents* and *substance* varies through the corpus of Thomas's writing. In the case of transubstantiation, I take it that accidents are what the senses perceive, and that substance is the form that imparts actuality.

6. See *The Renaissance*, 74.

7. *Platonic Theology*, in *Portable Renaissance Reader*, 387-92.

8. See V. P. Zubov, *Leonardo da Vinci*, trans. David H. Kraus (Cambridge, Mass.; Harvard University Press, 1968); Sherwin B. Nuland, *Leonardo da Vinci* (New York: Penguin, 2000).

9. This quotation derives from Leonard's notebooks, compiled during the sixteenth century and entitled "Treatise on Painting."

10. Zubov, *Leonardo da Vinci*, 4.

11. Nuland, *Leonardo da Vinci*, 31-33; Zubov, *Leonardo da Vinci*, 10-11; quoting from the *Codex Atlanticus*.

12. See Leo Steinberg, *Leonardo's Incessant Last Supper* (New York: Zone, 2001); Kenneth Clark, *Leonardo da Vinci. An Account of His Development as an Artist* (Baltimore: Penguin, 1961), 89-97.

13. See Lynn Picknett and Clive Prince, *The Templar Revelation* (New York: Simon & Schuster, 1998), 20-21.

14. Nuland, *Leonardo da Vinci*, 76-83. Zubov; *Leonardo da Vinci*, 37-38 dates the incident to 1514–1516.

15. See Edward MacCurdy, *The Mind of Leonardo da Vinci* (London: Jonathan Cape, 1952), 163.

16. *Storie fiorentine*.

17. Nuland, *Leonardo da Vinci*, 99.

18. See James D. Tracy, *Erasmus of the Low Countries* (Berkeley: University of California Press, 1996), 17.

19. See Albert Hyma, *The Youth of Erasmus* (Ann Arbor: University of Michigan Press, 1930), 3-35.

20. Ibid., 177, 167-81.

21. See Erika Rummel, *The Erasmus Reader* (Toronto: University of Toronto Press, 1990), 53.

22. Tracy, *Erasmus of the Low Countries*, 24.

23. Rummel, *Erasmus Reader*, 141.

24. Hyma, *Youth of Erasmus*, 22, quoting John Vos in 1424.

25. Rummel, *Erasmus Reader*, 144-46.

26. Ibid., 158.

27. Well described in Tracy, *Erasmus of the Low Countries*, 104-15.

28. Later editions reverted to the more conventional *Novum Testamentum*; see Tracy, *Erasmus of the Low Countries*, 74-86.

29. Rummel, *Erasmus Reader*, 216, discusses the issue of authorship.

30. See E. M. Jung-Inglessis, *St. Peter's*, trans. Graham Fawcett (Firenze: SCALA, 1980), 3-14.

31. For a good description, see Richard Friedenthal, *Luther*, trans. John Nowell (London: Weidenfelt and Nicolson, 1970), 127-43.

32. James K. Farge, *Orthodoxy and Reform in Early Reformation France. The Faculty of Theology of Paris, 1500–1543*, Studies in Medieval and Reformation Thought (Leiden: Brill, 1985).

33. James Anthony Froude, *The Life and Letters of Erasmus* (1894), 364 (in a letter to Botzemus written in 1529).

34. Owen Chadwick, *The Reformation* (Harmondsworth: Penguin, 1970), 42.

35. Friedenthal, *Luther*, 69.

36. Ibid.,128.

37. Ibid., 15-29.

38. John Dillenberger, *Martin Luther: Selections from His Writings* (New York: Doubleday, 1962), 490-91.

39. See H. G. Haile, *Luther: An Experiment in Biography* (Garden City, N.Y.: Doubleday, 1980), 191.

40. Chadwick, *Reformation*, 47-75.

41. Haile, *Luther*, 177.

42. Chadwick, *Reformation*, 56, prefers this account to the legendary statement, "Here I stand, I can do no other."

43. Ibid., 60.

44. Dillenberger, *Martin Luther*, 370.

45. See Roland H. Bainton, *The Reformation of the Sixteenth Century* (Boston: Beacon, 1952), 156-59.

46. Ibid., 185-210; Chadwick, *Reformation*, 97-136; Harold Grimm, *The Reformation Era 1500–1650* (New York: Macmillan, 1965), 289-308.

47. Chadwick, *Reformation*, 190-91.

48. Ibid., 153-54.

49. Bainton, *Reformation of the Sixteenth Century*, 77-94.

50. See Bernard Cottret, *Calvin: A Biography*, trans. M. Wallace McDonald (Grand Rapids: Eerdmans, 2000); Chadwick, *Reformation*, 82-96.

51. *Institutes* 3.11.23, from John Dillenberger, *John Calvin: Selections from His Writings*, American Academy of Religion—Aids for the Study of Religion (Ann Arbor: Edwards, 1975), 451.

52. *Institute* 3.14.3, from Dillenberger, *John Calvin*, 453-54.

53. Cottret, *Calvin*, 322, citing *Des scandals*, 123.

54. Erasmus, *On the Freedom of the Will* (epilogue), from *Luther and Erasmus: Free Will and Salvation*, The Library of Christian Classics XVII (Philadelphia: Westminster Press, 1969)

55. G. R. Elton, *Reformation Europe, 1517–1559: History of Europe* (New York: Harper & Row, 1963), 160-75.

56. Chadwick, *Reformation*, 114-17.

57. Ibid., 121-23.

58. Chadwick, *Reformation*, 269-73.

59. Ibid., 255-64.

60. Elton, *Reformation*, 200.

61. Ibid., 192.

62. Chadwick, *Reformation*, 271.

63. See Charles Howard McIlwain, *The Political Works of James I*, Harvard Political Classics I (Cambridge: Harvard University Press, 1918), 53-54. I have modernized the spelling and punctuation somewhat.

64. See Kishlansky, Geary, and O'Brien, *Civilization in the West*, 506-35.

65. See William Haller, "The Tenure of Kings and Magistrates," in *The Works of John Milton* (New York: Columbia University Press, 1932), 8-9. Again, I have smoothed out the spellings a bit, but left the wonderful turns of phrase.

66. The book has a complicated history of publication; see Peter Laslett, *John Lock: Two Treatises of Government*, Cambridge Texts in the History of Political Thought (Cambridge: Cambridge University Press, 1991). I quote from this facsimile edition.

67. See Isaac Kramnick, *The Portable Enlightenment Reader* (New York: Penguin, 1995), 81-82.

68. Ibid., 94-95.

69. Thomas Hobbes, *Leviathan*, A Norton Critical Edition, eds. Richard E. Flathman and David Johnston (New York: Norton: 1991), 390 in the original edition, re-spelled.

70. Kramnick, *Portable Enlightenment Reader*, 182.

71. See ibid., 45-47.

72. See Jean Mesnard, "The Revelation of God," *Blasé Pascal: Modern Critical Views*, ed. Harold Bloom (New York: Chelsea House, 1989), 105.

73. John E. Smith, ed., *The Works of Jonathan Edwards 2* (New Haven: Yale University Press, 1987), 266-68.

74. See Kramnick, *Portable Enlightenment Reader*, 1-7.

75. See Robert B. Pippin, "Kant," in *A Companion to Continental Philosophy*, ed. Simon Critchley and William R. Schroeder (Oxford: Blackwell, 1998), 35-56.

76. Kramnick, *Portable Enlightenment Reader*, 166-67.

77. Ibid., 109.

78. Richard B. Brandt, *The Philosophy of Schleiermacher: The Development of His Theory of Scientific and Religious Knowledge* (New York: Greenwood, 1968), 84-85.

79. G. W. F. Hegel, *Political Writings*, ed. Laurence Dickey and H. B. Nisbet, trans. H. B. Nisbet (Cambridge: Cambridge University Press, 1999), 225-26.

80. See Joel Kovel, *History and Spirit: An Inquiry into the Philosophy of Liberation* (Boston: Beacon, 1991).

81. See Hal Draper, *Karl Marx's Theory of Revolution* (New York and London: Monthly Review Press, 1977), 65.

82. See Kishlansky, Geary, and O'Brien, *Civilization in the West*, 734-40.

83. Steve Jones, *Darwin's Ghost: The Origin of Species Updated* (New York: Random House, 2000), 343.

84. Ernst Renan, *The Life of Jesus*, trans. Charles Edwin Wilbur (New York: Carlton, 1864), 363-64

85. See John Docker, *Postmodernism and Popular Culture: A Cultural History* (Cambridge: Cambridge University Press, 1994).

Chapter 13: The Modernization of Judaism

1. Benzion Dinur, "Emancipation," *Encyclopaedia Judaica* (Jerusalem: Encyclopaedia Judaica, 1971–72), 6:696-718

2. Jakob J. Petuchowski, "Reform Judaism," *Encyclopaedia Judaica*, 14:23-28.

3. Ibid., col. 25.

4. Ibid.

5. Max Wiener, *Abraham Geiger and Liberal Judaism: The Challenge of the Nineteenth Century*, trans. Ernest J. Schlochauer (Philadelphia: Jewish Publication Society of America, 1962).

6. Ibid., 11.

7. Ibid., 13.

8. Ibid., 40.

9. Ibid., 42.

10. Abraham Cronbach, *Reform Movements in Judaism* (New York: Bookman Associates, 1963), 7-9.

11. Ibid., 132.

12. Nathaniel Katzburg and Walter S. Wurzburger, "Orthodoxy," *Encyclopaedia Judaica*, 12:1486-1493. Professor Michael A. Meyer, Hebrew Union College-Jewish Institute of Religion, comments: There is no easy way of determining the first use of the term reform since it was used very broadly as a verb: for religion, education, and occupational structure as early as the late eighteenth century. The more significant development, to my mind, is when it was first used to designate a Jewish institution. That does not occur until 1845 when there is formed in Berlin the "Association for Reform in Judaism" (Genossenschaft fuer Reform im Judentum), which after a short time re-names itself the "Jewish Reform Congregation of Berlin" (Juedische Reformgemeinde in Berlin). For a brief time it also published a newspaper called *Reform-Zeitung. Organ fuer den Fortschritt im Judentum.* Thirty years earlier the distinction in the literature is often "Die Neuen" for reformers and "Die Alten" for traditionalists.

13. Ibid., 1487.

14. Ibid., 1488.

15. Ibid., 1490.

16. Moshe Shraga Samet, "Neo-Orthodoxy," *Encyclopaedia Judaica*, 12:956-58.

17. Ibid., 957.

18. Simha Katz, "Samson (ben) Raphael Hirsch," *Encyclopaedia Judaica*, 8:508-15.

19. Ibid., 512-13.

20. Ibid., 513.

21. Ibid., 514.

22. Samson Raphael Hirsch, *The Collected Writings* (New York: Philipp Feldheim, 1984), 1:388-389.

23. Ibid., 3:xiii-xiv.

24. Arthur Hertzberg, "Conservative Judaism," *Encyclopaedia Judaica*, 5:901-906.

25. Ibid., 902.

26. Ibid., 901.

27. Robert Gordis, *Understanding Conservative Judaism*, ed. Max Gelb. (New York: The Rabbinical Assembly, 1978), 26-27.

28. Ibid., 39-40.

29. Daniel J. Elazar and Rela Mintz Geffen, *The Conservative Movement in Judaism: Dilemmas and Opportunities* (Albany: State University of New York Press, 2000).

30. Ibid.

Chapter 14: The Modernization of Islam

1. See chapter 12.

2. John L. Esposito, "Pakistan: Quest for Islamic Identity," in *Islam and Development: Religion and Sociopolitical Change*, ed. John L. Esposito (Syracuse: Syracuse University Press, 1980), 139-62, esp. 146-47.

3. *International Journal of Middle East Studies* 1 (1970): 317-33. For recent studies on modern trends in Islam, see Charles Kurzman, ed., *Liberal Islam* (New York: Oxford University Press, 1998); his *Modernist Islam, 1840–1940: A Source Book* (New York: Oxford University Press, 2002); and Muhammad Arkoun, *The Unthought in Contemporary Islamic Thought* (London: Saqi Books, 2002).

4. It is now admitted by many educated Muslims that this development was made possible because direct or effective rule had passed to alien Western powers. Muslim governments, whether new "democratic authoritarians" or old despotic ones, feel that somehow they can ill-afford to create "frictions" as a result of free discussion and debate. Many Pakistanis think that since their state is "ideological," it can as little brook friction by free debate as, say, a Communist state. If this were true, all Muslim states would be, in fact, ideological even if not so constitutionally. Whereas, however, in the case of

a Communist state, the people in charge of affairs have certain definite objectives and also methods of realizing those objectives, which they push through by the force of the state machinery, this is obviously not the case with Muslim governments. In the case of the latter, it is their weakness vis-à-vis the conservative forces and, indeed, lack of an effective ideology that compels them to avoid friction by free debate of sociomoral issues.

5. See Gunnar Myrdal, *Asian Drama: An Inquiry into the Poverty of Nations* (New York: Pantheon, 1968), 3:1871.

6. Politics in Pakistan and to some extent in other countries, notably in Indonesia (and, of course, pre-Kemalist Turkey), are exceptions to this. In these countries, strong political conservative and revivalist organizations have been very active. One cannot help commenting, however, that the Islamic constitutional stand of these groups has been concerned with form rather than substance.

7. It should be remembered that bureaucracies in all these countries are, by and large, secular and hence out of touch with the ethos of the masses. Since, however, they are drawn from the old middle class strata of society, which are emotionally intensely Islamic, the bureaucrats act as an inhibitive force against reform because they do not want to appear to offend mass sentiments. See the last paragraph of this section.

8. Myrdal, *Asian Drama*, 2:894. Indeed, the whole of this and the following sections *et passim* his references to the "soft state."

9. In Persia, the government clashed in 1964 with the Mullahs over certain reforms; the Mullahs could not muster any large-scale mass support. This shows that in a determined reformist bid in which the government's genuine stand can be made to be understood by the people, religious conservatism can be successfully isolated from the masses. Generally, however, the governments labor under the vague apprehension that "masses are behind the Mullahs" and regard this proposition as a self-evident truth.

10. See note 4, above.

11. A remarkable fact about the intellectuals is that they hardly include any scientists at all. Even more than in the West, scientists in these countries are only technologists; under the circumstances it is out of the question to expect any intellectual effort at formulating a scientific worldview. But the scientists do not even feel the need to discern the social implications or requisites of their technology. They live in an isolated world of their own, or, rather, they live as technologists in their laboratories or their field work and as humans and perhaps even as Muslims in the society at large.

12. H. A. R. Gibb, in chapter 4 of his *Modern Trends in Islam* (New York: Octagon Books, 1972), has brought out the inner strains from which many representatives of Muslim Modernists suffer.

13. Professor Nikkie R. Keddie, in *An Islamic Response to Imperialism: Political and Religious Writings of Jamal al-Din 'al-Afghani'* (Berkeley: University of California Press, 1968), has also accused Jamal al-Din al-Afghani of this type of duplicity and sought to draw support there for her (otherwise formidably documented thesis that he was a Persian) contention that al-Afghani was a *Shi^{c}a*. It is, however, clear that one does not have to be a *Shi^{c}a* to practice duplicity. Like Shah Wali Allah of Delhi and others, however, al-Afghani may well have suffered from "double-mindedness" in the sense noted above and acted on the principle "You should talk to people according to their level of understanding." Duplicity is not easy to imagine on the part of a person who was capable of suffering exile from one country to another for the sake of what he preached.

14. Qur'an, IV, 3.

15. [Editor's note: *Ijma^c* is the "consensus" of the scholarly community on a matter, often involving law.]

16. [Editor's note: *Ijtihad* is independent reasoning generally in matters of law.]

17. Manfred Halpern quotes from Majid Khadduri's *From Religious to National Law* that al-Sanhuri, an eminent modern Arab legist, "wisely abstained from discussing controversial issues that might have brought him into conflict with the *^{c}Ulama*' and interrupted his work"— and that al-Sanhuri proceeded "without going into a theoretical discussion on how the *Shari^{c}a* generally should be modernized, or even trying to give a rationale to his scheme" (Manfred Halpern, *The Politics of Social Change in the Middle East and North Africa* ([Princeton, N.J.: University Press, 1963], 126.) While Halpern himself apparently approves of the salutary character of this procedure in general, he has certain reservations.

18. Max Thornburg, *People and Policy in the Middle East New York: A Study of Social and Political Change as a Basis for the United States Policy* (New York: Norton, 1964), 126.

19. Qur'an, II, 282.

20. [Editor's note: A *hadd/hudud* punishment is one explicitly mentioned in the Qur'an.]

21. See my article: "The Concept of *Hadd* in Islamic Law," in *Islamic Studies,* Journal of the Central Institute of Islamic Research 4, no. 3 (September 1965): 247 n. 10.

22. Halpern, *Politics of Social Change,*126.

23. Fazlur Rahman, "The Status of Women in Islam: A Modernist Interpretation," in *Separate Worlds: Studies of Purdah in South Asia*, ed. Hanna Papanek and Gail Minault (Delhi: Chanakya Publications, 1982), 285-310, esp. 286-87.

24. Ibid., 301. For more information on women and Islam, see Leila Ahmed, *Women and Gender in Islam* (New Haven: Yale University Press, 1992); Ruth Roded, ed., *Women in Islam and the Middle East* (London: I. B. Tauris, 1999); and Jane I. Smith, "Islam," in *Women in World Religions*, ed. Arind Sharma (Albany: State University of New York Press, 1987).

25. From *Women's and Men's Liberation*, ed. Leonard Grob, Riffat Hassan, and Haim Gordon (New York, Greenwood Press, 1991), 65-82.

26. Saiyyad: a descendant of the Prophet Muhammad.

27. *Ummah* (from *umm:* mother): community of Muslims.

28. Sunnah: practical traditions attributed to the Prophet Muhammad.

29. Hadith (plural: ahadith): oral traditions attributed to the Prophet Muhammad.

30. Fiqh: jurisprudence.

31. Surah 4: *An-Nisa':* 34.

32. Surah 4: *An-Nisa':* 11.

33. Surah 2: *Al-Baqarah:* 282.

34. Reference here is to the ahadith from *Sahih al-Bukhari*.

35. Leonard Swidler, *Biblical Affiliations of Women* (Philadelphia: Westminster Press, 1979), 76.

36. Muhammad Iqbal, *The Reconstruction of Religious Thought in Islam* (Lahore: Shaikh Muhammad Ashraf, 1962), 83.

37. Fazlur Rahman, *Islam* (Garden City, N.Y.: Doubleday and Company, 1968), 73.

38. Alfred Guillaume, *The Traditions of Islam* (Beirut: Khayats, 1966), 15.

39. Hamilton A. R. Gibb, *Studies on the Civilization of Islam*, ed. Stanford J. Shaw and William R. Polk (Boston: Beacon Press, 1966), 194.

40. Marshall G. S. Hodgson, *The Venture of Islam: Conscience and History in a World Civilization* vol. 1, *The Classical Age of Islam* (Chicago: University of Chicago Press, 1974), 332.

41. Hadith quoted in Jane I. Smith and Yvonne Y. Haddad, "Eve: Islamic Image of Woman," *Women's Studies International Forum* 5 no. 2 (1982): 136-37.

42. I. B. U. Ibn Kathir, *Tafsir Ibn Kathir* (Karachi: Nur Muhammad Karkhana Tijarate-e-Kutub, n.d.) 1:101.

43. A. A. Maududi, *The Meaning of the Qur'an* and *Tafhim ul-Qur'an*, 6 vols (Lahore: Maktaba-e-Ta'mir-e-Insaniyyat, 1974).

44. Ibid., 2:298, n. 1 (emphasis is mine).

45. Rasul: a Prophet sent by God with a message. Reference here is to the Prophet Muhammad.

46. M. M. Khan, translation with notes of *Sahih al-Bukhari* (Lahore: Kazi Publications, 1971), vol. 4 "Book of Prophets," chap. l, Hadith 548, p. 346.

47. *Sahih al-Bukhari* 7:33.

48. *Sahih al-Bukhari* (translation), vol. 7, "Book of Wedlock," chap. 80, Hadith 113, p. 80.

49. *Sahih al-Bukhari*, 7:33.

50. *Sahih al-Bukhari* (translation), vol. 7, "Book of Wedlock," chap. 81, Hadith 114, p. 81.

51. Muslim bin al-Hajjaj, *Sahih Muslim, 2 vols.* (Cairo: 'Isa al-Babi al-Halbi, n.d.), 1:625.

52. A. H. Siddiqui, translation with notes of *Sahih Muslim* (Lahore: Shaikh Muhammad Ashraf) vol. 2, "Book of Wedlock," chap. 576; Hadith 3466, p. 752.

53. *Sahih Muslim*, 1:625.

54. *Sahih Muslim* (translation), vol. 2, "Book of Wedlock," chap. 576, Hadith 3467, p. 752.

55. *Sahih Muslim*, 1:625.

56. *Sahih Muslim* (translation), vol. 2, "Book of Wedlock," chap. 576, Hadith 3468, pp. 752-53.

57. 'Abdul Wahab Ash-Shairani, *Al-Mizan al-Kubra* (Cairo), 1:59.

58. Ignaz Goldziher, *Muslim Studies*, trans. C. R. Barber and S. M. Stern, ed. S. M. Stern (Chicago: Aldine Publishing Company, 1971), 2:163.

59. See Muhammad bin 'Abd Allah al-Hakim, *Ma'rifat 'Ulum al-Hadith*, ed. Mu'azzam Hussain (Cairo: 1937), 62; and Ibn Hajar al-'Asqalani, *Sharh Nukhbat ul-Fikr fi Mustaleh Ahl al-Athar* (Cairo: 1934), 5.

60. See, for example, Shams ad-Din Adh-Dhahabi, *Mizan al-I'tidal fi Naqd ar-Rijal*, 4 vols. (Cairo: 'Isa al-Babi al-Halbi, n.d.). This is a highly authoritative work investigating the credentials of Hadith transmitters by a renowned Hadith critic (A.D. 1274–1348).

61. Hodgson, *Venture of Islam*, 2:480.

62. From *The Chronicle of Higher Education*, February 8, 2002, A48.

63. For further details on the case of Dr. Abu Zeid, see his *Voice of an Exile: Reflections on Islam*, written with Esther R. Nelson (Westport, Conn.: Praeger, 2004).

Chapter 15:
Judaism, Christianity, and Islam in Their Contemporary Encounters: Judaism Addresses Christianity

1. See chap. 4, above.

2. The theory of dialogue to which I adhere is laid out excellently in Leora Batnitzky, "Dialogue as Judgment, Not Mutual Affirmation: A New Look at Franz Rosenzweig's Dialogical Philosophy," *Journal of Religion* 79 (1999): 523-44, esp. 537-40. Contrary to what Batnitzky suggests, however, I do not adhere to the position that "it is best not to engage in dialogue on theological issues" (p. 540). My view, rather, is that we deeply compromise such dialogue when we make reconciliation or mutual affirmation its principal objective.

3. Quoted in Malcolm Hay, *Europe and the Jews: The Pressure of Christendom on the People of Israel for 1900 Years* (Boston: Beacon Press, 1950), 81.

4. Quoted from Martin Gilbert, *Exile and Return: The Emergence of Jewish Statehood* (Philadelphia and New York: J. B. Lippincott, 1978), 20.

5. Zech 8:16.

6. The authors are Tikva Frymer-Kensky (University of Chicago), David Novak (University of Toronto), Peter Ochs (University of Virginia), and Michael Signer (University of Notre Dame). Not long after the statement was issued, there appeared a supporting volume edited by these scholars and David Fox Sandmel, *Christianity in Jewish Terms* (Boulder, Colo.: Westview Press, 2000).

7. Ibid., xvii-xx. All citations from *Dabru Emet* in this article are taken from these pages.

8. Commentary on the Mishnah, *Abod. Zar.* 1:1.

9. See Jacob Katz, *Exclusiveness and Tolerance: Studies in Jewish-Gentile Relations in Medieval and Modern Times* (Springfield, N.J.: Behrman House, 1961), 18-19.

10. Peter Ochs, "The God of Jews and Christians," in *Christianity* (ed. Frymer-Kensky et al.), 60-61.

11. See Michael Goldberg, "God, Action, Narrative: Which Narrative, Action, God?" *Journal of Religion* 68 (1988): 39-56. Note also his book *Jews and Christians, Getting Our Stories Straight: The Exodus and the Passion-Resurrection* (Nashville: Abingdon Press, 1985).

12. Tos. to *b. Sanh.* 63b. See also Katz, *Exclusiveness*, 34-36; and David Ellenson, "A Jewish View of the Christian God: Some Cautionary and Hopeful Remarks," in *Christianity* (ed. Frymer-Kensky et al.), 72-75.

13. It is significant that Tosaphot here does not use the term "God of Israel," as *Dabru Emet* does, but restricts its language to the term "Maker of Heaven." I thank Rabbi Joel Poupko for bringing this to my attention.

14. Wolfhart Pannenberg, in "A Symposium on *Dabru Emet*," *Pro Ecclesia* 11, no. 1 (Winter 2002): 8.

15. Heinrich Denzinger, *The Sources of Catholic Dogma* (St. Louis: Herder, 1957), 50.

16. On the theological import of the terminology, see Jon D. Levenson, *The Hebrew Bible, the Old Testament, and Historical Criticism: Jews and Christians in Biblical Studies* (Louisville: Westminster John Knox, 1993), especially pp. 1-32.

17. See especially Luke 1:8-17.

18. See Jon D. Levenson, "Is Brueggemann Really a Pluralist?" *Harvard Theological Review* 93 (July 2000): 292.

19. 2 Cor 3:12-16. Unless otherwise noted, all quotations from the New Testament are drawn from the New American Bible.

20. See above, chap. 3.

21. *Tanh. ki-tissa'* 33.

22. Thus *Dabru Emet*: "Jews and Christians interpret the Bible differently on many points. Such differences must always be respected." See also Ellenson, "A Jewish," 76, who counsels Jews to "search . . . to affirm elements of commonality that mark these two faith traditions."

23. Gen 15:6. Unless otherwise noted, all Hebrew Bible translations are from the *Tanakh* (Philadelphia: Jewish Publication Society of America, 5748/1988).

24. I have explored this issue of Abraham as the putative common father in "The Conversion of Abraham to Judaism, Christianity, and Islam," in *The Idea of Biblical Interpretation: Essays in Honor of James L. Kugel*, ed. Hindy Najman and Judith H. Newman (Leiden and Boston: Brill, 2004), 3-40.

25. Rom 4:13. Departing from the New American Bible, I have capitalized "Law" to bring out the fact that Paul is speaking about the Torah.

26. Rom 9:6-8, quoting Gen 21:12.

27. Rom 9:30-33, quoting Isa 28:16. I have retained the New American Bible translation of the latter verse, which fits better with Paul's particular exegesis.

28. Katz, *Exclusiveness*, 4.

29. See Jubilees 21, e.g.

30. M. *Qidd.* 4:14.

31. See *b. Yoma* 28b and *Pes. Rab. Kah.* 12:1.

32. Heb 8:6, 8, 13.

33. Cited in Richard John Neuhaus, "The Public Square," *First Things* 134 (June/July 2003): 66. The statement comes from Knox Theological Seminary, which is associated with the Presbyterian Church in America (not to be confused with the Presbyterian Church USA).

34. E.g. Matt 5:21-48.

35. Heb 8:10, after Jer 31:33.

36. See *b. Sanh.* 56a-56b.

37. See David Novak, *The Image of the Non-Jew in Judaism: An Historical and Constructive Study of the Noahide Laws* (New York: Edward Mellen, 1983).

38. Gal 3:26, 28.

39. See Jon D. Levenson, "The Universal Horizon of Biblical Particularism," in *The Bible and Ethnicity*, ed. Mark G. Brett (Leiden: Brill, 1996), 143-69.

40. See Doris L. Bergen, *Twisted Cross: The German Christian Movement in the Third Reich* (Chapel Hill: University of North Carolina Press, 1996) and, more broadly, Richard Steigmann-Gall, *The Holy Reich: Nazi Conceptions of Christianity, 1919-1945* (Cambridge and New York: Cambridge University Press, 2003).

41. Rom 11:25-26, 28-29.

42. See Jack Wertheimer, "Surrendering to Intermarriage," *Commentary* 111, no.3 (March 2001): 25-32.

43. Pannenberg, in "A Symposium," 9.

Judaism, Christianity, and Islam in Their Contemporary Encounters: Christianity Meets Other Religions

1. See Sydney E. Ahlstrom, *A Religious History of the American People* (New Haven: Yale University Press, 1973), 812-16.

2. A recent article found an increase of commitment to the belief that "the Bible is the actual word of God" from 32 percent to 39 percent of respondents between 1994 and 1995; see John Williams, "More in Survey Say Religion a Big Part of Their Lives," *Houston Chronicle* (January 4, 1996).

3. See Raymond de Boyer de Sainte Suzanne, *Alfred Loisy, entre la foi de l'incroyance* (Paris: Centurion, 1968).

4. See D. R. Sharpe, *Walter Rauschenbusch* (New York: Macmillan, 1942).

5. For the use of this term to signal a disproportionate devotion to the papacy, see Garry Wills, "The Vatican Monarchy," *New York Review of Books* 45, no. 3 (February 1998): 20-25. In an earlier, less probing piece (which might be described as an assault *ad hominem*), Wills makes the connection between the papalism of John Paul II and fundamentalism; "The Tragic Pope?" *New York Review of Books* 41, no. 2 (December 1994): 4-7. Cf. Garry Wills, *Papal Sin: Structures of Deceit* (New York: Doubleday, 2000).

6. See James Barr, *Fundamentalism* (Philadelphia: Westminster Press, 1977) and his earlier work *The Semantics of Biblical Language* (London: Oxford University Press, 1961).

7. In fact, Augustine was not as committed to the notion of progress as the movement of biblical theology has been in our period. Indeed, part of Augustine's purpose was to cope with the reality of evident evil in the world in the period after Christ. *The City of God* was occasioned, after all, by the sack of Rome by Alaric in 410 C.E. See Bruce Chilton and Jacob Neusner, *Trading Places: The Intersecting Histories of Judaism and Christianity* (Cleveland: Pilgrim Press, 1996), 167-209.

8. Moreover, it is evident that, for all that Barr engaged in an attack on the biblical theology movement, his own commitment has been to a kind of biblical theology throughout. See D. A. Knight, "Barr, James," *Dictionary of Biblical Interpretation*, ed. J. Hayes (Nashville: Abingdon Press, 1999), 98-99.

9. In *The Anchor Bible Dictionary* 1, ed. D. N. Freedman et al. (New York: Doubleday, 1992), see John C. O'Neill, "Biblical Criticism," 725-30; and William Baird, "New Testament Criticism," 730-36

10. See Daniel Patte, *What Is Structural Exegesis? Guides to Biblical Scholarship* (Philadelphia: Fortress Press, 1976).

11. See Christopher Norris, *Deconstruction, Theory and Practice: New Accents* (London: Routledge, 1991).

12. See Ted Honderich, *Conservatism* (Boulder: Westview Press, 1991).

13. Within a single year, two books appeared with the title, *Liberalism and Its Discontents*, one by Alan Brinkley (Cambridge: Harvard University Press, 1998), and the other by Neal Patrick (Washington Square: New York University Press, 1997).

14. The fourth amendment to the Constitution states, "The right of the people to be secure in their persons, houses, papers, and effects, against unreasonable searches and seizures, shall not be violated."

15. See Francis Fukuyama, *The End of History and the Last Man* (New York: Free Press, 1992).

16. See William J. Bennett, *The Death of Outrage: Bill Clinton and the Assault on American Ideals* (New York: Macmillan, 1999).

17. See West Cornell, *Roots of Violence* (New York: Basic Books, 1997).

18. See W. M. Abbott, ed., *The Documents of Vatican II* (New York: Guild, 1966), 137.

19. See Stephen B. Oates, *Let the Trumpet Sound: The Life of Martin Luther King, Jr.* (New York: Harper & Row, 1982), 205-76.

Judaism, Christianity, and Islam in Their Contemporary Encounters: Islam and Pluralism

1. For an astute analysis of contemporary religious violence, see Mark Juergensmeyer, *Terror in the Mind of God: The Global Rise of Religious Violence*, 3rd ed. (Berkeley: University of California Press, 2003).

2. Malcolm X with Alex Haley, *The Autobiography of Malcolm X* (New York: Ballantine Books, 1964), 340-41.

3. W. Deen Muhammad, *An African American Genesis* (Calumet City, Ill.: Progressions Publications, 1987), 16-18.

4. Farid Esack, *Qur'an, Liberation & Pluralism* (Oxford: One World, 1997), 83.

5. Ibid., 162.

6. Ibid., 171.

7. Tariq Ramadan, *Western Muslims and the Future of Islam* (Oxford: Oxford University Press, 2004), 82.

8. Mohammed Abu-Nimer, *Nonviolence and Peace Building in Islam: Theory and Practice* (Gainesville: University of Florida Press, 2003), and his *Dialogue, Conflict Resolution, and Change: Arab-Jewish Encounters in Israel* (Albany: State of New York University Press, 1999). Also see Omid Safi, ed., *Progressive Muslims: On Justice, Gender, and Pluralism* (Oxford: Oneworld, 2003).

9. Dr. Asani's books include *Celebrating Muhammad: Images of the Prophet in Popular Muslim Poetry* (co-editor, Columbia, S.C.: University of South Carolina Press, 1995), and *Ecstasy and Enlightenment: The Ismaili Devotional Literature of South Asia* (New York: I. B. Tauris, 2002).

10. See Bruce B. Lawrence, *New Faiths, Old Fears: Muslims and Other Asian Immigrants in American Religious Life* (New York: Columbia University Press, 2002), esp. 33, 110-16. Also see Jack G. Shaheen, *Reel Bad Arabs: How Hollywood Vilifies a People* (New York: Olive Branch Press, 2001).

11. Ali S. Asani, "So That You May Know One Another," *Annals*, AAPSS 58 (July 2003): 40-51.

12. My understanding of the theological basis for pluralism within Islam has been greatly influenced by Abdulaziz Sachedina's pioneering study, *The Islamic Roots of Democratic Pluralism* (New York: Oxford University Press, 2001). I am also indebted to my colleague Roy Mottahedeh, whose 1992 article, "Towards an Islamic Theology of Toleration," I have found helpful. (The article appears in *Islamic Law Reform and Human Rights*, ed. T. Lindholm and K. [Vogt, Oslo, 1992]).

13. For the theological debates on the term *jihad* in early Islam, see R. Mottahedeh and R. Al-Sayyid, "The Idea of Jihad in Islam Before the Crusades," *The Crusades from the Perspective of Byzantium and the Muslim World*, ed. A. Laiou and R. Mottahedeh (Washington, D.C.: Dumbarton Oaks Research Library and Collection, 2001).

14. For a further discussion of this issues, see Khaled Abou El-Fadl, *The Place of Tolerance in Islam* (Boston: Beacon Press, 2002).

15. His Highness Prince Karin Aga Khan, Keynote Speech Concluding the Prince Claus Fund's Conference on Culture and Development, Amsterdam, 7 September 2002.

16. Salam al-Marayati, Founder and Director, Muslim Public Affairs Council, at the Islam in America 2003 conference held at the Harvard Divinity School on 9 March 2003.

CONTRIBUTORS

Alan J. Avery-Peck, Kraft-Hiatt Professor in Judaic Studies and Chair, Department of Religious Studies, College of the Holy Cross

James A. Brundage, Distinguished Professor Emeritus, History Department, University of Kansas

Amila Buturovic, Associate Professor, Division of Humanities; Noor Fellow in Islamic Studies; York University

Bruce D. Chilton, Bernard Iddings Bell Professor of Religion; Chaplain of the College; Director, Institute of Advanced Theology, Bard College

Olivia Remie Constable, Professor of History, University of Notre Dame

Seymour Feldman, Professor of Philosophy, Emeritus, Department of Philosophy, Rutgers University, New Brunswick, New Jersey

William Scott Green, Professor of Religion, Philip S. Bernstein Professor of Judaic Studies, Dean of the College, University of Rochester

Th. Emil Homerin, Professor of Religion, Department of Religion and Classics, University of Rochester

Jon D. Levenson, Albert A. List Professor of Jewish Studies, Harvard Divinity School, Harvard University

Jacob Neusner, Research Professor of Theology, Institute of Advanced Theology, Bard Center, Bard College

Elliot R. Wolfson, Judge Abraham Lieberman Professor of Hebrew Studies, Professor of Religious Studies, New York University

INDEX